INTRODUCTION TO CATALOGING AND CLASSIFICATION

Library Science Text Series

The Collection Program in Elementary and Middle Schools: Concepts, Practices, and Information Sources. By Phyllis J. Van Orden.

The Collection Program in High Schools: Concepts, Practices, and Information Sources. By Phyllis J. Van Orden.

Developing Library Collections. By G. Edward Evans.

The Humanities: A Selective Guide to Information Sources. 2nd ed. By A. Robert Rogers.

Immroth's Guide to the Library of Congress Classification. 3rd ed. By Lois Mai Chan.

Introduction to Cataloging and Classification. By Bohdan S. Wynar. Seventh edition by Arlene G. Taylor.

Introduction to Library Automation. By James Rice.

Introduction to Library Science: Basic Elements of Library Service. By Jesse H. Shera.

Introduction to Public Services for Library Technicians. 4th ed. By Marty Bloomberg.

Introduction to Technical Services for Library Technicians. 5th ed. By Marty Bloomberg and G. Edward Evans.

Introduction to United States Public Documents. 3rd ed. By Joe Morehead.

The Library in Society. By A. Robert Rogers and Kathryn McChesney.

Library Instruction for Librarians. By Anne F. Roberts.

Library Management. 2nd ed. By Robert D. Stueart and John Taylor Eastlick.

Micrographics. 2nd ed. By William Saffady.

Nonprint Cataloging for Multimedia Collections: A Guide Based on AACR 2. By JoAnn V. Rogers.

Online Reference and Information Retrieval. By Roger C. Palmer.

The School Library Media Center. 3rd ed. By Emanuel T. Prostano and Joyce S. Prostano.

BOHDAN S. WYNAR

INTRODUCTION TO CATALOGING AND CLASSIFICATION

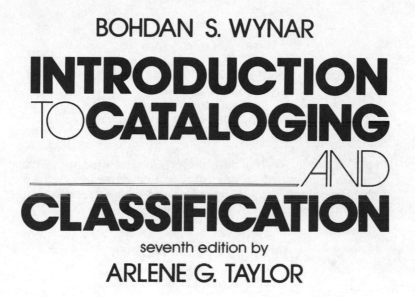

seventh edition by
ARLENE G. TAYLOR

1985

LIBRARIES UNLIMITED, INC.
Littleton, Colorado

LIBRARIES UNLIMITED, INC.
P.O. Box 263
Littleton, Colorado 80160-0263

Library of Congress Cataloging-in-Publication Data

Wynar, Bohdan S.
    Introduction to cataloging and classification.

    (Library science text series)
    Bibliography: p. 597
    Includes index.
    1. Cataloging. 2. Anglo-American cataloguing rules.
3. Classification--Books. I. Taylor, Arlene G.,
1941-   . II. Title.
Z693.W94   1985   025.3   85-23147
ISBN 0-87287-512-1
ISBN 0-87287-485-0 (pbk.)

Libraries Unlimited books are bound with Type II nonwoven material that
meets and exceeds National Association of State Textbook Administrators'
Type II nonwoven material specifications Class A through E.

Preface to the Seventh Edition

During the course of its six previous editions, this text has become widely known and used both as an introductory text for library science students and as a handy reference volume for practicing catalog librarians. In this seventh edition I have attempted to maintain the previously set standard for quality, accuracy, and timeliness.

Much has changed in the world of bibliographic control since the publication of the sixth edition in 1980. Cataloging via computer using the MARC format has become commonplace in all sizes and types of libraries—not just in academic libraries. Online catalogs are becoming more common. AACR 2 has been implemented, and the changes it brought have been, for the most part, absorbed. The controversy over closing card catalogs has died down as it has become apparent that closing card catalogs is the natural outgrowth of opening online catalogs. The *Library of Congress Subject Headings* (*LCSH*), ninth edition, has been published and is about to be superseded by the tenth edition. *Sears List of Subject Headings* is in its twelfth edition. The *Dewey Decimal Classification* is being supplemented with new schedules for a few notations at a time instead of waiting for a new edition to implement new schedules. New editions of several volumes of the LC classification schedules have been published. New filing rules have been published by both the American Library Association and the Library of Congress. Research into use of online catalogs has given us new insights about the importance of a subject approach to library materials, which has spurred new developments in the area of subject analysis. All of these changes, and more, have been incorporated into or have had an influence upon this edition.

In part I the chapters have been updated and examples have been expanded to include records in MARC format and displays from online catalogs. Part II, "Description and Access," no longer quotes heavily from *AACR 2*. Instead, the rules are explained and discussed. Part II now has fewer chapters than did part II in the sixth edition. Discussion of the rules for cataloging cartographic materials, manuscripts, music, sound recordings, motion pictures, graphic materials, machine-readable data files, and realia are combined into one chapter because of the great amount of repetition from chapter to chapter for each separate type of material. Examples of the different forms are still given, and problems peculiar to given types of material are still discussed. Also in part II the published revisions to AACR 2 are taken into account, and the many LC rule interpretations are discussed and illustrated. In addition, MARC coding information is given with many rules, and there are examples of fully coded MARC format records for each type of material.

Part III,. "Subject Analysis," is somewhat rearranged from what it was in the sixth edition. Chapter 15 is new. It contains a general introduction to subject analysis as a whole, including aspects of both classificatory and verbal approaches. An effort has been made to concentrate in part III on the fact that this text is intended to be, as titled, an introduction. Therefore, some of the more in-depth discussions of classification theory have been omitted. This is evident in chapter 16, "Classification of Library Materials," for example, although because the concept of faceting is entering more and more into subject analysis, a discussion of it is included in this chapter. The discussion of Universal Decimal Classification is completely updated and has been moved to chapter 17 with discussion of Dewey Decimal Classification, because these systems are so closely related. Discussion of LC Classification is also completely updated. There is a new chapter, "Creation of Complete Call Numbers." This is an effort to reflect the reality that "cuttering" is separate from the process of classification, and cuttering systems do not have to be tied to any particular classification scheme. The discussion of other classification schemes has been shortened, again reflecting the introductory nature of this textbook. (Those who wish a more extended treatment of these schemes should keep a copy of the sixth edition at hand.) However, because of the importance of special classification schemes in special libraries, an introduction to them has been added.

The verbal analysis section of part III remains structurally the same but reflects considerable updating. Because of many changes in LC subject heading policy, there is much new material in chapter 22. Even though the tenth edition of *LCSH* is anticipated within a year of publication of this text, the policies discussed will not be too out-of-date because of the use of the latest additions and changes to LCSH and use of the LC policy manual in writing this chapter. The *Sears* chapter has been updated to reflect the twelfth edition. Much new material replaces outdated material in the discussion of other types of verbal analysis.

Part IV, "Organization," is largely rewritten to reflect the tremendous changes that have come with automation. New material is given about networks and online systems. The new filing rules from ALA and LC required almost complete rewriting of that chapter. A new interest in authority work and advances in automated authority control, along with the new concepts brought about by online catalogs, are reflected in the chapter on catalog management.

A final change in this edition is worth noting here. A section called "Suggested Reading" has been added to each chapter. It is hoped the suggestions will assist those who wish to learn more about a particular topic.

There are a number of people whose assistance I wish to acknowledge. First, I would like to acknowledge the work done on the subject analysis and catalog management sections of the sixth edition by Jeanne Osborn. Although rapid change has dated some of her material, much of it is still in use in this edition.

Dr. Hans H. Wellisch, professor at the College of Library and Information Services, University of Maryland, provided immeasurable assistance in the revision of the subject analysis section of the text. Many of the suggestions for reorganization were his. In addition Dr. Wellisch wrote the following sections: the introductory paragraph to "Library Classification," page 369; "Faceted Classification," pages 372-374; "Universal Decimal Classification (UDC)," pages 399-401; "Special Classification Schemes," pages 441-444; "The NEPHIS Indexing System," pages 515-516; and "Automatic Indexing Methods," pages 516-520.

Professors of cataloging and classification were invited to make suggestions for this edition, and a number responded. Not all of these suggestions could be taken because some were in direct opposition to each other! But every suggestion was thoughtfully considered, and many were followed. Those who wrote and whose comments are greatly appreciated are Ann Allan, Associate Professor, School of Library Science, Kent State University; Esther G. Bierbaum, Assistant Professor, School of Library Science, University of Iowa; Larry G. Chrisman, Assistant Professor, Department of Library, Media and Information Studies, University of South Florida; Richard J. Hyman, Professor, Graduate School of Library and Information Studies, Queens College; Diane Podell, Adjunct Assistant Professor, Graduate School of Library and Information Studies, Queens College; Ted Samore, Professor, School of Library and Information Science, University of Wisconsin—Milwaukee; Mary Ellen Soper, Assistant Professor, Graduate School of Library and Information Science, University of Washington; and Francis J. Witty, Professor, Graduate Department of Library and Information Science, Catholic University of America.

I would like also to acknowledge the assistance of two people who answered many questions: Mary K. D. Pietris, Chief, Subject Cataloging Division, Library of Congress, who answered questions about LC practice; and Richard P. Smiraglia, Associate Professor and Music Catalog Librarian, University of Illinois at Urbana-Champaign, who taught me all I know about music cataloging.

OCLC's permission to reproduce MARC format records from the OCLC system is greatly appreciated.

I would like especially to thank Bohdan S. Wynar for his confidence in me in choosing me to complete this edition, and for his encouragement, advice, and patience throughout a project that took much longer than either of us anticipated.

I thank my children, Deborah and Jonathan, for their patience and understanding during the many hours that Mom spent seemingly glued to her desk or to the computer.

Finally, I wish to express appreciation to the editorial and production staffs of Libraries Unlimited for their valuable assistance.

September 1985   Arlene G. Taylor

Contents

Part I
INTRODUCTION

Part II
DESCRIPTION AND ACCESS

**Part III
SUBJECT ANALYSIS**

Part IV
ORGANIZATION

      Cataloging Routines...581
          Use of Work Forms, 582; Descriptive Cataloging, 584;
          Assigning Call Numbers, 584; Assigning Subject
          Headings, 585; Card Catalog Maintenance, 585;
          Maintenance of Other Types of Catalogs, 586;
          Reproducing Catalog Cards, 586; Reclassification
          and Recataloging, 586; Closing Card Catalogs, 587
      Notes..588
      Suggested Reading..590

      Cataloging and Classification Aids.........................591

      Bibliography 597

      Glossary of Selected Terms and Abbreviations...............601

      Author/Title/Subject Index................................615

Part I
INTRODUCTION

1
Principles of Cataloging

The purposes of this chapter are to introduce the basic concepts of cataloging and to provide a preliminary discussion of descriptive cataloging. The first section of the basic concepts part of this chapter defines some basic terms. The next section, "Characteristics of a Catalog," describes the differences between library catalogs and bibliographies and/or indexes. The physical formats and characteristic qualities of various types of catalogs are compared. This is followed by an examination of the concept of the unit record, with examples. The discussion of basic concepts of cataloging continues with a discussion of the ways to arrange entries in a catalog. Finally, there is a discussion of the purposes of a catalog.

The second part of this chapter serves as a basic introduction to descriptive cataloging. After a definition of descriptive cataloging and an explanation of its purpose, there is a section on how to examine the parts of an item that are essential to a catalog description—that is, how to read "technically" the item to be cataloged. The chief source of information and its component parts—the title proper and its various forms, the statement of responsibility, the edition, and the publication and distribution information—are all defined and described. This is an extremely important section, because it contains many technical definitions that are needed for an understanding of descriptive cataloging rules. The next section discusses the form of the catalog record and its eight separate parts: heading, body of the entry, physical description, series, notes, standard number, tracing, and call number. The last section of this first chapter is a preliminary introduction to the formats to be followed in typing catalog cards or creating MARC records.

BASIC CONCEPTS

DEFINITIONS

In order to provide access to the holdings of a library, an index or list of the materials in the collection must be maintained. In libraries the principal index or list of available materials is called the catalog. A catalog is a list of books, maps, coins, stamps, sound recordings, or materials in any other medium that constitute a collection. Its prime purpose is to record, describe, and index the holdings of a specific collection. The collection may be private or it may represent the resources of a museum or of a library. Cataloging is the process of preparing a catalog, or of preparing bibliographic records that will become entries in a catalog.

Why prepare catalogs? Catalogs are necessary whenever a collection grows too large to be remembered item for item. A small private library or a classroom library will have little need for a formal catalog; the user can recall each book, sound recording, map, or other such item by author, title, or subject. When such a collection becomes a little larger, an informal arrangement, such as grouping the items by subject categories, provides access to them. But when a collection becomes too large for such a simple approach, a formal record is necessary.

The use of a collection of any sort large enough to be cataloged depends upon the system by which each item is primarily identified in the catalog. In an art museum exhibition catalog the artist's name and the number assigned to each painting are of utmost importance. A catalog of musical phonograph records will be itemized by composer and often by performer. Ordinarily, a collection of books will be listed by author; if the author is unknown, listing will be by title, or by any other information that provides positive identification. Such information is called an entry.

In a library, each entry in the catalog is the representation of a bibliographic record at a particular point in the catalog. A bibliographic record is a transcription of the complete cataloging information for any item. The purpose of a bibliographic record is 1) to provide all the information necessary to describe an item accurately both physically and intellectually in order to distinguish it from every other item, and 2) to provide its location in the collection. When such a record is available in the catalog at each of several access points (e.g., author, title, subject), these entries then become an index to the collection. Thus, in the catalog the patron can find two important pieces of information: whether the library has the item wanted, and, if so, where it is located in the collection.

CHARACTERISTICS OF A CATALOG

Certain characteristics and functions of library catalogs distinguish them from other different but closely related forms of library tools – bibliographies and indexes. A bibliography, in simple terms, lists the literature on one subject – not only books but sometimes also pamphlets, articles in periodicals, documents, or other material not revealed in the ordinary library catalog. It may list the works of a certain author, describing all editions of those works. In contrast, a library catalog lists, arranges, and describes the holdings of a specific library or collection. The main functions of a library catalog are to enable a patron to determine

1) whether the library contains a certain item,
2) which works by a particular author are in the collection,
3) which editions of a particular work the library has, and
4) what materials the library has on a particular subject.

The rules for making catalog entries are, in general, standard rules that have national and, to a large extent, international acceptance. The current standard is the *Anglo-American Cataloguing Rules*, second edition, referred to hereinafter as *AACR 2*.[1] On the other hand, descriptive bibliographical practice fol-lows a variety of codes for recording authors' names, for capitalization and punctuation, etc.; this is because the bibliographer's concern is not so much with choice and form of entry as with a critical appraisal of the history of the edition and the format of the work.

A library catalog frequently is described as an "index." It may be more exact to say that a catalog leads the reader to a particular item in the collection, showing the user the location of the item, its physical description, and its subject content. (More detailed discussion of the problem of revealing the intellectual content of an item will be found in the chapters on subject headings.) An index, on the other hand, exhibits the analyzed contents of a single item, of the items in a certain class or collection, or of one or more periodicals, reports, or documents. The purpose of an index is to show in what particular book, periodical, document, etc., and at what specific place the information on a certain topic or subject can be found.

TYPES OF CATALOG ACCORDING TO FORMAT

Presently, the library catalog exists in one of several physical formats: book catalog, card catalog, microform catalog, or online computer catalog. The printed book or book catalog is the oldest type known in the United States; it was used by many American libraries as the most common form of catalog until the late 1800s. For example, the report of the Bureau of Education in 1876 gives a list of 1,010 printed book catalogs, 382 of them published from 1870 to 1876. Because the book catalogs were rather expensive to produce and quickly became outdated, they were gradually replaced by card catalogs. In a survey of 58 typical American libraries undertaken in 1893, 43 libraries had complete card catalogs and 13 had printed book catalogs with card supplements.[2] Thus, for many years book catalogs were out of favor in American libraries. It was only with more modern, cheaper methods of printing and with the advent of automation for quicker cumulation that book catalogs again became popular with certain types of libraries. An example of a book catalog produced by more modern production techniques is the Library of Congress *Catalog of Books Represented by Library of Congress Printed Cards*, known since 1956 as the *National Union Catalog*. This catalog is published monthly, with quarterly, semiannual, annual, and quinquennial cumulations. The *National Union Catalog* for many years was produced by photographic reduction of pre-existing catalog cards; hence, it was a by-product of a card catalog. A similar technique is used by a number of commercial publishers (e.g., G. K. Hall), who reproduce card catalogs of certain libraries in a book catalog format.

Beginning in the 1950s, a new type of book catalog appeared, based on the use of computers. These computer-produced catalogs, which use machine-readable cataloging records, vary widely in format, typography, extent of bibliographical detail, and pattern of updating. One example of a computer-produced book catalog is the *Current Catalog* of the National Library of Medicine, started in 1966. It is published biweekly, with quarterly, semiannual, and annual cumulations. The Library of Congress also now publishes its book catalog series via computer. Other examples are the New York Public Library Catalogs and several county system catalogs, e.g., Tulsa (Okla.) City-County Library System.

The card catalog is the library catalog most often found in the United States. Each entry is prepared on a standard 7.5x12.5 cm. card (roughly 3x5 inches); these cards are then filed, usually in alphabetical order, in trays. Entries on cards in the past were most often prepared by photo-reproduction of a printed or typed original. However, they are increasingly being computer-produced from machine-readable catalog records.

Microform catalogs have become much more popular with the development of computer-output microform (COM). COM catalogs are produced in either microfilm [i.e., "a length of film bearing a number of microimages in linear array" (*AACR 2*, p. 567)] or microfiche [i.e., "a sheet of film bearing a number of microimages in a two-dimensional array" (*AACR 2*, p. 567)]. It is feasible with this form of catalog to provide a completely integrated new catalog every three months or so, rather than providing supplements to be used with a main catalog. COM catalogs are possible even for small libraries, through commercial vendors to whom the library may send its new bibliographic records. The vendor processes the new bibliographic records, integrates them with the particular library's existing catalog and sends new COM catalogs at specified intervals. Many libraries now have COM catalogs, and there is a voluminous amount of literature on the subject.

The online computer catalog is still in the developmental stages. Bibliographic records stored in the computer memory are printed on a video screen (Cathode-Ray Tube, once commonly referred to as a CRT, but now usually called simply, a "terminal") in response to a request from a user. Entries may comprise the full bibliographic record or only parts of it, depending on the system and/or the desires of the user. Such systems are still costly, and only a few are fully operational as a "catalog," although several are working well as "finding lists" for acquisitions of recent years. An example of this is the Library Circulation System (LCS) of the University of Illinois System. A more detailed discussion of developments in computer cataloging is given in this text in the chapters on networks and online systems and on catalog management.

QUALITIES OF CATALOG FORMAT

An effective catalog in any format should possess certain qualities that will allow it to be easily consulted and maintained. If it is too difficult, too cumbersome, or too expensive, it is virtually useless. Hence the following comparative criteria exist for judging a catalog:

1) A catalog should be flexible and up-to-date. A library's collection is constantly changing. Since the catalog is a record of what is available in that library, entries should be added or removed as books are added to or discarded from the collection. The card catalog is totally flexible. Cards can be easily added to or removed from the trays whenever necessary. Changes can be made on cards and they can be refiled. However, especially in large libraries, filing backlogs often accumulate, resulting in long delays in entering current or changed records into the catalog. Book and COM catalogs are inflexible in

that once they have been printed, they cannot admit additions or deletions except in supplements or new editions of the catalog. On the other hand, because they are computer-produced, they can provide much more flexibility in making changes in existing entries. One instruction can be made to change many entries, while with a card catalog, each change must be made by hand. In addition, computer-produced catalogs can be more current in situations where large filing backlogs have existed. The online catalog is the most flexible and current. Additions, deletions, and changes can be made at any time, and the results are often instantly available to the user, or at least are available by the next day.

2) A catalog should be constructed so that all entries can be quickly and easily found. This is a matter of labeling, filing, and, in the case of online catalogs, simple and clear access codes. So far as the card catalog is concerned, the contents of each tray must be identified to the extent that a patron who wants to locate, for example, the works of Charles Dickens can find the Dickens entries easily. Labeling of each tray is essential; the patron must know exactly what part of the alphabet is contained in each one. Within the trays themselves, arrangement of entries must be such that items are not overlooked because the filing is not alphabetical, and guide cards should be sufficiently plentiful to identify coverage. Book catalogs are usually labeled on the spine, like encyclopedias. Often they have guides at the top of each page, indicating what entries are covered there. Microfilm catalogs typically are stored in readers that are equipped with alphabetic index strips designed to get the user to the desired part of the alphabet. Microfiche catalogs have at the top of each sheet of fiche eye-readable labels that indicate the part of the alphabet covered. Typically, each sheet of fiche has a microimage index in one corner that tells in which cross section of the fiche particular parts of the alphabet are found. Filing arrangement in computer-produced catalogs is not the same as in traditionally-filed card catalogs because of the difficulty of programming computers to arrange according to traditional library filing rules. As a result, traditional rules have been re-evaluated, and new filing rules closely resemble computer filing rules; but few card catalogs have been refiled according to the new rules.

Entries are located in online catalogs in a variety of ways. In some the computer must be told whether an author, title, or subject search is desired. Some systems, also, require the user to construct "search keys" made up of combinations of letters and/or words. For example, a title search key may consist of the first three letters of the first word that is not an article plus the first letter of each of the next three words. In other systems one can enter as much of the title, author, or subject as seems useful, starting at the left of the entry as it would appear in a card catalog. Still other systems allow users to input only the words they remember in any order, and the system searches for all records containing all the words input. These methods all have disadvantages, and it will take more time and experience before we know the best means of providing access to online catalogs.

3) A catalog should be economically prepared and maintained. The catalog that can be prepared most inexpensively and with greatest attention to currency has obvious advantages.

4)   A catalog should be compact. It should not only take up the least possible amount of space, but it should also be easily removable for consultation and prolonged study if possible. The catalog most closely fitting this description is the microfiche catalog, although its use requires a reader. With the development of small, portable microfiche readers, such catalogs could conceivably be taken to individual homes or offices. Microfilm catalogs take up little space, but readers are not portable. Because only one person at a time can use a microfilm catalog, multiple copies (including multiple readers) are usually required. Book catalogs are compact and can be removed for private study, but again, multiple copies may be required in a single location. An online catalog is as compact as the terminal used to gain access to it and can be accessible from any location having terminal access to the memory bank containing the catalog. It is becoming increasingly common for a library user to gain access to online catalogs via dial access from office or home using a personal computer and a modem. The card catalog is the least compact, and it cannot be removed for private consultation.

In summary, the following observations can be made about the major types of catalog:

Cards for the card catalog are easy to prepare and relatively inexpensive. The chief virtue of the card catalog is its flexibility. Though it is not compact and trays cannot ordinarily be removed for long intensive study, it should be remembered that many people can use it at the same time, as long as they do not need the same drawer.

The book catalog is expensive to prepare unless numerous copies of the catalog are required; library systems that need multiple copies will find the book catalog less costly than the card catalog. Entries can be found quickly in the book catalog, and it is compact, easy to store, and easy to handle. However, it lacks flexibility.

The microform catalog is much less expensive than the book catalog, and there is evidence that its maintenance is less expensive than for the card catalog, although the initial investment in catalog conversion to machine-readable form is high. It is compact and easy to store. It can be flexible if the library can afford to run new cumulations often.

The online catalog is the most flexible and current. It is also compact. Its entries can be found quickly. However, it is quite expensive, a drawback that may be overcome with continued development.

THE UNIT RECORD

The Library of Congress did not begin to sell its standard printed catalog cards to libraries until 1901. Before that, individual libraries had to devise their own sets of cards to identify and describe the contents of each book. Duplicating machines were comparatively rudimentary and very expensive; therefore, the cataloger usually typed the card information or wrote it out in longhand. Obviously, under these conditions, it was costly to duplicate every necessary detail on each card in the set. For the sake of economy, only one card (the main entry card) was likely to carry complete bibliographic information. All other cards (secondary entry cards) were highly abbreviated.

When the Library of Congress decided to print cards and to sell them, it discovered that the most economical method was to print all cards of one set exactly alike. In this way it was not necessary to have one set for main entry and other sets for each other entry. This was the genesis of the unit card system of cataloging; encouraged by the development of duplicating machines, this system became almost universal in American libraries. With the recent advent of book, COM, and online catalogs, however, the economical advantage of having a unit record reproduced at each entry point has been reversed. It is more economical to print only abbreviated entries at all but one entry point.

In a card catalog, the unit card system of providing multiple entries for an item is one in which a basic card, complete with all cataloging information, is used as a unit for identical duplication of all other necessary cards. After the reproduction of the unit card, all that is needed is the addition of appropriate added entries at the top of each card. This system has an important advantage for the patron: no matter what card is consulted—author, title, or subject—complete descriptive and bibliographical information for the item will be found. In most computer-produced catalogs, as already mentioned, abbreviated records are printed at all but one entry point. In printed catalogs, the fullest record is usually the main entry; in online catalogs, the user usually must ask for the full bibliographic record from whatever entry is found. In either case, finding complete information often requires two searches.

In an online catalog the unit record is fully coded according to the United States Machine Readable Cataloging Formats (USMARC, usually referred to simply as MARC). "User-friendly" versions of this record (usually resembling catalog card format) are constructed and displayed in response to a user's request. The form displayed is not stored in the computer's memory, however. Only the MARC record is stored—the ultimate unit record.

The main entry is the basic catalog entry; it is usually the author entry, and it ordinarily gives all the information that identifies the work. Generally, it carries a record of all secondary entries under which the work is entered in the catalog. This record is called the tracing, and it is an essential part of the system. The set of entries may have to be changed after it has been entered into the catalog or it may be necessary to remove it altogether. The set cannot be changed or removed unless all the entries of the set can be located. The tracing, usually found at the bottom of a printed main entry record (or sometimes on the reverse if in card format), gives this information. The record of secondary entries on a MARC record serves the function of the tracing that identifies all secondary entries that have been assigned to the record. But it is not necessary as a tool to locate those secondary entries, since there is only one copy of a MARC record stored in the system.

Secondary access points, or added entries, are any entries other than the main entry. They may reflect joint authors, editors, illustrators, translators, performers, etc.; titles; subjects; or any other information that is sufficiently important or memorable that the patron might use it for searching. Obviously, the number of added entries will vary from item to item. In a printed catalog there are usually at least four entries for every item: a main entry (author), a shelflist (for the library records), a title (added) entry, and a subject (added) entry. However, added title entries may not be made for such titles as *Works*, or *Selected Works*, because these are not distinctive enough to warrant a separate entry. Also, some items do not receive subject added entries (e.g., fiction, in many libraries). The topic of subject added entries is discussed under subject headings in the chapter on "Verbal Subject Analysis." In addition to the usual four entries for each item, added entries for subject, joint authors, etc., are made as needed. Some items may require seven or eight added entries; some may need just one or none at all.

There are three basic types of library catalog access points: main entry and added entry (both of which are prepared by descriptive cataloging rules), and subject added entry (prepared by subject cataloging procedures). In some catalogs the call number is also an access point — in online catalogs, for example, or in libraries where the shelflist is available to the public. In most cases the main entry is the author entry. For example, a copy of *The Logic of Aspect: An Axiomatic Approach*, by Antony Galton (*see* Figs. 1.1-1.2) will have as its main entry Galton, Antony. The title, *The Logic of Aspect: An Axiomatic Approach*, is an added entry. It describes the book by providing further identification apart from the author, whose name may not always be recalled. "Logic" is a subject added entry for this book; it describes the intellectual content of the book. When this subject entry is filed with similar ones, it indicates one of many possible items on a single topic. It must be remembered that a patron may not know the author or title of a book or other type of material on a certain subject. In such a case the only approach is to seek out information by subject. Another subject of this book is "Languages — Philosophy."

Figures 1.1-1.3 give the transcription of a title page of a book, a unit catalog record for that book as it might appear in a printed catalog, and a copy of the MARC record for the book as it appears on OCLC (Online Computer Library Center, one of the national data bases heavily used for cataloging via computer).

Fig. 1.1. Transcription of title page of a book.

THE LOGIC OF ASPECT

AN AXIOMATIC APPROACH

ANTONY GALTON

CLARENDON PRESS • OXFORD
1984

Fig. 1.2. The unit record—serves as the main entry record.

BC   Galton, Antony.
71   The logic of aspect : an axiomatic approach / Antony
.G33   Galton. – Oxford [Oxfordshire] : Clarendon Press,
1984   1984.
                 viii, 160 p. ; 23 cm. – (Clarendon library of logic
            and philosophy)

                 Bibliography: p. [157]-158.
                 Includes index.
                 ISBN 0-19-824430-4

                 1. Logic. 2. Languages–Philosophy. I. Title.
            II. Series.

Fig. 1.3. Unit record in MARC format.

(Symbols indicating the beginning of a subfield code
vary with different printers. Below the symbol appears
as "$." On an OCLC terminal it appears as "‡.")

```
OCLC: 10298901      Rec stat: p Entrd: 831220        Used: 850201
Type: a Bib lvl: m Govt pub:    Lang:  eng Source:   Illus:
Repr:    Enc lvl:   Conf pub: 0 Ctry:  enk Dat tp: s M/F/B: 10
Indx: 1 Mod rec:    Festschr: 0 Cont: b
Desc: a Int lvl:   Dates: 1984,
   1 010       83-25138
   2 040       DLC $c DLC
   3 020       0198244304 : $c L18.00 ($35.95 U.S.)
   4 039 0     2 $b 3 $c 3 $d 3 $e 3
   5 050 0     BC71 $b .G33 1984
   6 082 0     160 $2 19
   7 090       $b
   8 049       IVEA
   9 100 10    Galton, Antony.
  10 245 14    The logic of aspect : $b an axiomatic approach / $c Antony
Galton.
  11 260 0     Oxford [Oxfordshire] : $b Clarendon Press, $c 1984.
  12 300       viii, 160 p. ; $c 23 cm.
  13 440 0     Clarendon library of logic and philosophy
  14 504       Bibliography: p. [157]-158.
  15 500       Includes index.
  16 650 0     Logic.
  17 650 0     Languages $x Philosophy.
```

In a printed catalog, a copy of the unit record shown in Fig. 1.2 would be made for each access point listed in the tracing, and that access point would be added at the top of the copy so that it could be entered in the catalog at that point. Fig. 1.4 shows how the subject added entry would look.

Fig. 1.4. Subject heading added to unit record.

LANGUAGES--PHILOSOPHY

BC   Galton, Antony.
71   The logic of aspect : an axiomatic approach / Antony
 G33   Galton. -- Oxford [Oxfordshire] : Clarendon Press,
1984   1984.
              viii, 160 p. ; 23 cm. -- (Clarendon library of logic
          and philosophy)

              Bibliography: p. [157]-158.
              Includes index.
              ISBN 0-19-824430-4

              1. Logic. 2. Languages--Philosophy. I. Title.
          II. Series.

On the shelflist used for the inventory record, librarians make notations
(depending on individual practice) indicating number of copies, price,
accession number (if used), date when a copy was noted missing from the
shelves, etc. Fig. 1.5 illustrates such a use.

Fig. 1.5. Unit record used as shelflist.

BC   Galton, Antony.
71   The logic of aspect : an axiomatic approach / Antony
.G33   Galton. -- Oxford [Oxfordshire] : Clarendon Press,
1984   1984.
              viii, 160 p. ; 23 cm. -- (Clarendon library of logic
          and philosophy)

c.1 main Bibliography: p. [157]-158.
c.2 lit.   Includes index.
              ISBN 0-19-824430-4

              1. Logic. 2. Languages--Philosophy. I. Title.
          II. Series.

The label of a sound disc is used as the chief source for cataloging
information regarding the disc in the way that a title page is used for a book.
Figs. 1.6-1.8 show such a label and the unit record for that work as it would
appear in a printed catalog and in MARC format.

Fig. 1.6. Transcription of the label of a sound disc.

Fig. 1.7. The unit record (main entry).

M   Diamond, Neil
1527   Jonathan Livingston Seagull [sound recording] / Neil
D52   Diamond. -- New York, N.Y. : Columbia, p1973.
          1 sound disc (42 min., 35 sec.) : 33 1/3 rpm, stereo. ;
          12 in. + 1 pamphlet ([8] p. : ill. (some col.) ;
        31 cm.)

        Columbia: KS32550.
        Original motion picture sound track.
        Instrumental music, and songs sung by the
    composer.
        Contents: Prologue -- Be -- Flight of the gull -- Dear Father --
    Skybird -- Lonely looking sky -- The odyssey -- Anthem -- Be --
    Skybird -- Dear Father -- Be.

        1. Moving-picture music--Excerpts. 2. Music, Popular
    (Songs, etc.)--United States. I. Jonathan Livingston Seagull.
    Motion picture. II. Title.

Fig. 1.8. The unit record in MARC format.

```
OCLC: 8687227          Rec stat: n Entrd: 820813          Used: 850103
Type: j Bib lvl: m Lang:   eng Source:    Accomp mat: z
Repr:     Enc lvl: I Ctry:   nyu Dat tp: s MEBE: 1
          Mod rec: e Comp:   mp Format: n Prts: n
Desc: a Int lvl:     LTxt:   n    Dates: 1973,
    1 010       73-763017
    2 040       DLC $c SPP $d SPP
    3 007       s $b d $c r $d b $e s $f m $g e $h n $i n
    4 020        $c $8.98
    5 028 02    KS32550 $b Columbia
    6 043       n-us---
    7 050       [M1527]
    8 090        $b
    9 049       IVEA
   10 100 10    Diamond, Neil.
   11 245 10    Jonathan Livingston Seagull $h sound recording / Neil
Diamond.
   12 260 0     New York, N.Y. : $b Columbia, $c p1973.
   13 300       1 sound disc (42 min., 35 sec.) : $b 33 1/3 rpm, stereo. ;
$c 12 in. + $e 1 pamphlet ([8] p. : ill. (some col.) ; 31 cm.).
   14 500       Original motion picture sound track.
   15 511 0     Instrumental music, and songs sung by the composer.
   16 505 0     Prologue -- Be -- Flight of the gull -- Dear Father --
Skybird -- Lonely looking sky -- The odyssey -- Anthem -- Be --
Skybird -- Dear Father -- Be.
   17 650  0    Moving-picture music $x Excerpts.
   18 650  0    Music, Popular (Songs, etc.) $z United States.
   19 730 01    Jonathan Livingston Seagull. $h Motion picture.
```

ARRANGEMENT OF ENTRIES IN A CATALOG

A printed catalog (unlike an online catalog) must be arranged according to some definite plan. Depending on the subject and scope of the collection, many arrangements are possible. But no matter which one is used, it should cover the contents of the collection and guide the person who consults it to these contents.

Printed catalogs are ordinarily arranged according to one of three systems: dictionary, divided, or classified. The differences between them lie in the arrangement and filing of the entries.

Dictionary Catalogs

In the dictionary arrangement of entries, widely used in American libraries, all the entries—main, added, and subject—are combined, word by word, into one alphabetical file. This arrangement is said to be simple; undoubtedly it is, in the sense that only one file need be consulted. As the library grows, however, the dictionary arrangement becomes cumbersome and complex because all entries are interfiled. The problem becomes partly one of filing (are books by Charles Dickens, for example, filed before those about him?) and partly one of dispersion. The subject of "industrial relations" has many aspects. How can all these aspects be located if they are entered under headings from "A" for "arbitration" to "W" for "wages"? Two primary justifications are offered in favor of the dictionary arrangement: most patrons seek material on one aspect of a subject rather than upon the broad subject itself, and patrons are provided with ample *see* and *see also* references, which direct them to other aspects of their subjects.

Divided Catalogs

In the 1930s the realization that dictionary catalogs were becoming more and more complex led to a modification of the dictionary arrangement. The result was the divided catalog, which, in its most common form, is in reality two catalogs: one for main and added entries other than subject; the other for subject entries only. The divided catalog permits a simpler filing scheme than does the dictionary catalog. Thus it is easier to consult, although the problem of scattered subjects still exists. There is a further complication implicit in this arrangement. The patron must determine whether an author or title entry or a subject entry is wanted before knowing which part of the catalog must be checked. When this divided approach is used, books about Dickens and books by Dickens are not filed together in the catalog. Patrons will need some guidance and education in this matter.

There are a few libraries that use other types of divided catalogs, such as the three-way divided catalog consisting of separate sections for author, title, and subject entries. Although this system may simplify the filing of cards, it can be even more confusing for a patron than the two-way divided catalog. In this arrangement, entries for books by Dickens will be filed under Dickens' name in the author catalog, the titles of his individual novels will be filed in the title catalog, and books about Dickens will be filed in the subject catalog.

Another type of two-way divided catalog is a name/title catalog and a topical subject catalog. In such a divided catalog, names and titles that are used even as subject headings are filed in the name/title section. This type of divided catalog allows all the material by and about an author or a title to be filed together. Thus, to continue our previous example, books by and books about Dickens would be filed together in the same catalog. This system is potentially less confusing to the patron than any other form of divided catalog.

Classified Catalogs

The classified catalog has the longest history of all. Many American libraries used this form before they changed to the more popular dictionary form. It is based upon some special system of classification. For example, the shelflist, a record of the holdings of a library arranged by classification number, is a classified catalog of a kind. But in a true classified catalog, a bibliographic record may be entered under as many classification numbers as apply to its contents, not under just one number as in a shelflist. In addition, the shelflist lacks an alphabetical subject index, which a true classified catalog has. The major advantage of a classified catalog is that because it uses symbols or numbers it can keep up with changing terminology and thus be up to date. Perhaps its greatest disadvantage is that it is constructed on a particular classification scheme (even though this was an advantage as noted above). Since many patrons are not familiar with classification numbers, they would need special assistance when consulting the classified catalog. However, some fields – particularly the sciences – can make good use of such a catalog, inasmuch as science changes so rapidly, since the classified catalog is flexible and can be easily updated.

Classified catalogs are also of value in locations where the patrons may speak one of two or more languages. In such a case, an alphabetical subject index may be made in each language. In Quebec, for example, where both English and French are spoken, there would be one major classified catalog with French and English indexes.

Classified catalogs are actually only the subject part of a divided catalog. They must be accompanied by an author/title catalog.

PURPOSES OF A CATALOG

The multiple access point catalog, in whatever form it appears, records the holdings of a library in such a way as to offer the user a variety of approaches to the information sought. The objectives of this type of catalog as stated by Charles A. Cutter in his *Rules for a Dictionary Catalog* are still valid today, although modern practice indicates that they are incomplete. These objectives, first formulated in 1904, are as follows:

Objects

1) To enable a person to find a book when one of the following is known:
   a) The author
   b) The title
   c) The subject

2) To show what the library has
   d) By a given author
   e) On a given subject
   f) In a given kind of literature

3) To assist in the choice of a book
   g) As to the edition (bibliographically)
   h) As to its character (literary or topical).

Means

1) Author entry with the necessary references (for a and d)
2) Title entry or title reference (for b)
3) Subject entry, cross references, and classed subject table (for c and e)
4) Form entry and language entry (for f)
5) Edition and imprint, with notes when necessary (for g)
6) Notes (for h)[3]

Amplification of Cutter's Objects and Means

To conform to modern practice, the first objective needs to be rephrased as follows: To enable a person to find any intellectual creation whether issued in a print or nonprint format. Cutter's first object is inadequate even for printed materials inasmuch as "book" does not unambiguously encompass "periodical," "serial," or "pamphlet." In addition, as stated, the objective makes no provision for audiovisual materials (e.g., "filmstrip," "tape recording").

Cutter's object "e" is too simplistic. Rephrased, it should read "on given and related subjects." It is clearly a prime function of a dictionary catalog to guide patrons in using the system of subject headings that any particular library may have adopted. Cutter's apparent assumption that the user always has a clearly formulated "given" subject in mind is contrary to all observation of catalog users.

Cutter's objectives remained the primary statement of catalog principles until 1961, when the International Federation of Library Associations (IFLA) at the Paris Conference approved a statement about the purpose of an author/title catalog. It stated that the catalog should be an efficient instrument for ascertaining:

1) whether the library contains a particular book specified by:
   a) its author and title, *or*
   b) if no author is named in the book, its title alone, *or*
   c) if author and title are inappropriate or insufficient for identification, a suitable substitute for the title,

and 2) a) which works by a particular author *and*
   b) which editions of a particular work are in the library.[4]

These descriptions point out the dual functions that exist within the modern catalog causing it to be a finding list (see 1.a-c) for some purposes and a collocating device (see 2.a b) for others. The catalog is a finding list in that it can provide the user with the necessary access to an individual item, whether the user approaches the item by author, title, or subject. In this sense the catalog is a finding list made up of specific individual pieces of information. A simple type of finding list would be a list of the titles of all the books in a collection. In fact, the white pages of the telephone directory may be considered as a typical finding list. In 1936, Julia Pettee pointed out the meaning of the finding list theory:

> The identification of the literary unit and the attribution of author-
> ship in establishing the form of entry is so thoroughly ingrained in
> our catalogers [that] it may be a surprise to many to be told that
> these principles, in the long history of cataloging, are something
> very new and that they have not yet attained universal acceptance.
> The older working principle upon which all European rules have
> developed is that the catalog is a ready finding list for the particular
> book wanted, irrespective of its relation to any other book.[5]

A catalog constructed on this principle is efficient in showing whether or not a particular work by a certain author is in the collection. The deficiency is its failure to relate a particular work to other materials — that is, it does not fulfill functions 2.a-b stated above. The collocating (assembling) function provides means for bringing together in one place in a catalog all entries for like and closely related materials — e.g., for displaying together all the works of an author in the library collection. In 1977, Sally Hart McCallum discussed the meaning of the collocating function:

> Collocation is the arranging of elements in certain positions, particularly side by side. . . . It is usually found in the catalog in two forms: in the collocation of works of a single author, and in the collocation of editions of a work. The structure which this arrangement gives to the catalog helps to distinguish it from a simple list of items and extends the instrument's control over the documents in its domain.[6]

To achieve collocation, the main entry for a work must be in one "correct" form. Cataloging strictly from title pages, which is sufficient for a finding list, would result in scattering rather than collocating related works. For example, the works of an author writing under more than one name or using various forms of a name would not have the same main entry and would be filed in several different places in the catalog. The library dictionary catalog represents an attempt to combine both the finding list and collocating device principles in construction and arrangement of entries. The advantage of utilizing both features in one catalog is obvious; at the same time, however, it results in a complex instrument, difficult to construct and often frustrating to use. The function of the main entry, the choosing of this entry and the form to follow must be viewed in this relationship to basic properties of the catalog.

Several solutions are used to deal with this problem. Main entries may be arranged according to the form of the author's name as it appears on the title page, in which case the collocating of all works of the same author is achieved by using cross-references. The same approach may be used for titles. In this case, main entries are arranged according to the titles of the particular works; collocation of the various editions, translations, or literary forms of the same work is accomplished by using added entries.

The other method is to establish one "correct" form for an author's name, so that all publications by this author are automatically collocated in one place. Again, cross references are required to provide access from the form of name actually on the title page, or from variant forms widely known, for which some readers may search. In a similar manner, the title form is chosen according to the original, best known, or some other accepted uniform title; the result of this is that all editions, translations, etc., of the same work are automatically collocated in one place. In this case, references or added entries are provided for titles of the work that vary from the chosen heading.

Thus, a basic decision to be made, one of cataloging policy for the library, is whether uniform headings are to be adopted or headings are to follow the form of name and title as these appear on the title page of each work. *AACR 2* provides guidance in this matter; as can be seen from a study of rules for form of entry, *AACR 2* encourages uniform use of the author's name as commonly known, and of more uniform headings for certain entries. In either case, added entries and references of various types are essential if the objectives of the catalog are to be fulfilled. *AACR 2* consistently stresses that catalogers must consider added entries and references whenever a choice between two possible entries or forms of entry is necessary. The decision of how extensively to follow this practice is, of course, left to each individual library.

DESCRIPTION OF MATERIAL TO BE CATALOGED

DEFINITION AND PURPOSE OF DESCRIPTIVE CATALOGING

Descriptive cataloging is that phase of the cataloging process which is concerned with the identification and description of an item, the recording of this information in the form of a cataloging record, and the selection and formatting of access points—with the exception of subject access points. The term refers to the physical make-up of the item and to the responsibility for intellectual contents, without reference to its classification by subject or to the assignment of subject headings, both of which are the province of subject cataloging.

Identification and description are closely interrelated processes in descriptive cataloging. Identification consists of the choice of conventional elements, formulated by a set of rules that catalogers use to describe an item. When the cataloger has properly identified these conventions, they are described in a catalog record in such a fashion that the description is unique and can be applied to no other item in the collection.

What are the conventional elements that a cataloger tries to identify for the convenience of the patron? The majority of patrons will search for a specific item either by person(s) responsible for the contents or by title. This is universal. All catalogers, therefore, will ordinarily try to identify the person(s) responsible for the contents of an item and its title.

Many readers also wish to identify a particular edition of a work when there has been more than one; therefore, additional information must be added to the statements of title and responsibility. A particular edition may be identified by the number of the edition (e.g., 5th edition), the name of the edition (e.g., Student Edition), the name of the editor, the reviser, the illustrator, the translator, the performer, the producer, the publisher, the date of publication as well as the copyright date, or even the series of which the edition is a part. Even the size, the type or number of illustrations, or the extent of the item (e.g., number of pages of a book or number of frames of a microfiche) may be helpful information for a reader seeking a specific edition of a work.

TECHNICAL READING OF AN ITEM TO BE CATALOGED

In order to identify conventional elements of an item so that they can be described on a catalog record, it is necessary to know not only what to look for, but also how to look. Technical reading in this manner is scarcely the same as reading for information or for entertainment, when the entire item may be read, seen, or heard. Obviously, the cataloger will have no time for "reading" of this sort, and, therefore, must learn to read technically. Reading technically involves recognizing quickly certain devices peculiar to the particular type of item being cataloged. In this way, the cataloger can quickly determine what the item is about and how it can be described uniquely in such a way that this information can be passed on to the readers. The following discussion contains definitions useful to the cataloger in both descriptive cataloging and subject cataloging.

The first part of an item that the cataloger examines in detail is the chief source of information. This source varies according to the type of material. In books, manuscripts, printed music, and printed serials, it is the title page. In microforms and films it is the title frame. For sound recordings, it is the label and sometimes a container that is affixed to the item (e.g., cassette of a tape cassette). For cartographic and graphic materials and for three-dimensional artifacts and realia, the chief source of information is the object itself, including permanently affixed labels or unifying containers. If machine-readable data files have internal user labels, these are used as the chief source; otherwise accompanying printed documentation is used. In all these cases, the chief source of information may be absent for some reason, in which case cataloging rules prescribe alternate sources. But usually the chief source of information provides the most complete bibliographic information about the item: the author or other person responsible for the intellectual contents, the fullest form of the title, the name and/or number of the edition, the name of the publisher, distributor, etc., and the place and date of publication, distribution, etc.

The first element that the cataloger ordinarily notices is the title. The title from the chief source of information, which is generally the item's official title, is called the title proper; as such, it is used in all library records, in trade catalogs, and in bibliographies. It may or may not adequately describe the contents of the item. The book title, *A Short History of the United States*, is self-evident, but the title of the serial, *Toward Freedom*, needs an explanation. A glance through an issue will reveal that the serial discusses the development of new nations; this will be indicated as a subject heading on the catalog record.

In addition to the major part of the title, some items have secondary parts. The alternative title is introduced by "or" and was widely used in books published before the twentieth century. As in Gilbert and Sullivan's *Patience, or, Bunthorne's Bride*, it amplifies the title by telling the reader that "Patience," in this case, is a woman's name rather than the name of a specific virtue. The parallel title is the title proper written in another language or in another script. For instance, a bilingual book on snowmobiles in the Province of Quebec has its title proper in French, *La motoneige au Québec*, and its parallel title in English, *Snowmobiling in Quebec*. Other title information is often used to qualify the title proper. Such qualifications are often called subtitles. For example, the complete title of a tape cassette is *Behavior Control: The Psychologist as Manipulator*. "The Psychologist as Manipulator" is the subtitle. It explains the aspect of behavior control covered in the tape. There is also other title information that is not "subtitle" but does give further explanatory information. In the title, *Barbara Morgan Photography: Trisolini Gallery of Ohio University, Athens, Ohio, January 9-February 3, 1979*, the "other title" information tells where and when the show was held.

The title proper and other titles in the chief source of information, however, are not the only possible ones. Other titles exist, and the cataloger must note those that vary significantly from the title proper. When such titles are noted, the patron who knows a work only by a variant title can be directed to it. For example, Haydn's *Symphony 94 in G Major* is also known as the "Surprise Symphony"; many patrons would look for this popular form of the title instead of the title proper. Books may carry a cover title (i.e., title printed on the cover), binder's title (i.e., title lettered on the original spine of the book), or running title (i.e., title repeated at the top of each page or each alternate page of the book) that differs from the title proper. Sound recordings, motion pictures, or graphic materials may have titles on their containers that differ. Serials may have title variations on the cover or on an added title page.

The series title, however, is not a title variation, but indicates the series, if any, to which the item belongs. A series may be the work of one author, as in Will Durant's *The Story of Civilization*, which consists of several uniform volumes. This is called an author's series. A series may also be issued by a publisher who commissions several authors to write one or more volumes on a specified subject. Such is the case with the Rinehart *Rivers of America* series of many volumes. Or perhaps an author is not commissioned but submits a work that happens to fit into a category established by the publisher. Such is the case with Dodd, Mead's *Red Badge* series of mystery novels. Such series are called publishers' series.

The monographic series is a series that is usually issued with some regularity; each title in a monographic series ordinarily is given a number, usually in chronological order. For many patrons, the name of the series and the number of a title in it are the important identifying elements. Patrons often do not remember individual authors and titles but look for these under the series name. Thus, though author and title of an individual item are major identifying elements, the series title in a monographic series assumes a significant role.

The second element to be identified by the cataloger is the statement of responsibility. This is also found in the chief source of information and is usually the author, whose name is usually the main entry. According to *AACR 2*, an author is "the person chiefly responsible for the creation of the intellectual or artistic content of a work" (p. 568). In addition to writers of books and composers of music, this includes cartographers, artists, photographers, performers, etc. It may be necessary to locate some information about an unfamiliar author. For example, if the work is imaginative in nature, the author's nationality must be known since most classification schemes use the device of nationality to classify novels, drama, and poetry. This is discussed in the chapters on classification in this text. Information about an author may sometimes be found in the chief source of information, in an introduction, or in material accompanying the item, such as the dust jacket of a book or the container of a disc.

However, an author is not the only possibility for inclusion in a statement of responsibility. Any person or persons responsible for intellectual or artistic content or for performance, or any corporate body from which the content is issued, may need to be included in the catalog record.

The edition of the item, if named, is usually found in the chief source of information, but may also be found in other places. In a book, a piece of printed music, or a serial it may appear in the preliminaries [i.e., title page, verso (or back) of the title page, any pages preceding the title page, and the cover], in the preface to the work, or in a colophon (i.e., a statement at the end of the work). In cartographic or graphic material, sound recordings, motion pictures and videorecordings, machine-readable data files, and three-dimensional artifacts, the edition may appear in accompanying printed material. For those items with a container, the edition may be found there.

The edition is distinguished from a printing or issue in that a new edition indicates that certain specific changes — additions, deletions, modifications — have been made from earlier versions of the item. On the other hand, a new printing (or reprinting) or issue, means that more copies of the work were manufactured in order to keep up with demand. In the case of books and book-like materials, printings may have minor corrections or revisions, usually incorporated into the original type image. For other materials, a new issue may have slight variations from the original.

Editions may be named (e.g., "revised and enlarged," "abridged," "expurgated") or numbered (e.g., "5th edition"). Any of these edition statements indicates to the cataloger and the patron that some change in content or in form has been made. This information is very important to a scholar. To study the development of a poet, the literary scholar must have early and late editions of the poet's work. A physicist might want only the latest edition of a book on thermodynamics. More information concerning the verification of publication dates and of editions will be found in the chapters on descriptive cataloging.

Because the name of the publisher or distributor, etc., might indicate the type or quality of a work, this information might be important to the patron who must choose one item from several on a specific subject. If the publisher or distributor, etc., is noted for excellence in a certain area (e.g., Skira in art; McGraw-Hill in technology), publisher/distributor information has some value to the patron. This information, including place and date, is usually found in the chief source of information, but may also be found in the same other locations as the edition statement. If the item is copyrighted, the copyright date and the holders of the copyright must be listed in or on the item. This information is important when the publication date and the copyright date differ. In such a case, both dates are given in the catalog record.

The cataloger must learn to assess quickly the details of physical description. These include the extent of the item (e.g., number of pages or volumes, number of pieces, length of playing time), dimensions (e.g., height), and physical data other than extent or dimensions (e.g., presence of illustrations, playing speed, material of which made).

The cataloger must also be quick to identify other important and useful pieces of information about an item. Such information as variant titles of the same work (e.g., original title of a translation), language, edition history, accompanying materials, intended audience, contents of multi-volume items, and presence of bibliographies should often be noted in the catalog record. The standard number [e.g., International Standard Book Number (ISBN) and International Standard Serial Number (ISSN)] is becoming increasingly important as a means of unique international identification. It is often given in the catalog record.

If there is a preface, the cataloger should read it as an aid to determination of the author's plan or objective. This provides a key to the subject matter of the item. Similar aids are introductions, forewords, accompanying printed materials, and containers. The table of contents, with its listing of topics, is a valuable indication of the scope of a work. An index is a good source for determining subject content and special emphases. Bibliographies may also serve as an aid by indicating an author's point of view.

FORM OF THE CATALOG RECORD

Uniformity is necessary in the form of the catalog record. If certain standards are followed throughout, patrons will universally recognize all the elements that make up the record. They will know, for example, that the publisher information will always follow the rest of the body of the entry and that the physical description area consists of certain items arranged in a specific order. This information then becomes readily identifiable.

Although various arrangements are possible, most libraries follow the Library of Congress system, simply because LC printed cards have been so extensively used. When pre-existent records are not available, the cataloger devises a record very similar in form to that used by the Library of Congress. Doing this makes all the records as uniform as possible and therefore easy to consult.

Not all specific elements are present in every item to be cataloged, but all elements present should be recorded. Contemporary cataloging practice assumes that patrons are best served if these elements are recorded in the same order on all entries. This order is achieved in a manual system by recording elements in a specified order, ordinarily formatted in paragraph form. In a computer system, the elements must be tagged to give the system information about the element and its place in the record. The computer will format a properly tagged record in the order desired when printing it as entries on cards, in book or COM catalogs, or on a terminal screen. The order and usual paragraph formatting of a printed catalog entry are outlined below, followed by an example record shown in printed card format and in Machine-Readable Cataloging (MARC) format.

I.   HEADING
     A. Author or other person or corporate body chosen as main entry, *or*
     B. Title, if (A) cannot be ascribed.

II. BODY OF THE ENTRY (first paragraph)
     A. Title and statement of responsibility area
        1. Title proper (including alternative title, if any)
        2. General material designation (GMD)
        3. Parallel title(s), other title information, if any
        4. Statement(s) of responsibility
     B. Edition area
        1. Edition statement (named, numbered, or a combination of the two)
        2. Statements of responsibility relating to the edition, but not to all editions
     C. Material (or type of publication) specific details area
        1. For cartographic materials, statements of scale and projection

      2. For music, statement indicating physical presentation of the music
      3. For serial publications, numeric and/or alphabetic designation (e.g., No. 1-) and/or chronological designation (e.g., 1967-)
    D. Publication, distribution, etc., area
      1. Place of publication, distribution, etc.
      2. Name of publisher, distributor, etc.
      3. Statement of function of publisher, distributor, etc. (e.g., production company) when necessary for clarity
      4. Date of publication, distribution, etc., including copyright date, if necessary
      5. Place of manufacture, name of manufacturer, date of manufacture, if name of publisher is unknown

III. PHYSICAL DESCRIPTION AREA (second paragraph)
    A. Extent of item (e.g., number of pages, volumes, discs, frames, etc.)
    B. Other physical details (e.g., illustrative material, playing speed, material of which made)
    C. Dimensions (e.g., height, diameter)
    D. Accompanying material (e.g., teacher's guide, separate maps)

IV. SERIES AREA, if any (following physical description area as continuation of second paragraph)
    A. Title proper of series, parallel title(s), other title information
    B. Statement(s) of responsibility relating to series
    C. ISSN of series
    D. Numbering within series
    E. Subseries
    F. Second and following series, each in its own set of parentheses

V. NOTE AREA (each note is separate paragraph). Necessary data that cannot be incorporated in above parts of the record.

VI. STANDARD NUMBER AND TERMS OF AVAILABILITY AREA (paragraph following last note)
    A. Standard number (e.g., ISBN, ISSN)
    B. Key-title of a serial
    C. Terms of availability (e.g., price, or for whom available)

VII. TRACING (separate paragraph)
    A. Subject heading(s)
    B. Added entries for joint authors, editors, etc.
    C. Title added entry or entries
    D. Series added entry or entries

VIII. CALL NUMBER (formatted in upper left corner of entry or on line following tracing)
    A. Classification number
    B. Cutter number and work mark, if any

Fig. 1.9. Identification of information included in a catalog card.

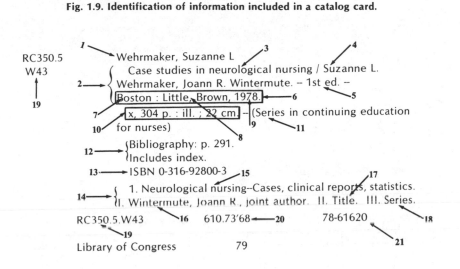

Key for figure 1.9.

1.	Heading: author's name	11.	Series statement
2.	Body of the entry	12.	Notes
3.	Title proper	13.	Standard number (ISBN)
4.	Statement of responsibility	14.	Tracing
5.	Edition statement	15.	Subject heading
6.	Publication, distribution, etc. area	16.	Added entry for personal name
7	Place of publication	17.	Title added entry
8.	Publisher	18.	Series added entry
9.	Date of publication	19.	Library of Congress call number
10.	Physical description area	20.	Dewey classification number
		21.	Library of Congress card number

Entries displayed to users of online catalogs are taking a variety of forms in experimental efforts to determine what form is most understandable to users. Most so far have chosen to display the records in a form that resembles the form that would be found on a catalog card. Fig. 1.11 shows such a display from LUIS, the public catalog module of NOTIS (Northwestern [University] Online Totally Integrated System). Fig. 1.12 is an example of the display used in the University of Chicago Libraries. In both examples, parts of the display are labeled (but different parts).

Fig. 1.10. Identification of information included in a MARC record.

```
OCLC: 4617812        Rec stat: c Entrd: 790329         Used: 850110
Type: a Bib lvl: m Govt pub:   Lang:  eng Source:    Illus: a
Repr:    Enc lvl:    Conf pub: 0 Ctry:  mau Dat tp: s M/F/B: 10
Indx: 1 Mod rec:     Festschr: 0 Cont: b
Desc: i Int lvl:     Dates: 1978,
    1 010       78-61620 ←21
    2 040       DLC $c DLC $d MQM $d m.c.
    3 020       0316928003 ←13
    4 050 0     RC350.5 $b .W43 ←19
    5 060       WY 160.3 W414c 1978
    6 082       610.73/68 ←20
    7 090       $b
    8 049       IVEA     /1
17 ←9 100 10    Wehrmaker, Suzanne L. $w cn        /3              /4        )
   10 245 00    Case studies in neurological nursing / $c Suzanne L. } 2
Wehrmaker, Joann R. Wintermute.
   11 250    7 1st ed. →5         /8          /9                              )
   12 260 0     Boston : $b Little, Brown, $c 1978. } 6
18 ←13 300     x, 304 p. : $b ill. ; $c 22 cm. } 10
   14 (440) 0   Series in continuing education for nurses ← 11
   15 504       Bibliography: p. 291. } 12
   16 500       Includes index.                     /15
   17 650 0     Neurological nursing $x Cases, clinical reports, statistics. )
   18 650 2     Nervous System Diseases $x nursing $x examination questions } 14
   19 650 2     Neurology $x nursing texts
   20 700 10    Wintermute, Joann R., $e joint author. $w cn               )
                        16        22
```

Key for figure 1.10.

1. Heading: author's name	12. Notes
2. Body of the entry	13. Standard number (ISBN)
3. Title proper	14. Tracing
4. Statement of responsibility	15. Subject heading
5. Edition statement	16. Added entry for personal name
6. Publication, distribution, etc., area	17. MARC indicator that tells computer that title will be added entry
7. Place of publication	
8. Publisher	18. MARC tag that indicates that series will be added entry
9. Date of publication	
10. Physical description area	19. Library of Congress call number
11. Series statement	20. Dewey classification number
	21. Library of Congress card number
	22. MARC subfield code

Fig. 1.11. Sample online catalog display from Northwestern University Library's NOTIS system.

```
LUIS SEARCH REQUEST:  A=WEHRMAKER
  BIBLIOGRAPHIC RECORD -- NO. 1 OF 1 ENTRIES FOUND
Wehrmaker, Suzanne L.
  Case studies in neurological nursing / Suzanne L. Wehrmaker, Joann R.
Wintermute. -- Boston : Little, Brown, 1978.
  x, 304 p. : ill. ; 22 cm. -- (Series in continuing education for nurses)
  SUBJECT HEADINGS (Library of Congress; use s= ):
      Neurological nursing--Cases, clinical reports, statistics.
  SUBJECT HEADINGS (Medical; use sm= ):
      Nervous System Diseases--nursing.
      Neurology--nursing texts.
  HOLDINGS IN NU MEDICAL LIBRARY:
  LOCATION:  hsl
  CALL NUMBER:  WY 160 W414c 1978 .
TYPE e TO START OVER.  TYPE h FOR HELP.
TYPE COMMAND AND PRESS ENTER
```

Fig. 1.12. Sample online catalog display from the University of
Chicago Libraries's Data Base Management System.

```
FULL EDITED BIBLIOGRAPHIC DISPLAY

     Wehrmaker, Suzanne L.
     Case studies in neurological nursing / Suzanne L Wehrmaker, Joann R.
Wintermute.
     1st ed.
     Boston : Little, Brown, 1978.
     x, 304 p. : ill. ; 22 cm.
      Series:  Series in continuing education for nurses
     Note:  Bibliography: p. 291.
     Note:  Includes index.
Other entries:
     Neurological nursing--Cases, clinical reports, statistics.
     Wintermute, Joann R., joint author.
      STATUS:   received; cataloged
      CALL NUMBER:   RC350.5.W43
      HOLDINGS:   c.1 [Gen]
      ICU NUMBER:   78-205 636
```

TYPED CARDS

There are still many libraries that find it necessary to type at least some
catalog cards locally. For these libraries, the following instructions illustrate a
simple and generally effective method for doing so. The sections on punctuation, spacing, capitalization, abbreviations, and numerals are useful in
creating original bibliographic records, whether they are input online in
MARC format or are to be hand-typed.

The following formalized rules may seem arbitrary, but they are essential
for uniformity. Practice will make a typist proficient within a short time. Indention rules are given first. These are followed by detailed explanations of the
typing rules (spacing, punctuation, capitalization, etc.) using ISBD format.

Indentions

Standard printed cards from the Library of Congress have the great
advantage of more than one style and size of type to help differentiate between
distinct items on the card. Lacking this advantage, typewritten cards must rely
upon a standardized system (as follows) of spacing and punctuation for
clarity.

The main entry heading begins nine spaces from the left margin of the
card. This segment of nine spaces is called the first indention.

Second indention begins four typewriter spaces to the right of the main
entry—or 13 spaces from the left margin. Second indention is used to align
title, collation, notes, and tracing. Any of this information that is too long to
be recorded on one line is brought back to first indention in standard
paragraph form. All added entries at the top of the card begin at the second
indention.

Occasionally there is need of a third indention (16 spaces from the left margin or seven spaces to the right of the beginning of the main entry). This will occur in three instances:

1) When the author entry is too long to be contained on one line, the overflow is carried to third indention. (To use second indention in this case would be confusing because the title begins at second indention.)

2) When an added entry is too long for one line, the second line will carry over to third indention.

3) In the cataloging of one volume or piece of a set that is in progress, the succeeding volumes or pieces must be allowed for. In this case the typist will space to third indention in the collation and type the specific material designation [e.g., "cassettes," "reels," or "v." (for "volumes")]. When the set is complete, it then becomes a simple matter to type the completed number of pieces directly to the left of the designation.

Card Format

The main entry heading begins on the fourth line from the top of the card. A typewritten catalog card is single-spaced throughout, with the following exceptions:

1) Double-space before the beginning of the first note.

2) Begin the tracing at the bottom of the card, but above the hole.

Figure 1.13 is a sample form showing the location of information on a catalog card, indentions, spacing after punctuation, and vertical spacing between parts of the card. The small numbers "1" and "2" have been inserted to clarify the exact number of spaces to be used in each instance. Fig. 1.14 illustrates the format for the second card, which is to be used when there is too much information to fit onto one card. Detailed instructions for spacing, punctuation, and capitalization in the International Standard Bibliographic Description (ISBD) format are given in the following sections.

The Library of Congress carries the tracing for the card set in paragraph form at the bottom of the card just above the hole (*see* Fig. 1.15). For typed cards the tracings, instead of being placed on the front, may be typed on the back of the main entry card. This is particularly true when the tracings are long. In any case, the form, once established, should not vary. The subject headings are typed first in order of importance. If they are equally important, the order does not matter, except that biographical headings, or others in which the person is the subject, always come first. Each subject heading is preceded by an arabic numeral. Here again uniformity must be maintained, depending on the kind of heading established.

Those entries that bring out descriptive elements of a book rather than its subject are preceded by roman numerals and come after all subject entries. As part of the tracing, they follow a specific order: joint author, editor, translator, or any other individual person who has helped to create the work; corporate entries or sponsoring agencies such as societies, university departments, bureaus and the like; title; series.

Detailed rules and examples pertaining to the elements that make up the catalog card and the specifications for personal names will follow in succeeding chapters on descriptive cataloging and rules for personal names.

Works entered under title are typed in the form called the hanging indention. The title begins at first indention and is continued at second indention. Physical description and notes are indented as for all other cards. *See* Fig. 1.13.

Fig. 1.13. Sample form for typed card.

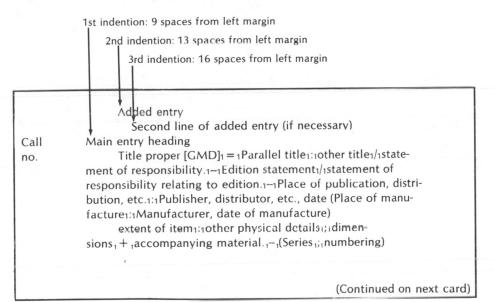

1st indention: 9 spaces from left margin

2nd indention: 13 spaces from left margin

3rd indention: 16 spaces from left margin

Added entry
        Second line of added entry (if necessary)
Call   Main entry heading
no.   Title proper [GMD]₁ = ₁Parallel title₁:₁other title₁/₁state-
        ment of responsibility.₁—₁Edition statement₁/₁statement of
        responsibility relating to edition.₁—₁Place of publication, distri-
        bution, etc.₁:₁Publisher, distributor, etc., date (Place of manu-
        facture₁:₁Manufacturer, date of manufacture)
             extent of item₁:₁other physical details₁;₁dimen-
        sions₁+₁accompanying material.₁—₁(Series₁;₁numbering)

(Continued on next card)

Fig. 1.14. Sample for supplementary typed card.

        Added entry
                Second line of added entry (if necessary)
Call   Main entry heading
no.   Title proper [GMD]₁...₁date of publication, etc.₂(Card 2)

        Notes.
        ISBN

             1.₁Subject heading–Subheading.₂ 2.₁Subject heading–
        Subheading.₂ I.₁Added entry.₂ II.₁Title.₂ III.₁Series.

Fig. 1.15. Typed form for hanging indention.

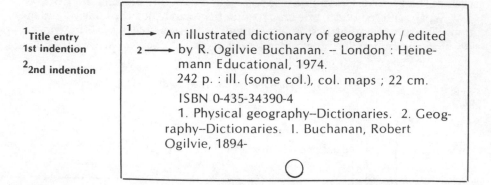

¹Title entry
1st indention

²2nd indention

1 ——▶ An illustrated dictionary of geography / edited
2 ——▶ by R. Ogilvie Buchanan. -- London : Heine-
        mann Educational, 1974.
        242 p. : ill. (some col.), col. maps ; 22 cm.
        ISBN 0-435-34390-4
        1. Physical geography--Dictionaries. 2. Geog-
        raphy--Dictionaries. I. Buchanan, Robert
        Ogilvie, 1894-

Spacing

1) The main entry heading begins on the fourth line from the top of the card.

2) Single space the lines, with the exceptions of double spaces before the first note and before the tracing.

3) The call number begins on the fourth line from the top of the card. Indent the call number one space from the left edge of the card.

4) Leave one space before and one space after
    a) Equals signs
        used to indicate parallel titles or other parallel information:
            La motoneige au Québec = Snowmobiling in Quebec
        used to separate alternative numbering systems in serials:
            Vol. 4, no. 1-   = No. 13-
        used to separate ISSN from key title:
            ISSN 0040-9898 = Toward freedom
    b) Colons
        used before other title information:
            On the contrary : articles of belief, 1946-1961.
        used between place of publication, etc., and publisher, etc.:
            New York : Macmillan
        used between the extent of item and other physical details
        in the physical description area:
            1 disc (45 min.) : 33 1/3 rpm, stereo
        used between standard number and terms of availability:
            ISBN 0-87287-153-3 : $15.00
        used between different parts of additions to corporate names:
            Alessandria (Italy : Province)

c) Diagonal slashes used to indicate a statement of responsibility:

    Instrument pilot's guide / by L. W. Reithmaier

d) Dashes used following the periods (full stops) that precede the edition area, the material specific details area, the publication, distribution, etc., area, and the series area:

    by L. W. Reithmaier. -- 2nd ed. -- Fallbrook, Calif.
    26 cm. -- (Oxford in Asia university readings)

e) Semicolons
used to indicate different functions of subsidiary responsibility:

    by W. W. Hellon ; photography, Woodward C. Helton
    and James McKinney ; illustrator, Pete Dykes

used to precede dimensions in the physical description area:

    219 p. : ill. ; 24 cm.
    1 score (8 p.) ; 31 cm.

used in the publication, etc., area to separate two places or two places and publishers, etc.:

    Toronto ; New York
    London : Oxford University Press ; Berkeley : University of California Press

used to precede numbering of a series or subseries:

    Studies in Nigerian languages ; no. 1

used to separate projection from statement of scale in cartographic materials:

    Scale 1:50,000 ; Transverse Mercator proj.

used to separate a new sequence of numbering from an old sequence of numbering in serials:

    No. 1 (Winter 1970)-no. 20 (Fall 1974) ; Vol. 1, no. 1
    (Jan. 1975)-

f) The plus sign used to separate accompanying materials from the dimensions in the physical description area:

    30 cm. + 1 atlas

g) The mark of omission (. . .) used to show omission of part of an element:

    by Jack P. Segal . . . [et al.]

5) Leave one space after

a) all commas, closing parentheses, and closing square brackets

b) periods (full stops) that end each area of the description or that are used after abbreviations

c) colons that follow the introductory wording in notes:

    Title on spine: Eighteenth century Franklin County
    deeds

6)   Leave two spaces after

a)   the period (full stop) separating the titles and statements of responsibility of works in an item lacking a collective title:
Henry Esmond : a novel / by Thackery.   Bleak house : a novel / by Dickens

b)   each item in the tracing:
I. Title.   II. Series.

7)   Omit the space before all commas, periods (full stops), hyphens, closing parentheses, and closing square brackets.

8)   Omit the space after all hyphens, opening parentheses, and opening square brackets.

NOTE: The peculiarities of ISBD spacing result from the dual use of punctuation marks: they can be used either as marks of punctuation or as marks of separation. The function of a mark in a particular instance determines the spacing around it. The ISBD rules for punctuation and spacing were designed for international standardization of bibliographic format so that records could be exchanged between countries, and would have clearly identifiable parts regardless of language differences or differences in meaning of punctuation marks. The ISBD rules also simplify the conversion of bibliographic records to machine-readable form.

Punctuation

1)   Use commas

a)   in the statement of responsibility between names of persons or bodies performing the same function but which are not connected with a conjunction in the chief source of information:
by Martin L. Bowers, Jon R. Carr, William Knight

b)   between the name of the publisher, etc., and the date of publication, etc., or between name of manufacturer and date of manufacture in the publication, distribution, etc., area:
American Library Association, 1978

c)   between variations in dates in the publication, etc., area:
1979, c1977

d)   between different pagination sections of a printed work:
xxi, 259, 27 p., 15 leaves of plates

e)   between the series or subseries and its ISSN:
Studies in biology, ISSN 0537-9024

f)   to separate a surname and a forename

g)   following personal names, when additions are made:
Smith, Paul, 1941-
John Paul II, Pope

h)   to separate a smaller place from its larger jurisdiction when both are used as an addition to a name:
        Hope Valley (Durham, N. C.)

i)   wherever required by grammar and there is no punctuation prescribed in the rules

2)   Use semicolons

    a)   to indicate different functions of subsidiary responsibility:
        by John Hinterberger ; illustrated by Jacques Rupp

    b)   preceding dimensions in the physical description area:
        ill. (some col.) ; 30 cm.
        1 score (28 p.) ; 28 cm.

    c)   preceding the numbering of a series or subseries:
        (Studies in Nigerian languages ; no. 1)
        (Studies in biology, ISSN 0537-9024 ; no. 102)

    d)   between a series of titles by the same author from a work lacking a collective title:
        Romeo and Juliet ; King Lear ; Macbeth / by
        William Shakespeare. --

    e)   between two places of publication, etc., in the publication, etc., area:
        London ; New York :

    f)   between two separate places of publication, etc., and publishers, etc.:
        London : Oxford University Press ; Berkeley : University of California Press

    g)   between two sequences of numbering, dates, etc.:
        1941-1943 ; 1944-1947
        Vol. 10, no. 3 (Mar. 1973)-vol. 12, no. 12 (Dec. 1975) ; no. 1 (Jan. 1976)-

    h)   between statement of scale and projection in cartographic materials:
        Scale 1:50,000 ; Transverse Mercator proj.

3)   Use periods (full stops)

    a)   at the end of the publication, distribution, etc., area unless the final mark of punctuation is a square bracket:
        Oxford University Press, 1979.
        Aero Publishers, 1979 [c1976]

    b)   at the end of each note:
        Includes index.
        Title from container.

    c)   at the end of each entry in the tracing:
        1. Sociology.
        I. Title.   II. Series.

d) between a series of separate titles and statements of respon-
    sibility from a work lacking a collective title:
    The sorcerer's apprentice / Dukas. Night on bald
    mountain / Mussorgsky.

e) preceding the title of a supplement or section:
    Journal of chemical engineering. Supplement

f) between the title of a series and the title of a subseries:
    Pacific linguistics. Series C

g) after abbreviations as indicated by the current usage of the
    language concerned:
    ill.
    min.

h) before subheadings of a corporate body heading:
    United States. Antarctic Projects Office

4) Use parentheses

a) to enclose the place and name of the manufacturer:
    (London : Wiggs)

b) to enclose the series area:
    (Books that matter)

c) to specify the number of components as part of the extent of
    an item:
    1 microfiche (140 fr.)
    1 tape (1 hr. 15 min.)
    3 v. (xix, 1269 p.)

d) in the physical description area to indicate some of the il-
    lustrative matter is in color:
    ill. (some col.)

e) for the physical details of accompanying material in the
    physical description area:
    2 v. ; 32 cm. + 1 atlas (159 leaves of plates : 25 col.
    maps ; 43 cm.)

f) to enclose statements of coordinates and equinox in car-
    tographic materials:
    (W 126° -- W 64° / N 49° -- N 23°)

g) to enclose a date following a numeric and/or alphabetic
    designation:
    No. 1 (Jan. 1978)

h) for designation of theses:
    Thesis (M.A.)--University of Denver, 1978.

i) to enclose qualifications to the standard number or terms of
    availability:
    ISBN 0-87287-161-4 (pbk.)
    $10.00 ($8.00 to students)

      j)   to enclose date, number, place, or other designation added to a corporate or geographic name:
           Franklin County Legal Journal (Corporation)

5)   Use colons

      a)   before other title information:
           Human action : a treatise on economics
           French rooster : [poem]

      b)   between place of publication, etc., or manufacture and the name of the publisher, etc., or manufacturer:
           New York : Macmillan

      c)   between the extent of item and other physical details in the physical description area:
           1 globe : col., plastic, mounted on metal stand

      d)   between standard number and terms of availability:
           ISBN 0-87287-153-3 : $15.00

      e)   between different additions to corporate names:
           WUNC (Radio station : Chapel Hill, N. C.)
           Symposium on Computer Applications in Medical Care
              (2nd : 1978 : Washington, D. C.)

      f)   between the introductory wording and the main content of notes:
           Bibliography: p. 190-191.
           Summary: A poetical journey into the unconscious of a woman in search of personal power
           First ed. published with title: Technical topics for the radio amateur.
           Credits: Script, Al DeZutter.

      g)   in the scale ratio in cartographic materials:
           Scale 1:250,000

Note that in f) there is no space before the colon, and in g) there is no space before or after the colon. In these cases, the colon is used as a mark of punctuation rather than a mark of separation.

6)   Use period (full stop) and dash

      a)   preceding the edition area, the material specific details area, the publication, distribution, etc., area, and the series area:
           / drawn by Robert Morgan. -- Rev. ed. -- Scale 1:500,000. -- London :
           ; 78 x 80 cm. -- (World climatology series)

In the cases in a) the format is period-space-hyphen-hyphen-space. The dash is represented by two hyphens on the typewriter.

7) Use dashes

    a)   for sequence in a contents note:
        Contents: The ethic of the group / L. C. Eisley -- Science
        and human values / G. Seldes -- Law and the limits /
        W. Hurst.

In this case, the format is space-hyphen-hyphen-space.

    b)   in thesis notes:
        Thesis (Ph.D.)--Yale, 1979.

        Note that there is no space before or after the dash.

8) Diagonal slashes are used before the statement of responsibility in
the title and statement of responsibility area, the edition area, the
series area, and the contents note:
    Introduction to sociology / Paul Sites
    (Reports / British Library, Research & Development ; no.
    5416)

9) Use equals signs

    a)   before parallel titles and other parallel information:
        La nuit : Etüde für Klavier = Night : piano study

    b)   before alternative numbering systems in serials:
        Vol. 4, no. 1-   = No. 13-

    c)   before a key title in the standard number area:
        ISSN 0190-1427 = AJS update

10) Plus signs are used to separate accompanying materials from the
dimensions in the physical description area:
    30 cm. + 1 disc

11) Question marks are used to denote

    a)   conjectural additions:
        [Pittsburg? Calif.]
        Pittsburg [Calif.?]

    b)   uncertain dates:
        [1892?]
        [189-?]
        [18--?]

12) Use hyphens to follow the numeric and/or alphabetic designation
and/or the date of first issue of a serial:
    No. 1 (Jan. 1978)-

13) Use square brackets

    a)   to show that the information enclosed has been supplied from a source other than the prescribed source of information according to *AACR 2*.

        Cristiana [Oslo]

        3^e [ed.]

        French rooster : [poem]

(The prescribed sources of information vary according to the specified area of the record and the type of material being cataloged. These are discussed in general in chapter 3 of this textbook, and more specifically in chapters 4-7.)

    b)   to enclose the general material designation (GMD):

        The curious campaign of the comma king [filmstrip]

It should be noted that adjacent elements in one area that require square brackets, should be enclosed in the same set, except for the GMD which is always enclosed in its own square brackets:

    -- [S.1. : s.n., 1974?]

Elements in different areas that require brackets are each enclosed in their own set of brackets:

    / [Compiler, Dencho Vlaev]. -- [Sofia] :

14) Omissions of parts of elements, such as an unimportant part of a long title, or all but the first responsible party when more than three are named, are indicated by three dots, called "the mark of omission":

    The Dickens concordance, being a compendium of names and characters and principal places in all the works of Charles Dickens . . .

    / [edited by] Henry P. David . . . [et al.]

It should be noted that omissions of *entire* elements or areas are not indicated by the mark of omission.

Capitalization

The rules for capitalization, in general, follow standard style for the language involved. Rules for capitalization are given extensive coverage in *AACR 2*, Appendix A, first covering rules in general and then giving specific rules by language. An important exception to normal usage is that a title is written like an ordinary sentence; the first word is capitalized, e.g.,

    The will to live.
    Act one.

If, however, the main entry of a work is its title proper, and if the first word of such a title is an article, the next word is also capitalized, e.g.,

    The Will to live.
    An Introduction to the physical sciences.

The capitalization of other words in the title is governed by ordinary rules for capitalization; e.g.,

> Across five Aprils.
> The Spirit of St. Louis.

The first word of every title, alternative title, or parallel title is capitalized, e.g.,

> Letters from the West, or, A caution to emigrants.
> El gato = The cat.

Abbreviations

Abbreviations are used except in the recording of titles and statements of responsibility wherever they fall in the description and in quoted notes. Acceptable abbreviations are those listed in *AACR 2*, Appendix B. Some abbreviations may be used only for the heading (*see* B.2), and single letter abbreviations are not used to begin a note. When in doubt, the cataloger should *not* abbreviate.

Numerals

Rules for numerals are given in *AACR 2*, Appendix C. There are rules prescribing when to substitute arabic for roman numerals; when to spell out numerals; when to substitute Western-style numerals for Oriental numerals; and how to record inclusive numbers, alternative dates, and ordinal numerals.

PRE-ISBD CATALOGING FORMAT

Before the introduction of ISBD in the United States in 1974, the cataloging differed from present cataloging in some ways. Less information was recorded, but what was given appeared in basically the same order as that information does now. The punctuation and spacing were simpler, in one sense, because punctuation was used only for punctuating, not also for separating areas and elements of description. In another sense, however, there was more difficulty in judging, for example, whether to use a comma, semicolon, or colon before a subtitle. And because "double punctuation" was strictly avoided, new catalogers often had difficulty learning, for example, not to precede or follow a square bracket with the comma or period called for by rules of grammar (e.g., the correct form was [New York] Macmillan[1961] *not* [New York], Macmillan, [1961]). A side-by-side comparison of ISBD punctuation and pre-ISBD punctuation may be found in *Cataloging with Copy*, Appendix F,[7] and many examples of pre-ISBD copy appear throughout the book.

CONCLUSION

This chapter has presented an overview of the entire cataloging process. Greater detail about the content of description is discussed in chapters 3-8. Choice and form of headings are covered in chapters 9-14. Subject analysis is given thorough treatment in Part III, with chapters 15-19 devoted to classification, and chapters 20-24 devoted to subject headings. The final part deals in more detail with networking, computer cataloging, and with cataloging routines and end processes.

NOTES

[1]*Anglo-American Cataloguing Rules*, 2nd ed. (Chicago, American Library Association, 1978); *Revisions* (Chicago, ALA, 1982); *Revisions 1983* (Chicago, ALA, 1984).

[2]A good discussion of the historical development of cataloging practices is presented in an article written by Charles Martel, "Cataloging: 1876-1926," reprinted in *The Catalog and Cataloging*, edited by A. R. Rowland (Hamden, Conn., Shoe String Press, 1969), pp. 40-50.

[3]Charles A. Cutter, *Rules for a Dictionary Catalog*, 4th ed. (Washington, D.C., GPO, 1904), p. 12.

[4]International Conference on Cataloguing Principles. Paris, 9th-18th October, 1961, *Report* (London, International Federation of Library Associations, 1963), p. 26.

[5]Julia Pettee, "Development of Authorship Entry and the Formulation of Authorship Rules as Found in the Anglo-American Code," *Library Quarterly* 6 (July 1936): 271.

[6]Sally Hart McCallum, "Some Implications of Desuperimposition," *Library Quarterly* 47 (April 1977): 114.

[7]Arlene Taylor Dowell, *Cataloging with Copy* (Littleton, Colo., Libraries Unlimited, 1976), pp. 258-266.

SUGGESTED READING

Avram, Henriette D. *MARC: Its History and Implications.* Washington, D.C., Library of Congress, 1975.

Carpenter, Michael, and Elaine Svenonius. *Foundations of Cataloging: A Sourcebook.* Littleton, Colo., Libraries Unlimited, 1985.

Dowell, Arlene Taylor. *Cataloging with Copy.* Littleton, Colo., Libraries Unlimited, 1976.

Dunkin, Paul S. *Cataloging U.S.A.* Chicago, American Library Association, 1969.

Hagler, Ronald, and Peter Simmons. *The Bibliographic Record and Information Technology.* Chicago, American Library Association, 1982.

2
Development of
Cataloging Codes

The *Anglo-American Cataloguing Rules*, second edition (*AACR 2*), is the result of a progression of ideas about how to approach the cataloging process in order to prepare catalogs that provide the best possible access to library collections. *AACR 2* represents the current agreements that have been reached in order to standardize cataloging practice and thereby facilitate cooperation among libraries. It expands on the agreements presented in earlier codes and forms the basis for further agreements that will be added to future codes.

The first cataloging rules were prepared by individuals. Panizzi's British Museum *Rules for the Compiling of the Catalogue* (1841) was the first major modern statement of principles underlying cataloging rules; as such, it has exerted an influence on every Western world code that has been published since its publication. Cutter's *Rules for a Dictionary Catalog*, in its fourth edition at his death in 1903, presented the first complete set of rules for a dictionary catalog. From the beginning of the twentieth century codes have been drawn up by committees, but the influence of those early farsighted individuals continued through LC *Rules on Printed Cards* (1903 through the 1930s), LC *Rules for Descriptive Cataloging* (1949), ALA *Rules* (1908, 1941, 1949), *AACR 1* (published in 1967), and the present *AACR 2*.

The ALA *Rules* of 1908 were the result of a seven-year study by a committee of ALA and the (British) Library Association. In 1901 the Library of Congress began its printed card service, with the result that libraries became interested in ways to use LC cards with their own cards. One of the important responsibilities of the committee was to formulate rules to encourage incorporation of LC printed cards into catalogs of other libraries. The committee attempted to reconcile the cataloging practices of LC with those of other research and scholarly libraries. The use of LC cards increased dramatically between 1908 and 1941; standardization of library catalogs progressed. However, the ALA *Rules* were not expanded during this 33-year period, drastically curtailing attempts of cataloging practice to stay in touch with cataloging done at the Library of Congress. In 1930 a subcommittee was appointed by ALA to begin work on a revision of cataloging rules, and the problems were outlined. Dissatisfaction with the 1908 code was expressed on the grounds of "omissions"; the basic rules were not in question. Expansion was required to meet the needs of large scholarly libraries or specialized collections:

> The preliminary edition, published in 1941, expanded the rules of 1908 to make more provision for special classes of material: serial publications, government documents, publications of religious bodies, anonymous classics, music and maps; to amplify existing rules to cover specific cases of frequent occurrence.[1]

The revised edition of 1949 states that

> the chief changes from the preliminary edition are a rearrangement of the material to emphasize the basic rules and subordinate their amplifications, and to make the sequence of rules logical as far as possible; reduction of the number of alternate rules; omission of rules for description; rewording to avoid repetition or to make the meaning clearer; and revision, where possible, of rules inconsistent with the general principles.[2]

The 1941 and 1949 rules were sharply criticized for being too elaborate and often arbitrary; emphasis had shifted from clearly defined principles to a collection of rules developed to fit specific cases rather than the conditions that the cases illustrated. Lubetzky commented that any logical approach to cataloging problems was blocked by the maze of arbitrary and repetitious rules and exceptions to rules.[3]

Because of the omission of rules for description from the 1949 ALA *Rules*, the Library of Congress published its *Rules for Descriptive Cataloging in the Library of Congress,*[4] also in 1949. This set of rules was much more simplified than had been the rules in Part II of the 1941 ALA preliminary edition. Therefore, these were not criticized, as were the rules for entry and heading, and were incorporated virtually intact into the next edition of rules published by ALA in 1967.

ANGLO-AMERICAN CATALOGING RULES, 1967 (AACR 1)

The Catalog Code Revision Committee that prepared the 1967 *Anglo-American Cataloging Rules* realized that revision must be a complete re-examination of the principles and objectives of cataloging, not merely a revision of specific rules. First, the objectives of the catalog were agreed upon; it was further decided that certain general principles should be the basis for rules of entry and heading. These general principles of the new code were based on the "Statement of Principles" approved by 53 countries at the International Conference on Cataloguing Principles in Paris, October 1961.[5] This was an important step toward international bibliographical standardization.

AACR 1 was oriented toward large research libraries, although in a few instances of obvious conflict, alternate rules were provided for use by non-research libraries. Unlike the 1949 ALA code which was only for entry and heading, *AACR 1* incorporated rules for entry and heading, description, and cataloging of non-book material. An important shift occurred in the philosophy underlying the rules for entry: "The entry for a work is normally based on the statements that appear on the title page or any part of the work that is used as its substitute."[6] This meant that information appearing only in the preface, introduction, or text was not to be considered unless title page information was vague or incomplete. Another basic shift in point of view was to that of cataloging by types of authorship rather than by types of works, and by classes of names rather than classes of people.

Unlike earlier codes, *AACR 1* emphasized that choice of entry was a completely separate activity from construction of the heading used for the entry chosen. General principles became the basis for the rules for choice of entry:

1) Entry should be under author or principal author when one can be determined.

2) Entry should be under title in the case of works whose authorship is diffuse, indeterminate, or unknown.

Application of rules based on these principles continued the practice of choosing a main entry, with other names and/or titles becoming added entries. However, the choice was no longer a result of first determining the type of work involved and then finding the specific rule for that type.

The construction of the headings for names that were to be main or added entries centered on two problems: choice of a particular name, and the form in which that name is presented in the heading. Rules for form of name became based on a general principle of using the form of name used by a person or corporate body rather than the full name or official name as the 1949 ALA *Rules* directed. Thus a person could be entered under an assumed name, nickname, changed name, etc. However, a person who used both his or her real name and an assumed name was still entered under the real name, and a person who used a full form of a forename, even though rarely, was entered under the fullest form ever used. Another change was to use a firmly established English form of name rather than the vernacular form for many well-known names (e.g., Horace, not Horatius Flaccus, Quintus).

Another very important area of change was in the form of entry for corporate bodies. The general rule followed the principle of using the form of name the body itself uses. Entry was usually under that form of name except when the rules provided for entry under a higher body or under the name of the government. However, the North American text gave exceptions exempting specified bodies of an institutional nature from the principle of entry under name; these were to be entered under place as in the old rules. These exceptions were contrary to the Paris Principles and to the British text of *AACR 1*, but they had been requested by the Association of Research Libraries, whose member libraries feared being overburdened with the necessity for changing thousands of entries already in catalogs.

The fear of the research libraries was also eased by the Library of Congress' January 1967 announcement of the policy of superimposition:

This means that the rules for choice of entry will be applied only to works that are new to the Library and that the rules for headings will be applied only to persons and corporate bodies that are being established for the first time. New editions, etc., of works previously cataloged will be entered in the same way as the earlier editions (except for revised editions in which change of authorship is indicated). New works by previously established authors will appear under the same headings.[7]

This policy continued throughout the duration of the application of *AACR 1*. As a result, thousands of headings were made between 1967 and 1981 in a form created under the 1949 ALA *Rules* or earlier rules on bibliographic records that were otherwise *AACR 1* records. The abandonment of the policy of superimposition with the implementation of *AACR 2* was a major step toward ultimate user convenience in finding entries and improved international cooperation; but for many large libraries, thousands of entries in pre-*AACR* form already in catalogs have had to be dealt with since January 1981.

In 1974 the rule in *AACR 1* for corporate entry under place was dropped. But because of superimposition, only new corporate bodies were established and entered under their own names. Besides this change, some 40 other rules were changed, and three chapters were totally revised in the years following publication of *AACR 1*. Perhaps the most significant change was the application of standards of bibliographic description, based on International Standard Bibliographic Description (ISBD), to descriptive cataloging of monographs, audiovisual media, and special instructional materials. ISBD facilitates the international exchange of bibliographic information by standardizing the elements to be used in the bibliographic description, assigning an order to these elements in the entry, and specifying a system of symbols to be used in punctuating these elements. (These symbols were discussed and illustrated in chapter 1 of this text.) In addition.

ISBD requires that a publication be totally identified by the description. It is independent of the provisions for headings, main or added, and of the provisions for the use of uniform titles; these were internationally standardized by the Paris Principles.[8]

ANGLO-AMERICAN CATALOGUING RULES, SECOND EDITION (AACR 2)

The numerous changes to rules in *AACR 1* and the progress toward an international standard for description not only of monographs, but of serials and all media, were two of the reasons for the meeting in 1974 of representatives of the national library associations and national libraries of Canada, the United Kingdom, and the United States to plan for the preparation of *AACR 2*. Two other reasons were a proliferation of other rules for nonbook materials that reflected dissatisfaction with *AACR 1* treatment of these materials and LC's announcement of intention to abandon the policy of superimposition.[9] The objectives established at that meeting were:

1) To reconcile in a single text the North American and British texts of 1967

2) To incorporate in the single text all amendments and changes already agreed and implemented under the previous mechanisms

3) To consider for inclusion in AACR all proposals for amendment currently under discussion between the American Library Association, the Library Association, the Library of Congress, and the Canadian Library Association; any new proposals put forward by these bodies and the British Library; and any proposals of national committees of other countries in which AACR is in use

4) To provide for international interest in AACR by facilitating its use in countries other than the United States, Canada, and the United Kingdom.[10]

The representatives at the 1974 meeting also agreed to establish a Joint Steering Committee for Revision of *AACR* (JSC) made up of one voting and one non-voting representative of each author organization. The JSC was to appoint an editor from each side of the Atlantic and was generally to oversee the process of revision through to publication.

The result of the revision process was what the preface to *AACR 2* calls a continuation of the first edition: "for, in spite of the changes in presentation and content which it introduces, these are still the *Anglo-American Cataloguing Rules*, having the same principles and underlying objectives as the first edition, and being firmly based on the achievement of those who created the work, first published in 1967."[11] However, *AACR 2*, published in late 1978 but not implemented by the major national libraries until January 1981, had some significant differences that are worth noting here.

In the process of reconciling the North American and British texts, it was decided to use British spelling of words if the British spelling appears as an alternative in *Webster's New International Dictionary*. In cases where terminology differs, British usages were chosen in some cases (e.g., "full stop" instead of "period"), while American usages appear in other cases (e.g., "parentheses" instead of the British "brackets").

One significant change is in the presentation of rules for description: one general chapter presents broad provisions that can be applied in many different situations. This chapter is followed by specific chapters for different types of materials and for different conditions and patterns of publication. The rules for description are deliberately less specific in legislating ways to handle certain phenomena. The cataloger is thereby encouraged to exercise judgment in interpreting the rules in light of the needs of the user being served. One possibility for such interpretation is that *AACR 2* provides three "levels" of description with increasing amounts of detail at each level. The cataloger may choose the level that provides the amount of detail relevant to the particular library's users, and, at the same time, meet the standards called for in a set of international cataloging rules.

In the rules for choice of access points, it is significant that less emphasis has been placed on "main" entry, although the concept is still present. However, many people believe that when multiple access points are readily available, and when the bibliographic description is complete by itself, there is no need to designate one of the access points as the "main" one. This concept, then, may disappear in future codes. A significant change in choice of main entry is that a corporate body is no longer considered to be an "author." Instead, there are now specified categories of works that are entered under corporate body. This concept greatly reduces the number of corporate main entries made, although those corporate bodies that would have had main entry under earlier rules are given added entry under *AACR 2*, and thus there is not a reduction in number of corporate entries.

Another important change in choice of access points is the abandonment of "form subheadings" (e.g., "Laws, statutes, etc.," "Treaties, etc.," "Liturgy and ritual") for legal and religious works. In some of these cases, the function of the form subheadings is now performed by uniform titles.

Rules for form of headings for personal names now emphasize using the form of name most often used by an author (e.g., Benjamin Disraeli instead of Earl of Beaconsfield; Bernard Shaw instead of George Bernard Shaw). If an author uses more than one name and is not known predominantly by one of them, multiple headings are made for that author. For persons who are not known as authors, emphasis is on using the name that is best known.

For corporate names, too, there is more emphasis on using the name as it is used by the body, removing provisions for inverting, amplifying, etc., that appeared in *AACR 1* (e.g., W. K. Kellogg Arabian Horse Center instead of Kellogg (W. K.) Arabian Horse Center). Geographic names are treated more internationally (e.g., states of Australia and counties of England are treated like states of the United States).

A detailed list of the changes in *AACR 2* may be found in the article "AACR 2: Background and Summary" cited in note 9. This article also points out some general advantages of *AACR 2*. First, *AACR 2* lays the groundwork for much more international and national cooperative cataloging, which is expected to improve greatly library service of a bibliographic nature and to result in considerable cost savings. Second, by providing the framework for standard description of all library materials, it makes possible an integrated, multimedia catalog. Third, it is expected to reduce user search time by providing headings that conform more often to the forms found in works and citations. Fourth, personal name headings are expected to be more stable than formerly, thus reducing catalog maintenance costs.[12]

Rule interpretations made by LC in their process of applying *AACR 2* are published regularly in *Cataloging Service Bulletin*. Official changes made to the rules are also published there. In an attempt to reduce costs of implementing *AACR 2*, LC chose during the first three years of using *AACR 2* to allow certain already established names to continue to be used in pre-*AACR 2* form when the change was relatively insignificant and did not affect the first entry element of any name and in some cases, later elements of a famous name. A list of these "compatible" headings was published in *Cataloging Service Bulletin*.[13] Other libraries had to decide whether to follow LC's lead in this implementation. Those libraries that use LC copy found, for the most part, that the cost of *not* following LC would be prohibitive. Even following LC, however, libraries found that there were administrative problems in applying new rules within a catalog based on several earlier sets of rules. There was a flurry of local *AACR 2* studies, among which was the author's dissertation.[14] The results of these studies (which are summarized in the aforementioned dissertation[15]) showed that somewhere between 14% and 20% of headings dealt with during the first year would be different under *AACR 2*, but only 7% to 13% of all headings would cause conflict in a catalog (depending upon the size of that catalog). A few libraries decided to close their existing card catalogs and to start new ones with the new rules. Most libraries, however, absorbed the 7% to 13% conflicting headings into existing catalogs by interfiling, providing *see also* references, or changing old headings to the new form.

It is hoped that chapters 3 through 14 of this text will prove helpful in illustrating the basic rules. The complete *AACR 2* should be consulted for additional rules covering aspects of problems too detailed for inclusion in this text, and for further explanations, definitions, and references.

NOTES

[1]*A.L.A. Cataloging Rules for Author and Title Entries* (Chicago, American Library Association, 1949), p. viii.

[2]*A.L.A. Cataloging Rules*, p. ix.

[3]Seymour Lubetzky, *Cataloging Rules and Principles: A Critique of the ALA Rules for Entry and a Proposed Design for Their Revision* (Washington, D.C., Processing Department, Library of Congress, 1953); also, by the same author, *Code of Cataloging Rules, Author, and Title; an Unfinished Draft ... with an Explanatory Commentary by Paul Dunkin* (Chicago, American Library Association, 1960).

[4]Library of Congress, Descriptive Cataloging Division, *Rules for Descriptive Cataloging in the Library of Congress: (adopted by the American Library Association)* (Washington, D.C., Library of Congress, 1949).

[5]International Conference on Cataloging Principles, Paris, 9th-18th October, 1961, *Report* (London, International Federation of Library Associations, 1963).

[6]*Anglo-American Cataloging Rules, North American Text* (Chicago, American Library Association, 1967), p. 9. (*AACR 1* was issued in two editions: the North American text and the British text.)

[7]Library of Congress, Processing Department, *Cataloging Service*, bulletin 79 (January 1967): 1.

[8]"International Standard Bibliographic Description," *Cataloging Service,* bulletin 105 (November 1972): 2.

[9]"AACR 2: Background and Summary," *Library of Congress Information Bulletin* 37 (October 20, 1978): 640.

[10]*Anglo-American Cataloguing Rules*, 2nd ed. (Chicago, American Library Association, 1978), pp. vi-vii.

[11]*AACR 2*, p. v.

[12]"AACR 2: Background and Summary," p. 652.

[13]"Implementation of AACR 2 at the Library of Congress," *Cataloging Service Bulletin*, no. 6 (Fall 1979): 5-8.

[14]Arlene Taylor Dowell, *AACR 2 Headings* (Littleton, Colo., Libraries Unlimited, 1982).

[15]Ibid., pp. 22-35.

SUGGESTED READING

Cutter, Charles Ammi. *Rules for a Dictionary Catalog.* 4th ed., rewritten. Washington, D.C., GPO, 1904.

Dowell, Arlene Taylor. *AACR 2 Headings: A Five-Year Projection of Their Impact on Catalogs.* Littleton, Colo., Libraries Unlimited, 1982.

International Conference on AACR 2, Florida State Univ., 1979. *The Making of a Code: The Issues underlying AACR 2.* Chicago, American Library Association, 1980.

Lubetzky, Seymour. *Cataloging Rules and Principles: A Critique of the ALA Rules for Entry and a Proposed Design for Their Revision.* Washington, D.C., Processing Dept., Library of Congress, 1953.

Osborn, Andrew. "The Crisis in Cataloging." *Library Quarterly* 11 (October 1941): 393-411.

Part II
DESCRIPTION AND ACCESS

3

General Rules for Description

INTRODUCTION

This chapter covers in some detail the rules for descriptive cataloging. (A basic introduction to description and basic definitions are given in the first chapter of this text.) Only the more general rules are covered here, however. The reader should carefully examine *AACR 2*, chapter 1, for more complex problems.

The first chapter of *AACR 2* covers description in general and is applicable to all types of materials (e.g., print, sound recordings, etc.) in all conditions (e.g., microform), and patterns (e.g., serial) of publication. Chapters 2 through 12 of *AACR 2* cover in detail various types of material and conditions and patterns of publication. These chapters often refer back to chapter 1 for rules that are generally applicable, but they also give specific guidance for situations that are peculiar to the type of material or condition of publication under discussion. Chapters 2 through 12 cover:

2   Books, Pamphlets, and Printed Sheets
3   Cartographic Materials
4   Manuscripts (including Manuscript Collections)
5   Music
6   Sound Recordings
7   Motion Pictures and Videorecordings
8   Graphic Materials
9   Machine-Readable Data Files
10   Three-Dimensional Artifacts and Realia
11   Microforms
12   Serials

Chapter 13, rather than dealing with a type of material or condition of publication, covers a special problem in cataloging: analysis. These *AACR 2* chapters are covered in chapters 4 through 8 of this text. There are purposely no chapters numbered 14 through 20 in *AACR 2*. These numbers were left vacant for later construction of rules for new types of material (e.g., holograms) as it becomes necessary to develop rules for cataloging them.

An important concept in using chapters 1 through 12 of *AACR 2* is that the rule numbers are mnemonic. In ISBD there are eight "areas" of description as follows:

1) Title and statement of responsibility area
2) Edition area
3) Material (or type of publication) specific details area
4) Publication, distribution, etc., area
5) Physical description area
6) Series area
7) Note area
8) Standard number and terms of availability area

Not all areas are used in describing all library materials, but in chapters 1 to 12 of *AACR 2*, all are mentioned, if only to say that the area in question is not used to describe the particular material (e.g., Rule 2.3, Material (or Type of Publication) Specific Details Area: "This area is not used for printed monographs."). The rules are numbered in such a way that the number preceding the period is the chapter number and the number following the period is the rule number. Rules 1 through 8 in each chapter represent the eight "areas" named above. Thus, Rule 1.2 deals with the edition area in general, while Rule 5.2 covers the edition area for music, and Rule 8.2 covers the edition area for graphic materials. Further, the rule numbers are subdivided by letters sometimes followed by numerals which are also mnemonic. In the general chapter, Rule 1.1D is the rule for parallel titles; for books, the comparable rule is 2.1D, and for serials it is 12.1D. In addition to the rules for "areas," all the chapters have general rules assigned the numeral "0." Chapters 1-2 and 5-12 also have rules 9 "Supplementary items," and 10 "Items made up of several types of materials." These rules do not all have exactly the same heading, but address the same concept (e.g., Rule 10 for serials is entitled, "Sections of Serials"). Chapters 1-3, 5, and 8 have a Rule 11 "Facsimiles, Photocopies, and Other Reproductions." However, Rule 11 for sound recordings is somewhat different, being entitled, "Nonprocessed Sound Recordings" and deals with unique recordings rather than reproductions. Chapter 2 has, in addition, Rules 12 through 18 that deal specifically with early printed monographs.

Throughout *AACR 2* there are "optional" rules that allow for adding or deleting information in certain instances, or that allow alternative methods of handling certain situations. Each cataloging agency must decide whether and how these options will be applied. Because so many libraries rely on the Library of Congress for cataloging data, this text includes, in this chapter and the ones on *AACR 2* that follow, a discussion of LC's decision about application of each option as it occurs in the rule sequence.

SELECTED RULES AND EXAMPLES

RULE 1.0.   GENERAL RULES

1.0A.   Sources of information

1.0A1.   A chief source of information is specified for each type of material or condition or pattern of publication. Information in the chief source is to be preferred to information found elsewhere. Some parts of the description may be taken from "prescribed" sources rather than the chief source. In either case information that is not from the chief source, where required, or from prescribed sources in the other instances, must be enclosed in square brackets.

1.0A2.   Lack of a chief source of information may be a problem with such items as locally produced sound recordings. If the item cannot be used as a basis for description, take the information from any available source and give a note explaining the source of the supplied data.

1.0C.   Punctuation

Punctuation is covered in detail in the first chapter of this text and so is not discussed here or at the beginning of each "area" of the description. Most areas in most chapters have a rule numbered "A1" (1.1A1, 1.2A1, 1.4A1, etc.) in which detailed guidance for punctuation of specific areas of the description is given.

1.0D.   Levels of detail in the description

AACR 2 is the first to provide three recommended levels of description. The minimum requirements for each level are specified in this rule. The rules in chapters 1-12 of *AACR 2* provide guidance for every element of level 3. The examples in this text, for the most part, follow LC practice in cataloging at level 2. Figs. 3.1 and 3.2 illustrate the first and second levels for the same item. The third level includes every possible element set out in the rules and is likely to be used only in cataloging such things as rare items.

Fig. 3.1. Rule 1.0D1. First level of description.

Facing zero population growth. -- Duke University Press, 1978.
    xiv, 288 p.

    Bibliography: p. [241]-277.
    Includes indexes.
    ISBN 0-8223-0412-0

Note: Cataloging to the first level of description requires use of only Rules 1.1B, 1.1F, 1.2B, 1.3, 1.4D, 1.4F, 1.5B, 1.7, and 1.8B.

Fig. 3.2. Rule 1.0D2. Second level of description.

Facing zero population growth : reactions and interpretations, past and present / Joseph J. Spengler. – Durham, N.C. :
Duke University Press, 1978.

   xiv, 288 p. ; 25 cm. – (Studies in social and economic
demography ; 1)

   Bibliography: p. [241]-277.
   Includes indexes.
   ISBN 0-8223-0412-0 : $18.75

1.0E.   Language and script of the description
   In general, information given in the title and statement of responsibility,
edition, publication, and series areas is transcribed in the language as given in
the item. Elements in other areas generally are given in the language of the
cataloging agency.

1.0F.   Inaccuracies
   Inaccuracies and misspellings are transcribed as they appear in the chief
or prescribed source from which they are taken. Inaccuracies may be followed
by "[sic]" (*see* Fig. 3.3) or they may be followed by "i.e." and the correction in
square brackets (*see* Fig. 3.4). If the error is a missing letter or letters, they may
be supplied in square brackets (e.g., mis[s]pelled).

Fig. 3.3. Rule 1.0F. Correction of inaccuracies.

Obvious error
indicated by
[sic]

The Lekwa family = Familien Lekva / written
and published by Verl L. Lekwa from material
gathered by he [sic] and Barbara Jean Lekwa
Sansgaard and James Ernest Sansgaard. -- Columbus Junction, Iowa : V. L. Lekwa, 1973.

   129 p. : ill. ; 23 cm.

Fig. 3.4. Rule 1.0F. Correction of inaccuracies.

Abbreviation,
"i.e." with cor-
rection in square
brackets

The 1860 census records of Jackson and Kan-
nebec [i.e. Kanabec] Counties, Minnesota / Sher-
man Lee Pompey. – Independence, Calif. :
Historical and Genealogical Pub. Co., c1965.

   [6] leaves ; 28 cm.

   Cover title.

1.0H.   Items with several chief sources of information

Single part items. An item that has more than one chief source of information should generally be described from the first one, with a few major exceptions outlined in this rule. For example, in cataloging sound recordings, two or more chief sources of information (e.g., labels on both sides of a disc) should be treated as a single source. Also, the chief source with the latest date of publication, distribution, etc., should be preferred. In addition, *AACR 2* prescribes preferences to follow by language, if there are different languages in the chief source. (*See AACR 2*, pp. 16-17 and the revision to 1.0H published in *AACR 2: Revisions 1983*.)

Multipart items. The chief source of information for the first part of a multipart item should be used for the basic description, with variations in later parts shown in notes. If the first part is missing, use the first part that is available. If there is no "first" part, use the part that gives the most information or the unifying container.

RULE 1.1.   TITLE AND STATEMENT OF RESPONSIBILITY AREA
         (MARC field 245)

1.1A.   Preliminary Rule

1.1A2.   Sources of information
     Title and statement of responsibility information is to be taken from the chief source of information. There is a prescribed order for data, regardless of their order in the chief source. The prescribed order should be followed except when grammatical construction does not allow it.

1.1B.   Title proper (subfield a of MARC field 245)

**1.1B1.   The exact wording, order, and spelling of the title proper should be followed in the transcription, but punctuation and capitalization may be changed. *See* Fig. 3.5.

> **Fig. 3.5. Rule 1.1B1. Transcription of title using exact words,
> but inserting commas and changing capitalization.**

> Chief source of information: Feeling Mad
>   Feeling Sad
>   Feeling Bad
>   Feeling Glad
>
> Transcription: Feeling mad, feeling sad, feeling bad, feeling glad.

An alternative title (*see AACR 2* Glossary, Appendix D) is transcribed as part of the title proper rather than as other title information. The word "or" (or its equivalent) is set off with commas and the first word of the alternative title is capitalized. *See* Fig. 3.6.

Fig. 3.6. Rule 1.1B1. Transcription of alternative title as part of title proper.

Alternative   Maria, or, The wrongs of woman / by Mary
title   Wollstonecraft ; with an introduction by Moira
                 Ferguson. – New York : Norton, [1975]

1.1B2. A statement of responsibility that is connected to the title proper with a grammatical construction (such as a case ending) is transcribed as part of the title proper. *See* Fig. 3.7.

Fig. 3.7. Rule 1.1B2. Transcription of title proper including author's name.

Bill Collins' Book of movies. – Stanmore, N.S.W. : Cassell Australia, 1977.

236 p. : ill. ; 30 cm.

ISBN 0-7269-1376-6(bound). – ISBN 0-7269-1369-3(pbk.)

1.1B4. Very long titles may be abridged if this can be done without giving up important information. The first five words may not be abridged, however. The mark of omission (i.e., ". . .") shows where omissions have been made. *See* Fig. 3.8.

Fig. 3.8. Rule 1.1B4. Abridgement of long title proper.

Hearings before the Subcommittee on the Rules and Organization of the House of the Committee on Rules, House of Representatives, Ninety-fifth Congress, second session . . . – Washington, D.C. : G.P.O., 1979.

1.1B7. If the chief source of information (or its substitute) lacks a title proper, one may be supplied from some other source, or may be constructed by the cataloger, if none can be found. Square brackets are used in such a case. *See* Fig. 3.9.

Fig. 3.9. Rule 1.1B7. Devised title proper enclosed in square brackets.

[Map of Kerr Lake Recreation Area, North Carolina]

1.1B10. When a chief source includes a collective title and also the titles of the separate works of the collection, the collective title is transcribed as the title proper. The separate individual titles are given in a contents note. *See* Fig. 3.10.

The shorter novels of Herman Melville / introduction by Raymond Weaver. – New York, N.Y. : Fawcett World Library, [196-?], c1928.

271 p. ; 18 cm.

Contents: Benito Cereno – Bartleby, the scrivener – The encantadas, or Enchanted isles – Billy Budd, foretopman.

1.1C. *Optional addition.* **General material designation** (subfield h of MARC field 245)

1.1C1. *AACR 2* gives two lists of general material designations (GMDs). List 1 is for British use and list 2 is for North American use.

LIST 1	LIST 2
cartographic material	map
	globe
	art original
	chart
	filmstrip
graphic	flash card
	picture
	slide
	technical drawing
	transparency
machine-readable data file	machine-readable data file
manuscript	manuscript
microform	microform
motion picture	motion picture
multimedia	kit
music	music
	diorama
	game
object	microscope slide
	model
	realia
sound recording	sound recording
text	text
videorecording	videorecording

The Library of Congress uses the North American list. The examples given in this text will do likewise. The only GMDs currently supplied by LC are:

filmstrip
slide
transparency
microform
motion picture
kit
sound recording
videorecording[1]

Some of the others would be used if LC were to begin cataloging those kinds of materials. However, the decision has been made *not* to use the GMDs for maps, manuscripts, music, and text.

It should be noted that by making the North American list more detailed, *AACR 2* sometimes causes a problem for North American catalogers. Because terms are very specific, there is no term for some items. For example, a toy is not really a "game" or a "model" nor do any other terms fit. Yet the British term "object" would fit nicely.

1.1C2.   When the GMD is used, it is added to the description in square brackets immediately after the title proper. For example:

Fig. 3.11. Rule 1.1C2. GMD following the title proper.

Scared straight! [motion picture]

Basic concepts of humanistic psychology [sound recording]

Great musicals of the American theatre [text]

1.1C3.   When an item is a reproduction of a work that originally appeared in a different form (e.g., microform of a map, or sound tape of an original sound disc), the GMD for the reproduction, not the original, is given. For example, this videorecording, although originally issued as a 16mm motion picture, would be entered as:

The Americans, 1776 [videorecording]

This set of 105 slides which was originally issued as a filmstrip would be entered as:

Blood pressure [slide]

1.1C4.   Some items consist of parts that fall into more than one category of the list of GMDs chosen. If one of these is predominant in the item, that form is given as the GMD. If none is predominant, the GMD used is "kit." (*See also* 1.10.) For example, the following item contains one book, one sound cassette, one poster, two puppets, and an activity guide, and would be entered as:

Why mosquitoes buzz in people's ears [kit]

1.1D. **Parallel titles** (subfield b of MARC field 245)

1.1D1. Parallel titles are recorded in the order found in the chief source of information. *See* Fig. 3.12.

Fig. 3.12. Rule 1.1D1. Transcription of parallel title.

[1]Sign for   La motoneige au Québec $\overset{1.}{=}$ Snowmobiling in
parallel title   Quebec. – Québec : Direction générale du [2]
              tourisme, [1972]

[2]Parallel   70 p. ; 18 cm.
title
              Cover title.
              French and English.
              Includes index.

1.1D2. In third-level descriptions, all parallel titles from the chief source of information are to be included. In second-level descriptions, the first parallel title from the chief source is always included, and if another parallel title is in English, it also is given. The Library of Congress records all parallel titles for items issued in the United States.[2] *See* Fig. 3.13.

Fig. 3.13. Rule 1.1D2. Transcription of a second parallel title
that is in English.

Divertimento a flauto traverso con fagotto = Divertimento für Querflöte und Fagott = Divertimento for flute
and fagott.

1.1D4. Parallel titles that are not in the chief source of information are recorded in a note. LC does this only if such parallel titles are considered to be important.[3]

1.1E. **Other title information** (subfield b of MARC field 245)

1.1E1. Other title information is transcribed using the same rules as for the title proper. Other title information includes, but is not limited to, subtitles. *See* Figs. 3.14, 3.15, and 3.16.

Fig. 3.14. Rule 1.1E1. Transcription of other title information.

Subtitle   The midnight patrol : the story of a Salvation
                     Army lass who patrolled the dark streets of Lon-
                     don's west end on a midnight mission of mercy /
                     by Phyllis Thompson. -- London : Hodder and
                     Stoughton, 1974.

                     155 p. ; 21 cm.

                     Bibliography: p. 157.
                     ISBN 0-340-17896-5 : £2.10

Fig. 3.15. Rule 1.1E1. Transcription of two kinds of other title information.

[1]Subtitle   The American view : art from 1770 to 1978 :
                     Kennedy Galleries, December 6, 1978 to January
[2]Other title   6, 1979. -- New York : The Galleries, [c1978]
information

                     [88] p. : ill. (some col.) ; 28 cm.

                     Includes index.

Fig. 3.16. Rule 1.1E1. Transcription of other title information following GMD.

[1]GMD   The Scales of justice [filmstrip] : our court sys-
                     tem / Center for Humanities, Inc. -- White
[2]Other title   Plains, N.Y. : Guidance Associates, 1979.
information

1.1E3.   Lengthy other title information
     Very long other title information may be either abridged or given in a
note. *See* Fig. 3.17.

Fig. 3.17. Rule 1.1E3. Abridgement of lengthy other title information.

Amtrak authorization : hearings before the Subcommittee on Transportation and Commerce of the Committee on Interstate and Foreign Commerce, House of Representatives, Ninety-fifth Congress, second session, on H.R.

Abridged other title information 11493 ... H.R. 11089 ... March 20, 21, and April 5, 1978. – Washington, D.C. : G.P.O., 1978.

v, 221 p. ; 24 cm.

"Serial no. 95-125."

1.1E5. When parallel titles are involved, other title information follows the title proper or the parallel title that it accompanies. *See* Fig. 3.18.

Fig. 3.18. Rule 1.1E5. Transcription of other title information following title proper or parallel title to which it is appropriate.

La nuit : Etüde für Klavier = Night : piano study : op. 31, Nr. 3 / Alexander Glasunow. – Frankfurt : M. P. Belaieff, [1975]

7 p. ; 31 cm.

"M. P. Belaieff, Nr. 111."

1.1E6. In cases where a title proper needs explanation, an explanatory term or phrase is added in brackets as other title information in the same language as the title proper. *See* Fig. 3.19. Such additions are preceded by a colon so as to distinguish them from GMDs.

Fig. 3.19. Rule 1.1E6. Addition of explanatory term as other title information.

Addition to title Beginnings : [poems] / by Carol Lynn Pearson ; illustrated by Trevor Southey. – Garden City, N.Y. : Doubleday, 1975, c1967.

63 p. : ill. ; 24 cm.

ISBN 0-385-07711-4 : $3.95

1.1F. **Statements of responsibility** (subfield c of MARC field 245)

1.1F1. Statements of responsibility that appear prominently in an item are recorded as they appear. Just as for title information, statements of responsibility that do not come from the chief source of information must be enclosed in square brackets. LC prefers to record non-prominent statements of responsibility (i.e., those not in the chief source of information) in the note area.[4] *See* Figs. 3.20-3.22.

Fig. 3.20. Rule 1.1F1. Statements of responsibility recorded as they appear in chief sources of information.

And then there's always the possibility of disappearing altogether [motion picture] / Pegarty Long. – Malibu, Calif. : Long, 1978.

Fig. 3.21.

Dear Dr. Stopes : sex in the 1920s / edited by Ruth Hall. –
    London : Deutsch, 1978.
    218 p. ; 24 cm.
    ISBN 0-233-97027-4 : £6.50

Fig. 3.22. Rule 1.1F1. Statement of responsibility taken from outside chief source of information.

Statement of   Ben Oliel and Seeley / [Dorothy Wood Ewers].
authorship   – [Crete? Ill.] : D. W. Ewers, [1966]

                          ca. 200 p. : 30 cm.

1.1F2.   Unlike titles proper, a statement of responsibility is not essential to a description, and if one is not prominent in the item, one is not constructed. *See* Fig. 3.23.

Fig. 3.23. Rule 1.1F2. Item bearing no prominent statement of responsibility.

Blood pressure [slide]. – Garden Grove, Calif. : Trainex
    Corp., [1979?]

    105 slides : col. + 1 sound cassette (29 min. ; mono.), instructor's guide, and vis-u-test.

It should be noted that serials and other items often have identical titles proper (e.g., Bulletin). When no statement of responsibility is given, non-distinctive titles become a problem when the title is the main entry and when it is necessary to make an added entry for that title on the record for another work. This problem is being solved with uniform titles. (*See* discussion in chapter 13.)

1.1F5.   Occasionally an item names more than three persons or corporate bodies that have all performed the same function or had the same degree of responsibility for the work. If there are three such persons or bodies, all are given in the statement of responsibility. If there are more than three, only the first person or corporate body of each group is listed. The omission of the others is indicated by " ... [et al.]" (or the equivalent of "et al." in nonroman scripts). *See* Fig. 3.24.

Fig. 3.24. Rule 1.1F5. Transcription of statement of responsibility with more than three persons performing the same function.

[1]First named author of a group of more than three subsidiary authors

        Studies in modality / Nicholas Rescher ; with the collaboration of Ruth Manor ... [et al.]. – Oxford : Blackwell, 1974.

        xi, 156 p. : 22 cm. – (American philosophical quarterly monograph series , no. 8)

[2]Mark of omission and [et al.]

        Includes bibliographical references and indexes.
        ISBN 0-631-11520-X : £2.30

1.1F6.   Multiple statements of responsibility (i.e., for different kinds of responsibility for a work) are transcribed in the order in which they appear in the information source. If the layout is such that the statements are not in an obvious order, the cataloger is instructed to use "the order that makes the most sense." *See* Fig. 3.25.

Fig. 3.25. Rule 1.1F6. Transcription of more than one statement of responsibility.

Persons with different kinds of responsibility

        Looking backwards / Colette ; translated from the French by David Le Vay ; with an introduction by Maurice Goudeket. – Bloomington : Indiana University Press, 1975.

        214 p. ; 24 cm.

        Translation of: Journal a rebours and De ma fenetre.
        ISBN 0-253-14900-2

1.1F7.   Most titles of address, honor, and distinction, initials of societies, qualifications, etc., are omitted from statements of responsibility. There are four exceptions:
   1)   when the title is necessary grammatically

   2)   when only a given name or only a surname is accompanied by a title

   3)   when a title is necessary for identification

   4)   when a title of nobility or British title of honor is involved.

See Fig. 3.26.

Fig. 3.26. Rule 1.1F7. Transcription of a title of address in a
statement of responsibility.

Title "Mrs."   Suppression of Mutiny, 1857-1858 / Mrs. Henry
necessary to   Duberly. – New Delhi : Sirjana Press ; Ludhiana :
identify author   distributors, Book Center, 1974.

                              168 p. : maps ; 23 cm.

                              Originally published as: Campaigning ex-
                              periences in Rajpootana and Central India dur-
                              ing the suppression of the Mutiny, 1857-58. 1859.
                              "First edition: India - August, 1974."
                              Rs35.00

1.1F8.   In instances where the relationship of the person or body in the statement of responsibility to the work is not clear, a word or phrase of explanation may be added in brackets. This does not allow, however, for the former practice of adding "by" and/or "and" in statements of authorship. *See* Figs. 3.27 and 3.28.

Fig. 3.27. Rule 1.1F8. Explanatory phrase added to statement of responsibility
for clarity.

Necessary   Modern literary manuscripts, acquired with
addition   the aid of the Arts Council of Great Britain : an
                              exhibition held in the King's Library in the British
                              Museum, 2 July-29 September 1974 / [catalogue
                              compiled] by W. H. Kelliher. -- London : British
                              Museum for the British Library Board, 1974.

                              20 p. : ill., facsims. ; 25 cm.

                              Includes index.
                              ISBN 0-7131-0489-2 : £0.30

Fig. 3.28. Rule 1.1F8. Omission of explanatory words in statement of responsibility.

1   2

^{1}[by] not
added   Potters of Southern Africa / G. Clark, L. Wag-
^{2}[and] not   ner. – 1st ed. – Cape Town : C. Struik, 1974.
added   200 p. : ill. (some col.) ; 29 cm.

Includes index.
ISBN 0-86977-046-2

Note: In cataloging prior to 1974, both "[by]" and "[and]" would have been added to this example.

1.1F12.   Noun phrases sometimes appear between titles and statements of responsibility that are not clearly part of either. One has to decide whether such a noun or noun phrase seems to indicate the nature of the work or the role of the person or body responsible. If it seems to indicate the nature of the work, it is transcribed as other title information. Otherwise it is transcribed as part of the statement of responsibility. Preference is given the latter treatment when in doubt. LC has commented that generally, nouns indicate other title information, while verbs indicate responsibility.[5] *See* Figs. 3.29 and 3.30.

Fig. 3.29. Rule 1.1F12. Noun phrase transcribed as other title information.

Noun phrase   Walt Whitman's poetry : a study & a selection
indicative of   / by Edmond Holmes. – Philadelphia : R West,
nature of the work   1978.

132 p. ; 23 cm.

"Selections from Leaves of grass": p. [77]-132.
Originally published: London : J. Lane, 1902.
ISBN 0-8492-5220-2(bound) : $12.50

Fig. 3.30. Rule 1.1F12. Noun phrase transcribed as part of statement of responsibility.

Copyright, working within the revision law : pro-
Noun phrase   ceedings of the Spring Copyright Conference,
indicating role   Seven Springs Resort, Champion, Pa., May 27-
of corporate body   28, 1977 / conference sponsored by Pennsylvania Learning Resources Association ... [et
al.]. – [S.l.] : The Association, 1977.

168 p. ; 29 cm.

Bibliography: p. 165.
Includes index.

1.1F13.   The rules for transcription of title information include instructions to give statements of responsibility as part of the title when they are inseparable grammatically. When this has been done, no separate statement of responsibility is given unless there is a separate statement in the chief source of information. *See* Figs. 3.31 and 3.32.

Fig. 3.31. Rule 1.1F13. Person responsible is transcribed as part of the title proper and thus is not repeated as a statement of responsibility.

Horowitz in concert [sound recording] : recorded at his 1966 Carnegie Hall recitals. -- [New York] : Columbia Master works, 196-.

2 sound discs (81 min.) : 33 1/3 rpm, stereo ; 12 in.

Fig. 3.32. Rule 1.1F13. Person responsible is repeated because the chief source of information bears a separate statement of responsibility.

[1]Author's name
as part of the
title

1 McGuffey's New third eclectic reader for young learners / by Wm. H. McGuffey. – New York : Gordon Press, 1974.
[2]

[2]Separate
author
statement

242 p. : ill. ; 24 cm.

Originally published: New York : American Book Co., 1885. (Eclectic educational series)
ISBN 0-87968-142-X

1.1G.   Items without a collective title

Items that lack a collective title may or may not have a predominant part. If such a predominant part is present, the title of that part is given as the title proper for the work, and other titles are given in a note. If there is no predominant part, the cataloger is given a choice between describing the item as a unit, or describing each part separately and linking the separate descriptions with notes. If the item is described as a unit, the titles are transcribed in the order given in the chief source of information (or in the order in which they appear, if there is no chief source). If the parts are all by the same person(s) or body(ies), their titles are separated by semicolons, and the statement of responsibility follows the last one. *See* Figs. 3.33 and 3.34.

Fig. 3.33. Rule 1.1G. Transcription of titles of two sides of a recording
by the same person. Each title is taken from a separate label,
and there is no linking word.

African politics ; More songs from Kenya [sound record-
ing] / David Nzomo.

Fig. 3.34. Rule 1.1G. Transcription of titles of two works that are published
in the same book. The title page gives the linking word "and."

Fantazias ; and, In nomines / by Henry Purcell ; edited
with a foreword by Anthony Ford.

If different persons or bodies were responsible for the various parts, or if it is
not known whether all parts were by the same person(s) or body(ies), each title
is followed by its other title information, statement of responsibility, and a
period. *See* Fig. 3.35.

Fig. 3.35. Rule 1.1G. Transcription of separate titles and
statements of responsibility for work that
lacks a collective title.

[1]Separate title
and statement of
responsibility

1. The suicide meet / Mary Humphrey Baldridge
Pickle / by Sheila Junor-Moore.   The saga of the
elk / by Jim Taylor.   What it means to me to be a
Canadian / compiled from Calgary School chil-
dren, grades 6 and 7. -- Toronto : Playwrights
Co-op, 1977.

[2]Name-title add-
ed entries for sep-
arate titles

34 p. ; 28 cm.

ISBN 0-88754-067-8 : $3.00

2——► I. Junor-Moore, Sheila.   Pickle. 1977.   II. Tay-
lor, Jim, 1937-   The saga of the elk. 1977.
III. What it means to me to be a Canadian.
IV. Title.

RULE 1.2.   EDITION AREA (MARC field 250)

1.2B.   **Edition statement** (subfield a of MARC field 250)

1.2B1.   If there is an edition statement, it is transcribed as found on the
item with the exception that standard abbreviations found in Appendix B of
AACR 2 and numerals as found in Appendix C of *AACR 2* are used in place
of the actual words from the source of information. *See* Figs. 3.36 and 3.37.

Fig. 3.36. Rule 1.2B1. Transcription of edition statement.

Edition with abbreviations

Export/import traffic management and forwarding / by Alfred Murr. – 3rd ed., rev. and enl. — Cambridge, Md. : Cornell Maritime Press, 1974. ix, 603 p. : forms ; 24 cm.

Bibliography: p. 594-595.
Includes index.
ISBN 0-87033-023-3 : $14.00

Fig. 3.37. Rule 1.2B1. Transcription of edition statement.

Edition with foreign abbreviations

Heidegger / Pierre Trotignon. – 2e éd. revue et corr. – [Paris] : Presses universitaires de France, 1974, c1965.

128 p. ; 18 cm. – (Collection SUP. Philosophes)

Bibliography: p. [124]-126.

1.2B4.   As an option *AACR 2* allows addition of an edition statement in square brackets when a work is known to have significant changes from earlier editions, but does not include an edition statement in a prescribed source of information.

The Library of Congress originally chose not to apply this option because of the "danger of bibliographic 'ghosts.'" [6] However, after using *AACR 2* for a while, LC chose to follow the option in instances where two catalog records would be exactly the same in the description from title through series, and "if differences are *manifest*." [7]

1.2C.   **Statements of responsibility relating to the edition** (subfield b of MARC field 250)

1.2C1.   A statement of responsibility that applies to the edition in hand, but not to all editions of a work, is given following the edition statement, if there is one. *See* Fig. 3.38.

Statement
of authorship
in edition
area

The Oxford school dictionary / compiled by
Dorothy C. Mackenzie. – 3rd ed. / revised by Joan
Pusey. -- Oxford [England] : Clarendon Press,
1974.

xii, 371 p. ; 21 cm.

ISBN 0-19-910208-2 : £0.75

1.2C2.   When there is no edition statement, when there is doubt about whether a statement of responsibility applies to all editions, or when one is describing a first edition, all statements of responsibility are transcribed into the title and statement of responsibility area.

RULE 1.3. MATERIAL (OR TYPE OF PUBLICATION) SPECIFIC DETAILS AREA (MARC field 255 for cartographic materials, field 254 for music, and field 362 for serials)

This area, so far, has been used only for cartographic materials, music, and serials. Therefore, the content of this area is discussed in the chapters specifically devoted to the description of these materials.

RULE 1.4. PUBLICATION, DISTRIBUTION, ETC., AREA (MARC field 260)

1.4B.   **General rules**

1.4B1.   All details about place(s), name(s), and date(s) of the activities involved in publishing, distributing, issuing, and/or releasing are recorded in this area.

1.4B6.   When the work in hand is a reproduction, the original publication details may be covered by a label giving reproduction details. In such a case the information from the label is recorded in the publication, distribution, etc., area, and the publication details for the original are given in a note (if they can be determined easily).

LC applies this rule whether or not a "reproduction" is involved.[8] *See* Fig. 3.39.

Fig. 3.39. Rule 1.4B6. Publication details from label transcribed in publication,
distribution, etc., area with original publication details in a note.

¹**Publisher**   Human potentialities [sound recording] / Her-
information   bert A. Otto. – New York : J. Norton Publishers,
relating to   [1974?]   ↘₁
reproduction
                         1 tape reel (27 min.) : 3 3/4 ips, mono. ; 5 in.

²**Publication**   Publisher information under label reads:
details of   ↗New York : McGraw-Hill, 1968
original   2↗

1.4C.   **Place of publication, distribution, etc.** (subfield a of MARC field
                 260)

1.4C1.   The place of publication (or production, etc.) is recorded as it
appears in a prescribed source of information.

1.4C3.   The name of the country, state, province, etc., is added to the
name when necessary to distinguish between places or if necessary for
identification. *See* Figs. 3.40-3.42.

Fig. 3.40. Rule 1.4C3. Addition of country in brackets where city alone
appeared in prescribed source of information.

Name of Coun-   Vanished fleets : sea stories from old Van Die-
try added   man's land / by Alan Villiers. – Cambridge
              ——→[Cambridgeshire] : P. Stephens, 1974.

LC adds larger jurisdictions that appear with a place name in the source
of information even when identification is not needed. When the larger
jurisdiction does not appear together with the place name, LC adds it in
brackets when the place is obscure. The larger jurisdiction is also added when
there is more than one place with the same name and the one in the cataloged
item is not the best known. Such additions are made according to the
provisions for geographic names in chapter 23 of *AACR 2*.⁹

Fig. 3.41. Rule 1.4C3. Addition of state to name of city.
Name of state appeared in prescribed source of information.

Name of   Hans in luck [motion picture]. -- Santa Monica,
State added   ——→Calif. : Bosustow Productions, 1978.

Fig. 3.42. Rule 1.4C3. Name of state not added to city because it was not on the title page and was not considered necessary to identify the city.

Name of
State not
added

Troll tales of Tumble Town [filmstrip] / Don Arthur Torgersen. – Chicago : Coronet Instructional Media, 1978.

1.4C5. When more than one place is given in the item for a publisher, distributor, etc., the first-named place is transcribed. If another place is in the home country of the cataloging agency, and the first is not, it is also transcribed. In addition, if a place other than the first is typographically prominent, it is also transcribed. *See* Fig. 3.43.

Rule 1.4D5 treats two or more places that relate to two or more publishers, etc.

Fig. 3.43. Rule 1.4C5. Transcription by a U.S. cataloging agency of U.S. city following foreign city.

[1]Foreign city

[2]U.S. city

Educational theory : an introduction / [by] T. W. Moore. – London ; Boston : Routledge and K. Paul, 1974.

1.4C6. A probable place is given in brackets with a question mark when the place of publication, etc., is uncertain. *See* Fig. 3.44.

Fig. 3.44. Rule 1.4C6. Transcription of probable place of publication with question mark.

Place
uncertain

A century in Singapore : 1877-1977 / Hongkong and Shanghai Banking Corporation. – [Singapore? : Hongkong and Shanghai Banking Corp., 1977?]

If the place is unknown but the country, state, province, etc., is known or probable, the country, state or province, etc., is given in brackets (with a question mark if uncertain). *See* Fig. 3.45.

Fig. 3.45. Rule 1.4C6. Transcription of country in lieu of city
for place of publication, etc.

Name of   Out of the writers' workshop / edited by Kwabe-
Country   na Asiedu. – [Ghana] : National Association of
               Writers, c1974.

               79 p. ; 21 cm.

               Selections from 2 workshops organized by the
               National Association of Writers held at Wesley
               College, Kumasi, Ghana, May 16-19, and at Girl
               Guides Training Centre, Accra, June 4-8, 1974.

LC supplies the name of the country in this situation, except for
Australia, Canada, and the United States, for which state or province is
preferred if known or probable. For Great Britain, the names "England,"
"Scotland," "Wales," or "Northern Ireland" are preferred, if known or
probable. For all other situations, the country or probable country is given if
known and the local place of publication is not known.[10]

If no country, etc., or probable country can be given, the abbreviation
"s.l." (sine loco), or its equivalent in nonroman scripts, is given. *See* Fig. 3.46.

Fig. 3.46. Rule 1.4C6. Transcription of abbreviation "s.l."
when no place or probable place is known.

Place   Precious cargo / by Ralph Byrne. -- [S.l. : R.
unknown   Byrne], c1978.

Note: Upper case "S.l." results from its beginning an area of the description.

1.4C7.   An option allows transcription in parentheses, after the place
name, of the full address of a publisher, distributor, etc. Such an addition
should not be made for major trade publishers.

LC has a strict set of provisions for applying this option. The basic ones
are that it applies only to monographs published in the U.S., issued in the
current year or one of the previous two years, and not bearing ISBNs or
ISSNs.[11] *See* Fig. 3.47.

Fig. 3.47. Rule 1.4C7. Addition of address of publisher to the
place of publication, etc.

Journey into small groups / William Bangham. – Memphis, Tenn.
(1548 Poplar Avenue, Memphis, 38104) : Lay Renewal,
c1974.

1.4D. **Name of publisher, distributor, etc.** (subfield b of MARC field 260)

1.4D1. The name of the publisher, distributor, etc., follows the name of the place.

1.4D2. The name of the publisher, distributor, etc., is given in the shortest form it can take to be understood internationally. *See* Fig. 3.48.

Fig. 3.48. Rule 1.4D2. Transcription of name of publisher
in shortest identifiable form.

Publisher's
name abbre-
viated
  The Basic book of antiques / by George
Michael. – New York : Arco Pub. Co., [1974]

It is important to note the term "internationally." Because there is now more emphasis on creating bibliographic records for an international audience, the publisher, distributor, etc., area sometimes needs fuller information than was adequate in the past.

LC does not omit parts of a hierarchy for any corporate bodies except commercial publishers. Also, such words as "Inc." that appear after a serial title being recorded as a publisher are retained.[12]

1.4D3. Two restrictions are placed on omissions from names of publishers, distributors, etc.:

 a) Words that indicate function other than only a publishing function are included. *See* Figs. 3.49 and 3.50.

Fig. 3.49. Rule 1.4D3a. Transcriptions of name of publisher, distributor,
etc., including words and phrases indicating functions performed.

Published
for ...
by ...
  At the edge of megalopolis : a history of Salem, N. H., 1900-1974 / [Noyes, Turner]. – Canaan,
N. H. : Published for the Town of Salem, N. H., by
Phoenix Pub., c1974.

Fig. 3.50.

Distributor
indicated
  The National labor relations act : a guidebook
for health care facility administrators / Dennis D.
Pointer and Norman Metzger. – New York : Spectrum Publications : distributed by Halsted Press,
[1975]

b) Parts of a name that distinguish between publishers, etc., are retained. For example:

Encyclopaedia Britannica Educational Corp.
Encyclopaedia Britannica, Inc.

(These are separate bodies and cannot be identified simply as Encyclopaedia Britannica).

1.4D4.   A person or corporate body that appears in both the statement of responsibility and the publication area may be given in the publication area in a shortened form if the name is in a recognizable form in the title and statement of responsibility area. *See* Fig. 3.51.

Fig. 3.51. Rule 1.4D4. Transcription of shortened form of name
that appears in full form in the title and
statement of responsibility area.

Shortened   The Dexter Avenue Baptist Church, 1877-1977 /
name   edited by Zelia S. Evans, with J. T. Alexander.
                         – 1st ed. -- [Montgomery, Ala.] : The Church,
                         c1978.

When a person is both author and publisher, the form used in the publisher, etc., area is the initial(s) and surname of the person. LC places some restrictions on use of this rule. If an initialism appears in the statement of responsibility and the full form is in the item's imprint, the full form is used. The shortened form must create no doubt that it is referring to a name already mentioned and to which name it refers if there is more than one.[13] Brackets are not required for this shortened form unless the name is in brackets in the title and statement of responsibility area. *See* Fig. 3.52.

Fig. 3.52. Rule 1.4D4. Transcription in brackets of abbreviated form of name
that appears in brackets in the statement of responsibility.

Statement of   Federal funds in Maine : a second look / [pre-
responsibility   pared for the Governor by the Dept. of Finance
                         and Administration, Bureau of the Budget]. – Au-
Shortened   gusta : [The Bureau], 1974.
name placed
in brackets

1.4D5.   There are four situations in which the transcription of a subse-quently named publisher, distributor, etc. (and its place, if different from the first) is to be added after the first named body:

a) when the two bodies are linked in a single statement, e.g.,

London: Published for the Institute of Mediaeval Studies
by Sheed & Ward.

b) when a distributor, etc., is named first, while a publisher is named later,

c) when a publisher, distributor, etc., is clearly the principal one (as shown by layout or typography) but is not named first,

d) when the first body is not in the country of the cataloging agency, while a later one is. *See* Fig. 3.53.

Fig. 3.53. Rule 1.4D5. Transcription by a U.S. cataloging agency of U.S. city and publisher following foreign city and publisher.

[1]Foreign city and publisher

[2]U.S. city and publisher

Genetics of forest ecosystems / Klaus Stern, Laurence Roche. – London : Chapman and Hall ; New York : Springer-Verlag, 1974.

An option allows addition of the name (and place if different) of a distributor when the first name is for a publisher. LC is applying this option.[14] *See* Fig. 3.54.

Fig. 3.54. Rule 1.4D5. Transcription of names of both producer and distributor.

The Plow that broke the Plains [videorecording] / United States Resettlement Administration – Washington, D.C. : National Archives and Records Service : distributed by National Audiovisual Center, 1978.

LC, in applying Rule 1.4D5, records both entities when two are named. The situations prescribed in the rule, then, are used as guidelines when three or more names are given.[15]

1.4D6. When the name of the publisher, etc., is not known, the abbreviation s.n. (sine nomine) is given in brackets. *See* Fig. 3.55.

Fig. 3.55. Rule 1.4D6. Transcription of "s.n." to indicate that the name of the publisher is unknown.

Publisher unknown

The story of Lanark / prepared and written by Elizabeth L. Jamieson. – [S.l. : s.n.], c1974.

1.4E.   *Optional addition.* **Statement of function of publisher, distributor, etc.**

An option allows addition of "distributor," "publisher," "producer," or "production company" to the name of a publisher, distributor, etc., unless the function of the agency is clear (e.g., because the phrase naming the publisher includes words indicating function). *See* Figs. 3.50 under Rule 1.4D3 and 3.56 below.

Fig. 3.56. Rule 1.4E. Transcription in brackets of function performed following name of agency.

Term show-   Live or die [motion picture] / E. C. Brown Founda-
ing function   tion. – [Illinois?] : Wexler Film Productions,
                      Inc. ; Highland Park, Ill. : Perennial Education
                  ⟶ [distributor], 1978.

LC is applying this option, but only when there is a publisher and a distributor and the distributor's name does not indicate this function, or when there is only one entity named and this entity performs the distributing function.[16]

1.4F.   **Date of publication, distribution, etc.** (subfield c of MARC field 260)

1.4F1.   The date of publication of the edition in hand is the next element of this area.

1.4F2.   The date given in the item is used even if it is known to be incorrect, in which case the correct date is added in brackets and an explanation is given in a note if necessary. *See* Fig. 3.57.

Fig. 3.57. Rule 1.4F2. Transcription of a date known to be incorrect, followed by the correct date in brackets.

[1]Imprint   New Industrial polymers : a symposium sponsor-
date on   ed by the Division of Organic Coatings and
title page   Plastics Chemistry at the 167th meeting of the
[2]Corrected   American Chemical Society, Los Angeles,
imprint date   Calif., April 1-2, 1974 / Rudolph D. Deanin, ed-
                     itor. -- Washington, D.C. : American Chemical
                     Society, 1972 [i.e., 1974] ⟵2
                  1 ⟋⎯⎯⎯⎯⎯⎯⎯⎯⎯

1.4F3.   If an edition has been reissued, the reissue date is given only if the edition area identifies the item as a reissue. Otherwise the original issue date is given. *See* Figs. 3.58 and 3.59.

Fig. 3.58. Rule 1.4F3. Transcription of original date.
No mention is made of the fact that the item in hand is a
1974 reissue of the 1959 work.

Original
date

The rebellion of 1914-15 : a bibliography /
compiled by Gerald Dennis Quinn. – [Cape
Town] : University of Cape Town Libraries, 1959.

1.4F4. If publication and distribution dates differ, the distribution date
is added only if thought to be significant. When both dates are given, each is
given after the name to which it applies. If the dates are the same, the date is
given after the publisher or distributor named last. *See* Fig. 3.56.

1.4F5. An option allows adding the latest copyright date to the publication, distribution, etc., date if it is different. LC is applying this option.[17] *See*
Fig. 3.59. NOTE: A copyright date is always preceded by a "c," and a
phonogram copyright date is preceded by a "p."

Fig. 3.59. Rule 1.4F5. Transcription of copyright date that varies
from publication date.

[1]Date of
reissue specified
in edition
area
[2]Copyright date

A pocket guide to chess endgames / David
Hooper. – 1st ed. reprinted. – London : G. Bell,
1973, c1970.

1.4F6. If there is no known date of publication or distribution, the
copyright date is used. If there is no copyright date, a manufacturing date, if
present, is given. In the latter case, a word such as "printing" or "pressing" is
added, e.g., 1985 pressing. *See* Fig. 3.60.

Fig. 3.60. Rule 1.4F6. Use of copyright date when publication date is unknown.

Copyright
date

How to deal with a horse / Patricia Stillwagon.
– South Brunswick : A. S. Barnes, c1974.

LC has found it necessary to issue a lengthy rule interpretation for when to use
copyright date, probable date of publication, and/or date of manufacture.[18]

1.4F7. If no date of publication, etc., copyright, or manufacture can be
found, the cataloger is instructed to give an approximate date. *See* Figs. 3.61
and 3.62. *See also* examples in *AACR 2*, chapter 1, page 36.

Fig. 3.61. Rule 1.4F7. Transcriptions of approximate dates of publication.

Believed to   A genealogy of the Beeson family / compiled
be 1974   by Margaret Ailene Beeson. – Greensboro, N. C. :
                     M. A. Beeson, [1974?]

Fig. 3.62.

Uncertain   This is Hungary / by Zoltán Halász. – [Rome :
date   Hungarian Press Office, between 1970 and 1974]

An option allows giving an approximate date if it is significantly different
from the dates given according to Rule 1.4F6. LC is applying this option within
the limits of the rule interpretation issued for 1.4F6.[19] *See* Fig. 3.10 on page 57.

1.4F8.   When a multipart item has been published during more than one
year and thus two or more dates are found on different parts, the earliest and
latest dates are given. Give only the earliest date and a hyphen followed by
four spaces when a multipart item is incomplete. Many libraries then add the
latest date when the item is complete. *See* Fig. 3.63.

Fig. 3.63. Rule 1.4F8. Transcription of earliest and latest dates
of a multipart item.

[1]Inclusive   The German colonies in South Russia 1804 to
dates   1904 / by P. Conrad Keller ; translation A. Beck-
                     er. – [Saskatoon : Western Producer], c1968-1973. ◄——1
[2]Two vol-   2 ——► 2 v. : ill., maps ; 22 cm.
ume work

**1.4G.   Place of manufacture, name of manufacturer, date of manu-
               facture** (subfields e, f, and g of MARC field 260)

1.4G1.   If the name of the publisher, distributor, etc., is not known and
the place and name of the manufacturer are given in the item, the latter are
transcribed into the record after the date. (The date given in the publication
date position is often the date of manufacture in this situation; if so, it is not
repeated here.) *See* Fig. 3.64.

Fig. 3.64. Rule 1.4G1. Transcription of place and name of manufacturer
following date when publisher is unknown.

¹Place of publi-
cation unknown

²Name of pub-
lisher unknown   The offensive side of Lou Holtz / by Lou Holtz.
                   – [S.l. : s.n.], c1978 (Little Rock, Ark. : Parkin
³Manufactur-   Printing Co.)   ₃
er's imprint

1.4G4.   An option allows giving the place, name, and date of manufacture when they are different from those given as place, name, and date of
publication, etc., if they are considered to be important.

LC is applying this option on a case-by-case basis, with emphasis on the
importance of the data.[20]

RULE 1.5. PHYSICAL DESCRIPTION AREA (MARC field 300)

1.5A3.   This preliminary rule calls for giving the physical description for
the item in hand if the work is available in different formats. Optionally, notes
are made to describe the other physical formats in which an item is available.

The part of this rule that calls for describing text on microfilm as
microfilm has caused much controversy in the library community. It is
believed by many librarians that the importance of text on microfilm is as a
version of the text. The fact that the version is in microform rather than
regular print is, to these persons, less important than the description of the
original in terms of number of pages of text. On the other side, there are those
who say that the purpose of bibliographic description is to describe the item in
hand. If it is two sheets of microfiche, it is not the same as a 350-page bound
volume.

This debate has been temporarily resolved by LC's decision to catalog
microreproductions of certain printed items by transcribing the physical
details of the original work in the body of the description while giving the
details of the microreproduction in a note. This practice has not been adopted
as a rule revision because the other countries involved in responsibility for
AACR 2 have not had as much discussion and/or as much problem about the
issue. (*See also* chapter 6 of this text.)

In describing the item in hand the cataloger should also be careful to
describe the item as published, not what it will be after binding or other
processing for the library's shelves.[21]

The option of making a note describing other formats is being applied by
LC. They believe it helpful to library users to be able to see information about
other existing forms of the same item.[22] *See* Fig. 3.65.

Fig. 3.65. Rules 1.5A3 and 1.5B1. Transcription of extent of item in hand
with note of other physical formats in which
the work is available.

[1] Number of
physical units
[2] Note of
other existing
forms of same
item

Benjamin and the miracle of Hanukah [videore-
cording] / Benjamin & Associates. – Wilmette,
Ill. : Films Inc., 1978.

1 videocassette (30 min.) : sd., col. ; 3/4 in.

1 — U standard.

Also issued as Betamax or VHS cassette and as
2 — motion picture.

1.5B.   **Extent of item (including specific material designation)** (subfield a of MARC field 300)

1.5B1.   The extent of item consists of the number of physical units in
arabic numerals followed by the specific material designation. *See* Fig. 3.65
above.

How to record the extent of item for different types of materials is
covered in detail in each chapter on a type of material. Where appropriate,
additions in parentheses are made following the number of physical units (e.g.,
number of frames on a filmstrip, playing time), and these are explained fully in
the following chapters.

1.5B5.   A multipart item that is not yet complete is described with the
specific material designation preceded by three spaces. An option allows
adding the number of physical units after completion of the item. *See* Fig.
3.66.

Fig. 3.66. Rule 1.5B5. Transcription of designation preceded by
three spaces for incomplete item.

Designation
for incomplete
multipart
item

Deaths, marriages, and much miscellaneous
from Rhinebeck, New York newspapers,
1846-1899 / [compiled by Arthur C. M. Kelly]. –
Rhinebeck, N.Y. : Kelly, 1978-

———→ v. ; 30 cm.

Includes index.
Contents: v. 1. Deaths.

The Library of Congress is applying the option; so if the work in Fig. 3.66 becomes complete in, say, 3 volumes, the physical description area will read: 3v. ; 30 cm.

1.5C.   Other physical details (subfield b of MARC field 300)

1.5C1.   Physical details other than extent of item or dimensions are given following the extent. These vary by type of material. Details are discussed in later chapters. *See* Fig. 3.67.

Fig. 3.67. Rule 1.5C1. Transcription of other physical details following extent of item.

Physical   Reactive intermediates. -- Vol. 1 (1978)-   . --
data about   New York : John Wiley & Sons, c1978-
presence of
illustrations   v. : ill. ; 24 cm.

1.5D.   Dimensions (subfield c of MARC field 300)
     The dimensions of an item serve as an aid in finding it on the library shelves. Dimensions are especially valuable for libraries with separate storage areas for oversized items. They also serve the user who wishes to borrow an item through interlibrary loan.

     As is true for other parts of the physical description, instructions for giving dimensions vary by type of material. *See* Fig. 3.68.

Fig. 3.68. Rule 1.5D. Transcription of dimensions following extent of item, there being no "other" physical details.

Height in   Repartee : for orchestra / Eric Wild. -- Toronto
centimeters   : Clark & Cruickshank, c1974.

                              1 score (21 p.) ; 28 cm. ◂——

1.5E.   Accompanying material (subfield e of MARC field 300)
     Accompanying material includes answer books, teacher's manuals, atlases, portfolios of plates, slides, phonodiscs, booklets explaining audio-visual materials, and other such items. These materials often are placed in pockets inside the cover of the work being cataloged, or they may be loose inside the container. Their description may make up the fourth element of the physical description area.

1.5E1.   Four methods are suggested for handling accompanying material: a) It may be described in a separate entry. b) It may be described in a multi-level description as outlined in chapter 13 of *AACR 2*. c) Details may be given in a note. d) Details may be given as the last element of the physical description area.

See Fig. 3.69.

Fig. 3.69. Rule 1.5E1d. Transcription of the name of accompanying material as the last element of the physical description area.

| Accompany-ing material | The reading process : the teacher and the learner / Miles V. Zintz. – 2nd ed. – Dubuque, Iowa : W. C. Brown Co., [1975]

xi, 575 p. : ill. ; 24 cm. + instructor's manual. |

If the fourth method is used, an option allows addition in parentheses of further physical description of the accompanying material. *See* Fig. 3.70.

Fig. 3.70. Rule 1.5E1d. Transcription of physical description for accompanying material.

| Accompany-ing material with its physical description | There is no such phenomenon / Rita Arditi Volk. – San Francisco : Sedarsky-Besse Associates, 1974.

158 p. : ill. ; 29 cm. + 1 sound disc (5 min. : 33⅓ rpm : 7 in.) |

LC is applying this option on a case-by-case basis to items that are substantial in extent or are significant for some reason (e.g., nonprint items accompanying text).[23]

RULE 1.6.   SERIES AREA (MARC field 4xx)

The first definition of "series" as it appears in the *AACR 2* Glossary is: "A group of separate items related to one another by the fact that each item bears, in addition to its own title proper, a collective title applying to the group as a whole."

1.6B.   Title proper of series (subfield a of MARC field 4xx)

1.6B1.   The title proper of a series is transcribed according to the rules for transcribing the title proper of the item. *See* Fig. 3.71.

Series
title

Peaches : for flute and piano / André Previn.
–New York : Edition W. Hansen/Chester Music,
[c1978]

1 score (8 p.) + 1 part ; 30 cm. – (The Chester
woodwind series)

Other title information is seldom recorded for series. It is recorded only if
valuable for identifying the series. When other title information or parallel
titles for series are recorded, they are transcribed according to the same rules
used for the title and statement of responsibility area.

1.6B2.   This rule gives a hierarchy for choice among variant series titles
that may appear in an item. A title in the chief source of information is preferred. If variants appear in the chief source, the one that identifies most adequately and succinctly is used. The same criterion is applied to variant titles,
none of which is in the chief source of information.

        LC prefers a series title given on a series title page if it differs from the
series title in the chief source of information.[24]

1.6E.   **Statements of responsibility relating to series** (subfield a of
        MARC field 4xx)

1.6E1.   Statements of responsibility that appear "in conjunction with the
series title" are to be recorded if "they are considered to be necessary for identification." LC has issued a rule interpretation stating that this means statements
that are in close proximity for titles that are essentially meaningless without
such a statement (e.g., Report).[25] *See* Fig. 3.72.

[1]Generic
title

[2]Statement
of responsi-
bility

The Cooper River environmental study / by Frank
    P. Nelson, editor. -- Cayce : South Carolina
    Water Resources Commission, 1974.
    164 p. : ill. ; 28 cm. – (Report / South Carolina
Water Resources Commission ; no. 117)

1.6F.   **ISSN of series** (subfield x of MARC field 4xx)

The ISSN is the International Standard Serial Number, assigned to a serial as an internationally agreed-upon unique identifier. It is useful for identification and ordering purposes. It is recorded in the series area if it appears in the item. *See* Fig. 3.73.

Fig. 3.73. Rule 1.6F. Transcription of ISSN following series title.

¹Series title   Report on social security for Canada / Leonard
²ISSN   Marsh ; with a new introduction by the author ;
³Series   and a preface by Michael Bliss. – Toronto ; Buf-
number   falo : University of Toronto Press, [1975]   ₁

                     xxxi, 330 p. ; 23 cm. – (The Social history of
                     Canada, ISSN 0085-6207 ; 24) ◄——3
                 2

1.6G.   **Numbering within series** (subfield v of MARC field 4xx)

1.6G1.   Numbering given with the series in the item is recorded as part of the series area. Abbreviations as found in Appendix B of *AACR 2* are used and arabic numerals are substituted for nonarabic numerals. *See* Fig. 3.74.

**Fig. 3.74, Rule 1.6G1. Transcription of series numbering
as given in the item.**

¹Series   Administrative process : a guide to practice
title   before administrative agencies. -- [Harrisburg] :
²Series   Pennsylvania Bar Institute, c1978.   ₁   ²
number
                     vi, 161 p. ; 28 cm. – (PBI publication ; no. 95)

LC has found it necessary to issue a lengthy rule interpretation concerning transcription of series numbering.[26]

1.6H.   **Subseries** (subfield p of MARC field 4xx)

AACR 2 defines subseries: "A series within a series; that is, a series which always appears in conjunction with another, usually more comprehensive, series of which it forms a section. Its title may or may not be dependent on the title of the main series."

Such a subseries, if present, is transcribed after the details of the main series. Parallel titles, other title information, statements of responsibility, ISSN, and numbering are transcribed for subseries in the same way as for series. *See* Fig. 3.75.

Fig. 3.75. Rule 1.6H. Transcription of subseries information
following series title.

^{1}Series
title
^{2}Subseries
title
^{3}ISSN for
subseries
^{4}Numbering
for subseries

Children's language at four and six : a longitu-
dinal and multivariable study of language abili-
ties among children / Barbro Eneskär. – Lund :
LiberLäromedel/Gleerup, 1978.   _1

69 p. : tables ; 25 cm. – (Studia psychologica et
paedagogica. Series altera, ISSN 0346-5926 ; 42)
2   3   4

1.6J.   More than one series statement

1.6J1.   If there is more than one series, each series is recorded in a
separate series statement in its own set of parentheses. If one series is more
specific than the other(s), it is recorded first. *See* Fig. 3.76.

Fig. 3.76. Rule 1.6J1. Transcription of two series statements,
each in its own set of parentheses.

^{1}First
series
^{2}Second
series

History of the western Gangas / B. Sheik Ali.
–1st ed. – Mysore : Prasaranga, University of Mysore, 1976.   _1

xiii, 416 p., [31] leaves of plates . ill., maps ; 26
cm. – (Comprehensive history of Karnataka ; v. 1)
(Other publications / University of Mysore ; 61)

                                                          2

RULE 1.7.   NOTE AREA (MARC fields 5xx)

Many works require description beyond that presented formally in the
title and statement of responsibility area through the series area. Notes qualify
or amplify the formal description. Some notes contribute to identification of a
work (e.g., a note giving the original title of a translated work). Some contribute to the intelligibility of the record (e.g., a note explaining the relationship to the work of a person who has been given an added entry). Other notes
aid the reader who does not have in hand an exact citation (e.g., a summary or
contents note). Still other notes characterize an item (e.g., a thesis note), or
give its bibliographic history (e.g., notes giving previous titles).

1.7A.   Preliminary rule

1.7A3.   Form of notes
This rule gives general guidelines for the formulation of notes.

Order of information. In any one note, data that correspond to data found in descriptive areas preceding the notes area are transcribed in the same order in the note. The prescribed punctuation is used with the exception that a period (full stop), space, dash, space is replaced simply by a period (full stop). *See* Fig. 3.77.

Fig. 3.77. Rule 1.7A3. Transcription of information in the note in the same order it would be transcribed above, but without any period, space, dash, space separating areas.

Priceless pearls : [poems] / by A. S. H. Hossain. – Calcutta : M.S.S. Hossain, 1890.

iv, ix, 147 p. ; 18 cm.

With: The lament of Islam / A. S. H. Hossain. Calcutta: [s.n.], 1894.

Quotations. Quotations in notes are given in quotes followed by an indication of the source, unless the chief source of information is the source of the quotation.

Formal notes. Standard format is used for certain notes because uniformity can assist in recognition of some types of information and because it allows for space economy.

Informal notes. Informal notes should be as brief as they can be without sacrificing clarity, understandability, or good grammar.

1.7A4.   Notes citing other editions and works
     When notes are made citing other works or other manifestations of the same work, the notes should give enough information to identify the work cited. When giving a note for an original work from which the work in hand is reproduced, all notes relating to the original are combined into one note.

1.7B.   Notes
     A general outline of notes is given here followed by some examples (*see* Figs. 3.78-3.83 on pages 88-90). More specific applications are discussed in the following chapters where notes applicable to the various types of material are discussed in detail.
     Notes are to be given in the order listed here. Upon examination, one can determine the logic of the order. First come notes concerning the nature and language of the item. Then come notes that relate to the areas of description from title through series in the order in which they appear in the body of the entry. These are followed by notes that characterize and summarize the item.
     [Note: MARC field 500 is used unless otherwise noted.]

1.7B1.	**Nature, scope, or artistic form of the item**
1.7B2.	**Language of the item and/or translation or adaptation** (MARC field 546)
1.7B3.	**Source of title proper**
1.7B4.	**Variations in title**
1.7B5.	**Parallel titles and other title information**
1.7B6.	**Statements of responsibility** (MARC fields 500, 508, 511, and 570)
1.7B7.	**Edition and history** (MARC fields 500 and 503)
1.7B8.	**Material specific details**
1.7B9.	**Publication, distribution, etc.** (MARC field 550)
1.7B10.	**Physical description**
1.7B11.	**Accompanying materials and supplements**
1.7B12.	**Series**
1.7B13.	**Dissertations** (MARC field 502)
1.7B14.	**Audience**
1.7B15.	**Reference to published descriptions** (MARC field 510)
1.7B16.	**Other formats available** (MARC field 530)
1.7B17.	**Summary** (MARC field 520)
1.7B18.	**Contents** (MARC fields 504 and 505)
1.7B19.	**Numbers borne by the item (other than those covered in 1.8)** (MARC fields 023-030, 036, 037)
1.7B20.	**Copy being described and library's holdings** (MARC field 590)
1.7B21.	**"With" notes** (MARC field 501)
1.7B22.	**Combined notes relating to the original** (MARC field 534)

Fig. 3.78. Rule 1.7B. Transcriptions of notes.

Title varia-
tion (1.7B4)

American dainties and how to prepare them / by an American lady. – London : R. Jackson, [190-?]

iv, 92 p. ; 19 cm.

Cover title: American fancy groceries and recipes by an American lady for 170 dainty dishes.

[1]Statement of
responsibility
(1.7B6)
[2]Physical
description
(1.7B10)
[3]Audience
(1.7B14)

[4]Other formats
available
(1.7B16)
[5]Contents
(1.7B18)

Fig. 3.79. Rule 1.7B. Transcriptions of notes.

Troll tales of Tumble Town [filmstrip] / Don Arthur Torgersen. – Chicago : Coronet Instructional Media, 1978.

6 filmstrips : col. ; 35 mm. + 6 sound cassettes
1 (102 min.) and program guide.
2 Illustrations, Tom Dunnington.
Sound accompaniment compatible for manual and automatic operation.
3 For elementary grades.
4 Also issued with sound accompaniment on disc.
5 Contents: 1. Muddlepuddle, the troll who lived in the lake (51 fr.) – 2. Rumplegrumple, the trickiest troll (49 fr.) – 3. Tamtammy MacTroll and the scariest night in Troll Forest (51 fr.) – 4. Terrabulous Troll goes to school (52 fr.) – 5. Ravencraven, the wicked witch of Troll Cave (47 fr.) – 6. Frozenose and Snozenose, the angry giants of Troll Mountain (48 fr.).

Fig. 3.80. Rule 1.7B. Transcriptions of notes.

[1]Quoted note
on history
(1.7B7)
[2]Edition and
history note
(1.7B7)
[3]Contents
(1.7B18)

Annals of Athens, Georgia, 1801-1901 / by Augustus Longstreet Hull ; with an introductory sketch by Henry Hull. -- Danielsville, Ga. : Heritage Papers, c1978.

xiv, 568 p., [6] leaves of plates : ill. ; 23 cm.

1 ——► "These sketches ... were for the most part first published in the Southern watchman in 1879."
2 ——►Reprint with additions and corrections. Originally published: Athens, Ga. : Banner Job Office, 1906.
3 ——►Includes index.

Fig. 3.81. Rule 1.7B. Transcriptions of notes.

[1]History
note (1.7B7)
[2]Summary
(1.7B17)

Arson : fire for hire [motion picture] / ABC News. – New York : McGraw-Hill Films, 1978.

1 film reel (27 min.) : sd., col. ; 16 mm. + teacher's guide.

1 ——►Originally broadcast on the ABC television program Close-up.
2 ——►Summary. Explains that arson is the fastest growing crime in America, and that in many places it has become a big and profitable business. Points out that one of the reasons for the increase in arson is the lack of effective law enforcement and prosecution.

Fig. 3.82. Rule 1.7B. Transcriptions of notes.

[1]Physical
description
(1.7B10)
[2]Contents
(1.7B18)
[3]Contents
(1.7B18)

Air law / Shawcross and Beaumont. -- 4th ed. / Peter Martin ... [et al.]. – London : Butterworths, 1977-

v. : ill., forms ; 26 cm.

1 ——►Loose-leaf (v. 2) for updating.
2 ——►Includes bibliographical references and index.
3 ——►Contents: v. 1. General text -- v. 2. Noter-up, treaties, and legislation.

Fig. 3.83. Rule 1.7B. Transcriptions of notes.

¹Thesis note
for doctoral
work (1.7B13)
²Institution
granting degree
(1.7B13)
³Contents
(1.7B18)

Robert Harley as secretary of state, 1704-1708
/ by John Henry Davis. – Chicago : [s.n.], 1932.

xiv, 218 leaves ; 32 cm.   2

1——→Thesis (Ph.D.)–University of Chicago.
3 ——→Bibliography: leaves 198-218.

RULE 1.8.   STANDARD NUMBER AND TERMS OF AVAILABILITY AREA (MARC fields 020 and 022)

1.8B.   **Standard number** (subfield a of MARC field 020 or 022)

1.8B1.   An internationally agreed-upon standard number for the item in hand is given in the standard number area following the notes. The numbers usually given here are the International Standard Book Number (ISBN) or the International Standard Serial Number (ISSN). *See* Fig. 3.84.

Fig. 3.84. Rule 1.8B1. Transcription of standard number for the
item being described.

Standard
number

Angel makers / by Penny Kemp. – 1st ed. – Toronto : Playwrights Co-op, 1978.

41 p. ; 28 cm.

——→ISBN 0-88754-089-9

1.8B2.   If there are two or more standard numbers, the one that applies to the item being described should be given. An option allows recording more than one number and adding a qualification (as prescribed in 1.8E). LC is applying this option. There are many possible situations that involve multiple ISBNs. These are discussed in detail in an LC rule interpretation.[27] *See* Fig. 3.85.

Fig. 3.85. Rule 1.8B2, option. Transcription of more than one
standard number on a record.

¹Standard
number for hard
back edition   1
²Standard
number for
paperback edition 07-X(pbk.)

Bean Street : poems / by John S. Morris. -- Fay-
etteville, Ark. : Lost Roads Pub. Co., 1977.

32 p. ; 22 cm. – (Lost roads ; no. 4)

ISBN 0-918786-06-1 – ISBN 0-918786-07-X(pbk.)
                                          2

When ISBNs are inserted into a MARC record, each is input into its own 020 field, and each number is recorded as a block without hyphens.

1.8C. **Key-title** (MARC field 222)

1.8C1. The key-title of a serial, if found on the item, is added after the ISSN, even if it is the same as the title proper. A key-title is not recorded if there is no ISSN, however. *See* Fig. 3.86.

Fig. 3.86. Rule 1.8C1. Transcription of key-title of a serial
following ISSN.

Italian-American identity. – Vol. 1 (Jan. 1977)-
   . – [New York : Identity Enterprises for the Ameri-
can-Italian, 1977-   ]

    v. . ill. , 28 cm.

Monthly.
Running title, Jan. 1977-   : Identity.
ISSN 0163-0423 = Italian-American identity

1.8D. *Optional addition.* **Terms of availability** (subfield c of MARC field 020)

1.8D1. This option allows giving the price of an item if it is for sale, or a brief statement of other terms if it is not for sale.

LC is applying this option only for monographs cataloged according to *AACR 2* chapters 2, 5, 6, 7, or 8 and published in either the current year or one of the preceding two years. Various situations that might occur with respect to price information are elaborated upon in a rule interpretation.[28] *See* Fig. 3.87.

Fig. 3.87. Rule 1.8D1. Transcription of terms of availability
following standard number.

[1]Standard
number
[2]Price

    Plot counter-plot / Anna Clarke. -- London :
    Collins [for] the Crime Club, 1974.

    192 p. ; 21 cm. – (Crime club)

    1——ISBN 0-00-231637-4 : £2.00 ——2

1.8E. **Qualification** (subfield a of MARC field 020)

1.8E1. A brief qualification is added after the standard number or terms of availability when there are two or more (*see* Fig. 3.85), and an option allows qualifying any statement of terms of availability when it needs explanation. LC is applying the option.[29]

RULE 1.9.   SUPPLEMENTARY ITEMS

Many supplementary items are described as separate entities and are given complete independent bibliographic records. The rule that identifies which supplementary works should be cataloged separately is 21.28.

In the cases where a supplementary work is described dependently, one of three methods may be chosen: 1) the supplementary item may be recorded as accompanying material (Rule 1.5E); (*see* Figs. 3.69 and 3.70 on page 82); 2) the item may be described in the note area (Rule 1.7B11); 3) multilevel description may be used (Rule 13.6).

RULE 1.10.   ITEMS MADE UP OF SEVERAL TYPES OF MATERIALS

1.10A.   Some items have components that belong to more than one group or type of material (e.g., printed text and slides). This rule deals with their description.

1.10B.   If one of the components is so predominant that the item is of no use without that component (e.g., a slide set with an accompanying script that has little value without seeing the slides), the item should be described in terms of the predominant component with details of the other component(s) given as accompanying material or in a note. *See* Fig. 3.88.

Fig. 3.88. Rule 1.10B. Description of item made up of two components, one of which is predominant.

¹**Predominant component**   Alcohol and your body [filmstrip]. — Kansas City, Mo. : McIntyre Productions, 1978.

²**Subsidiary component**   1 filmstrip (96 fr.) : col. ; 35 mm. + 1 sound cassette (27 min.). — (Health)

Writer, Al DeZutter.
Sound accompaniment compatible for manual and automatic operation.

Summary: Deals with the increasing problem of teenage alcoholism, helping students understand the nature of alcohol and its physical effects on the body.

1.10C.   If there is no predominant component, the item is cataloged as a kit as described below.

1.10C1.   General material designation
The instructions in 1.1C4 are followed except when an item has no collective title. Then the appropriate GMD is given after each individual title.

1.10C2.   Physical description
The cataloger is instructed to choose the most appropriate of three methods of providing the physical description:

a) listing the extent of each of the individual parts and ending with "in container" and its dimensions, if there is a container. *See* Fig. 3.89.

Fig. 3.89. Rule 1.10C2a. Transcription of parts of a kit as a listing of extent of item of each part.

Sharks [kit] / National Geographic Society. – Washington,
  D. C. : The Society, c1978.

  3 study prints, 1 filmstrip (4 fr.), 1 sound cassette (15
min.), 30 narration scripts, 1 teacher's guide, 2 duplicating masters, 2 worksheets; in container, 34 x 30 x 5 cm. –
(Learning shelf kit)

b) giving separate physical descriptions on separate lines for each type of component. *See* Fig. 3.90.

Fig. 3.90. Rule 1.10C2b. Transcription of separate lines of physical description for parts of a kit.

The Bingo Long Traveling All-Stars & Motor Kings [kit]. –
  New Rochelle, N.Y. : Spoken Arts, 1978.

  4 filmstrips : col. ; 35 mm.
  4 sound cassettes (44 min.) : 2 track, mono.
  1 teacher's guide (28 p.) ; 24 cm.
  8 duplicating masters ; 28 x 22 cm. – (Black culture
against the odds)

(The Library of Congress never uses this method.)[30]

c) giving a general term with the number of pieces as the extent of item for items with a large number of different types of materials. *See* Fig. 3.91.

Fig. 3.91. Rule 1.10C2c. Transcription of physical description using a general term for an item with a large number of heterogeneous pieces.

Safety begins with you [kit]. – New York : Children's Media
  Productions, c1979.

  24 various pieces. – (School craft kits)

RULE 1.11. FACSIMILES, PHOTOCOPIES, AND OTHER REPRODUCTIONS

Facsimiles, photocopies, or other reproductions of printed texts, maps, manuscripts, printed music, and graphic items are described in such a way that the details of the facsimile, etc., are given in all areas except the note area. If the title of the facsimile, etc., is different, the title of the facsimile, etc., is given as title proper. The same is true for edition, publication details, or series. In these cases, the details of the original are given in a single note in the notes area. The details of the original are given in the same order as they would appear in the main part of the description.

If the facsimile, etc., is in a different form of material than the original, the chapter relating to the form of the facsimile, etc., is used. For a manuscript reproduced as a book, the chapter on description of books would be used. For maps reproduced on microfilm, the chapter on description of microforms would be used. *See* Fig. 3.92.

Fig. 3.92. Rule 1.11. Description of a photoreproduction as a reproduction with details of the original given in a note.

The Expert gardener. – Amsterdam : Theatrum Orbis Terrarum ; Norwood, N.J. : W. J. Johnson, 1974.

54 p., [2] leaves of plates : ill. ; 21 cm. – (The English experience, its records in early printed books published in facsimile ; no. 659)

Photoreprint of: The Expert gardener, or, A treatise containing certaine necessary, secret, and ordinary knowledges in grafting and gardening ... faithfully collected out of sundry Dutch and French authors. London : Printed by Richard Herne, 1640.

NOTES

[1]*Cataloging Service Bulletin*, no. 11 (Winter 1981): 6-7.

[2]Ibid., p. 7.

[3]Ibid.

[4]*Cataloging Service Bulletin*, no. 12 (Spring 1981): 5.

[5]Ibid., pp. 6-7.

[6]"AACR 2 Options to Be Followed by the Library of Congress, Chapters 1-2, 12, 21-26," *Library of Congress Information Bulletin* 37 (July 21, 1978): 423.

[7]*Cataloging Service Bulletin*, no. 13 (Summer 1981): 7.

[8]*Cataloging Service Bulletin*, no. 11 (Winter 1981): 8.

[9]*Cataloging Service Bulletin*, no. 23 (Winter 1983): 8-9.

[10]*Cataloging Service Bulletin*, no. 15 (Winter 1982): 2.

[11]Ibid., p. 3.

[12]*Cataloging Service Bulletin*, no. 25 (Summer 1984): 25.

[13]*Cataloging Service Bulletin*, no. 13 (Summer 1981): 10-11.

[14]*Cataloging Service Bulletin*, no. 25 (Summer 1984): 26.

[15]Ibid., pp. 27-30.

[16]*Cataloging Service Bulletin*, no. 12 (Spring 1981): 11.

[17]*Cataloging Service Bulletin*, no. 25 (Summer 1984): 30.

[18]Ibid., pp. 30-32.

[19]Ibid., p. 32.

[20]*Cataloging Service Bulletin*, no. 12 (Spring 1981): 11.

[21]*Cataloging Service Bulletin*, no. 17 (Summer 1982): 7-8.

[22]"AACR 2 Options to Be Followed by the Library of Congress, Chapters 1-2, 12, 21-26," *Library of Congress Information Bulletin* 37 (July 21, 1978): 423.

[23]Ibid., p. 424.

[24]*Cataloging Service Bulletin*, no. 13 (Summer 1981): 11.

[25]*Cataloging Service Bulletin*, no. 22 (Fall 1983): 16.

[26]*Cataloging Service Bulletin*, no. 25 (Summer 1984): 37-40.

[27]*Cataloging Service Bulletin*, no. 16 (Spring 1982): 9-22.

[28]Ibid., pp. 22-31.

[29]Ibid., pp. 26-27.

[30]*Cataloging Service Bulletin*, no. 11 (Winter 1981): 12.

SUGGESTED READING

Chan, Lois Mai. *Cataloging and Classification: An Introduction*. New York, McGraw-Hill, 1981. Chapter 3.

Hagler, Ronald. *Where's That Rule? A Cross-Index of the Two Editions of the Anglo-American Cataloging Rules*. Ottawa, Canadian Library Association, 1979. pp. 7-13.

Hagler, Ronald, and Peter Simmons. *The Bibliographic Record and Information Technology*. Chicago, American Library Association, 1982. Chapters 3-4.

Maxwell, Margaret F. *Handbook for AACR 2*. Chicago, American Library Association, 1980. Chapter 1.

4

Description of Books, Pamphlets, and Printed Sheets

INTRODUCTION

This chapter and the three following ones each discuss application of the general rules for description to books (and other printed monographic material), non-book materials, microforms, and serials. Emphasis in each chapter is upon those areas where the description of a type of material must be unique to that type: chief and prescribed sources of information, material specific details, physical description, and notes. For each type of material one or more items has been chosen as an example to demonstrate a bibliographic record for that type of item. For each item, the chief source of information is illustrated, followed by a complete bibliographic record in card format and coded in MARC format. Because no one item can demonstrate every eventuality, other examples of particular instances are also given throughout each chapter.

SELECTED RULES AND EXAMPLES

RULE 2.0. GENERAL RULES

2.0A.   Scope
This chapter covers what *AACR 2* calls "printed monographs"—all printed texts except serials, which are covered in *AACR 2* chapter 12 (chapter 7 of this text), and microform reproductions of printed texts, which are covered in *AACR 2* chapter 11 (chapter 6 of this text).

2.0B.   Sources of information

2.0B1.   Chief source of information
For most printed monographs there is a title page that serves as the chief source of information. If there is no title page, then the part of the item that gives the most complete information is used as a substitute for the title page.

In this case, the part used as a substitute is specified in a note, and the information from the substitute is treated as if it were from a title page. That is, brackets are not used for information from a substitute title page. If the item has no part that can substitute, information may be taken from any available source.

If information that would ordinarily appear on a title page is given on facing pages, both pages are treated as "the title page."

2.0B2.   Prescribed sources of information
Each area of the description has a prescribed source or sources from which information should be taken. If information in an area is from a non-prescribed source, it should be enclosed in square brackets.

The prescribed sources for printed monographs are:

AREA	PRESCRIBED SOURCES OF INFORMATION
Title and statement of responsibility	Title page
Edition	Title page, other preliminaries, and colophon
Publication, distribution, etc.	Title page, other preliminaries, and colophon
Physical description	The whole publication
Series	The whole publication
Note	Any source
Standard number and terms of availability	Any source

Figures 4.1-4.3 illustrate the title page and "other preliminaries" for the book that is used in this chapter to illustrate building a description. "Preliminaries" is defined in *AACR 2* as "the title page or title pages of an item, together with the verso of each title page, any pages preceding the title page(s), and the cover."[1] "Colophon" is defined as "a statement at the end of an item giving information about one or more of the following: the title, author(s), publisher, printer, date of publication or printing...."[2] The book used here has a plain front cover, with the information on the spine duplicating that on the title page. It has no colophon. Colophons are not common in English language books but are found more often in books in other languages.

Fig. 4.1. Title page.

Handbook of
Data Processing for Libraries

Second Edition

SPONSORED BY THE COUNCIL
ON LIBRARY RESOURCES

Robert M. Hayes
University of California, Los Angeles

Joseph Becker
Becker and Hayes, Inc.
Los Angeles, California

A WILEY BECKER & HAYES SERIES BOOK

MELVILLE PUBLISHING COMPANY
Los Angeles, California

Fig. 4.2. Verso of title page.

Copyright © 1970, 1974, by John Wiley & Sons, Inc.
Published by **Melville Publishing Company**,
a Division of John Wiley & Sons, Inc.
All rights reserved. Published simultaneously in Canada

No part of this book may be reproduced by any means, nor transmitted, nor translated into a machine language without the written permission of the publisher.

Library of Congress Cataloging in Publication Data:

Hayes, Robert Mayo, 1926-
    Handbook of data processing for libraries.
    (Information sciences series)
    "A Wiley-Becker & Hayes series book."
    Includes bibliographies.
    1. Libraries--Automation. 2. Electronic data processing--Library science.
I. Becker, Joseph, joint author. II. Title.
Z678.9.H36   1974   025'.02'02854   74-9690
ISBN 0-471-36483-5

Printed in the United States of America

10 9 8 7 6 5 4 3 2 1

Fig. 4.3. Recto and verso of leaf preceding title page.

Information Sciences Series

Editors
ROBERT M. HAYES
University of California
Los Angeles, California

JOSEPH BECKER
President
Becker and Hayes, Inc.

Consultant
CHARLES P. BOURNE
University of California
Berkeley, California

Joseph Becker and Robert M. Hayes:
INFORMATION STORAGE AND RETRIEVAL

Charles P. Bourne:
METHODS OF INFC

Harold Borko:
AUTOMATED LAN(

Russell D. Archibald
NETWORK-BASED

Launor F. Carter:
NATIONAL DOCUM
AND TECHNOLOG`

Perry E. Rosove:
DEVELOPING COM

F. W. Lancaster:
INFORMATION RE

Ralph L. Bisco:
DATA BASES, CON

Charles T. Meadow:
MAN-MACHINE CC

Gerald Jahoda:
INFORMATION ST(

Robert S. Taylor:
THE MAKING OF A LIBRARY

Herman M. Weisman:
INFORMATION SYSTEMS, SERVICES, AND CENTERS

Jesse H. Shera:
THE FOUNDATIONS OF EDUCATION FOR LIBRARIANSHIP

Charles T. Meadow:
THE ANALYSIS OF INFORMATION SYSTEMS, Second Edition

Stanley J. Swihart and Beryl F. Hefley:
COMPUTER SYSTEMS IN THE LIBRARY

F. W. Lancaster and E. G. Fayen:
INFORMATION RETRIEVAL ON-LINE

Richard A. Kaimann:
STRUCTURED INFORMATION FILES

Thelma Freides:
LITERATURE AND BIBLIOGRAPHY OF THE SOCIAL SCIENCES

Manfred Kochen:
PRINCIPLES OF INFORMATION RETRIEVAL

Robert M. Hayes and Joseph Becker:
HANDBOOK OF DATA PROCESSING FOR LIBRARIES, Second Edition

2.0D.-2.0H.

Levels of description, language and script, inaccuracies, accents and other diacritical marks, and items with several title pages are treated as discussed in the general chapter on description.

RULE 2.1. TITLE AND STATEMENT OF RESPONSIBILITY AREA (MARC field 245)

2.1B.   Title proper (MARC subfield a)

The title proper is transcribed as instructed in 1.1B. *See* Fig. 4.4.

Fig. 4.4. Rule 2.1B. Transcription of title proper.

Handbook of data processing for libraries

2.1C.   *Optional addition.* General material designation (MARC subfield d)

As discussed in the general chapter, the GMD "[text]" that is appropriate to the material of this chapter is not displayed in eye-readable forms of records from the Library of Congress. Its use is not illustrated in this chapter.

2.1D.-2.1E.

Parallel titles and other title information are transcribed as instructed in 1.1D.-1.1E. (MARC subfield b)

2.1F.   Statements of responsibility (MARC subfield c)

Statement(s) of responsibility are transcribed according to the instructions in 1.1F. *See* Fig. 4.5.

Fig. 4.5. Rule 2.1F. Addition of statements of responsibility.

Handbook of data processing for libraries / Robert M. Hayes, Joseph Becker ; sponsored by the Council on Library Resources

2.1G.   If an item lacks a collective title, titles of parts are transcribed as instructed in 1.1G.

RULE 2.2. EDITION AREA (MARC field 250)

2.2B.   Edition statement (MARC subfield a)

AACR 2 specifies that if a work contains an edition statement and if the work is different from other editions of the work or the edition in hand is a named reissue of the work, the edition statement is transcribed as instructed in

1.2B. In practice editions are not compared during cataloging, and edition statements are taken at face value and transcribed. *See* Fig. 4.6.

Fig. 4.6. Rule 2.2B. Addition of edition statement.

> Handbook of data processing for libraries / Robert M.
> Hayes, Joseph Becker ; sponsored by the Council on Library
> Resources. – 2nd ed.

_____

2.2C.   Statements of responsibility relating to the edition (MARC subfield b)

Statements of responsibility that relate to the edition in hand, but not to all editions of a work, are transcribed according to instructions in 1.2C. An example of this is Fig. 3.38 in the preceding chapter of this text.

RULE 2.3. MATERIAL (OR TYPE OF PUBLICATION) SPECIFIC DETAILS AREA

Area 3 is not currently used in the cataloging of printed monographs.

RULE 2.4. PUBLICATION, DISTRIBUTION, ETC., AREA (MARC field 260)

2.4B-2.4F. Place of publication, name of publisher, date of publication (MARC subfields a, b, and c)

Details of place, publication, distribution, etc., and date(s) are transcribed as instructed in 1.4. *See* Fig. 4.7.

Fig. 4.7. Rule 2.4. Addition of publication details.

> Handbook of data processing for libraries / Robert M.
> Hayes, Joseph Becker ; sponsored by the Council on Library
> Resources. – 2nd ed. – Los Angeles, Calif. : Melville Pub. Co.,
> c1974.

_____

Note that there are two copyright dates on the verso of the title page (Fig. 4.2). The date that corresponds to the edition statement is the one chosen for transcription.

As described under 1.4E, LC is adding a statement of function to the name of a distributor where needed. For example:

> – [Leicester] : Leicester University Press ; Atlantic Highlands,
> N.J. : Humanities Press [distributor], 1977.

2.4G. **Place of printing, name of printer, date of printing** (MARC sub-fields e, f, and g)

If the publisher is unknown, the place and name of the printer are given. Optionally, the place and name of the printer are given in addition to the publisher if they are found in the item and are considered to be important. As discussed with 1.4G, LC is applying the option. An example of the transcription of place and name of printer is Fig. 3.64 in the preceding chapter.

RULE 2.5. PHYSICAL DESCRIPTION AREA (MARC field 300)

2.5B. **Number of volumes and/or pagination** (MARC subfield a)

Single volumes

2.5B1. The following terms are used in recording the number of pages or leaves in a publication.

Term used	Situation
pages (abbreviated "p.")	[volume with leaves printed on both sides]
leaves	[volume with leaves printed on only one side]
columns	[volume with more than one column to a page and numbered in columns]
leaves, pages, and/or columns (in sequence)	[volume that contains sequences of leaves, pages, and/or columns]
broadside	[broadside]
sheet	[folder and other single sheets]
case	[case]
portfolio	[portfolio]

2.5B2. Numbers of pages, leaves, or columns are recorded in accord with the numbered or lettered sequences represented. The number on the last page, leaf, or column of each sequence is recorded, followed in each case by the appropriate term or abbreviation. Examples:

92 p.	[46 leaves printed on both sides]
62 leaves	[62 leaves printed only on one side]
ix, 289 p.	[last numbered page in roman numerals sequence and in arabic numerals sequence]
iv leaves, 224 p.	[last numbered leaf and last numbered page]

See Fig. 4.8 (following Rule 2.5D1).

2.5B3.   Unnumbered sequences are disregarded unless the whole item or a substantial part of a publication is unnumbered (*see* 2.5B7 and 2.5B8). An exception is made when pages in an unnumbered sequence must be referred to in a note, in which case either the estimated number is given preceded by "ca.," or the exact number is given enclosed in square brackets. Examples:

79, [1], 64 p.   [unnumbered page referred to
                                                        in note]

Bibliography: p. [80]   [note requiring use of unnumbered
                                                        page]

2.5B5.   When a single sequence is numbered in more than one way (e.g., when numbering changes from roman to arabic numerals), the first numbering scheme is ignored, and only the last number of the sequence is recorded. Example:

252 leaves   [item numbered i-vii followed by
                                                        leaves 8-252, for a total of 252
                                                        leaves—not 7 leaves followed by
                                                        252 leaves as would be indicated
                                                        by: vii, 252 leaves]

2.5B7.   When an entire volume is unnumbered, if it is not too large, the pages are counted and given in square brackets. The number of pages of larger items are estimated and recorded following "ca." Examples:

[12] p.   [unnumbered pages counted]

ca. 200 p.   [unnumbered pages approximated]

2.5B8.   Three options are given for dealing with complicated or irregular paging:

1) The total number of pages or leaves may be given followed by "in various pagings" or "in various foliations." (Blank pages, advertising matter, and other inessential sequences are excluded from this total.)

2) The number of pages or leaves in major sequences may be recorded followed by the total number of pages or leaves in remaining sequences. This total is given in square brackets.

3) The volume may be described as "1 v. (various pagings)," "1 case," or "1 portfolio."

Examples:

86 p. in various pagings	[total number of pages]
273 leaves in various foliations	[total number of leaves]
128, ix, [48] p.	[two main sequences followed by number of pages in several smaller sequences]
1 v. (various pagings)	[indication of many sequences — perhaps some are numbered, some are not, some may be lettered — too complicated for use of alternatives "1" or "2"]

2.5B10.   Leaves or pages of plates

The number of leaves or pages of plates is recorded at the end of the numbers given for paging sequences regardless of whether the plates are placed together or are scattered through the publication. If there is only one plate, it is described as "1 leaf of plates." If plates are unnumbered, follow 2.5B7. If paging is complex, follow 2.5B8. If there are both leaves and plates, use the term that is predominant. Examples:

vi, 224, [9] p., 26 leaves of plates	[numbered leaves of plates]
176, p., [16] p. of plates	[unnumbered pages of plates]
74 leaves, [33] leaves of plates	[unnumbered leaves of plates]
398, [1] p., [1] leaf of plates Bibliography: p. [399]	[unnumbered page with bibliography note referring to it and an unnumbered plate]

Publications in more than one volume

2.5B17.-2.5B18.

A printed monograph in more than one physical part is described with the number of whichever of the following terms is appropriate:

volumes — each bibliographic unit in its own binding

parts — bibliographic units bound several to a volume

pamphlets — collections of pamphlets bound together or assembled in a portfolio

pieces — items of varying character, assembled for cataloging as a collection

(Example continues on page 106.)

case(s)—box(es) containing bound or unbound material

portfolio(s)—container(s), usually consisting of two covers joined at the back and tied at the front, top, and/or bottom, holding loose papers, illustrative materials, etc.

Examples:

5 v.	[each of five bibliographic units bound separately]
25 pts.	[each part issued separately but specified by the publisher that they should be bound several to a volume when complete]
2 cases	[unbound material held together as a bibliographic unit in two boxes]

2.5B19.   When the number of bibliographic volumes is different from the number of physical volumes, the number of bibliographic volumes is given first followed by "in" and the number of physical volumes. Example:

3 v. in 1

2.5B20.   When the volumes of a multi-volume set are paged so that the first page numbers of a succeeding volume follow the last page number of the preceding volume (ignoring any preliminary pages in the succeeding volume that may be separately paged), the total number of pages or leaves is given in parentheses after the number of volumes. Example:

2 v. (ix, 1438 p., 32 leaves of plates)

2.5B21.   An option allows giving the pagination of each volume of a separately paged set of volumes in parentheses after the number of volumes. Example:

3 v. (vi, 49; 62; 58 p.)

The Library of Congress is applying this option only when the information is especially significant as, for example, in the case of early printed books.[3]

2.5B23.   Braille or other raised types
If appropriate, add to the number of volumes or leaves one of the following phrases:

of braille	of press braille
of Moon type	of print/braille [eye-readable print and
of jumbo braille	braille]
of microbraille	of print/press braille

Examples:

  3 v. of jumbo braille

  484 leaves of braille

2.5C.   **Illustrative matter** (MARC subfield b)

2.5C1.   If a monograph has illustrations, the abbreviation "ill." is given in the physical description unless all of the illustrations belong to one of the groups mentioned in 2.5C2. Tables are not treated as illustrations. Illustrated title pages and minor illustrations (e.g., decorations) are ignored. The Library of Congress treats graphs and diagrams as illustrations and uses "ill." when they are present.[4] *See* Fig. 4.8 (following Rule 2.5D1).

2.5C2.   Illustrations of the following types that are considered to be important are given in the following order:

TERM	ABBREVIATION (IF ALLOWED)
charts	
coats of arms	
facsimiles	facsim., facsims.
forms	
genealogical tables	geneal. table(s)
maps	
music	
plans	
portraits (use for both single and group portraits)	port., ports.
samples	

  If there are illustrations in addition to these types, they are described as "ill.," and "ill." precedes the other types in the list. Examples:

47 p. : ill., ports.	[contains illustrations, some of which are portraits]
280 p. : facsims.	[the only illustrations are facsimiles]
176 p., [24] p. of plates : ill., coats of arms, maps, plans	[illustrations include three of the specific types in rule 2.5C2, in addition to other illustrations]

Library of Congress practice is that if a quick examination reveals that the illustrations are all of one or two types, the one or two types are specified. If the illustrations are chiefly of one or two types, they are given after "ill." In all other cases, "ill." alone is used.[5]

2.5C3.   If illustrations are in two or more colors, they are described as "col." or "some col." Examples:

48 p. : ill. (some col.)	[some illustrations in color]
216 p. : ill., maps (some col.), col. ports.	[some maps in color, all portraits in color]
xiv, 182 p. : col. ill.	[all illustrations in color]

2.5C4.-2.5C8.

Treatment of special cases (e.g., number of illustrations known, special locations of illustrations, works consisting of all or nearly all illustrations) is delineated in these rules in *AACR 2* which should be consulted when such special cases arise.

2.5D.   **Size** (MARC subfield c)

2.5D1.   Size of printed monographs is given in terms of the height of volumes in centimeters. The height of the binding (or the height of the item, if unbound) is measured and recorded as the *next* whole centimer *up* (*not* the *nearest* centimeter). Size of volumes that measure less than 10 centimeters is given in millimeters. *See* Fig. 4.8.

Fig. 4.8. Rule 2.5. Addition of physical description.

Handbook of data processing for libraries / Robert M. Hayes, Joseph Becker ; sponsored by the Council on Library Resources. – 2nd ed. – Los Angeles, Calif. : Melville Pub. Co., c1974.
   xvi, 688 p. : ill. ; 24 cm.

Note: Book actually measures 23.4 centimeters but is recorded as 24.

2.5D2.   Width of a volume is recorded only when it is less than half the height or greater than the height. Examples:

ca. 150 p. : ill. ; 34 x 16 cm.	[width less than half the height]
ii, 97 p. : ill., ports. ; 18 x 21 cm.	[width greater than the height]

2.5D3.-2.5D5.

These rules in *AACR 2* cover unusual cases and should be consulted when one is cataloging sets with items of varying sizes, or single sheets.

2.5E. **Accompanying material** (MARC subfield e)

2.5E1. As explained in 1.5E, material that is issued with an item and is intended to be used with it may be recorded as the last element of the physical description area. Example:

> 142 p. : ill., maps ; 39 cm. + 1 overlay grid

An option allows addition of the physical description of the accompanying material. The Library of Congress is applying this option on a case-by-case basis to items that are substantial in extent or that are significant for some reason.[6]

2.5E2. The location of accompanying material that is issued in a pocket inside the cover of an item is specified in a note as instructed in 2.7B11. Example of note:

> Overlay grid in pocket inside back cover.

RULE 2.6. SERIES AREA (MARC field 4xx)

2.6B. **Series statements**

Each series statement is transcribed as instructed in 1.6. *See* Fig. 4.9.

Fig. 4.9. Rule 2.6B. Addition of series statements.

> Handbook of data processing for libraries / Robert M. Hayes, Joseph Becker ; sponsored by the Council on Library Resources. – 2nd ed. – Los Angeles : Melville Pub. Co., c1974.
> xvi, 688 p. : ill. ; 24 cm. – (Information sciences series) (A Wiley-Becker & Hayes series book)

Note: It will be noticed that in the CIP (i.e., Cataloging in Publication) on the verso of the title page (Fig. 4.2, page 99), "A Wiley-Becker & Hayes series book" is given as a quoted note rather than as a series. The interpretation by LC was that it was a characterization of books of that publisher, rather than a series. This was an interpretation in *AACR 1* that has been omitted from *AACR 2*. "A Wiley-Becker & Hayes series book" fits the *AACR 2* definition of "series."

RULE 2.7.   NOTE AREA (MARC field 5xx)

2.7B.   Notes (MARC field 500 unless otherwise specified)

As noted in the preceding chapter, notes for all materials are given in the same order. The ones particularly applicable to printed monographs are illustrated here.

2.7B1.   Nature, scope, or artistic form
When nature, scope, or artistic form of a work is not apparent from the rest of the description, notes may be made. *See* Fig. 4.10.

Fig. 4.10. Rule 2.7B1. Addition of note about nature of publication.

George Robert Bonfield, Philadelphia marine painter, 1805-1898. -- [Philadelphia] : Philadelphia Maritime Museum, c1978.
78 p. : ill. (some col.) ; 22 x 29 cm.

⟶ Catalog of an exhibition.
Bibliography: p. 76-77.

The Library of Congress generally restricts this type of note for books to works in certain classifications (i.e., AM, ACN, HE, AJ, AK, NE, SA) that contain one or more literary works by one personal author. This type of note may also record the literary forms of belles lettres when their titles are misleading.[7]

2.7B2.   Language of item and/or translation or adaptation
If the language is not evident from the description or if the fact of translation or adaptation is not apparent, notes may be made. *See* Figs. 4.11 and 4.12.

Fig. 4.11. Rule 2.7B2. Addition of note about language of publication.

Pastoral : mediaeval into Renaissance / Helen Cooper. – Ipswich : Brewer ; Totowa, N.J. : Rowman & Littlefield, 1977.
257 p., [2] leaves of plates : ill. ; 24 cm.

⟶Verse passages in Latin and medieval French.
Bibliography: p. [235]-248.
Includes index.
ISBN 0-87471-906-2 (Rowman & Littlefield) : £8.50

Fig. 4.12. Rule 2.7B2. Addition of note about translation.

Weather and climate : in colour / Svante Bodin ; ill. by
Studio Frank. – Poole [Eng.] : Blanford Press, 1978.
    272 p. : col. ill. ; 19 cm. – (Blanford colour series)

——►Translation of: Vader och vind.
    Includes index.
    ISBN 0-7137-0858-1 : £4.95

2.7B3.   Source of title proper
The source of the title proper is noted if the title is not taken from the
chief source of information. *See* Fig. 4.13.

Fig. 4.13. Rule 2.7B3. Addition of note on source of title proper.

Unbranched dorsal-fin rays and subfamily classification
in the fish family Cyprinidae / by William A. Gosline. – Ann
Arbor : University of Michigan, 1978.
    21 p. ; 23 cm. – (Occasional papers of the Museum of
Zoology, University of Michigan ; no. 684)

——► Caption title.
    Bibliography: p. 19-21.

2.7B4.   Variations in title
Titles on an item that differ from the title proper should be noted. *See*
Fig. 4.14.

Fig 4 14 Rule 2 7B4 Addition of note on variant title.

Starring pelicans, cats, and frogs : from the award win-
ning ABC television children's series / a creation of ABC
News ; written by Lester Cooper ; edited by Julie Duffy ;
illustrated by Ed Cage and Novle Rogers ; photography by
H. Michael Stewart. – 1st ed. – Dallas : Handel, 1978.
    63, [1] p. : col. ill. ; 29 cm. – (Animals, animals, animals /
Lester Cooper ; no. 1)

——►Cover title: ABC TV's award winning animals, animals,
animals.
    Bibliography: p. [64]
    Summary: Text and illustrations introduce pelicans,
cats, frogs, and toads. Based on the television series "Animals, animals, animals."
    ISBN 0-917080-03-3

2.7B5.   Parallel titles and other title information

This rule allows the cataloger to record parallel titles and other title information not recorded in the title area if they are thought to be important. A Library of Congress rule interpretation comments that this rule applies only to such information not already covered in other rules. It is pointed out that lengthy other title information from the chief source must be abridged or given in a note regardless of its importance.[8] *See* Fig. 4.15.

Fig. 4.15. Rule 2.7B5. Addition of note on other title information
not recorded above.

Travels of a latter-day Benjamin of Tudela / Yehuda Amichai ; [translated from the Hebrew by Ruth Nevo]. -- Webster Groves, Mo. : Webster review ; Berkeley, Calif. : distributed by Serendipity Books Distribution, 1977.

64 p. ; 22 cm. -- (Webster review ; v. 3, no. 3)

——▶At head of title: A special issue.
ISBN 0-917146-10-7 : $1.25

2.7B6.   Statements of responsibility

Here is a place for statements of responsibility (e.g., significant persons or bodies connected with previous editions, or persons or bodies not named in the chief source) that were not given in the title and statement of responsibility area. *See* Fig. 4.16.

Fig. 4.16. Rule 2.7B6. Addition of note on responsible bodies,
combined with note on nature of work.

Statewide coordination and governance of postsecondary education : quality, costs, and accountability : the major issues of the '80s / [editors, Robert Berdahl, Martha Levin, John Ziegenhagen]. -- Wayzata, Minn. : Spring Hill Center, c1978.

46 p. ; 28 cm.

——▶Papers from a conference held Dec. 11-13, 1977, at Spring Hill Center, and sponsored by the Center and the Education Commission of the States.
Includes bibliographical references.
ISBN 0-932676-05-7

Note: The statement of responsibility incorporated in the note above did not appear in the chief source of information but was composed by the cataloger from information that appeared elsewhere. Had it appeared in the chief source of information it would have been transcribed in the statement of responsibility area (*see* Fig. 4.5, page 101).

2.7B7.   Edition and history

Bibliographic history notes and notes relating to the edition in hand are recorded here. A Library of Congress rule interpretation is helpful for constructing notes about reprint editions.[9] *See* Figs. 4.17 and 4.18.

**Fig. 4.17. Rule 2.7B7. Addition of note on original of
edition being described.**

The English Lake District as interpreted in the poems of Wordsworth / by William Knight. – Norwood, Pa. : Norwood Editions, 1978.

viii, xvi, 270 p. : port. ; 23 cm.

⟶ Reprint. Originally published: 2nd ed. Edinburgh : D. Douglas, 1891.
Includes bibliographical references.
ISBN 0-8482-1426-9 : $30.00

**Fig. 4.18. Rule 2.7B7. Addition of note about previous
closely related work.**

"Steam and petticoats" : the early railway era in south-western Ontario / by Wayne Paddon. -- [S.l. : s.n.], c1977 (London : M. Kelly)

304 p. : ill. ; 24 cm.

⟶ Sequel to; Story of the Talbot settlement.
Includes bibliographical references and index.

The Library of Congress gives special instructions for notes describing "limited editions" of 500 or fewer copies. The note is to be succinct and phrased so that the number does not come first (so that it will not have to be spelled out) unless it is within quotation marks.[10] *See* Fig. 4.19.

Fig. 4.19. Rule 2.7B10. Addition of note giving limited edition details.

Lessons & complaints / James Purdy. – New York : Nadja Editions, [1978]

[5] p. ; 25 cm.

"Limited to 174 numbered copies and 26 lettered."
Library has copy no. 103.

2.7B9.   Publication, distribution, etc.

Important publication, distribution, etc., details that cannot be given in the publication, distribution, etc., area are recorded in a note. *See* Fig. 4.20.

Fig. 4.20. Rule 2.7B9. Addition of note on printing and distribution.

Proteus / Morris West ; illustrated by Robert Heindel. –
Limited 1st ed. – Franklin Center, Pa. : Franklin Library,
1979.
   305 p. : ill. ; 24 cm.
──►Printed for members of the First Edition Society.

The Library of Congress interprets a date that consists of month and year or month, day, and year, and that appears in a prominent position, to be a date of release or transmittal and records it in a note in quotation marks. It is not considered to be a publication date, although the publication date may be inferred from it and given in brackets.[11] Example:

"March 1985."

2.7B10.   Physical description

Important physical details not given in the physical description area may be recorded here. *See* Fig. 4.21.

Fig. 4.21. Rule 2.7B10. Addition of note giving further physical details.

Strengthening deterrence : NATO and the credibility of
Western defense in the 1980s : the Atlantic Council's Working
Group on the Credibility of the NATO Deterrent / Kenneth
Rush, and Brent Scowcroft, co-chairmen ; Joseph J. Wolf,
rapporteur and editor. – Cambridge, Mass. : Ballinger Pub. Co.,
[1982]
   xvii, 270 p. : ill., maps ; 24 cm.
──► Maps on lining papers.
Includes bibliographical references and index.

2.7B11.   Accompanying material

Notes on the location of accompanying material may be needed. *See* example under 2.5E2.

2.7B12. Series
Series data that cannot appropriately be given in the series area may be recorded in a note. Example:

> Originally issued in series : Research studies in library science.

2.7B13. Dissertations
Dissertations or theses are described with a formal note. The English word "thesis" is followed by the degree for which the author was a candidate (e.g., Ph.D., M.A., Master's), the name of the institution or faculty, and the year the degree was granted (MARC field 502). *See* Fig. 4.22.

Fig. 4.22. Rule 2.7B13. Addition of notes to description of a master's thesis.

[1]Thesis note for M.A. degree
[2]Institution granting degree

The character of Mencius / by Albert Felix Ver-wilghen. – [Seattle : s.n.], 1964.
xviii, 152 leaves ; 29 cm.   [2]
Thesis (M.A.)–University of Washington.
Bibliography: leaves [129]-152.

Revisions, abridgements, edited editions, and publications lacking formal thesis notes are also noted (MARC field 500). *See* Fig. 4.23.

Fig. 4.23. Rule 2.7B13. Addition of note to description of a revised Ph.D. thesis.

Television fraud : the history and implications of the quiz show scandals / Kent Anderson. -- Westport, Conn. : Greenwood Press, 1978.
xii, 226 p ; 22 cm – (Contributions in American studies, ISSN 0084-9227 ; no. 39)
Based on the author's thesis (Ph.D.)–University of Washington.
Bibliography: p. [209]-215.
Includes index.
ISBN 0-313-20321-0 : $18.95

2.7B14. Audience
If the intended audience is stated in the publication, it may be noted here. Example:

> For adults learning to read.

2.7B17.   Summary (MARC field 520)

Summary notes may be given when the contents of an item are not specified in the rest of the description. Library of Congress practice has generally limited such summary notes on printed monographs to children's books. Since 1984, however, some summary notes created by LC's overseas offices have been included in LC bibliographic records.[12] *See* Fig. 4.24.

Fig. 4.24. Rule 2.7B14. Addition of summary note.

Angels and me / written by Carolyn Nystrom ; illustrated by Dwight Walles. – Carol Stream, Ill. : Creation House, c1978.

32 p. : ill. (some col.) ; 26 cm. – (The Mustard seed library)

──→ Summary: Text and suggested Biblical verses discuss the importance of God's angels.
ISBN 0-88419-128-1 : $4.95

2.7B18.   Contents (MARC field 500 or 504 or 505)

When parts of an item are titled and would be useful to the user of a bibliographic record, they are brought out in notes. The Library of Congress rule interpretation is lengthy and should be consulted when contents notes seem appropriate.[13] LC takes titles from the table of contents rather than from the head of the parts as *AACR 2* directs. *See* Figs. 4.25-4.31.

Fig. 4.25. Rule 2.7B18. Addition of selective contents notes.

Creative quilting / by Elsa Brown. -- New York : Watson-Guptill Publications, 1975.

[1]Bibliography note

1──→ 144 p. : ill. ; 27 cm.
Bibliography: p. 141-142.

[2]Index note

2──→ Includes index.
ISBN 0-8230-1105-4

Fig. 4.26.

Human sexuality in health and illness / Nancy
Fugate Woods ; with a chapter by James S.
Woods. – Saint Louis : Mosby, 1975.

x, 232 p. ; 23 cm.

Includes bibliographies and index.
ISBN 0-8016-5620-6

**Bibliography
and index
notes
combined**

Fig. 4.27.

Political dynamics : impact on nurses and
nursing / Grace L. Deloughery, Kristine M. Geb-
bie. – Saint Louis : Mosby, 1975.

ix, 236 p. ; 27 cm.

Includes bibliographical references and index.
ISBN 0-8016-1245-4

The criteria for distinguishing between "bibliographies" and "bibliographical references" changed at LC in 1984. For many years a list of citations or
works grouped together in a single list had to be arranged in some logical order
(e.g., alphabetically or chronologically) in order to be designated a
"bibliography." If the arrangement was footnote-type numbering in the order
referred to in the text, the designation "bibliographical references" was used.
Starting in 1984 the definition of "bibliography" was changed to include a list
of works or citations grouped together regardless of arrangement. If there is
one major list at the end of a book, it is recorded in the form:

Bibliography: p.[109]-111.

If there are chapter or section bibliographies, but no major bibliography, the
note becomes:

Includes bibliographies.

Only when the only bibliographic citations are in the form of true footnotes at
the bottom of pages is the note given:

Includes bibliographical references.[14]

Fig. 4.28. Rule 2.7B18. Addition of contents note for collection of works
of one author.

At peace : stories / by Ann Copeland. – [Ottawa] : Oberon
Press, c1978.
    164 p. ; 23 cm.
———► Contents: Siblings – The Lord's supper – Higher learn-
ing – The golden thread – Cloister – Jubilee – At peace.
    ISBN 0-88750-270-9 – ISBN 0-88750-271-7 (pbk.)

Fig. 4.29. Rule 2.7B18. Addition of contents note for collection of works
by different authors.

Classics of organization theory / edited by Jay M. Shafritz,
    Philip H. Whitbeck. – 1st ed. – Oak Park, Ill. : Moore Pub.
    Co., c1978.
    xi, 323 p. : ill. ; 23 cm.
    Includes bibliographical references.
———► Contents: Of the division of labour / Adam Smith – The principles of scientific management / Frederick Winslow Taylor –
General principles of management / Henri Fayol – Bureaucracy /
Max Weber – The giving of orders / Mary Parker Follett – Notes
on the theory of organization / Luther Gulick – The scalar
principle / James D. Mooney.

Fig. 4.30. Rule 2.7B18. Addition of contents note for
multi-volume work.

The collected works of Sir Winston Churchill. – Centen-
ary limited ed. – London : Library of Imperial History, 1973-

    v. : ill. ; 24 cm.

———► Contents: v.1. My early life. My African journey – v.2. The
story of the Malakand field force.
    ISBN 0-903988-01-1 (v. 1)

Fig. 4.31. Rule 2.7B18. Addition of partial contents note.

Voices of the Black theatre / by Loften Mitchell. – Clifton,
N.J. : J. T. White, [1975]
   ix, 238 p. : ill. ; 24 cm.
   Contains taped individual recollections of Black theatrical
figures with introductory essays and comments by L. Mitchell.
   Includes index.
   →Partial contents: The words of Eddie Hunter – The words
of Regina M. Andrews – The words of Dick Campbell – The
words of Abram Hill – Interlude: Paul Robeson – The words
of Frederick O'Neal – The words of Vinette Carroll – The words
of Ruby Dee.
   ISBN 0-88371-006-4

2.7B19. Numbers borne by the item

Numbers borne by the item other than ISBNs (which are given in the
standard number area) are recorded as notes—often quoted. *See* Fig. 4.32.

Fig. 4.32. Rule 2.7B19. Addition of note giving number of the item.

Uranium mill tailings control : hearings before the Subcommittee on Energy and the Environment of the Committee on Interior and Insular Affairs, House of Representatives, Ninety-fifth Congress, second session ... held in
Washington, D.C. ... – Washington, D.C. : G.P.O.,
1978.
   v, 716 p. : graphs ; 24 cm.
  → "Serial no. 95-30."

2.7B20. Copy being described and library's holdings (MARC field 590)

Notes are made about any imperfections of the copy in hand. Also, if a
library has only part of a multi-volume set, the details of holdings are noted.
These notes are "copy-specific." That is, a note made under this rule will be
applicable only to the copy held by the cataloger who is creating the
description. This is fine in an individual library. However, if the library
belongs to a network and creates online original cataloging that other libraries
eventually use as a basis for their cataloging, this type of note can be a source
of difficulty, as is known by libraries that have had to change LC's copy-
specific notes to reflect local cataloging. Such notes are tagged 590 in a MARC
record and thus are readily identifiable. Examples:

Library's copy autographed by the author.

Library lacks v. 3.

2.7B21.   "With" notes (MARC field 501)

For items lacking a collective title and described separately, a note is given beginning "With:" and then listing the other separately titled parts of the item. *See* Fig. 3.77 in the preceding chapter.

The only notes required by the book whose title page and other preliminaries are shown in Figs. 4.1-4.3 are bibliography and index notes. *See* Fig. 4.33.

RULE 2.8. STANDARD NUMBER AND TERMS OF AVAILABILITY AREA (MARC field 020)

2.8B.   International Standard Book Number (ISBN) (MARC subfield a)

ISBNs are transcribed as instructed in 1.8B. *See* Fig. 4.33.

2.8C.   *Optional addition*. Terms of availability (MARC subfield c)

It is optional to add the price or other terms of availability. The Library of Congress exercises this option for current items. *See* Fig. 4.33.

Fig. 4.33. Rule 2.7-2.8. Addition of note, ISBN, and price.

Handbook of data processing for libraries / Robert M.
Hayes, Joseph Becker ; sponsored by the Council on Library
Resources. – 2nd ed. – Los Angeles, Calif. : Melville Pub.
Co., c1974.
      xvi, 688 p. : ill. ; 24 cm. – (Information sciences series) (A
Wiley-Becker & Hayes series book)
      Includes bibliographies and index.
      ISBN 0-471-36483-5 : $30.00

The complete bibliographic record in MARC format for the book whose title page and other preliminaries are shown in Figs. 4.1-4.3 is shown in Fig. 4.34.

RULES 2.9-2.11.

Supplementary items, items made up of several types of material, facsimiles, photocopies, and other reproductions are described as instructed in the general chapter under Rules 1.9-1.11.

EARLY PRINTED MONOGRAPHS

RULES 2.12-2.18.

These rules give instructions for describing early printed monographs. In general, description follows the general rules, but necessary additions, modifications, and differences are given in these rules. The ISBD(A) — the

Fig. 4.34. Complete bibliographic record in MARC format
for a printed monograph.

```
OCLC: 922738        Rec stat: c Entrd: 740517        Used: 850205
Type: a Bib lvl: m Govt pub:    Lang:  eng Source:   Illus: a
Repr:    Enc lvl:   Conf pub: 0 Ctry:  cau Dat tp: s M/F/B: 10
Indx: 1 Mod rec:    Festschr: 0 Cont: b
Desc: a Int lvl:    Dates: 1974,
   1 010      74-9690
   2 040      DLC $c DLC $d OCL $d m.c. $d OCL $d DLC
   3 020      0471364835 : $c $30.00
   4 050 0    Z678.9 $b .H36 1974
   5 082      025/.02/02854
   6 090        $b
   7 049      IVEA
   8 100 10   Hayes, Robert Mayo, $d 1926-
   9 245 10   Handbook of data processing for libraries / $c Robert M.
Hayes, Joseph Becker ; sponsored by the Council on Library Resources.
  10 250      2nd ed.
  11 260 0    Los Angeles, Calif. : $b Melville Pub. Co., $c c1974.
  12 300      xvi, 688 p. : $b ill. ; $c 24 cm.
  13 440 0    Information sciences series
  14 490 0    A Wiley-Becker & Hayes series book
  15 504      Includes bibliographies and index.
  16 650 0    Libraries $x Automation.
  17 650 0    Library science $x Data processing.
  18 700 10   Becker, Joseph.
```

International Standard Bibliographic Description for Ancient Books—had not been completed before publication of *AACR 2*, and the *AACR 2* rules have been found to be inadequate by rare book catalogers. LC has compiled rules for the bibliographic description of early printed books and later books that need special treatment. The compilation is based primarily on *AACR 2*, but includes provisions from the ISBD(A) and a few rules appearing in neither place.[15] These rules are applied to books published before 1801.

NOTES

[1]*AACR 2*, p. 569.

[2]*AACR 2*, p. 565.

[3]*Cataloging Service Bulletin*, no. 8 (Spring 1980): 9.

[4]*Cataloging Service Bulletin*, no. 15 (Winter 1982): 6.

[5]Ibid.

[6]"AACR 2 Options to Be Followed by the Library of Congress, Chapters 1-2, 12, 21-26," *Library of Congress Information Bulletin* 37 (July 21, 1978): 424.

[7]*Cataloging Service Bulletin*, no. 12 (Spring 1981): 17-18.

[8]*Cataloging Service Bulletin*, no. 11 (Winter 1981): 13.

[9]*Cataloging Service Bulletin*, no. 21 (Summer 1983): 14-15.

[10]Ibid., pp. 15-16.

[11]*Cataloging Service Bulletin*, no. 17 (Summer 1982): 14.

[12]*Cataloging Service Bulletin*, no. 24 (Spring 1984): 11.

[13]*Cataloging Service Bulletin*, no. 25 (Summer 1984): 40-43.

[14]Ibid., p. 43.

[15]*Bibliographic Description of Rare Books* (Washington, D.C., Library of Congress, 1981).

SUGGESTED READING

Bibliographic Description of Rare Books. Washington, D.C., Library of Congress, 1981.

Manual of AACR 2 Examples. Compiled by the Minnesota AACR 2 trainers; edited by Edward Swanson and Marilyn H. Jones. Lake Crystal, Minn., Soldier Creek Press, 1980.

Maxwell, Margaret F. *Handbook for AACR 2*. Chicago, American Library Association, 1980. Chapter 2.

5
Description of Nonbook Materials

INTRODUCTION

This chapter covers the description of materials that have been variously called "nonbook," "nonprint," "audiovisual," or "media"—the last term often including monographic materials, as in "School Media Center." Often these special materials are not handled in the same way as monographs are handled. An administrative decision within each library determines whether to catalog and/or classify each of these special materials; because of the dimensions many cannot be shelved with corresponding monographic materials. The dimensions of such materials, then, become quite significant in bibliographic descriptions because this directly influences their location in a given collection, a consideration that often makes classification relatively insignificant and description of greater importance.

If the librarian cannot easily remember the contents of the collection, then cataloging control is needed. If the library has only six maps, for instance, there is little need to catalog them. Sixty maps, however, or even sixteen, may well need to be cataloged. The disadvantage of failing to catalog descriptively any special materials is that the patron must look somewhere other than in the main catalog for the record of the material. It is strongly recommended that as many special materials as possible be cataloged descriptively and thus recorded in the main catalog. Past problems in doing this have been greatly eased by the publication of *AACR 2* with its integrated approach to the description of special materials. In *AACR 2* all materials are described according to the same set of principles.

The materials specifically addressed in this chapter are: cartographic materials (covered in chapter 3 of *AACR 2*), manuscripts (*AACR 2*, chapter 4), published music (*AACR 2*, chapter 5), sound recordings (*AACR 2*, chapter 6), motion pictures and videorecordings (*AACR 2*, chapter 7), graphic materials (*AACR 2*, chapter 8), machine-readable data files (*AACR 2*, chapter 9), and three-dimensional artifacts and realia (*AACR 2*, chapter 10). Each of these kinds of material presents some interesting challenges to the descriptive cataloger.

The challenge of cataloging manuscripts is that each is unique. The manuscript or the manuscript collection does not exist in another library, except perhaps in reproduction. It is not the kind of material for which catalogers can find cataloging copy already in existence. In addition, such materials often do not have any clearly defined chief source of information, and, indeed, they often do not have clearly defined titles. There may be difficulty even reading the handwriting in which a manuscript is written. It may be difficult to know whether one is dealing with an original or with a hand-written copy, and if a copy, the date it was copied and by whom. The manuscript cataloger is often dealing with events and names of persons not recorded elsewhere.

A musical composition in written form normally appears as a series of staves upon which notes are printed, but occasionally other systems of notation are used. The description of music written for a solo instrument, such as the piano, is relatively straightforward. The description of music written for several instrumental or vocal parts (i.e., scores) presents some special problems, especially in the title and statement of responsibility area, in the physical description area and in the notes area.

Both classification and description of sound recordings are affected by the fact that extremely disparate materials often appear on a single physical item. This problem is addressed for description in *AACR 2*, Rule 6.1G, described below.

Two of the complications encountered in describing motion pictures and videorecordings involve the source of information and the large numbers of people responsible for them. Titles and other information, as they appear in the item itself, in accompanying materials or on containers, often vary considerably. The large number of people involved presents problems for deciding how many "credits" will provide useful description of an item. Another problem is concerned with the ease with which videorecordings may be made, thus complicating the concepts of "copy" and "edition." These and other problems are addressed in the rules that follow, but ultimately the cataloger must use some judgment based upon general principles.[1]

Graphic materials include: art originals, art prints, art reproductions, filmstrips and filmslips, flash cards, flip charts, photographs, pictures, postcards, posters, radiographs, slides, stereographs, study prints, technical drawings, transparencies, and wall charts. Many of these materials are not cataloged and/or classified in many libraries. An administrative decision within each library determines whether to catalog and/or classify these materials. Because most of them cannot be physically shelved with corresponding monographic materials, a book classification system often is not used. Rather, use is made of a simple accession or serial number to keep them in order. On the other hand, catalog records of the materials can easily be interfiled in the catalog with records for monographic or serial material, because, in *AACR 2*, all materials are described according to the same standard—i.e., ISBD(G). Some libraries provide some identification, such as color coding of catalog records that represent the materials listed above when they are interfiled in the main catalog. Other libraries provide separate catalogs for special materials.

The cataloging of machine-readable data files (MRDF) is a very recent addition to the cataloging field. The need for standards for cataloging these materials was recognized in 1970 when ALA's Cataloging and Classification Section established a subcommittee to develop rules for cataloging MRDFs. Since then, steady progress has been made, but the form in which bibliographic information for MRDFs can be found varies so greatly, that cataloging them is somewhat more of a challenge than for most other materials. The state of the art of production of MRDFs is comparable to that of books in the early days of printing. A short time ago there was no source of data comparable to a title page. Program files now usually have such a source, with non-standard and varying amounts of information, but data files still usually have no such source. As with videorecordings there is the problem of ease of duplication, complicating the ideas of "copy" and "edition." Micro-computer software has developed since the publication of *AACR 2*. As a result it was necessary to develop some supplementary interpretations for the rules in *AACR 2*, chapter 9. These guidelines have been published as a separate booklet.[2] These interpretations are used in this text where applicable. Where the guidelines and *AACR 2*, chapter 9, are in conflict, the guidelines are given preference because of the rapid development in this area that has made some statements in *AACR 2* obsolete.

Prior to the advent of *AACR 2*, three-dimensional artifacts and realia were not cataloged or classified except in a few museum libraries. With a method of description consistent with that of describing other materials, however, we are seeing more cataloging of these materials—especially in media centers where emphasis is no longer on the "book" as the principal means of transmitting knowledge.

A number of manuals have been written that supplement *AACR 2* in the area of nonbook materials. They are listed in the "Suggested Reading" at the end of this chapter. They should be consulted for more detailed discussion of the problems of cataloging these materials, for definitions of terms unique to these types, and for in-depth examples of cataloging.

SELECTED RULES AND EXAMPLES

RULE [Chapter #].0.   GENERAL RULES

[Chapter #].0A.   Scope

This rule in each chapter identifies the kinds of materials covered in that chapter. It also sometimes points out certain kinds of items *not* covered or not covered completely and suggests the chapter that should be consulted instead or in addition. For example, Rule 4.0A directs that for the cataloging of manuscript cartographic items, one should also consult chapter 3.

[Chapter #].0B   Sources of information

[Chapter #].0B1.   Chief source of information
The following chief sources of information are prescribed in this rule in each chapter:

TYPE OF MATERIAL	CHIEF SOURCE OF INFORMATION
Atlases	Title page (same as for books).
Other cartographic items	a) cartographic item itself, or, if a) is inappropriate, b) container or case, or the cradle and stand of a globe.

Manuscript	The manuscript itself.
	
	    If information is scattered the order of preference is: title page if there is one and it was originally part of the manuscript, colophon, caption, heading, text itself.
	
	    If information cannot be taken from the manuscript, use, in this order: another manuscript copy of the item, a published edition of the item, reference sources, and other sources.

Published music	a) List title page, cover, or caption— whichever furnishes the fullest information. b) If information cannot be taken from a), use, in this order: caption, cover, colophon, other preliminaries, other sources.

Sound recordings:
Disc	Label
Tape (open reel-to-reel)	Reel and label
Tape cassette	Cassette and label
Tape cartridge	Cartridge and label
Roll	Label
Sound recording on film	Container and label

Two or more labels are treated as one chief source

    If textual material has a collective title while the chief sources above do not, then the source of the collective title may be treated as a chief source.

    If information cannot be taken from a chief source above, use, in this order: accompanying textual material, a container, other sources. Prefer printed data to sound data.

Motion pictures and videorecordings	Film itself (e.g., title frames) and, if in a permanent container (e.g., a cartridge), the container and its label. If information cannot be taken from the chief source, use, in this order: accompanying textual material, container that is not an integral part of the piece, other sources.
Graphic materials	Item itself, including permanently affixed labels or containers. For an item consisting of two or more parts (e.g., slide set), use a container that provides a collective title if the items do not. If information cannot be taken from the chief source, use, in this order: non-integral container, accompanying textual material, other sources.
Machine-readable data files	Internal user label. For an item consisting of two or more parts use a container that provides a collective title if the items do not. If information cannot be taken from the chief source, use, in this order: label on the storage medium itself (e.g., disk, cassette), label on non-integral container, accompanying documentation, other sources.
Three-dimensional artifacts and realia	Object itself along with any accompanying textual material and container issued with the item. Information on the item or permanently affixed to it is preferred.

[Chapter #].0B2.   Prescribed sources of information

There are prescribed sources of information for each of the areas of description. These prescribed sources are fairly standard from medium to medium, although there are a few variations. A table of the most common prescribed sources is set out below, with the variations noted.

AREA	PRESCRIBED SOURCES OF INFORMATION
Title and statement of responsibility	Chief source of information*
Edition	Chief source of information, accompanying printed material**
Area 3	Chief source of information***
Publication, distribution, etc.	(Same as for edition area)†
Physical description	Any source
Series	(Same as for edition area)††
Note	Any source
Standard number and terms of availability	Any source††

Figures 5.1-5.20 show the chief sources of information and some of the prescribed sources for a map, a manuscript, a piece of music, a sound recording, a videotape, a set of stereograph reels, a machine-readable data file, and a game. Complete descriptions for these items are given at the end of this chapter.

---

*For manuscripts, published copies of the item may also be used.

**For those types of materials where the container is not regarded as chief source, the container may be used for this area. For music, the caption, cover, or colophon may also be used.

***Area 3 is used only for cartographic materials and for music. Accompanying materials may also be used for this area for cartographic materials.

†For manuscripts only the date is given in this area and it may be taken from anywhere in the manuscript or from published copies.

††This area is not used for manuscripts.

Fig. 5.1. Upper right corner of map.

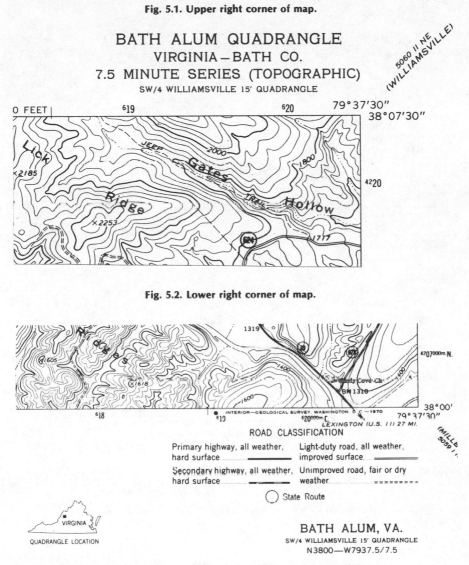

BATH ALUM QUADRANGLE
VIRGINIA — BATH CO.
7.5 MINUTE SERIES (TOPOGRAPHIC)
SW/4 WILLIAMSVILLE 15' QUADRANGLE

Fig. 5.2. Lower right corner of map.

ROAD CLASSIFICATION

Primary highway, all weather, hard surface ▬▬▬▬	Light-duty road, all weather, improved surface ════
Secondary highway, all weather, hard surface ▬ ▬	Unimproved road, fair or dry weather ═══════

◯ State Route

VIRGINIA

QUADRANGLE LOCATION

BATH ALUM, VA.
SW/4 WILLIAMSVILLE 15' QUADRANGLE
N3800—W7937.5/7.5

1968

AMS 5060 II SW—SERIES V834

Fig. 5.3. Lower left corner of map.

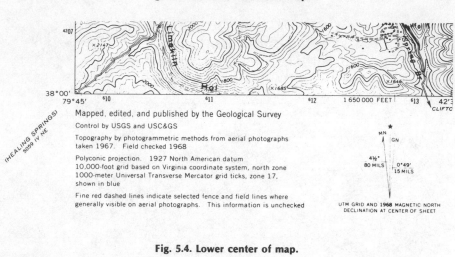

Mapped, edited, and published by the Geological Survey

Control by USGS and USC&GS

Topography by photogrammetric methods from aerial photographs
taken 1967.   Field checked 1968

Polyconic projection.   1927 North American datum
10,000-foot grid based on Virginia coordinate system, north zone
1000-meter Universal Transverse Mercator grid ticks, zone 17,
shown in blue

Fine red dashed lines indicate selected fence and field lines where
generally visible on aerial photographs.   This information is unchecked

UTM GRID AND **1968** MAGNETIC NORTH
DECLINATION AT CENTER OF SHEET

Fig. 5.4. Lower center of map.

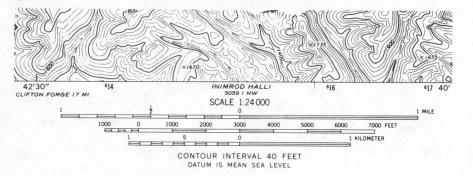

SCALE 1:24 000

CONTOUR INTERVAL 40 FEET
DATUM IS MEAN SEA LEVEL

THIS MAP COMPLIES WITH NATIONAL MAP ACCURACY STANDARDS
FOR SALE BY U. S. GEOLOGICAL SURVEY, WASHINGTON, D. C. 20242
AND VIRGINIA DIVISION OF MINERAL RESOURCES, CHARLOTTESVILLE, VIRGINIA 22903
A FOLDER DESCRIBING TOPOGRAPHIC MAPS AND SYMBOLS IS AVAILABLE ON REQUEST

Fig. 5.5. Outside of letter shown in Fig. 5.6.

Windsor 3ᵃ: Feb.ʸ 1793.

Note from the King.

Fig. 5.6. Letter from George III to Henry Dundas.
[Reproduced by permission of the Manuscript Department, William R. Perkins Library, Duke University.]

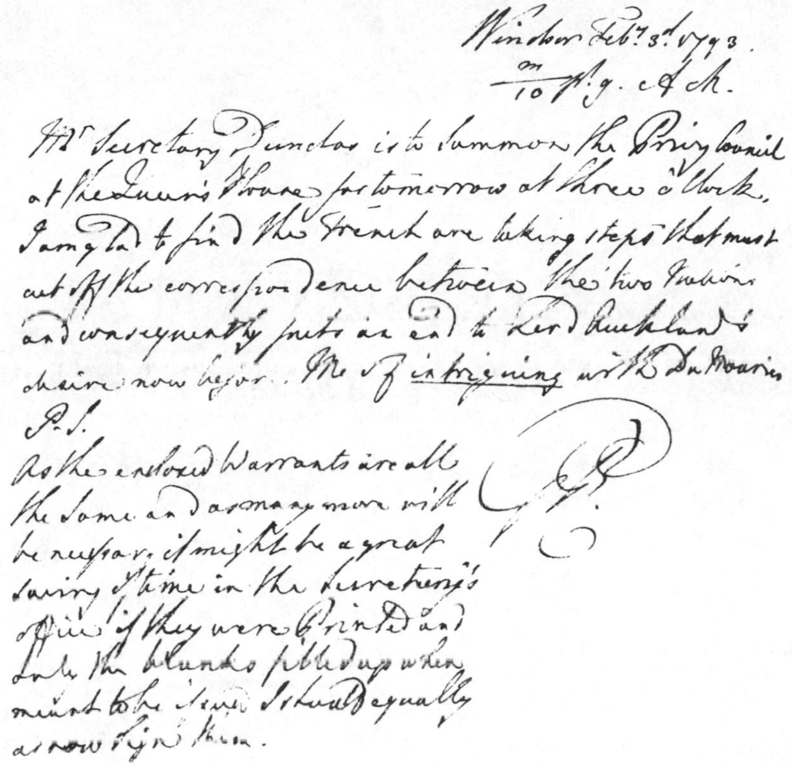
Windsor Feb.y 3.d 1793.
10 m p.t 9. A.M.
Mr Secretary Dundas is to summon the Privy Council
at the Queen's House for tomorrow at three o'Clock.
I am glad to find the French are taking steps that must
cut off the correspondence between the two Nations
and consequently puts an end to Lord Auckland's
desire now before Me of intriguing with Du Mourier
GR.
P.S.
As the enclosed Warrants are all
the Same and as many more will
be necessary it might be a great
saving of time in the Secretary's
office if they were Printed and
only the blanks filled up when
meant to be issued I should equally
as now Sign them.

Fig. 5.7. Transcription of letter shown in Fig. 5.6.

[*Windsor, 3 Feb. 1793, 9:10 a.m.*] Mr. Secretary Dundas is to summon the Privy Council at the Queen's House for tomorrow at three o'Clock. I am glad to find the French are taking steps that must cut off the correspondence between the two Nations, and consequently puts an end to Lord Auckland's desire now before Me of intriguing with Du Mourier.

GR.

P.S. As the enclosed Warrants are all the Same and as many more will be necessary it might be a great saving of time in the Secretary's office if they were Printed and only the blanks filled up when meant to be issued I should equally as now Sign them.

Fig. 5.8. Chief source of information for a score.

COLLEGIUM MUSICUM: YALE UNIVERSITY · SECOND SERIES · VOLUME VII

Christoph Schaffrath

CONCERTO IN B-FLAT FOR CEMBALO AND STRINGS

Edited by Karyl Louwenaar

A-R EDITIONS, INC. · MADISON

**Fig. 5.9. Series and availability information found in a preliminary
to the score shown in Fig. 5.8.**

Collegium Musicum, a series of publications of the
Department of Music, Yale University, was initiated by
the late Leo Schrade in 1955. The continuing aim of the
series, as set forth by Professor Schrade in the first
volume, is to "present compositions which, through
neglect or lack of knowledge, have been ungraciously
forgotten or overlooked, despite their artistic value and
historical importance." The series is prepared under the
general editorship of Leon Plantinga; materials for
publication are chosen and editorial policy is established
by a committee of the Yale music faculty.

Subscribers to this series, as well as patrons of
subscribing institutions, are invited to apply for
information about the "Copyright-Sharing Policy" of A-R
Editions, Inc., under which the contents of this volume
may be reproduced free of charge for performance use.

Correspondence should be addressed to:

A-R Editions, Inc.
315 West Gorham Street
Madison, Wisconsin 53703

Fig. 5.10. Chief source of information from disc.
Both labels are treated as a single chief source.

Fig. 5.11. Information from container of disc.

℗ & © 1979 Midsong International Records, Inc.,
Unauthorized Duplication is a Violation of Applicable Laws.

Fig. 5.12. Transcription of title frames at beginning of videotape.

Automated Check-in

— — —

Locating check-in records

— — —

Using check-in records

Fig. 5.12a. Transcription of credit frames at end of videotape.

by
Anne Marie Allison
and
Harry Kamens

— — —

Prepared under the auspices
of Hyman W. Kritzer
Asst. Provost and Director
of Libraries
Kent State University

— — —

directed by
John Dannley

— — —

Produced by
Television Services
Kent State University

Fig. 5.13. Photocopy of cassette label.

AMPEX
VIDEOCASSETTE

OCLC #6

Automated Check-in

Time - 14:45

MONO · STEREO
COLOR · BLACK & WHITE

AMPEX CORPORATION · REDWOOD CITY, CA 94063   PLAY LENGTH_____

Fig. 5.14. Chief source of information for set of stereograph reels.

Fig. 5.15. Unifying container for stereograph reel set.

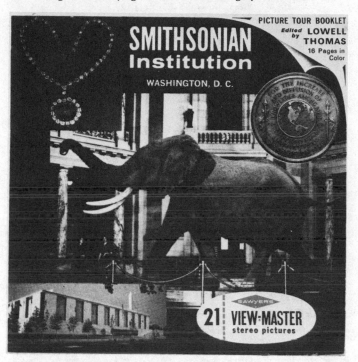

Fig. 5.16. First page of accompanying booklet.

Fig. 5.17. Transcription of first screen of information for a
machine-readable data file.

```
WordStar Release 3.31p ID # 123456Q7-001
Copyright (c) 1979, 1984, MicroPro International Corp.
All rights reserved.



            IBM PC, XT and 3270 Computers
               IBM Graphics Printer
```

Fig. 5.18. Label on storage medium of a machine-readable data file.

Fig. 5.19. Top of container of game.

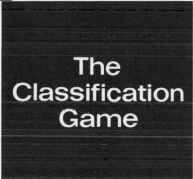

Fig. 5.20. End panel of game's container.

Instructo® **ACTIVITY KIT**

REORDER NO.
1014

The Classification Game

Fig. 5.20a. Top and bottom of page of accompanying textual material.

INSTRUCTO® TEACHING GUIDE

Instructo educational materials undergo careful testing and evaluation under actual and varying classroom teaching conditions.

No. 1014 THE CLASSIFICATION GAME

© 1969 THE INSTRUCTO CORPORATION • PAOLI. PENNSYLVANIA 19301

RULE [Chapter #].1.   TITLE AND STATEMENT OF RESPONSIBILITY AREA (MARC field 245)

[Chapter #].1B.   Title proper (MARC subfield a)

[Chapter #].1B1.   This rule in each chapter directs that the title proper be transcribed as instructed in 1.1B of the general chapter. Examples:

> Saturday night Fiedler
>
> Automated check-in
>
> Smithsonian Institution, Washington, D.C.

A rule revision combining and revising 5.1B1 and 5.1B2 has made this rule in the chapter for music more extensive. The cataloger is directed to transcribe as title proper a title consisting of name(s) of a type of composition and medium of performance, key, date, and/or number. In other cases medium, key, date, and number are treated as other title information. Examples:

> Concerto in B-flat for cembalo and strings
>
> Drei Sonaten für Klavier zu vier Händen

A Library of Congress rule interpretation for the films chapter (7.1B1) states that credits for performer, director, etc., that precede the title in the chief source are not considered part of the title proper unless they are within the title or represented by a possessive immediately preceding the title.[3] Examples:

> Chief source:
>   Twentieth Century Fox presents Star Wars
>
> Title proper:
>   Star Wars

This applies only to chapter 7 and thus could not be applied to a title on a sound recording reading, for example, "Armstrong presents Lerner & Loewe's Brigadoon."

[Chapter #].1B2.   Rule .1B2, and sometimes .1B3 and following, in each chapter presents special instructions for titles proper for that type of material. For example in cartographic materials one is instructed to include statement of scale if it is part of the title proper. Example:

> Arabian peninsula 1:500,000 / prepared by ...

In most cases .1B2 gives instructions for supplying a title when the item lacks one. Examples:

[Letter] 1793 Feb. 3, Windsor [to Henry] Dundas

[Public library advertisement]

[Harris 1967 public opinion survey, no. 1702]

Rule 3.1B3 gives directions to the cataloger on how to choose from more than one title in the chief source for cartographic materials. Choice is made on the basis of language, sequence, or layout, and if these are insufficient, then the most comprehensive title is chosen. Thus the title proper for the map whose chief source is illustrated in Figs. 5.1 to 5.4 would be:

Bath Alum quadrangle, Virginia–Bath Co.

[Chapter #].1C. *Optional addition.* **General material designation** (MARC subfield h)

The Library of Congress is applying GMDs to only some of the materials covered in this chapter. The following table sets out the GMD appropriate to the materials covered by each chapter and indicates which GMDs are being used by LC.[4]

TYPE OF MATERIAL	APPROPRIATE GMD	GMD USED BY LC
Cartographic	[map] [globe] [text] (for atlases)	none
Manuscripts	[manuscript]	none
Music	[music]	none
Sound recordings	[sound recording]	[sound recording]
Motion pictures and videorecordings	[motion picture] [videorecording]	[motion picture] [videorecording]
Graphics	[art original] [chart] [filmstrip] [flash card] [picture] [slide] [technical drawing] [transparency]	does not catalog* does not catalog [filmstrip] does not catalog does not catalog [slide] does not catalog [transparency]
Machine-readable data files	[machine-readable data file]	does not catalog**

(Table continues on page 142.)

TYPE OF MATERIAL (cont'd	APPROPRIATE GMD (cont'd)	GMD USED BY LC (cont'd)
Three-dimensional artifacts and realia	[diorama] [game] [microscope slide] [model] [realia]	does not catalog***

Examples:

Saturday night Fiedler [sound recording]

Automated check-in [videorecording]

Smithsonian Institution, Washington, D.C. [slide]

Perfect writer [machine-readable data file]

The classification game [game]

---

*The Library of Congress would use "chart" and "flash card" if it were to start cataloging such material. If it were to start cataloging art originals, pictures, and technical drawings, it would decide then whether or not to display the GMD.

Four special rules appear in a footnote to the North American list in 1.1C, and three of them apply to the material covered by the chapter on graphics: "(2) for material treated in chapter 8, use *picture* for any item not subsumed under one of the other terms in list 2; (3) use *technical drawing* for items fitting the definition of this term in the Glossary, appendix D; for architectural renderings, however, use *art original* or *picture*, not *technical drawing*; (4) use *kit* for any item containing more than one type of material if the relative predominance of components is not easily determinable and for the single-medium packages sometimes called 'lab kits.' "[5]

**The Library of Congress has said that if it ever catalogs MRDFs, it will decide then whether to display the GMD.

Because the GMD is the most direct way to distinguish between the cataloging for the file itself and the cataloging for the documentation, it seems to be a highly desirable addition. It will be illustrated in this chapter.

There has been some disagreement about the applicability of the term "machine-readable data file" to describe microcomputer files. However, in the absence of any acceptable alternative, that GMD is the only one presently available.[6]

***The Library of Congress has said that for all these types, it would use the GMD if it does start cataloging the material. The British GMD for all three-dimensional artifacts and realia is "object." British catalogers are thus saved having to decide into which category to place such items as toys (including dolls intended for instruction as well as play), quilts, puppets, etc.

[Chapter #].1D – [Chapter #].1E. (MARC subfield b)

Parallel titles and other title information are recorded as instructed in the general chapter under 1.1D-1.1E. Examples:

> Zwei- und dreistimmige Inventionen = Two and three part inventions
>
> State of California : south half
>
> Teatro del mondo [sound recording] : symphonic rotations in four scenes for large orchestra
>
> American women artists [slide] : the twentieth century

In the case of cartographic materials, manuscripts, and motion pictures, there are specific instructions for additions to be made as other title information. In the case of maps, if the title does not indicate the geographic area, this is added as other title information. Example:

> Land use and industry : [in East Germany]

For manuscripts there are extensive directions in 4.1B2 for creating supplied titles. If a manuscript item has a title and it lacks information required for a supplied title for that type of document, the information is added as other title information. Example:

> The duty of communicating in the Lord's Supper enforced : [sermon]

In the case of motion pictures, a direction is given to add [*trailer*] as other title information when the item is a trailer containing extracts from a larger film. Example:

> Breaking away [motion picture] : [trailer]

[Chapter #].1F.   **Statements of responsibility** (MARC subfield c)

Statements of responsibility are recorded as instructed in 1.1F in the general chapter. Examples:

> Bath Alum quadrangle, Virginia–Bath Co. / mapped, edited, and published by the Geological Survey
>
> Concerto in B-flat for cembalo and strings / Christoph Schaffrath ; edited by Karyl Louwenaar
>
> American movie [motion picture] / [written and produced by] Jan Peterson
>
> Slugathon [machine-readable data file] : the slime game / Paul Pomerleau
>
> Family portrait [game] / by Sandy Miller

The rule in chapter 6 for recording statements of responsibility is somewhat different from that for other materials. The cataloger must make a decision as to whether the participation of the person(s) or body(ies) involved in the recording goes beyond that of performance, execution, or interpretation of a work. If so, the statement is given as statement of responsibility. If not, the statement is given as a note. Thus, the statement on the chief source of information shown in Fig. 5.10, "Arthur Fiedler and the Boston Pops," must be relegated to note position because participation seems to be "confined to performance, execution, or interpretation." However, writers of spoken words, composers of music, and collectors of field material for sound recordings are included in statements of responsibility. Examples:

> Individual differences in susceptibility to hypnosis [sound recording] / E. R. Hilgard

> (This is a lecture given by its author. In the case of a group of poems by E. E. Cummings read by Spencer Tracy, for example, only E. E. Cummings would be given in the statement of responsibility.)

> The new moon [sound recording] / Sigmund Romberg ; [lyrics by] Oscar Hammerstein

A Library of Congress rule interpretation for giving statements of responsibility for films and graphics states that names should be given in the statement of responsibility when a person or body has had some degree of overall responsibility. When a person or body has been responsible for only segments or one aspect of a work, the name(s) should be given in the note area.[7]

[Chapter #].1G.   Items without a collective title

As explained in the general chapter, items that lack collective titles may be described either as a unit or by making a separate description for each separately titled part. For cartographic materials, there is also a rule allowing the cataloger to supply a collective title for an item that consists of a large number of physically separate parts. A collective title may also be supplied for manuscript collections, but is authorized in rule 4.1B2 rather than under 4.1G. Examples:

> Rhapsody in blue ; An American in Paris [sound recording] / Gershwin

> [Maps of the United States]

> [Papers] / William Alexander Smith

The Library of Congress has made a decision to describe a sound recording as a unit in all cases.[8]

[Chapter #].2. EDITION AREA (MARC field 250)

Elements of the edition area are transcribed for materials in this chapter, with the exception of manuscripts, in the same manner as instructed in the general chapter. Examples:

> World atlas / Rand McNally. – Imperial ed.
>
> Brigadoon [sound recording] / book & lyrics by Alan Jay Lerner ; music by Frederick Loewe. – Collector's ed.
>
> The Braniff Concorde [motion picture] / Braniff Airways, Inc. – Spanish ed.

Two of the materials, music and machine-readable data files, have special problems in interpreting whether certain statements are edition statements or not.

A Library of Congress rule interpretation discusses the care that must be taken with music publications to distinguish between edition statements and musical presentation statements. The latter often include the word "edition," but should not be taken as edition statements. Musical presentation statements indicate the version, arrangement, music format, etc., in which a work is presented. These go in the statement of responsibility when the music itself is meant (i.e., a version, arrangement, or transposition of the music) because an "author" is responsible for changing the original work, even if such a person is not named. When the music format is meant (e.g., edition as a set of parts), the statement is transcribed in Area 3 (see below).[9] Only when edition statements of the book type appear, are they transcribed into the edition area. Example:

> Drei Sonaten für Klavier zu vier Händen / Johann Christian Bach ; herausgegeben von Wilhelm Weismann. – Ed. Peters

It is also difficult to interpret "edition" when cataloging MRDFs. Many changes can be made to a MRDF very quickly and easily. For example, format can be changed from punched card to tape to disk; data can be added or changed or deleted; "translations" can be made of program statements from one program language to another; data elements can be reformatted. When changes are made, there is usually no standard internal label to carry a record of the changes. Documentation may or may not be revised when changes are made to the file. In the case of microcomputer software, there may be a statement of change in a new issue of a program. This statement may or may not contain the word "edition" but should be interpreted as such. Other common words are: version, level, release, update.[10] Examples:

> WordStar [machine-readable data file]. – Release 3.31
>
> The CPS 1974 American national election study [machine-readable data file] / principal investigators, Warren E. Miller, Arthur H. Miller, F. Gerald Kline ; The Center for Political Studies, The University of Michigan. – ICPR ed.

**[Chapter #].3   MATERIAL (OR TYPE OF PUBLICATION)
                        SPECIFIC DETAILS AREA** (MARC fields 255
                        [cartographic materials] and 254 [music])

Two types of material covered by this chapter have special rules in this area: cartographic materials and music.

RULE 3.3.   MATHEMATICAL DATA AREA (MARC field 255)

3.3B.   Statement of scale (MARC subfield a)

3.3B1.   The first part of this area is "Statement of scale." Scale is given as a representative fraction expressed as 1:_____ and preceded by the word "scale." If a verbal statement of scale is on the item, it is given as a representative fraction in square brackets. If any statement of scale is found outside the item, it also is given as a representative fraction in square brackets. If no statement is found, the scale is computed and given preceded by "ca." If it cannot be computed, the statement "scale indeterminable" is used.

3.3B2.   An option allows giving additional scale information found on the item. LC is applying this option.[11] Example:

> West Indies and Central America / compiled and drawn in the
>   Cartographic Division of the National Geographic Society,
>   for The National geographic magazine. – Scale 1:4,815,360.
>   1 in. to 76 miles.

3.3B3.-3.3B8.
Detailed instructions for recording more than one scale value, and for handling other problems, are given in these rules, which should be consulted when one is doing in-depth map cataloging.

3.3C.   Statement of projection (MARC subfield b)

If a statement of projection is found on the item or any of the accompanying materials, it is given following the scale, using abbreviations and numerals in place of words. Example:

> Bath Alum quadrangle, Virginia–Bath Co. / mapped, edited,
>   and published by the Geological Survey. – Scale 1:24,000 ;
>   Polyconic proj.

3.3C2.   An option allows addition of associated phrases, such as statements about meridians, or parallels, if these phrases are connected with the projection statement. LC is applying this option.[12] For example:

> Lambert conformed conic proj. based on standard parallels
>   33° and 45°.

3.3D. *Optional addition.* **Statements of coordinates and equinox (MARC subfields c, d, and e)**

These rules for adding coordinates and equinox to the description will be applied by LC when the information is readily available although they are not illustrated here.[13]

5.3. *Optional area.* **MUSICAL PRESENTATION STATEMENT (MARC field 254)**

This area for music was added to *AACR 2* in 1984. It calls for recording a statement found in the chief source that indicates the physical presentation of the music. As discussed above under the edition area, it is necessary to distinguish among statements that are true edition statements, those that are statements of responsibility, and those that indicate the physical presentation. LC is applying this optional area.[14] Example:

> Aubade, trio for flute, oboe & clarinet in B^b / DeWailley ;
> [edited by] Jerry Kirkbride. – Score and parts

The remaining nonbook materials chapters (except 3 and 5) state that area 3 is not used for the types of material covered by those chapters. The implication is that use of this area is not permitted for the type of material in question. In the chapter on microforms, however, there is instruction in this area to follow the instructions in Rule 3.3 for microforms of cartographic materials and Rule 12.3 for serial microforms. For most types of material, need for this area is rare; but MRDFs are often produced serially, and occasionally the content of a MRDF is cartographic. The scope note for the chapter on description of serials says that the rules in that chapter are to be used for serial publications of all kinds in all media. Clearly, then, it is permissible, and certainly desirable, to use area 3 when describing a MRDF. All bibliographic data bases (e.g., the MARC data base), that are available on a subscription basis so that new records are added regularly, require serial cataloging. For example:

> Specialized textile information service [machine-readable
> data file] / compiled in collaboration with British Launderer's
> Research Association ... [et al.]. – 1970-

[Chapter #].4. **PUBLICATION, DISTRIBUTION, ETC., AREA (MARC field 260)**

For the most part the details in this area are recorded in the same manner as discussed in the general chapter under Rule 1.4.

This area in the manuscripts chapter is called the "Date Area." It omits details of place and name of publisher (this being unpublished material) and includes only date, and then only if it is not already in the title. The date of a single manuscript is given as a year, optionally followed by the month and day. LC will follow the option when the information is readily available.

For a manuscript collection, inclusive years are given. Example:

[Papers] / William Alexander Smith. – 1765-1949.

In the music chapter there is an instruction to record plate numbers and publishers' numbers in the note area. The sound recordings chapter deals with the issue of trade names, brand names, or subdivision names used by recording companies. In cases where these are used, they are recorded as the name of the publisher. Example:

Label on disc reads:
SUNSET, a product of Liberty Records
A division of Liberty Records, Inc., Los Angeles,
California

Description should read:
Los Angeles : Sunset

However, if a trade name seems to be a name of a series, it is recorded as a series rather than as the name of a publisher.

In 1984 (p) dates were added by example to the (c) dates already given as examples, thus authorizing use of these dates that appear on sound recordings. Example:

"Saturday night Fiedler" [sound recording]. –
New York : Midsong International Records, p1979.

Note: In Fig. 5.10 (page 134) the (p) date is 1979 while the (c) date is 1978. However, in Fig. 5.11 (page 134) the date, 1979, is preceded by "(p) & (c) ." Considering that the performance was recorded in 1979, the 1978 date seems to be an error and is ignored in the catalog record.

In the film and machine-readable data files chapters, "producer" (and in the case of films and videorecordings "production agency") has been added as a name that can be used for "name of publisher." The cataloger of a MRDF may have some difficulty distinguishing a publisher of documentation from a producer or distributor of the data file. In addition, the roles of producers and distributors in the data community are not always clearly differentiated, nor are they exactly comparable to "publishers."

For the materials covered by the films and graphics chapters, LC has chosen not to apply the option allowing one to give the full address of a publisher, distributor, etc.[15] Also for these chapters there is a provision for giving in a note a date of original production that differs from the date in area 4. LC is applying this option when the difference is greater than two years.[16] Example:

Washington, [D.C.] : Division of Audiovisual Arts : distributed
by National Audiovisual Center, 1979.

The record on which the above imprint appears would have the following note:

Made in 1975.

The graphics chapter has four types of material for which only the date is given in this area: Art originals, unpublished photographs, other unpublished graphic materials, and collections of graphic materials. Examples:

> [Polar bears] [art original] / Dorothy S. Taylor. – 1975.

> [Photographs of blue ribbon pigs, Iowa State Fair] [picture]. – 1927-1947.

The realia chapter also has types of material that are treated somewhat differently. For "naturally occurring objects" that are not mounted for viewing or packaged for presentation, place, publisher, and date are not recorded. For artifacts not intended primarily for communication (e.g., clothing, money, furniture), no place or publisher is recorded. For these items the date of manufacture is given as the first element of this area. Example:

> [White treadle sewing machine] [realia]. – 1890.

If the person or body that has manufactured an object is named in the statement of responsibility (as is the case with hand-made items such as hand-woven tapestries or hand-made pottery), the place and name are not repeated in this area. In such a case, the place, if known, may be part of the cataloger-constructed title proper.

Examples of application of rules for the publication, distribution, etc., area:

> West Indies and Central America / compiled and drawn in the Cartographic Division of the National Geographic Society, for The National geographic magazine. – Scale 1:4,815,360. 1 in. to 76 miles ; Oblique Mercator proj. – Washington, [D.C.] : The Society, 1970.

> Concerto in B-flat for cembalo and strings / Christoph Schaffrath ; edited by Karyl Louwenaar. – Madison (315 West Gorham Street, Madison, Wis., 53703) : A-R Editions, c1977.

> Whither MARC and Mann? [sound recording]. – Chicago : American Library Association, 1978 (Evanston, Ill. : Produced by Cebar Communications, Inc.)

> Automated check-in [videorecording] / by Anne Marie Allison and Harry Kamens ; directed by John Dannley. – [Kent, Ohio] : Produced by Television Services, Kent State University, [1977]

> Note: The date of publication was taken from advertising matter.

Smithsonian Institution, Washington, D.C. [slide]. – Portland, Ore. : Sawyer's, Inc., [196-?]

Note: The date is presumed to be in the 1960s because reference is made in the
booklet to a new building projected for completion in 1969.

The classification game [game]. – Paoli, Pa. : Instructo
Corp., c1969.

[Chapter #].5.   PHYSICAL DESCRIPTION AREA (MARC field 300)

[Chapter #].5B.   Extent of item (including specific material designation)
(MARC subfield a)

Each of the chapters for nonbook materials gives a direction to record the
number of physical units in arabic numerals followed by a term from the
chapter's list of specific material designations. The following lists are
provided:

Cartographic materials:

aerial chart	map section
aerial remote sensing image	orthophoto
anamorphic map	photo mosaic (controlled)
atlas	photo mosaic (uncontrolled)
bird's-eye view *or* map view	photomap
block diagram	plan
celestial chart	relief model
celestial globe	remote-sensing image
chart	space remote-sensing
globe	image
(for globes other than	terrestrial remote-sensing
celestial globes)	image
hydrographic chart	topographic drawing
imaginative map	topographic print
map	
map profile	

Music:

score	vocal score
condensed score	piano score
close score	chorus score
miniature score	part
piano [violin, etc.] conductor	
part	

Sound recordings:

sound cartridge	sound tape reel
sound cassette	sound track film
sound disc	

Films and videorecordings:

film cartridge	videocartridge
film cassette	videocassette
film loop	videodisc
film reel	videoreel

Graphics: (as distributed by LC among the GMDs
appropriate to this chapter[17])

Art original	photograph
art original	picture
Chart	postcard
chart	poster
flip chart	radiograph
wall chart	study print
Filmstrip	Slide
filmslip	slide
filmstrip	stereograph
Flash card	Technical drawing
flash card	technical drawing
Picture	Transparency
art print	transparency
art reproduction	

Machine-readable data files:

data file
program file

Three-dimensional artifacts
and realia:

diorama	microscope slide
exhibit	mock-up
game	model

Normally, specific material designations are given to different classes of materials that represent different kinds of physical objects. In the case of published music, specific material designations vary under different circumstances, one of them being whether the music is written for a solo instrument or for several instruments. The physical extent of a piece of music written for a solo instrument is described, as for any monograph, in terms of leaves, pages, or volumes. If the option of using the GMD [music], is not applied, then the term *music* is incorporated in the extent of item statement. Example:

36 p. of music.

A specific material designation using the terms *score(s)* and/or *part(s)* is to be given to a piece of music written for several instrumental or vocal parts. The type of score it is — miniature, piano, vocal, etc. — as well as its pagination and the number of copies of it issued by the publisher are to be recorded. (Definitions of different types of scores are given in *AACR 2*, Appendix D.) If the score is accompanied by parts, the number of these issued by the publisher is to be recorded.

The rules for music, sound recordings, graphics, MRDFs, and realia allow the cataloger to use terms other than those listed if needed. Examples:

Music	Realia
choir book	jigsaw puzzle
table book	simulation
Sound recordings	hand puppet
piano roll	quilt
organ roll	tapestry
MRDFs	statue
hierarchical file	sculpture
object program	bowl (or cup, jar, candle holder, etc.)
	dress (or coat, belt, suit, etc.)

The manuscript chapter directs the cataloger to record the extent of single manuscripts as one would for books. The term "bound" is added if the manuscript has been bound. Example:

128 leaves, bound

A collection that occupies one linear foot or less of shelf space is described in terms of the number of items or the number of containers or volumes. LC is applying the option to add the number of items if the collection is described in number of volumes or containers.[18] Examples:

1 v. (208 items)

2 boxes (110 items), 2 v. (68 items)

ca. 600 items

A collection that occupies more than one linear foot of shelf space is described in terms of the number of linear feet occupied. LC is applying the option to add the number of items or containers or volumes.[19]

Various pieces of information may be added in parentheses after the statement of extent if easily ascertainable from the item in hand. Numbers of pages are added after statements of extent of atlases and music. Examples:

1 atlas (20 leaves)

1 score (35 p.) + 4 parts

Numbers of items may be given for collections of manuscripts, some kinds of graphics, and realia. Examples:

2 ft. (ca. 300 items)

1 transparency (3 overlays)

3 flip charts (10 sheets each)

1 game (various pieces)

1 jigsaw puzzle (ca. 500 pieces)

Running/playing time may be given for sound recordings, films, and video-recordings. Examples:

2 sound cassettes (ca. 150 min.)

1 videocassette (15 min.)

A trade name or other technical specification may be added for videorecord-ings that can only be used on certain equipment. Example:

1 videodisc (MCA DiscoVision) (ca. 35 min.)

The number of frames may be given for filmstrips, filmslips, or stereographs. Example:

4 filmstrips (ca. 40 fr. each)

For MRDFs the number of logical records, the programming language, and/or specifications of the machine on which a program has been designed to run, may be given. Examples:

2 data files (1,500, 800 logical records)

1 program file (OBASIC, KAYPRO 4)

In a few cases the number of intellectual items may differ from the number of physical items, and this may be specified. Examples:

8 maps on 2 sheets

1 aerial chart in 6 sections

3 program files on 1 computer disk

Specific rules in *AACR 2* for any of the above situations should be consulted when cataloging nonbook materials.

[Chapter #].5C.   Other physical details (MARC subfield b)

Different kinds of "other physical details" (besides extent of item and dimensions) are given for each of the materials covered in this chapter. The following outlines indicate the kinds of details specified for each type of material. These details are called for only where appropriate. Where there are several kinds of details for one type of material, they are to be given in the order specified in the list.

Cartographic materials:
    number of maps in an atlas
    color
    material
    mounting
    Examples:

        1 atlas (5 v.) : 250 col. maps

        1 relief model : col., plastic

        1 globe : col., plastic, mounted on wooden stand

        1 map : col., mounted on linen

Manuscripts:
    material other than paper for a single manuscript
    illustrations (as instructed in 2.5C or 8.5C)
    Example:

        42 leaves : parchment, col. ill.

Music:
    illustrations (as instructed in 2.5C).
    Example:

        1 score (x, 77 p., [1] leaf of plates) : facsim.

Sound recordings:
    type of recording
    playing speed
    groove characteristics (discs)
    track configuration (sound track films)
    number of tracks (tape cartridges, cassettes, and reels)
    number of sound channels
    recording and reproduction characteristics (tapes) [optional addition]
    Examples:

        1 sound disc (31 min.) : analog, 33 1/3 rpm, stereo.

        2 sound cassettes (ca. 150 min.) : 1 7/8 ips, mono.

        1 sound disc : analog, 78 rpm, microgroove, mono.

        1 sound disc (42 min.) : digital, stereo.

Films and videorecordings:
    aspect ratio and special projection characteristics (motion pictures)
    sound characteristics
    color
    projection speed (motion pictures)
    playing speed (videodiscs)

Examples:

2 film reels (25 min.) : multiprojector, multiscreen

1 videocassette (15 min.) : sd., col.

1 videodisc (MCA DiscoVision) (ca. 35 min.) : sd., b&w, 1800 rpm

Graphics:
The other physical details required in the description depend upon the kind of graphic material being cataloged. Some require only an indication of color (e.g., col., b&w, sepia). These are:

flash cards	stereographs
pictures	study prints
postcards	transparencies
posters	wall charts

Others require some description of a characteristic in addition to color. These are:

art prints—process in general terms (e.g., engraving, lithograph) or specific terms (e.g., copper engraving) and color

art reproductions—method of reproduction (e.g., photogravure, collotype) and color

filmstrips and filmslips—indication of sound if it is integral (if sound is not integral, it is described as accompanying material) and color

flip charts—indication of double-sided sheets (if applicable) and color

photographs—indication if photograph is a transparency not designed for projection or if it is a negative print and color. Optionally, the process used may be given. LC will apply this option on a case-by-case basis.

slides—treat sound as it is for filmstrips, and in addition, add the name of the system if the sound is integral. Also indicate color.

Two kinds of items require description of a characteristic, but no indication of color. These are:

art originals — medium (chalk, oil, pastel, etc.) and base (board, canvas, fabric, etc.) are given.

technical drawings — method of reproduction if any (blue-print, photocopy, etc.) is given

One kind of graphic item requires no description for other physical details:

radiograph

Examples:

8 study prints : col.

5 filmstrips : sd., col.

1 art original : oil on board

Machine-readable data files:
AACR 2 calls for giving other physical details in the note area. However, the guidelines published by ALA for cataloging microcomputer software suggest identification of sound and color in this position.[20]

Three-dimensional artifacts and realia:
material
color
Examples:

1 jar : clay, brown and red

1 statue : stone, grey

1 diorama (various pieces) : plastic, col.

[Chapter #].5D.   Dimensions (MARC subfield c)

For book-like materials, dimensions are given as instructed in 2.5D. This applies to atlases, single manuscripts, and music.

For large, flat items the height x width is given in centimeters; and if the item is stored folded, the dimensions of the folded item follow the dimensions of the extended item. This applies to maps, plans, large manuscripts, technical drawings, and wall charts. Example:

1 map : col. ; 67 x 97 cm. folded to 15 x 22 cm.

Round items are described in terms of the diameter, specified as such. Sound discs and videodiscs are measured in inches, while other items are measured in centimeters. Exception: No measurements are given for stereographs, including stereograph reels. Example:

1 globe : col., cardboard, mounted on metal stand ; 32 cm. in diam.

The gauge (width) is given for motion pictures, videotapes, filmstrips, and filmslips. All are given in millimeters except for videotapes, which are given in inches. Examples:

1 film cartridge (4 min.) : si., col. ; super 8 mm.

1 film reel (12 min.) : sd., col. with b&w sequences ; 16 mm.

1 videocassette (15 min.) : sd., col. ; 3/4 in.

5 filmstrips : col. ; 35 mm.

Most other items are measured in terms of height x width or height x depth. This is true for relief models; manuscript collections when the containers are uniform; sound cartridges and cassettes when the dimensions are other than the standard ones; art originals, prints, and reproductions; transparencies; slides, if the dimensions are other than 5 x 5 cm. (2 x 2 in.); three-dimensional artifacts and realia. Examples:

1 relief model : col., wood ; 50 x 35 x 4 cm.

2 ft. (ca. 300 items) ; 44 x 30 x 9 cm.

1 diorama (various pieces) : plastic, col. ; 75 x 125 x 50 cm.

For three-dimensional artifacts and realia it may be necessary to give only one dimension. In such a case the dimension being given is specified. Examples:

1 jar : clay, brown and red ; 32 cm. high

1 paperweight : glass, col. ; 8 cm. in diam.

Three-dimensional artifacts and realia in containers should have the name of the container and its dimensions given after the dimensions of the object or as the only dimensions. Dimensions of a container are an optional addition for cartographic materials. LC is applying the option.[21] Examples:

1 relief model : col., wood ; 50 x 35 x 4 cm. in box, 26 x 19 x 9 cm.

1 jigsaw puzzle (ca. 60 pieces) : cardboard, col. ; 18 cm. in diam. in box, 11 cm. in diam. x 4 cm.

No dimensions are given for stereographs, for sound recordings on rolls, or for cartridges or cassettes that are of standard dimensions.

There is no rule in the MRDF chapter in *AACR 2* for dimensions. However, the ALA guidelines for microcomputer software suggest showing the size of a disk in inches to the nearest ¼ inch, showing the length of the face of a cartridge that is to be inserted in inches, also to the nearest ¼ inch, and giving the dimensions of a cassette (only if it is of non-standard size) by giving length and width in inches to the nearest ⅛ inch. Example:

1 program file (OBASIC, KAYPRO 4) on 1 computer disk ; 5 1/4 in.

[Chapter #].5E.   Accompanying material (MARC subfield e)

Material issued with an item is treated, by both *AACR 2* and LC, as described in the general chapter in 1.5E1. Graphic materials and MRDFs are more likely than other materials to have accompanying documentation. In the case of MRDFs, if an item has both data files and program files, and it is clear that one is subordinate to the other, the number of subordinate files is given as accompanying material. Eye-readable text that is issued with a MRDF, that is by the same author as the file, and that has a general term for a title, is also given as accompanying material. Otherwise the accompanying documentation is described in a note.[22] The MRDF rule for accompanying material is numbered "9.5D" because there is no rule for dimensions. There is no rule for accompanying material in the manuscripts chapter. Examples:

> on 1 side of 1 sound disc (ca. 22 min.) : 33 1/3 rpm, stereo. ; 12 in. + 1 program notes booklet ([8] p. : ill. ; 23 cm.)

> 1 videocassette (50 min.) : sd., col. ; ½ in. + 1 script booklet

> 3 stereograph reels (View-master) (7 double fr. each) : col. + 1 booklet (16 p. : col. ill. ; 11 cm.)

> 1 program file (400 statements, FORTRAN IV) + 2 data files (300, 700 logical records)

> 1 data file (900 logical records) + 1 machine-readable code-book (4,200 logical records) + 1 codebook (364 p. ; 25 cm.)

> 5 filmstrips : col. ; 35 mm. + 5 sound cassettes (60 min. : 1 7/8 ips, 2 track, mono.) + 1 teacher's guide (25 p. ; 23 cm.)

[Chapter #].6   SERIES AREA (MARC field 4xx)

Series statements are recorded as instructed in the general chapter in Rule 1.6. This area is not used for manuscripts. Examples:

> 1 map section : col. ; 58 x 43 cm. – (7.5 minute series : topographic)

> 1 score (x, 77 p., [1] leaf of plates) : facsim. ; 28 cm. – (Collegium Musicum / Yale University, ISSN 0147-0108. Second series ; v. 7)

> 2 sound discs (84 min.) : analog, 33 1/3 rpm, stereo. ; 12 in. – (RCA classique)

> 1 videocassette (15 min.) : sd., col. ; 3/4 in. – (OCLC ; no. 6)

1 data file (1,575 logical records) + 1 codebook (675 p. ; 24
cm.) – (SRC/CPS American national election series ; no. 13)

1 game (various pieces) : cardboard, col. ; in box,
24 x 28 x 8 cm. + 1 teacher's guide (2 p. ; 28 cm.). – (Instructo
activity kit)

[Chapter #].7.   NOTE AREA (MARC field 5xx)

Each chapter gives rules for giving notes for the kind of materials covered
by that chapter. The rule numbers are mnemonic, for the most part, from
chapter to chapter — that is, rules with the same number are generally for the
same kind of note, although the details of what to record in the notes
sometimes differ.

[Chapter #].7B1.   Nature and scope of the item (MARC field 500 [520 for
manuscripts])

This kind of note is made if the nature, scope, etc., of the item are not
apparent from the rest of the description. Examples:

Map:

Shows locations of important historical events.

Sound recording:

Organ music to demonstrate the instrument; various
organists and organs.

Film:

Newsreel.

MRDF:

Records cover the science and technology of textiles, plus
all relevant patent literature in the United Kingdom and United
States dating from 1970 to the present.

This note for manuscripts prescribes terms to be used for originals and
copies. The word "signed" is added if appropriate. Examples:

Typescript signed.

Mss. (photocopies)

Ms. signed (carbon copy)

Holograph (photocopy)

For collections of manuscripts, the cataloger is instructed to name the types of items that compose the collection and to mention any other characterizing features. Example:

> [Papers] / William Alexander Smith. -- 1765-1949.
> 51 boxes (11,573 items), 101 v. ; 44 x 30 x 9 cm.
>
> Mss.
> Capitalist and businessman operating mainly in North Carolina from ca. 1866 to 1934. Includes correspondence, reports, financial statements, writings, legal papers, volumes, clippings, genealogy, pictures, bills, receipts, and promissory notes.

This note for music is called "Form of composition and medium of performance." Musical form not apparent from the rest of the description is given briefly. Examples of forms of composition are carol, opera, concerto, and symphony. The medium of performance is given unless it has been given earlier in English or in an easily understood term in a foreign language. Example:

> For harpsichord, 2 violins, viola, and violoncello.

[Chapter #].7B2.   Language (MARC field 500)

A note about the language is made when the language of the textual content is not apparent from the rest of the description. Examples:

Map:
> Place names in Arabic and English.

Manuscript:
> In French.

Music:
> German and English words.

Sound recording:
> Sung in Latin.

Film:
> In English; also issued in Portuguese and Spanish.

[Chapter #].7B3.   Source of title proper (MARC field 500)

Examples:

Sound recording:
Title from publisher's catalog.

Graphic:
Title from later reproductions.

MRDF:
Title from title page of codebook.

Realia:
Title from label.

[Chapter #].7B4.   Variations in title (MARC field 500)

Examples:

Map:
Title in lower right hand corner: Bath Alum, Va.

Sound recording:
Title on container: The last sixteen piano trios.
[Label reads: The last sixteen trios.]

Filmstrip:
Title on container: Saint Pierre of the Cluniac Abbey of Moissac.
[Title proper reads: Moissac, the Romanesque abbey church
and its sculpture.]

MRDF:
Also known as: 1974 American national election study.
[Title proper reads: The CPS 1974 American national election
study.]

An LC rule interpretation for this rule in the chapters on motion pictures
and videorecordings and graphic materials indicates that LC will make this
note for these materials only when a title added entry is needed for the variant
title. This decision is made by consulting Rule 21.2 and determining if the
variation in title is as great as the title differences described there.[23]

[Chapter #].7B6.   Statement of responsibility (MARC fields 500, 508, and 511)

This note is for persons or bodies that bear some responsibility for the item and are necessary to the description but cannot be named in the title and statement of responsibility area. Examples:

Map:

Grid and marginal information added by the Army Map Service.

Manuscript:

Holograph signed note by William Pitt appended to letter.

Music:

Text founded on the drama of the same name by Pushkin.

Sound recordings:

Hollywood Bowl Pops Orchestra ; Carmen Dragon, arranger-conductor.

Violoncello: Raphael Wallfisch ; piano: Richard Markham.

Barbara Rondelli, soprano ; Nürnberger Symphoniker, Ljubomir Romansky, conductor.

Film:

Cast: John Howard Davies, Alec Guinness, Robert Newton.

Credits: Editor, Lars Floden ; voices, Hans Conreid, June Forray ; music, Larry Wolff.

Graphic:

Booklet edited by Lowell Thomas.

An LC rule interpretation lists (in prescribed order) the functions for which persons or bodies will be given in a "credits" statement. It also lists the functions that will not be given.[24]

[Chapter #].7B7.   Edition and history (MARC fields 500 and 503)

Examples:

Map:

First published under title: Geographic map of the ... Kingdom of Saudi Arabia.

Manuscript: [note called "Donor, source, etc., and previous owner(s)" in the manuscripts chapter]

Gift of the estate of Mrs. Theodora Cabot, 1955.

Music:

Edited from ms. sources in the National Library of Turin.

Sound recordings:

Recorded in San Francisco in 1971.

Originally issued: New York : McGraw-Hill, 1968. (Sound seminars)

Reissue of: Capitol SW-1804.

Videorecording:

Originally produced as motion picture in 1960.

Filmstrip:

Edited from episodes of the television program entitled The undersea world of Jacques Cousteau.

MRDF:

Data collected Nov., Dec. 1974, and Jan. 1975.

Puzzle:

Based on a painting by Mather Brown.

[Chapter #].7B8.   Material specific details (MARC field 500)

Four of the types of material covered by this chapter have this rule for notes that are specific to the type of material being cataloged: cartographic materials, manuscripts, music, and machine-readable data files. The graphic materials chapter originally had this rule, but it has been officially deleted.
Examples:

Maps [called "Mathematical and other cartographic data"]
"Contour interval 50 feet."

Relief shown by hachures, shading, spot heights, etc.

Manuscripts [called "Place of writing"]
At top of letter: Brooklyn.

Music [called "Notation"]
Shape-note notation.

MRDF [called "Program"]
OSIRIS version.

[Chapter #].7B9.   Publication, distribution, etc. (MARC field 500)

Examples:

Map:
Based on 1972 data.

Manuscript: [note called "Published versions"]
Published in: Some letters of George III / W.B. Hamilton.
p. 416. *In* The South Atlantic quarterly. Vol. 68, no. 3 (Summer 1969).

Film:
A foreign film (France)

Graphic:
Issued in 3 parts.

[Chapter #].7B10.   Physical description (MARC field 500)

Examples:

Map:
Maps issued in envelopes bearing copies of inset maps
of cities.

Manuscript:
Paper watermarked: 1834.

Music:
Duration: 13:20.

> [given only if stated in the item; a cataloging deci-
> sion made in the Music Section, Special Materials
> Cataloging Division, Library of Congress, indi-
> cates that for music and sound recordings, hours,
> minutes, and seconds are to be expressed in the
> note area as numerals separated by colons.[25]]

Each copy signed by the composer.

Sound recording:

Impressed on pliable surface with rectangular edge
attached to hard paper cover for support.

Videorecording:

U standard.

Graphic:

´For flannel board.

MRDF [note called "File description and physical description"]

Weighted sample size is 2523.

Puzzle:

Vertical sides in straight lines; horizontal sides form
wavy lines.

Diorama:

Contains four background scenes and 72 figures of
animals, people, and plants.

[Chapter #].7B11.   Accompanying material. (MARC field 500)

Rule 1.5E1 gives four options for treating accompanying material. When
giving details in a note is chosen, the details are recorded here. Examples:

Map:

Accompanied by: Index to maps of Arabia / issued by
Army Map Service. 1 sheet ; 25 x 36 cm.

Sound recordings:

Program notes by Anthony Hodgson on container.

Film:

With teacher's guide and supplementary material.

MRDF:

Codebook numbered: ISBN 0-89138-111-2.

[Chapter #].7B12.   Series (MARC field 500)

Examples:

Originally issued in series: Musica viva Bohemica.

Part 1 in a series.

Series statement supplied by producer.

[Chapter #].7B14.   Audience (MARC field 500 [540 for manuscripts])

Manuscript [note called "Access and literary rights"]:
Information on literary rights available in the repository.

Film:
For dental personnel.

Flash card:
For primary grades.

Slide:
For nurses' training.

MRDF:
Restrictions: available by lease arrangement. Also available through commercial online vendors.

[Chapter #].7B15.   (MARC field 510 [manuscripts] or 538 [MRDFs])

This note number appears in only two chapters. It is called "Reference to published descriptions" in the manuscripts chapter. Example:

Described in: Manuscripts for research / report of the director, 1961-1974, North Country Historical Research Center, Feinberg Library, State University College, Plattsburgh, New York. 1975. p. 31-32.

This note is called "mode of use" in the MRDF chapter. It is here that the "Guidelines" for microcomputer software recommend giving information about the make and model of the computer(s) required (unless this was given in the file description area), the amount of memory required, the operating system, the software requirements, and the characteristics of any peripherals needed. This note is to begin with the phrase "System requirements."[26] Example:

System requirements: IBM PC, XT, or 3270; DOS 1.1/2.0

[Chapter #].7B16.   Other formats available (MARC field 500)

Examples:

Sound recording:
Issued also on reel (60 min. : 3 3/4 ips, mono. or stereo. ; 5 in.)

Videorecording:
Available as cartridge or disc.

Slide:

Issued also as filmstrip.

Filmstrip:

Issued also with sound accompaniment on disc.

[Chapter #].7B17. Summary (MARC field 520)

Summary notes are often given for nonbook materials because of the difficulty of browsing them (as can be done with books) to determine what they contain. Examples:

Sound recording:

Summary: The author presents an overview and introduction to the area of human potentialities and its implications for humankind.

Film:

Summary: A sports documentary covering three snowmobile races.

Flash card:

Summary: Aids young children in developing number and money concepts.

Puzzle:

Summary: The picture shows a battle scene on the deck of a British war ship during the Revolutionary War. The officers are in full dress uniforms for 1787-1795 period.

[Chapter #].7B18. Contents (MARC fields 500, 504, and 505)

Examples:

Maps:

Each sheet includes: "Index to adjoining sheets," glossary, and "Sources of base compilation."

Inset: Area west of Apalachicola River.

Music:

Contents: Sonate C dur, op. 15, Nr. 15 – Sonate A dur, op. 18, Nr. 5 – Sonate F dur, op. 18, Nr. 6.

Film:

   Contents: The black league (20 min.) – Doing your own
   thing (22 min.) – Teamwork against the odds (18 min.) –
   A new era (15 min.)

Filmstrip:

   Contents: Return to the sea (130 fr.) – To save a living
   sea (153 fr.) – The liquid sky (120 fr.) – A sea of motion
   (133 fr.) – Invisible multitudes (147 fr.)

An LC rule interpretation allows addition after the number of frames,
slides, etc., of the duration of the accompanying sound.[27] Example:

   Contents: Return to the sea (130 fr., 25 min., 15 sec.) –
   To save a living sea (153 fr., 30 min., 25 sec.) ...

[Chapter #].7B19.   Numbers (other than Standard Numbers) (MARC fields
                     023-030, 036-037, and 500)

Examples:

Maps:

   Supt. of Docs. no.: I 19.2:V88/4.

   Publisher's no.: AMS 5060 II SW-Series V834.

Music:

   Pl. no.: B.S.I. no. 31.

   Publisher's no.: Nr. 4516.

Sound recordings:

   Big Sur Recordings: 7110.

   Angel: S 37309.

Graphic:

   Packet no. A 792.

MRDF:

   Original study number: CPS study 495441.

Realia:

   "No. 1014."

An LC rule interpretation for this note for music calls for recording both
a plate number and a publisher's number even though *AACR 2* calls for only
the plate number if both are given. LC also calls for transcribing the

publisher's number as it appears, even though it includes a publisher's name already given in the publication, distribution, etc., area.[28]

An LC rule interpretation for the transcription of a label name and number of a sound recording calls for making this note the first one.[29]

[Chapter #].7B20. Copy being described and library's holdings (MARC field 590)

Examples:

Music:

Library has 2 copies of the score and 1 copy of each part.

MRDF:

Data set name: CIPERRS.

[Chapter #].7B21. "With" notes (MARC field 501)

When a separately titled part of an item that lacks a collective title is being described as a separate entity, the other separately titled parts are listed in a note that begins "With:". Examples:

Music:

With: La plus que lente / Claude Debussy.

Sound recording:

With: Suite italienne / Igor Stravinskii – Vocalise, op. 34, no. 14 / Sergei Rachmaninoff.

Note: A problem in the "With" note has been noted by music librarians. Because the rules for notes call for referring to another bibliographic item by its title proper and statement of responsibility, musical works that are entered under a uniform title may be "lost" to a user of the "With" note. Such musical works seldom have added entries for title proper, and the filing arrangement under the main entry is by uniform title, not title proper.

[Chapter #].7B22. (MARC fields 500 and 534)

Two chapters have a rule "7B22." This rule in the manuscripts chapter is called "Ancient, medieval, and Renaissance manuscripts" and gives instructions for more detailed notes for these manuscripts.

This rule in the graphic materials chapter is called "Notes relating to original" and calls for description of the original of a reproduced art work.

**[Chapter #].8.   STANDARD NUMBER AND TERMS OF AVAIL-
ABILITY AREA** (MARC fields 020 and 022)

Details of this area are recorded as instructed in the general chapter under 1.8. Most of the materials covered by this chapter currently are not given international standard numbers, leaving the terms of availability to stand alone.

[Chapter #].9.   SUPPLEMENTARY ITEMS

All chapters except that for manuscripts have this rule for describing supplementary items as instructed in the general chapter under 1.9.

**[Chapter #].10.   ITEMS MADE UP OF SEVERAL TYPES OF
MATERIAL**

All chapters except that for manuscripts have this rule for describing "kits" made up of different types of materials. The reader should take note of the possible ways for describing kits given in the general chapter under Rule 1.10. See the examples given there.

**[Chapter #].11.   FACSIMILES, PHOTOCOPIES, AND OTHER
REPRODUCTIONS**

The chapters for cartographic materials, music, motion pictures and videorecordings, and graphics have this rule for describing facsimiles, photocopies, and other reproductions as instructed in Rule 1.11.

There is a rule numbered 6.11 in the sound recordings chapter called "NONPROCESSED SOUND RECORDINGS." This rule is intended for use for the cataloging of such locally produced sound recordings as oral history interviews, addresses recorded in local auditoriums, lectures by local professors, or recordings of concerts or plays. The rules for processed sound recordings should be followed as much as possible. However, such recordings may have no title proper and will need to have one formulated. No information is given in the publication, etc., area. The date of recording is given in a note. Notes should also give participants and details of the event recorded as well as other notes prescribed in Rule 6.7. *See* Fig. 5.21.

Fig. 5.21. Rule 6.11. Description of a nonprocessed sound recording.

[Interview with Hattie McDonald on her 100th birthday] / interviewed by Susan Hall.
1 sound cassette (50 min.) : 1 7/8 ips, mono.

Recorded in Durham, N.C., July 29, 1979.
Summary: A discussion of life's impressions on the daughter of parents who had been born slaves.

The problem with this rule is the inconsistency of treatment of date here with the way it is treated in other parts of *AACR 2*. There is no comparable rule for treating nonprocessed motion pictures and videorecordings, yet these are nearly as common as nonprocessed sound recordings. Homemade video-recordings were rare at the time of publication of *AACR 2*, but "home movies" have been around for many years. In the chapter for motion pictures and sound recordings the only reference to nonprocessed materials is in the title and statement of responsibility area where one is instructed to supply a title that includes the date of shooting of the film. If one tries to follow precedents that appear in *AACR 2* and thus uses the rules for cataloging manuscripts, art originals, unpublished photographs and other unpublished graphic items, and artifacts not intended primarily for communication, one would record a date in the publication, distribution, etc., area. However, if one uses the rule for "nonprocessed sound recordings," there are no details at all in the publication, distribution, etc., area, and the date is given in a note. These treatments seem unnecessarily inconsistent. Because it is useful to have a date in the fixed field of the MARC record, and because that date is taken from the publication, distribution, etc., area, it is recommended that a date be given in the publication, distribution, etc., area for all nonprocessed materials except naturally occurring objects.

Figures 5.22 through 5.29 give the *AACR 2* descriptions for the items whose sources of information are shown in Figs. 5.1 through 5.20. Figs. 5.30 through 5.37 illustrate the MARC records for the same items.

Fig. 5.22. AACR 2 description of the map.

Bath Alum quadrangle, Virginia–Bath Co. / mapped,
    edited, and published by the Geological Survey. – Scale
    1:24,000 ; Polyconic proj. – Washington, D.C. : For sale by
    U.S. Geological Survey, 1968.
    1 map section : col. ; 58 x 43 cm. – (7.5 minute series :
topographic)

    Title in lower right corner: Bath Alum, Va.
    "Topography by photogrammetric methods from aerial
photographs."
    Publisher's no.: AMS 5060 II SW-Series V834.

Fig. 5.23. AACR 2 description of the single manuscript.

[Letter] 1793 Feb. 3, Windsor [to Henry] Dundas / G.R.
[George III].
   1 leaf ; 38 x 46 cm. folded to 23 x 19 cm.

   Holograph signed.
   Purchase, 1961.
   Published in: Some letters of George III / W.B. Hamilton.
p. 416. *In* The South Atlantic quarterly. Vol. 68, no. 3 (Summer 1969).

Fig. 5.24. AACR 2 description of the score.

   Concerto in B-flat, for cembalo and strings / Christoph
Schaffrath ; edited by Karyl Louwenaar. – Madison (315
West Gorham Street, Madison, Wis. 53703) : A-R Editions,
c1977.
   1 score (x, 77 p., [1] leaf of plates) : facsim. ; 28 cm. –
(Collegium musicum. Second series ; v. 7)

   Edited from ms. parts (partly holograph) in the Deutsche
Staatsbibliothek, Berlin (Am.B.492)
   Includes bibliographical references.
   ISBN 0-89579-100-5 : May be reproduced free of charge
for performance use by applying to A-R Editions, Inc.

Fig. 5.25. AACR 2 description of the sound disc.

   Saturday night Fiedler [sound recording]. – New York : Midsong International Records, p1979.
   1 sound disc (31 min.) : analog, 33 1/3 rpm, stereo. ;
12 in.

   Midsong International Records: MSI-011.
   Arthur Fiedler and the Boston Pops.
   Side 2: "Based on Toccata and Fugue in 'D' minor and
air for the 'G' string [by J. S. Bach]."
   Recorded June 9, 1979.
   Contents: Saturday night fever medley (18:47) –
Bachamania (11:32)

Fig. 5.26. AACR 2 description of the videorecording.

Automated check-in [videorecording] / by Anne Marie
Allison and Harry Kamens ; directed by John Dannley. –
[Kent, Ohio] : Produced by Television Services, Kent State
University, [1977]
1 videocassette (15 min.) : sd., col. ; 3/4 in. – (OCLC ;
no. 6)

"Prepared under the auspices of Hyman W. Kritzer..."
Summary: Presents an introduction to use of the serials
check-in subsystem of the OCLC system.
Contents: Locating check-in records – Using check-in
records.
$55.00

Fig. 5.27. AACR 2 description of the stereograph reel.

Smithsonian Institution, Washington, D.C. [slide]. – Portland, Or. : Sawyer's Inc., [196-?]
3 stereograph reels (View-master) (7 double fr. each) : col.
+ 1 booklet (16 p. : col. ill. ; 11 cm.). – (View-master
guided picture tour)

Booklet edited by Lowell Thomas.
Summary: Shows and describes some of the major exhibits
housed in three of the buildings of the Smithsonian.
Contents: Reel 1. Air and space exhibits – Reel 2. Natural
history exhibits – Reel 3. History & technology exhibits.
"Packet no. A 792."
$2.25

Fig. 5.28. AACR 2 description of the machine-readable data file.

WordStar [machine-readable data file]. – Release 3.31. – San
Rafael, Calif. : MicroPro International Corp., c1984.
1 program file on 1 computer disk ; 5 1/4 in. + 1 binder
(3 manuals) + 1 command card + 1 key fronts card.

Reference manual, training guide, and installation
manual: c1983; training guide: 2nd ed., rev.
Manual may not be reproduced.
System requirements: IBM PC, XT, or 3270; DOS 1.1/2.0.

Fig. 5.29. AACR 2 description of the game.

The Classification game [game.] – Paoli, Pa. : Instructo
    Corp., c1969.
    1 game (various pieces) : cardboard, col. ; in box,
24 x 28 x 8 cm. + 1 teacher's guide (2 p. ; 28 cm.). – (Instructo activity kit)

Contains 4 store interiors (3 interlocking pieces each), 4
store floors, and 48 picture cards.
    For primary grades.
    Summary: Helps students improve organizing and classi-
fying skills by learning to place the appropriate items in
each of four stores: clothing store, food store, pet store, and
toy store.
    "No. 1014."
    $4.95

Fig. 5.30. MARC record for the map.

```
Type: e Bib lvl: m Lang: eng Source: d Form:      Relief: a
RecG: a Enc lvl: I Ctry:  dcu Dat tp: s Govt pub: f Indx: 0
Desc: a Mod rec:    Base:  cp Dates: 1968,
    1 010
    2 040      IVE $c IVE
    3 034 1    a $b 24000
    4 043      n-us-va
    5 052      3883 $b B3
    6 090      G3883.B3 1968 $b .U5
    7 049      IVEA
    8 245 00   Bath Alum quandrangle, Virginia--Bath Co. / mapped, edited,
and published by the Geological Survey.
    9 255      Scale 1:24,000 ; $b Polyconic proj.
   10 260 0    Washington, D.C. : $b For sale by U.S. Geological Survey, $c
1968.
   11 300      1 map section : $b col. ; $c 58 x 43 cm.
   12 490 0    7.5 minute series : topographic
   13 500      Title in lower right corner: Bath Alum, Va.
   14 500      "Topography by photogrammetric methods from aerial
photographs."
   15 500      Publisher's no.: AMS 5060 II SW-Series V834.
   16 650      Bath Alum (Va.) $x Maps.
   17 710 20   Geological Survey (U.S.)
```

Fig. 5.31. MARC record for the manuscript.

```
Type: b Bib lvl: m Coll st:    Lang:  eng Source: d Illus:
Repr:    Enc lvl: I Con lvl:   Ctry:  ncu Dat tp: s Pr st:
Desc: a Mod rec:    File:              Dates: 1790,
    1 010
    2 040      IVE $c IVE
    3 045 0    v9v9 $b d17930203
    4 090      DA506.A2 $b 1793
    5 049      IVEA
    6 100 0    George $b III, $c King of Great Britain, $d 1738-1820.
    7 245 00   [Letter] 1793 Feb. 3, Windsor [to Henry] Dundas / $c G. R.
[George III].
    8 300      1 leaf ; $c 38 x 46 cm. folded to 23 x 19 cm.
    9 520      Holograph signed.
   10 590      Purchase, 1961.
   11 500      Published in: Some letters of George III / W. B. Hamilton.
p. 416. In The South Atlantic quarterly. Vol. 68, no. 3 (Summer 1969).
   12 651 0    Great Britain $x History $y George III, 1760-1820.
```

Fig. 5.32. MARC record for the score.

```
Type: c Bib lvl: m Lang:   N/A Source:   Accomp mat: b
Repr:    Enc lvl: I Ctry:  wiu Dat tp: s MEBE: 1
         Mod rec: m Comp:  co  Format: a Prts:
Desc: a Int lvl:    LTxt:  n   Dates: 1977,
    1 010      78-771520/M
    2 040      DLC $c IVE
    3 020      0895791005 $c May be reproduced free of charge for performance
use by applying to A-R Editions, Inc.
    4 048      $b kc01 $a oc
    5 050 0    M2 $b .C64362 vol. 7 $a M1010
    6 049      IVEA
    7 100 10   Schaffrath, Christoph, $d 1709-1763.
    8 240 10   Concertos, $m harpsichord, string orchestra, $r Bb major
    9 245 00   Concerto in B-flat, for cembalo and strings / $c Christoph
Schaffrath ; edited by Karyl Louwenaar.
   10 260 0    Madison (315 West Gorham Street, Madison, Wis. 53703) : $b A-R
Editions, $c c1977.
   11 300      1 score (x, // p., [1] leaf of plates) : $b facsim. ; $c 28 cm.
   12 440 0    Collegium musicum. $p Second series ; $v v. 7
   13 500      Edited from ms. parts (partly holograph) in the Deutsche
Staatsbibliothek, Berlin (Am.B.492)
   14 504      Includes bibliographical references.
   15 650 0    Concertos (Harpsichord with string orchestra) $x Scores.
   16 700 10   Louwenaar, Karyl.
```

Fig. 5.33. MARC record for the sound recording.

```
Type: j Bib lvl: m Lang:   N/A Source: d Accomp mat:
Repr:    Enc lvl: I Ctry:  nyu Dat tp: s MEBE: 0
         Mod rec:   Comp:  pp  Format: n Prts: n
Desc: a Int lvl:    LTxt:  n   Dates: 1979,
    1 010
    2 040      IVE $c IVE
    3 007      s $b d $d h $e s $f m $g c $h n $i n $j m $k p $l l $m n
    4 028 02   MSI-011 $b Midsong International Records
    5 090      ML102.P66 $b S27
    6 049      IVEA
    7 100 10   Fiedler, Arthur, $d 1894-1979.
    8 245 10   Saturday night Fiedler $h sound recording
    9 260 0    New York : $b Midsong International Records, $c p1979.
   10 300      1 sound disc (31 min.) : $b analog, 33 1/3 rpm, stereo. : $c
12 in.
   11 511 0    Arthur Fiedler and the Boston Pops.
   12 500      Side 2: "Based on Toccata and Fugue in 'D' minor and air for
the 'G' string [by J. S. Bach]."
   13 518      Recorded June 9, 1979.
   14 505 0    Saturday night fever medley (18:47) -- Bachamania (11:32)
   15 650 0    Popular music.
   16 710 20   Boston Pops Orchestra.
```

Fig. 5.34. MARC record for the videorecording.

```
Type: g Bib lvl: m Govt pub: s Lang:   eng Source: d Leng: 015
InLC: u Enc lvl: I Type mat: v Ctry:   ohu Dat tp: s MEBE: 1
Tech: l Mod rec:         Accomp mat:
Desc: a Int lvl: f Dates: 1977,
   1 010
   2 040      IVE $c IVE
   3 007      v $b f $ c r $d b $ e n $f a $g h $h r
   4 020        $c $55.00
   5 090      Z699.S4 $b A44 1977
   6 049      IVEA
   7 100 1    Allison, Anne Marie.
   8 245 10   Automated check-in  $h videorecording / $c by Anne Marie
Allison and Harry Kamens ; directed by John Dannley.
   9 260      [Kent, Ohio] : $b Produced by Television Services, Kent State
University, $c [1977]
  10 300      1 videocassette (15 min.) : $b sd., col. ; $c 3/4 in.
  11 490 1    OCLC ; no. 6
  12 500      "Prepared under the auspices of Hyman W. Kritzer ..."
  13 520      Presents an introduction to use of the serials check-in
subsystem of the OCLC system.
  14 505      Locating check-in records -- Using check-in records.
  15 650  0   Serials control systems $x Automation.
  16 610 20   Ohio College Library Center.
  17 700 11   Kamens, Harry.
  18 710 11   Kent State University. $b Television Services.
  19 830  0   OCLC (Series) ; $v no. 6.
```

Note: The name of OCLC was not changed from "Ohio College Library Center" until the end of December 1977.

Fig. 5.35. MARC record for the stereograph reel.

```
Type: g Bib lvl: m Govt pub:   Lang:   eng Source: d Leng: 021
InLC: u Enc lvl: I Type mat: s Ctry:   oru Dat tp: q MEBE: 0
Tech: n Mod rec:         Accomp mat:   m
Desc: a Int lvl:   Dates: 1960,1969
   1 010
   2 040      IVE $c IVE
   3 007      g $b s $c r $d c $e n $h z
   4 020        $c $2.25
   5 043      n-us-dc
   6 090      Q11.S8 $b S64
   7 049      IVEA
   8 245 00   Smithsonian Institution, Washington, D.C. $h slide
   9 260      Portland, Or. ; $b Sawyer's, Inc., $c [196-?]
  10 300      3 stereograph reels (View-master) (7 double fr. each) : $b col.
+ $e 1 booklet (16 p. : col. ill. ; 11 cm.)
  11 440  0   View-master guided picture tour
  12 500      Booklet edited by Lowell Thomas.
  13 520      Shows and describes some of the major exhibits housed in three
of the buildings of the Smithsonian.
  14 505      Reel 1. Air and space exhibits -- Reel 2. Natural history
exhibits -- Reel 3. History & technology exhibits.
  15 500      "Packet no. A 792."
  16 610 20   Smithsonian Institution.
```

Fig. 5.36. MARC record for the machine-readable data file.

```
Type: m Bib lvl: m Govt pub:   Lang:   eng Source: d Frequn: n
File: u Enc lvl: I Machine:  a Ctry:  cau Dat tp: c Regulr:
Desc: a Mod rec:    Dates: 1984,
   1 010
   2 040      IVE $c IVE
   3 090      HF5548.2.T4 $b W6 1984
   5 049      IVEA
   6 245 00   WordStar $h machine-readable data file
   7 250      Release 3.31.
   8 260      San Rafael, Calif. : $b MicroPro International Corp., $c c1984.
   9 300      1 program file on 1 computer disk ; $c 5 1/4 in. + $e 1 binder
(3 manuals) + 1 command card + 1 key fronts card.
  10 500      Reference manual, training guide, and installation manual:
c1983; training guide: 2nd ed., rev.
  11 506      Manual may not be reproduced.
  12 538      System requirements: IBM PC, XT, or 3270; DOS 1.1/2.0.
  13 650  0   Word processing $x Computer programs.
  14 710 20   MicroPro International Corp.
```

Fig. 5.37. MARC record for the game.

```
Type: n Bib lvl: m Govt pub:   Lang:   eng Source: d Leng: ---
InLC: u Enc lvl: I Type mat: g Ctry:  pau Dat tp: s MEBE: 0
Tech: n Mod rec:        Accomp mat:  r
Desc: a Int lvl: b Dates: 1969,
   1 010
   2 040      IVE $c IVE
   3 020      $c $4.95
   4 090      LB1029.G3 $b C52
   5 049      IVEA
   6 245 04   The Classification game $h game
   7 260      Paoli, Pa. : $b Instructo Corp., $c c1969.
   8 300      1 game (various pieces) : $b cardboard, col. ; $c in box, 24 x
28 x 8 cm. + $e 1 teacher's guide (2 p. ; 28 cm.)
   9 490 0    Instructo activity kit
  10 500      Contains 4 store interiors (3 interlocking pieces each), 4
store floors, and 48 picture cards.
  11 500      For primary grades.
  12 520      Helps students improve organizing and classifying skills by
learning to place the appropriate items in each of four stores: clothing
store, food store, pet store, and toy store.
  13 500      "No. 1014."
  14 650  0   Educational games.
  15 650  0   Categorization (Psychology)
```

NOTES

[1]A discussion of these problems in relation to *AACR 2* may be found in Michael Gorman, "Cataloging and Classification of Film Study Material," in Nancy Allen, *Film Study Collections* (New York, F. Ungar Publishing, 1979), pp. 113-123.

[2]American Library Association, Committee on Cataloging: Description and Access, *Guidelines for Using AACR 2 Chapter 9 for Cataloging Microcomputer Software* (Chicago, American Library Association, 1984).

[3]*Cataloging Service Bulletin*, no. 13 (Summer 1981): 15.

[4]LC decisions about use of GMDs are recorded in "Display of General Material Designations under AACR 2," *Cataloging Service Bulletin*, no. 6 (Fall 1979): 4-5.

[5]*AACR 2*, p. 20.

[6]ALA, CC:DA, *Guidelines for ... Microcomputer Software*, p. 3.

[7]*Cataloging Service Bulletin*, no. 13 (Summer 1981): 15-16.

[8]*Cataloging Service Bulletin*, no. 11 (Winter 1981): 15.

[9]*Cataloging Service Bulletin*, no. 26 (Fall 1984): 12.

[10]ALA, CC:DA, *Guidelines for ... Microcomputer Software*, p. 4.

[11]*Cataloging Service Bulletin*, no. 8 (Spring 1980): 10.

[12]Ibid.

[13]*Cataloging Service Bulletin*, no. 25 (Summer 1984): 44.

[14]Ibid., pp. 46-47.

[15]*Cataloging Service Bulletin*, no. 13 (Summer 1981): 16.

[16]*Cataloging Service Bulletin*, no. 15 (Winter 1982): 6.

[17]*Cataloging Service Bulletin*, no. 25 (Summer 1984): 48.

[18]*Cataloging Service Bulletin*, no. 8 (Spring 1980): 10.

[19]Ibid.

[20]ALA, CC:DA, *Guidelines for ... Microcomputer Software*, p. 7.

[21]*Cataloging Service Bulletin*, no. 8 (Spring 1980): 10.

[22]ALA, CC:DA, *Guidelines for ... Microcomputer Software*, p. 8.

[23]*Cataloging Service Bulletin*, no. 13 (Summer 1981): 16.

[24]*Cataloging Service Bulletin*, no. 22 (Fall 1983): 21.

[25]Richard P. Smiraglia, *Cataloging Music* (Lake Crystal, Minn.: Soldier Creek Press, 1983), p. 36.

[26]ALA, CC:DA, *Guidelines for ... Microcomputer Software*, pp. 9-10.

[27]*Cataloging Service Bulletin*, no. 13 (Summer 1981): 17.

[28]*Cataloging Service Bulletin*, no. 14 (Fall 1981): 16-17.

[29]Ibid., p. 17.

SUGGESTED READING

Cartographic Materials: A Manual of Interpretation for AACR 2. Chicago, American Library Association, 1982.

Dodd, Sue A. *Cataloging Machine-Readable Data Files.* Chicago, American Library Association, 1982.

Frost, Carolyn O. *Cataloging Nonbook Materials: Problems in Theory and Practice.* Littleton, Colo., Libraries Unlimited, 1983.

Maxwell, Margaret F. *Handbook for AACR 2.* Chicago, American Library Association, 1980. Chapters 3-8.

Olson, Nancy B. *Cataloging of Audiovisual Materials: A Manual Based on AACR 2.* 2nd ed. Mankato, Minn., Minnesota Scholarly Press, 1985.

Rogers, JoAnn V. *Nonprint for Media Collections: A Guide Based on AACR 2.* Littleton, Colo., Libraries Unlimited, 1982.

Smiraglia, Richard P. *Cataloging Music: A Manual for Use with AACR 2.* Lake Crystal, Minn., Soldier Creek Press, 1983.

Weihs, Jean, with Shirley Lewis and Janet Macdonald. *Nonbook Materials: The Organization of Integrated Collections.* 2nd ed. Ottawa, Canadian Library Association, 1979.

6
Description of Microforms

INTRODUCTION

The cataloging of microforms requires knowledge of a number of different types of material. Books, manuscripts, maps, music, and graphic materials all can be reproduced in microform. In addition, microform can be the original means for publication of some kinds of content — especially data stored in a computer. According to *AACR 2*, all microforms, whether original publications or reproductions, are described in terms of the microform format with details of the original, when applicable, given in a note. As mentioned earlier in this text under discussion of Rule 1.5A3, this is a controversial method for handling microforms. Those who oppose it say that the user is misled by being given a modern date in the publication, distribution, etc., area when the intellectual content of the item is much older. They are also concerned about short-entry catalogs in which the notes are not printed. Publishers that specialize in reproducing older printed material in microform say that the purpose of the reproduction is to make older materials available for scholarly study and research, not to create a new edition of it as a printed reprint of the text would do. Earlier rules called for description of the original in the major part of the record with microform details in a note. Those opposed to this method point out that the physical form of the item is important. A user who comes into the library wanting to borrow an item to take elsewhere to read needs to know whether it is in book form or microform. There are also potential problems for the cataloger in determining what the original was and what its physical description should be. A microform of a dissertation, for example, may be a positive copy of a negative master that is a copy of a photocopy of a printout of text originally held in a machine-readable data file. Two articles that discuss the issues involved should be read for further information.[1] Americans have tended to prefer the method of describing the original, with details about the microform in a note; but Europeans have espoused describing the original in a note. In 1980 a subcommittee of ALA's Committee on Cataloging: Description and Access was appointed to examine this question again and put forth a recommendation; its recommendation was that the original be described in the body of the entry, with details of the microform given in a note. The rules have not been revised, but the Library of Congress has issued a policy decision to this effect.[2] Both methods are illustrated in this text.

SELECTED RULES AND EXAMPLES

RULE 11.0.   GENERAL RULES

11.0A.   Scope

This chapter covers all kinds of microforms, including those that are themselves original publications, those that are microreproductions of previous publications, and those that are microreproductions of material assembled for the purpose of bringing out an original edition in microform.

11.0B.   Sources of information

11.0B1.   Chief source of information
The following are the chief sources of information for the different types of microform:

TYPE	CHIEF SOURCE
microfilm	title frame, usually at the beginning of the item giving full title and publication details
aperture cards:	
set of cards	title card
single card	card itself
microfiches and microopaques	title frame, or, if there is none, the eye-readable data at the top of the fiche or opaque

Information that is usually presented on one title frame or card may be presented on successive frames or cards. In this case, treat the successive frames or cards as one chief source.
Information not available in the chief source is taken from other sources. The order of preference is:

the remainder of the item
container
accompanying material
other sources

11.0B2.   **Prescribed sources of information**

AREA	PRESCRIBED SOURCES OF INFORMATION
Title and statement of responsibility	Chief source of information
Edition	Chief source of information, the rest of the item, the container
Special data for cartographic materials and serials	[same as edition area]
Publication, distribution, etc.	[same as edition area]
Physical decription	Any source
Series	[same as edition area]
Note	Any source
Standard number and terms of availability	Any source

Two items, one in microfilm format and the other in microfiche format, are used in this chapter to illustrate the building of description for microforms. The item illustrated in Figs. 6.1-6.2 is one that was assembled and filmed specifically for the purpose of bringing out an original edition in microform. The item illustrated in Figs. 6.3-6.5 is a microform of a previously existing work.

Fig. 6.1. Transcription of the first five frames of a microfilm.

Frame 1

WOMEN AND/IN HEALTH

filmed by the
WOMEN'S HISTORY RESEARCH CENTER
JULY 1974

Frame 2

WOMEN'S HISTORY RESEARCH CENTER

2325 Oak Street
Berkeley, California 94707

Frame 3

© Women's History Research Center, Inc. 1974

Reproduction of the material contained herein
may not be reproduced in any form except by express permission from Women's History
Research Center, Inc. and the Publisher(s).

Frame 4

THIS FILM WAS MADE POSSIBLE BY A
REVENUE SHARING GRANT FROM THE
ALMEDA COUNTY BOARD OF SUPERVISORS.

Frame 5

Filmed at a reduction ratio of 15:1

Fig. 6.2. Transcription of label on container of first reel of microfilm.

WOMEN AND HEALTH/MENTAL HEALTH
Reel No. 1   Positive
Section I
Women's History Research Center

Fig. 6.3. Transcription of title frame of microfiche.

77-28,548

HANSON, John Frederick, 1949-
THE TRIAL OF LIEUTENANT GENERAL
MASAHARU HOMMA.

Mississippi State University, Ph.D., 1977
History, United States

Xerox University Microfilms, Ann Arbor, Michigan 48106

© 1977
JOHN FREDERICK HANSON

ALL RIGHTS RESERVED

_____

Fig. 6.4. Transcription of eye-readable data at top of fiche.

77-28548   HANSON, John F   THE TRIAL OF LIEUTENANT   1 of 3
                                      GENERAL MASAHARU HOMMA
                Ann Arbor, MI. : University Microfilms International 1978

_____

**Fig. 6.5. Copy of title page of original dissertation
(second frame of microfiche).**

THE TRIAL OF LIEUTENANT GENERAL MASAHARU HOMMA

by
JOHN F. HANSON

A Dissertation
Submitted to the Faculty of
Mississippi State University
in Partial Fulfillment of the Requirements
for the Degree of Doctor of Philosophy
in the Department of History

Mississippi State, Mississippi
August 1977

_____

RULE 11.1. TITLE AND STATEMENT OF RESPONSIBILITY AREA
(MARC field 245)

11.1B.-11.1F.

Titles proper, parallel titles and other title information, and statements of responsibility are transcribed as instructed in the general chapter. The GMD for the material covered in this chapter is "microform." LC has decided to add the GMD for microform materials under *AACR 2*, although it was not added in the past.[3] *See* Figs. 6.6-6.8.

Fig. 6.6. Rule 11.1. Transcription of title and statement of responsibility area for the microfilm.

Women and/in health [microform] / filmed by the Women's History Research Center.

Fig. 6.7. Transcription of title and statement of responsibility area for the microfiche according to AACR 2.

The trial of Lieutenant General Masaharu Homma [microform] / John Frederick Hanson

Fig. 6.8. Transcription of title and statement of responsibility area for the microfiche according to LC policy.

The trial of Lieutenant General Masaharu Homma [microform] / by John F. Hanson

11.1G.   Items without a collective title

Like other materials, a microform that lacks a collective title can be described either as a unit or by making a separate description for each separately titled part. It is common to find several different serial titles on the same roll of microfilm. These are given separate descriptions in most libraries.

RULE 11.2. EDITION AREA (MARC field 250)

A statement relating to an edition of a microform, rather than the edition of an original that is being reproduced, is called for in this rule. However, for reproduction of previously existing materials under current policy, LC would reverse this rule. *See* Fig. 6.9.

Fig. 6.9. Rule 11.2. Transcription of a statement relating to the edition of a microform, according to AACR 2.

Die Kataloge der Frankfurter und Leipziger Buchmessen 1759-1800 [microform] / hrsg. von Bernhard Fabian. – Microfiche-Ed.

RULE 11.3. SPECIAL DATA FOR CARTOGRAPHIC MATERIALS AND SERIALS (MARC field 255 or 362)

Material specific details for cartographic materials and for serials are recorded as instructed in the chapters for those materials. When reproductions of previously existing works are cataloged, this area will contain data relating to the original regardless of the policy being followed. Examples:

> Bulletin of the American Economic Association [microform]. — 4th ser., no. 1 (Mar. 1911)–no. 6 (Dec. 1911)

> Viewpoint [microform]. — Vol. 1 (1976)–

RULE 11.4. PUBLICATION, DISTRIBUTION, ETC., AREA (MARC field 260)

The details of this area are recorded as instructed in the general chapter. Again, if one is following *AACR 2* policy, it should be remembered that the details recorded here are those of the publication of the *microform*, not those of an original being reproduced. *See* Figs. 6.10-6.12.

Fig. 6.10. Rule 11.4. Addition of publication details to descriptions of microfilm and microfiche, according to AACR 2.

> Women and/in health [microform] / filmed by the Women's History Research Center. — Berkeley, Calif. : The Center, 1974.

Fig. 6.11

> The trial of Lieutenant General Masaharu Homma [microform] / John Frederick Hanson. — Ann Arbor, Mich. : Xerox University Microfilms, 1978, c1977.

It will be noted that the name of the publisher for the microfiche is given differently in the title frame (chief source, Fig. 6.3), and in the eye-readable data (Fig. 6.4). Therefore, the name in the chief source is given in Fig. 6.11. However, the date given in the eye-readable data appears to be the publication date, while the date in the title frame is the copyright date; so both are given. If one is following LC policy, the details of the original are given here for a microform of a previously existing work. *See* Fig. 6.12.

Fig. 6.12. Rule 11.4. Addition of publication details, according to LC policy.

> The trial of Lieutenant General Masaharu Homma [microform] / by John F. Hanson. — 1977.

RULE 11.5.   PHYSICAL DESCRIPTION AREA (MARC field 300)

11.5B.   **Extent of item (including specific material designation)** (MARC
              subfield a)

11.5B1.   The number of physical units of a microform item is followed
by one of this chapter's specific material designations:

> aperture card
> microfiche
> microfilm
> microopaque

The option to drop the prefix "micro" when the GMD "microform" is used is
not being followed by LC in order to make the bibliographic description
complete so that libraries using LC's records will not be obligated to use the
GMD.[4]

   If the item is described in terms of "microfilm," one of the following
terms is added: "Cartridge," "cassette," or "reel." If the item is described in
terms of "microfiche," the term "cassette" may be added if appropriate. *See*
Fig. 6.13.

   If the item is described in terms of "microfiche," the number of frames is
added in parentheses if the number can be determined easily. *See* Fig. 6.14.

11.5C.   **Other physical details** (MARC subfield b)

   A negative microform is indicated here, followed by a statement of
illustrations. If illustrations are in color, the term "col. ill." is used. If the
microform itself is colored, terms used are "col. & ill." Example:

> 15 microfiches : negative, ill.

11.5D.   **Dimensions** (MARC subfield c)

   The dimensions of a microfiche, a microopaque, and an aperture card
mount are given as height x width in centimeters to the next whole centimeter
up. *See* Fig. 6.14.

   The diameter of a microfilm reel is given in inches, to the next whole inch
up, if the diameter is other than three inches. In addition, the width of a microfilm is given in millimeters. *See* Fig. 6.13.

11.5E.   **Accompanying material** (MARC subfield e)

   Accompanying material is described as instructed in the general chapter.
The option to give also the physical description of the accompanying material
is being applied by LC as discussed in the general chapter under 1.5E.
Example:

> 10 microfilm reels ; 35 mm. + 1 guide (v, 14 p. ; 23 cm.)

Fig. 6.13. Rule 11.5. Addition of physical description to
description of microfilm.

Women and/in health [microform] / filmed by the
Women's History Research Center. – Berkeley, Calif. : The
Center, 1974.
    13 microfilm reels on 14 ; 35 mm.

Note: The 14 physical reels are numbered consecutively except that number
"3A" falls between "3" and "4." Therefore the extent of item is given with the
number of bibliographic entities preceding the number of physical ones.

Fig. 6.14. Rule 11.5. Addition of physical description to
description of microfiche, according to AACR 2.

The trial of Lieutenant General Masaharu Homma [micro-
form] / John Frederick Hanson. – Ann Arbor, Mich. : Xerox
University Microfilms, 1978, c1977.
    3 microfiches (231 fr.) : maps ; 11 x 15 cm.

If one is following LC policy, the physical description area for a
reproduction of a previously existing work contains details relating to the
original. *See* Fig. 6.15.

Fig. 6.15. Rule 11.5. Addition of physical description
to description of microfiche, according to LC policy.

The trial of Lieutenant General Masaharu Homma [micro-
form] / by John F. Hanson. – 1977.
    vii, 223 leaves : maps ; 28 cm.

RULE 11.6.   SERIES AREA (MARC field 4xx)

11.6B.   Series statements

Series statements are recorded as instructed in Rule 1.6. When cataloging
reproductions a series statement for an original is recorded with other details
of the original. If one is following *AACR 2*, this means placing the original
series in a note. If one is following LC, the original series is transcribed in the
series area. Examples:

    116 microfilm reels ; 35 mm. – (British publishers' archives
    on microfilm)

    7 microfiches ; 11 x 15 cm. – (Columbia University oral
    history collection ; pt. 2, no. 24)

RULE 11.7.   NOTE AREA (MARC field 5xx)

11.7B.   Notes

Following are some typical notes used for microforms. For further details consult *AACR 2*, pages 243-245.

11.7B1.   Nature, scope or artistic or other form of an item (MARC field 500)

Example:

> Extensive collection of feminist serial literature published 1956 through June, 1974.

11.7B4.   Variations in title (MARC field 500)

See Fig. 6.16.

11.7B6.   Statements of responsibility (MARC field 500)

Example:

> Collected by the Women's History Research Center, 1968-1974 ; transferred to the Special Collections Dept., Northwestern University Library, 1974.

11.7B7.   Edition and history (MARC fields 500 and 503)

Example:

> Filmed from the H.G. Wells collection in the Bromley Public Libraries.

11.7B10.   Physical description (MARC field 500)

Reduction ratio. Reduction ratio is given if it is outside the 16X-13X range, using one of the following terms:

Low reduction	*For less than 16X*
High reduction	*For 31X-60X*
Very high reduction	*For 61X-90X*
Ultra high reduction	*For over 90X; for ultra high reduction give also the specific ratio, e.g.,* Ultra high reduction, 150X
Reduction ratio varies	

See Fig. 6.16.

Reader. If a particular brand of reader is needed for reading a cassette or cartridge, it should be noted.

11.7B11.   **Accompanying material** (MARC field 500)

Example:

> With printed index: Index to the archives of Richard Bentley & Son, 1829-1898 / compiled by Alison Ingram. 1977. 128 p. ; 26 cm.

See also Fig. 6.16.

11.7B12.   **Series** (MARC field 500)

Example:

> Originally issued in series: Archives on microfilm.

11.7B13.   **Dissertations** (MARC field 502)

See Fig. 6.17.

11.7B16.   **Other formats available** (MARC field 500)

Example:

> Library also has volumes in printed form and on microfilm.

11.7B17.   **Summary** (MARC field 520)

Example:

> Summary: Pamphlets relating to conditions in South Carolina, 1866-1892.

11.7B18.   **Contents** (MARC fields 504 and 505)

See Figs. 6.16 and 6.17.

11.7B22.   **Notes relating to original** (MARC field 534)

Example:

> Reproduction of original: New York : Teachers College, Columbia University, 1927. xix, 166 p. : ill. ; 24 cm. Bibliography: p. 157.

See also Fig. 6.17.

Fig. 6.16. Description of the microfilm.

Women and/in health [microform] / filmed by the
Women's History Research Center. – Berkeley, Calif. : The
Center, 1974.
13 microfilm reels on 14 ; 35 mm.

Collection of microfilmed clippings from newspapers,
professional journals, alternative newspapers, academic
research papers, theses, and conference speeches. Includes
leaflets, poetry and graphic material.
Title on reel containers: Women and health/mental
health.
Low reduction.
Guide issued under title: Guide to the microfilm edition
of the women and health collection.
Contents: Section 1. Physical and mental health of
women – Section 2. Physical and mental illnesses of
women – Section 3. Biology, women and the life cycle –
Section 4. Birth control/population control – Section 5.
Sex and sexuality – Section 6. Black and Third World
women–health – Section 7. Special issues of mass
periodicals.

Fig. 6.17. Description of the microfiche, according to AACR 2.

The trial of Lieutenant General Masaharu Homma [micro-
form] / John Frederick Hanson. – Ann Arbor, Mich. : Xerox
University Microfilms, 1978, c1977.
3 microfiches (231 fr.) : maps ; 11 x 15 cm.

Thesis (Ph.D.)–Mississippi State University, 1977.
Includes bibliography.
"77-28,548."
Reproduction of original: vii, 223 leaves ; 28 cm.
Typescript. Bibliography: leaves [220]-223.

If one is following LC policy, the description shown in Fig. 6.17 would
appear as in Fig. 6.18.

The trial of Lieutenant General Masaharu Homma [micro-
form] / by John F. Hanson. – 1977.
vii, 223 leaves : maps ; 28 cm.

Typescript.
Thesis (Ph.D.)–Mississippi State University, 1977.
Bibliography: leaves [220]-223.
Microfiche. Ann Arbor, Mich. : Xerox University Micro-
films, 1978, c1977. 3 microfiches (231 fr.) ; 11 x 15 cm.
"77-28,548."

The MARC records for the items shown in Figs. 6.16-6.18 are shown in
Figs. 6.19-6.21.

Fig. 6.19. MARC record for the microfilm.

```
Type: a Bib lvl: m Govt pub:   Lang:  eng Source: d Illus:
Repr: a Enc lvl: I Conf pub: 0 Ctry:  cau Dat tp: s M/F/B: 10
Indx: 0 Mod rec:    Festschr: 0 Cont:
Desc: a Int lvl:    Dates: 1974,
   1 010
   2 040      IVE $c IVE
   3 007      h $b d $d a $e f $f a015 $g b $h u $i c $j u
   4 090      HQ1426 $b .W68 1974
   5 049      IVEA
   6 110 20   Women's History Research Center.
   7 245 10   Women and/in health $h microform / $c filmed by the Women's
History Research Center.
   8 260 0    Berkeley, Calif. : $b The Center, $c 1974.
   9 300      13 microfilm reels on 14 ; $c 35 mm.
  10 500      Collection of microfilmed clippings from newspapers,
professional journal·, alternative newspapers, academic research papers,
theses, and conference speeches.  Includes leaflets, poetry and graphic
material.
  11 500      Title on reel containers: Women and health/mental health.
  12 500      Low reduction.
  13 500      Guide issued under title: Guide to the microfilm edition of the
women and health collection.
  14 505 0    Section 1.  Physical and mental health of women -- Section 2.
Physical and mental illnesses of women -- Section 3.  Biology, women and the
life cycle -- Section 4.  Birth control/population control --  Section 5.  Sex
and sexuality -- Section 6.  Black and Third World women--health -- Section 7.
Special issues of mass periodicals.
  15 650  0   Women $z United States $x Addresses, essays, lectures.
  16 650  0   Birth control.
  17 650  0   Minority women.
  18 650  0   Women $x Health and hygiene.
  19 650  0   Women $x Psychology.
  20 650  0   Women $x Sexual behavior.
  21 740 01   Women and health/mental health.
```

Fig. 6.20. MARC record for the microfiche, according to AACR 2.

```
Type: a Bib lvl: m Govt pub:    Lang:  eng Source: d Illus: b
Repr: b Enc lvl: I Conf pub: O Ctry:   miu Dat tp: r M/F/B: 10
Indx: O Mod rec:    Festschr: O Cont: b
Desc: a Int lvl:    Dates: 1978,1977
   1 010
   2 040       IVE $c IVE
   3 007       h $b e $d a $e m $f b--- $g b $h u $i c $j u
   4 037       77-28548
   5 090       U55.H62 $b H3572 1978
   6 049       IVEA
   7 100 10    Hanson, John Frederick, $d 1949-
   8 245 14    The trial of Lieutenant General Masaharu Homma $h microform / $c
John Frederick Hanson.
   9 260 0     Ann Arbor, Mich. : $b Xerox University Microfilms, $c 1978,
c1977.
  10 300       3 microfiches (231 fr.) : $b maps ; $c 11 x 15 cm.
  11 502       Thesis (Ph.D.)--Mississippi State University, 1977.
  12 504       Includes bibliography.
  13 500       "77-28,548."
  14 534 0     Reproduction of original: $e vii, 223 leaves ; 28 cm.  $n
Typescript.   $n Bibliography: leaves [220]-223.
  15 600 10    Homma, Masaharu, $d 1887-1946.
```

Fig. 6.21. MARC record for the microfiche, according to LC policy.

```
Type: a Bib lvl: m Govt pub:    Lang:  eng Source: d Illus: b
Repr: b Enc lvl: I Conf pub: O Ctry:   miu Dat tp: r M/F/B: 10
Indx: O Mod rec:    Festschr: O Cont: b
Desc: a Int lvl:    Dates: 1978,1977
   1 010
   2 040       IVE $c IVE
   3 007       h $b e $d a $e m $f b--- $g b $h u $i c $j u
   4 037       77-28548
   5 090       U55.H62 $b H36 1977
   6 049       IVEA
   7 100 10    Hanson, John Frederick, $d 1949-
   8 245 14    The trial of Lieutenant General Masaharu Homma $h microform / $c
by John F. Hanson.
   9 260 0       $c 1977.
  10 300       vii, 223 leaves : $b maps ; $c 28 cm.
  11 500       Typescript.
  12 502       Thesis (Ph.D.)--Mississippi State University, 1977.
  13 504       Bibliography: leaves [220]-223.
  14 533       Microfiche. $b Ann Arbor, Mich. : $c Xerox University Microfilms,
$d 1978, c1977. $e 3 microfiches (231 fr.) ; 11 x 15 cm. "77-28,548."
  15 600 10    Homma, Masaharu, $d 1887-1946.
```

RULE 11.8.   STANDARD NUMBER AND TERMS OF AVAILABILITY AREA (MARC fields 020 and 022)

This area is treated as described under 1.8 in the general chapter. It should be remembered that only a standard number assigned to the *microform* is placed here. A standard number of the original should be included in the note on details of the original.

[RULE 11.11.   NONPROCESSED MICROFORMS]

There is no Rule 11.11 in *AACR 2*, but it has come to the attention of ALA's Committee on Cataloging: Description and Access that there is a need for an interpretation to cover cataloging the many microforms that are created (usually by libraries or archives) for the purpose of preservation rather than for commercial purposes. These are comparable to nonprocessed sound recordings covered in Rule 6.11. Both nonprocessed microforms and nonprocessed sound recordings bear the same relationship to commercial products that manuscripts bear to books. The principles found in the manuscripts chapter and in Rule 6.11 should be applied to nonprocessed microforms.

NOTES

[1]Janet Swan Hill, "Descriptions of Reproductions of Previously Existing Works: Another View," *Microform Review* 11 (Winter 1982): 14-21; and Nancy R. John, "Microforms," *Journal of Library Administration* 3 (Spring 1982): 3-8.

[2]*Cataloging Service Bulletin*, no. 14 (Fall 1981): 56-58.

[3]"Display of General Material Designations under AACR 2," *Cataloging Service Bulletin*, no. 6 (Fall 1979): 4-5.

[4]"AACR 2 Options Proposed by the Library of Congress: Chapters 2-11," *Library of Congress Information Bulletin* 38 (August 10, 1979): 316.

SUGGESTED READING

Frost, Carolyn O. *Cataloging Nonbook Materials: Problems in Theory and Practice.* Littleton, Colo., Libraries Unlimited, 1983. Chapter 9.

Hill, Janet Swan. "Descriptions of Reproductions of Previously Existing Works: Another View," *Microform Review* 11 (Winter 1982): 14-21.

John, Nancy R. "Microforms," *Journal of Library Administration* 3 (Spring 1982): 3-8.

Maxwell, Margaret F. *Handbook for AACR 2.* Chicago, American Library Association, 1980. Chapter 9.

Rogers, JoAnn V. *Nonprint for Media Collections: A Guide Based on AACR 2.* Littleton, Colo., Libraries Unlimited, 1982. Chapter 8.

7
Description of Serials

INTRODUCTION

A serial is a publication in any medium issued in successive parts at regular or irregular intervals and intended to continue indefinitely. Serials include both periodicals and non-periodicals. A periodical may be defined as a serial that has a distinctive title and that is issued more frequently than once a year and at regular intervals, with each issue containing articles by several contributors. Non-periodicals are all other forms of serials, such as yearbooks, annuals, memoirs, transactions and proceedings of societies, and any series cataloged together instead of separately.

A clear distinction should be made between serials and monographs. A monograph represents a complete bibliographic unit; it may be issued in successive parts at regular or irregular intervals, but it is *not* intended to continue indefinitely. In most cases, of course, a monographic publication is completed in one volume. However, there are certain types of monographs that are often treated as serials by libraries because they are not complete in one volume. These include continuations of sets, provisional serials, and pseudo-serials. A continuation of a set is a nonserial—i.e., monographic—set in process of publication. The *Oxford History of English Literature* and the *Dictionary of the Middle Ages* are examples of continuations of sets. Neither publication is presently complete although many individual volumes have been issued. Such publications require a special order record—i.e., a standing order—for follow-up purposes; if such works are cataloged as sets, this creates problems of accurate records in the library's holdings record for the set. Provisional serials are those publications which are treated as serials while in the process of publication and as nonserials when complete. The justification for such treatment is often a particularly lengthy period of publication and/or a complicated numbering of individual issues. Either of the two previous examples of continuations of sets could be treated by individual libraries as provisional serials. A pseudo-serial is a frequently reissued and revised publication that is generally treated as a monographic work at first publication but that is often treated as a serial after numerous successive editions have appeared. Serial numbering may be taken from the edition number or from the date of publication. Examples of pseudo-serials are Sir John Bernard Burke's *Genealogical and Heraldic History of the Peerage* (commonly called Burke's *Peerage*) or the *Guide to Reference Books* edited successively by Alice Bertha Kroeger, Isadore Mudge, Constance Winchell, and Eugene P. Sheehy. Monographic treatment of a pseudo-serial requires individual descriptive cataloging for each new edition as well as additional added entries for previous editors or compilers. If a pseudo-serial is treated as a serial, the main entry is made under the title instead of the author and will require only one set of catalog entries.

The principles for cataloging serials are generally the same as those for cataloging monographic publications. On the other hand, certain physical characteristics of serial publications (e.g., numerous changes in bibliographic descriptions, including changes of titles) necessitate some special rules. The aim of these special rules is to prepare an entry that will stand the longest time and will allow necessary changes to be made with a minimum of modification. If the serial is still being published or if the library has only part of the set and hopes to complete it, an open entry is prepared according to the rules that are presented in this chapter.

The descriptive cataloging of serials is generally more complex than that of monographs because of their greatly varied and possibly intricate bibliographic structure. On the other hand, classification and subject headings are likely to be somewhat more general, therefore simpler. Indeed, in many libraries, periodicals are not classified at all but are shelved alphabetically by main entry. The detail with which serials are described may vary widely from library to library. Some consider a highly analytic description essential, while others reduce serials cataloging to the title and statement of responsibility area and a holdings note, a method most suitable for computer-produced catalogs.

The serials cataloger is likely to be faced with the problem of describing a full set completely although all that may be at hand are a few volumes or current issues. The most important sources of additional information are the *Union List of Serials, New Serial Titles, British Union Catalogue of Periodicals*, and *Ulrich's International Periodicals Directory*, with its companion publication, *Irregular Serials and Annuals: An International Directory*.[1] Other important sources are the Library of Congress catalogs and national and trade bibliographies, as well as publishers' catalogs. *Titles in Series* is useful for its lists of titles in monographic series, especially those published by university presses, and Bowker's *Books in Series in the United States 1966-1975* lists monographs distributed in popular, scholarly, and professional series.[2] In addition, a Library of Congress publication, *Monographic Series*, lists all monographs cataloged by the Library of Congress that appeared as parts of series between 1974 and 1983, as well as all revised records, regardless of the date of publication.[3] Series access has been incorporated in the *National Union Catalog* since 1982. OCLC and other data bases would prove sources of additional information, as would published state union lists of serials.

SELECTED RULES AND EXAMPLES

RULE 12.0. GENERAL RULES

12.0A. Scope

The scope of this chapter is serial publications of all kinds regardless of form. That is, nonbook materials as well as printed text can appear serially. A rule interpretation from LC gives guidelines for distinguishing between monographic and serial publications.[4]

12.0B. Sources of information

12.0B1. Sources of information. Printed serials

Chief source of information. The title page (or title page substitute) of the first issue of a serial is used as its chief source of information. If the first issue is not available, the first issue that is available is used. This is a break from pre-*AACR 2* practice that called for using the latest issue. While there is some objection to using the first issue because of all the changes that can occur in such areas as the publication area, the pre-*AACR 2* practice could not, in fact, be followed because of the physical impossibility of examining every new issue.

If a printed serial lacks a title page, the following substitutes are to be used in this order: cover, caption, masthead, editorial pages, colophon, other pages. LC gives a rule interpretation that makes the following exception: if an item has two or more different titles and the title on the preferred source is known to be less stable than another title, then the source with the stable title is to be used as the title page substitute.[5]

Prescribed sources of information. As it does for other materials, *AACR 2* prescribes sources of information for the various areas of description for printed serials. Information taken from outside these sources is enclosed in square brackets.

AREA	PRESCRIBED SOURCE OF INFORMATION
Title and statement of responsibility	Chief source of information
Edition	Chief source of information, other preliminaries, colophon
Numeric and/or alphabetic, chronological, or other designation	[same as edition area]
Publication, distribution, etc.	[same as edition area]
Physical description	The serial itself
Series	Anywhere in the serial
Note	Any source
Standard number and terms of availability	Any source

12.0B2. Sources of information. Nonprinted serials

The prescribed sources of information for nonprinted serials are those called for in the chapter for a particular type of material. The sources for a serial machine-readable data file, for example, are named in chapter 9 of *AACR 2* [chapter 5 of this text]. In these cases, too, the source in the first issue of the nonprint serial should be used.

The example to be used in this chapter to illustrate the building of the description of a serial is a journal whose title has changed. The chief source of information and preliminaries are given for each of the two titles as Figs. 7.1-7.4.

Fig. 7.1. Title page of first issue of serial.

THE LIBRARY OF CONGRESS

Quarterly Journal

OF CURRENT ACQUISITIONS

Contents

Coöperative Scholarship · Archibald MacLeish 1

Toward a Rare Book Policy in the Library of Congress
Lawrence C. Wroth 3

A "New" Washington Letter · David C. Mearns 12

"My Much Loved America" · Sidney Kramer 17

Serial Publications in India · Horace I. Poleman 23

News Out of Ethiopia · James B. Childs 30

The First Protestant Hymn Book · Richard S. Hill 32

American Painter-Etchers · Leicester B. Holland 37

In Honor of the Constitution · Frederick R. Goff 39

Recent Americana · Donald Mugridge 42

PUBLISHED AS A SUPPLEMENT TO THE ANNUAL REPORT OF THE LIBRARIAN OF CONGRESS

July ✦ August ✦ September

1943

Fig. 7.2. Title page of first issue with changed title.

The Quarterly Journal

OF THE LIBRARY OF CONGRESS

Volume 21   JANUARY 1964   Number 1

CONTENTS

Sarah L. Wallace, *Editor*   Janice B. Harrington, *Assistant Editor*

Published as a Supplement to the Annual Report of the Librarian of Congress

Fig. 7.3. From page facing title page of Volume 21, Number 1.

Cover design: *The Miraculous Image of Our Lady of the Pine Tree.* Anonymous Mexican wood-cut, probably from the late 18th century. (The Prints and Photographs Division)

For sale by the Superintendent of Documents, United States Government Printing Office, Washington, D.C., 20402. Price $2.00 per year, including the *Annual Report of the Librarian of Congress*, domestic; 50 cents additional for foreign mailing; single copies vary in price. This issue is priced at 50 cents.

Fig. 7.4. Editor's note about title change from Volume 21, Number 1.

EDITOR'S NOTE

Maxims to guide him who would make a change are many and conflicting. To Confucius, credited with so many epigrams, is attributed the saying: "Only the very wisest and the very stupidest never change." A German proverb observes that "Man changes often, but gets better seldom." There are other cautions to make one pause: that change never answers the end, that it is seldom made for the better, and that it "doth unknit the tranquil state of men."

Nevertheless, despite these warnings, with this issue the editors have changed the cover, the title, the format, and the date of *The Quarterly Journal of Current Acquisitions*. The change in the first is obvious, even to the casual reader. The second is neither startling nor radical, for which we hope the catalogers in the Nation's many libraries will thank us. The name *The Quarterly Journal of Current Acquisitions* has been exchanged for the one it has always used in popular parlance, *The Quarterly Journal of the Library of Congress*. The format has been altered slightly and will continue on a flexible basis, layouts changing to meet the spirit of the subject and the demands of the materials described.

As to dates, this issue is number one of volume 21. Normally, it would appear in December 1963. Under the new plan, volumes will coincide with calendar years. Therefore, all four issues of volume 21 will appear in 1964, the January 1965 issue beginning volume 22.

To return to the maxims, while change may be sweet, there is also a certain virtue in constancy. The *Journal* continues to be a supplement to the *Annual Report of the Librarian of Congress* describing acquisitions more fully than is possible within the confines of that yearly document. The new title, however, allows authors of these supplemental reports a wider scope. As an example, acquisitions no longer current can be related to new additions and the collections discussed as a whole. Opportunity will be offered to report the use of the collections, the tangible values gained from them through study and research. A miser only counts his gold and stories it away, but a foundation uses its fortune to further mankind. In like manner, the *Quarterly Journal* will report on how the Nation uses the gold in its treasurehouse of knowledge.

Disraeli also had a word on change. He said it is constant. The editors expect to continue the change and growth of this periodical within its basic outlines. Comments from the readers will be welcome.

SLW

RULE 12.1.   TITLE AND STATEMENT OF RESPONSIBILITY AREA
(MARC field 245)

12.1B.   **Title proper** (MARC subfield a)

12.1B1.   The title proper is given as instructed in the general chapter. *See* Figs. 7.5 and 7.6.

Fig. 7.5. Rule 12.1B. Transcription of title proper of the original title of the serial.

Quarterly journal of current acquisitions

Fig. 7.6. Rule 12.1B. Transcription of title proper of the
later title of the serial.

The Quarterly journal of the Library of Congress

12.1B2. A corporate body's name is considered to be part of the title proper only when it consistently appears as part of the title in various locations in the serial. LC applies this criterion to any word, phrase, etc., that may or may not be part of the title proper.[6]

On the title page shown in Fig. 7.1, there could be a question as to whether the title ought to be "The Library of Congress quarterly journal of current acquisitions." However, it is elsewhere referred to in that first issue as "Quarterly journal of current acquisitions."

12.1B3.-12.1B5.

These rules cover transcription of titles that are sections of, or supplements to, other serials. In general if the title common to all sections appears with the section or supplement title, both are transcribed as title proper. Examples:

Solar energy. Cumulative index

Major studies of the Congressional Research Service.
Supplement

If the common title is not present with the section or supplement title, the section or supplement title is treated as title proper. Example:

Bibliography of Utah geology
[Note reads:]
Supplement to: Utah geology.

12.1B6. When the title proper of a serial includes a date or numbering that changes from issue to issue, the date or numbering is omitted. It is replaced by the mark of omission unless it is at the beginning. LC uses the mark of omission at the end of the title proper only if there is a grammatical reason to do so.[7] Examples:

Sport in ...

Proceedings of the ... annual meeting

12.1C. *Optional addition.* **General material designation** (MARC subfield h)

The GMDs appropriate to serials are governed by the type of material being cataloged. As discussed in the general chapter under 1.1C, LC will display only some GMDs in its printed records. The reader should consult the discussion in this text of the GMD rule for the medium in which a serial is produced. For example, the discussion of Rule 2.1C indicates that "[text]" is not used for printed serials, and the application of Rule 9.1C indicates that "[machine-readable data file]" should be used for cataloging serial MRDFs.

12.1D.-12.1E. (MARC subfield b)

Parallel titles and other title information are transcribed as instructed in the general chapter.

> Canadian journal of psychiatry = Revue canadienne de
>   psychiatrie

> DNR : daily news record

> Pesticide residues in food : report

> Index to Title 40 of the Code of federal regulations : protec-
>   tion of environment

LC has decided to catalog serials using an augmented first level description, rather than the second level description used for other materials. The first level description is augmented with: GMD (when appropriate); parallel title(s); first statement of responsibility; first place of publication, etc., with first publisher, etc.; other physical details and dimensions; series. Therefore, other title information is usually omitted. Two exceptions occur when the title consists of both an initialism and a full form of the name, in which case one is chosen as title proper and the other is recorded as other title information; and when a statement of responsibility is inseparable from the other title information.[8]

12.1F.   **Statements of responsibility** (MARC subfield c)

Statements of responsibility are transcribed as instructed in the general chapter. *See* Fig. 7.7 which treats the original journal title.

**Fig. 7.7. Rule 12.1F. Addition of statement of responsibility
after the title proper.**

> Quarterly journal of current acquisitions / The Library of
>   Congress

The changed title includes statement of responsibility as part of the title proper and therefore has no separate statement. *See* Fig. 7.8 for entry of the journal under its new title.

The Quarterly journal of the Library of Congress. –

Personal editors are not recorded in statements of responsibility. If considered important they may be given in a note.

RULE 12.2.   EDITION AREA (MARC field 250)

12.2B.   Edition statement

AACR 2 prescribes specific types of edition statements that are to be recorded in the edition area for serials:

a)   local edition statements

b)   special interest edition statements

c)   special format or physical presentation statements

d)   language edition statements

e)   reprint or reissue statements indicating a reissue or revision of a serial as a whole

For example:

Taft Foundation reporter. – Regional ed.

Taft Foundation reporter. – National ed.

Sea. – Eastern ed.

See also examples in *AACR 2*. Edition statements are relatively rare in the cataloging of serials.

RULE 12.3.   NUMERIC AND/OR ALPHABETIC, CHRONOLOGICAL, OR OTHER DESIGNATION AREA (MARC field 362)

12.3B.   Numeric and/or alphabetic designation (MARC subfield a)

The numeric and/or alphabetic designation of a serial is given as it appears in the first issue of the serial, using standard abbreviations and numerals. The numeric and/or alphabetic designation of the original is used when a facsimile or reprint is in hand. When a serial changes title but continues its previous numbering, the numbering of the first issue with the new title is used. LC comments that numbering recorded in this area should be unique to the issue. If such a designation is exactly the same for more than one issue, it should be given in a note.[9]

Rules 12.3B1-12.3B3 provide for transcription of a numeric and/or alphabetic designation. Rules 12.3C1-12.3C3 treat the transcription of a chronological designation when there is no numeric or alphabetic designation. Rule 12.3C4 covers transcription of both numeric and/or alphabetic designation *and* chronological designation. It would have been clearer if this rule had been accorded a boldface rule heading. There are relatively few instances in which there is a numeric and/or alphabetic designation without also having a chronological designation; however, it is relatively common for serials of the "advances in" and "progress in" type to be dated only with an imprint date (*see* Fig. 7.9). Such a date is recorded as part of the publication area rather than part of the numeric, alphabetic, chronological area (*see* Fig. 7.10). For other examples of numeric designations see the examples under 12.3C4.

Fig. 7.9. Title page of serial showing date in imprint only.

ADVANCES IN CHEMICAL PHYSICS

Edited by I. PRIGOGINE

University of Brussels, Brussels, Belgium

With a Preface by P. DEBYE

Cornell University, Ithaca, New York

VOLUME I

INTERSCIENCE PUBLISHERS, INC., NEW YORK

INTERSCIENCE PUBLISHERS LTD., LONDON   1958

Fig. 7.10. Rule 12.3B1. Transcription of numeric designation of the first issue of a serial.

Advances in chemical physics. – Vol. 1 -   . – New York : Interscience Publishers, 1958-

12.3C.   **Chronological designation** (MARC subfield a)

12.3C1.   A chronological designation that identifies the first issue of a serial is recorded as it appears, using standard abbreviations and numerals. For example:

> Index to Title 40 of the Code of federal regulations : protection of environment. – 1978-

> HRA, HSA, CDC, OASH, & ADAMHA public advisory committees : authority, structure, functions, members. – Mar. 1978-

12.3C4.   When the first issue of a serial has both numbering and a chronological designation, both are given, with the numbering given first. For example:

> Developmental medicine and child neurology. – Vol. 4 (1962)-

> Gas turbine electric plant construction cost and annual production expenses. Annual supplement / Office of Energy Data and Interpretation, Energy Information Administration, U.S. Dept. of Energy. – 2nd (1974)-

See also Figs. 7.11 and 7.13.

Fig. 7.11. Rule 12.3C4. Addition of both numbering and chronological designation to the description of the original title.

> Quarterly journal of current acquisitions / The Library of Congress. – [Vol. 1, no. 1] (July/Sept. 1943)-

Note: It could be argued that because the first issue in this example (Fig. 7.11) does not bear the numbering, "Vol. 1, no. 1," it should not be added to the example. Rule 12.3D, if taken literally, applies only when there is neither numbering nor date on an issue. This could lead to including only the date in Fig. 7.11. However, because the second issue is clearly marked "Volume 1, number 2" (*see* Fig. 7.12), the intended numbering of the first issue seems obvious. Therefore, combining logic with Rule 12.3D yields the solution of the bracketed number. However, the Library of Congress seems inclined to interpret first issue cataloging strictly and therefore would probably transcribe the information in Fig. 7.11 as:

> – July/Sept. 1943-

A difficulty with this rule is that it does not refer to the potential confusion caused by a situation in which the numbering sequence is repeated every year so that there is no overall numbering, but only the dates to distinguish issues (e.g., issues published in 1978 are numbered 1 through 4, issues for 1979 are also numbered 1 through 4, etc.). If the numbering is given first, as is called for in the rules, the implication is that the numbering is continuous and a completed serial could appear to have published only a few numbers over a span of many years [e.g., No. 1 (Winter 1940)-no. 4 (Fall 1979)].

An LC rule interpretation says that in such a case the date should be followed by the number as if both were a single numeric designation. Example:

– 1940, no. 1-1979, no. 4

In such a case a chronological designation would be recorded only when a separate one also appears on the issue.[10]

Fig. 7.12. Title page of second issue, showing numerical designation.

THE LIBRARY OF CONGRESS

Quarterly Journal

OF CURRENT ACQUISITIONS

Contents

Mr. Jefferson to Dr. Rush, with Affection · Julian P. Boyd . .   3
Architects and Poets and Prophets · David C. Mearns   9
Movable Type Printing in China · Arthur W. Hummel . . . 18
A Rare Agnese Atlas · Lawrence Martin 25
The Elizabeth Madox Roberts Papers · Allen Tate 29
The World's Largest Theater Library · Kurt Pinthus 32
A Lost Volume of Bentham's Constitutional Code
                                               David Baumgardt . . 40
Pictorial Wood Blocks of the American Nineteenth Century
                                               Sidney Kramer . . 42
Italian Legal Codes on the Eve of the Allied Invasion
                       Vladimir Gzovsky and Elio Gianturco . . 44
The Archive of Hispanic Culture · Robert C. Smith 53
Posters and News Bulletins in Wartime China
                                               Arthur W. Hummel . . 58
"Know Thy Enemy" · Max Lederer 60
Review of the Quarter · Verner W. Clapp and the Staff . . . 64

PUBLISHED AS A SUPPLEMENT TO THE ANNUAL
REPORT OF THE LIBRARIAN OF CONGRESS

October + November + December
1943
Volume 1 + Number 2
Washington

1944

Fig. 7.13. Rule 12.3C4. Addition of both numbering and chronological
designation to the designation of the later title.

The Quarterly journal of the Library of Congress. – Vol. 21,
no. 1 (Jan. 1964)-

12.3D.   No designation on first issue

When a serial lacks any designation, the cataloger is instructed to record
"[No. 1]-" or its equivalent in the language of the title proper; and then if later
issues appear with numbering, one is to change to the later form. If an item
lacks a numerical designation, but has a date, 12.3C1 should be applied.

LC does not use this rule because it has decided that items that lack any
designation will be treated as monographs. If such publications appear later
with numbering, they can be recataloged as serials.[11]

12.3E.   More than one system of designation

More than one separate system of designation in a serial is indicated by
recording the systems as parallel statements with an equal sign preceding the
alternative numbering. For example:

The Durham research review / The Institute of Education,
University of Durham. – [Vol. 1] (July 1950)-v. 8
(Spring 1977) = No. 1-38

Opinions latinoamericanas. – Vol. 1 (July 1978)-   = No.
1-

Although the rule does not say whether the chronological designation is
repeated following the alternative numbering, an LC rule interpretation
suggests recording it with the first numeric system. The same rule
interpretation prescribes recording a second or third numbering system in Area
3 only if it appears on the same source as the first system. If not on the same
source, it may be given in a note if considered important.[12]

12.3F.   Completed serials

When the serial is completed (e.g., ceases publication, or its title changes)
the designation of the last issue is given following the designation of the first.
See Fig. 7.14.

Fig. 7.14. Rule 12.3F. Addition of designation of last issue to the
description of the original title.

Quarterly journal of current acquisitions / The Library of
Congress. – [Vol. 1, no. 1] (July/Sept. 1943)-v. 20,
no. 4 (Sept. 1963)

12.3G.   Successive designations (MARC subfield a)

When the designation system of a serial changes without a change in title proper, the new designation is recorded after the designations of the first and last issues under the old system. Examples:

> International rehabilitation review. – Vol. 1 (1962)-v. 26
>   (1975) ; 1976-

> Triquarterly. – Vol. 1 (Fall 1958)-v. 6 (Spring 1964) ;
>   No. 1 (Fall 1964)-

> American journal of digestive diseases. – Vol. 5 (1938)-v. 22
>   (1955) ; New ser., v. 1 (1956)-v. 23 (1978)

LC's interpretation for this rule is that normally a new numbering system that involves repeating (e.g., using "1" again) suggests that other changes have taken place, and therefore, one is probably dealing with a new serial.[13]

RULE 12.4. PUBLICATION, DISTRIBUTION, ETC., AREA (MARC field 260)

Details of the publication, distribution, etc., area are transcribed as instructed in the general chapter. If one is following LC policy, this means transcribing only the first place and the first publisher, distributor, etc.

The date of publication is recorded as instructed in 1.4F even if it coincides with the date given as the chronological designation in the preceding area. The date of first issue is followed by a hyphen and, if the serial is completed, the date of publication of the last issue. *See* Figs. 7.15 and 7.16.

**Fig. 7.15. Rule 12.4. Addition of publication, distribution, etc., information
to the description of the original title.**

> Quarterly journal of current acquisitions / The Library of
>   Congress. – [Vol. 1, no. 1] (July/Sept. 1943)-v. 20,
>   no. 4 (Sept. 1963). – Washington, D.C. : The Library,
>   1943-1963.

**Fig. 7.16. Rule 12.4. Addition of publication, distribution, etc., information
to the description of the later title.**

> The Quarterly journal of the Library of Congress. – Vol. 21,
>   no. 1 (Jan. 1964-   . – Washington, D.C. : For sale by
>   the Supt. of Docs., U.S. G.P.O., 1964-

RULE 12.5. PHYSICAL DESCRIPTION AREA (MARC field 300)

12.5B. **Extent of item (including specific material designation) (MARC subfield a)**

12.5B1. A printed serial still in progress is described as "v." preceded by three spaces. For a serial still in progress that is of a type of material other than print, the specific material designation relevant to that type of material, preceded by three spaces, should be used. *See* Fig. 7.18.

12.5B2. When the serial is completed, the specific material designation is preceded by the number of issues or parts in arabic numerals. Example:

> The Christian's magazine [microform]. – Vol. 1 (1806)-v. 4
> (1811). – Ann Arbor, Mich. : University Microfilms,
> 1946-1949.
> 2 microfilm reels ; 35 mm.

See also Fig. 7.17.

12.5C. **Other physical details (MARC subfield b)**

Other physical details are recorded according to the rule numbered "5C" in the appropriate chapter for the type of material being treated.

The term most often used here for printed serials is "ill." The first issue may not be totally representative of details that may be found later, but one cannot expect to keep returning to the record with more details. It is better to be more general with this area of a serial. *See* Figs. 7.17 and 7.18.

12.5D. **Dimensions (MARC subfield c)**

Dimensions are recorded according to the rule numbered "5D" in the appropriate chapter for the type of material being treated. *See* Figs. 7.17 and 7.18.

Fig. 7.17. Rule 12.5. Addition of physical description to the description of the original title.

> Quarterly journal of current acquisitions / The Library of
> Congress. – [Vol. 1, no. 1] (July/Sept. 1943)-v. 20,
> no. 4 (Sept. 1963). – Washington, D.C. : The Library,
> 1943-1963.
> 20 v. : ill. ; 24 cm.

Fig. 7.18. Rule 12.5. Addition of physical description to the description
of the new title.

The Quarterly journal of the Library of Congress. – Vol. 21,
no. 1 (Jan. 1964)-   . – Washington, D.C. : For sale by
the Supt. of Docs., U.S. G.P.O., 1964-
v. : ill. ; 27 cm.

12.5E.   Accompanying material (MARC subfield e)

Accompanying material is described only if it is intended to be issued
regularly and used with the serial. Its frequency is given in a note. If issued
only once or irregularly, such material could be described in a note, ignored,
or cataloged separately if it is important enough.

RULE 12.6.   SERIES AREA (MARC field 4xx)

12.6B.   Series statements (MARC subfield a)

Series statements are transcribed as instructed in the general chapter with
the exception that series numberings are not given when each issue has a
separate series number. Example:

Wage chronology : Ford Motor Company / U.S. Bureau of
Labor Statistics....
v. ; 28 cm. – (Bulletin / Bureau of Labor Statistics)

RULE 12.7.   NOTE AREA (MARC fields 310, 5xx, and 7xx)

12.7B.   Notes

Notes are made as instructed in subrules 12.7B1 to 12.7B22. Many notes
refer to another serial. *AACR 2* gives instructions for citing another serial in a
note. It suggests using the title or heading-title that is the catalog entry for the
serial. If the serial is not in the catalog, or if main entry is not used, the title
proper and statement of responsibility are to be cited. An LC rule
interpretation expands these instructions to include uniform title of the series
when this is appropriate.[14]

Following are some typical notes used for serials. For further details
consult *AACR 2*, pages 262-268.

12.7B1.   Frequency (MARC field 310)

AACR 2 prescribes making a frequency note unless frequency is apparent
from the title and statement of responsibility area or is unknown. However, an
LC rule interpretation calls for a note on the known frequency even if it is
apparent from the rest of the item.[15]

Examples:

Eight issues yearly.

Bimonthly.

Semiannual.

12.7B2.   Languages (MARC field 546)

Examples:

Text and summaries in English or French.

Text in Afrikaans and English.

Summaries in English, 1977-Mar./Apr. 1978; summaries in
English and Spanish, May/June 1978-

12.7B4.   Variations in title (MARC field 500)

Examples:

Running title: Chemical engineering catalog census.
[Title proper is: CEC census of buyers in the chemical
process industries.]

Each issue has a distinctive title.

12.7B5.   Parallel titles and other title information (MARC field 500)

Example:

"An international journal of palaeobotany, palynology and
allied sciences."

12.7B6.   Statements of responsibility (MARC fields 500 and 570)

Examples:

Official journal of: the American Academy for Cerebral
Palsy and Developmental Medicine.

Issued by graduate students in the Dept. of French at the
Pennsylvania State University.

Editor: A. C. Strasburger.

12.7B7.   Relationships with other serials

Continuation. When a serial changes title and a new record is created, a note is made for the preceding title whether or not the numbering continues or is different. (MARC field 780). For example:

> Continues: Cerebral palsy bulletin.

Continued by. The record for the serial before the title change should have a note added that names the succeeding title. Optionally, the date of change may also be added. (MARC field 785). For example:

> Continued by: Industrial vegetation, turf and pest management.

Note: The Library of Congress is applying the options for adding dates under "continued by" and "absorption" when the information is readily available without having to search.[16]

Merger. When two or more serials are merged, the names of the previously separate serials are given on the record for the new serial. (MARC fields 580 and 787). For example:

> Merger of: Mariah; and, Outside.

Each of the serials that were merged should have a note added to give the title of the new serial and the title(s) with which it has merged. (MARC fields 580 and 787). For example:

> Merged with: Outside, to become: Mariah/Outside.

Split. A note is made on the record for a serial that is the result of a split of a serial into two or more parts. The note should name the serial that was split. (MARC fields 580 and 787). For example:

> Continues in part: Transportation research.

An option allows also naming the other serial(s) resulting from the split. LC is not applying the option.[17] The serial that was split should have a note added that gives the names of the resulting serials. (MARC field 580). For example:

> Split into: Transportation research. Part A, General; and, Transportation research. Part B, Methodological.

Absorption. The record for a serial that has absorbed another serial should have added to it a note giving the title of the serial that has been absorbed. An option allows giving also the date of the absorption. (MARC fields 580 and 787). (*See* note on option under "Continued by.") For example:

> Absorbed: American Association of Stratigraphic Palynologists. Proceedings of the annual meeting.

The record for the serial that has been absorbed should have a note added that gives the title of the serial that absorbed it. Again, an option allows adding the date. (MARC field 580). For example:

Absorbed by: Palynology.

Reproduction. (MARC field 580). Example:

Reprint. Originally published: Washington, D.C. : International Monetary Fund.

Supplements. (MARC fields 580 and 770). Examples:

Supplement to: International financial statistics, 1958-1963; Direction of Trade, 1964-

Supplements, including laws, ordinances, bills, etc., accompany some numbers.

12.7B8.   Numbering and chronological designation (MARC field 515)

Examples:

Report year ends Mar. 31.

Numbering begins each year with no. 1.

12.7B9.   Publication, distribution, etc. (MARC field 500 or 550)

Example:

Published: Midland, Mich. : Agricultural Products Dept., Dow Chemical U.S.A., 1977-1978. [Publisher area reads: Midland, Mich. : Ag-Organics Dept., Dow Chemical U.S.A., 1969-1978.]

12.7B17.   Indexes (MARC field 555)

Example:

Indexes: Vols. 4 (1962)-8 (1966) published separately.

12.7B19.   Numbers [other than ISSNs] (MARC fields 023-030, 036, 037, and 500)

Example:

Catalogue 34-217.

12.7B21.   "With" notes (MARC field 501)

Example:

Filmed with: BYU studies.   Vol. 11, no. 1-v. 13.

See also Figs. 7.19 and 7.20.

12.7B22.   Item described (MARC field 500)

This note is to be used when the description is not based on the first issue. Example:

Description based on: Vol. 36, no. 1 (Winter 1979)

RULE 12.8.   STANDARD NUMBER AND TERMS OF AVAILABILITY AREA (MARC fields 022 and 222)

The ISSN and key-title are recorded as instructed in 1.8. *See* Fig. 3.86 under that rule in chapter 3 of this text; *see also* Figs. 7.19 and 7.20.

RULE 12.9.   SUPPLEMENTS (MARC field 525 or separate record)

Supplements are described as instructed in the general chapter.

RULE 12.10.   SECTIONS OF SERIALS

Sections of a serial should be described as separate serials rather than using the "multilevel" structure described in the analysis chapter [chapter 8 of this text]. Rules 12.1B3-12.1B5 give instructions for recording separate titles proper for sections of a serial.

Fig. 7.19. Rules 12.7 and 12.8. Addition of notes, standard number, and key-title to the description of the original title.

Quarterly journal of current acquisitions / The Library of
   Congress. – [Vol. 1, no. 1] (July/Sept. 1943)-v. 20,
   no. 4 (Sept. 1963). – Washington, D.C. : The Library,
   1943-1963.
   20 v. : ill. ; 24 cm.

   Quarterly.
   Continued by: The Quarterly journal of the Library of
Congress.
   Supplement to: Library of Congress. Annual report of the
Librarian of Congress for the fiscal year ending ...
   Vol. 3, no. 2 (Oct. 1945)-v. 20, no. 4 (Sept. 1963) for sale
by the Supt. of Docs., U.S. G.P.O.
   ISSN 0090-0095 = Quarterly journal of current
acquisitions

Fig. 7.20. Rules 12.7 and 12.8. Addition of notes, standard number, and key-title to the description of the later title.

The Quarterly journal of the Library of Congress. – Vol. 21, no. 1 (Jan. 1964)- . – Washington, D.C. : For sale by the Supt. of Docs., U.S. G.P.O., 1964-

v. : ill. ; 27 cm.

Quarterly.
Continues: Quarterly journal of current acquisitions.
Supplement to: Library of Congress. Annual report of the Librarian of Congress for the fiscal year ending ...
ISSN 0041-7939 = Quarterly journal of the Library of Congress.

MARC records for the items whose descriptions are shown in Figs. 7.19 and 7.20 are shown in Figs. 7.21 and 7.22.

Fig. 7.21. MARC record for the original title.

```
Type: a Bib lvl: a Govt pub: f Lang:   eng Source: d S/L ent: 0
Repr:    Enc lvl: I Conf pub: 0 Ctry:   dcu Ser tp: p Alphabt: a
Indx: u Mod rec:    Phys med:    Cont: ^   Frequn: q Pub st:   d
Desc: a Cum ind: u Titl pag: u ISDS:      1 Regulr: r Dates: 1943-1963
   1 010
   2 040       IVE $c IVE
   3 022       0090-0095
   4 043       n-us-dc
   5 086       LC 1.17:
   6 090       Z881.U49 $b A3
   7 049       IVEA
   8 222 00    Quarterly journal of current acquisitions
   9 245 00    Quarterly journal of current acquisitions / $c The Library of
Congress.
  10 260 01    Washington, D.C. : $b The Library, $c 1943-1963.
  11 300       20 v. : $b ill. ; $c 24 cm.
  12 310       Quarterly.
  13 362 0     [Vol. 1, no. 1] (July/Sept. 1943)-v. 20, no. 4 (Sept. 1963).
  14 500       Vol. 3, no. 2 (Oct. 1945)-v. 20, no. 4 (Sept. 1963) for sale
by the Supt. of Docs., U.S. G.P.O.
  15 580       Supplement to: Library of Congress. Annual report of the
Librarian of Congress for the fiscal year ending ... , ISSN 0083-1565.
  16 693 20    Library of Congress $x Periodicals.
  17 710 20    Library of Congress.
  18 772 1     Library of Congress. $t Annual report of the Librarian of
Congress for the fiscal year ending ... $x 0083-1565
  19 785 00     $t Quarterly journal of the Library of Congress $x 0041-
7939
```

Fig. 7.22. MARC record for the later title.

```
Type: a Bib lvl: s Govt pub: f Lang:  eng Source: d S/L ent: 0
Repr:    Enc lvl: I Conf pub: 0 Ctry:  dcu Ser tp: p Alphabt: a
Indx: u Mod rec:    Phys med:    Cont: ^    Frequn: q Pub st:  c
Desc: a Cum ind: u Titl pag: f ISDS:    1 Regulr: r Dates: 1964-9999
    1 010
    2 040      IVE $c IVE
    3 022      0041-7939
    4 043      n-us-dc
    5 074      788
    6 086 0    LC 1.17:
    7 090      Z881.U49 $b A3
    8 049      IVEA
    9 222 00   Quarterly journal of the Library of Congress
   10 245 04   The Quarterly journal of the Library of Congress.
   11 260 00   Washington, D.C. : $b For sale by the Supt. of Docs., U.S.
G.P.O., $c 1964-
   12 265      Library of Congress, 10 First St., S.E., Washington, D.C.
20540
   13 300          v. : $b ill. ; $c 27 cm.
   14 310      Quarterly.
   15 362 0    Vol. 21, no. 1 (Jan. 1964)-
   16 580      Supplement to: Library of Congress. Annual report of the
Librarian of Congress for the fiscal year ending ... , ISSN 0083-1565.
   17 510 2    Abstracts of English studies $x 0001-3560
   18 510 2    Library & information science abstracts $x 0024-2179
   19 510 0    Index to U.S. government periodicals $x 0098-4604
   20 510 2    Public Affairs Information Service bulletin $x 0033-3409
   21 510 2    Recently published articles $x 0145-5311
   22 510 2    Writings on American history $x 0364-2887
   23 693 20   Library of Congress $x Periodicals.
   24 710 20   Library of Congress.
   25 772 1    Library of Congress. $t Annual report of the Librarian of
Congress for the fiscal year ending ... $x 0083-1565
   26 780 00    $t Quarterly journal of current acquisitions $x 0090-0095
```

NOTES

[1]*Union List of Serials in Libraries of the United States and Canada*, 3rd ed. (New York, H. W. Wilson, 1965); coverage through 1949. *New Serial Titles: A Union List of Serials Commencing Publication after December 31, 1949* (Washington, D.C., Library of Congress, 1953-). *Ulrich's International Periodicals Directory* (New York, Bowker, 1965-). *Irregular Serials & Annuals: An International Directory* (New York, Bowker, 1967-). *British Union Catalogue of Periodicals* (London, Butterworths, 1955-58; 4v.). *British Union Catalogue of Periodicals. New Periodical Titles* (London, Butterworths, 1964- ; quarterly).

[2]*Titles in Series: A Handbook for Librarians and Students* (Metuchen, N.J., Scarecrow Press, 1953-). *Books in Series in the United States 1966-1975: Original, Reprinted, In-Print, and Out-of-Print Books Published or Distributed in the U.S. in Popular, Scholarly, and Professional Series* (New York, Bowker, 1977; suppl.).

[3]Library of Congress, *Library of Congress Catalogs: Monographic Series* (Washington, D.C., 1974-1982).

[4]*Cataloging Service Bulletin*, no. 20 (Spring 1983): 8-10.

[5]*Cataloging Service Bulletin*, no. 16 (Spring 1982): 33-34.

[6]*Cataloging Service Bulletin*, no. 15 (Winter 1982): 7.

[7]*Cataloging Service Bulletin*, no. 14 (Fall 1981): 17.

[8]*Cataloging Service Bulletin*, no. 11 (Winter 1981): 16-17.

[9]*Cataloging Service Bulletin*, no. 23 (Winter 1983): 19.

[10]Ibid., p. 20.

[11]*Cataloging Service Bulletin*, no. 20 (Spring 1983): 9.

[12]*Cataloging Service Bulletin*, no. 23 (Winter 1983): 20.

[13]*Cataloging Service Bulletin*, no. 26 (Fall 1984): 12.

[14]*Cataloging Service Bulletin*, no. 23 (Winter 1983): 21.

[15]*Cataloging Service Bulletin*, no. 21 (Summer 1983): 16.

[16]*Cataloging Service Bulletin*, no. 8 (Spring 1980): 12.

[17]Ibid.

SUGGESTED READING

Cannan, Judith Proctor. *Serial Cataloguing: A Comparison of AACR 1 and 2.* New York, New York Metropolitan Reference & Research Library Agency, 1980.

Maxwell, Margaret F. *Handbook for AACR2.* Chicago, American Library Association, 1980. Chapter 10.

Soper, Mary Ellen. "Description and Entry of Serials in AACR2." *Serials Librarian*, 4 (Winter 1979): 167-176.

Tseng, Sally C. "Serials Cataloging and AACR 2: An Introduction." *Journal of Educational Media Science*, 19 (Winter 1982): 177-216.

8
Analysis

INTRODUCTION

Whether or not to describe parts of a work is an ever-present problem in cataloging. When does a part of a larger work deserve description of its own? When such description is warranted, how is it accomplished in relation to the larger work? These are questions addressed by *AACR 2* chapter 13, "Analysis."

In the Glossary of *AACR 2*, "analytical entry" is defined as "an entry for a part of an item for which a comprehensive entry has been made." "Analytical note" is defined as "the statement in an analytical entry relating the part being analyzed to the comprehensive work of which it is a part." Analytical entries vary from complete bibliographic descriptions to simple added entries for parts mentioned in the description of the larger work. Obviously, preparing additional entries requires time. Usually, the decision in this matter depends on the administrative policy of an individual library and the local needs. In deciding whether analytical entries are needed, certain general principles may be taken into consideration:

1) The availability of printed indexes, bibliographies, and abstracting services that will locate the material to be analyzed.

2) The availability of LC analytics.

3) The quantity and quality of material on the given subject already in the catalog.

4) The quantity of material by the same authors already in the catalog. The best example in this category is provided by the library's policy regarding books in sets that usually represent various types of collections or compilations of one or more authors—e.g., Harvard Classics or Harvard Shelf of Fiction. If the library has little material by an author, the need for analytics may be greater.

5) The parts to be analyzed have a special significance for a given library (e.g., parts written by local noted authors, etc.).

6) The parts occupy the major portion of a given work.

In addition, the rules in *AACR 2* give some guidance in deciding when and how analysis should be accomplished.

However, a basic descriptive question that must be answered before making the decision to analyze a multipart item, and one for which there is no guidance in *AACR 2*, is: What is to be considered a multipart item rather than two or more separate bibliographical entities for cataloging purposes?

A publication issued in two or more volumes may be defined as a set. Usually, monographs in collected sets represent various types of collections or compilations by one or more authors. Many reference books are examples of monographs in collected sets. The number of physical volumes making up such a set may cause problems in cataloging and classification. If the works of a single author are collected in several volumes, the cataloger may be tempted to class each volume separately. On the other hand, the cataloger may only have one volume of a multi-volume set to catalog, and may consider classing it as if the library had the entire set. Although both of these approaches are arguable, the fact remains that neither is really right or wrong. There are no established codes for cataloging and classifying monographs in sets. The principles presented below are provided merely for the consideration of the cataloger; they are not meant to be followed slavishly.

One usually catalogs and classes a set of monographs together if,

1) they are issued in a uniform format,
2) the individual volumes are numbered in consecutive order, and
3) there is a general index to the entire set.

Two additional criteria are,

1) if patrons are likely to expect to find the monographs together as a set, and
2) if there is a possibility that supplements and/or additional volumes will appear at a later date.

However, one usually catalogs and classes a set of monographs separately if,

1) not all the volumes of the set are in the library, nor are likely to be added to the library's collection, and
2) each volume has a separate title, especially in the case of literary works.

Obviously, these two sets of principles are somewhat contradictory and demand individual application in actual practice. The following examples are designed to clarify these problems. First, it should be quite obvious that a set of books comprising an encyclopedia should be cataloged and classed together. An encyclopedia is uniform in format; the individual volumes are

consecutively numbered; there is usually a general index to the entire encyclopedia; patrons do expect to find these books together as a set; and supplements and/or yearbooks often appear at a later date. Second, it similarly
follows that a set of monographs that is a collection of great works (such as the
Harvard Classics or the *Great Books of the Western World*) should be both
cataloged and classed together. In both of these examples, however, individual
volumes have one or more separate titles. Should individual volumes in either
of these two sets (both of which, for example, include the plays of William
Shakespeare) be classed with other collections of Shakespeare's plays or not?
Should the non-literary material in either of these two sets be classed separately in its appropriate location? Either choice will create some problems. It is
unwise in either case to try to avoid a record in the catalog for each separate
bibliographical unit. The catalog may be the only key the patron uses for
discovering the library's holdings. Analysis is one method of solving this
particular problem. The use of analytical entries in Figs. 8.7 through 8.10
(under Rules 13.5A, 13.5B, and 13.6) allows these sets of monographs to be
cataloged and classed together while also providing separate entries for
individual bibliographical units.

The collected or complete works of one author present another problem
of monographs in sets. This is particularly apparent if the author writes in
more than one discipline. For example, Will Durant's *Story of Civilization*
may be cataloged together or separately. If this work is cataloged together as a
set, the individual parts or volumes are listed in a contents note, and the set
receives general subject added entries and a general subject classification
number. *See* Fig. 8.1. On the other hand, if each of the parts of this work is
cataloged separately, the relationship of each part to the main work is shown
by a series note. This latter approach allows for a complete publication area,
including the date, for each part, and for separate specific subject added
entries. *See* Fig. 8.2. Cataloging each part separately allows the cataloger to
choose whether to classify each part separately or in the more general number.
There are many advantages to the separate cataloging of parts—advantages in
both descriptive and subject cataloging—but it must be remembered that this
approach requires the production of more bibliographic records and catalog
entries. An advantage of the second example (Fig. 8.2) is that this method
provides separate subject headings for each individual volume.
The classification problems will be dealt with on pages 377-378 of this
textbook.

Fig. 8.1. Durant's *Story of Civilization* cataloged as a set using a
contents note for the individual bibliographical units.

Durant, Will, 1885-

Title of ————→The story of civilization / by Will Durant. –
entire set   New York : Simon and Schuster, 1935-
                       v. : ill., maps, ports. ; 28 cm.

Includes bibliographies and indexes.
Contents: pt. 1. Our oriental heritage – pt.
2. The life of Greece – pt. 3. Caesar and
Christ – pt. 4. The age of faith – pt. 5. The
Renaissance – pt. 6. The Reformation.

General sub- ————→1. Civilization 2. World history I. Title.
ject added
entries

Fig. 8.2. One part of Durant's work cataloged as a separate bibliographical unit
using a series note to relate to the collected set.

[1]Title of   Durant, Will, 1885-
individual   1 ——→Caesar and Christ : a history of Roman civili-
volume   zation and of Christianity from their beginnings
                 to A.D. 325 / by Will Durant. – New York : Simon
                 and Schuster, 1944.
                       751 p. : ill., maps, ports. ; 28 cm. – (The
[2]Title of   2 ——→ story of civilization / by Will Durant ; pt. 3)
set

               3 ——→ 1. Rome–History. 2. Rome–Antiquities. 3.
[3]Specific sub-   Christianity. 4. Church history. I. Title. II. Ser-
ject added   ies: Durant, Will, 1885-   . The story of civiliza-
entries   tion.

SELECTED RULES AND EXAMPLES

RULE 13.1. SCOPE

The scope of the analysis chapter in *AACR 2* is to give instructions for describing an item that constitutes a part or parts of a larger item. Various methods are suggested for doing this. Some of the suggestions here are also referred to in other chapters, but the point of this chapter is to gather together all the methods and to give suggestions for choosing one over another.

RULE 13.2. ANALYTICS OF MONOGRAPHIC SERIES AND MULTIPART MONOGRAPHS

The suggested criterion for deciding to describe a part of a monographic series or a multipart monograph independently concerns title. If the title of the part is not dependent on the title of the whole, a complete description of the part should be created, giving the title (and statement of responsibility, if applicable) of the whole set in the series area. The volume number of the part is also given in the series area. *See* Fig. 8.3.

Fig. 8.3. Rule 13.2. Complete independent description of a monographic series with the title of the comprehensive series given in the series area.

Chateaubriand : composition, imagination, and poetry / Charles A. Porter. – Saratoga, Calif. : Anma Libri, 1978.

145 p. ; 24 cm. – (Stanford French and Italian studies ; v. 9)

Bibliography: p. 141-145.
ISBN 0-915838-37-0

The rule does not go on to say what one should do if the title of an individual part is dependent on the comprehensive title or if there is no individual title. The implication is that such works would not be described separately. However, when such items appear as parts of series that are analyzed in full or that are classified separately, a separate record is necessary. An LC rule interpretation gives rules and examples for handling such situations; it should be consulted when needed.[1] Its basic idea is that the comprehensive title becomes part of the title proper, no series statement is given, and an explicitly traced series added entry is made.

RULE 13.3. NOTE AREA

If it is decided to describe the comprehensive work as a set, individual parts may be named in the note area. This is usually done in a formal contents note. *See* Fig. 8.4.

**Fig. 8.4. Rule 13.3. Display of individual parts of a work in the
description for the comprehensive work.**

Early development and conceptualization of the field of
marketing / edited by Henry Assael. – New York : Arno
Press, 1978.

161 p. in various pagings : ill. ; 24 cm. – (A Century of
marketing)

A collection of selections reprinted from various sources
published 1901-1960.
Contents: Appraisal of contributions to marketing
thought by late nineteenth-century liberal economists /
F. G. Coolsen – Report of the Industrial Commission on the
distribution of farm products / U.S. Industrial Commission – The elements of marketing / P. T. Cherington – Modern distribution / J. F. Johnson – Some problems in market
distribution / A. W. Shaw.
ISBN 0-405-11188-6 : $15.00

RULE 13.4. ANALYTICAL ADDED ENTRIES

When the title of a part appears either in the title and statement of
responsibility area or in the note area, an added entry may be made to provide
direct access to the part without having to make a separate bibliographic
record for the part. Such an added entry is composed of the main entry
heading and title, if title is not main entry. The title used is the uniform title if
there is one, otherwise it is the title proper. *See* Figs. 8.5 and 8.6.

RULE 13.5. "IN" ANALYTICS

Another possible way to describe a part is to provide an "In" analytic
record. This is useful when one wishes to provide more information than can
be given in the note area of the record for the set.
LC makes "In" analytics only in very special cases.[2]

13.5A. An "In" analytic shows first a description of the part. This is
followed by a short description of the comprehensive work.
The description of the part contains all the elements of the eight areas of
description that apply to the part, with the exception that in the publication,
distribution, etc., area, only those elements that differ from the whole item are
given.

**Fig. 8.5. Rule 13.4. Unit record for a comprehensive work with
analytical added entries made for the parts.**

Memories of old Dorking / edited by Margaret K. Kohler. –
   Dorking : Kohler and Coombes, 1977.
   252 p. in various pagings, [8] p. of plates : ill., facsims. ; 23
cm.
   Rose's work 1st published in the West Surrey times during 1876 and 1877; Attlee's article 1st published in Dorking
advertiser, 1912; Dinnage's articles 1st published in Dorking
advertiser, 1963.
   Includes index.

[1] Parts listed
in the note
area

1 ⟶ Contents: Recollections of old Dorking / Charles
Rose – Reminiscences of old Dorking / John Attlee – Recol-
lections of old Dorking / William Henry Dinnage.
   ISBN 0-903967-08-1 : £3.90

[2] Analytical
added entries
for the parts

   1. Dorking (Surrey)–Description. I. Kohler, Margaret K. II.
2 ⟶ Rose, Charles, 1818-1879. Recollections of old Dorking.
1977. III. Attlee, John, 1828-1913. Reminiscences of old
Dorking. 1977. IV. Dinnage, William Henry, 1870-1963.
Recollections of old Dorking. 1977.

**Fig. 8.6. Rule 13.4. Unit record to be filed under analytical added entry
for one of the parts.**

Analytical ⟶ Attlee, John, 1828-1913. Reminiscences of old Dork-
added   ing. 1977.
entry

Memories of old Dorking / edited by Margaret K. Kohler. –
   Dorking : Kohler and Coombes, 1977.
   252 p. in various pagings, [8] p. of plates : ill., facsims. ; 23
cm.
   Rose's work 1st published in the West Surrey times during 1876 and 1877; Attlee's article 1st published in Dorking
advertiser, 1912; Dinnage's articles 1st published in Dorking
advertiser, 1963.
   Includes index.
   Contents: Recollections of old Dorking / Charles
Rose – Reminiscences of old Dorking / John Attlee – Recollections of old Dorking / William Henry Dinnage.
   ISBN 0-903967-08-1 : £3.90

   1. Dorking (Surrey)–Description. I. Kohler, Margaret K. II.
Rose, Charles, 1818-1879. Recollections of old Dorking.
1977. III. Attlee, John, 1828-1913. Reminiscences of old
Dorking. 1977. IV. Dinnage, William Henry, 1870-1963.
Recollections of old Dorking. 1977.

The description of the whole item begins with the word "In," emphasized in some manner (e.g., underlining), followed by: the main entry heading; uniform title (if appropriate); title proper; edition statement; and numeric or other designation (if a serial), or publication details (if a monographic item). *See* Figs. 8.7 and 8.8.

Fig. 8.7. Rule 13.5A. "In" analytic where the part is contained in a monographic item.

Ethelinda : an English novel / done from the Italian of Flaminiani. -- p. [79]-124 ; 17 cm.
——➤In Croxall, S. A select collection of novels and histories. -- 2nd ed. -- London : [J. Watts], 1729. -- Vol. 5.

Fig. 8.8. Rule 13.5A. "In" analytic where the part is contained in a serial item.

Library administration in its current development / L. Quincy Mumford and Rutherford D. Rogers. -- p. 357-367 ; 23 cm. -- Includes bibliographical references.
——➤ In Library trends. -- Vol. 7 (1958-59)

13.5B. Parts of "In" analytics

If an "In" analytic record is to be made for a part of a part already cataloged as an "In" analytic, the description following the word "In" should first give information about the part containing the part being analyzed. The information about the comprehensive work is then given as a series statement. *See* Fig. 8.9.

Fig. 8.9. Rule 13.5B. "In" analytic where the part is contained in a work that is itself part of a larger work.

The school for scandal / Richard Brinsley Sheridan. -- p. [107]-197 ; 22 cm.
——➤In Modern English drama. -- New York : Collier, 1961, c1937. -- (The Harvard classics ; v. 18)

RULE 13.6. MULTILEVEL DESCRIPTION

An alternative to "In" analytic records is a technique called multilevel description. It is useful when one wishes to provide complete identification of both part and whole in a single record.

The first level of descriptive information shows the description of the whole item. The second level contains description (not repeating information given at the first level) of an individual part or group of parts. If the second level describes a group of parts, then a third level may describe an individual part. *See* Fig. 8.10.

Fig. 8.10. Rule 13.6. Multilevel description showing three levels from most to least comprehensive.

The Harvard classics / [edited by Charles W. Eliot] – Registered ed. – New York : Collier, 1961, c1937-1938. – 50 v. : ill., ports. ; 23 cm. – "The five-foot shelf of books."

Vol. 18 : Modern English drama / Dryden. . .[et al.]. – 450 p., [1] leaf of plates.

The school for scandal / Richard Brinsley Sheridan. – p.[107]-197.

LC does not use the technique of multilevel description.[3]

NOTES

[1]*Cataloging Service Bulletin*, no. 21 (Summer 1983): 16-18.

[2]*Cataloging Service Bulletin*, no. 11 (Winter 1981): 17.

[3]Ibid.

SUGGESTED READING

Bloomberg, Marty, and G. Edward Evans. *Introduction to Technical Services for Library Technicians.* 4th ed. Littleton, Colo., Libraries Unlimited, 1981. pp. 190-191.

Hagler, Ronald, and Peter Simmons. *The Bibliographic Record and Information Technology.* Chicago, American Library Association, 1982. pp. 102-104.

9
Choice of Access Points

INTRODUCTION

The rules in *AACR 2*, chapter 21, deal with the choice of access points and not the form of entry. "Choice of access points" means choosing all names and titles under which the description of an item may be sought by a user. For any one item, one of the access points is chosen as a main entry, and the others become added entries. In the introduction to *AACR 2* there is a recognition that choice of one entry to be the main one may not be considered important in some libraries.[1] There is lack of agreement on this point in the cataloging community. Proponents of main entry assert that one of the major outcomes of cataloging is to identify the work contained therein. This can best be done, they say, by choosing the major entry point for the work and then using it to collocate all editions, translations, criticisms, etc., of that work that may appear. Proponents of the idea that all access points for an item are basically equal question the number of works that need such a collocating device. It is probably a very small proportion; yet a great deal of time is spent choosing main entries for many works that will never have editions, translations, etc. Those in favor of equal access points also refer to the reduced need for entry as a filing element. In online catalogs there is usually only one copy of any bibliographic record, and it is retrieved equally by any one of its access points. Much has been written about this controversy.[2]

This chapter covers basic choice of main entry under personal author, corporate body, and title (Rule 21.1). More specific guidance is then given for choice of entry for 1) works where there have been changes in title proper (Rule 21.2) or in persons or bodies responsible for the work (Rule 21.3), 2) works of single responsibility (Rules 21.4-21.5), 3) works of shared responsibility (Rule 21.6), 4) collections and works produced under editorial responsibility (Rule 21.7), 5) works of mixed responsibility (Rules 21.8-21.27), and 6) works that are related to other works (Rule 21.28). General rules for added entries are given (Rules 21.29-21.30), followed by special rules for certain legal and religious publications (Rules 21.31-21.39).

The rules covered in this text deal only with basic or general instances; for more complex problems and special cases, the student should consult *AACR 2*, chapter 21. Examples in this text allow the student to see not only the choice of main entry, but also the form of entry and the added entries. The following chapters deal with the rules for these specific forms.

SELECTED RULES AND EXAMPLES

RULE 21.0.   INTRODUCTORY RULES

21.0B.   Sources for determining access points

Access points for the item being cataloged are determined from the chief source of information or its substitute (*see* Rule 1.0A). Other statements appearing formally in one of the prescribed sources of information should be taken into account, but the emphasis is to be on the chief source of information, making it unnecessary for the cataloger to search in the contents or outside the item for potential access points. A rule interpretation from LC indicates that when information in the prescribed sources is ambiguous, information may be taken from the contents or from outside the item.[3]

21.0D.   *Optional additions.* Designations of function

This option allows for abbreviated designations of function, such as "ed." for "editor" and "tr." for "translator," to be added to a heading for a person. The Library of Congress has decided not to apply this option, with one exception: the abbreviation "Ill." is added to the headings for illustrators that appear as added entries on bibliographic records in the annotated cards (AC) series (i.e., for children's books).[4]

RULE 21.1.   BASIC RULE

21.1A.   Works of personal authorship

"Personal author" is defined as "the person chiefly responsible for the creation of the intellectual or artistic content of a work."[5] This can include composers, cartographers, photographers, performers, and others, as well as writers. The general rule is to enter works by one or more persons under the heading for the personal author according to the specific instructions given in Rules 21.4A, 21.5B, 21.6, and 21.8-21.17, and to make added entries as instructed in 21.29-21.30. For example, the sound recording entitled "Where the Blue of the Night Meets the Gold of the Day," which includes songs from the original sound tracks of Bing Crosby's early films, would be entered under the heading:

Crosby, Bing, 1904-1977.

There would be an added entry for the title.

21.1B. Entry under corporate body

A corporate body is defined as "an organization or a group of persons that is identified by a particular name and that acts, or may act, as an entity."[6] Guidelines dictate that a corporate body should be considered to have a name: if the words referring to it are a specific appellation, not just a description; if the initial letters of important words are capitalized; and/or if the words are associated with a definite article. Corporate bodies include, for example, associations, institutions, business firms, governments, conferences, ad hoc events (e.g., exhibitions, festivals), and vessels (e.g., spacecraft).

LC has issued a rule interpretation that gives assistance in determining whether a conference is named. This interpretation should be consulted when needed.[7]

21.1B2. The general rule states that a corporate body may be chosen as main entry if it falls into one or more of six categories:

a) A work that deals with the body itself, such as a report on finances or operations, or a listing of staff, or a catalog of the body's resources.

b) Certain legal, governmental, or religious types of works listed in this rule with rule numbers to consult for more guidance.

c) Works that deal with official pronouncements that represent the body's position on matters other than those covered in a) above.

d) Works of a *collective* nature that report on activities of conferences, expeditions, or events that can be defined as corporate bodies and whose names appear prominently in the publication.

e) Sound recordings, films, or videorecordings in which the responsibility of the group for the existence of the performance is more than a performance or execution of a previously existing script, score, etc. (e.g., improvized jazz or drama).

f) Cartographic materials for which a body does more than merely publish or distribute the materials.

A lengthy LC rule interpretation on this rule gives guidance in applying this rule and should be consulted for more information.[8] *See* Figs. 9.5-9.7 under Rule 21.4B.

21.1B3. If a work falls outside the above categories, the main entry is chosen as if no corporate body were involved, but added entries may be made. Thus, the report of an exhibition entitled "130 Years of Ohio Photography" sponsored by and held in the Columbus Museum of Art would be entered under the heading "Columbus Museum of Art," and an added entry would be made under the title. However, a monograph entitled "Benue through Pictures" that has been put together in the Information Division of Benue, Nigeria, does not fall under one of the five categories of 21.1B2; therefore, the main entry would be under the title, with an added entry under the heading: Benue (Nigeria). Information Division.

21.1B4.   If a subordinate unit of a corporate body is involved for a work that falls in a category in 21.1B2, the heading for the subordinate unit is used if the responsibility of that unit is stated prominently. Otherwise, the heading for the parent body is used. For example, the staff directory of the Women's Bureau of the Ministry of Labour in Ontario would be entered under the heading for the Women's Bureau, not that for the Ministry of Labour.

21.1C.   **Entry under title**

Entry under title is prescribed when there is no known personal author, or personal authorship is diffuse (*see* Rule 21.6C2), *and* the work is not eligible for entry under corporate body; when the work is a collection of multiple authorship or is produced under editorial direction; or when the work is a text that a religious group accepts as sacred scripture.

An LC rule interpretation adds a case for title entry that is not listed in *AACR 2*. It is the situation where a work seems to give technical credit of more than one kind to several persons, and the position and typography of the statement indicates lesser importance in relation to the title.[9]

RULE 21.2.   CHANGES IN TITLES PROPER

This rule and the next one fill a need for guidance about when separate main entries should be chosen for different parts of a multipart monograph or of a serial. The cataloger is instructed to choose separate main entries (and thus make separate records) for each edition when the title proper of a monograph changes between editions. However, if the title proper of a multipart monograph changes between *parts*, one title proper (the one that predominates) is to be used for the whole monograph. If the title proper of a serial changes, a separate main entry is chosen for each title, and separate records are made.

21.2A.   The three cases in which a title proper is considered to have changed occur when:

1)   any of the first five words (except an initial article) changes;

     e.g., the change of *Federal Education Program Guide* to *Federal Education Grants Directory* constitutes a change in title proper.

2)   any important words are added, deleted, or changed;

     e.g., *Cataloging Service* changed to *Cataloging Service Bulletin*.

3)   the order of words changes;

     e.g., *Census of Public Water Supplies in Missouri* changed to *Census of Missouri Public Water Supplies.*

According to this definition, change of *Report of the Department of Community Affairs, Division of Veterans Affairs to the Governor* to *Report of the Department of Community Affairs of the Division of Veterans Affairs to the Governor* would not qualify as a change in title proper; the change is not in the first five words, the added words "of the" are not important words, and there is no change in the order of words.

A rule interpretation from LC indicates that the title of a serial is not considered to be changed if the only differences are in abbreviated words, numbers, signs, or symbols as opposed to their spelled-out forms, or are in initialisms with as opposed to without punctuation, or consist of such things as hyphenated as opposed to unhyphenated words. Guidance is also given for treatment of fluctuating titles.[10]

RULE 21.3. CHANGES OF PERSONS OR BODIES RESPONSIBLE FOR A WORK

Monographs that have been modified by a person or body different from the one responsible for the original edition are to be treated according to Rules 21.9-21.23. This means that in some cases, when the nature and/or content has been changed, the main entry will be different from that of the original; while in other cases, when the modification abridges, rearranges, or updates, for example, the main entry of the original will be used. An example of the first case is shown in Fig. 9.1.

Fig. 9.1. Rule 21.3. Entry of a work whose nature has been changed from that of the original.

Bambi's fragrant forest : based on the original story by Felix
    Salten / Walt Disney Productions.

Make added entries for persons or bodies responsible for the original and the modification:
    1. Salten, Felix, 1869-1945. Bambi. II. Walt Disney
Productions.

An example of the second case is shown in Fig. 9.2.

Fig. 9.2. Rule 21.3. Entry of an abridged work.

Salten, Felix, 1869-1945.
    Bambi [sound recording] / abridged by Marianne Mantell.
Read by Glynis Johns.

Make added entries for persons or bodies responsible for the modification:
    I. Mantell, Marianne. II. Johns, Glynis. III. Title.

If responsibility in a multipart monograph changes between parts, the heading appropriate to the first part is used unless a later one predominates, just as with a change of title proper. However, if more than three persons or bodies are finally responsible for a multipart monograph, with none predominant, main entry is changed to title.

There are two conditions under which changes in persons or bodies could require a new entry for a serial:

1)   when the serial has a corporate body main entry and the name of that body changes, or

2)   when the serial has a corporate body or personal author as main entry, and the responsibility for the serial changes.

The first case is where the serial has a corporate body as the main entry and the name of that body is later changed to a new form. An example of this is the *Financial Report* of the Board of Trustees of the Firemen's Pension Fund, formerly the Firemen's Pension and Relief Fund. The second case is where the serial has a person or body as the main entry and later a different person or body takes over responsibility for the publication.

RULE 21.4.   WORKS FOR WHICH A SINGLE PERSON OR CORPORATE BODY IS RESPONSIBLE

21.4A.   Works of single personal authorship

An item that contains a work or works by one personal author should have the heading for that person as its main entry. For example, the following title page is from a work of single personal authorship. The choice of main entry should be the single author, Pamela Bennetts (*see* Figs. 9.3 and 9.4).

Fig. 9.3. Title page.

Title   ⎯⎯➤ **MY DEAR LOVER ENGLAND**

Single author   ⎯⎯➤ Pamela Bennetts

New York

St. Martin's Press
1975

Fig. 9.4. Rule 21.4A. A work of single personal authorship.

Personal   ⟶ Bennetts, Pamela.
author main   My dear lover England / Pamela Bennetts.
entry
Make added entry for title:
        I. Title.

21.4B.   Works emanating from a single corporate body

An item that contains a work or works that emanate from one corporate body should have the heading for that body as its main entry if one or more of the categories given under 21.1B2 applies. *See* Figs. 9.5, 9.6, and 9.7.

Fig. 9.5. Rule 21.4B. A work of single corporate responsibility.

Corporate   ⟶ Al-Anon Family Group Headquarters.
body main   World directory of Al-Anon Family Groups
entry (21.1B2,   and Ala-teens.
type a)
Make added entry for title:
        I. Title.

Fig. 9.6. Rule 21.4B. A work of single corporate responsibility.

Corporate   ⟶ United States. Congress. Senate. Select Com-
body main   mittee on Indian Affairs.
entry (21.1B2,   Consolidating Alaska natives governing bod-
type c)   ies : hearings before the United States Senate,
    Select Committee on Indian Affairs, Ninety-fifth
    Congress, first session, on S. 1920 ... S. 2046. ...
Make added entry for title:
        I. Title.

Rule 9.7. Rule 21.4B. A work of single corporate responsibility.

Corporate   ⟶ AIAA Communications Satellite Systems Confer-
body main   ence (7th : 1978 : San Diego, Calif.)
entry (21.1B2,   A collection of technical papers : AIAA 7th
type d)   Communications Satellite Systems Conference,
    San Diego, California, April 24-27, 1978.
Make added entry for title:
        I. Title.

21.4C.   **Works erroneously or fictitiously attributed to a person or corporate body**

When a publication erroneously or fictitiously attributes responsibility to a person or body, enter it under the heading for the actual person or body responsible if possible and appropriate, or else under the title. Make an added entry under the heading for the person or body attributed responsibility if such person or body is real. *See* Fig. 9.8.

Fig. 9.8. Rule 21.4C. Entry under the real author rather than
the attributed author.

Actual   ⟶ Farmer, Philip Jose.
author as   The adventure of the peerless peer / by John
main entry   H. Watson : edited by Philip Jose Farmer.

Note explaining statement of responsibility:
                  Written by P. J. Farmer in imitation of A. C.
                  Doyle.

Make added entry for title:
                  I. Title.

Note: No added entry is made for the attributed author, John H. Watson, since he is a fictional character created by A. C. Doyle in his series of detective stories about Sherlock Holmes and Dr. Watson.

21.4D.   **Works by heads of state, other high government officials, popes, and other high ecclesiastical officials**

21.4D1.   Official communications

Two categories of official works are entered under the corporate heading (*see* 24.20 and 24.27B) for the official:

"a)   official communications from heads of state, heads of government, and heads of international bodies (e.g., messages to legislatures, proclamations, and executive orders other than those covered by 21.31)

b)   official communications from popes, patriarchs, bishops, etc. (e.g., orders; decrees; pastoral letters; official messages to councils, synods, etc.; bulls; encyclicals; and constitutions)."[11]

An added entry is made under the personal heading for the person. *See* Fig. 9.9.

Fig. 9.9. Rule 21.4D1. Official communication entered under corporate heading.

Main entry
under corpor-   →Maine. Governor (1975-1979 : Longley)
ate heading   Budget message address of James B. Longley,
                Governor of Maine, to the One hundred and
                seventh Legislature, State of Maine, February 6,
                1975.
Make added entries:
                I. Maine. Legislature. II. Longley, James B. ←——
Added entry   III. Title: Budget message address of James B.
under personal Longley, Governor of Maine ...
heading

21.4D2.   Other works

Other works by a government or religious official are given the personal heading for the person as main entry. One explanatory reference is made under the corporate heading rather than making an added entry under the corporate heading for each such work. *See* Fig. 9.10. For examples of explanatory references see chapter 14 of this text.

Fig. 9.10. Rule 21.4D2. Other works entered under personal heading.

Main entry
under per-   ——→Jefferson, Thomas, 1743-1826.
sonal heading   The portable Thomas Jefferson / edited and
                with an introduction by Merrill D. Peterson.

Make added entry for person responsible for this edition of the work:
                I. Peterson, Merrill D.

21.4D3.   Collections of official communications and other works

A collection of official communications *and other works* by *one* person is entered under the personal heading, with an added entry under the corporate heading. A collection of official communications and other works by *more than one* person is entered as a collection (*see* 21.7), with an added entry for the heading for the office held, if all the persons held the same office.

A collection of official communications *only* of *more than one* holder of *one* of the offices listed in 21.4D1 is entered under the heading for the office, with an added entry for an openly named compiler.

There is no rule here for a collection of official communications *only* of more than one holder of *more than one* of the offices listed. Such a work should be treated as a collection and entered as instructed in Rule 21.7.

RULE 21.5. WORKS OF UNKNOWN OR UNCERTAIN AUTHORSHIP OR BY UNNAMED GROUPS

21.5A.   Enter under the title a work of unknown or uncertain responsibility or one that emanates from a body that lacks a name. *See* Fig. 9.11.

Fig. 9.11. Rule 21.5A. Work of unknown authorship entered under title.

Main entry ——→ Davis, Noble, and Kinder reunions, 1945-1975,
under title   and family trees. – 6th ed. – [S.l. : s.n.], c1978
                         (Baltimore : P. M. Harrod Co.)

Note providing bibliographic history:
                         Edition for 1941 published under title: Davis,
                         Kinder, and Noble reunions, 1930-1935-1940, and
                         family trees.

Make added entry for earlier title:
                         I. Davis, Kinder, and Noble reunions, 1930-
                         1935-1940, and family trees.

21.5C.   Enter a work under a characterizing word or phrase or under a phrase naming another work by the person, if that is the only clue to authorship and it appears in the chief source of information. For example, the title page shown in Fig. 9.12 is from a work with an unknown author, but provides a "characterizing phrase." It would be entered in the form given in Fig. 9.13.

Fig. 9.12. Title page.

Title ——————→ THE MANUAL OF FRENCH COOKERY
Subtitle ————————→ Dedicated to the Housekeepers and
                          Cooks of England who Wish to
                                 Study the ART
                          simplified for the benefit of the
                                most unlearned by
Unknown
author   ——————→ One who has tested the receipts
Place   ——————→ London
Publisher   ——————→ Chapman and Hall

Fig. 9.13. Rule 21.5C. A work of unknown authorship entered under characterizing phrase.

Entry under
characterizing
phrase

One who has tested the receipts.
    The Manual of French cookery : dedicated to
the housekeepers and cooks of England who
wish to study the art : simplified for the benefit
of the most unlearned / by one who has tested
the receipts.

Make added entry for title:
    I. Title.

RULE 21.6.   WORKS OF SHARED RESPONSIBILITY

21.6A.   Scope

This rule is used for situations in which two or more persons or corporate
bodies have made the same kind of contribution to a work. It also applies
when the same kinds of contributions come from one or more persons *and* one
or more corporate bodies.

Special types of collaborations are covered by rules on mixed responsibility (Rules 21.8-21.27), but when those rules prescribe main entry under the
heading for an adapter, for example, and when there is shared responsibility
among two or more adapters, then this rule of shared responsibility is applied.
This rule does not apply to works produced under editorial direction or to
works that are collections of previously existing works.

21.6B.   Principal responsibility indicated

21.6B1.   Enter a work of shared responsibility under the heading for the
principal person or body if one is indicated by wording or typography. Make
added entries under the headings for other persons or bodies involved, if there
are not more than two. Always make an added entry under the heading for the
person or body, other than the principal one, whose name appears first on the
title page. *See* Figs. 9.14 and 9.15. Since the principal author, Connie Haynes,
is indicated on the title page of this work by the wording of the subsidiary
authorship statement, the choice of main entry is the principal author.

Fig. 9.14. Title page.

Title   ⟶ **SPEED, STRENGTH, AND STAMINA**
Subtitle   ⟶ **Conditioning for Tennis**
                                by
Principal   ⟶ Connie Haynes
author   with
Subsidiary   ⟶ Eve Kraft and John Conroy
authors   illustrated by
Illustrator   ⟶ George Janes

                             1st edition
                             Doubleday
                     Garden City, New York
                              1975

Fig. 9.15. Rule 21.6B1. Principal author indicated.

Main entry ⟶ Haynes, Connie.
under princi-   Speed, strength, and stamina : conditioning
pal author   for tennis / by Connie Haynes, with Eve Kraft and
                John Conroy ; illustrated by George Janes.

Make added entries for subsidiary authors:
                I. Kraft, Eve. II. Conroy, John, 1908-   . III.
                Title.

21.6B2.   When the chief source of information indicates that two or three persons or bodies have principal responsibility, main entry is made for the first named of these. Added entries are made under headings for the other principal author(s), and for a collaborator if there are two principal authors and one collaborator (i.e., there may be no more than two added entries).

21.6C.   **Principal responsibility not indicated**

21.6C1.   If principal responsibility is not indicated and if there are not more than three names, enter under the one that is named first and make added entries under the others. *See* Figs. 9.16 and 9.17.

Fig. 9.16. Title page.

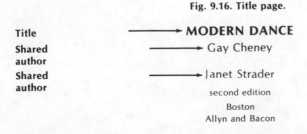

Title   ⟶ **MODERN DANCE**
Shared   ⟶ Gay Cheney
author
Shared   ⟶ Janet Strader
author
                          second edition
                              Boston
                         Allyn and Bacon

In this case of shared authorship, the principal author is not indicated; further, there are not more than three authors listed (i.e., two in this example), so the choice of main entry is the first named author (*see* Fig. 9.17). If there had been more than three authors on the title page, the choice of entry would have been the title (*see* Fig. 9.18).

Fig. 9.17. Rule 21.6C1. Principal author not indicated, and not more than three authors.

Main entry ⟶ Cheney, Gay.
under first
named author   Modern dance / Gay Cheney, Janet Strader.

Make added entry for second named author:
     I. Strader, Janet.

21.6C2.   If principal responsibility is not indicated and there are more than three persons or bodies, enter the work under the title and make an added entry under the heading for the person or body named first in the chief source of information. *See* Fig. 9.18.

Note: If the work is produced under the direction of an editor named in the chief source of information, apply Rule 21.7.

Fig. 9.18. Rule 21.6C2. Principal author not indicated.

Title main ⟶ Europe reborn : the story of Renaissance civiliza-
entry   tion / contributors, Julian Mates ... [et al.].

Make added entry for first named author:
     I. Mates, Julian, 1927-

21.6D.   **Shared pseudonyms**

When two or more persons have used a single pseudonym for the result of their collaboration, the pseudonym is given as the heading in the appropriate place (either main entry or added entry). References are made from the real names to the pseudonym and, if the persons are also established singly, from the pseudonym to the real name(s) (*see* 26.2D1). *See* Figs. 9.19 and 9.20.

Fig. 9.19. Rule 21.6D. Shared pseudonyms.

Main entry ⟶ Ashe, Penelope
under shared   Naked came the stranger / Penelope Ashe
pseudonym

It should be noted that Penelope Ashe is the shared pseudonym of 25 writers who wrote the book in collaboration. Because a number of unnamed persons were involved, explanatory references cannot be made. Such a reference might be made for Lillie Young, one of the contributors, who posed as Penelope Ashe, and who has since published a work under her own name.

Fig. 9.20. Rule 21.6D. Shared pseudonyms.

Coles, Manning.
    A toast to tomorrow / Manning Coles

In this case, the name is the shared pseudonym of Adelaide Frances Oke Manning and Cyril Henry Coles. References would be made from these names to the pseudonym.

RULE 21.7.   COLLECTIONS AND WORKS PRODUCED UNDER EDITORIAL DIRECTION

21.7A.   Scope

This rule is used for situations in which independent contributions by different persons or corporate bodies are brought together either as collections of previously existing works (or extracts from those works) or as contributions produced under editorial direction or as combinations of the two preceding situations.

Do not apply this rule to works that emanate from a corporate body and fall in the scope of 21.1B2 (including papers or proceedings of named conferences).

21.7B.   With collective title

Main entry for a work covered by this rule is title if there is a collective title. Added entries are made under the headings for prominently named editors or compilers if there are not more than three, or for the principal one or the one named first if there are more than three. *See* Figs. 9.21 and 9.22.

Fig. 9.21. Rule 21.7B. Collections and works produced under editorial direction with collective titles. Added entries are made for the first-named editors.

Title main   ———►Altruism, morality, and economic theory / edited
entry   by Edmund S. Phelps.

Note expanding upon statement of responsibility:
          Based on the proceedings of a conference
          held March 3-4, 1972, sponsored by the Russell
          Sage Foundation.

Make added entries for persons or bodies responsible for the item:
          I. Phelps, Edmund S. II. Russell Sage Founda-
          tion, New York.

Fig. 9.22.

Title main ———▶ The New Cassell's French dictionary : French-
entry   English, English-French / completely revised by
                         Denis Girard ; with the assistance of Gaston
                         Dulong, Oliver Van Oss and Charles Guinness.

Make added entry for editor:
                         I. Girard, Denis. II. Title: Cassell's French
                         dictionary.

Name-title added entries are made if there are only two or three contributions or independent works included in a work covered by this rule. A name-
title added entry is composed of the name of a person or corporate body
followed by the title of an item for which the person or body is responsible. *See*
Fig. 9.23 for an example of name-title added entries.

An added entry is made for each contributor when only two or three have
contributed four or more works. In this case if one or two contributors have
contributed only one work each, a name-title added entry is made for each.

An added entry is made for the first contributor named when more than
three are named in the chief source of information.

A rule interpretation from LC indicates that the above provisions for
added entries for contributors are to be followed when the work is a collection,
but not when it is produced under editorial direction. In the latter case LC
makes the name added entries prescribed but does not make name-title added
entries.[12]

21.7C.   Without collective title

The main entry for a work that falls under this rule but does *not* have a
collective title is the heading appropriate for the first work or contribution
named in the chief source of information. If a chief source is lacking, the first
work in the item is used. Added entries are made as instructed in 21.7B. The
LC rule interpretation is also like that under 21.7B. *See* Fig. 9.23.

Fig. 9.23. Rule 21.7C. Collections without a collective title.

Main entry ———▶ Ellsworth, Ralph E., 1907-
under first   Buildings / by Ralph E. Ellsworth. Shelving / by
named author   Louis Kaplan. Storage warehouses / by Jerrold
                     Orne.

Make name-title added entries:
                     I. Kaplan, Louis, 1909-   Shelving. II. Orne,
                     Jerrold, 1921-   Storage warehouses. III. Title.
                     IV. Title: Shelving. V. Title: Storage ware-
                     houses.

Note: The rule does not mention separate title added entries for the separate titles in a collection without a collective title, nor does Rule 21.30J suggest such title added entries. However, an LC rule interpretation gives instructions to trace separate title added entries for each of the titles listed in the title and statement of responsibility area if there are not more than three.[13]

WORKS OF MIXED RESPONSIBILITY:

SELECTED RULES AND EXAMPLES

21.8A.   Scope

In many works the responsibility is divided. This occurs when different persons or bodies have contributed to the intellectual or artistic content performing different kinds of functions, e.g., writing, adapting, illustrating, translating, etc. Determination of main entry depends to a large extent on the relative importance of such contributions.

The rules in this section are divided into two basic categories of mixed responsibility:

1) a modification of a previously existing work, such as a revised edition, an adaptation, or a translation, and

2) a new work that consists of different kinds of contributions, such as an illustrated text or a musical work with words by a person other than the composer.

WORKS THAT ARE MODIFICATIONS OF OTHER WORKS

RULE 21.9.   GENERAL RULE

Works that are modifications of other works may be entered under the heading appropriate to the new work or that appropriate to the original, depending upon the nature of the modification. If the modification has changed the nature or content of the original in a substantial way, or if the medium of expression is different, the new heading is chosen. However, if the modification is an updating, rearrangement, abridgment, or revision where the original person or body is still represented as being responsible, the original heading is chosen. Rules 21.10-21.23 give specific guidance in applying this general rule.

Modifications of Texts (Rules 21.10-21.15)

RULE 21.10. ADAPTATIONS OF TEXTS

Adaptations of texts are entered under the heading for the adapter, or under title if the adapter is unknown. A name-title added entry is made for the original work. Examples of adaptations are paraphrases, changes of literary form (e.g., dramatization), and adaptations for children. *See* Fig. 9.24.

Fig. 9.24. Rule 21.10. Entry under adapter.

Adapter as ⟶ Taylor, Helen L.
main entry   Little Pilgrim's progress / by Helen L. Taylor.

Note expanding upon statement of responsibility:
         Adaptation for children of: The Pilgrim's
         progress / John Bunyan.

Make name-title added entry for original author:
         I. Bunyan, John. The Pilgrim's progress. II.
         Title.

RULE 21.11. ILLUSTRATED TEXTS

21.11A.   General rule

When an illustrator has added illustrations to a text, the main entry is under the heading appropriate to the text. *See* Fig. 9.25. An added entry for the illustrator may be made if appropriate (*see* 21.30K2). Works of collaboration between an artist and a writer are treated in 21.24.

Fig. 9.25. Rule 21.11. Illustrated text entered under author.

Main entry ⟶ Day, Jenifer W.
under author   What is a bird? / by Jenifer W. Day ; illustra-
         ted by Tony Chen.

Make added entry for artist:
         I. Chen, Tony. II. Title.

RULE 21.12. REVISIONS OF TEXTS

21.12A.   The main entry for the original work is used for a revision if the wording of the chief source of information indicates that the original person or body is still considered to be responsible for the work. Such revisions include condensations, enlargements, abridgments, revisions, and updates. The reviser, condenser, etc., is given an added entry. *See* Fig. 9.26.

Fig. 9.26. Rule 21.12A. Revised work entered under original author.

Main entry ———➤ Darwin, Charles, 1809-1882.
under original   The origin of species / Charles Darwin ;
author   abridged and introduced by Philip Appleman.

Make added entry for reviser:
                        I. Appleman, Philip, 1926-   II. Title.

21.12B. The reviser, etc., is given as main entry, however, when according to the chief source of information the original person or body is no longer considered to be responsible. *See* Fig. 9.27.

Fig. 9.27. Rule 21.12B. Revised work entered under reviser.

Main entry ———➤ Bedingfeld, A. L.
under reviser   Oxburgh Hall, Norfolk : a property of the National Trust / by A. L. Bedingfeld. – 2nd ed.

Note expanding upon statement of responsibility:
                        "First edition, 1953, by Professor F. de Zulueta."

Make name-title added entry for original author:
                        I. Zulueta, Francis de. Oxburgh Hall, Norfolk.
                        II. Title.

RULE 21.13. TEXTS PUBLISHED WITH COMMENTARY

This rule applies to items comprising a text or texts by one person or body and a commentary or interpretation by another person or body. In essence, the rule calls for entry under the heading appropriate to the commentary if the chief source of information presents the work as a commentary, and entry under the heading for the original work if the chief source of information presents the work as an edition of the original. If the chief source is ambiguous, entry is determined by (in order of preference) emphasis in the preface, the typographic presentation of the text and commentary, or the relative extent of text and commentary. If there is still doubt, the work is treated as an edition with an added entry appropriate to the commentary. *See* Fig. 9.28.

Fig. 9.28. Rule 21.13. Text with commentary
entered under commentator.

Main entry ──────► Fischer, John L.
under named   Annotations to the Book of Luelen / translated
commentator   and edited by John L. Fischer, Saul H. Riesenberg
                        and Marjorie G. Whiting.

Note explaining the statement of responsibility:
                        Annotations by J. L. Fischer, S. H. Riesenberg,
                        and M. G. Whiting.

Make added entries appropriate to the text:
                        I. Riesenberg, Saul H. II. Whiting, Marjorie G.
                        III. Bernart, Luelen. The book of Luelen.

RULE 21.14. TRANSLATIONS

A single translation is entered under the heading appropriate to the
original. An added entry for the translator may be made in accordance with
21.30K1. *See* Fig. 9.29.

Fig. 9.29. Rule 21.14. Translation entered under original author.

Main entry ──────► Flohr, Salo, 1908-
under origi-   Twelfth chess tournament of nations / Salo
nal author   Flohr ; [translated from the Russian by W.
                       Perelman].

A collection of translations of works by different authors is treated as a
collection (*see* rule 21.7).

RULE 21.15. TEXTS PUBLISHED WITH BIOGRAPHICAL/CRITICAL MATERIAL

Works that consist of a writer's work or works accompanied by biographical or critical material written by someone else are treated according to the
way they are represented in the chief source of information. If the chief source
presents the work as biography and/or criticism, the main entry is the
biographer/critic. If the chief source presents the work as an edition with an
editor, compiler, etc., then the original writer is used as main entry. In either
case an added entry is made for the one not chosen as main entry. *See* Figs.
9.30 and 9.31.

Fig. 9.30. Rule 21.15. Biographical work entered under biographer.

Main entry ——→ Morse, John T. (John Torrey), 1840-1937.
under   Life and letters of Oliver Wendell Holmes / by
biographer   John T. Morse.

Make added entries for author as subject of the biography and as personal author:
           1. Holmes, Oliver Wendell, 1809-1894.
           I. Holmes, Oliver Wendell, 1809-1894. II. Title.

Fig. 9.31. Rule 21.15. Edited biographical work.

Main entry ——→ Dover, Thomas, 1660-1742.
under author   Thomas Dover's life and Legacy / edited and
                 introduced by Kenneth Dewhurst

Make added entry for editor:
           I. Dewhurst, Kenneth, ed. II. Title.

Art Works (Rules 21.16-21.17)

RULE 21.16. ADAPTATIONS OF ART WORKS

AACR 2 defines "Art works" as "paintings, engravings, photographs, drawings, sculptures, etc., and any other creative work that can be represented pictorially (e.g., ceramic designs, tapestries, fabrics)."[14]

21.16A. When an art work is adapted from one medium to another, the main entry is the adapter, or the title if the adapter is unknown. A name-title added entry is made for the original. *See* Fig. 9.32.

21.16B. When an art work is reproduced, however, the main entry is the heading for the original, with an added entry for the person or body responsible for the reproduction. *See* Fig. 9.33.

RULE 21.17. REPRODUCTIONS OF TWO OR MORE ART WORKS

21.17A.   **Without text**

If a work consists of reproductions of an artist's works, and there is no text, the main entry is the artist.

21.17B.   **With text**

When text accompanies reproductions of an artist's works, entry is under the personal heading for the author of the text if that person is represented as author in the chief source of information; an added entry is made under the heading for the artist. Otherwise, or in case of doubt, entry is made under the heading for the artist with an added entry for the person mentioned in the chief source of information as having written the text. *See* Figs. 9.34 and 9.35.

**Fig. 9.32. Rule 21.16A. Adaptation entered under heading
for title because adapter is unknown.**

1

[1]Main entry
under title
(adapter
unknown)

[Mona Lisa] [picture] / [computer representation
of the original by Leonardo da Vinci, produced via program written at IBM]

Copies distributed at demonstrations of IBM
equipment.   2

[2]Name-title
added entry for
original work

I. Leonardo, da Vinci, 1452-1519. Mona Lisa.

[3]Added entry for
responsible
corporate body

II. IBM.

3

**Fig. 9.33. Rule 21.16B. Reproduction of art work entered under
heading for the artist.**

Main entry ⟶ Hobbema, Meindert, 1638-1709.
under artist   View on a high road [picture] / Hobbema ; National Gallery of Art.

Make added entry for body responsible for reproduction:
            I. National Gallery of Art (U.S.).
            II. Title.

**Fig. 9.34. Rule 21.17B. Art reproductions with text entered under
author of text.**

Main entry ⟶ Cassou, Jean, 1897-
under author   Rembrandt / par Jean Cassou
of text

Make added entry for artist:
            I. Rembrandt Harmenszoon van Rijn, 1606-1669.

Fig. 9.35. Rule 21.17B. Art reproductions with text entered under artist.

Main entry ⟶ Rembrandt Harmenszoon van Rijn, 1606-1669.
under artist   More drawings of Rembrandt / introduction
by Stephen Longstreet.

Make added entry for author of text:
            I. Longstreet, Stephen, 1907-   II. Title.

Musical Works (Rules 21.18-21.22)

RULE 21.18.   GENERAL RULE

21.18A.   Scope

This rule applies to all kinds of arrangements of musical works where medium of performance has been changed; the original has been simplified; the new work is described as "based on," etc.; new material has been incorporated; or the harmony or style of the original has been changed.

21.18B.   A musical arrangement is defined as a "musical work, or a portion thereof, rewritten for a medium of performance different from that for which the work was originally intended."[15] A "simplified version of a work for the same medium of performance" is also regarded as an arrangement. The general rule for a musical arrangement is to enter it under the heading for the original composer whenever possible. An added entry is made for the name of the arranger. *See* Fig. 9.36.

Fig. 9.36. Rule 21.18. Arrangement of musical work entered under original composer.

Main entry ———► Mozart, Wolfgang Amadeus, 1756-1791.
under   Eighth quintet, k. 614, fourth movement / W.
composer   A. Mozart ; arranged for 2 B♭ trumpets, horn,
                              trombone & tuba by Ralph Lockwood.

Make added entry for arranger:
                              I. Lockwood, Ralph.

21.18C.   A musical work that is an adaptation represents a more serious departure from the original work than does an arrangement. Thus, generally, the main entry is made under the heading for the adapter, with an added entry given to the author of the original work. Three types of adaptations of music are specified for entry under adapter:

   "1)   a distinct alteration of another work (e.g., a free transcription)

   2)   a paraphrase of various works or of the general style of another composer

   3)   a work merely based on other music (e.g., variations on a theme)."[16]

In case of doubt about whether a work is an adaptation, it is to be treated as an arrangement, transcription, etc. *See* Fig. 9.37.

Fig. 9.37. Rule 21.18. Adaptation of musical work
entered under adapter.

Main entry   ⟶ Brahms, Johannes, 1833-1897.
under   Variations and fugue on a theme by Handel,
adapter   op. 24 / Johannes Brahms.

Note explaining the scope of the item:
        The theme is that of the Aria con variazioni
        from Handel's Suite for harpsichord, 2nd collec-
        tion, no. 1.

Make name-title added entry for original work:
        I. Handel, George Frideric, 1685-1759. Suite,
        harpsichord, 2nd collection, no. 1, B♭ major. Aria
        con variazioni.

RULE 21.19.   MUSICAL WORKS THAT INCLUDE WORDS

21.19A.   General rule

If a musical work includes words, the main entry is for the composer with
an added entry for the writer of the words, if the writer's work is represented,
as in a full score or a vocal score, for example. A name-title added entry is
made for an original text upon which the words may have been based.
Librettos are treated under another rule: 21.28. *See* Fig. 9.38.

Fig. 9.38. Rule 21.19A. Musical comedy entered under composer.

Main entry   ⟶ Adler, Richard
under composer   The pajama game : a musical comedy / music
        and lyrics by Richard Adler and Jerry Ross ; book
        by George Abbott.

Note expanding statement of responsibility:
        "Based on the novel '7½ cents' by Richard
        Bissell."

Make added entries for shared composer and for writer, and an added name-title entry for
original text:
        I. Ross, Jerry. II. Abbot, George. III. Bissell,
        Richard. 7½ cents. IV. Title.

21.19C.   Writer's works set by several composers

If the work or works of one writer are set in a collection of songs, etc., by two or more composers, entry is made according to the rule for collections, 21.7. *See* Fig. 9.39.

Fig. 9.39. Rule 21.19C. Collection of songs with words by one writer and music by several composers; entered as a collection under title.

Title main   ⟶ A Shakespeare song book / edited by H. A.
entry   Chambers.

Make added entry for writer of words and for editor:
            I. Shakespeare, William, 1564-1616. II. Chambers, H. A.

RULE 21.20.   MUSICAL SETTINGS FOR BALLETS, ETC.

Main entry for the musical setting for ballets, etc., is the composer. Added entries are made for writers of librettos, choreographers, etc., if their names appear in the chief source of information. *See* Fig. 9.40.

Fig. 9.40. Rule 21.20. Music for a ballet entered under composer.

Main entry   ⟶ Nabokov, Nicolas.
for composer   Don Quichotte : ballet en 3 actes / Nicolas
                 Nabokov ; libretto par Nicolas Nabokov et
                 Georges Balanchine.

Make added entry for shared author of libretto:
            I. Balanchine, Georges. II. Title.

RULE 21.21.   ADDED ACCOMPANIMENTS, ETC.

If accompaniment or parts have been added to a musical work, main entry is made for the original work, with an added entry for the composer of the accompaniment or parts.

RULE 21.22.   LITURGICAL MUSIC

Music that is officially part of a liturgy is treated under the rules for religious publications. *See* 21.39.

Sound Recordings (Rule 21.23)

RULE 21.23.   ENTRY OF SOUND RECORDINGS

It should be noted that this rule applies only to sound recordings that are modifications of other works. This includes readings of texts and perform-ances of musical works. There is no rule specifically for sound recordings con-sidered to constitute new works, such as recordings of improvisations and lec-tures. These items would be entered according to the principles of responsibility found in the basic rules. Such works as interviews made as oral history could be entered according to the principles in 21.25.

It should be noted also that this rule must be used in conjunction with Rule 6.1G. If under 6.1G it is decided that a sound recording lacking a collec-tive title should be described as a unit, then one of Rules 21.23B-21.23D will be applied. If, however, it is decided to make a separate description for each separately titled work, Rule 21.23A will be applied.

21.23A.   One work

Main entry for a sound recording of one work is the heading appropriate to that work. The rule specifically calls for added entries for the principal performers unless there are more than three, in which case an added entry is made for the first-named principal performer. A rule interpretation from LC points out that added entries should also be made for those prescribed by the rules under which the choice of main entry for the work is made.[17] *See* Fig. 9.41.

Fig. 9.41. Rule 21.23A. Sound recording entered under author of original work.

Main entry ⟶ Rey, Margret.
under author   Curious George learns the alphabet [sound re-
                             cording] / Margret & H. A. Rey.

Note expanding statement of responsibility:
                             Read by Julie Harris.

Make added entry for shared author and for reader:
                             I. Rey, H. A. (Hans Agusto), 1898-   II.
                             Harris, Julie. III. Title.

21.23B.   Two or more works by the same person(s) or body(ies)

Main entry for a sound recording of works that are all the responsibility of the same person(s) or body(ies) is the heading appropriate to those works. Added entries are made for performers and for additional responsible persons or bodies as explained above under 21.23A. *See* Fig. 9.42.

Fig. 9.42. Rule 21.23B. Sound recording entered under composer
of the several works performed.

Main entry ———▸ Chopin, Frédéric, 1810-1849.
under   The 24 preludes [sound recording] / Chopin.
composer

Note expanding statement of responsibility:
              Alexander Brailowsky, pianist.

Make added entry for performer:
              I. Brailowsky, Alexander. II. Title.

21.23C.   Works by different persons or bodies. Collective title

Main entry for a sound recording of works by different persons or bodies
that has a collective title is the person or body represented as principal
performer. If there are two or three principal performers, main entry is the
first named, with added entries for the others. A rule interpretation from LC
gives guidance in deciding whom to consider "principal performers." This rule
interpretation should be consulted for further detail.[18] *See* Fig. 9.43.

Fig. 9.43. Rule 21.23C. Sound recording entered under principal performer.

Main entry ———▸ Boston Pops Orchestra.
under princi-   Greatest hits of the '50s [sound recording].
pal performer
Note expanding statement of responsibility:
              Boston Pops Orchestra; Arthur Fiedler,
           conductor

Make added entry under principal performer:
              I. Fiedler, Arthur, 1894-1979. II. Title.

A sound recording with four or more principal performers or no principal
performers is given main entry under title. *See* Fig. 9.44.

Fig. 9.44. Rule 21.23C. Sound recording entered under title.

Main entry ———▸ Firestone presents your favorite Christmas music
under title   [sound recording]

Note expanding statement of responsibility:
              Julie Andrews; Vic Damone; Dorothy Kirsten;
           James McCracken; The Young Americans; with
           the Firestone Orchestra, conducted by Irwin
           Kostal.

21.23D.   Works by different persons or bodies. No collective title

This rule applies to a sound recording that contains works by different persons or bodies, that has no collective title, and that is to be cataloged as a unit. Treatment depends upon the decision about whether participation of the performer(s) goes beyond mere performance, execution, or interpretation.

Popular, rock, and jazz music are usually considered to have participation of performers beyond execution or interpretation. In these cases main entry is under principal performer, if there is one; under the first of two or three principal performers; or under the heading appropriate to the first work if there are four or more principal performers. Added entries are made for the performers not named as main entry if there are not more than three. *See* Figs. 9.45 and 9.46.

Fig. 9.45. Rule 21.23D. Sound recording entered under principal performer.

Main entry ──────▶ Holmes, Rupert.
under principal   Escape : (the pina colada song) [sound recording] /
performer   [written and sung by] Rupert Holmes. Drop it /
                        [written and sung by] Rupert Holmes.

Fig. 9.46. Rule 21.23D. Sound recording entered under heading for first work.

Main entry ──────▶ Little white duck. Mary had a little lamb [sound
under title   recording].
of 1st work

Note expanding statement of responsibility:
                        Recording sung by Betty Wells, Bill Marine and The
                        Playmates with orchestra directed by Maury Laws
                        (side A), The 4 Cricketones with orch. and chorus
                        (side B).

Classical and other "serious" music is usually considered to have participation of performers that does not go beyond execution or interpretation. For these works, main entry is under the heading appropriate to the first work with added entries for the other works if appropriate as explained under 21.7C.

MIXED RESPONSIBILITY IN NEW WORKS

RULE 21.24. COLLABORATION BETWEEN ARTIST AND WRITER

If a work appears to be a collaborative effort between an artist and a writer, rather than an artist's illustrations of a writer's text (covered by 21.11A), main entry is under the one named first in the chief source of information, unless the other one is given greater prominence by typography, etc. *See* Fig. 9.47.

Fig. 9.47. Rule 21.24. Collaborative work entered under artist.

Main entry
under artist
named first
on title page

⟶ Mair, A. J. (Alice Joy).
    More homes of the pioneers and other build-
ings : pen and wash drawings / by A. J. Mair ;
with text by J. A. Hendry. –

Make added entry for author:
    I. Hendry, J. A. (John A.). II. Title.

RULE 21.25.   REPORTS OF INTERVIEWS OR EXCHANGES

Whether to give main entry to the reporter or to one of the other participants in an interview or exchange depends upon how much the words are those
of the reporter and how much those of the other participant(s). If the report
gives essentially the words of the interviewee or other participant, main entry is
the principal participant, first-named participant, or title, if there are more
than three equal participants. An added entry is made for an openly named
reporter. If the report, for the most part, consists of the words of the reporter,
main entry is for the reporter, with added entry(ies) for the persons
interviewed (or for only the first if there are more than three). *See* Figs. 9.48
and 9.49.

Fig. 9.48. Rule 21.25A. Interview entered under the first named participant.

Main entry
under first-
named partici-
pant

⟶ Scott, David Randolph.
    Interview from deep space [sound recording] /
by David Randolph Scott, Alfred Merrill
Worden, and James Benson Irwin.

Make added entries for other participants:
    I. Worden, Alfred Merrill. II. Irwin, James
Benson. III. Title.

Fig. 9.49. Rule 21.25B. Interview entered under reporter.

Main entry
under
reporter

⟶ Schneider, Duane.
    An interview with Anaïs Nin / Duane
Schneider.

Make added entry for person interviewed:
    I. Nin, Anaïs, 1903-

RELATED WORKS:

SELECTED RULES AND EXAMPLES

RULE 21.28.   RELATED WORKS

21.28A.   Scope

According to Rule 1.9, supplementary items may be described separately or dependently (i.e., described as accompanying material; or in a note; or in a multilevel description, further described in 13.6). This rule (21.28) applies only to separately cataloged works that are related to another work. It includes continuations, sequels, supplements, indexes, concordances, incidental music to dramatic works, cadenzas, scenarios, screenplays, choreographies, subseries, special numbers of serials, and collections of extracts from serials. It does not apply to works that have only subject relationship to other works, or to the particular types of relationship covered in 21.8-21.27.

In *AACR 2* proper, this rule includes librettos, but an alternative rule for librettos is given in a footnote. The Library of Congress has decided to apply the alternative rule for librettos because "librettos are normally sought as an adjunct to the music."[19] Therefore, librettos are entered by LC under the heading for the musical work, with an added entry under the personal heading for the librettist. A name-title added entry is also made under the heading for the original text on which the libretto is based, if this applies. *See* Fig. 9.50.

Fig. 9.50. Rule 21.28A, footnote 7. Libretto entered under heading appropriate to the musical work.

Main entry   ⟶ Laderman, Ezra.
for composer   [Galileo Galilei. Libretto. English]
           Galileo Galilei : an opera-oratorio in three acts
      / libretto by Joe Darion ; music by Ezra
      Laderman.

Note providing other title information:
           Original title: The trials of Galileo.

Make added entry for librettist:
           I. Darion, Joseph. II. Title. III. Title: The trials
      of Galileo.

21.28B.   General rule

Main entry for a related work is the heading appropriate to it as if it were an independent work. An added entry is made for the name-title or title (whichever is main entry) of the related work. An added entry is not made, however, for the related work in the case of a sequel by the same author. LC has made some other exceptions to making added entries for the related works that apply to excerpts from serials, indexes, and census data.[20] *See* Figs. 9.51-9.54.

**Fig. 9.51. Rule 21.28B. Supplement cataloged separately and
entered under author.**

Main entry   ——▸ Gore, Marvin.
for author   Elements of systems analysis for business data
of   processing. Instructional supplement / Marvin
supplement   Gore, John Stubbe.

Make added entry for co-author of supplement:
               I. Stubbe, John.   II. Title.

Note that a name-title added entry is not made because it would, in essence, be
a duplication of the main entry and title given before the words "Instructional
supplement."

Fig. 9.52. Rule 21.28B. Concordance entered under its own author.

Entry under   ——▸ Williams, Mary.
compiler of   The Dickens concordance, being a compen-
the   dium of names and characters and principal
concordance   places mentioned in all the works of Charles
               Dickens ... / by Mary Williams.

Make added entry for author of works to which this work is related:
               I. Dickens, Charles, 1812-1870.   II. Title.

**Fig. 9.53. Rule 21.28B. Collection of extracts from a serial
entered as a collection. [Joyce is the subject of these essays].**

Main entry appro- James Joyce essays / by Brian O'Nolan ... [et al.].
priate to related
work in hand

Note providing bibliographic history:
             "These essays were first published in Envoy,
             1951."

Make added entry for first-named author and for serial from which essays were extracted:
               I. O'Nolan, Brian, 1911-1966.   II. Envoy
             (Dublin)

Fig. 9.54. Rule 21.28B. Index entered under its own author.

Main entry   ——▸ Schneider, Ben Ross, 1920-
for compiler   Index to The London stage, 1660-1800 / com-
of index   piled, with an introduction by Ben Ross Schneider, Jr. ;
               foreword by George Winchester Stone, Jr.

Make added entry for serial indexed:
               I. The London stage, 1660-1800.   II. Title.

ADDED ENTRIES:

SELECTED RULES AND EXAMPLES

RULE 21.29.   GENERAL RULE

The preceding rules have indicated the added entries required in typical circumstances to supplement the main entry by providing additional bibliographical access to materials represented in the catalog. In general, added entries are suggested to provide access to other names of persons or titles under which a work may be known and under which catalog users might reasonably search. Persons, corporate bodies, and works related to the work at hand are considered, providing these are openly stated in the work. It is a matter of local library policy to establish certain administrative procedures to make all required added entries, which in turn must be related to the extent of the collection, the needs it serves, and some economic considerations.

It is prescribed here that if the cataloger believes an added entry is needed, and if the reason for an added entry is not clear from the body of the description, a note should be provided to justify the added entry.

An option provides for explanatory references in place of certain added entries (as in 26.5); the Library of Congress is not applying this option.[21]

LC prescribes the following order for added entries:

"1)   Personal name;

2)   Personal name/title;

3)   Corporate name;

4)   Corporate name/title;

5)   Uniform title (all instances of works entered under title);

6)   Title traced as Title-period;

7)   Title traced as Title-colon, followed by a title;

8)   Series."[22]

LC has given guidelines in addition to those in *AACR 2* for making added entries for audiovisual materials and for sound recordings. These should be consulted when appropriate.[23]

RULE 21.30.   SPECIFIC RULES

21.30A-21.30H, 21.30K, 21.30M.

These specific rules for added entries for collaborators, writers, editors and compilers, corporate bodies, other related persons or bodies, related works, other relationships, translators, illustrators, and analytical entries have been touched on in the rules for choice of main entry. When particular guidance is needed for one of these cases, these rules in *AACR 2* should be consulted. One should also consult LC rule interpretations for 21.30E, Corporate bodies; 21.30G, Related works; 21.30H, Other relationships; and 21.30M, Analytical entries.[24] *See* Figs. 9.55 and 9.57.

Two added entry rules are used with such frequency that they warrant special mention:

21.30J.   Titles

There are only four instances in which an added entry for a title proper (that is not a main entry) should not be made:

"1)   the title proper is essentially the same as the main entry heading or a reference to that heading

or   2)   the title proper has been composed by the cataloguer

or   3)   in a catalogue in which name-title and subject entries are interfiled, the title proper is identical with a subject heading, or a direct reference to a subject heading used for the work

or   4)   a conventionalized uniform title has been used in an entry for a musical work (*see* 25.25-25.36)."[25]

See Figs. 9.55-9.57.

Added entries should also be made for any other title (e.g., cover title) that differs significantly (according to 21.2A) from the title proper.

LC does not apply restrictions 1) and 3) in the above list. An extensive rule interpretation gives guidelines for making title added entries, and for tracing them. Guidance is also given for tracing spelled-out forms of abbreviations, numerals, etc., as well as the non-spelled-out forms.[26]

21.30L.   Series

An added entry is made for a series on each record for each work in the series if it is judged to be a useful access point. Adding the numeric or other designation to each added entry is optional. This option is applied at the Library of Congress.[27] *See* Fig. 9.56.

Fig. 9.55. Rule 21.30D. Added entry for editor.

───► Hollindale, Peter.

Shakespeare, William, 1564-1616.
    As you like it / [by William Shakespeare] ; edited by Peter
Hollindale.

Added entry noted in tracing:
    I. Hollindale, Peter. II. Title.

Fig. 9.56. Rule 21.30L. Added entry for series.

───► Studies in folklore ; 2.

Dundes, Alan.
    Analytic essays in folklore / by Alan Dundes.

Use of series area:
    – (Studies in folklore ; 2)

Added entry noted in tracing:
    I. Title. II. Series.

Fig. 9.57. Rule 21.30K1. Added entry for translator.

───►Wiemann, Rudolph.

Busch, Wilhelm, 1832-1908.
    The bees : a fairy tale / by Wilhelm Busch ; translated by
Rudolph Wiemann.

Notes providing information on translation and summary:
    Translation of: Schnurrdiburr.
    Verse.
    Summary: Relates in verse the adventures and misadven-
tures of a hive of bees and the bee keeper, his daughter, and
their neighbors.

Added entry noted in tracing:
    I. Wiemann, Rudolph. II. Title.

Series added entries are not made if the series shares only common physical characteristics or if the series numbering appears to be only publisher's stock control numbers.

LC has added two categories for which it will not make added entries: commercially published series in which the title is only indicative of a literary genre, and commercially published series in which the title gives no indication of the content, genre, audience, or purpose. Guidance is also given in LC's rule interpretation as to which types of series should always be traced and for the form of the series added entry tracing.[28]

SPECIAL RULES:

SELECTED RULES AND EXAMPLES

CERTAIN LEGAL PUBLICATIONS

RULE 21.31.   LAWS, ETC.

21.31A.   Scope

This rule is applied to legislative enactments and decrees that have the force of law except for the following cases, which are treated in later rules: administrative regulations (21.32), constitutions and charters (21.33), court rules (21.34), and treaties (21.35).

21.31B.   Laws of modern jurisdictions

21.31B1.   Laws governing one jurisdiction

Laws governing one jurisdiction are entered under the heading for the jurisdiction they govern, with added entries for persons and corporate bodies (other than legislative bodies) that compiled or issued the laws. A uniform title is added as instructed in 25.15A (*see* chapter 13 of this text). *See* Fig. 9.58.

Fig. 9.58. Rule 21.31B1. Laws governing a single jurisdiction.

Name of ⎯⎯⎯⎯➤United States.
jurisdiction   ⎯[Tax reduction act of 1975]
Uniform title,⎯⎯⎯   Tax reduction act of 1975, P.L. 94-12, as signed
see Rule 25.15A   by the President on March 29, 1975 : law and ex-
                              planation. – Chicago : Commerce Clearing
                              House, [1975]

Make added entry for corporate body issuing or compiling the law:
                              I. Commerce Clearing House.   II. Title.

21.31B2.   Laws governing more than one jurisdiction
A compilation of laws governing more than one jurisdiction is treated as a collection (*see* 21.7).

RULE 21.32.   ADMINISTRATIVE REGULATIONS, ETC.

The purpose of this rule is to distinguish between administrative regulations that are promulgated by government agencies under authority granted by one or more laws (as in the United States) and those that are from jurisdictions in which such regulations are laws (as in the United Kingdom and Canada). The former are entered under the promulgating agency, while the latter are entered as instructed in 21.31. *See* Figs. 9.59 and 9.60.

Fig. 9.59. Rule 21.32. U.S. administrative regulation entered under promulgating agency.

Main entry ———▶ United States. Internal Revenue Service.
under promulgat-   Estate tax regulations under the Internal
ing agency   Revenue Code of 1954 / [United States Treasury
        Department, Internal Revenue Service]

Make added entry under heading for uniform title for authorizing law:
        I. United States. [Internal Revenue Code of
        1954]. II. Title.

Fig. 9.60. Rule 21.32. U.K. administrative regulation entered under the jurisdiction.

Main entry ———▶ Great Britain.
under   [Army Code No. 13206]
jurisdiction   The Queen's regulations for the Army, 1975 /
        United Kingdom, Ministry of Defence

Make added entry for promulgating agency:
        I. Great Britain. Ministry of Defence. II. Title.

It should be noted that although *AACR 2* uses "United Kingdom" instead of "Great Britain" in all its examples, LC and other national libraries have decided to continue using "Great Britain" on their records. See the discussion in chapter 11 on page 296.

RULE 21.33.   CONSTITUTIONS, CHARTERS, AND OTHER FUNDA-
        MENTAL LAWS

21.33A.   Main entry for a constitution, charter, or other fundamental law of a jurisdiction is the jurisdiction. *See* Fig. 9.61.

Fig. 9.61. Rule 21.33. Entry for constitution.

Political   ──────► Wyoming.
jurisdiction   Constitution of the State of Wyoming,
adopted in convention at Cheyenne, Wyoming,
September 30, 1889, including all amendments
adopted to Nov. 2, 1976 / compiled by Linda
Mosley.

Make added entry for compiler:
           I. Mosley, Linda.

RULE 21.35. TREATIES, INTERGOVERNMENTAL AGREEMENTS, ETC.

21.35A.   **International treaties, etc.**

A treaty between one national government and two others is given main
entry for the government that is the only one on its side. Other types of treaties
between two or three national governments are given main entry for the
government whose heading is first in English alphabetic order. (*See* Rule 24.3E
for establishment of each heading.) Added entries are made for the other
governments. A uniform title is also made according to 25.16B1.

A treaty between more than three national governments is given main
entry under title—either title proper or uniform title according to 25.16B2. *See*
Fig. 9.62.

Fig. 9.62. Rule 21.35A1. Treaty involving two countries.

¹Entry under   Singapore. ◄──── 1
country alpha-   [Treaties, etc. Switzerland, 1969 Feb. 28]
betically first   Diplomatic notes modifying the annex to the
²Uniform title   2 air services agreement between the Government
for main and   of the Republic of Singapore and the Govern-
added entries   ment of the Swiss Confederation signed at
Singapore on 28th February, 1969.

Make added entry for the second-named country: 2
           I. Switzerland. [Treaties, etc. Singapore. 1969
Feb. 28]. II. Title: Diplomatic notes modifying
the annex to the air services agreement.

CERTAIN RELIGIOUS PUBLICATIONS

RULE 21.37. SACRED SCRIPTURES

Main entry for a work that is accepted as sacred scripture by a religious
group is title. The uniform title is constructed according to 25.17-25.18. An
added entry is made for a person associated with the work. *See* Fig. 9.63.

Fig. 9.63. Rule 21.37. Sacred scripture entered under uniform title.

Uniform title ───►Tipiṭaka. Suttapiṭaka. English. Selections.
main entry   Some sayings of the Buddha, according to the
                  Pali canon / translated [from the Pali] by F. L.
                  Woodward ; with an introduction by Christmas
                  Humphreys.

Make added entries for persons associated with the work:
          I. Woodward, F. L. (Frank Lee), 1870 or 71-
          1952. II. Humphreys, Christmas, 1901-   III.
          Tipiṭaka. Vinayapiṭaka. English. Selections. IV.
          Title.

RULE 21.39.   LITURGICAL WORKS

21.39A.   General rule

Liturgical works include "officially sanctioned or traditionally accepted texts of religious observance, books of obligatory prayers to be offered at stated times, and calendars and manuals of performance of religious observances."[29] These are to be entered under the heading for the church or denomination that uses them. An appropriate uniform title, using 25.19-25.23, is added to the main entry. *See* Fig. 9.64.

Fig. 9.64. Rule 21.39A. Liturgical work entered under heading for the church.

Corporate head-   Catholic Church.
ing for specific   [Rite of ordination. English]
church   The ordination of deacons, priests, and bish-
Uniform title   ops : provisional text prepared by the Interna-
                  tional Committee on English in the Liturgy, ap-
                  proved for interim use by the Bishops' Commit-
                  tee on the Liturgy, National Conference of
                  Catholic Bishops, and confirmed by the
                  Apostolic See.

Make added entry for title:
          I. Title.

21.39C.   Jewish liturgical works

Main entry for a Jewish liturgical work is title, with the uniform title being constructed according to 25.21-25.22. An added entry is made for a body that makes special use of the work. *See* Fig. 9.65.

Fig. 9.65. Rule 21.39C. Jewish liturgical work entered under uniform title.

Main entry ──────▶ Maḥzor (1972). English & Hebrew.
under uniform   Maḥzor for Rosh Hashanah and Yom Kippur :
title   a prayer book for the Days of Awe / edited by
                  Jules Harlow. – New York : Rabbinical Assembly,
                  [1972]

Make added entry for editor and make added entry for body that uses the work:
                  I. Harlow, Jules. II. Rabbinical Assembly of
                  America.

───────────────

NOTES

[1]*AACR 2*, p. 2 (paragraph 0.5).

[2]For example, see Seymour Lubetzky, "The Fundamentals of Bibliographic Cataloging and *AACR 2*," *in* International Conference on AACR 2, Florida State University, 1979, *The Making of a Code* (Chicago, American Library Association, 1980), pp. 18-23; Michael Gorman, "*AACR 2*: Main Themes," in ibid., pp. 45-46; Elizabeth L. Tate, "Examining the 'Main' in Main Entry Headings" in ibid., pp. 109-140.

[3]*Cataloging Service Bulletin*, no. 12 (Spring 1981): 21.

[4]*Cataloging Service Bulletin*, no. 18 (Fall 1982): 29-30.

[5]*AACR 2*, p. 284.

[6]Ibid.

[7]*Cataloging Service Bulletin*, no. 22 (Fall 1983): 21-23.

[8]*Cataloging Service Bulletin*, no. 25 (Summer 1984): 51-55.

[9]*Cataloging Service Bulletin*, no. 18 (Fall 1982): 34-35.

[10]*Cataloging Service Bulletin*, no. 25 (Summer 1984): 55-57.

[11]*AACR 2*, p. 292.

[12]*Cataloging Service Bulletin*, no. 13 (Summer 1981): 20.

[13]*Cataloging Service Bulletin*, no. 27 (Winter 1985): 20-22.

[14]*AACR 2*, p. 308.

[15]Ibid., p. 563.

[16]Ibid., p. 310.

[17]*Cataloging Service Bulletin*, no. 25 (Summer 1984): 57.

[18]Ibid., pp. 58-61.

[19]"AACR 2 Options to Be Followed by the Library of Congress, Chapters 1-2, 12, 21-26," *Library of Congress Information Bulletin*, 37 (July 21, 1978): 425.

[20]*Cataloging Service Bulletin*, no. 24 (Spring 1984): 12.

[21]*Cataloging Service Bulletin*, no. 8 (Spring 1980): 12.

[22]*Cataloging Service Bulletin*, no. 12 (Spring 1981): 24.

[23]*Cataloging Service Bulletin*, no. 13 (Summer 1981): 24-26.

[24]Rule interpretations for the following added entry rules are found in the following issues of *Cataloging Service Bulletin* (*CSB*): Rule 21.30E—*CSB* 13 (Summer 1981): 26-27; Rule 21.30G—*CSB* 20 (Spring 1983): 11; Rule 21.30H—*CSB* 20 (Spring 1983): 12; Rule 21.30M—*CSB* 20 (Spring 1983): 12-14.

[25]*AACR 2*, p. 324.

[26]*Cataloging Service Bulletin*, no. 27 (Winter 1985): 20-29.

[27]*Cataloging Service Bulletin*, no. 8 (Spring 1980): 13.

[28]*Cataloging Service Bulletin*, no. 22 (Fall 1983): 23-26.

[29]*AACR 2*, p. 343.

SUGGESTED READING

Chan, Lois Mai. *Cataloging and Classification*. New York, McGraw-Hill, 1981. Chapter 4.

Hagler, Ronald, and Peter Simmons. *The Bibliographic Record and Information Technology*. Chicago, American Library Association, 1982. pp. 217-220.

Maxwell, Margaret F. Handbook for *AACR 2*. Chicago, American Library Association, 1980. Chapter 11.

Tate, Elizabeth L. "Examining the 'Main' in Main Entry Headings," *in* International Conference on AACR 2, Florida State University, 1979, *The Making of a Code* (Chicago, American Library Association, 1980), pp. 109-140.

10
Form of Headings for Persons

INTRODUCTION

The previous chapter dealt with choice of access points; this chapter and the next three chapters will present rules for the form of entry regardless of whether the access point is to be a main entry or an added entry. Once it has been decided what is to be the main entry or heading and what are to be added entries, it must be determined how those entries are to be displayed or written on the record. Choice of entry rules deal with who or what is to be the entry; form of entry rules deal with how an entry is to be written or recorded.

Most headings in American library catalogs consist of a personal name entered under the surname followed by forenames (like the white pages of a telephone directory). However, as the following rules for headings for persons show, there are certain complexities that must be considered in a library catalog. Rules—i.e., principles and practices—must be followed consistently for those persons known by more than one name. There are many possible instances when a person may be known and/or even write under more than one name. Some authors deliberately disguise their real names and write under a pseudonym or pen name—such as Charles Lutwidge Dodgson, who wrote his children's fantasies under the pseudonym of Lewis Carroll. Others consistently write under initialized forenames (e.g., H. G. Wells), while still others, such as Bernard Shaw, consistently omit one of their forenames. If someone's original name is written in a nonroman alphabet, different romanization systems may create different spellings of the name (such as Chekhov, Chekov, or Tchekhov). A married woman has two possible surnames—her birth surname and her husband's surname. Further, compound surnames—i.e., surnames consisting of two or more parts—create problems. Granville-Barker is an example of a compound, hyphenated English surname. Prefixes to surnames create another type of compound surname. De Gaulle and von Goethe are examples of surnames with prefixes; O'Brien and MacPherson are other examples. Individuals who are members of nobility may have two names—a titled name and a common surname (such as Lord Byron, George Gordon Byron). Certain individuals are known under their bynames or forenames rather than their surnames; these include royalty (Elizabeth II), saints (Joan of Arc), popes (Paul VI), and individuals in ancient and medieval periods prior to the development of surnames (Horace). Bynames or forenames often exist in different forms in different languages (such as Horace in English, but Horatius in Latin). The purpose of this chapter is to demonstrate the general rules used to resolve all of these problems. For more complicated problems of personal names, the student should carefully examine *AACR 2*, chapter 22.

The *AACR 2* chapter is divided into four sections, the first three of which suggest the order of the steps taken by the cataloger to establish the form in which the name will appear as a heading in the catalog. The first section, Rules 22.1-22.3, is entitled "Choice of name." This "choice" is a separate action from "choice of access points," discussed in the preceding chapter. Once it has been decided through choice of access points that a person will be given an access point, Rules 22.1-22.3 prescribe the choice of name when that person has used more than one name or different manifestations of the same name. After making a choice of name, the cataloger uses the next section, Rules 22.4-22.11, "Entry element," to decide which element of the chosen name will be the first, and in what order the other elements will follow. The third step is to make any additions to the name that may be necessitated because of the kind of name involved (Rules 22.12-22.17), or because two or more names are identical (Rules 22.18-22.20). The fourth section of *AACR 2*, chapter 22, is "Special Rules for Names in Certain Languages." These are for selected languages in which heading form does not follow the typical "western" style.

It should be noted that the rules in this chapter apply to the choice and form of personal names whether they are access points because of some kind of responsibility for the creation of a work or because they are the subject of a work. That is, a personal name subject heading is constructed in the same manner and according to the same rules as is a personal name main or added entry heading for an author, painter, performer, etc.

The Library of Congress adopted *AACR 2* for new names beginning January 2, 1981. It also abandoned the policy of superimposition at that time so that a number of already established name forms were changed to agree with the prescribed *AACR 2* form. Superimposition was a policy established with the adoption of *AACR 1* in 1967. Under that policy any name that had been established prior to *AACR 1* continued to be used on new cataloging as already established, even if its form according to *AACR 1* would have been different. Even though this policy was officially abandoned with the adoption of *AACR 2*, in certain defined categories, established names were considered to be "*AACR 2* compatible," and the established form continued to be used even on new records. However, after the initial impact of adopting *AACR 2* was over, it became counterproductive to continue the "compatible" policy, because it took more time to decide on such headings than to change the old forms. Therefore, the "compatible" policy was abandoned on September 1, 1982.[1] All pre-*AACR 2* headings coded as compatible between January 2, 1981, and September 1, 1982, remain in that form at LC. Thus, it is useful to be aware of some of the major cases. These are summarized with examples in an issue of *Cataloging Service Bulletin*, which should be consulted by anyone who works with cataloging copy from LC.[2]

A heading created using this chapter is coded 100, 600, 700, or 800 in the MARC format, depending upon whether it functions as a main entry, a subject heading, or an added entry, or begins a series tracing.

CHOICE OF NAME:

SELECTED RULES AND EXAMPLES

RULE 22.1. GENERAL RULE

22.1A. The name by which a person is commonly known is the one that should be chosen, whether that name be the person's real name, nickname, pseudonym, shortened form of name, or other form of name customarily used by a person. Thus the following choices might be made:

Pseudonym

Mathew James

not birth name: James D. Lucey

Nickname

Billy Graham

not William Franklin Graham

Name in religion

Maria Teresa dell'Eucaristia

not birth name: Maria Teresa Tosi

Short form of name

Virginia Knight Nelson

not Alyce Virginia Knight Nelson

Real name

Sally Benson

not pseudonym: Esther Evarts

22.1B. The name by which a person is commonly known is to be determined from chief sources of information of works in that person's language. This, of course, may not be possible if the person is only a subject of works or creates only nonverbal works (e.g., unsigned paintings). In these cases the name is to be determined from reference sources in the person's language or from the person's country of residence or activity.

A rule interpretation from LC indicates that chief sources used for this rule may be from works published both during and after a person's lifetime. The same rule interpretation also indicates that "reference sources" include books and articles written about a person. There are special instructions, also, about treatment of music composers, names without forenames, names containing abbreviations rather than initials, and other more unusual situations.[3]

Throughout this chapter of *AACR 2* there are references to "commonly known" and "predominant" when referring to choosing one name or one form of name. *AACR 2* defines predominant name as, "The name or form of name of a person or corporate body that appears most frequently (1) in the person's works or works issued by the corporate body; or (2) in reference sources, in that order of preference." We are told by the framers of *AACR 2* that "most frequently" should not be taken to mean 51 percent of the instances; yet nowhere is there any firm guideline. For a number of years, the Library of Congress used 75 percent in interpreting the "fullness of name" rule. That is, until a name appeared in a different form in an author's works 75 percent of the time (counting works by the person issued after the person's death as well as during the person's lifetime), the form of heading was not changed. They are continuing to apply this concept with *AACR 2*, except the percentage was changed to 66⅔ percent during the early years of *AACR 2* and later was changed to 80 percent. A note with the interpretation that gives the figure of 80 percent to be used with the rule for fullness (22.3A) cautions that this figure is to be applied only to 22.3A—that no formula has been assigned to the other rules.[4] However, other libraries might still use this as a guideline for changes. When a name is first established, "predominant" could be 51 percent or more; but a change would not be called for until the name had appeared differently 80 percent of the time.

22.1C.-22.1D.   Terms and punctuation associated with a name

These rules refer to inclusion of titles of nobility or honor, diacritical marks, and hyphens. At first glance it may not be clear how these relate to choice of name. However, the intention here is to give rules for choosing those elements that should be included in the heading. The order in which these elements appear is the subject of Rules 22.4-22.17.

The principle again is to follow the form customarily used by the person. Include titles, words, or phrases that commonly appear with the name. Include accents, other diacritical marks, and hyphens used by the person, except do not include a hyphen that is used between a forename and a surname.

RULE 22.2.   CHOICE AMONG DIFFERENT NAMES

Rules 22.2 and 22.3 give more specific guidelines for adhering to the principle stated in 22.1. Rules in 22.2 help choose among different names for the same person, and those in 22.3 help in the choice among different forms of the same name. Both may have to be used in a particular instance, because a name chosen from among different names may itself appear in varying degrees of fullness or with variant spellings. For example, once it has been decided that the name used should be George Novack, not William Warde, one then has to decide whether to use George Novack, George E. Novack, or George Edward Novack.

LC has noted that this rule applies to authors who have used both a nickname and the real name (e.g., Lucille/Luci). The name first should be tested for predominance; if none is found then the latest form is used, unless there is evidence that the nickname is being used as a pseudonym, in which case 22.2C3 may be considered. Once the real or nickname is established, it should not be changed until a different form appears in 80 percent of the author's works.[5]

22.2A. Predominant name

If a person is *known* by more than one name, and if there is a name that is clearly most common, it is used. If not, the following order of preference is used in making a choice:

"1)   the name that appears most frequently in the person's works

2)   the name that appears most frequently in reference sources

3)   the latest name."[6]

LC has noted that 22.2A or 22.3A, not 22.2C, should be used for an author who simultaneously uses different forms of a *real* name.[7] The same source notes that if a person's name is shown with a nickname in quotation marks or parentheses, the nickname should be omitted in the heading.

22.2B. Change of name

When a person has changed his or her name or has acquired and become known by a title of nobility, the latest name should be used for the heading. *See* Fig. 10.1.

Fig. 10.1. Rule 22.2B. Entry under latest name used.

Latest name
used
    Jackson, Barbara Ward, Lady, 1914-
       A new creation? : Reflections on the environ-
    mental issue / Barbara Ward (Lady Jackson).

Note: Refer from[8] Ward, Barbara, birth name used in writings before author's marriage.

22.2C. Pseudonyms

22.2C1. One pseudonym
When a person has used one pseudonym on all works or is predominantly shown in reference sources under one pseudonym, it is used for the heading, with a reference from the real name, if known. *See* Fig. 10.2.

Fig. 10.2. Rule 22.2C1. Entry under the one pseudonym
used by the author.

Ford, Ford Madox, 1873-1939.
     It was the nightingale / Ford Madox Ford.

Note: Refer from real name: Hueffer, Ford Madox.

22.2C2.   Predominant name

When a person has used several pseudonyms (and possibly also a real
name), it should be determined whether one of the names has become
predominant in 1) later editions of the person's works, 2) critical works, or 3)
other reference sources (in that order). If so, the heading is under the
predominant name with references under the other names. The cataloger is
instructed here to ignore reference sources that always enter persons under
their real names. *See* Fig. 10.3.

Fig. 10.3. Rule 22.2C2. Entry under pseudonym by which author
is predominantly known.

Carroll, Lewis, 1832-1898.
     The hunting of the snark / by Lewis Carroll ;
illustrated by Edward A. Wilson.

Note: Refer from real name: Dodgson, Charles Lutwidge.

22.2C3.   No predominant name

When no name predominates, each name is used as the heading for each
item that uses that name. References are made to connect the names according
to 26.2C and 26.2D. *See* Fig. 10.4.

Fig. 10.4. Rule 22.2C3. Entry under each pseudonym
for the same author.

McBain, Ed.
     The sentries / Ed McBain

Hunter, Evan.
     The blackboard jungle / Evan Hunter

Collins, Hunt.
     Cut me in / Hunt Collins

Marsten, Richard.
     Murder in the navy / Richard Marsten

Note: The author never wrote using his birth surname, Lombino. He changed
his name legally to Hunter. Make explanatory references to connect the various pseudonyms.

LC has restricted the application of this rule to situations in which an author has written two or more works under each of two or more names and no name is predominant. Otherwise, one is to apply 22.2C2.[9]

22.2C4.   Different names in editions of the same work
When different editions of a work have appeared with different names of the author, the name most often used should be the heading for all editions. If no one name is predominant, one should use the name that appears in the latest editions. In all cases name-title references are made from the other name(s) used for editions of that work.

RULE 22.3. CHOICE AMONG DIFFERENT FORMS OF THE SAME NAME

22.3A.   Fullness

When a name is found in forms that vary in fullness, the form most commonly found should be used as the heading, with references from the other forms when they would be useful. *See* Fig. 10.5.

Fig. 10.5. Rule 22.3A. Name entered under form most commonly found.

Hamilton, John P.
    Predominant form: John P. Hamilton
    Occasional form: J. P. Hamilton
    Rare form: "Bud" Hamilton

Note: Because Hamilton is a common surname, the second forename, Peter, may be required in parentheses to distinguish between two identical names (*see* 22.16). Also, references may be needed from the two forms of name not chosen.
    When a form cannot be decided upon as most common, *AACR 2* prescribes using the latest form; but if the latest form is in doubt, then use the fullest form. LC skips the possibility of "latest form" and goes directly to fullest form if one form cannot be determined to be most common.[10]
    LC's rule interpretation also suggests that if the name appears in two or more forms in the same work, one should choose the form in the chief source. If the name does not appear in the chief source, then a form in another prominent source should be used, if the name appears only once in a prominent source. Otherwise, the fullest form should be chosen.[11]
    LC applies the "80% rule" when a heading is already coded as "AACR" but subsequent items are received showing the name in a different form. If an established heading is coded "AACR 2 compatible" LC will not reconsider the heading.[12] *See* Figs. 10.6 and 10.7.

Fig. 10.6. Rule 22.3A. Fullness—LC practice.

Established heading: Nechitaĭlo, A. L.
    Has written later as: Annetta Leonidovna Nechitaĭlo
    Heading coded "AACR 2 compatible"
    Established heading retained.

Fig. 10.7. Rule 22.3A. Fullness—LC practice.

Established heading: Sánchez E., Rodrigo
    Has now written over 80% as: Rodrigo Sánchez Enríquez
    New heading: Sánchez Enríquez, Rodrigo

22.3B.   Language

22.3B1.   Persons using more than one language
    The heading for a person who writes in more than one language should be
the form that corresponds to the language of most of the works. *See* Fig. 10.8.

Fig. 10.8. Rule 22.3B1. Entry for person using more than one language.

Names found on works: William More
                       Guillermo Mora
Lived and worked in both U.S. and Venezuela.
Most works in Spanish.
Entry: Mora, Guillermo

    If there is doubt about which language is used in most of the works, the
form found most in reference sources of the person's country of residence or
activity should be used. LC practice when reference sources cannot be found,
or the person is not listed, is to use the form of the name in the person's native
language.[13]

Note: The choice made according to this rule may be altered by application of
22.3B2, 22.3B3, or 22.3C.

22.3B2.   Names in vernacular and Greek or Latin forms
    The heading for a name that appears in both Latin or Greek and the
vernacular in reference sources and/or in the person's works should be given in
the form found most often in reference sources. For cases of doubt, the Latin
or Greek is chosen for persons active before 1400 A.D. and the vernacular for
persons active after 1400. *See* Fig. 10.9.

Fig. 10.9. Rule 22.3B2. Entry of name found in both the
vernacular and Latin.

Name in vernacular: Dante Alighieri (with various
  spellings)
Name in Latin: Dantes Aligerius
Form most commonly found in reference sources:
  Dante Alighieri
Entry: Dante Alighieri, 1265-1321.

22.3B3.   Names written in the roman alphabet established in an English form

The heading for a person entered under given name according to 22.8 or for a Roman of classical times should be the English form if an English form is well established in English-language reference sources. The vernacular or Latin is used in cases of doubt. *See* Fig. 10.10.

Fig. 10.10. Rule 22.3B3. Entry of name with established English form.

Name of saint in Latin: Justinus
Name in English language reference sources: Justin
Entry: Justin, Saint.

22.3B4.   Other names

The heading for all other names found in two or more languages is the form found most often in reference sources of the person's country of residence or activity. *See* Fig. 10.11.

Fig. 10.11. Rule 22.3B4. Entry of name that is found in
different language forms.

Name on original work: John Boyer Noss
Name on translation of original work: Jān B. Nūs
Place of author's residence: U.S.
Entry: Noss, John Boyer

22.3C.   Names written in a nonroman script

Names that must be romanized or transliterated present many problems. Some languages have a number of systems for romanization, and use of the different systems results in different spellings. In addition, there may be one or more English language forms of some better known names. The rules in 22.3C give some guidance.

22.3C1.   Persons entered under given name, etc.

This rule, like 22.3B3, calls for entry under an English language form, if one exists. (If more than one exists, choose the one that appears most frequently.) *See* Fig. 10.12. If there is no English form, or if one romanization cannot be determined to be predominant, the name should be romanized according to the cataloging agency's adopted romanization table.

Fig. 10.12. Rule 22.3C1. Entry of name originally in nonroman script—given name.

Romanizations of name: Movses Khorenaꞇsi
                        Moses Xorenc'i
English language form of name: Moses of Chorene
Entry: Moses, of Chorene

22.3C2.   Persons entered under surname

Unlike the preceding rule, this one directs the cataloger to romanize a name entered under surname according to the table adopted by the cataloging agency. References are made from other romanized forms. If a name is found only in romanized form in the works involved, that form is used.

An alternative rule is given for 22.3C2: An English form, well established in English-language reference sources, may be used for the heading. This corresponds to the treatment of persons entered under given name, but is counter to the principle of entry under the name elements most commonly found in writers' works, or in reference works in the language or country of residence or activity for persons other than writers. The Library of Congress is following the alternative rule. The policy is to search the name in *Collier's Encyclopedia, The Encyclopedia Americana*, and *Encyclopaedia Britannica*. If the name is in all three sources in a single form, that form is used. If it varies, the form in *Encyclopaedia Britannica* is used. If it is not found in all three sources, the systematic romanization is used. An exception is made for persons of specialized fame. In such cases major specialized encyclopedias, such as *New Catholic Encyclopedia*, are used. Another exception is for persons of recent fame. For these, yearbooks to the encyclopedias and indexes to major newspapers are consulted.[14] *See* Fig. 10.13.

Fig. 10.13. Rule 22.3C2. Entry of name originally in nonroman script—surname.

Entry in romanized form found in English language reference sources

Scriabin, Alexander N.
  12 Etüden für Klavier, op. 8 = 12 studies for piano / Alexander Skrjabin ; hrsg. von Günter Philipp. –

Note: Romanized form appearing in the item:
    Alexander Skrjabin

Systematic romanization according to LC's adopted tables:
    Skriabin, Aleksandr N.

Form most often found in English-language reference sources:
    Scriabin, Alexander N.

Refer from:
    Skriabin, Aleksandr N.
    Skrjabin, Alexander

It should be noted that the alternative rule makes no provision for names for which there are no entries in English-language reference sources. Presumably, as the LC rule interpretation indicates, one should use the provision given in 22.3C1 for persons entered under given name: "If no English romanization is found ... romanize the name according to the table for the language adopted by the cataloguing agency."[15] See Fig. 10.14.

Fig. 10.14.

Romanizations found in chief sources of information, but not in reference sources:
    Matsiute, Regina
    Maciūte, Regina [romanization according to adopted table]
Entry: Maciūte, Regina
Refer from: Matsiute, Regina

22.3D.   Spelling

If variant spellings occur that are not the result of different romanizations, the form that represents an official orthodox change should be used, if this is applicable. Otherwise, one should choose the predominant spelling, or, in case of doubt, the spelling found in the first item cataloged. See Fig. 10.15.

Fig. 10.15. Rule 22.3D. Entry of name with variant spellings.

Variant spellings found: Thomas Decker
                        Thomas Dekker
                        Thomas Deckar
Predominant spelling: Thomas Dekker
Entry: Dekker, Thomas, ca. 1572-1632.

ENTRY ELEMENT:

SELECTED RULES AND EXAMPLES

RULE 22.4. GENERAL RULE

22.4A.   When a person's name consists of more than one part, a choice must be made about which part will be the entry element. In general the entry element is the one that would usually be used in authoritative alphabetic lists in the person's own country or language. "Authoritative" is defined as meaning "who's who" type publications, not telephone directory type. However, if it is known that the person prefers some other entry element than would be the usual usage for that language or country, the person's preference is followed.

22.4B.   **Order of elements**

The entry element is chosen according to Rules 22.5-22.9, but the order of other elements is given here.

22.4B2.   If the entry element is the first element, the name is entered in direct order. If that first element is a surname, it is followed by a comma. *See* Fig. 10.16.

Fig. 10.16. Rule 22.4B2. Name entered under first element, which is surname.

Name on chief source of information: Wu Hsin-chung
Surname: Wu
Entry: Wu, Hsin-chung

22.4B3.   If the entry element is not the first one, the names preceding it are transposed to follow the entry element and a comma. *See* Fig. 10.17.

Fig. 10.17. Rule 22.4B3. Name entered under third element,
which is surname.

Name on chief source of information: Jill S. Slattery
Surname entry element: Slattery
Entry: Slattery, Jill S.

22.4B4.   If the entry element is the proper name in a title of nobility, according to 22.6, the personal name follows in direct order, and the term of rank follows last. *See* Fig. 10.18.

Fig. 10.18. Rule 22.4B4. Name entered under proper name of a
title of nobility.

Name on chief source of information: Thomas Pitt,
   2nd Baron Camelford
Entry element: Camelford
Entry: Camelford, Thomas Pitt, Baron, 1775-1804.
Refer from: Pitt, Thomas, Baron Camelford

Note: The part of the term of rank denoting that this is the second person with this title and same common name is not included. Instead, birth and death dates distinguish otherwise identical names.

RULE 22.5.   ENTRY UNDER SURNAME

22.5A.   General rule

If a name contains a surname, the entry element should be the surname unless one of the following rules provides for a different entry element. (*See also* Rules 22.6, 22.17, and 22.28.) When a surname is represented by an initial, and another element of the name is in full, the initial is treated as a surname. This is in contrast with the provisions of Rule 22.10 for entry of names that consist only of initials. *See* Figs. 10.16 and 10.17.

22.5B.   Element other than the first treated as a surname

A name that functions as a surname, even though it is not really a surname, is treated as if it were. *See* Fig. 10.19.

Fig. 10.19. Rule 22.5B. Entry under element treated as a surname.

Name on chief source of information: Muhammad Sa'īd Bāyirlī
Entry: Bāyirlī, Muhammad Sa'īd
Refer from: Muhammad Sa'īd Bāyirlī

22.5C.   Compound surname

22.5C1.   Preliminary rule
Compound surnames consist of two or more proper names. The rules under 22.5C treat these and also some names that appear to be compound surnames. The rules are applied in the order given. References should be made from elements of a compound surname not chosen for entry.

22.5C2.   Preferred or established form known
The entry element for a compound surname of a person with a known preference should be the person's preferred entry element. Otherwise, the entry element should be the element under which it is given in reference sources from the person's country or in the person's language. *See* Fig. 10.20 below and Fig. 10.25 under Rule 22.5C5.

Lloyd George, David, 1863-1945.
    War memoirs of David Lloyd George.

Note: Refer from: George, David Lloyd. George is his correct paternal surname.

22.5C3.   Hyphenated surnames
    Compound surnames that are hyphenated (even if only sometimes) should be entered under the first element. *See* Fig. 10.21.

Entry under   Ward Lock's encyclopedia / edited by Harold
first part of   Boswell-Taylor
hyphenated   ⟶ I. Boswell-Taylor, Harold
surname

Note: Refer from: Taylor, Harold Boswell-

**22.5C4.   Other compound surnames, except those of married women
                whose surname consists of a combination of maiden name
                and husband's surname**
    Compound surnames remaining, if the foregoing rules have not sufficed, should be entered under the first element, with the exception of Portuguese names, which should be entered under the last element. *See* Fig. 10.22.

Torres Ramírez, Blanca
    Las relaciones cubanosovieticas / por Blanca Torres
Ramírez.

Note: Refer from: Ramírez, Blanca Torres

**22.5C5.   Other compound surnames. Married women whose surname
                consists of maiden name and husband's surname**
    If the woman's language is Czech, French, Hungarian, Italian, or Spanish, the entry element is the first element of the compound surname. In all other cases, the husband's surname (usually the last element) is the entry element. Hyphenated names, however, are treated above under 22.5C3. *See* Figs. 10.23 and 10.24.

Fig. 10.23. Rule 22.5C5. Entry of married French-speaking woman.

Entry under
maiden name

Mendès France, Joan.
    L'anglais juridique et le droit anglais : textes
bilinques et exercises / joan Mendès France et
Hélène Bourrouilhou.

Note: Refer from: France, Joan Mendès

Fig. 10.24. Rule 22.5C5. Entry of married English-speaking woman.

Graves, Kathleen George
    Our Union County heritage : a historical and
biographical album of Union County, people,
places, and events / by Kathleen George Graves

Entry under
husband's
name

and Winnie Palmer McDonald.
    I. McDonald, Winnie Palmer

However, if a married woman is known to prefer some other entry element
than prescribed here, 22.5C2 takes precedence. *See* Fig. 10.25.

Fig. 10.25. Rule 22.5C2. Entry of married English-speaking woman under
preferred entry element.

Entry under
maiden name

Rutherford Carr, Deborah
    Individuals / by Deborah Rutherford Carr and
Thomas J. Carr.

Note: Author is known to prefer combination of maiden name and husband's
surname as compound surname.
    Refer from: Carr, Deborah Rutherford

22.5D. Surnames with separately written prefixes

LC's rule interpretation should be consulted for guidance on placement of
constituent parts of a name in headings and references once the appropriate
entry element has been determined according to the following rules.[16]

22.5D1. Articles and prepositions

Names that contain an article or a preposition or a combination of the
two as part of the surname should be entered under the element that would
normally be used in lists from the person's country or in the person's language.

In *AACR 2* this rule contains many specific examples of names in
different languages. Only the most basic of those rules are cited here.

DUTCH. Dutch names are entered under the part following the prefix
with one exception: a name with the prefix "ver" is entered under the prefix.
See Fig. 10.26.

Fig. 10.26. Rule 22.5D1. Entry of Dutch name.

Schuit, Steven R.
    Dutch business law : legal, accounting, and
Entry under   tax aspects of business in the Netherlands / by
part follow-   Steven R. Schuit and Jan M. van der Beek.
ing prefix

——➤ I. Beek, Jan M. van der

Note: Refer from: Van der Beek, Jan M.

ENGLISH. English names are entered under the prefix. *See* Fig. 10.27.

Fig. 10.27. Rule 22.5D1. Entry of English name beginning with prefix.

Nuclear or not? : choices for our energy future :
a Royal Institution forum / edited by Gerald
Foley and Ariane van Buren.

Entry under
prefix   I. Van Buren, Ariane

Note: Refer from: Buren, Ariane van

FRENCH. French names in which the prefix is an article or a contraction
of an article and a preposition are entered under the prefix. *See* Fig. 10.28.

Fig. 10.28. Rule 22.5D1. Entry of French name beginning with article.

Entry under   Le Bihan, Alain.
the article   Francs-maçons   et ateliers parisiens de la
Grande Loge de France au XVIIIᵉ [i.e.
dix-huitième] siècle : 1760-1795 / Alain Le Bihan.
– Paris : Bibliothèque nationale, 1973.

Note: Refer from: Bihan, Alain le

All other French names with prefixes are entered under the element
following the prefix. *See* Figs. 10.29 and 10.30.

Fig. 10.29. Rule 22.5D1. Entry of French names that include prepositions.

Entry under   Richemont, Jean de.
part of   L'intégration du droit communautaire dans
name follow- l'ordre juridique interne : article 177 du Traité de
ing the   Rome / Jean de Richemont ; préf. par Marcel
preposition   Ancel.

Fig. 10.30.

Entry under the article following the preposition	La Fontaine, Jean de, 1621-1695. Fables / La Fontaine ; préface et commentaires de Pierre Clarac.

Note: Refer from: Fontaine, Jean de la

GERMAN. German names are entered like French names. Articles or contractions of articles and prepositions are entry elements. *See* Fig. 10.31.

Fig. 10.31. Rule 22.5D1. Entry of German name under prefix.

Vom Scheidt, Jürgen, 1940-
    Alles über Rauschdrogen / Jürgen vom Scheidt, Wolfgang Schmidbauer.

Note: Refer from: Scheidt, Jürgen vom

All other German names with prefixes are entered under the element following the prefix. *See* Fig. 10.32.

Fig. 10.32. Rule 22.5D1. Entry of German name with preposition.

Entry under part of name following the preposition	Weizsäcker, Carl Christian von. Modern capital theory and the concept of exploitation / Carl Christian von Weizsäcker.

ITALIAN. Modern Italian names are entered under the prefix. *See* Fig. 10.33.

Fig. 10.33. Rule 22.5D1. Entry of modern Italian name.

Entry under the prefix	De Filippo, Peppino. La lettera di mammà : farsa in due parti / Peppino De Flippo.

Note: Refer from: Filippo, Peppino de.

In order to determine the correct entry element for medieval and early modern Italian names, reference sources should be consulted. Example:

Medici, Lorenzo de'

SPANISH. Spanish names that have a prefix that consists only of an article are entered under the prefix. Otherwise, a name is entered under the element following the prefix. *See* Fig. 10.34.

Fig. 10.34. Rule 22.5D1. Entry of Spanish name.

Entry under part of name following prefix	Lorenzo, Pedro de. Libros de la vocación / Pedro de Lorenzo.

22.5D2.   Other prefixes

In all languages, when the prefix is not an article or a preposition or a combination of the two, the entry element should be the prefix. *See* Fig. 10.35.

**Fig. 10.35. Rule 22.5D2. Entry under the prefix. "Mac"
is an attributive prefix.**

MacIntyre, Elisabeth.
    The purple mouse / by Elisabeth MacIntyre. – 1st ed. –

RULE 22.6.   ENTRY UNDER TITLE OF NOBILITY

If a person is commonly known by a title of nobility, the proper name in that title should be the entry element. This rule applies to persons who use titles rather than surnames in their works, or, if there are no textual works to consult, to those persons who are listed by title in reference sources that do not list all members of the nobility under title. The proper name in the title is followed by the personal name in direct order; and the personal name is followed by the term of rank. Unused forenames are not included. A reference is made from the personal surname unless it is the same as the proper name in the title. *See* Fig. 10.18. If the person does not use a term of rank, and the proper name in the title is used as a surname, then the personal surname is omitted (e.g., John Julius Norwich was born John Julius Duff Cooper and became Viscount Norwich, but the name appears as John Julius Norwich). If the title includes a territorial designation that is an integral part of the title, it should be included. *See* Fig. 10.36.

This rule is closely related to 22.4B4 and 22.12. The three result in the same form of name, but they approach this type of name from the three viewpoints of order of elements, entry element, and additions to names.

Fig. 10.36. Rule 22.6. Entry under title of nobility.

Joint Advisory Committee on Pets in Society.
    Dogs in the United Kingdom : report of the Joint Advisory Committee on Pets in Society

Note clarifying statement of responsibility:
    Chairman: Lord Houghton of Sowerby

Make added entry under title of nobility with territorial designation:
    I. Houghton of Sowerby, Douglas Houghton, Baron

RULE 22.8.   ENTRY UNDER GIVEN NAME, ETC.

If a person is not identified by a title of nobility and the name does not include a surname, the entry element should be the part of the name that is the entry element in reference sources. Any words or phrases that are commonly associated with the name in that person's works or in reference sources should be included, preceded by a comma. *See* Fig. 10.37.

Fig. 10.37. Rule 22.8. Entry of a name under given name.

Paul, of Aleppo.
    The travels of Macarius, patriarch of Antioch / written by his attendant archdeacon, Paul of Aleppo.

Given names that are combined with a patronymic are entered in direct order. Library of Congress rule interpretations give guidelines for more complicated given name entries and should be consulted for more guidance.[17]

22.10-22.11.

These rules give instructions for entry elements when all one has for a name are initials, letters, numerals, or phrases. These are to be entered in direct order if they do not contain a real name. Example: One who has tested the receipts (*see* Fig. 9.12 in the preceding chapter). More specialized rules cover entry of phrases that contain names, and these should be consulted when needed.

ADDITIONS TO NAMES:

SELECTED RULES AND EXAMPLES

GENERAL

RULE 22.12.   TITLES OF NOBILITY AND TERMS OF HONOR AND ADDRESS, ETC.

22.12A.   If a nobleman or noblewoman is not entered under title according to 22.6, but the title or a part of the title usually appears with the name, the title of nobility should be added in the vernacular to the personal name. *See* Fig. 10.38.

Fig. 10.38. Rule 22.12A. Addition of title of nobility to given name entry.

Title of   John, of Gaunt, Duke of Lancaster, 1340-1399.
nobility   John of Gaunt's register, 1379-1383 / edited from the orig-
              inal record by the late Eleanor C. Lodge and Robert
              Somerville.

22.12B.   **British titles of honor**

There are four British titles of honor that are to be added to a name if they usually appear with the name in the person's works or in reference sources. They are: Sir, Dame, Lord, Lady. Note that the terms "Hon." and "bart." formerly used in headings are not now authorized. LC no longer uses them and revises existing headings that contain them.[18]

In *AACR 2* this rule goes on to distinguish the times when such terms should be added after the forenames and when they should be inserted before forenames. However, the Library of Congress, because of the incapability of their computer system to handle these as nonfiling characters, places all terms of honor and address after the forenames.[19] *See* Figs. 10.39 and 10.40.

Fig. 10.39. Rule 22.12B. Addition of title of honor.

Term of   Stephen, James Fitzjames, Sir, 1829-1894.
honor   A digest of the law of evidence / by Sir James Fitzjames
              Stephen. – 5th ed. / by Sir Herbert Stephen and Harry
              Lushington Stephen.

Note: Position of title is LC practice. According to *AACR 2*, heading should be:

Stephen, Sir James Fitzjames, 1829-1894

Fig. 10.40. Rule 22.12B. Addition of title of honor.

Term of   Hepworth, Barbara, Dame, 1903-
honor   Barbara Hepworth / J. P. Hodin. – London : Lund
           Humphries

Note: Position of title is LC practice. *AACR 2* form:

Hepworth, Dame Barbara, 1903-

RULE 22.13.   SAINTS

The word "Saint" is added after a saint's given name unless the person was a pope, emperor, empress, king, or queen. In those cases the latter epithet takes precedence over "Saint," and one follows Rules 22.17A-22.17B. *See* Fig. 10.41.

Fig. 10.41. Rule 22.13. Addition of "Saint."

Addition   Jeanne d'Arc eine Heilige? : Sceptische Studien
of designa-   gelegentlich des Canonisation-processes.
tion "Saint"
               I. Joan, of Arc, Saint, 1412-1431.

RULE 22.15.   ADDITIONS TO NAMES ENTERED UNDER SURNAME

22.15A.   When a name consists only of a surname with an accompanying word or phrase in the person's works or in reference sources, the associated word or phrase should be added after the surname. A reference is made from the name in direct order if it would be useful. LC generally makes the direct order reference only when such a heading is a pseudonym or assumed name.[20] *See* Fig. 10.42.

Fig. 10.42. Rule 22.15A. Addition of phrase associated with surname alone.

Jefferson, Mr., of Gray's Inn.
    Tales of old Mr. Jefferson, of Gray's Inn / collected by
young Mr. Jefferson, of Lyon's Inn.

Note: Refer from: Mr. Jefferson of Gray's Inn.

22.15B.   **Terms of address of married women**

When a woman is identified only by "Mrs." with her husband's name, the term "Mrs." is added. *See* Fig. 10.43.

Fig. 10.43. Rule 22.15B. Entry for married woman identified only by
husband's name.

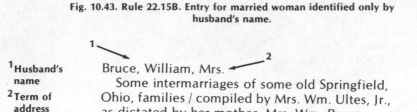

¹Husband's   Bruce, William, Mrs.
  name   Some intermarriages of some old Springfield,
²Term of   Ohio, families / compiled by Mrs. Wm. Ultes, Jr.,
  address   as dictated by her mother, Mrs. Wm. Bruce.

Note: Form above is LC practice. *AACR 2* form:

   Bruce, Mrs. William

22.15C.   Titles or terms other than those in the preceding rules are not
added to names entered under surname except when necessary to distinguish
between otherwise identical names for which dates are not available. *See* Figs.
10.44 and 10.46.

Fig. 10.44. Rule 22.15C. Omission of unneeded term of address.

   Name on chief source of information: Dr. Mary Lyon
   Entry: Lyon, Mary

RULE 22.16. ADDITIONS TO NAMES CONSISTING OF OR CONTAINING INITIALS

   When two identical names consist wholly or in part of initials, and the full
form of one or both names is known, the full form is added in parentheses in
order to distinguish between the two names. The rule calls for a reference from
the full form. However, in many catalogs such references are superfluous,
especially when the initial in the name is for a second or later forename. *See*
Figs. 10.45 and 10.46.

Fig. 10.45. Rule 22.16. Addition to name containing initials.

Full form   Roberts, J. O. (Jack O.)
of name   Coal and nuclear : a comparison of the cost of
added in   generating baseload electricity by region / J. O.
parentheses   Roberts.

Note: Refer from: Roberts, Jack O.

Fig. 10.46. Rule 22.16. Addition to name containing initials.

Full form
of name
added in
parentheses

Rouse, John E. (John Edward), 1942-
    Urban housing / by John E. Rouse, Jr.

Note: In addition to use of forenames in parentheses, note that the term
"Jr." was omitted from the heading in favor of addition of the birth date.

This rule allows the option of making the above additions even when not
necessary to distinguish identical names. LC is following the option when the
information is known with certainty. A rule interpretation gives guidelines for
how much of the name to include in the parenthetical statement and where to
place it. Once a heading has been established without the names in
parentheses, they are not added if they become known later unless the heading
must be changed for some other reason (e.g., it comes in conflict with another
heading).[21]

Birthdates also are used to distinguish between names that are otherwise
identical (*see* 22.18). LC does not search for full forenames if the birthdate is
readily available to make the distinction. That is, when two names are
identical, readily available forenames and/or birthdates can be used to
distinguish them. Only if neither is available does LC then make a search to
identify the names for which forename initials stand.[22]

RULE 22.17. ADDITIONS TO NAMES ENTERED UNDER GIVEN NAME, ETC.

22.17A.   Royalty

This rule in *AACR 2* has many specific subsections with accompanying
examples. The essence of the rule is that royal persons are entered under the
names by which they are known. These are usually only given names, but if a
house, dynasty, or surname is involved, it follows the given name or forename.
If there is a roman numeral, it follows the appropriate name. A phrase (in
English, if possible) consisting of title and state governed follows next. Other
epithets are not added, but are referred from. Consorts, children, and grand-
children of rulers have a title added to their names (again in English, if possible) plus the name of the ruler to whom related. *See* Figs. 10.47 and 10.48.

Fig. 10.47. Rule 22.17A. Entry of royalty.

Entry under
royal forename

Title and
name of state

Nikolaĭ Mikhaĭlovich, Grand Duke of Russia,
    1859-1919.
    [Pis'ma vysochaishikh osob k grafinie A. S.
    Protasovoĭ]
        Письма высочайшихъ особъ къ графинѣ А. С. Прота-
    совой / Великій князь Никогай Михайловичъ. — С.
    -Петербургъ : Экспедиція заготовленія гос. бумагъ,
    1913.

Fig. 10.48. Rule 22.17A. Addition to names of royalty.

Governess.
My life with Caroline / by a governess.

Addition of name of ruler to whom related
1. Caroline, Princess, daughter of Rainier II,
Prince of Monaco, 1957-

22.17B.   **Popes**

22.17C.   **Bishops, etc.**

22.17D.   **Other persons of religious vocation**

These rules call for addition of the words *Pope, Bishop, Archbishop, Cardinal*, and other titles in English (if there is an English equivalent) to the names of persons who are high ecclesiastical officials. The name of the latest see is also added to some titles. For other persons of religious vocation who are entered under given name, titles or terms of address are added in the vernacular. Initials of a Christian religious order regularly used by the person are also added. *See* Figs. 10.49 and 10.50.

Fig. 10.49. Rule 22.17B. Additions to names of popes.

Title   John Paul II, Pope, 1920-
added in   Easter vigil and other poems / translated from
English   the Polish by Jerzy Peterkiewicz

Fig. 10.50. Rule 22.17D. Additions to names of persons of
religious vocation.

Mead, Jude.
Dove in the cleft : the life of Mother Mary
Crucified of Jesus, C.P., the first Passionist nun,
1713-1787 / Jude Mead.
Title added in vernacular
1. Maria Crocifissa di Gesu, madre, 1713-1787

ADDITIONS TO DISTINGUISH IDENTICAL NAMES

RULE 22.18. DATES

Birth and death dates are added as the last element of a heading in order to distinguish between two otherwise identical headings. *See* Figs. 10.51-10.56.

Fig. 10.51. Rule 22.18. Addition of dates for a living person.

Parkinson, Cyril Northcote, 1909-

Fig. 10.52. Rule 22.18. Addition of dates when references differ as to year of birth; 1496 is probable.

Fox, Edward, Bishop of Hereford, 1496?-1538.

Fig. 10.53. Rule 22.18. Addition of dates when year of birth unknown.

Timberlake, Henry, d. 1626.

Fig. 10.54. Rule 22.18. Addition of dates when years of birth and death unknown, but date of activity is known. (Not used for twentieth century.)

Gardiner, Richard, fl. 1599-1603.

Note: "fl." is the *AACR 2* abbreviation for "flourished."

Fig. 10.55. Rule 22.18. Day, month, and year of birth added to distinguish from others of same name, and same year of birth.

Fischer, John, 1910 Apr. 27-

Fig. 10.56. Rule 22.18. Addition of probable dates.

Ford, John, ca.1586-1640.

An option to this rule allows adding the date(s) even when there is no conflict. LC is applying this option when the date is known at the time the heading is first established, or later if a conflict arises. For persons living in the twentieth century, LC only adds precise dates. Less precise dates may be added to the headings for pre-twentieth century persons.[23]

RULE 22.19. DISTINGUISHING TERMS

RULE 22.20. UNDIFFERENTIATED NAMES

When dates are not available to distinguish between identical names, certain other additions may be made following Rule 22.19. For given names, a brief term may be devised (e.g., "poet") and added in parentheses. For surname entries, a term of address, title of position, initials of academic degree, etc., that appear with the name in works or reference sources may be added. *See* Fig. 10.57. Otherwise, according to Rule 22.20 the same heading is used for all persons with the same name.

Fig. 10.57. Rule 22.19. Distinguishing term added.

Chapman, William H., M.A.

22.21-22.28.

These are special rules for names in certain languages and should be consulted as needed.

NOTES

[1]*Cataloging Service Bulletin*, no. 17 (Summer 1982): 31.

[2]*Cataloging Service Bulletin*, no. 18 (Fall 1982): 49-51.

[3]*Cataloging Service Bulletin*, no. 26 (Fall 1984): 13-16.

[4]*Cataloging Service Bulletin*, no. 18 (Fall 1982): 52-53.

[5]Ibid., p. 52.

[6]*AACR 2*, p. 350.

[7]*Cataloging Service Bulletin*, no. 14 (Fall 1981): 30.

[8]For examples of references, see the chapter on references in this text.

[9]*Cataloging Service Bulletin*, no. 23 (Winter 1983): 31.

[10]*Cataloging Service Bulletin*, no. 18 (Fall 1982): 52.

[11]Ibid., p. 53.

[12]Ibid.

[13]*Cataloging Service Bulletin*, no. 11 (Winter 1981): 22.

[14]*Cataloging Service Bulletin*, no. 27 (Winter 1985): 29.

[15]*AACR 2*, p. 355.

[16]*Cataloging Service Bulletin*, no. 23 (Winter 1983): 31-33.

[17]*Cataloging Service Bulletin*, no. 11 (Winter 1981): 25; no. 13 (Summer 1981): 29; no. 15 (Winter 1982): 17-18; no. 25 (Summer 1984): 64-65.

[18]*Cataloging Service Bulletin*, no. 11 (Winter 1981): 25.

[19]*Cataloging Service Bulletin*, no. 18 (Fall 1982): 55.

[20]*Cataloging Service Bulletin*, no. 22 (Fall 1983): 30.

[21]*Cataloging Service Bulletin*, no. 23 (Winter 1983): 33-35.

[22]Ibid.

[23]*Cataloging Service Bulletin*, no. 22 (Fall 1983): 30-31.

SUGGESTED READING

Chan, Lois Mai. *Cataloging and Classification*. New York, McGraw-Hill, 1981. pp. 99-107.

Hagler, Ronald, and Peter Simmons. *The Bibliographic Record and Information Technology*. Chicago, American Library Association, 1982. pp. 188-197.

Maxwell, Margaret F. *Handbook for AACR 2*. Chicago, American Library Association, 1980. Chapter 12.

11
Form of Headings for Geographic Names

INTRODUCTION

This chapter covers chapter 23 in *AACR 2* which treats the form of heading for any geographic name that may be used as a main or added entry heading. This includes names for places that are now or once were jurisdictional entities. It does not include names that cannot be jurisdictions, such as continents, mountains, and rivers. Yet there is an attempt in *AACR 2* to separate rules for place names that are "only" geographic names from those that are names of jurisdictions. Therefore, one rule in chapter 24, "Headings for Corporate Bodies" (Rule 24.6), deals with what seem to be geographic names; but the rule actually deals with jurisdictions. Another rule, 24.3E, covers "conventional" names of governments and gives instructions to use the geographic name as constructed in chapter 23. Other rules throughout chapter 24 cover additions of geographic names to corporate names for the purpose of identification or distinction. It can be seen, then, that the cataloger cannot rely solely on chapter 23 for the construction of names that appear to be geographic.

In this chapter there are rules for choice of name (23.2-23.3), additions to place names (23.4), and modification of place names (23.5). Problems involved in choice of name generally involve choice between an English form and a form in some other language. Choice may also involve which name to use when the name of a place has changed. For additions to place names, problems involve decisions about which larger place names are most useful for identification. (For example, should the name of the county, state, and/or country be added to the name of a town?) A problem that may require modification of a name involves the use of a term indicating type of jurisdiction. The problem is whether that term comes first, while the name is commonly known or listed under another element of the name (e.g., Kreis Lippe, a county in West Germany, is commonly listed under Lippe). The purpose of this chapter is to demonstrate the rules used to resolve these problems.

A heading created according to the rules in this chapter is coded 110, 651, 710, or 810 in the MARC format, depending upon whether it functions as a main entry, subject heading, or added entry, or begins a series. Codes 110, 710, and 810 are for corporate names, and in these cases the name of a jurisdiction alone is coded as a corporate name. However, in the subject fields there are separate numbers for corporate names (610) and geographic names (651). Jurisdictions that stand alone are coded as geographic names.

SELECTED RULES AND EXAMPLES

RULE 23.2. GENERAL RULES

These general rules involve choice of a name from among variant forms of a name that may be found.

23.2A.   English form

AACR 2 calls for use of the English form of a place name and specifies that this form should be determined from gazetteers and other reference sources from English-speaking countries. When there is doubt as to whether the English form is generally used, the vernacular form is to be used. *See* Fig. 11.1.

Fig. 11.1. Rule 23.2A. Geographic name entered under
English form of name.

[1]English form   Forms of name found: Brasil
in general use   Brazil ◄——————[1]
                      AACR 2 heading: Brazil

                      Forms of name found: Bucharest ◄——————[1]
                                             Bucuresti
                                             Bucuresci̬
                                             Bukharest
                                             Bucarest
                      AACR 2 heading: Bucharest (Romania)

                      Forms of name found: Rome ◄——————[1]
                                             Roma
                      AACR 2 heading: Rome (Italy)

The Library of Congress bases headings for United States names on the *Rand McNally Commercial Atlas and Marketing Guide.* Names from Great Britain, Australia, and New Zealand are based on the form found in a recently published gazetteer. For names in Canada, LC uses headings provided by the National Library of Canada. For other names the official source used by LC is the U.S. Board on Geographic Names (BGN). However, if the BGN authorizes only a vernacular form when an English form can be determined to be in general use, the English form is used.[1]

Certain of the examples given in *AACR 2* for geographic names are not being followed by LC. BGN approves both "Union of Soviet Socialist Republics" (the form used in *AACR 2*) and "Soviet Union" (the form used by LC in the past). LC is continuing to use "Soviet Union." *AACR 2* uses "United Kingdom" in examples where "Great Britain" has been used in the past. However, "Great Britain" can be thought of as the conventional name for "United Kingdom of Great Britain and Northern Ireland." In addition, libraries in Britain wish to continue using "Great Britain." Therefore, LC continues to use the heading "Great Britain." Other decisions include use of "Germany (West)" for Federal Republic of Germany, "Germany (East)" for German Democratic Republic, "Korea (North)" for Democratic People's Republic of Korea, "Korea (South)" for Republic of Korea. For Washington, D.C., LC will use "District of Columbia" as the heading for the government of this name, with "Washington (D.C.)" used only as a location qualifier or as the entry element for cross references from place. In dealing with London, LC uses "Corporation of London" or "Greater London Council" for jurisdictional headings and "London (England)" as the qualifier added to corporate names or as the entry element for a cross reference from place.[2]

23.2B.   Vernacular form

23.2B1.   If there is no English form in general use, the form in the official language of the country is used. *See* Fig. 11.2.

Fig. 11.2. Rule 23.2B1. Geographic name entered under vernacular form of name.

AACR 2 headings: [no English form in use]	Pistoia (Italy) Tétaigne (France) Tromsø (Norway)
AACR 2 heading: [English form not in general use]	Braunschweig (West Germany) [English form: Brunswick]

23.2B2.   In cases where there is more than one official language in a country, the most common form found in English-language reference sources is used. *See* Fig. 11.3.

Fig. 11.3.

Forms of name found: Bruxelles
Brüssel
Brussels

Form most often found in English-language sources:
Brussels

AACR 2 heading: Brussels (Belgium)

Note: There is no rule for variations of spelling of the name in the same language. Because of the close association in the rules of geographic names and corporate names, it is assumed that needed rules, such as the one for spelling, may be taken from chapter 24 and applied to geographic names. Rule 24.2C states that for a name with variant spellings, the one that represents an official change in orthography should be used if this applies, or else the predominant spelling should be used. *See* Fig. 11.4.

Fig. 11.4. Entry of name with variant spellings.

Original spelling: Tandjungpinang, Indonesia
New official spelling: Tanjungpinang, Indonesia
Variants also found: Tandjoengpinang
Tandjung Pinang
Tanjung Pinang
AACR 2 heading: Tanjungpinang (Indonesia)

RULE 23.3. CHANGES OF NAME

The essence of this rule is that like corporate bodies, if the name of a place changes, the old name is used for items to which that name is appropriate, and the new name is used for items appropriate to it. The old and new names are connected with *see also* references. *See* Figs. 11.5 and 11.6.

Fig. 11.5. Rule 23.3. Use of more than one name for the same place.

In 1971, the Town of Whitchurch-Stouffville was created, incorporating the Village of Stouffville in Ontario.
An item requiring Stouffville as a heading prior to 1971 would use the heading:
Stouffville (Ont.)
An item requiring Stouffville as a heading in 1971 or later would use the heading:
Stouffville (Whitchurch-Stouffville, Ont.)

RULE 23.4.   ADDITIONS TO PLACE NAMES

23.4A.   Punctuation

Additions to place names that are used as entry elements are made in parentheses.

> e.g., Staunton (Va.)

When the whole place name is used as an addition, it is enclosed in parentheses with a comma preceding the larger place.

> e.g., Second Presbyterian Church (Staunton, Va.)

23.4B.   General rule

When two or more places have the same name, they are differentiated by adding to each the name of a larger place according to the instructions in Rules 23.4C-23.4J. Place names used as additions may be abbreviated as instructed in Appendix B.14 of *AACR 2*.

Two options are appended to this rule; the first allows application of Rules 23.4C-23.4J even when there is no conflict between names. The second option gives certain areas for which the name of a larger geographic area may be omitted when these areas are being used as additions: states, provinces, or territories of Australia, Canada, and the United States; British counties; constituent states of Malaysia, the U.S.S.R., and Yugoslavia; islands.

These two options are being applied selectively by the Library of Congress. The first is applied to all cities and towns, and to all other entities except those named in the second option, with the addition of regions and islands areas in the British Isles (the second option includes only British counties). LC also adds that islands must be jurisdictions to be excluded from application of the first option. Then, the second option is applied as stated.[3] The effect of these applications is that all U.S., Canadian, etc., cities have a larger place name added (state, province, etc.), but the larger place name itself does not have yet a larger place name added to *it*.

e.g., San Francisco (Calif.)
not   San Francisco (Calif., U.S.)
and   California
not   California (U.S.)

It should be noted that if a larger place falling under the second option has a smaller place of the same name within it, a term should be added to the larger place according to 24.6.

e.g., heading for the city:
New York (N.Y.)

e.g., heading for the state:
New York (State)

The examples in this section are given according to LC's use of the options.

23.4C.   Places in Australia, Canada, or the United States

Add the name of the state, province, or territory of Australia, Canada, or the United States to a place located there. Places located in cities are treated according to 23.4G.

e.g., Delmont (Pa.)
Montreal (Québec)
Melbourne (Vic.)

23.4D.   Places in the British Isles

23.4D1.   Counties, etc.

When the name of a county, region, or islands area in the British Isles is used as an entry element, one of the following names is added to the heading, as appropriate: England, Ireland (for the Republic of Ireland), Northern Ireland, Scotland, Wales.

e.g., Antrim (Northern Ireland)
Warwickshire (England)
Ayrshire (Scotland)

23.4D2.   Other places (other than places in cities, *see* 23.4G)

For places other than counties in the British Isles, additions are made as follows:

The name of the county is added to a place in England,
Wales, or the Republic of Ireland.

e.g., Cambridge (Cambridgeshire)
Mold (Flintshire)
Tralee (Kerry)

The name of the region or islands area is added to a place in Scotland.

e.g., Kirkwall (Orkney Islands)

"Northern Ireland" is added to a place in that country.

> e.g., Londonderry (Northern Ireland)

23.4E.   Places in Malaysia, the U.S.S.R., or Yugoslavia

The name of the constituent state is added to a place in Malaysia, the U.S.S.R., or Yugoslavia.

> e.g., Moscow (R.S.F.S.R.)
>   Kiev (Ukraine)
>   Tbilisi (Georgian S.S.R.)

Note: For the constituent republics of the Soviet Union, use the following headings:[4]

Armenian S.S.R.	Lithuania
Azerbaijan S.S.R.	Moldavian S.S.R.
Byelorussian S.S.R.	Russian S.F.S.R.
Estonia	Tajik S.S.R.
Georgian S.S.R.	Turkmen S.S.R.
Kazakh S.S.R.	Ukraine
Kirghiz S.S.R.	Uzbek S.S.R.
Latvia	

23.4F.   Places on islands

When the name of an island or island group is predominantly associated with the name of a place there, the name of that island or island group is added to the place name.

> e.g., Palermo (Sicily)
>   Palma (Majorca)
>   Mount Stewart (Prince Edward Island)

Note that local places on islands that have previously been established with the name of the country or other jurisdiction as qualifier should now be qualified with the name of the island or island group. A rule interpretation from LC indicates that for places in Hawaii, the name of the state, not the name of an individual island, is used.[5]

23.4G.   Places in cities

Named places in cities are established under the name followed by the name of the city and its qualifier. A reference is made from the names of the city followed by the name of the place.

e.g., Bregninge (Svendborg, Denmark)
Refer from: Svendborg (Denmark). Bregninge

Georgetown (Washington, D.C.)
Refer from: Washington (D.C.). Georgetown

23.4H.   Other places

If a place is not covered by 23.4C-23.4G, the name of the country in which it lies is added.

e.g., Lund (Sweden)
Siena (Italy)
Rio de Janiero (Brazil)

RULE 23.5. PLACE NAMES INCLUDING A TERM INDICATING A TYPE OF JURISDICTION

23.5A.   When the first element of a place name indicates a type of jurisdiction, but the place is usually listed under another name element in reference sources of the country, the term indicating type of jurisdiction should be omitted.

e.g., Kreise Lippe in West Germany is commonly listed
under Lippe in German lists.
Heading: Lippe (West Germany)

Note: The examples in *AACR 2*, as mentioned earlier, "are illustrative and not prescriptive" (Rule 0.14). It is worth mentioning that examples in chapter 23 that show "(Germany)" as an addition, are not correct because of the division of the country into two areas that need to be distinguished. For correct example *see* Fig. 11.2 in this text.

The type of jurisdiction is included in all cases that do not fit the above criteria.

e.g., Dutchess County (N.Y.)

Note: The term "county" should be included for U.S. counties, even though many U.S. atlases list counties by name only under the caption "counties" and therefore omit the word "county" with the name. Note that "county" is now spelled out. Most U.S. counties have been established by LC and other librar- ies in the past using "Co." and are being changed by LC as new occasions for use of each county name arise.

23.5B.   Occasionally a place name does not include a term indicating type of jurisdiction, but such a term is required for differentiating between two identical names. If this is the case, Rule 24.6 should be applied.

e.g., Chimaltenango (Guatemala : Department)

[there is also a municipality named Chimaltenango]

Note: LC continues to abbreviate "Department" as "Dept.," even though it is not allowed in *AACR 2*, Appendix B, "Abbreviations."

NOTES

[1]*Cataloging Service Bulletin*, no. 18 (Fall 1982): 61-64.

[2]Ibid., pp. 64-65.

[3]*Cataloging Service Bulletin*, no. 13 (Summer 1981): 32-33.

[4]*Cataloging Service Bulletin*, no. 18 (Fall 1982): 64.

[5]*Cataloging Service Bulletin*, no. 14 (Fall 1981): 43.

SUGGESTED READING

Chan, Lois Mai. *Cataloging and Classification*. New York, McGraw-Hill, 1981. pp. 107-108.

Hagler, Ronald, and Peter Simmons. *The Bibliographic Record and Information Technology*. Chicago, American Library Association, 1982. pp. 208-209.

Maxwell, Margaret F. *Handbook for AACR 2*. Chicago, American Library Association, 1980. Chapter 13.

12
Form of Headings for Corporate Names

INTRODUCTION

This chapter covers the rules for construction of names of corporate bodies. "Corporate body" is defined in 21.1B1. In general, entry of a corporate body is under the name the body itself uses except when the rules specify entry under a higher or related body or under the name of a government. Like the principle in use for personal names, the principle for corporate names is to choose the name the corporate body generally uses (including conventional names), even if that name is not the official one. Unlike personal names, however, when the name of a corporate body changes, a new heading is made under that name with cross references to and from various other former and related names.

Following the general rule (24.1) in this chapter, there are rules for choice of names (24.2-24.3), and for additions, omissions, and modifications (24.4-24.11). These are followed by rules for subordinate and related bodies in general (24.12-24.16), for government bodies and officials (24.17-24.26), and for religious bodies and officials (24.27). Problems involved in choice of name include choice among variant forms found in items issued by a body, such as official name or acronym or short form, choice among variant spellings (including differences in romanization), and choice among different languages. Problems requiring additions, omissions, or other modifications include the need to distinguish between two or more bodies with the same name, the need to provide adequate identification for a name that does not convey the idea of a corporate body, and the desire to omit unnecessary or excess terms such as "incorporated" or "biennial." In dealing with a subordinate body, the cataloger must decide whether the body can be entered directly under its own name or must be entered under a higher body, and because government and religious bodies present special problems in this area, the cataloger must know whether a subordinate body belongs in one of these two groups before applying the rules. The purpose of this chapter is to demonstrate only the most important problems of corporate entry. For more detail, the cataloger should consult *AACR 2*, chapter 24.

As with personal names, there are certain previously established headings for corporate bodies that LC considered "*AACR 2* compatible" from January 2, 1981, to September 1, 1982 (see discussion on page 268 in the chapter on form of headings for persons). These are summarized with examples in *Cataloging Service Bulletin*.[1]

A heading created according to the rules in this chapter is coded 110, 111, 610, 611, 710, 711, 810, or 811 in the MARC format, depending upon whether it functions as a main entry, subject heading, or added entry, or begins a series. The codes ending in "11" are for conference names. The codes ending in "10" are for all other corporate names.

GENERAL RULES:

SELECTED RULES AND EXAMPLES

RULE 24.1.   BASIC RULE

A corporate body is to be entered directly under its own name unless later rules instruct that it be entered subordinately to a higher body or to a government. Although the rule does not say so, there are also religious bodies that must be entered subordinately. Therefore, the cataloger must first determine whether a body is a government or religious body and start with those rules if it is: Rules 24.17-24.26 for government bodies; Rule 24.27 for religious bodies. If a body is neither government nor religious but is subordinate to another body, Rules 24.12-24.16 must be consulted. In many cases one will be referred back to this rule (24.1), because the body can be entered under its own name even though it is a subordinate body.

The form of the name of a corporate body is determined from items issued by the body in its language, if possible, or from reference sources. The punctuation usage of the body should be followed (e.g., whether or not periods are included after initials depends upon the predominant usage by the body).

References from different forms of a corporate body name are prescribed in the reference chapter, Rule 26.3.

> e.g., Lawyer's Committee for Civil Rights Under Law.

> W.K. Kellogg Arabian Horse Center.
>   Refer from: Kellogg Arabian Horse Center

> Nelliston Community Group.

> Symposium "Pro Musica Antiqua" Prag.

A rule interpretation from LC gives guidance for punctuating and spacing corporate names.[2]

It should also be noted here that for a corporate name that includes the name of a place at the end, the punctuation used by the body will be retained. This means that some names may be established ending with a place preceded by a comma and a space, and others may be established with a place enclosed in parentheses. These have nothing to do with the additions prescribed in 24.4 and should not be interpreted as "errors,"

> e.g., University of California, San Diego
> *not* University of California (San Diego)

24.1A.   Romanization

The name of a body that is written in a nonroman script is romanized using the table adopted by the cataloging agency. This means that even if a romanized form of the name appears in items issued by a body, that form may be used only if it corresponds to the table adopted by the cataloging agency. References are made from other romanizations.

A footnote in *AACR 2* allows an alternative to this rule: a romanized form appearing in items issued by the body is used with references from other romanizations. The Library of Congress is not applying the alternative rule.[3] *See* Fig. 12.1.

**Fig. 12.1. Rule 24.1A. Romanization of names originally in nonroman script.
Also illustrates Rule 24.3A: Use of the form in the official language
of the body. Refer from the English form of the names.**

Corporate
names entered
under roman-
ized form

Akademiī͡a nauk SSSR. ◀

   Noctilucent clouds : optical properties / Academy of Sciences of the U.S.S.R., Soviet Geophysical Committee, and Institute of Physics and Astronomy of the Academy of Sciences of the Estonian S.S.R.

Make added entries for romanized forms of names:

   I. Akademiī͡a nauk SSSR. Mezhduvedomstvennyĭ geofizicheskiĭ komitet. II. Eesti NSV Teaduste Akadeemia. Füüsika ja Astronoomia Instituut.

24.1B.   Changes of name

When a corporate body changes its name, a new heading is established for the new name. A bibliographic record for an item relating to the old name is given the old name as a heading, while a bibliographic record for an item relating to the new name is given the new name as a heading. References are made referring to each name from the other. *See* Fig. 12.2.

Fig. 12.2. Rule 24.1B. Entry under each name a
corporate body has used.

Entry under   The Long Range Planning Service of the Stanford Research
three names   Institute became the Business Intelligence Program in April
1976. On May 19, 1977, the Institute changed its name to
S.R.I. International.

        Works by these bodies are found under the following head-
ings according to the name used at the time of publication:

   ⟶ Stanford Research Institute. Long Range Planning Service.

   ⟶ Stanford Research Institute. Business Intelligence Program.

   ⟶ S.R.I. International. Business Intelligence Program.

RULE 24.2.   VARIANT NAMES. GENERAL RULES

     Variant names here do not include those resulting from official changes of
names. Such changes are covered by 24.1B.

24.2B.   When different name forms are found in various places in items
issued by a corporate body, the form found in chief sources of information
should be used. *See* Fig. 12.3.

Fig. 12.3. Rule 24.2B. Entry of name having variant forms.

Name on title page: Michael Bradner Associates
Forms of name found elsewhere in work:
    Mike Bradner & Associates
    Mike Bradner and Associates
AACR 2 heading: Michael Bradner Associates
Refer from: Mike Bradner and Associates
        Bradner Associates

24.2C.   When there are variant spellings of a name in items issued by
the body, the one that represents an official change in orthography should be
used, if this applies, or if not, the predominant spelling should be chosen. *See*
Fig. 12.4.

Fig. 12.4. Rule 24.2C. Entry of name having variant spellings.

Name on some title pages:
    Allgemeines deutsches Commersbuch
Name on most title pages:
    Allgemeines deutsches Kommersbuch
AACR 2 heading: Allgemeines deutsches Kommersbuch
Refer from: Allgemeines deutsches Commersbuch

24.2D. When different name forms appear in the chief source of information, the one presented formally should be used if that is applicable, or the predominant form should be used if no form is presented formally or all are equally presented. *AACR 2* prescribes that if no form is predominant, a short form that distinguishes this body from others with a similar name should be used in preference to a longer form. However, a rule interpretation from LC indicates that if a body's initials or acronym appear formally with the full form, the full form should be chosen for the heading.[4] *See* Fig. 12.5.

Fig. 12.5. Rule 24.2D. Entry under brief form of name.

Names on title page: GAAG, the Guerrilla Art Action
   Group
Neither form formally presented. No predominant form.
AACR 2 heading: GAAG.
Refer from: Guerrilla Art Action Group
LC choice of heading: Guerrilla Art Action Group.

RULE 24.3. VARIANT NAMES. SPECIAL RULES

24.3A.   Language

This rule sets up an order of precedence to follow when the name of a body appears in different languages:

1)   the form in the official language of the body

2)   an English language form if there is more than one official language and one is English

3)   the predominant language

4)   English, French, German, Spanish, or Russian, in that order

5)   the language that comes first in English alphabetic order

An LC rule interpretation inserts another criterion between 3) and 4): if one does not know the official language of the body, the official language of the country in which the body is located is used (if the country has a single official language).[5] *See* Fig. 12.6.

Fig. 12.6. Rule 24.3A. Entry of name found in different languages.

Names on publications:
    Schweizerische Hochschulrektoren-Konferenz,
        Kommission für Hochschulplanung
    Commission de planification de la Conférence
        des recteurs des universités suisses
Official language: German
AACR 2 heading: Schweizerische Hochschulrektoren
    -Konferenz. Kommission für Hochschulplanung.
Refer from French form.

An alternative to this rule allows use of a form of language appropriate to the catalog's users if the application of the rule results in a language not familiar to the users. LC is not following this alternative because a national library cannot cater to individual library users.[6]

24.3B.   Language. International bodies

The English form of an international body is used if the name appears in English in its publications. Otherwise, the preceding rule, Rule 24.3A, is used. *See* Figs. 12.7 and 12.8.

Fig. 12.7. Rule 24.3B. Entry of international body when the
name appears in English.

Names on title page:
    al-Maṣrif al-'Arabī lil-Tanmiyah al-Iqtiṣādīyah
        fī Afrīqiyā
    Arab Bank for Economic Development in Africa
    Banque Arabe de développement économique en
        Afrique
AACR 2 heading: Arab Bank for Economic Development
    in Africa
Refer from the names in Arabic and French.

Fig. 12.8. Rule 24.3B. Entry of international body when the
name is not in English on its publications.

Forms of name used on publications:
    Nederlandse Vereniging voor Internationaal
        Recht
    NVIR [full form predominant]
English equivalent: Netherlands Branch of the International
    Law Association
    [English not used on its publications]
AACR 2 heading: Nederlandse Vereniging voor
    Internationaal Recht
Refer from English equivalent.

24.3C.   Conventional name

24.3C1.   General rule

A conventional name that is often used to identify a corporate body in reference sources in its own language should be used in place of an official name. *See* Fig. 12.9.

Fig. 12.9. Rule 24.3C1. Entry under conventional name.

[1]Conventional name   Abbey of Bury St. Edmunds.
                           The customary of the Benedictine Abbey of Bury St.
[2]Official name   Edmunds in Suffolk : (from Harleian MS. 1005 in the
                           British Museum) / edited by Antonia Gransden.

24.3C2.   Ancient and international bodies

When an English form of name of an ancient body or of a body of inter-national character has become very well known in English language usage, this form should be used. A footnote comments that this rule applies to such bodies as religious bodies, fraternal and knightly orders, church councils, and diplomatic conferences. *See* Fig. 12.10.

Fig. 12.10. Rule 24.3C2. Entry under English form of conventional names of international bodies

Orthodox Eastern Church.
[Hēmerologion tēs Ekklēsias tēs Hellados]
Ἡμερολόγιον τῆς Ἐκκλησίας τῆς Ἑλλάδος.

English form of names

Catholic Church. Canadian Catholic Conference.
Messages des évêques canadiens à l'occasion de la Fête du travail (1956-1974) / présentation de Richard Arès.

24.3D.   Religious orders and societies

The best-known form of name for a religious order or society should be used. An English form is preferred, if one exists. Otherwise, the language of the country of origin is used. *See* Fig. 12.11.

Fig. 12.11. Rule 24.3D. Entry of religious orders and societies.

Name of religious order or society

White Fathers.
Annexes des Archives de la Maison généralice des Pères blancs = Documents in the Annexe of the Archives of the Generalate of the White Fathers.

24.3E.   Governments

The conventional name of a government is preferred unless there is an official name in more common use. The name of the geographic area over which the government has jurisdiction serves as the conventional name.

> e.g., Jersey City (N.J.)
> *not*   City of Jersey City
>
> Korea (North)
> *not*   Democratic People's Republic of Korea
>
> San Marino
> *not*   Most Serene Republic of San Marino

24.3F.   Conferences, congresses, meetings, etc.

When variant forms of a conference name appear in the chief source of information, one that includes the name (or initials) of a body associated with the conference should be chosen, if possible. If, however, the meeting is *subordinate* to the body, Rule 24.13 should be applied. *See* Fig. 12.12.

Fig. 12.12. Rule 24.3F. Entry of a conference under form of name that includes initials of the bodies associated with the meeting.

Name of meeting: ALI-ABA Course of Study: Legal
    Issues in the Coal Industry
Name appears both with and without the initials of the
    American Law Institute and the American Bar
    Association
AACR 2 heading: ALI-ABA Course of Study: Legal Issues
    in the Coal Industry (1978 : Washington, D.C.)
Refer from: Course of Study: Legal Issues in the Coal
    Industry (1978 : Washington, D.C.)

24.3G.   Local churches, etc.

Names of local churches, like those of most other corporate bodies, are established using a predominant form of name. This rule in *AACR 2* gives a preferred order of criteria to use in case there is no predominant form. Rule 24.10 provides for additions to such names.

ADDITIONS, OMISSIONS, AND MODIFICATIONS:

SELECTED RULES AND EXAMPLES

RULE 24.4.   ADDITIONS

24.4A.   General rule

The subrules under 24.4 give general directions for making additions to corporate names. Special types of corporate names may need more specialized types of additions, which are covered in Rules 24.6-24.11. All additions to corporate names are enclosed in parentheses.

24.4B.   Names not conveying the idea of a corporate body

When a corporate name does not sound like that of a corporate body, a designation is added in English. A rule interpretation from LC that gives guidance in determining when such designations are needed (e.g., for ships, performing groups, etc.) should be consulted when needed.[7]

> e.g., ABBA (Musical group)
>
> Prévention routière internationale (Association)
>
> But (Yacht)

24.4C.   Two or more bodies with the same or similar names

24.4C1.   General rule
When two or more corporate name headings are identical or so similar that they could be easily confused, a word or phrase must be added to each according to the subrules under 24.4C. An option allows making these additions even when not necessary for distinguishing between bodies. An extensive rule interpretation explains how LC is applying this option. In general additions are made to every government body name that is entered under its own name unless the government's name (or an understandable substitute for it) is already part of the name. An exception is made for government institutions (e.g., schools, libraries, hospitals) that have very distinctive names. For non-government names, qualifiers are added unless the qualifier is already part of the name, the name represents a business firm, the body is international, or the name is very distinctive. A very distinctive name is one that usually has proper nouns or adjectives that are not likely to be repeated in the name of another body. The rule interpretation goes on to elaborate upon the forms qualifiers should take, choice of qualifiers, and resolution of conflicts in qualifiers.[8]

24.4C2.-24.4C10.

Rules 24.4C2-24.4C7 authorize addition of place names—country, state, province, etc.—for a body that is national, provincial, etc., in character, or of local place names for a body whose character is essentially local. If a place is not appropriate, 24.4C8-24.4C10 provide for addition of the name of an institution, the inclusive years of existence, or some other appropriate general designation in English. *See* Fig. 12.13.

Fig. 12.13. Rule 24.4C2. Addition of country to corporate name.

National Committee on the Status of Women (India).
  Status of women : report to the Government / National Committee on the Status of Women.

Note: This name could be held by similar groups in several countries. Therefore the name of the country is added.

It should be noted that when a place is used as a qualifier, if it is a place that is itself qualified by a larger place according to chapter 23, the smaller and the larger place are both used in the qualifier of the corporate body. Thus, for a corporate body in Oklahoma City, the name of the city alone cannot be used as qualifier. It must be: (Oklahoma City, Okla.). *See also* Fig. 12.14.

RULE 24.5.   OMISSIONS

24.5A.-24.5C.

These rules require omission of certain elements from corporate names: initial articles are omitted unless required for grammatical reasons (LC does not retain an initial article even for grammatical reasons[9]); terms indicating incorporation, etc., are omitted unless they are an integral part of the name or are needed to clarify the fact that the name is that of a corporate body. Other required omissions occur in rare instances, and the cataloger should consult *AACR 2* for them. *See* Figs. 12.14-12.16.

Fig. 12.14. Rule 24.5A. Entry of name omitting initial article.

Initial   News (New York, N.Y.)
article   ╱   European round trip / The News.
omitted   ╱

Fig. 12.15. Rule 24.5C1. Entry of name omitting term indicating incorporation.

Name appearing on publications:
    Firestone Tire and Rubber Company, Inc.
Judgment: "Inc." not necessary for clarification as a
    corporate body
Heading: Firestone Tire and Rubber Company

**Fig. 12.16. Rule 24.5C1. Entry of name retaining term
indicating incorporation.**

Term of
incorporation
retained

A Week full of Saturdays [motion picture]

      [Produced and distributed by Alternate Choice, Inc.]

I. Alternate Choice, Inc.

RULE 24.6. GOVERNMENT ADDITIONS

As mentioned in the chapter on geographic names, this rule is an attempt to give directions for entry of names of jurisdictions – distinct from the rules given for strictly geographic names. However, they are not totally separate, because this rule says that if names have not been differentiated by use of Rule 23.4, then further addition according to this rule should be made.

LC has elaborated upon how it will interpret this rule, because it is not clear from the rule whether additions should be made to *both* conflicting names in all cases:

A succession of jurisdictions that have had the same name are all entered under one heading, e.g.:

> North Carolina   Hawaii
>
> *not* North Carolina (Colony) *not* Hawaii (Kingdom)
>   North Carolina (State)   Hawaii (Republic)
>   Hawaii (State)

The name of a sovereign nation that is the same as the name of another place is not qualified, e.g.:

> Italy
> Italy (Tex.).

A third elaboration on this rule distinguishes between situations where the name of a place within a jurisdiction conflicts with the name of the jurisdiction, and situations where the name of a jurisdiction conflicts with the name of a place in another jurisdiction. In the first situation, the name of the larger jurisdiction is qualified with the name of the type of government, e.g.:

> Québec (Québec)   [name of city]
> Québec (Province)   [name of larger jurisdiction]

In the second situation, only the name of the place in another jurisdiction is qualified, e.g.:

> Alberta (Va.)
> Alberta
> *not* Alberta (Province)

An exception is made for the state of Washington. It is entered:

> Washington (State)[10]

24.6B.   If a jurisdiction is not a city or town and must have an addition because of conflict with another name, the type of jurisdiction is given in English, if there is an English equivalent; otherwise it is given in the vernacular, e.g.:

> São Paulo (Brazil)
> São Paulo (Brazil : State)
> Alessandria (Italy : Province)
> Esberg (Denmark : Kommune)
> Detmold (Germany : West : Landkreis)

RULE 24.7.   CONFERENCES, CONGRESSES, MEETINGS, ETC.

24.7A.   Omissions

Words that express number, frequency, or year of meeting are omitted from the name of a conference. *See* Fig. 12.17.

Fig. 12.17. Rule 24.7A. Omission of number from name of conference.

Name on title page: II Jornadas de Derecho Natural
Heading: Jornadas de Derecho Natural ...

24.7B.   Additions

The number of a conference, etc., the year, and the place in which it was held are added to the name in parentheses. If any of these elements are not known, they are omitted. *See* Figs. 12.18 and 12.19.

Fig. 12.18. Rule 24.7B. Additions to names of conferences.

[1]Name of
conference   Symposium on Viral Hepatitis (2nd : 1978 : University
[2]Number   of California San Francisco) ◄—— 4
[3]Date   Second Symposium on Viral Hepatitis, University
[4]Place   of California San Francisco, Mar. 16-19, 1978.

Fig. 12.19. Rule 24.7B. Additions to names of conferences.

[1]Name of   International Congress on Ocular Trauma (1976 : Boston,
conference   Mass.)
[2]Date   1   Ocular trauma : International Congress on Ocular
[3]Place   Trauma at Boston

For further guidance in selecting qualifiers for conferences, etc., the LC rule interpretation on this rule should be consulted.[11]

RULE 24.10.   LOCAL CHURCHES, ETC.

24.10A.   A designation in English is added to the name of a local church, if needed, to clarify that the name is that of a church.

> e.g., Santa Maria Bianca della Misericordia (Parish
>   church : Milan, Italy)

24.10B.   The name of the place or ecclesiastical jurisdiction in which a church is located is added using Rules 24.4C4-24.4C6, unless the location is already evident in the name.

> e.g., Mt. Enon Baptist Church (Mitchell County, Ga.)

LC has noted that it will use any rules in 24.4, not just 24.4C4-24.4C6, in choosing the qualifier to be added to the name of a local church, etc.[12]

SUBORDINATE AND RELATED BODIES

The problem of entry of corporate bodies that are subordinate to or closely related to other bodies is a difficult one. No completely unambiguous set of rules (including *AACR 2*) has yet been devised to handle it. The remainder of chapter 24 of *AACR 2* (Rules 24.12-24.27) deals with such rules; yet even with this exhaustive treatment the end result may still depend upon the judgment of the individual cataloger.

There are three parts to this section: general rules, government body rules, and religious organization rules. The cataloger must first know if a body is a government or religious body. This is important because, in some cases, the results of applying the non-government rules to a government body yield a heading not intended by the makers of the code (e.g., "University of Natal," entered in direct order according to the sequence of government body rules, would be entered "Natal. University" if the general sequence of rules were applied). However, once into the sequence for government or religious bodies, the cataloger may be referred back to the general sequence for further instructions.

If it is determined that a body is a government body, Rules 24.17-24.26 must be consulted before any others in chapter 24, because a government body is always a subordinate body—that is, it is always subordinate to a jurisdiction. Once into the rules, the result may be the same as if subordination were not involved—that is, the body may be entered under its own name. (For example, the University of California, Los Angeles, a state institution, and the University of Southern California, a private institution, both end up entered under "University of. . . .") But if the body is one of the types listed in 24.18, it will be entered subordinately. If it *is* one of the types listed, then Rule 24.19 for direct or indirect subheading must be consulted; and if it is one of Types 5 through 10, one of Rules 24.20-24.26 must also be consulted. The cataloger must also be concerned with the level of subordinate body involved. If it is subordinate to another government body that is entered under its *own name* because it is not one of the types listed in 24.18, then general Rules 24.12-24.14 must be consulted for formulation of the heading for the subordinate body. If it is subordinate to another body that is entered under *jurisdiction*, then the cataloger continues to use government body Rules 24.17-24.19 for formulation of the heading for the subordinate body.

If it is determined that a body is a religious body, Rule 24.27 and its subparts are consulted first. Certain kinds of religious subordinate bodies are specified for subordinate entry in these rules. All others are to be treated according to general Rules 24.12-24.14.

For all subordinate bodies other than government or religious, the cataloger uses general Rules 24.12-24.16, which refer back to 24.1-24.3 for construction of headings for subordinate bodies that should be entered under their own names.

SELECTED RULES AND EXAMPLES

RULE 24.12.   GENERAL RULE

If a subordinate body is not a government body entered under jurisdiction, it is to be entered under its own name according to Rules 24.1-24.3 unless it is one of the types listed under 24.13. A reference is made from the name formulated as a subheading of its higher body to the name as an independent heading. *See* Figs. 12.20 and 12.21. (Note the similarity of this rule to 24.17 for government bodies.)

Fig. 12.20. Rule 24.12. Entry of subordinate body under its own name.

Information on title page of exhibition catalog:
    Baxter Art Gallery, California Institute of Technology,
        Pasadena
AACR 2 heading: Baxter Art Gallery.
Refer from: California Institute of Technology, Pasadena.
    Baxter Art Gallery

Fig. 12.21.

Information on title page: National Affiliation for Literacy
    Advance, Laubach Literacy International's pro-
        gramming arm in the U.S. and Canada.
AACR 2 heading: National Affiliation for Literacy Advance.
Refer from: Laubach Literacy International. National
    Affiliation for Literacy Advance

RULE 24.13. SUBORDINATE AND RELATED BODIES ENTERED SUBORDINATELY

When a subordinate or related body's name belongs to one of Types 1-5 below, the heading for that body is constructed so that the higher body is named first, followed by the name of the subordinate or related body. If the name or abbreviation of the higher body is included in the name of the subordinate body in noun form, it is omitted from the subheading, unless it does not make sense to omit it. There may or may not be names of intervening bodies that are part of the hierarchy, depending on the application of Rule 24.14. (Note the similarity of this rule to 24.18 for government bodies. Note also that Types 1-3 in the two rules are nearly identical, but that the other types are quite different.)

Type 1. If a name contains a term that implies the body is part of another body, it is entered subordinately. Examples of such terms: department, division, section, branch, and their equivalents in other languages. *See* Fig. 12.22.

Fig. 12.22. Rule 24.13, Type 1. Subordinate entry of body that is part of another.

Current legal aspects of doing business in the Far
    East / Section of International Law, American Bar
    Association.

    I. American Bar Association. Section of International Law.

A major LC departure from *AACR 2* affects headings constructed by many rules, but it can be illustrated here. LC continues to abbreviate Department as "Dept." even though this is not authorized by *AACR 2* Appendix B, "Abbreviations."[13] *See* Fig. 12.23.

Fig. 12.23. Rule 24.13. Illustration of LC's decision on use of the abbreviation "Dept."

Previously established heading: Notre Dame, Ind.
    University. Dept. of Economics
LC's new heading under *AACR 2*: University of Notre
    Dame. Dept. of Economics.
Note: Even though the heading must be reconstructed for
    other reasons, the abbreviation "Dept." is retained.

Type 2. If a name contains a term that implies that the body is subordinate to another in an administrative sense, it is entered subordinately *if* the name of the higher body is required to identify the subordinate body. *See* Fig. 12.24. *AACR 2* gives two words as examples: committee, commission. LC

has created lists of words in English, French, and Spanish that imply administrative subordination.[14] For the second part of the rule, judgment is to be used
by LC's catalogers to determine whether the name of the higher body is
required for identification.

**Fig. 12.24. Rule 24.13, Type 2. Subordinate entry of body that is
administratively subordinate to another.**

Information on title page: NAIS Teacher Services
      Committee.
Heading: National Association of Independent Schools.
      Teacher Services Committee.
Refer from: NAIS Teacher Services Committee.

Type 3. If a name is "general in nature" or indicates only that it is a
geographic, chronological, numbered, or lettered subdivision of a higher
body, it is entered subordinately. For LC "general in nature" means that the
name has no distinctive elements, such as proper names, nor does it have
subject words.[15] *See* Fig. 12.25.

**Fig. 12.25. Rule 24.13, Type 3. Subordinate entry of body that has a name
that is general in nature.**

Name in credits of motion picture: Brigham Young Univer-
      sity, Media Productions.
Judgment: "Media Productions" is general in nature.
Heading: Brigham Young University. Media Productions.

Type 4. If a name of a unit of a university simply indicates that it
encompasses a particular field of study, it is entered subordinately. A rule
interpretation adds "college" as well as "university" and also adds "interest"
and "activity" to "field of study" as criteria for the type of field encompassed
by the unit.[16] *See* Fig. 12.26.

**Fig. 12.26. Rule 24.13, Type 4. Subordinate entry of body that has a name
that simply indicates a field of study.**

Name on title page: School of Graduate and Professional
      Studies, Emporia State University
Heading: Emporia State University. School of Graduate
      and Professional Studies.

Type 5. If the name of a subordinate or related body includes the entire
name of the higher or related body, it is entered subordinately. LC's rule
interpretation states that "entire name" is to be understood as the name that
was selected for use in the heading for the higher or related body, not
necessarily its catalog-entry form.[17] *See* Fig. 12.27.

Name on title page: Chaucer Group of the Modern
    Language Association
Heading: Modern Language Association of
    America. Chaucer Group.
Note: "of America" is determined from other sources to
    be included in the predominant usage of the higher
    body.

LC considers "U.S." to be equivalent to "United States" when determining whether the entire name is included. LC also considers the name to be included if it is in another language. LC does not apply Type 5 when the subordinate body's name includes a location not included in the higher body's name, when a state university institution contains the name of a statewide university system, or when the name of a local church contains the name of its related denomination.[18]

RULE 24.14.   DIRECT OR INDIRECT SUBHEADING

A body that belongs to one of the types listed in Rule 24.13 and that, therefore, is to be entered subordinately is entered as a subdivision of the element closest above it in its hierarchy that is entered under its own name. If there are elements in the hierarchy that fall between the subdivision and the name that is to be the entry element, they are omitted unless they are needed to distinguish this body from another that does or might have the same entry form (e.g., several sections of the same institution might have an office called the "Personnel Office"). A reference is made from the form that includes the name of an intervening body that has been omitted from the heading. (Note the similarity of this rule to 24.19 for government bodies.) *See* Figs. 12.28 and 12.29.

Name on title page: University of Washington Libraries,
    Manuscripts Section
Heading: University of Washington. Libraries.
    Manuscript Section.

Note: Even though the University of Washington is a government body, its subordinate bodies are entered according to 24.12-24.14 because the University is entered under its own name, not under jurisdiction.

Fig. 12.29. Rule 24.14. Direct subordinate entry of a laboratory.

Name on title page: Radiological Research Laboratory,
    Department of Radiology, Columbia University, New
    York, N.Y.
Heading: Columbia University. Radiological Research
    Laboratory.
Refer from: Columbia University. Dept. of Radiology.
    Radiological Research Laboratory

Omission of elements of a hierarchy is another area where the results of various catalogers' judgments may vary. The words "or is likely to be" often mean differences in judgment. The Library of Congress has identified for its catalogers two categories where judgment should not vary. In the first category, names of bodies performing functions common to many higher bodies (e.g., Personnel Office; Planning Dept.), the hierarchy should be included. In the second category, names of bodies performing major functions unique to the higher body (e.g., Division of Fisheries; Division of Transport [under the Ministry of Transport, Industry, and Engineering]), intervening elements of the hierarchy should be omitted. Common sense must dictate the inclusion of hierarchy for the great middle ground. The cataloger should consider whether the name would be appropriate for another subordinate body within the same higher body structure and whether some word or phrase in a name in the hierarchy expresses an idea necessary to the identification of the subordinate body.[19]

GOVERNMENT BODIES AND OFFICIALS:

SELECTED RULES AND EXAMPLES

RULE 24.17.   GENERAL RULE

A government body that is not one of Types 1-10 below is entered under its own name according to Rules 24.1-24.3, or is entered subordinately to a higher body that is entered under its own name according to Rules 24.12-24.14. A reference is made from the form the name would have if it were a subheading under the name of the government. *See* Fig. 12.30.

Fig. 12.30. Rule 24.17. Entry of a government body under its own name.

Heading: National Institutes of Health (U.S.)
Refer from: United States. National Institutes of Health
            N.I.H.
            United States. Public Health Service.
                National Institutes of Health
            United States. Federal Security Agency.
                National Institutes of Health

The Library of Congress treats the United Nations as a government body when applying these rules.[20]

RULE 24.18. GOVERNMENT AGENCIES ENTERED SUBORDINATELY

When a government body's name belongs to one of Types 1-10 below, it is entered subordinately. If the name or abbreviation of the government is included in the name of the subordinate body in noun form, it is omitted from the subheading, unless it does not make sense to omit it. There may or may not be names of intervening bodies between the name of the government and the name of the subordinate body being established, depending on the application of Rule 24.19.

A rule interpretation from LC should be consulted for guidance in the more unusual situations that arise when a name lacks a term indicating that it is a corporate body or when a government agency name contains the entire name of its parent body (there is no equivalent to Rule 24.13, Type 5, under Rule 24.18).[21]

Type 1. If a name contains a word that implies the body is part of another body, it is entered subordinately. The same terms given as examples under Rule 24.13, Type 1, apply here. *See* Fig. 12.31.

Fig. 12.31. Rule 24.18, Type 1. Entry of subordinate government body
that has a name implying it is part of another body.

Name on title page: Division of Planning, City of Jersey
    City
Heading: Jersey City (N.J.). Division of Planning.

Type 2. If a name contains a word that implies that the body is subordinate to the government in an administrative sense, it is entered subordinately *if* the name of the government is required to identify the agency. *See* Fig. 12.32.

Fig. 12.32. Rule 24.18, Type 2. Entry of subordinate government body
that has a name implying administrative subordination.

Information on title page: Legislative Commission on
    Medical Cost Containment, Raleigh; [seal]:
    The Great Seal of the State of North Carolina.
Heading: North Carolina. Legislative Commission on
    Medical Cost Containment.

LC has issued a rule interpretation for catalogers at LC. There are two tests to be applied here. One is a judgment as to whether the name contains a word that implies "administrative subordination." The cataloger should ask whether the word is commonly used in a particular jurisdiction for names of government subdivisions. If in doubt, the word is considered *not* to have such an implication. The same list of terms in English, French, and Spanish, given for Rule 24.13, Type 2, is given under the rule interpretation for this rule and should be consulted when needed.[22]

If the name passes the first test, it is then evaluated as to whether the name of the government is required for identification. "If the name of the government is stated explicitly or implied in the wording of the name, enter it independently; in all other cases, enter the name subordinately."[23] Thus, the United States Travel Service, which includes the government in its name, is entered independently: United States Travel Service. The Soil Conservation Service, however, is entered subordinately: United States. Soil Conservation Service.

If the body is entered independently according to this interpretation, the name of the government is added as a qualifier unless the name or an understandable surrogate for the name of the government (e.g., "American" for U.S.) appears in the name.[24] *See* Fig. 12.30 (page 320).

Type 3. If a name is "general in nature" or indicates only that it is a geographic, chronological, numbered, or lettered subdivision of a government or a government agency, it is entered subordinately. *See* Fig. 12.33.

Fig. 12.33. Rule 24.18, Type 3. Entry of subordinate government body that has a name that is general in nature.

Name on title page: U.S. Public Health Service. Region V

Judgment: Region V is a name that is general in nature.

Heading: United States. Public Health Service. Region V.

LC policy for interpreting this rule states that if the body is at the national level, it is to be considered general and entered subordinately if the name contains neither distinctive words nor subject words or if the name contains only a general phrase and the term "national" or "state" or their foreign language equivalents.[25] For example, enter subordinately:

> Research Center
> Library
> Technical Laboratory
> National Gallery

but enter independently:

> Population Research Center (U.S.)
> Nuclear Energy Library (U.S.)
> Technical Laboratory of Oceanographic Research (U.S.)
> National Gallery of Art (U.S.)

If the body is below the national level, and it is not any of the other types under 24.18, LC enters it under the name of the government unless that name is explicitly or implicitly included in the subordinate body's name or the name contains some other word that tends to make it absolutely unique (e.g., a proper noun).[26]

As under 24.18, Type 2, a body entered independently under Type 3 will have the name of the government added as a qualifier unless it is already part of the body's name.[27]

Type 4. If the name represents a major executive agency (as defined by official publications of the government) it is entered subordinately. *See* Fig. 12.34.

Fig. 12.34. Rule 24.18, Type 4. Entry of a major executive agency.

Name on title page: Oyo State Executive Council.
Heading: Oyo (Nigeria : State). Executive Council.

LC restricts application of this rule to major executive agencies of *national* governments.[28]

Type 5. Government legislative bodies are entered subordinately according to the provisions in Rule 24.21. *See* Fig. 12.38 (page 325).

Type 6. Government courts are entered subordinately according to the provisions in Rule 24.23. *See* Fig. 12.39 (page 325).

Type 7. Principal armed services are entered subordinately according to the provisions in Rule 24.24. *See* Fig. 12.40 (page 326).

Type 8. Chiefs of state and other heads of government are entered subordinately according to the provisions in Rule 24.20. *See* Fig. 12.37.

Type 9, Embassies, consulates, etc., and Type 10, Delegations to international and intergovernmental bodies, are also entered subordinately.

RULE 24.19. DIRECT OR INDIRECT SUBHEADING

This rule is the same as 24.14 except that the body is entered under the heading for the government instead of the lowest element in the hierarchy that is entered under its own name. Other elements in the hierarchy are interposed or omitted in the same way and with the same difficulties in judgment. (*See* discussion under 24.14.) *See* Figs. 12.35 and 12.36.

Fig. 12.35. Rule 24.19. Indirect subordinate entry of an office.

Name on title page: Office of the Executive Director,
    Colorado Department of Natural Resources.
Heading: Colorado. Dept. of Natural Resources. Office
    of the Executive Director.

Fig. 12.36. Rule 24.19. Direct subordinate entry of an office.

Name on title page: U.S. Department of Commerce
    Maritime Administration, Office of Port and
    Intermodal Development.
Heading: United States. Office of Port and Intermodal
    Development.
Refer from: United States. Maritime Administra-
    tion. Office of Port and Intermodal Development.

SPECIAL RULES

RULE 24.20.   GOVERNMENT OFFICIALS

24.20B.   Heads of state, etc.

The heading for a head of state who is acting in an official capacity is
made up of the name of the government followed by the title of the office in
English, if possible, the inclusive years the person held that office, and a brief
form name of the person in the language used for the person's personal
heading. Use non-sexist terminology, e.g., "Sovereign," not "Queen" or
"King." *See* Fig. 12.37.

Fig. 12.37. Rule 24.20B. Entry of governor as an official.

	1	2	3	4
[1]Government				

[1]Government   New Jersey. Governor (1974-1982 : Byrne)
[2]Title   A plan for education and tax reform in New Jersey :
[3]Dates   special message to the Legislature, June 13, 1974 / Brendan
[4]Surname   T. Byrne, Governor.

An explanatory reference should be made to the incumbent as a person (*see*
26.3C1).

24.20C.   Heads of governments and of international governmental bodies

For heads of governments who are not also heads of state and for heads
of international intergovernmental organizations, the subheading is the title of

the office in the vernacular or in the official language of the organization, without dates or names.

RULE 24.21. LEGISLATIVE BODIES

Chambers of legislative bodies are entered subordinately to the legislative body, and committees are entered subordinately to the legislature or to a chamber, whichever is appropriate. A subcommittee of the U.S. Congress is entered as a subheading of the committee to which it is subordinate. If legislatures are numbered, the number and year(s) are added [e.g., United States. Congress (95th : 1977-1978).]. Session numbers may also need to be added. *See* Fig. 12.38.

Fig. 12.38. Rule 24.21. Entry of a state legislative committee.

Name on title page. Committee on Motor Vehicles,
    Illinois House of Representatives
Heading: Illinois. General Assembly. House of
    Representatives. Committee on Motor Vehicles.

It should be noted that, although *AACR 2* shows in its examples "United States. Congress. House of Representatives," which is the official name of that body, the Library of Congress continues to use the conventional name "House" in its headings for the body.[29]

RULE 24.23. COURTS

Civil and criminal courts are entered as subheadings of the jurisdiction. A place name for the place a court sits or the area it serves is omitted but added as a conventional addition if needed to distinguish it from others of the same name. *See* Fig. 12.39.

Fig. 12.39. Rule 24.23. Entry of a court under jurisdiction with addition of area it serves.

Name on title page: Franklin County branch of the
    Court of Common Pleas of the 39th Judicial
    District of Pennsylvania
Heading: Pennsylvania. Court of Common Pleas (39th
    Judicial District).

RULE 24.24. ARMED FORCES

A principal service of the armed forces of a government is entered as a subheading of the government. A branch, district, or unit is entered as a subheading for the principal service; and if it is numbered, the numbering in the style used in the name follows the name. *See* Fig. 12.40.

Fig. 12.40. Rule 24.24. Entry of an armed service branch under the principal service.

Name on chief source of information:
  Air Defense Command, U.S. Air Force
Heading: United States. Air Force. Air Defense Command.

A rule interpretation from LC indicates that for a branch, district, or unit to be entered as a subheading of the service, it must be subject to combat, an administrative unit over a combat unit, or a unit that serves as a direct support unit to the preceding two types. Thus, research agencies, schools, hospitals, etc., would be entered using the general rules.[30]

RELIGIOUS BODIES AND OFFICIALS:

SELECTED RULES AND EXAMPLES

RULE 24.27.   RELIGIOUS BODIES AND OFFICIALS

24.27A.   Councils, etc., of a single religious body

Councils, etc., of a single religious body are entered as subheadings of that body. Appropriate additions may be made as for conferences, etc. (24.7B). General councils are entered according to the general rules for subordinate bodies (24.12-24.13). *See* Fig. 12.41.

Fig. 12.41. Rule 24.27A. Entry of a religious council.

Name on title page: Il Concilio romano del 1725
Heading: Catholic Church. Concilio romano (1725).

24.27B.   Religious officials

The heading for a religious official acting in an official capacity looks very much like the heading for a head of state (24.20B). It consists of the heading for the diocese, order, patriarchate, etc., followed by the title in English (unless there is no English equivalent), the inclusive years of incumbency, and the name of the person. *See* Fig. 12.42.

Fig. 12.42. Rule 24.27B. Entry of a religious official.

Name on title page: His Holiness John Paul II
Heading: Catholic Church. Pope (1978-   : John
    Paul II)
Refer in an explanatory reference to the personal head-
    ing for John Paul II.

24.27C.   Subordinate bodies

Provinces, dioceses, synods, and other subordinate units having jurisdiction over geographic areas are entered as subheadings of the religious body. For the Catholic Church, the English form of name should be used. *See* Fig. 12.43.

Fig. 12.43. Rule 24.27C. Entry of religious subordinate body.

Name on title page: Arzobispado del Cuzco
Heading: Catholic Church. Archdiocese of Cuzco (Peru).
Refer from: Catholic Church. Arzobispado del Cuzco
(Peru).

NOTES

[1]*Cataloging Service Bulletin*, no. 18 (Fall 1982): 67-68, 69, 71.

[2]Ibid., pp. 65-67.

[3]*Cataloging Service Bulletin*, no. 11 (Winter 1981): 34.

[4]*Cataloging Service Bulletin*, no. 18 (Fall 1982): 68.

[5]*Cataloging Service Bulletin*, no. 26 (Fall 1984): 17.

[6]"AACR 2 Options to Be Followed by the Library of Congress: Chapters 1-2, 12, 21-26," *Library of Congress Information Bulletin* 37 (July 21, 1978): 427.

[7]*Cataloging Service Bulletin*, no. 18 (Fall 1982): 68-70.

[8]Ibid., pp. 70-74.

[9]*Cataloging Service Bulletin*, no. 11 (Winter 1981): 37.

[10]*Cataloging Service Bulletin*, no. 16 (Spring 1982): 44-45.

[11]*Cataloging Service Bulletin*, no. 21 (Summer 1983): 29-30.

[12]*Cataloging Service Bulletin*, no. 11 (Winter 1981): 39.

[13]*Cataloging Service Bulletin*, no. 25 (Summer 1984): 78.

[14]*Cataloging Service Bulletin*, no. 20 (Spring 1983): 21-22.

[15]*Cataloging Service Bulletin*, no. 25 (Summer 1984): 67-68.

[16]*Cataloging Service Bulletin*, no. 15 (Winter 1982): 26.

[17]*Cataloging Service Bulletin*, no. 23 (Winter 1983): 22-23.

[18]Ibid., pp. 23-24.

[19]*Cataloging Service Bulletin*, no. 18 (Fall 1982): 76-78.

[20]*Cataloging Service Bulletin*, no. 23 (Winter 1983): 38.

[21]*Cataloging Service Bulletin*, no. 17 (Summer 1982): 22-23.

[22]*Cataloging Service Bulletin*, no. 20 (Spring 1983): 22-23.

[23]Ibid., p. 23.

[24]Ibid., p. 24.

[25]*Cataloging Service Bulletin*, no. 25 (Summer 1984): 68-69.

[26]Ibid., p. 69.

[27]Ibid., p. 70.

[28]*Cataloging Service Bulletin*, no. 14 (Fall 1981): 48.

[29]*Cataloging Service Bulletin*, no. 18 (Fall 1982): 79.

[30]*Cataloging Service Bulletin*, no. 24 (Spring 1984): 21-22.

SUGGESTED READING

Chan, Lois Mai. *Cataloging and Classification*. New York, McGraw-Hill, 1981. pp. 108-113.

Hagler, Ronald, and Peter Simmons. *The Bibliographic Record and Information Technology*. Chicago, American Library Association, 1982. pp. 198-213.

Maxwell, Margaret F. *Handbook for AACR 2*. Chicago, American Library Association, 1980. Chapter 14.

13
Uniform Titles

INTRODUCTION

When a work has appeared under more than one title, a uniform or conventional title may be used for cataloging purposes in order to bring all editions of the work together. Uniform titles are commonly used for sacred scriptures, creeds, liturgical works, and anonymous classics. "Bible" is a very common example of a uniform title in library catalogs; similarly, editions of the Mother Goose verses are assembled under the uniform title "Mother Goose." In these cases the uniform titles represent main entry headings. In other instances the uniform title is bracketed and placed between the main entry and the body of the entry, as in the case of music, laws, liturgical works, and translations. *AACR 2*, chapter 25, contains many further suggestions for extending these rules to other instances. The Library of Congress, on its printed cards, has used uniform titles consistently only in those instances listed above; so libraries that apply these rules fully must also assume responsibility for revising many LC printed cards. MARC records formulated by LC according to *AACR 2*, however, contain all uniform titles provided by the rules. These do not all appear on LC's printed cards, but may be available to a library depending upon the type of access the library has to machine-readable records.[1]

One of the problems faced in constructing uniform titles is the choice of a title when titles of a work appear in more than one form. Titles may be in different languages, in one or more long forms and one or more short forms, or in two simultaneous versions (as when a work is published simultaneously in England and the United States under different titles). Some works may be published in parts and need identification of the part *without* identification of the whole (as in the case of one title from a trilogy), or *with* identification of the whole (as in the case of a book from Homer's *Iliad*, called only "Book 1"). Further additions may be needed to distinguish uniform titles from each other or from other headings, to identify the language in which the work appears, to identify the version, or to date the particular edition. The purpose of this chapter is to demonstrate the general rules used to resolve these problems. Much more detail can be found in *AACR 2*, chapter 25.

In addition to the first rule, which sets down the conditions for use of uniform titles, the *AACR 2* chapter comprises three groups of rules: basic rules for choice and form of the title itself (Rules 25.2-25.4, and 25.12), rules for additions to uniform titles (Rules 25.5-25.11), and special rules for certain materials (Rules 25.13-25.36). The materials given special treatment are manuscripts (25.13), incunabula (25.14), legal materials (25.15-25.16), sacred scriptures (25.17-25.18), liturgical and other religious works (25.19-25.24), and music (25.25-25.36).

A heading created using this chapter is coded 130, 240, 630, 730, or 830 in the MARC format, depending upon whether it functions as a main entry, a supplementary title between main entry and the title proper, a subject heading, an added entry, or a series tracing.

RULE 25.1. USE OF UNIFORM TITLES

Whether or not uniform titles are needed depends on the type and size of catalog one has. *AACR 2* gives five criteria to use in deciding whether to use uniform titles:

"a) how well the work is known

b) how many manifestations of the work are involved

c) whether the main entry is under title

d) whether the work was originally in another language

e) the extent to which the catalogue is used for research purposes."[2]

In essence this rule states that the entire set of rules on uniform titles is optional, and a policy decision should be made in each cataloging agency as to whether some or all of the rules should be applied.

GENERAL RULES:

SELECTED RULES AND EXAMPLES

RULE 25.2. BASIC RULE

25.2A.   The basic rule gives an instruction to choose one title from among various ones that may appear on different manifestations of a work. (Revised editions are not included when considering variant titles of a work. *See* Rule 25.2B.)

On the bibliographic record for a particular item the uniform title should be used if:

1) the title proper differs from the uniform title;

2) an addition of another element must be made because the title proper is not sufficient to organize the file (e.g., a uniform title is identical in form to the heading for a person);

3) a title main entry or a title added entry must be differentiated from that of another work (e.g., two different serials are entered under their titles, which are identical); or

4) the title proper contains elements that obscure the title of the work (e.g., there are introductory words about the presentation of the work that precede the title proper but must be transcribed in grammatical order).

The uniform title is given before the title proper and enclosed in square brackets. If the main entry is title, *AACR 2* calls for it also to be enclosed in brackets, but an option allows omitting the brackets if the uniform title is used as main entry.

The Library of Congress is following the option, which is a continuation of LC's past practice. In addition it is LC practice not to enclose uniform titles in brackets when used in added entries.[3] The examples in this text follow LC practice.

It is also LC practice in the case of anonymous classics that have been published in many editions, translations, and differing titles, to use the uniform title for all editions, even when it does not differ from the title proper.[4] *See* Fig. 13.1.

Fig. 13.1. Rule 25.2A. Uniform title as main entry without square brackets — LC practice.

Uniform title
as main
entry
→ Beowulf.
      Beowulf : an edition with manuscript spacing notation and graphotactic analyses / Robert D. Stevick.

25.2B.   Uniform titles are not used for revisions or updated versions of a work in the same language as the original. Instead, these are related by giving a note about the earlier edition in the bibliographic record for the later edition. *See* Fig. 13.2.

Fig. 13.2. Rule 25.2B. New title, not uniform title, is used for new edition in the same language.

Note giving
title of
earlier
edition
Hawker, Pat.
      Amateur radio techniques / Pat Hawker. – 6th ed. -- London : Radio Society of Great Britain, 1978.

      336 p. : ill. ; 25 cm.

      First ed. published with title: Technical topics for the radio amateur.

INDIVIDUAL TITLES

RULE 25.3.   WORKS CREATED AFTER 1500

25.3A.   For a work created after 1500 the title in the original language by which the work has become known is used as its uniform title. The "known" title is judged from its use in manifestations of the work or in reference sources. *See* Fig. 13.3.

Fig. 13.3. Rule 25.3A. Uniform title in original language.

Suder, Joseph, 1892-
   [Dona nobis pacem]
   Festmesse in D [sound recording] / Joseph Suder.

  Other titles given to this work:
    Messe Dona nobis pacem
    Grosse Messe Dona nobis pacem

LC catalogers delete the initial article from a uniform title if it is in the nominative case, even when the uniform title is under a name. This provision also applies to Rule 25.4A.[5] With this provision, the first, third, and fifth examples under this rule in *AACR 2* would not begin with "The" (e.g., [Pickwick papers], not [The Pickwick papers]).

25.3B.   If none of the titles in the original language can be established as being the "best known," the title proper of the original edition is used. In using such original titles, one should omit introductory phrases, statements of responsibility that can be grammatically separated, and initial articles. LC also omits alternative titles.[6]

25.3C.   Simultaneous publication under different titles

25.3C1.   When a work is published in two or more editions simultaneously in the same language with different titles, the cataloger should use as uniform title the one for the edition published in the cataloging agency's country, if this applies. If it does not apply, the title of the edition received first should be used. *See* Fig. 13.4.

Fig. 13.4. Rule 25.3C. American title used as uniform title for work whose British title is different.

Mansfield, Peter, 1928-
   [Arab world]
    The Arabs / Peter Mansfield. -- Harmondsworth : Penguin,
  1928.
Note explaining uniform title:
    American ed. published under title: The Arab world.

RULE 25.4. WORKS CREATED BEFORE 1501

25.4A.   If a work was created before 1501, the title in the original language by which the work is identified in modern reference sources is used. If none of the titles can be established in reference sources, the title found most frequently in modern editions, early editions, or manuscript copies (in that order of preference) is used. This rule, however, is superseded by Rules 25.4B-25.4C and 25.14, if they apply. *See* Fig. 13.5.

LC is deleting all initial articles as described under 25.3A.

Fig. 13.5. Rule 25.4. Uniform title for pre-1501 work as identified in reference sources.

Uniform ——————▶ Gawain and the Grene Knight.
title   Sir Gawain and the Green Knight / translated
                        with an introduction by Brian Stone.

25.4B-25.4C.

In general, a well-established English title, if there is one, is used for a pre-1501 Greek work or anonymous work in nonroman script. *See* Fig. 13.6.

Fig. 13.6. Rules 25.4 and 25.5D. Anonymous pre-1501 work originally in nonroman script entered under established English title with the language of the translation in hand added.

[1]Uniform
title   Arabian nights. English.
                   More fairy tales from the Arabian nights /
[2]Language   edited and arranged by E. Dixon ; illustrated by
                   J.D. Batten.

RULE 25.5. ADDITIONS TO UNIFORM TITLES

25.5B.   If uniform titles used as main entries are identical to each other or to the form used as the heading for a person, corporate body, or reference, additions are made in parentheses to the uniform title. *See* Fig. 13.7.

Fig. 13.7. Rule 25.5B. Additions in parentheses to distinguish between two otherwise identical uniform titles.

Jungle book (1942)
   Jungle book [motion picture]

Jungle book (1967)
   The jungle book [motion picture]

For this rule LC has made a lengthy rule interpretation that prescribes the kinds of additions that are to be made to distinguish between otherwise identical titles of different serials, including monographic series.[7] In general such conflicts are handled by adding a uniform title to the bibliographic record for the serial in hand, not to the one cataloged earlier.

Place of publication is LC's preferred qualifying term for conflicting serial titles, e.g.,

> Times (Charleston, S.C.)

> Times (Kansas City, Mo.)

However, if the title consists only of an indication of type and/or periodicity of publication, or if the place is inadequate to resolve the conflict, or if the conflicting titles include initials of their issuing bodies' names, then the heading for the body that originated or issued the serial is used as the qualifying term, e.g.,

> Occasional paper (Canberra College of Advanced Education.
>   Library)

> Occasional paper (London Public Library and Art Museum (Ont.))

> European physics series (McGraw-Hill)

> European physics series (Wiley)
> [both works published in New York, N.Y.]

Other qualifiers may be added when the above provisions do not suffice. Other qualifiers may be place and date, corporate body and date, date, edition statement, other title information, etc. The LC rule interpretation should be consulted for elaboration on these qualifiers and on other special situations.

In the case of radio and television programs, LC adds the qualifier "(Radio program)" or "(Television program)" to all such titles even if there is no conflict. LC also has special provisions for U.S. census publications, comics, and motion pictures.[8]

25.5C.   Identical uniform titles that are entered under the same personal or corporate heading also need additions in parentheses to distinguish them.

> e.g., United States.
>   [Census (1960)]

> United States.
>   [Census (1970)]

25.5D.   When the item in hand is in a different language from the original, the name of the language of the item is added to the uniform title. LC catalogers use the language name as established in *Library of Congress Subject Headings*.[9] *See* Figs. 13.6 and 13.8.

Fig. 13.8. Rule 25.5D. Modern translation with original title as uniform title, followed by language of translation.

¹Uniform
title   Leys, Simon.
                                      [Les habits neufs du président Mao. English]
²Language   The Chairman's new clothes : Mao and the
                                  cultural revolution / Simon Leys ; translated by
                                  Carol Appleyard and Patrick Goode.

AACR 2 Rule 25.5D and LC's rule interpretation on multilingual works should be consulted when this situation arises.[10]

25.5E.   An option allows addition of GMDs at the end of uniform titles. LC is not applying this option.[11]

RULE 25.6.   PARTS OF A WORK

This rule is not applied to parts of the Bible and certain other sacred scriptures (*see* Rules 25.17-25.18) or to parts of musical works (*see* Rule 25.32).

25.6A.   Single parts

25.6A1.   When a separately cataloged part of a work has a title that is not dependent for its meaning upon the title of the collected work, the title of the part alone is used as the uniform title. A reference is made from the form the heading would have if the title of the part were a subheading of the title of the whole work. *See* Fig. 13.9.

Fig. 13.9. Rule 26.6A1. Separately cataloged part with its own title as uniform title.

Hesse, Hermann, 1877-1962.
[Tractat vom Steppenwolf. English]
Treatise on the Steppenwolf / Hermann Hesse ; [translated from the German] ; paintings by Jaroslav Bradac.

Note: The title of the whole work is *Der Steppenwolf.*
Refer from: Hesse, Hermann, 1877-1962.
          Steppenwolf. Tractat vom Steppenwolf. English

25.6A2.   When a separately cataloged part of a work has a title that *is* dependent for its meaning upon the title of the whole work, the uniform title is the title of the whole work followed by the title of the part as a subheading. Arabic numerals are used to record part numbers. *See* Fig. 13.10.

Fig. 13.10. Rule 25.6A2. Separately cataloged part given as subheading
of the title of the whole work.

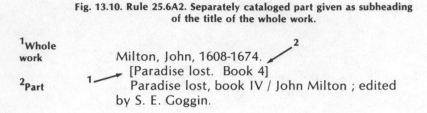

¹Whole
work   Milton, John, 1608-1674.
                        [Paradise lost. Book 4]
²Part   Paradise lost, book IV / John Milton ; edited
                        by S. E. Goggin.

25.6B.   Several parts

When an item consists of consecutively numbered parts, the designation
of the parts in the singular is used as a subheading of the title of the whole
work and is followed by the inclusive numbering of parts. *See* Fig. 13.11.

Fig. 13.11. Rule 25.6B. Separately cataloged consecutive parts of a work
given as subheading of the title of the whole work.

¹Whole
work   Milton, John, 1608-1674.
                        [Paradise lost. Book 9-10]
²Singular   Paradise lost, books IX and X / John Milton ;
form of   edited by Cyril Aldred.
name of part

When an item has two parts not consecutively numbered, the uniform title
is made for the first part, and a name-title added entry is made for the second.
When an item has three or more parts not consecutively numbered, the
uniform title of the whole work is used, followed by "Selections."

COLLECTIVE TITLES

Collective titles can be general (e.g., "Works," "Selections") or more
specific (e.g., "Novels," "Poems," "Laws, etc."). When these are used alone,
the effect is to separate originals from translations, different editions from
each other, etc., if the titles proper are different. They also are inadequate
when being used in added entries. Therefore, LC has emphasized using Rule
25.5C in conjunction with collective titles when needed to bring together items
with different titles proper or to refer to a work in an added entry. The
designation to be enclosed in parentheses may be title proper, editor,
translator, publisher, etc. — whichever best fits each case. Two of the examples
given are:

        United States.
            [Laws, etc. (U.S. code)]
            United States code . . .

Maugham, W. Somerset (William Somerset), 1874-1965.
[Short stories (Heinemann)]
Complete short stories . . .

This technique is applied only after the need arises; thus, earlier entries must be revised.[12]

RULE 25.8. COMPLETE WORKS

If an item contains the complete works of a person, the collective title "Works" is used as uniform title. *See* Fig. 13.12.

Fig. 13.12. Rule 25.8. Collective title "Works" used as uniform title.

Posada, José Guadalupe, 1852-1913.
[Works. English & German. 1976]
Das Werk von Jose Guadalupe Posada = The works of José Guadalupe Posada / edited and with an introduction by Hannes Jähn.

A rule interpretation from LC indicates that "Works" occurs so frequently that there should always be additions made to such uniform titles to make them distinctive. The interpretation outlines the additions to be made.[13]

RULE 25.9. SELECTIONS

When an item contains three or more works in various forms, all by the same person, the collective title "Selections" is used as uniform title. *See* Fig. 13.13.

Fig. 13.13. Rule 25.9. Collective title "Selections" used as uniform title.

Twain, Mark, 1835-1910.
[Selections. 1972]
The best of Twain / selected and introduced by Mike Kalmbach.

LC calls for the same additions here that are made to the collective title "Works."[14]

RULE 25.10. WORKS IN A SINGLE FORM

The following collective titles are used for a collection of the works of a person all in one form:

Correspondence	Poems
Essays	Prose works
Novels	Short stories
Plays	Speeches

LC applies this rule only when the title proper of the collection is not distinctive or when there is no collective title proper.[15]

SPECIAL RULES FOR CERTAIN MATERIALS:

SELECTED RULES AND EXAMPLES

LEGAL MATERIALS

RULE 25.15. LAWS, ETC.

25.15A.   **Modern laws, etc.**

25.15A1.   **Collections**
A collection of legislative enactments is given the uniform title "Laws, etc.," unless the compilation is on a particular subject. *See* Fig. 13.14.

Fig. 13.14. Rule 25.15A1. Collective title "Laws, etc." used as uniform title.

India.
   [Laws, etc.]
   The Code of civil procedure, 1908 (5 of 1908), as modified up to the 1st May 1977.

When a compilation of laws is on a particular subject, a citation title, if there is one, should be used as uniform title. If there is no citation title, a uniform title should be constructed according to Rule 25.3. LC adds that if a subject compilation lacks both a citation title and a collective title, the uniform title of the first law in the collection should be used.[16]

25.15A2.   **Single laws, etc.**
Single laws are assigned as uniform title one of the following (in order of preference): an official citation title (or official short title), an unofficial short or citation title used in legal literature, the official title, or any other official designation. *See* Fig. 13.15.

Fig. 13.15. Rule 25.15A2. Official short title used as uniform title.

[1]Government
[2]Uniform title
[3]Language

Québec (Province).
   [Labour code. English & French]
      Code du travail : Titre 1, des relations du travail = Labour code : Title, labour relations.

RULE 25.16. TREATIES, ETC.

The uniform title for treaties is "Treaties, etc." Various additions are made depending upon the circumstances: the second party for a collection or single treaties between two parties; the date or earliest date of signing (in the form: year, abbreviated name of the month, number of the day) for a single treaty. A single treaty between four or more parties is entered under the name by which the treaty is known (in English, if possible) followed by the year of signing in parentheses. Added entries for individual signers, if made, are formulated with the uniform title "Treaties, etc." followed by date of signing. *See* Fig. 13.16.

Fig. 13.16. Rule 25.16. Uniform title for a treaty between two parties.

```
1Conven-
tional uniform      United States.                    2          3
title                 [Treaties, etc.  Vietnam, 1972 Oct. 2]
2Second         1     Agricultural commodities : agreement be-
Country               tween the United States of America and Viet-
3Date                 Nam signed at Saigon October 2, 1972.
```

SACRED SCRIPTURES

RULE 25.17. GENERAL RULE

The uniform title for a sacred scripture should be the title that is usually used in English language reference sources that discuss the particular religious group that uses the scripture.

RULE 25.18. PARTS OF SACRED SCRIPTURES AND ADDITIONS

25.18A.   Bible

When appropriate, the testaments (designated O.T. and N.T.) are added after the word "Bible." Then books are designated. If the books are numbered, the number is given as an ordinal arabic numeral after the name. The name of a group of books may also be a subdivision of the testament (e.g., Minor Prophets, Apocrypha, Gospels). Next are added, as appropriate: 1) language; 2) version, translator, name of manuscripts or repository, or reviser; and 3) year. Examples are:

Bible.   *N.T. Gospels . . .*
Bible.   *O.T. Historical books . . .*
Bible.   *O.T. Genesis XII, 1 — XXV, 11 . . .*
Bible.   *N.T. Corinthians, 1st . . .*

Bible.   [parts] [language] [versions] [selections] [date]
Bible.   English. Knox. 1956.
Bible.   *N.T.* English. Goodspeed. 1943.
Bible.   *O.T. Leviticus.* Hebrew. Samaritan. 1959.
Bible.   English. Authorized. Selections. 1947.

Note: Enter combinations of selections or excerpts under the most specific
Bible heading and insert subheading "Selections" after language and version
but before date (Rule 25.18A9). *See* Figs. 13.17 and 13.18.

Fig. 13.17. Rule 25.18A. Uniform title entries for the Bible.

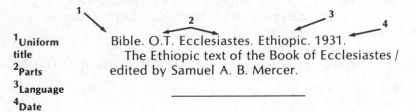

^{1}Uniform   1
title   Bible. English. Selections. 1931.
^{2}Language   Readings from the Bible.

Contents note to clarify subheading:
^{3}Selections   Contents: The birth of Jesus.–The Lord's
^{4}Date   Prayer.–XXIII Psalm.–Ten Commandments.

Fig. 13.18.

^{1}Uniform   Bible. O.T. Ecclesiastes. Ethiopic. 1931.
title   The Ethiopic text of the Book of Ecclesiastes /
^{2}Parts   edited by Samuel A. B. Mercer.
^{3}Language
^{4}Date

25.18B.-25.18M.

These are special rules for the Talmud, Mishnah and Tosefta, Midrashim,
Buddhist scriptures, Vedas, Aranyakas, Brahmanas, Upanishads, Jaina
Āgama, Avesta, and Koran. Rules are given for parts and additions as for the
Bible.

LITURGICAL WORKS

RULE 25.19.   FORM AND LANGUAGE OF TITLE OF LITURGICAL WORKS

When a liturgical work is entered under an English language corporate body name, the uniform title should also be in English if there is an established English title; if not, the uniform title is given in the language of the liturgy. LC restricts use of English language titles, however, to the most famous works that are represented by fixed English titles in existing bibliographic descriptions.[17] *See* Fig. 13.19.

Fig. 13.19. Rule 25.19. Uniform title for a liturgical work.

[1]Corporate name   Catholic Church. ← 1

                      [Mass, Epiphany. German] ← 3

[2]Uniform title   2 ⟋   Messe an Epiphanias.

[3]Language

RULES 25.20-25.23.

These are special rules for Catholic and Jewish liturgical works, for variant and special texts, and for parts of liturgical works.

MUSIC

RULE 25.25.   GENERAL RULE

"Formulate a uniform title for a musical work as instructed in 25.26-25.36. Use the general rules 25.1-25.7 insofar as they apply to music and are not contradicted by the following rules."

RULE 25.26.   DEFINITIONS

AACR 2 carefully distinguishes here between the use of the word "title" and the use of the word "work" in these rules. Essentially, "title" refers to the words used to name the "work," which refers to a whole unit, a set of works with a group title, or a group of works with a single opus number.

RULES 25.27-25.31.

Uniform titles are frequently used in cataloging music because the same musical composition is often issued in numerous editions with variations in the language and the wording of the title pages. Composer-title cross references are made from forms of the title not used as uniform title, as needed. The following examples are typical:

Beethoven, Ludwig van, 1770-1827.
  Battle of Vitoria
  see
Beethoven, Ludwig van, 1770-1827.
  Wellingtons Sieg.

Beethoven, Ludwig van, 1770-1827.
  Cantata on the death of Emperor Joseph II
  see
Beethoven, Ludwig van, 1770-1827.
  Kantate auf den Tod Kaiser Josephs II.

In the selection and construction of uniform titles the most reliable bibliographical sources are consulted, such as thematic indexes, bibliographies, music encyclopedias, etc. Information given in the work cataloged is not used without an attempt at verification. The Library of Congress catalogs are certainly useful in constructing a uniform title, but only after the cataloger has identified the work in thematic or other musical sources.

Rules 25.25-25.33 give the principles for construction of a uniform title for a single work. The basic rule for choice of uniform title instructs the cataloger to use the composer's original title unless a later title in the same language has become better known. If the title is distinctive, it is left unmodified unless there is a conflict. If the title is distinctive and there *is* a conflict, the title is followed by some modification as instructed under Rule 25.31B1. For example:

Bach, Johann Sebastian, 1685-1750.
  [Kunst der Fuge]
  The art of the fugue

Bach, Johann Sebastian, 1685-1750.
  [Lobet den Herrn, alle Heiden]
  Motet no. 6 : Praise the Lord, all ye heathen

However, if the title consists solely of one type of composition, the title is modified as instructed under Rule 25.27. Additions are then made according to Rule 25.29: the medium of performance (the instruments for which it was written). This is followed by further identifying elements to distinguish the work from other compositions by the same composer, generally the serial number, opus (or thematic index) number, and the key (Rule 25.31A). Examples:

Haydn, Joseph, 1732-1809.
  [Quartets, strings, no. 83, op. 77, no. 2, F major]
  Quartet, op. 77, no. 2, in F major

Dvořák, Antonín, 1841-1904.
  [Symphonies, no. 8, op. 88, G major]
  From the new world: symphony no. 8 by Dvořák.

Further additions are made to distinguish arrangements of a musical work, translations of texts of vocal works, etc. (Rule 25.31B). Example:

> Cowell, Henry, 1897-1965.
> [Concerto brevis; arr.]
> Concerto brevis for accordion and orchestra

Titles of works in the larger vocal forms (operas, oratorios, etc.) generally require additional modification because of the various versions in which they are likely to be issued. For example:

> Puccini, Giacomo, 1858-1924.
> [Manon Lescaut]
> [Manon Lescaut. Vocal score]
> [Manon Lescaut. Libretto. English]

RULE 25.32. PARTS OF A MUSICAL WORK

A separately published part of a musical work uses the title of the whole work, followed by the title of the part. This is counter to 25.6A1 for other types of works. Examples:

> Arne, Thomas Augustine, 1710-1778.
> [Artaxerxes. The soldier tir'd]

> Schumann, Robert, 1810-1856.
> [Fantasierstücke, piano, op. 12. Nr. 7. Traumes Wirren]

RULES 25.33-25.36.

These rules give principles for construction of a uniform title for items containing more than one work. Two works published together are treated as in Rule 25.7. Complete works are treated as in Rule 25.8. A collection of selections of various types of compositions originally composed for various instrumental and/or vocal media are assigned a uniform title according to the instructions in Rule 25.9. However, if a collection contains works of various types all in a broad or specific medium, the designation of that medium is used; e.g.,

> [Instrumental music]
> [Vocal music]
> [Brass music]
> [Piano music]
> [Violin, piano music]

If the collection contains works of one type, the name of that type is used, with the addition of medium in appropriate cases; e.g.,

> [Operas]
> [Quartets, strings]
> [Sonatas, piano]

NOTES

[1]"AACR 2 Options to Be Followed by the Library of Congress: Chapters 1-2, 12, 21-26," *Library of Congress Information Bulletin*, 37 (July 21, 1978): 427.

[2]*AACR 2*, p. 442.

[3]*Cataloging Service Bulletin*, no. 27 (Winter 1985): 31.

[4]Ibid.

[5]*Cataloging Service Bulletin*, no. 11 (Winter 1981): 45-46.

[6]*Cataloging Service Bulletin*, no. 13 (Summer 1981): 44.

[7]*Cataloging Service Bulletin*, no. 25 (Summer 1984): 70-75.

[8]Ibid., p. 76.

[9]Ibid., p. 77.

[10]Ibid.

[11]*Cataloging Service Bulletin*, no. 11 (Winter 1981): 49.

[12]*Cataloging Service Bulletin*, no. 16 (Spring 1982): 49-50.

[13]*Cataloging Service Bulletin*, no. 22 (Fall 1983): 34-35.

[14]Ibid., pp. 35-36.

[15]Ibid., pp. 36-37.

[16]*Cataloging Service Bulletin*, no. 28 (Spring 1985): 20.

[17]*Cataloging Service Bulletin*, no. 11 (Winter 1981): 52.

SUGGESTED READING

Maxwell, Margaret. *Handbook for AACR 2*. Chicago, American Library Association, 1980. Chapter 15.

Smiraglia, Richard P. *Cataloging Music*. Lake Crystal, Minn., Soldier Creek Press, 1983. Chapter 3.

14
References

INTRODUCTION

All the rules in the preceding four chapters have referred to "references" needed when one name or form of heading is chosen from among more than one possible name or form of heading. This chapter is a summary of all those situations where cross references are called for explicitly or implicitly in the earlier rules. This chapter also gives examples of the different types of references. Chapter 26 of *AACR 2*, "References," begins with introductory notes that define different kinds of references, explain the form to use, and set up the conditions under which references should be made. Following this introduction are specific rules for and examples of references for persons, corporate bodies and geographic names, and uniform titles. Finally, there is a rule allowing references instead of certain added entries that are common to many editions.

References are not included in the bibliographic records for the items being cataloged when the references are made. Instead they are recorded in a record called an "authority record." An authority record is a separate record for each name or title established as a heading to be used in the library's public catalog. It contains the established form for the heading, the forms from which references should be made to the established form, and often, notes about the sources of information used in establishing the heading. In manual authority files the forms from which references are to be made are preceded by x's—one x precedes a *see* reference, and two x's precede a *see also* reference. In a machine-readable authority file headings and references are preceded by codes similar to those used in bibliographic records. There is a separate MARC format for authority records. In this format 1xx codes precede headings, 4xx codes precede *see* references, and 5xx codes precede *see also* references. Sample authority records and further information about authority files are given on pp. 577-579 in chapter 27 of this text.

SELECTED RULES AND EXAMPLES

RULE 26.0. INTRODUCTORY NOTES

There are two basic types of references: *see* references and *see also* references. Also discussed in this chapter are *name-title* references and *explanatory* references. These are more complicated versions of *see* and *see also* references.

See references are used to direct users from a form of name or title of a work that they have looked under to the form that has been chosen as the heading for that name or title. A *see* reference says to the user, "No, you won't find what you're looking for here; but if you'll look under _____, you will find something."

See also references are used to direct users from a name or uniform title heading to a related name or uniform title heading. A *see also* reference says to the user, "Yes, there is some information here, and you may also be interested in related information that you can find under _____ ."

Name-title references are used when a title has been entered under a personal or corporate name and either *see* or *see also* references are needed from another form of the title. When such references are needed, the name is given before the title in both the form referred from and the form referred to.

Explanatory references are used when more guidance or explanation than can be given in simple references is necessary.

Terminology used in references is undergoing change with the expansion of online catalogs. In an online environment the codes 4xx and 5xx can be translated into other words or phrases than *see* and *see also*, if the creator of the system believes that other terminology would be more understandable to users. Popular substitutes are "search under" or "the heading used in this catalog is" for *see*, and "search also under" or "related information may be found under" for *see also*. Because *AACR 2* uses *see* and *see also*, these terms are used in the remainder of this chapter for ease of explanation.

Forms of references.   *AACR 2* suggests that the form of name from which a reference is made should have the same structure it would have if it were the heading rather than a reference to the heading. *AACR 2* also calls for making only one reference rather than two or more when one form is used to refer to more than one catalog heading. For example:

> Taylor, J. R.
>   see also
> Taylor, James Robly, 1925-
> Taylor, John Roberts.

> ACU
>   see
> Arbeitskreis Computer im Unterricht.
> Arbeitskreis Computer-Unterstützter Unterricht.
> Association of Commonwealth Universities.

However, the Library of Congress makes individual references rather than combined references in these instances.[1] Presumably this is because of the difficulty of maintaining records of such combined references in an automated system.

Conditions for making references. Certain points should be kept in mind when making references. A heading must appear in a catalog in order for a reference to be made to it. References made to headings that are not there are called *blind references* because they direct a user to something that cannot be seen, which is a frustrating experience for anyone using a catalog. Normally, there should be an entry under both the name referred from and the name referred to when a *see also* reference is made. Note the word "normally" here. Few libraries with manual catalogs find it feasible to make a *see* reference where a *see also* reference would be made if the catalog contained the heading referred from, only to change to a *see also* reference when that heading is added to the catalog. A record should be kept of every reference made. This record is kept, as mentioned earlier, on an authority record for the heading that is being referred to, in order to be able to correct or delete a reference when the heading is changed or deleted. If there is doubt about whether a reference is needed, it probably should be made.

The wording of the examples of explanatory references in *AACR 2* and in this text is not intended to be prescriptive, but only to provide examples.

RULE 26.1. BASIC RULE

A reference is made from a form not used to the one that is used unless the form is so similar as to make the reference unnecessary. Appropriate additions are made to distinguish the form in the reference from other headings or references.

RULE 26.2. NAMES OF PERSONS

26.2A. "See" references

26.2A1. Different names
When a person has used a name different from that chosen for the heading for that person, or when a different name is found in reference sources, a reference is made from the different name to the heading. (*See also* Rule 26.2C1 and Rule 26.2D1.) For example:

Tosi, Maria Teresa
　　see
Maria Teresa dell'Eucaristia, suor, 1918- .

Beyle, Marie Henri
　　see
Stendhal, 1783-1842.

Sklodowska, Marie
　　see
Curie, Marie, 1867-1934.

26.2A2.   Different forms of the name

If a form of name used by a person is significantly different from the form used for the heading for the person, a reference is made. For LC catalogers the policy for normal inverted headings is to make references from forms that have any variations to the left of the comma or in the first element to the right of the comma.[2] For example:

> Burt, Stanley G.
>   see
> Burt, S. G. (Stanley G.).

> Abe, Suehisa
>   see
> Abe, Suenao, 1622-1709.

> Ruth, George Herman
>   see
> Ruth, Babe, 1895-1948.

> Homerus
>   see
> Homer.

26.2A3.   Different entry elements

A reference should be made from any element of a name heading under which a user might reasonably look for a name. For example:

> Van Zuidam, R. A.
>   see
> Zuidam, R. A. van.

> Buren, Ariane van
>   see
> Van Buren, Ariane.

> Damas, Bernardo Valverde
>   see
> Valverde Damas, Bernardo.

> Ram Acharya
>   see
> Acharya, Ram.

> Wellesley, Arthur, Duke of Wellington, 1769-1852
>   see
> Wellington, Arthur Wellesley, Duke of, 1769-1852.

26.2B.   Name-title references

Name-title references involving personal name differences are prescribed in four cases. The most common of these is a name-title reference from the inverted form of initials for each item entered under initials in direct order. For example:

> N., A. R.
>   The right way and the wrong way
>   see
> A. R. N.

It is LC policy in such cases to make a reference from the inverted form alone, not a name-title reference.[3] For example:

> N., A. R.
>   see
> A. R. N.

26.2C.   "See also" references

When a person is entered under two headings (e.g., two pseudonyms), *see also* references are made at each heading to direct the user also to search under the other heading. For example:

> Baker, Ray Stannard
>   see also
> Grayson, David
>
> Grayson, David
>   see also
> Baker, Ray Stannard

LC also makes a *see also* reference from a form of name from which a *see* reference should be made but which is exactly the same as another heading already established in the catalog and there are no data to resolve the conflict. For example:

> Goldstein, Charles
>   see also
> Goldstein, Chaim Itsl.
> [Goldstein, Charles is already established][4]

26.2D.   Explanatory references

26.2D1.   General rule
Explanatory references are provided when more information is needed for guidance than can be given with a *see* or *see also* reference. For example:

Stone, Rosetta
   The joint pseudonym of Michael K. Frith and Dr. Seuss.
For separate works entered under each name see
   Frith, Michael K.
   Seuss, Dr.

Hunter, Evan
   For works of this author written under pseudonyms, see
   Collins, Hunt
   McBain, Ed
   Marsten, Richard

26.2D2.   An option allows making an explanatory reference under each separately written prefix that can be used in a number of surnames. The purpose of such a reference is to explain how names with this prefix are entered in the catalog. For example:

Van
   Names beginning with this prefix are also entered under the
   name following the prefix (e.g., Zuidam, R. A. van)

The Library of Congress is not applying this option because it is felt that such references provide the user with less help than do specific references.[5]

RULE 26.3.   NAMES OF CORPORATE BODIES AND GEOGRAPHIC NAMES

26.3A.   "See" references

26.3A1.   Different names
   When a corporate body or place has appeared in works or reference sources with a different name or names than that used for the catalog heading, a reference is made from the different name. If, however, the name represents a name *change*, use Rule 26.3C1. For example:

God Squad
   see
Detroit (Mich.). Police Dept. Chaplain Corps.

26.3A3.   Different forms of the name
   If a different form of name for a body or place is found in works or reference sources or if different romanizations result in different forms, references are made from the differing form(s). For example:

A.B.E.D.I.A.
   see
Arab Bank for Economic Development in Africa.

Wien (Austria)
    see
Vienna (Austria)

Pharmaceutical Society of Korea
    see
Taehan Yakhakhoe.

Carlsruhe (West Germany)
    see
Karlsruhe (West Germany)

Kellogg Arabian Horse Center
    see
W.K. Kellogg Arabian Horse Center.

General Aniline and Film Corp. Ansco
    see
Ansco.

Jesus, Society of
    see
Jesuits.

Bradner Associates
    see
Michael Bradner Associates.

Torup (Denmark)
    see
Hammer-Torup (Denmark)

26.3A5.   Numbers

If the catalog is filed so that numbers expressed as words are in a different place than numbers expressed as numerals, make references from the opposite form to the one used in the heading, if the number is in a position to affect the filing. For example:

Three M Company
    see
3M Company

3 Bridges Reformed Church (Three Bridges, N.J.)
    see
Three Bridges Reformed Church (Three Bridges, N.J.)

26.3A6.   Abbreviations

If the catalog is filed so that abbreviations are in a different place than the equivalent words, refer from the full form to an abbreviation, if the abbreviation is in a position to affect the filing. For example:

> Mount Auburn Cemetery (Cambridge, Mass.)
>   see
> Mt. Auburn Cemetery (Cambridge, Mass.)

LC includes ampersands or other symbols that represent "and" here. If such a symbol occurs in the first five words, a reference from the name using "and" or its equivalent in the language of the heading is made. For other abbreviations to get a reference, LC requires that they be in the first five words, not be listed in Appendix B.9 of *AACR 2*, *and* not represent a proper name.[6]

26.3A7.   Different forms of heading

References are made from different forms of a corporate name that seem to be reasonable forms under which a user might search. For example:

> Cambridge. University
>   see
> University of Cambridge.

> California Institute of Technology, Pasadena. Baxter Art
> Gallery
>   see
> Baxter Art Gallery.

> Virgin Islands of the United States. Division of Curriculum
>   & Instruction. Project Introspection
>   see
> Project Introspection.

> United States. Maritime Administration. Office of
>   Commercial Development. Office of Port and Intermodal
>   Development
>   see
> United States. Office of Port and Intermodal
>   Development.

> Concilio romano (1725)
>   see
> Catholic Church. Concilio romano (1725).

26.3B.   "See also" references

26.3B1.   *See also* references are made between corporate headings that are related. This includes names that represent corporate name changes. LC calls these "earlier/later heading references," and instead of reading *see also*, the message of the reference reads "search also under the earlier heading" or "search also under the later heading."[7] For example:

> Amsterdam (Holland). Gemeentelijke-Archiefdienst
>   see also
> Amsterdam (Holland). Gemeente-Archief.

> Treaty of Versailles, 1919
>   see also
> Paris Peace Conference, 1919.

> Automotive Transport Association of Ontario
>   search also under the later heading
> Ontario Trucking Association.

> Ontario Trucking Association
>   search also under the earlier heading
> Automotive Transport Association of Ontario.

26.3C.   Explanatory references

26.3C1.   General rule

Explanatory references are made when more guidance is required. For example:

> United Nations. Missions.
>   Delegations, missions, etc. from member nations to the United Nations and to its subordinate units are entered under the name of the nation followed by the name of the delegation, mission, etc., e.g.
> United States. Mission to the United Nations.
> Uruguay. Delegación en las Naciones Unidas.

> A. Harris & Co.
>   Sanger Brothers was established in 1857. A. Harris & Co. was established in 1886. In 1961 they merged to form Sanger-Harris.
>   Works by these bodies are found under the following headings according to the name used at the time of publication:
>   Sanger Brothers.
>   A. Harris & Co.
>   Sanger-Harris.

Oceans '78 Conference (4th : 1978 : Washington, D.C.)

Publications of this series of meetings are found under the following headings or titles:
1970: IEEE International Conference on Engineering in the Ocean Environment (1970 : Panama City, Fla.)
1971: Conference on Engineering in the Ocean Environment (1971 : San Diego, Calif.)
1972: IEEE International Conference on Engineering in the Ocean Environment (1972 : Newport, R.I.)
1974: IEEE International Conference on Engineering in the Ocean Environment (1974 : Halifax, N.S.)
1975: Conference on Engineering in the Ocean Environment (1975 : San Diego, Calif.)
1976: Oceans '76.
1977: Oceans '77 conference record.
1978: Oceans '78 Conference (4th : 1978 : Washington, D.C.)

The Library of Congress no longer makes references of this type. Instead each related body is connected with the earlier or later name by a *see also* reference. References like the "United Nations. Missions" example above are handled by tracing specific *see* references on each applicable authority record.[8]

26.3C2.   Acronyms
When a filing system files initials separated by periods in a different place from initials not separated by periods, *AACR 2* allows for making an explanatory reference. For example:

N.A.C.
    see
Naval Avionics Center.
Neighbourhood Advice Council.
    In this catalog, titles and other entries may be found under the acronym filed as a word.

Note: Make the same explanatory reference under NAC.

The Library of Congress no longer makes explanatory references for acronyms. They are converted to simple *see* references on the authority record for each name involved.[9]

RULE 26.4.   UNIFORM TITLES

26.4A.   "See" references

26.4A1.   Different titles or variants of the title
When different titles have been used in other editions of a work than the one(s) held by the library, or when variant titles have been used to cite a work in reference sources, references may be made from these variants. When it is appropriate, these references are in the form of name-title references. For example:

Laderman, Ezra.
   The trials of Galileo
      see
Laderman, Ezra.
   Galileo Galilei

Córdoba (Argentina : Province).
   Ley no. 4051
      see
Córdoba (Argentina : Province).
   Ley orgánica del poder judicial (1942)

Suder, Joseph, 1892-
   Festmesse, in D
      see
Suder, Joseph, 1892-
   Dona nobis pacem

Revueltas, Silvestre, 1899-1940.
   Chit-chat music
      see
Revueltas, Silvestre, 1899-1940.
   Música para charlar
[Title page title: Música para charlar = Chit-chat music. Title added entries would be made for both titles. In the other cases, a title added entry would be made for the title proper of the edition being cataloged.]

When translated titles are involved, the reference is made from the translated version of the title to the uniform title followed by the appropriate language subheading. For example:

Song of Roland
   see
Chanson de Roland. English

Naft, Stephen, 1878-1956.
   Kyōsanshugi ni taisuru nijū no shitsumon
      see
Naft, Stephen, 1878-1956.
   Answer please! Questions for communists. Japanese

26.4A2.   Titles of parts of a work cataloged independently
   When a part of a work is cataloged so that the part is entered independently, a reference is made from the uniform title of the whole work with the part as a subheading to the title of the part as an independent entry. For example:

Hesse, Hermann, 1877-1962.
   Steppenwolf. Tractat vom Steppenwolf
      see
Hesse, Hermann, 1877-1962.
   Tractat vom Steppenwolf

26.4A3.   Titles of parts cataloged under the title of the whole work
   When a part of a work is cataloged so that the part is a subheading of the
whole work, and if the title of the part is distinctive, a reference is made from
the title of the part to the uniform title of the whole work with the part as a
subheading. For example:

Strauss, Richard, 1864-1949.
   Breit über mein Haupt dein schwarzes Haar
      see
Strauss, Richard, 1864-1949.
      Lieder, op. 19. Breit über mein Haupt dein
      schwarzes Haar

al-Mu'awwidhatān
   see
Koran. al-Mu'awwidhatān.

26.4A4.   Collective titles
   If a collection or selection of works of one person has been given a
collective uniform title, and if the title proper is distinctive, a name-title
reference is made from the title proper to the uniform title. For example:

Shepp, Archie.
   Further fire music
      see
Shepp, Archie.
      Instrumental music. Selections

NOTES

[1]*Cataloging Service Bulletin*, no. 21 (Summer 1983): 37-38.

[2]*Cataloging Service Bulletin*, no. 27 (Winter 1985): 32.

[3]*Cataloging Service Bulletin*, no. 15 (Winter 1982): 30-31.

[4]*Cataloging Service Bulletin*, no. 28 (Spring 1985): 20-21.

[5]*Cataloging Service Bulletin*, no. 12 (Spring 1981): 34.

[6]*Cataloging Service Bulletin*, no. 21 (Summer 1983): 45.

[7]*Cataloging Service Bulletin*, no. 27 (Winter 1985): 41-42.

[8]Ibid., pp. 41-51.

[9]Ibid., pp. 51-52.

SUGGESTED READING

Chan, Lois Mai. *Cataloging and Classification: An Introduction*. New York, McGraw-Hill, 1981. pp. 117-121.

Part III
SUBJECT ANALYSIS

15
Subject Arrangement of Library Materials

INTRODUCTION

Subject analysis is the part of cataloging that deals with determining what the intellectual content of an item is "about." The cataloger must observe and translate an item's characteristics of discipline, topic, form, etc., into the conceptual frame of the system. The subject analyzer must usually determine first the subject, then the form of an item, except in literature where form might be of more importance. An item entitled *History of Mathematics* is about mathematics, not about history. Similarly, *Nature in Italian Art, a Study of Landscape Backgrounds from Giotto to Tintoretto* is about landscape painting, not about Italian art history. In some cases, however, the subject is elusive and the cataloger must rely on judgment. The problem has been elaborated upon by Sayers:

> If the book on Scotland is not mainly geographic and historical, but consists of descriptive and narrative chapters together with a melange of literary and scientific observations and reflections on the national traits and institutions, also considerable social philosophy in the last chapters, the judgment is indeed complex and the decisions may be uncertain.[1]

Much has been written on subject analysis and classification theory. The subject has been pursued much more vigorously in Great Britain and in countries that have been under British influence in the last century than has been the case in the United States.[2]

A useful text on the subject of determining the "aboutness" of an item has been written by A. G. Brown.[3] Once this "aboutness" has been determined, the cataloger then usually chooses a classification notation from the classification scheme used by the library and one or more verbal subject terms from the subject heading list used by the library. The classification notation is usually used as the basis for a call number, which will determine the position of the item on the library's shelves. The subject term(s) most often appear as access points for the item in the library's catalog.

CLASSIFIED VERSUS ALPHABETIC APPROACH TO INFORMATION

During cataloging, the cataloger must take into account the dual manifestations of the items to be added to the collection. Items are both intellectual and physical entities. In descriptive cataloging the physical description addresses the physical entity while access points are constructed to allow for approach to the intellectual work. In subject analysis, classifiers traditionally choose only one classification, which will place in one location on the shelves all copies of a given item. On the other hand, catalogers may choose more than one subject term or classification under which to represent an item in a catalog or index. Classifiers strive for the optimum location in view of the content of the item, the accepted classification schedule, and the needs of the clientele. Such decisions are not always easy to make. For instance, the same historical treatise might go equally well into political or economic history, or perhaps under social history or biography. In the choice of subjects to be represented in the catalog or index for this hypothetical treatise, all the aspects can be brought out through choice of multiple access points.

Inquirers who want information on a certain subject will approach the catalog with questions formulated in their own words. These terms must be translated into the predetermined access categories of the catalog. Such communication between inquirer and catalog, with the possible intervention of a librarian, must take place regardless of the type of catalog consulted or the arrangement of its entries. Three systems of arranging entries in a library catalog were discussed in chapter 1. Classified catalogs were said to be the oldest of the three, although in present-day libraries they are less numerous than alphabetical catalogs of either the dictionary or the divided type. In the case of the classified catalog, the user's search terms must be converted to retrieval by means of classification. More than one category of the schedules may represent a significant aspect of the same item, thus allowing more than one entry or access point for that item. Skilled users may know the schedules well enough to go directly to those categories which correspond to their needs. However, all classified catalogs must be accompanied by an alphabetical index, to help users translate their search terms into classification notations that represent them in the catalog.

The alphabetical catalog might facilitate the information retrieval process for most users, but it is similar in principle to the classified catalog index. In either case, the search for relevant information usually starts with an alphabetical list of subject terms. If the user's terminology coincides with that of the list, the search process will be quite direct. If not, the user must follow cross references, or try to adjust his or her vocabulary to that of the accepted system.

Still, each type of catalog requires a different pattern of communication. The classified catalog offers a "vertical" (hierarchical) approach to the collection through its closely related classes and categories, under which materials can be identified by means of logical, orderly sequences from general to specific. The alphabetical catalog gives a "horizontal" approach through its random scattering of access points throughout the entire linguistic finding apparatus.

Classified Arrangement

Certain advantages of a classified catalog were cited in chapter 1. They include:

1. *A controlled order of academic disciplines, as well as of popular topical sequences.* This order fosters direct, efficient searching at either catalog or shelf for those users familiar with the classification scheme. A reader interested in psychology, for instance, can initially consult and study a single section of the catalog with assurance of its relevance.

2. *Extensive opportunities for in-depth searching.* Based on logical relationships rather than linguistic associations, this arrangement not only offers a better comprehension of subject matter, but also directly stimulates the learning experience. It expands the frequently discussed values of browsing in an open-shelf library.[4] Directly related is the opportunity to search in both directions, from general to specific as well as from specific to general.

3. *Denotative symbols (notation) objectively signifying topics and categories.* They reduce to a minimum the connotative implications and prejudices often associated with linguistic terms. The notation further allows one class number to be used for shelving, while others may designate supplementary entries in the catalog.

There are, on the other hand, disadvantages which account for the relatively few classed catalogs in modern libraries in the United States:

1. *Much of our cultural heritage, as recorded in documentary collections, cannot be satisfactorily systematized.* Any classification scheme has inherent deficiencies. The most effective classed catalogs are in special libraries, chiefly those for one or more scientific or technological disciplines. These areas are the most susceptible to rigid logical systematization. Even traditional academic disciplines tend to crumble nowadays before the onslaught of inter- and multi-disciplinary studies. Systems of arrangement within any subject field can be made obsolete by the advancing frontiers of knowledge.

2. *Systematic arrangements are almost never such ready vehicles of common knowledge as is the alphabet.* While factual information, study, and research slowly became less and less the province of aristocrats alone, due to the spread of democracy and popular education, the older, more esoteric patterns of organization,

however worthy, were often sacrificed to the rote mechanisms of arithmetic and alphabetic progression.

The alphabetic index accompanying a classified catalog usually gives access only to spans and categories of classification, unlike an alphabetical catalog, which identifies specific titles. It points the user to both the classified catalog, where *all* the library's holdings are recorded, and the shelves, where actual documents can be examined, but where items may be inadvertently missing, being at the moment in use elsewhere. It may be a published index to a particular classification scheme, e.g., the "relative index" of the Dewey Decimal Classification. It may be a list of separately published subject headings that are locally associated with class numbers from a given system, e.g., *Library of Congress Subject Headings*, which carries many LC classification numbers, although it is not specifically designed to be a classification index. Or it may be a specially generated index, such as a chain index, based on the extracted vocabulary of the classification used. The major advantage of a chain index in this context is that specific rules for controlling the index vocabulary may be based on the classification scheme being used. For example, the concept "alcoholic beverages" is classed in at least four places in the Dewey classification schedules. These four contexts are outlined below:

100	Philosophy
170	Ethics
172-179	Applied ethics
178	Ethics of consumption
178.1	In use of alcoholic beverages
300	Social sciences
390	Customs, etiquette, folklore
394	General customs
394.1	Drinking
394.13	Alcoholic beverages
600	Technology
610	Medical sciences
613	Hygiene
613.8	Addictions
613.81	Alcoholic beverages
640	Home economics
641	Food and drink
641.2	Beverages
641.21	Alcoholic beverages

From these sequences and categories, the following chain index entries could result:

Addictions: medical science 613.8
Alcoholic beverages: addictions: medical science 613.81
Alcoholic beverages: applied ethics 178.1
Alcoholic beverages: customs 394.13
Alcoholic beverages: home economics 641.21
Applied ethics 172-179
Beverages: home economics 641.2
Customs 394
Customs, etiquette, folklore 390
Drinking: customs 394.1
Ethics of consumption: philosophy 178
Ethics: philosophy 170
Food and drink: home economics 641
Home economics 640
Hygiene: medical science 613
Medical sciences 610
Philosophy 100
Social sciences 300
Technology 600

Alphabetical Arrangement

Some of the more obvious advantages of an alphabetical catalog or index are:

1. *Simplicity and popularity.* The apparent simplicity of alphabetical filing can be deceptive, however. Filing problems inevitably arise, especially in dictionary catalogs, where interfiling personal and corporate authors, titles, subjects, cross references, etc., becomes something like the old dilemma of adding apples and oranges to pears. (The filing of LC subject headings is discussed in chapter 22, and chapter 26 addresses general filing systems and problems.)

2. *Direct access to bibliographic data and holdings.* In spite of its filing pitfalls, a consolidated, single-strike catalog is in many ways more efficient. The "double look-up," and even more extended serial searching, are reduced to a minimum. The user may in most cases move directly from the catalog to the shelves.

3. *Greater freedom in introducing new groupings.* Descriptive subject headings need not bear the same logical relationship to one another as do classes in a systematic arrangement.

On the other hand, the alphabetic approach has serious drawbacks:

1. *Fragmentation of subject matter.* Most published subject heading lists for libraries indulge in a kind of surreptitious "classing" through the use of inversions, subdivisions, and the like. The urge to group like topics in one place, to make subject searching more efficient, is almost irresistible.

2.   *Exacerbation of semantic problems.* In the absence of short,
      specific words for many subject concepts, awkward compound and
      prepositional phrase headings soon appear, to complicate the filing
      and confound the user.

3.   *Inherent weakness in the conceptual structure of subject headings.*
      With no systematic framework to regulate its growth, an alphabetic
      subject list inevitably stumbles over the problems of the plurality
      and specificity of its terms. The concept of specific entry is difficult
      to control, as we shall see in a later chapter.

CONCLUSION

This chapter has discussed the topic of subject analysis and arrangement
of library materials both by classification and by verbal/alphabetical
approaches. In the chapters that follow these two approaches are considered
separately along with systems and schemes for implementing each approach.
The student should remember, however, that these are two sides of the same
coin and that both are attempts to provide users access to the intellectual
contents of the items being analyzed.

NOTES

[1]W. C. Berwick Sayers, *Sayers' Manual of Classification for Librarians*, 3rd
ed. rev. by Arthur Maltby (London, Andre Deutsch, 1955), pp. 235-236.

[2]Among those who have written on the subject in the last two decades are
R. S. Angell, D. Austin, K. G. B. Bakewell, A. G. Brown, E. J. Coates, A. C.
Foskett, D. J. Foskett, F. W. Lancaster, A. Maltby, C. D. Needham, W. C. B.
Sayers, B. C. Vickery, and H. Wellisch.

[3]A. G. Brown, *An Introduction to Subject Indexing: A Programmed Text*
(London, C. Bingley, 1976).

[4]Unfortunately, the problems and values of browsing have not been
sufficiently researched. One can also raise the question why, in most libraries,
the shelflist, which functions as a limited classed catalog, is not made readily
accessible to the users. Precisely because of its usefulness to the entire library
staff, the shelflist is often sequestered away from public reach. But patrons
who have a sufficient grasp of their fields of interest, and who are willing to
learn something about the classification scheme, surely would reap similar
benefits from having access to it.

SUGGESTED READING

Brown, A. G. *An Introduction to Subject Indexing: A Programmed Text.* London, C. Bingley, 1976.

Chan, Lois Mai. *Cataloging and Classification: An Introduction.* New York, McGraw-Hill, 1981. Chapter 3.

Foskett, A. C. *The Subject Approach to Information.* 4th ed. London, C. Bingley; Hamden, Conn., Linnet Books, 1982.

Wellisch, Hans, ed. *Subject Retrieval in the Seventies: New Directions: Proceedings of an International Symposium*, edited by Hans Wellisch and Thomas D. Wildon. Westport, Conn., Greenwood, 1972.

16
Classification of Library Materials

INTRODUCTION

Collections in libraries of any appreciable size are arranged according to some system, and the arrangement is generally referred to as classification. Classification provides formal, orderly access to the shelves.

No matter what scheme is chosen, or how large the library, the purpose of classification is to bring related items together in a helpful sequence from the general to the specific. Ease of access is especially important if the collection is heterogeneous. It is convenient and desirable—particularly in the open-shelf collections to which many libraries in the United States are committed—to have, for example, all histories of the United States together, or all books on symbolic logic, or all symphony scores, so that the patron, who may or may not have one title in mind, can find related works in one location.

The ultimate aim of any classification system is to lead the patron to the items required, either through direct search of the shelves (open stacks), or through the help of a library attendant whose duty it is to retrieve the materials on demand (closed stacks). Each system has its virtues. Open stacks encourage browsing, and thus stimulate intellectual awareness and foster serendipity. They work best with a logical, fairly comprehensible system of classification that encourages the patron's self-reliance in seeking items on a particular subject or its specific aspects. Closed stacks lessen the chances that materials will be mishandled, misplaced, or stolen, but they force the patron to limit his or her own searching to the catalog (and perhaps the shelflist), and to wait for a library employee to bring items specifically requested. Closed stacks still have a use in a storage library situation where items may not be shelved in subject groups at all, but ranged in more or less fixed location by size, with consecutive numbers assigned as addresses. "Fixed location" means that each item has one specific, fixed position on the shelf in the library as was the case in many libraries prior to the mid-nineteenth century. "Relative location" is a fluid, constantly changing arrangement of items according to their relationship to one another and resulting from the addition of new materials or the removal of old, weeded, or lost materials. In this system items may be moved from shelf to shelf without altering or disturbing their classified sequence.

No matter what the classification scheme or the type of shelving, the library catalog, as primary source of reference, must be complete and current. It provides information about particular items or types of items through various access points—usually by author(s) or other names associated with an item, by any title given to a work, and by subject headings. Along with information found via these access points is usually a call number (i.e., the shelf address where an item may be found). One element of the call number is usually the classification.

LIBRARY CLASSIFICATION

Organized documentary collections have existed since early civilizations learned to convert their spoken languages to written form. Even before the codex book appeared, early record depositories received some form of utilitarian arrangement. Groupings were made by title, by broad subject, by chronology, by author, by order of acquisition, by size, etc. One of the earliest catalogs was the one known as *Pinakes* (Greek for "tablets") compiled for the great Alexandrian library by the poet Callimachus in the third century B.C. Though this catalog did not survive, it is known that it arranged the entries in at least ten (and possibly more) main classes, subdivided alphabetically by author. In the Middle East and in the Byzantine Empire it served as a model for other catalogs and bibliographies until the early Middle Ages. The monastery libraries of that time in Western Europe were mostly small and had almost no need for classification, but the university libraries of the late Middle Ages arranged books corresponding to the Trivium and Quadrivium, the traditional seven subject fields taught. Within the classes, books had fixed locations on the shelves. Beginning in the sixteenth century, librarians devised many different classification schemes for the arrangement of books, but fixed locations predominated in most European and early American libraries until the mid-nineteenth century. The most substantive developments in the arrangement of library collections were concurrent with the rapid growth of libraries and their use during the nineteenth century. At that time librarians felt a definite need for better methods of arrangement, so that the content of their holdings would be available, and more apparent, to the user.

The history of modern library classification corresponds to the various attempts to adapt and modify existing philosophical systems of knowledge to the arrangement of materials and to users' needs. One of the best known early American classifiers was Thomas Jefferson, third President of the United States. He adapted certain elements of Francis Bacon's outline of knowledge, not only to his own library, but also to his plans for the organization of the University of Virginia and the reorganization of the College of William and Mary.

Bacon's system classified materials as functions of the three basic faculties: history (natural, civil, literary, ecclesiastical) as the function of memory; philosophy (including theology) as that of reason; and poetry, fables, and the like, as that of imagination.[1] Its influence was widespread.

Jean Le Rond d'Alembert used the Baconian system for the arrangement of the famous *Encyclopédie ou dictionnaire raisonné des sciences des arts et des métiers* of the French Enlightenment (1751-1765). Jefferson's classification was based on that modification as was the *Catalogue* of Benjamin Franklin's Library Company of Philadelphia (1789). Three years before Jefferson's *Catalogue of the Library of the United States* was installed at the Library of Congress, a variant of the Philadelphia scheme was used to produce the 1812 *Catalogue of the Library of Congress.*[2]

Among other early followers of the Baconian system were Thaddeus Mason Harris, librarian at Harvard (1791-1793); Edward William Johnson, librarian of the College of South Carolina and later of the St. Louis Mercantile Library; and, finally, Johnson's successor, William Torrey Harris, a Hegelian who inverted the Baconian system, creating an independent American classification. At the same time, various adaptations of the Brunet utilitarian classification scheme existed in several American libraries as a direct result of its use to arrange parts of the British Museum and the Bibliothèque Nationale.

In 1876 Melvil Dewey devised his famous Dewey Decimal Classification (DDC), based in large part on W. T. Harris's system, with a decimal notation. Soon DDC was spreading its influence throughout the world. At about the same time, Charles A. Cutter began his work at the Boston Athenaeum. Cutter sought to achieve, not a classification of knowledge, but a practical, useful method for arranging library materials. Nevertheless, his Expansive Classification shows the definite influence of Spencer and Comte, especially in the development of its subordinate classes.

At the beginning of the present century, when the Library of Congress had grown from several thousand books to nearly one million, it was apparent that the library would need a new classification system. After much deliberation, J. C. M. Hanson and Charles Martel decided to design an independent system governed by the actual content of the collection (literary warrant). This form of classification differs from a purely philosophical approach in that it is based on the books as entities. For this reason it is enumerative. An *enumerative* classification is one that attempts to assign designations for (to enumerate) all the single and composite subject concepts required in the system. *Hierarchical* classification is based on the assumption that the process of subdivision and collocation must exhibit as much as possible the "natural" organization of the subject, proceeding from classes to divisions to subdivisions and following, at least in part, the rules of division as set down by "logic." *Synthetic* classifications confine their explicit lists of designations to single, unsubdivided concepts, giving the local classifier generalized rules with which to construct headings for composite subjects (see below, "Faceted Classification," pp. 372-374.

In summary, established philosophical systems of knowledge, with various modifications, underlie most traditional library classifications. The frequent distinction between classification of knowledge and classification of materials seems to have confused the thinking of many librarians. The two processes have important interactions. Even cursory examination of any library classification, including those purporting to organize "the items themselves," reveals an intellectual concept of the item as an expression of certain ideas in one of many available media. Philosophical classification organizes knowledge itself—registering, evaluating, and classifying thoughts, ideas, and concepts for the universal purpose of adequately representing the field of human learning. Library classification arranges the records which express and preserve knowledge, making adjustments as needed because of the physical format of such records.

TRADITIONAL CLASSIFICATION SCHEMES

Most traditional classification systems are basically enumerative. By contrast, the more recent schemes tend to be synthetic. In this introductory text the discussion will apply quite generally to both kinds of order. All printed schedules of library classifications reflect adjustments for the media in which the information may appear and provide detailed analysis of the scope and sequence of topics covered. But it is well to remember that materials on shelves or in files are arranged in a single order. Most items can be requested by author, title, subject, or form, but they can be organized by only one of these at a time. Linear arrangement imposes certain limitations on the classifier. Over the years efforts to meet such limitations have resulted in techniques or features which are characteristic of nearly every worthwhile library classification.

One such feature is a generalia or general works class, which accommodates items that are too broad in scope for inclusion in any single class. Such works usually overlap several traditional disciplines or "classes," e.g., encyclopedias, dictionaries, general periodicals, etc.

In addition, form classes organize materials according to their form of presentation rather than to their subject content. Literary works, e.g., poetry, drama, fiction, etc., are the most obvious, but books of etchings, photographs, musical scores, etc. also fall into this group.

Form divisions group items dealing with different subjects in the same mode of presentation. The "standard subdivisions" of the Dewey Decimal Classification, for instance, can be used to subdivide most disciplines or topics. It should be recognized, however, that some are "modes of treatment" rather than "form divisions." So, for example, "compends," "outlines," "dictionaries," or "periodicals" belonging to a subject do embody physical forms. Other groups such as philosophical or theoretical treatments, works dealing with study and teaching or research in a subject, histories, and biographies, etc., are classified rather by their "inner form."

A notation translates the meaning of a specific class, division, or subdivision into a shorthand symbol or code to be used as a shelf or file address and a convenient reference to the arrangement and identification of the parts of the system. It must be simple, brief, and flexible. It may be composed of letters, numerals, arbitrary signs, or a mixture of these. In general, there are two basic types of notation. Pure notation uses one kind of symbol, such as the Roman alphabet or Arabic numerals, consistently and exclusively, or nearly so (although one might question whether a pure letter notation would permit both upper and lower case symbols denoting variations of signification). The

Dewey Decimal Classification is known for its "pure" notation, but it employs a decimal point as well as the ten digits. Mixed notation uses two or more kinds of symbols, e.g., a combination of letters and numerals. Notation plays an important role in any classification scheme, especially with the modern emphasis on relative location. A notation that serves as a guide to the arrangement of items on the shelf helps to preserve orderly sequence by topic, or form, or whatever the principle of organization may be.

Another feature of the library classification is the index, which provides a means of efficient alphabetical reference to all the terms used in the classification schedules. Most indexes are relative, in that they not only provide alphabetical references to all terms used in the schedules, but also show the relation of each specific subject to other related subjects or their aspects. Perhaps the best known of this type is the relative index to the Dewey Decimal Classification, where the disciplinary organization makes it likely that a single topic will be subordinated under more than one class or subclass, according to its different features or characteristics. No doubt a relative index is a useful aid for the beginning student of classification; in the classification process it is important not only to locate specific topics in the index and the schedules, but also to learn how to relate specific items to the rest of the collection. The key to successful classification is realization that library materials are arranged according to specific subjects or forms, but are also arranged in relation to the subject and forms of other materials.

FACETED CLASSIFICATION

A faceted classification differs from a traditional one in that it does not assign fixed and preconceived slots to subjects in an enumerative sequence, but uses clearly defined, mutually exclusive, and collectively exhaustive aspects, properties, or characteristics of a class or specific subject. Such aspects, properties, or characteristics are called *facets* of a class or subject, a term introduced into classification theory and given this new meaning by the Indian librarian and classificationist S. R. Ranganathan and first used in his Colon Classification in the early 1930s. Though the term was then new to classification, the idea was not (as Ranganathan freely admitted). It had its roots in Dewey's device of place indication by means of a standard notation (e.g., the United States always being 73) appended to any class notation for a subject by means of digits 09, a device now known as a *facet indicator*. Dewey recognized three things: 1) that certain characteristics such as "belonging to a place," "being in the form of a periodical," and some others are general and should be applicable to all subjects so as to express a geographical aspect or a physical form, etc.; 2) that such an appended class notation must be clearly distinguished from the class notation for the main subject to avoid confusion; and 3) that two or more facets, including class notations for different subjects, could be combined to express a complex subject—his "number building" device (e.g., the subject "frost damage to oranges" can be expressed by adding to the class notation 643.31 for oranges the facet indicator 9 and the last two digits taken from the subject "plant injuries: low temperatures" 632.11, to result in 634.31911).

Most other classification schemes designed after Dewey also provided generally applicable facets for places and time periods, and often also for forms. Even LCC, which is an entirely enumerative scheme, included such facets, although they were specially developed for each class as a part of the enumerative structure and are not uniformly applicable in all classes (*see* pp. 416-418). The Universal Decimal Classification expanded Dewey's "standard subdivisions" to about a dozen generally applicable "auxiliaries" (*see* p. 400). Finally, the Colon Classification introduced the fully faceted approach by means of synthetic class notations, that is, those constructed entirely from individual facets in a prescribed sequence from the most specific to the most general.

Originally, Ranganathan postulated five basic facets: personality (that is, the focal or most specific subject), material, energy (that is, any activity, operation, or process), space, and time, known as the "PMEST formula." These basic facets were used to analyze a class or subject and to construct a composite class notation for it. For example, the subject "the design of metal ploughshares in the 19th century U.S." shows all five facets: from the most general to the most specific, 19th century is the time facet; U.S. is the space (or place) facet; design (an activity) is the energy facet; metal is the material facet; and ploughshares, the focal subject, is personality. It was soon found that these five basic facets were too broad, and that most classes or disciplines needed tailor-made facets; e.g., the field of education can be broken down into facets for educands, educators, teaching methods, subjects taught, level of instruction, etc.; agriculture has the facets crops, operations (sowing, harvesting, etc.), implements and tools, etc.

Each facet must have a distinctive notation and a facet indicator to show the sequence of facets unambiguously. Thus, in an imaginary faceted scheme the notation of the example given above might be

AfsM3d5U13Z18

where Afs is the class notation for ploughshares (in the tool facet of agriculture), M3 stands for iron in the material facet, d5 is the class notation for design, U13 means U.S., and Z18 stands for the 19th century.

Thus, a faceted structure relieves a classification scheme from the procrustean bed of rigid hierarchical and excessively enumerative subdivision which resulted in the assignment of fixed "pigeonholes" for subjects that happened to be known or were foreseen when a system was designed but often left no room for future developments and made no provision for the expression of complex relationships and their subsequent retrieval. Enumeration is, however, not entirely absent from faceted schemes: the Colon Classification has some 50 main classes, largely corresponding to traditional disciplines, and an astronomy classification would certainly list the planets of the sun in their order of distance.

While all traditional schemes are essentially based on the strictly hierarchical genus-species relationship for most of their subdivisions, faceted schemes, while recognizing this relationship where warranted, also display others, such as whole-part, operations and processes, agents and tools, substances, physical forms, organizational aspects, and many more, as needed for each specific field or subject. The design of faceted classification schemes is treated in detail by Vickery[3] and Foskett.[4]

A faceted class notation such as the one in the example above is not necessarily meant to serve as a shelving device or "call number" (though all or part of it may be so used) but rather for the arrangement of items in bibliographies and access service data bases, where the synthetic notation provides a helpful sequence, and the individual facets can be accessed and retrieved either alone or in any desired combination. This feature is especially important for computerized retrieval, which has been successfully applied to faceted classification,[5] and in online retrieval as a complement to verbal retrieval methods by subject headings or keywords.[6] The faceted approach is indeed not limited to the construction and assignment of class notations. It is clearly discernible also in verbal subject indication, e.g., a subject heading such as NEWSPAPERS--UNITED STATES--BIBLIOGRAPHY shows "United States" as the place facet and "bibliography" as the form facet. The "List of subdivisions" in the *Sears List of Subject Headings* is actually a list of generally applicable facets (though it is not arranged systematically as it would be in a faceted classification).

Since the 1960s all major classification schemes (with the exception of LC Classification) either have been partially restructured on a faceted basis or display a fully faceted structure. The influence of faceted classification theory has been most conspicuous in DDC, which now offers facets not only for its traditional "standard subdivisions" and areas, but also for individual literatures and languages, for racial, ethnic, and national groups, and for persons, and discusses faceting in its introduction. Special faceted classifications have been designed for broad fields such as education or business management, as well as for more specialized ones such as occupational safety, the diamond industry, library and information science, and many others (*see* pp. 441-444).

CRITERIA FOR A
SUCCESSFUL CLASSIFICATION SCHEME

Classification schemes, as indicated earlier, vary widely. Besides providing for the subject organization of the collection, a successful classification scheme may also contain devices for indicating method of treatment or form of materials treated, time periods, places, peoples, various types of persons, and other special categories.

Any or all of these devices may be justifiably and successfully used for a special situation such as a rare book collection or a collection concerned with a particular subject area or period. Following is a list of a few criteria which may be generally applied to judge a successful classification system:

1.   It must be inclusive as well as comprehensive. That is, it must encompass the whole field of knowledge as represented in collectible media of communication and information. It must therefore include all subjects that are, have been, or may be recognized, allowing for possible future additions to the body of knowledge. It must make provision, not only for the records themselves, but for every actual and potential use of the records.

2. It must be systematic. Not only must the division of subjects be exhaustive, but it must bring together related topics in logical, comprehensible fashion, allowing its users to locate easily whatever they want that is available. It must be so arranged that each aspect of a subject can be considered a separate, yet related, part of the scheme, and it must be so arranged that new topics and aspects can be added in a systematic manner.

3. It must be flexible and expansible. It must be constructed so that any new subject may be inserted without dislocating the general sequence of classification. It must allow for recognized knowledge in all its ramifications, and it must be capable of admitting new subjects or new aspects of well-established subjects. The flexibility of the notation is of first importance if the classification scheme is to be expansive and hospitable in the highest degree. It should also be current. Both the Dewey Decimal Office and the Library of Congress send subscribing libraries periodic lists of all changes in their schedules, noting additions and deletions. These notices and revisions are especially important in subject areas in which a great deal of new work is being done.

4. It must employ terminology that is clear and descriptive, with consistent meaning for both the user and the classifier. The arrangement of terms in the schedule and the index should help reveal the significance of the arrangement. The terms themselves should be unambiguous and reasonably current, correctly identifying the concepts and characteristics present in the materials being classified.

BROAD AND CLOSE CLASSIFICATION

Close classification means classing each work as specifically as possible, using all available subdivisions in the classification scheme. Broad classification groups works under the main divisions and subdivisions of the scheme, without using its minute breakdowns into narrower concepts. The classifier using the schedules should understand that when a library has relatively few items in a given subject area, broad classification might actually be more useful than isolating each item under its own specific call number, since many graduated progressions of the full scheme are not represented in the collection. A library using the Dewey Decimal Classification with a large collection of Bibles, for example, may need to classify the King James Version in 220.5203, whereas a smaller collection might cut back to the broad number 220. Generally speaking, DDC provides small libraries with more opportunities than does the LC Classification to cut back to broader notations, because its enumeration stresses logical progress through the natural hierarchies of subject matter, while the Library of Congress bases its enumeration more on the large quantities of materials represented on its shelves and has relatively few notations that signify broad categories. Larger libraries, having more titles to arrange in a given subject area, often prefer the LC opportunities for close classification. However, specific practices can result in broad classification even though the scheme allows for close classification. The Library of Congress, for example, often classifies all volumes of a monographic series together in the broad notation that exemplifies the theme of the series as a whole. This results in individual volumes not being shelved with others on the same specific subject.

GENERAL PRINCIPLES OF CLASSIFYING

Most of this chapter has been directed to the broad principles, methods, and problems of constructing classification systems. Some attention should now be given to the application of any one such system to the ordering of a library collection and to the necessity of choosing the optimum location for each item.

When classifying an item with respect to a particular library's holdings, it may be necessary to bypass existing minute or narrow concepts and class notations, or to insert new ones into the existing schedules. Both of these modifications are usually possible in some degree, but classification schemes vary in their hospitality to local manipulation. It is assumed that such possibilities and difficulties were considered when the choice was made of one scheme over all others for use in a local library.

Once the particular system of arrangement is chosen, certain general precepts enable the classifier to apply it meaningfully and consistently to the separate items and groups of items acquired by the library. The following summary is designed to aid that process of continuous, cumulative application. These principles apply primarily to such linear (shelf) classifications as the Dewey Decimal and the Library of Congress schemes.[7]

1. **Class the item first according to subject, then by the form in which the subject is represented, except in the generalia class and in literature, where form might be paramount.** In most cases the classifier has to determine the subject matter of the item using the classification schedules as the matrix. This is no easy task, especially when the item does not cover a specific, easily recognized topic. Chapter 1 of this text provides a short summary of procedures used by catalogers in "reading an item technically." The technique is helpful in subject, as well as in descriptive, cataloging. Such features as the preface, introduction, table of contents, or index of a book; the slipcase of a sound recording; the documentation for a machine-readable data file; etc., may help the classifier to recognize the subject matter.

2. **Class an item where it will be most useful.** The classifier has to consider the nature of the collection (see the previous discussion of broad versus close classification) and the needs of the user. Generally speaking, this second principle is a part of the fundamental rule that characteristics chosen for classification are essential to the purpose for which the scheme was developed. At least two questions can be raised in this context:

a.   What is the subject matter of the item and how does it relate to the nature of the collection? The procedures in a highly specialized library with a professional clientele will be different from those used in a public library.

b.   What is the form in which the subject is presented, or its method of treatment? For example, subject bibliographies can be classed in one of two ways. If they are put with related subject materials they will be more useful to a patron who wants titles on a given subject already represented in the library's holdings. If, as in both the DDC and LC classifications, the preferred location is in a separate bibliography section which is further subdivided into author bibliographies, national bibliographies, subject bibliographies, etc., then the "user" who benefits most is the librarian doing bibliographic verification, book order preparation, and the like.

3. **Place the item in the most specific subject division that will contain it, rather than with the general topic.** In this respect it is helpful to study the morphology of the entire scheme, in order to answer such questions as:

a.   What is the specific heading embracing the subject?

b.   How is this subject subdivided in the classification schedule?

Obviously if most libraries of any size would assign a single number to all books dealing with the history of France, failing to subdivide them by time periods and places, the result would be a discouragingly large assortment of volumes under one number. On the other hand, the uses of broad classification for definite, clearly recognized objectives, should not be overlooked.

4. **When the book deals with two or three subjects, place it with the predominant subject or with the one treated first. When the book deals with more than three subjects, place it in the general class that combines all of them.** This principle requires little explanation. The subject that is treated most fully should take predominance over secondary subjects. If two subjects are coordinate (e.g., electricity and magnetism treated equally in the same volume) the item should be placed with whichever topic comes first.

There are some refinements to this general principle. For example, if the work covers two subjects, one of which is represented as acting upon or influencing the other, such a work should be classed under the subject influenced or acted upon. Thus a work discussing French influence on English literature should be classed with English literature. On similar grounds a work such as *Religious Aspects of Philosophy* should be classed under philosophy, not religion, since a treatment of some particular aspect of a subject should be classed with the subject, not with the aspect.

Another, perhaps more involved difficulty arises with the monographic series or collected set. (*See* pages 220-221.) Will Durant's *Story of Civilization* can be classed as an author's collection of twelve related volumes under a broad "history of civilization" number. Or the classifier can place volume 1 with other works on oriental civilization, volume 2 with those on Greek civilization, and so on. The Library of Congress, as mentioned earlier, often classifies series and collected sets together, but has in recent years provided, for optional use by other libraries, an alternative, volume-specific class number in brackets on most of its separate records for monographs belonging to serial sets.

CONCLUSION

Critics have noted limitations in existing classification systems used by most libraries today.[8] A few are summarized here only as a basis for further study. There is a long-standing argument over the logical arrangement of various systems. Though a scheme may be logical within itself, it can also have inconsistencies. For example, in Dewey Decimal Classification, language is separated from literature, and history from social sciences. In the Library of Congress scheme language is classified with literature, and history is shelved close to the social sciences. Arguments can be advanced for both approaches. Language is closely related to literature, but it is also an essential to all disciplines. History throws much light on the social sciences, but every discipline and every literature has its own history which influences, and is influenced by, general social history. There is some evidence that the current trend away from hierarchical enumeration toward synthesis has lessened concern over achieving the one incontestably correct logical arrangement.

Again, DDC and LC, the two most popular library classifications, are both linear, and therefore uni-dimensional. Yet the relationships among works are multi-dimensional and cannot be represented as the projection of a straight line. Linear arrangement, plus the expense and potential confusion of classing different copies of the same item in different places, requires that one classification number be assigned to each title whether it covers one subject or many. A supplementary subject approach to classified materials through separate subject lists with references was developed in an attempt to solve this and related problems. *See* chapters 21-24 for extended discussions of the technique.

Other limitations include problems of reorganization and relocation arising from the need to keep any classification scheme up to date. One of the most obvious of these problems is the tendency of the notation to become more complex and awkward as the schedules are expanded to include new subjects and to define old topics more specifically.

In chapters 17-20 some of the better-known modern classifications devised by librarians and used in various contexts are discussed. Their resemblances and differences are briefly examined, to show their actual and possible uses, strengths, and limitations.

NOTES

[1]Cf. Bacon's *Advancement of Learning* (1605) and *De augmentis scientarium.*

[2]Leo E. LaMontagne, "Historical Background of Classification," in *The Subject Analysis of Library Materials* (New York, Columbia University School of Library Service, 1953), p. 20.

[3]B. C. Vickery, *Faceted Classification: A Guide to the Construction and Use of Special Schemes.* London, Aslib, 1960.

[4]A. C. Foskett, *The Subject Approach to Information*, 4th ed. London, Bingley, 1982, pp. 150-175.

[5]R. R. Freeman, "The Management of a Classification Scheme: Modern Approaches Exemplified by the UDC Project of the American Institute of Physics." *Journal of Documentation* 23 (1967): 304-320.

[6]Karen Markey, "Subject Searching Experiences and Needs of Online Catalog Users: Implications for Library Classification." *Library Resources & Technical Services* 29 (January/March 1985): 34-51.

[7]This discussion summarizes the principles stated by several authors, including William Stetson Merrill, *Code for Classifiers, Principles Governing the Consistent Placing of Books in a System of Classification*, 2nd ed. (Chicago, American Library Association, 1939) and W. C. Berwick Sayers, *A Manual of Classification for Libraries and Bibliographers*, 3rd ed. (London, Andre Deutsch, 1955). The reader will observe that for the purpose of this discussion we selected Sayers' third edition rather than more recent ones.

[8]A helpful list of articles and books on classification theory can be found in the brief bibliography: Phyllis A. Richmond, "Reading List in Classification Theory," *Library Resources & Technical Services* 16 (Summer 1972): 364-382.

SUGGESTED READING

Buchanan, B. *Theory of Library Classification.* London, Bingley, 1979.

Dunkin, Paul S. *Cataloging U.S.A.* Chicago, American Library Association, 1969. Chapter 6.

Foskett, A. C. *The Subject Approach to Information.* 4th ed. London, Bingley, 1982. Chapter 8.

Herdman, M. M. *Classification: An Introductory Manual.* 3rd ed., revised by Jeanne Osborn. Chicago, American Library Association, 1978.

17
Decimal Classification

INTRODUCTION

Of modern library classification schemes, the Dewey Decimal Classification (DDC) is both the oldest and the most widely used in the United States. It also has a substantial following abroad. Such widespread use is a tribute to Melvil[le Louis Kossuth] Dewey, whose original plan was adaptable enough to incorporate new subjects as they emerged, and flexible enough to withstand the changes imposed by the passage of time. Born on December 10, 1851, and graduated from Amherst in 1874, Dewey became assistant college librarian. He developed the first draft of his system for arranging books at that time. He soon became a leader in American librarianship, helping to found both the American Library Association and the first American library school at Columbia University. Being a man of many interests, he was also an advocate of spelling reform. He shortened his forename to "Melvil," dropped his two middle names, and even attempted to change the spelling of his surname to "Dui." Throughout his career he promoted librarianship by his teaching, writing, and speaking. In recognizing and acting upon the need to systematize library collections for effective use, he knew of various previous attempts, but found them inadequate.

Dewey never claimed to have originated decimals for classification notation, but earlier systems used them merely as shelf location devices with no significant relation to the subject matter. What Dewey did claim as original, and with some justification, was his "relative index," compiled as a key to the "diverse material" included in his tables. His most significant contribution was perhaps the use of decimals for hierarchical divisions. Combined with the digits 0 to 9, decimals provide a pure notation which can be subdivided indefinitely. Through the inclusion of lead zeros, the decimal principle dominates even the three notational places to the left of the decimal point.

The first edition of Dewey's scheme, prepared for the Amherst College Library, was issued anonymously in 1876 under the title *A Classification and Subject Index for Cataloguing and Arranging the Books and Pamphlets of a Library*. It included schedules to 1,000 divisions numbered 000-999, together with a relative index and prefatory matter—a total of forty-four pages. The second, "revised and greatly enlarged" edition was published under Dewey's name in 1885. Since that time seventeen more full editions and eleven abridgments have appeared. The fourteenth edition, published in 1942, remained the standard edition for many years because an experimental index to the fifteenth edition, published in 1951, was unsuccessful. In 1958 the sixteenth edition appeared with many changes and additions, including a complete revision of sections 546-47, "Inorganic and Organic Chemistry." Since that time each successive edition has carried, besides other, less sweeping changes, one or more "phoenix schedules," which are totally new developments of targeted portions of the system. The present nineteenth edition and the associated eleventh abridged edition were published in 1979.[1]

DDC notations are assigned the tag 082 in the MARC format when they have been created for a particular item by the Library of Congress. A DDC notation created by a local library participating in a network is placed in MARC field 092. DDC complete call numbers are also placed in field 092, regardless of who assigned the DDC notation to the item involved.

Closely related to DDC is the Universal Decimal Classification (UDC), which was based on DDC. It is discussed briefly at the end of this chapter.

BASIC CONCEPTS

The system is called "decimal" because it arranges all knowledge as represented by library materials into ten broad subject classes numbered from 000 to 900. Using Arabic numerals for symbols, it is flexible only to the degree that numbers can be expanded in linear fashion to cover special aspects of general subjects. Theoretically, expansions may continue indefinitely. The more specific the work being classified, the longer the number combination will tend to grow. At least one Library of Congress record carries a suggested Dewey number containing twenty-one digits, i.e., eighteen decimal places (cf. LC card number 72-90701—*American Indian Art: Form and Tradition*). But such long numbers, however accurate, are unwieldy; it is hard to crowd them onto book spines and catalog cards, and dangers of miscopying and misshelving are multiplied. For these and related reasons many larger libraries have turned from DDC to some other system, such as LC, which has a more economical notation.

Nevertheless, the Dewey Decimal Classification System has many advantages. Its content is compact, consisting in the eighteenth and nineteenth editions of a volume for introductory matter, auxiliary tables, a list of relocations and schedule reductions, and a series of three schedule summaries, plus a second volume for schedule development and a third for the relative index. It incorporates many mnemonic devices that can be transferred from one class to another (e.g., "-03" at the end of a class number of any length often indicates a dictionary of the subject at hand). The classifier, once familiar with the system, can apply it to incoming materials quite rapidly. It provides a limited number of optional alternative locations and allows for great detail of specification. The patron is likely to be familiar with it, because it is the system most frequently used in school and small public libraries. Furthermore, it arranges subjects from the general to the specific in a logical order, which often can be traced by analogy through more than one class. It is philosophical in conception, being based on a systematic outline of knowledge that allows for subjects not yet known to man. Even so, the overall arrangement is not preemptively theoretical or logical. Dewey's intent was to provide a practical system for classifying books. This primary application to the books generally found in American libraries remains one of its notable limitations, although efforts have been made in later editions to rectify that bias.

The basic concepts of the system are covered in two "official" sources: the introduction in volume 1 of the 19th edition,[2] and a manual published by the publisher of DDC in 1982.[3] The DDC introduction gives detailed explanations of the schedules and tables and detailed instructions in classifying and building numbers with DDC. The manual repeats basic points from the DDC introduction, but most of the volume is devoted to a discussion of the tables and schedules by number, pointing out areas of difficulty and explaining what should or should not be included in certain numbers.

SCHEDULE FORMAT

At the close of volume 1, DDC provides three summaries, showing successively the ten main classes, the 100 divisions, and the 1,000 sections of the basic scheme. Each class from 100 to 900 consists of a group of related disciplines. The 000 class is reserved for materials too general to fit anywhere else.

The Ten Main DDC Classes

000   Generalities
100   Philosophy & related disciplines
200   Religion
300   Social sciences
400   Language
500   Pure sciences
600   Technology (Applied sciences)
700   The arts
800   Literature (Belles-lettres)
900   General geography & history

Each main class is separated into ten divisions, although a few of these, as well as some further subdivisions, may seem to be rather artificially located within the class:

The Divisions of a Typical DDC Class

600-609	Technology (Applied sciences)
610-619	Medical sciences Medicine
620-629	Engineering and allied operations
630-639	Agriculture and related technologies
640-649	Home economics and family living
650-659	Management and auxiliary services
660-669	Chemical and related technologies
670-679	Manufactures
680-689	Manufacture of products for specific uses
690-699	Buildings

As a hierarchical classification, DDC applies the principle of developing disciplinary and subject relationships sequentially, from the general topic to the special/specific subdivision. Within most subdivisions the first portion covers general works on the given topic:

The Sections of a Typical DDC Division

610	Medical sciences Medicine
611	Human anatomy, cytology, tissues
612	Human physiology
613	General & personal hygiene
614	Public health & related topics
615	Pharmacology & therapeutics
616	Diseases
617	Surgery & related topics
618	Other branches of medicine
619	Experimental medicine

In volume 2 the full schedules present in detail those subjects identified by the primary sections:

The Subdivisions of a Typical DDC Section

612	Human physiology
612.1	Blood and circulation
612.2	Respiration
612.3	Nutrition
612.4	Secretion, excretion, related functions
612.6	Reproduction, development, maturation
612.7	Motor functions and integument
612.8	Nervous and sensory functions
612.9	Regional physiology

Decimals may of course be, and usually are, further subdivided, although, as in the section subdivisions listed above, there are often asymmetrics attesting to the fact that the phenomena of the world cannot always be subdivided and re-subdivided into groups of ten:

Extended Decimal Subdivision of a DDC Topic

612	Human physiology
612.1	Blood and circulation
612.11	Blood
612.12	Blood chemistry
612.13	Blood vessels and vascular circulation
612.14	Blood pressure
612.17	Heart
612.18	Vasometers

Successive lengthening of the base number by one (occasionally two or three) digit(s) achieves step-wise division. This pyramidal structure means that, in subject relationships, what is true of the whole is true of the parts. For instance, the medical sciences are a branch of technology; physiology is a medical science, etc.

A Typical DDC Hierarchical Sequence

600	Technology (Applied sciences)
610	Medical sciences Medicine
612	Human physiology
612.1	Blood and respiration
612.11	Blood
612.112	White corpuscles

As the notation expands beyond the decimal point, DDC editors introduce a space after every third number. Thus the schedules show "331.873 2 Membership and membership policies in labor unions," or "001.644 04 Electronic data processing network systems." The schedules rarely display numbers with more than four decimal places, although the relative index sometimes expands numbers to eight or even nine decimals. Thus in the index we find "Radiations—biophysics—terrestrial—med. sci.—animals 636.089 201 448." Yet the schedules proper expand "636 - Animal husbandry" only as far as "636.089 Veterinary sciences; veterinary medicine." (Instructions at 636.089 in the schedules allow the building of the longer number found in the index. The concept of building numbers is explained later in this chapter.) The spaces are inserted merely to facilitate reading the closely listed digits. On library materials and bibliographic records they should be omitted, so that the number will occupy no more space than is absolutely necessary.

Certain places in the schedules where fully symmetrical expansion cannot be maintained are given centered headings, which represent concepts for which there is no specific number in the notational hierarchy, and which, therefore, cover an abbreviated span of numbers. These appear with centered inch-long lines immediately above them, and with triangular arrow-head indicators at their left margins, e.g.,

A Typical DDC Centered Heading

▶   439.7-439.8   East Scandinavian languages

If the sequential development of subdivisions is spread over several pages in such a way that the original broad relationships are obscured, a summary introduces the governing steps of the sequence, e.g.,

Summary

332.1	Banks and banking
332.2	Specialized banking institutions
332.3	Credit and loan institutions
332.4	Money
332.5	Other mediums of exchange
332.6	Investment and investments
332.7	Credit
332.8	Interest and discount
332.9	Counterfeiting, forgery, alteration

Other useful formatting devices are the section numbers and running titles at the top of each page of volume 2 (the schedules), the use of bold-face and light-face type in various sizes, plus lefthand marginal indentions, to indicate hierarchical structure, the use of square brackets for numbers from which a topic has recently been shifted (or "relocated") and the use of italics for "reused" numbers. In the nineteenth edition there are only eleven individually reassigned topics for which italics warn the user that the number has been only recently vacated (*see* DDC edition 19, Editor's Introduction, volume 1, sections 14.23 and 2.4).

PHOENIX SCHEDULES

In the nineteenth edition there are also three relatively confined but significant areas which have undergone complete remodeling. Sociology, which in edition 18 occupied number 301, is now recast into the span 301-307. Similarly, topics covering the political process (formerly subdivisions of "324 Electoral process" and "329 Practical politics. Political parties") have now been combined and reordered under 324 alone, leaving 329 vacated. The third broad change is in area notations -41 and -42, where subdivisions are revised to conform to the reorganized local administrative pattern of the United Kingdom. All these changes are summarized at the close of volume 1, where the edition 18 and 19 numbers are listed in parallel columns.

A fourth phoenix schedule was at one time contemplated for "560-590 Life sciences" but it was postponed, to allow more careful study, and to concentrate efforts in the three areas cited above.

CLASSIFICATION BY DISCIPLINE

A basic premise of the Dewey approach is that there is no one class for any given subject. The primary arrangement is by discipline. Any specific topic may appear in any number of disciplines. Various aspects of such a topic are usually brought together in the relative index. For example, a work on "families" may be classed in one of several places depending on its emphasis. Moreover, the phoenix schedule for sociology included in edition 19 has significantly changed some of these assignments, as can be seen in the table below. Besides the aspects shown there, other material on families may be found in still different DDC numbers. Use of the relative index would lead the classifier to some of them.

Some DDC Class Numbers Pertaining to the Family

19th ed.		18th ed.
155.924	Psychological influences of family members	155.924
173	Ethics of family relationships	173
241.63	Christian family ethics	241.63
261.835	Christian attitudes on sex, marriage, family	261.8342
294.3563	Buddhist attitudes on family relationships	294.3563
296.4	Religious family rites, celebrations, services	296.7
304.66	Population control, including family planning	301.426
306.8	Marriage and family	301.42
306.85	Types of families, patriarchal, nuclear, etc.	301.421
346.015	Domestic relations (Family law)	346.015
362.82	Families with specific problems	362.82
392.3	Customs of the home and domestic arts	392.3
616.89156	Family psychotherapy	616.8915
640.42	Family budgeting, expenditure control, etc.	640.42
790.191	Recreational activities for families	790.191
796.0191	Sports for families	796.0191
929.2	Family histories	929.2

SCOPE NOTES AND "ADD" INSTRUCTIONS

The schedules employ several instructional devices that will aid the classifier. One such device is the scope note, which appears frequently under a specific classification category, identifying what is to be classed in that number, or what should be classed elsewhere. For instance, under the centered heading 913-919 are found a cluster of scope notes and classing instructions as follows:

913-919   Geography of and travel in ancient world; specific continents, countries, localities; extraterrestrial worlds
If preferred, class elementary geography textbooks on ancient world, on specific continents, countries, localities in 372.8913-372.8919

Class interdisciplinary works on geography and history of ancient world, of specific continents, countries, localities [*all formerly* 913-919] in 930-990

Class comprehensive works, geography of and travel in more than one continent in 910; geography of and travel in areas, regions, places not limited by continent, country, locality in 910.09; historical geography in 911; graphic representations in 912

Another type of scope note is the definition which helps the classifier understand the meaning of a particular topic, e.g.,

330   Economics
The science of human behavior as it relates to utilization of scarce means for satisfaction of needs and desires through production, distribution, consumption

For commerce, see 380.1

Still other headings are followed by notes enumerating specific qualifications, such as:

331   Labor economics
Class here industrial relations

Class sociology of laboring classes in 305.56, economic conditions of laboring classes in 330.9; personnel management in 658.3

331.1   Labor force and market
Class labor force and market with respect to workers with specific personal characteristics in 331.3-331.6

"Add" instructions appear under some simple numbers or sequences of numbers to serve as means of further subdivision through analogy. They refer the classifier to still another number or number sequence where subdivisions are spelled out, and give instructions on how to transfer the subdivisions into the analogue number or sequence. The following example will illustrate:

574.921-.928   Marine biology (Biological oceanography)
Add to base number 574.92 the numbers following 551.46 in 551.461-551.468, e.g. Mediterranean Sea life 574.922; however, class Antarctic waters of Atlantic Ocean in 574.924, of Pacific Ocean in 574.9258, of Indian Ocean in 574.927; comprehensive works on Antarctic waters in 574.924

Under "551.46   Oceanography" we find that the full sequence referred to may be summarized as follows:

551.461	Atlantic Ocean
551.4611	North Atlantic
551.4612-.4614	Northeast and northwest Atlantic
551.462	Mediterranean Sea
551.463	Caribbean Sea and Gulf of Mexico
551.464	South Atlantic Ocean
551.465	Pacific Ocean
551.466	East Pacific Ocean
551.467	Indian Ocean
551.468	North Polar Sea (Arctic Ocean)

A more complicated add instruction may take the following form:

616.99411-.99415   Malignant neoplasms (Cancers) of cardiovascular organs
Add to base number 616.9941 the numbers following
611.1 in 611.11-611.15, e.g. cancer of heart 616.99412;
then add further as instructed under 618.1-618.8

This process of number building is explained in detail in the Editor's Introduction to DDC edition 19 (volume 1, section 8.542, pp. xlv-xlvi).

Several other types of notes help to determine a needed classification number, and occasionally clarify a given terminology with helpful examples. Under "693.98   Construction in nonrigid materials" we find the note "Example: pneumatic construction." There are also numerous "class here" notes throughout the schedules, e.g.,

711.6   Plans and planning of structural elements in civic art
Adaptation to site and use
Class here comprehensive works on plans and planning of
specific elements
For utilities, see 711.7

To meet the increasing use of the Dewey Decimal Classification on an international scale a greater number of optional provisions has characterized recent editions. In the nineteenth edition new options emphasize favored languages, religions, and the like. This edition also returns to conventional American spelling from the earlier efforts to retain some vestige of simplified spelling forms, such as "divorst," "publisht," and the like. Even these few remnants of Dewey's preferences tended to perplex users whose native language was not English, say the editors.

AUXILIARY TABLES

Auxiliary tables 1 through 7 give the classifier still another way to expand existing numbers in the schedules. In many instances the use of these tables eliminates the "add" instructions (formerly called "divide-like notes") which usually require frequent back-and-forth paging to determine an appropriate number sequence. Note that in either case a base number is always provided, to which the indicated sequence of numbers is to be added.

STANDARD SUBDIVISIONS

As was noted under the "General Principles of Classifying" section of chapter 16, all shelf classifications provide a dual approach. Some items are grouped on the basis of their subject content, while others are placed according to their format. The standard subdivisions supplied in auxiliary Table 1 of the Dewey Decimal Classification derive from what was called in earlier editions a table of "form divisions." The present-day "standard subdivisions" include examples other than form. Some actually do treat format (e.g., dictionaries, encyclopedias, periodicals, etc.). Others represent "modes of treatment," covering theoretical or historical aspects of the subject, such as philosophy and theory, history, etc. To show that none can stand alone as a complete class number, each is preceded in the table by a dash, which should be omitted when that number is attached to a bona fide class notation. The following illustrates some of the categories to be found in Table 1 as presented in volume 1 of DDC edition 19:

-01   **Philosophy and theory.** An exposition of any subject treated from the theoretical point of view.
    Example: 701   Philosophy of the arts

-03   **Dictionaries, encyclopedias, concordances.**
    Example: 720.3   Dictionary of architecture

-05   **Serial publications.** Used for publications of a literary nature or in which the subject is treated in articles, papers, etc.
    Example: 720.5   Architectural Record

-08   **History and description of the subject among groups of persons.** This number is italicized in edition 19, signifying that its use for collections has been discontinued.

-09   **Historical and geographical treatment.**
    Example: 720.9   Fletcher's History of Architecture

Most of the standard subdivisions are further subdivided in Table 1. For example, under "-01   Philosophy and theory" the following subtopics are listed:

-012   Classification
-013   Value
-014   Languages (Terminology) and communication
-015   Scientific principles
-016   Indexes
-018   Methodology
-019   Psychological principles

The -09 can be geographically divided, through the addition of area digits from Table 2, e.g., "720.973   History of architecture in the United States." This type of complex number building is explained later in this chapter in the section titled "Area Tables."

Unless specific instructions indicate otherwise, standard subdivisions may be used with any number if such application is meaningful. Although in the table each is preceded by a single zero, e.g., "-03   Dictionaries, etc.," it is sometimes necessary in the schedules to apply a double or triple zero to introduce the subdivision. This happens when single zero subdivisions are already appropriated in the schedules for special purposes. The instructions which cover such situations are explicit and should be follqwed carefully. A few examples will illustrate certain basic principles:

a)   **Standard subdivisions contained as a part of a complete heading**
In some parts of the schedules a concept that is ordinarily expressed as a standard subdivision has its own number, e.g., a dictionary of literature is classed in 803 (800 for literature, 803 for dictionary), rather than in 800.3 or 800.03.

b)   **0-divisions utilized for a specific purpose; standard subdivision to be introduced by a double-0**
An example of the double-0 appears at "271   Religious congregations and orders in church history." Here the instruction is to use 271.001-271.009 for standard subdivisions. Single-0 subdivisions are used for specific kinds of religious congregations, e.g., "271.01   Contemplative," "271.03   Teaching," "271.04   Preaching," etc. Therefore, a dictionary of religious congregations and orders in general is classed in 271.003.

c)   **00-divisions utilized for special purposes; standard subdivisions to be introduced by a triple-0**
An example of the triple-0 appears at "350   Public administration." Here the instruction is to use 350.0001-350.0009 for standard subdivisions of this general subject. 350.001-350.009 are reserved for bureaucracy and specific aspects of the chief executive, while 350.01-350.08 are used for specific executive departments and ministries of cabinet rank. 350.1-350.9 encompass specific aspects of public administration such as personnel management, lists of officials and employees, civil service examinations, etc. Therefore, a dictionary of public administration in general is classed 350.0003.

AREA TABLES

When a given heading can be subdivided geographically and the library has many books dealing with that subject, it is recommended that the classifier use Table 2 (the area table) which allows one to expand the number systematically by region or site. Until the seventeenth edition of DDC, geographic subdivision was indicated by means of a note to "Divide like 930-999." However, as the schedules grew the use of their historical sequences to form geographic aspects for other numbers became cumbersome and confusing. In the seventeenth edition the area table replaced 930-999 for number building, leaving the history numbers solely for history. It is by far the bulkiest of the seven auxiliary tables accompanying the DDC schedules. Its general arrangement is as follows:

-1	Areas, regions, places in general
-2	Persons regardless of area, region, place
-3	The ancient world
-4	Europe Western Europe
-5	Asia Orient Far East
-6	Africa
-7	North America
-8	South America
-9	Other parts of world and extraterrestrial worlds Pacific Ocean islands (Oceania)

Area -1 is used for the treatment of any subject geographically, but not limited by continent, country, or locality. It allows diverse elements that have natural ties to regions or groups (e.g., frigid zones, temperate zones, land forms, or types of vegetation) to be brought together under certain subjects. Area -2 permits subdivision by biography, diaries, reminiscences, correspondence, and the like of persons associated with any subject for which the schedule instructions say to add the "areas" notation directly instead of adding "standard subdivision" notation -092 from Table 1. Area -3 offers specific subdivisions for ancient countries and areas up to the fall of the Roman Empire. Area notations -4 through -9 are for specific continents, and modern countries. For example, area number "-4 Europe" has the following summary subtopics:

-41	British Isles
-42	England and Wales
-43	Central Europe Germany
-44	France and Monaco
-45	Italy
-46	Iberian Peninsula and adjacent islands Spain
-47	Union of Soviet Socialist Republics (Soviet Union)
-48	Scandinavia
-49	Other parts of Europe

The area notations -41 and -42 have been extensively revised in the nine-teenth edition to reflect a thorough reorganization of British local administra-tion. The area concepts of "British Isles," "United Kingdom," and "Great Britain" were at the same time relocated from area -42 to area -41. For the con-venience of those wishing to compare the edition 19 table with the one it replaces, a list of the number changes between the eighteenth and nineteenth editions is printed near the close of volume 1. The primary divisions, with a few illustrative subtopics, may now be summarized as follows (notice the failure of the notation to reflect hierarchical equivalencies precisely, as where Scotland requires a longer number than does England):

-41	British Isles
-411	Scotland
-412	Northeastern Scotland
-4127	City of Dundee district. Including Monifieth
-42	England and Wales
-421	Greater London
-4213	West London
-42132	Westminster. Including Paddington, Saint Marylebone
-422	Southeastern England

For example, a general treatise on higher education in Dundee, Scotland, will be classed in 378 in the Dewey Decimal Classification. The schedule at 378.4-.9 instructs "Add 'Areas' notation 4-9 from Table 2 to base number 378." The index refers to "*area*-4127" as the number for "Dundee Tayside Scot." This number is therefore applied to 378, giving 378.4127, as the follow-ing analysis shows:

378	Higher education
378.4	Europe
378.41	British Isles
378.412	Northeastern Scotland
378.4127	Dundee, Scotland

There is no provision in Table 2 for separating Dundee from Monifieth or the rest of Tayside, so this is the most specific number which can be applied.

Where specific instructions (as in 378.4-.9) are not given for geographical treatment in the schedules, the classifier can apply the standard subdivision "-09   Historical and geographical treatment" to any number which lends itself to that approach, unless localized instructions mandate a double- or triple-0 in place of the single-0. For example, the specific DDC number for savings banks is 332.21. To class a work on savings banks in Westminster, London, the schedule gives no specific direction to use Table 2, nor does it give direction to use single -0 for specific subdivisions. So the standard subdivision -09 may be used directly. In Table 1 a note under "-093-099   Treatment by specific con-tinents, countries, localities; extraterrestrial worlds" says to "Add 'Areas' notation 3-9 from Table 2 to base number -09." So books on savings banks in Westminster, London, will be classed in 332.210942132. The number may be analyzed to show:

332.21	Savings banks
332.2109	Standard subdivision for historical and geographical treatment
332.21094	In Europe
332.210942	In England and Wales
332.2109421	In Greater London
332.21094213	In West London
332.210942132	In Westminster

It should be noted by the beginning student that although these examples result in long numbers, they are quite simple to construct.

INDIVIDUAL LITERATURES

In Table 3, "Subdivisions of Individual Literatures," a detailed and specialized development of subdivision "-08 Collections" makes use of a supplementary Table 3-A, which is new in edition 19. The notation "-09 History, description, critical appraisal" is adapted from the Table 1 standard subdivision -09, and developed for use with divisions 810-890 from the full schedules. In addition, numbers "-1-8 Specific forms" develop and expand the summary form numbers which appear in the full schedules under "810 American literature in English." These mnemonic form divisions for kinds of literature are:

-1	Poetry	(e.g., 831 German poetry)
-2	Drama	(e.g., 842 French drama)
-3	Fiction	(e.g., 839.313 Dutch fiction)
-4	Essays	(e.g., 869.4 Portuguese essays)
-5	Speeches	(e.g., 845 French speeches)
-6	Letters	(e.g., 836 German letters)
-7	Satire and humor	(e.g., 869.7 Portuguese satire & humor)
-8	Miscellaneous writings	(e.g., 839.318 Dutch miscellaneous writings)

INDIVIDUAL LANGUAGES

Table 4, "Subdivisions of Individual Languages," is used with base numbers for individual languages, as explained under 420-490. In a fashion similar to that of Table 3 it provides mnemonic form divisions for languages, e.g.,

-1   Written and spoken codes of the standard form of the language.
         (e.g., 431   Written and spoken codes of standard German)
-2   Etymology of the standard form of the language.
         (e.g., 442   Etymology of the standard form of French)
-3   Dictionaries of the standard form of the language.
         (e.g., 439.313   Dictionaries of the standard form of Dutch)

-5   Structural system (Grammar) of the standard form of the language.
        (e.g., 469.5   The grammar of the standard form of Portuguese)
-7   Nonstandard forms of the language.
        (e.g., 437   Nonstandard German)
-8   Standard usage of the language.
        (e.g., 448   Standard French usage)

RACIAL, ETHNIC, NATIONAL GROUPS

Table 5, "Racial, Ethnic, National Groups," is used according to specific instructions at certain places in the schedules, or through the interposition of "-089   Treatment among specific racial, ethnic, national groups" from Table 1. These applications are exactly parallel to the use of Table 2, which is used either on direct instructions in the schedule, or on interposition of "-09 Historical and geographical treatment" from Table 1. The Table 5 summary is:

-1   North Americans
-2   Anglo-Saxons, British, English
-3   Nordics
-4   Modern Latins
-5   Italians, Romanians, related groups
-6   Spanish and Portuguese
-7   Other Italic peoples
-8   Greeks and related groups
-9   Other racial, ethnic, national groups

An example to illustrate the use of Table 5 could be a work dealing with special education for American blacks. The number for special education, as found in the index and the schedules, is 371.9. An instruction under sub-division "371.97   Students exceptional because of racial, ethnic, national origin" says "Add 'Racial, Ethnic, National Groups' notation 01-99 from Table 5 to base number 371.97." The number in Table 5 for "United States blacks (Afro-Americans)" is -96073. Thus the full class number 371.9796073 may be analyzed as follows:

371.9	Special education
371.97	Students exceptional because of racial, ethnic, national origin
371.979	Racial, ethnic, national groups other than North American or major European nationalities
371.9796	Africans and people of African descent
371.97960	Digit used to expand the notation, here geographically
371.979607	In North America
371.9796073	In the United States

LANGUAGES

Table 6, "Languages," is a basic mnemonic table used to indicate the particular language of a work, or which is the subject matter of a work. It is used as instructed in the tables, and is particularly relevant to classes 400 and 800. The summary is:

-1   Indo-European (Indo-Germanic) languages
-2   English and Anglo-Saxon languages
-3   Germanic (Teutonic) languages
-4   Romance languages
-5   Italian, Romanian, Rhaeto-Romanic
-6   Spanish and Portuguese
-7   Italic languages
-8   Hellenic languages
-9   Other languages

To illustrate the application of this table let us class a Bible in French, starting from the entry given in both index and schedules "220.5 Modern versions and translations of the Bible." For "220.53-59 Other languages than English" the schedule direction says "Add 'Languages' notation 3-9 from Table 6 to base number 220.5." The notation for French in Table 6 is -41. The resulting whole number for a modern French Bible may be analyzed as follows:

220   The Bible
220.5   Modern versions
220.54   In the Romance languages
220.541   In modern French

PERSONS

Table 7, "Persons," is used when the schedules say to add the "Persons" notation to a base number, or through interposition of "-088 Treatment among groups of specific kinds of persons" from Table 1. This table deals with various characteristics of persons, as the following summary shows:

-01   Individual persons
-02   Groups of persons
-03-08   Persons by various nonoccupational characteristics
           -03   Persons by racial, ethnic, national background
           -04   Persons by sex and kinship characteristics
           -05   Persons by age
           -06   Persons by social and economic characteristics
           -08   Persons by physical and mental characteristics
-09-99   Persons by various occupational characteristics
           -09   Generalists and novices

-1-9   Specialists
-1   Persons occupied with philosophy and related
          disciplines
-2   Persons occupied with or adherent to religion
-3   Persons occupied with the social sciences and
          socioeconomic activities
-4   Persons occupied with linguistics and lexicography
-5   Persons occupied with pure sciences
-6   Persons occupied with applied sciences (Technologists)
-7   Persons occupied with the arts
-8   Persons occupied with creative writing and speaking
-9   Persons occupied with geography, history, related
          disciplines and activities

Obviously, from -09 to -9 this table is based on the ten main classes of DDC. A book on Shakers as a social group furnishes the following example. The number for adherents of religious groups in social contexts is now 305.6. This number represents a phoenix schedule change in the nineteenth edition from "301.452   Adherents to religious organizations" in the eighteenth edition. The directions in the schedule at the new number say "Add to base number 305.6 the numbers following 2 in 'Persons' notation 21-29 from Table 7." The Table 7 number for Shakers is -288. Thus our book would be classed 305.688. The analysis of the number proceeds as follows:

305   Social stratification (Social structure)
305.6   Adherents of religious groups
305.68   Nondominant Christian churches
305.688   Shakers

THE RELATIVE INDEX

The "relative" index is so-called because it is claimed to show relationships of each specific topic to its discipline, and to other topics. Terminological subdivisions are indicated by lists of entries successively indented from the left margins of each column. Many *see also* references are given in italics (e.g., "Organizations ... *s.a. spec. kinds e.g.* Labor unions; Corporations"). There are also *see* references to "other aspects" (e.g., "Prairies ... *other aspects see* Plane regions"). Geographic name entries usually refer the user to the appropriate area table (e.g., "Macerata Italy *area*-45673"). A few referrals occur to the standard subdivisions and to other auxiliary tables (e.g., "Repairs & repairing ... *s.a. s.s.*-0288").

The DDC "relative" index enumerates alphabetically all the main headings in the classification schedules, plus certain other specific entries not actually listed in the schedules. One such instance was discussed on page 384. In another, the index carries the subordinated entry "Halogenated compounds — synthetic drugs pharm. 615.312." Yet there is no 615.312 listed as such in the schedules. Only an "add to" instruction under 615.31 shows how to expand the schedules to obtain the more specific 615.312.

In other places index terminology varies from that found in the schedules for the same class number, although the general meanings coincide. Thus, the schedule entry "612.7921 Glands and glandular secretions, including perspiration" is a generalized representation of the index entry "Sebaceous glands — biochemistry — human phys.   612.7921." Synonyms which appear in the schedules in scope notes or parentheses are represented by *see* references in the index. For example, the index has the entry "Blackjack (game) *see* Twenty-one (game)," as well as "Twenty-one (game) — recreation   795.42." The corresponding entry in the schedules is "795.42   Games based chiefly on chance. Examples: baccarat, faro, twenty-one (blackjack)."

The classifier should, of course, consult the index, especially in cases in which the location of the desired topic, or the precise nature of its relation to other topics, is in doubt. Yet the relative index should never become a substitute for the schedules. It is coordinated with them, but is limited for reasons of space, and cannot show hierarchical progressions or topical groupings. It will guide the classifier to some, but not necessarily all, aspects of a given subject. The next important step in the classification process is to consult the schedules for verification, perspective, and possible further instructions. Only by using the two types of display together can the full potential of the scheme be realized.

BROAD AND CLOSE CLASSIFICATION

Because it offers a wide variety of techniques and nearly limitless expansions in number building, Dewey Decimal Classification is hospitable to all the titles which a large library might add in any subject. It also offers various ways to meet the limited needs of smaller libraries. The classifier must remember that, in general, when there are relatively few books in a given subject area, DDC encourages broad classification. Digits in class notations after decimal points may be cut off at any appropriate place. The present policy of the Library of Congress is to provide bibliographic records with Dewey Decimal numbers of from one to three segments. The segments are indicated by prime marks, e.g., "513'.93'028," which stands for "Arithmetic — Business mathematics — Techniques, procedures, apparatus, etc." A small public library with a limited collection of mathematics books might prefer to keep them all together under 513. If the library has several dozen books on mathematics, it might keep the business-oriented ones together by using the number 513.93. If it maintains a separate resource collection for use by business and commercial clients, it could add the standard subdivision -028 to distinguish the "how-to-do-it" manuals. When a library decides to retain one or more of the DDC segments to achieve close classification at a particular point in the collection, it omits the prime marks, which were used in the LC record merely to suggest break-points.

UPDATING

New editions of Dewey Decimal Classification have been published every eight years or so. Between editions, updating is accomplished via the publication of *Dewey Decimal Classification Additions, Notes and Decisions* (affectionately known as "DC&," "&" being the symbol for "AND," the acronym for "Additions, Notes and Decisions").[4] DC& is published every 12-16 months, although a more frequent schedule has been promised. It contains corrections of errors, clarifications, updating, expansions, and possible new schedules for the next edition. A policy for "continuous revision" has been adopted by Forest Press, which means that in the future, phoenix schedules and major revisions will be released as separates between editions, and new editions will appear as cumulations. It is also anticipated that new editions will appear less often.[5]

ABRIDGED EDITIONS

The first *Abridged Decimal Classification and Relativ Index for Libraries, Clippings, Notes, etc.* appeared in 1894, the year in which the fifth edition of the full schedules was published. Abridged edition 11 is based on DDC edition 19, and followed its publication in 1979 by only a few months. Like its predecessors, it is designed primarily for general collections of 20,000 titles or less, such as are found in small public and school libraries. Abridged edition 10 was an adaptation, using not only shorter, but some slightly different numbers than its companion eighteenth edition. But the widespread use of segmentation marks for Dewey class numbers in Library of Congress records and other centrally produced bibliographic entries vitiated the usefulness of this approach. Abridged edition 11 is therefore once again a true abridgment of its parent nineteenth edition. Yet it continues the trend in the ninth and tenth abridged editions toward fewer entries, while the full seventeenth, eighteenth, and nineteenth editions increase their entries, as the following brief table shows:

Edition	Total entries
DDC 17th edition	22,355
DDC abridged 9th edition	2,838
DDC 18th edition	26,141
DDC abridged 10th edition	2,542
DDC 19th edition	29,528
DDC abridged 11th edition	2,516

CONCLUSION

Among the difficulties built into the Dewey Decimal Classification System are its long numbers, which increase rather than diminish as the system grows, nullifying much of the mnemonic character of the basic system. Thus the number 636.089201448, which was cited on page 384 as coming from the relative index entry for medical radiation of terrestrial animals is so long that any mnemonic associations between it and the number 612.01448 (from which it was built) are obscured. Librarians who wish to retain these long numbers because of extensive holdings in one or more fields should write them on cards and items to be shelved in several lines. The above numbers could be written in short meaningful segments as follows:

```
636 and 612
.089    .01
201     448
448
```

Related to the long number difficulties are the rapid, often sweeping, topical relocations from one edition to another. Such drastic surgery is forced upon the system by its limited notational base and the swift growth and change in the world of knowledge and of publication. DDC 19 suggests in volume 1, section 14, pages lxxii-lxxiv, various ways of adjusting to its expansions, reductions, relocations, reused numbers, and phoenix schedules. Its relative index is designed to facilitate updated classification by containing an entry for every significant term in the schedules and tables, with numerous cross references to assist the user who is not familiar with the terminology. While the big rush, particularly in academic libraries, to change from Dewey to the Library of Congress classification seems to have run its course, no library can afford to ignore all efforts to keep shelf arrangement contemporary with the shifts in knowledge as reflected in the literature.

UNIVERSAL DECIMAL CLASSIFICATION
(UDC)

The UDC was developed in 1885 by two Belgian lawyers, Paul Otlet and Henri LaFontaine, for the classification of a huge card catalog of the world's literature in all fields of knowledge. It was based on the DDC (then in its fifth edition) but was, with Dewey's permission, expanded by the addition of many more detailed subdivisions and the use of typographical signs to indicate complex subjects and what we know today as facets. DDC's decimal notation was retained (except for final zeros), and the ten main classes as well as some subdivisions are still the same in UDC as they are in DDC, but class 4 (i.e., DDC 400) has been amalgamated with class 8 and is currently vacant. Many major and almost all minor subdivisions are now quite different from those in DDC. The main difference lies, however, in the synthetic structure of UDC. Thus, a work dealing with two or more subjects can be classed by two or more

UDC class notations, linked by a colon sign (the most commonly used of the typographical symbols), as in the following example:

362.1 : 658.3 : 681.31 Hospital : Personnel management : Computers

for a work on the use of computers in the management of hospital personnel. Such a class notation is, however, not a "call number" but is intended for a classified catalog in which each of the three class notations may serve as an access point, while the other two are shown in rotation, e.g.,

658.3 : 681.31 : 362.1 and *681.31* : 362.1 : 658.3

If UDC is to be used for shelf classification, one of the three class notations may be chosen as a call number for a book on this complex subject.

UDC's faceted structure has its roots in DDC's device for indication of place, namely, the intercalation of -09 followed by the class notation for a country or region, e.g., -0973 for the United States. UDC uses largely the same place notations as DDC but encloses them in parentheses. Thus, "plant cultivation in the U.S." is 631.50973 in DDC but 631.5(73) in UDC (note that the main class notation is the same in both). In addition to the place facet UDC has also specific symbols and notations for the language of a work, its physical form, races and peoples, time periods, materials, persons, specific points of view, and recurring subdivisions in certain classes, all of which can be appended to basic notations either alone or in combination, as in the following example:

631.5 = 82	Plant cultivation – written in Russian
631.5(038)	– Glossary
631.5"17"	– 18th century
631.5(= 97)(85)	– By American Indians in Peru

Due to this highly faceted structure and largely expressive notation the UDC has been used successfully in computerized information retrieval.[6]

UDC schedules were first published in 1905 in French, followed later by full editions (each one containing about 150,000 class notations) in English (published as British Standards in several dozens of separate booklets for main classes and their major subdivisions), German, Japanese, Russian, Spanish, and eight other languages. Medium-sized editions containing about 30 percent of the full schedules exist in 11 languages, the most recent one being in English.[7] Abridged editions are published in 17 languages and five scripts, including Hebrew, Japanese, and Korean.[8] In addition, there are special editions for certain subject fields, e.g., geology, building construction, and agriculture.

UDC is managed by the International Federation of Documentation (FID) in The Hague (Netherlands), which coordinates a continuous revision and expansion process by means of a network of committees and experts, the results of which are published annually.[9] UDC is widely used in many European countries, in Latin America, Japan, and the Soviet Union. In the United States it is used mainly in some scientific and technical libraries and by one abstracting data base.[10] A U.S. Information Center for the UDC exists at the College of Library and Information Services of the University of Maryland in College Park, Maryland, where a complete collection of current English UDC editions and their updating as well as pending proposals for revision are available. More detailed descriptions of the UDC, its development, and its application may be found in a number of publications.[11]

NOTES

[1]Melvil Dewey, *Dewey Decimal Classification and Relative Index*, 19th ed., edited under the direction of Benjamin A. Custer (Albany, N.Y., Forest Press, 1979), 3v.; Melvil Dewey, *Abridged Dewey Decimal Classification and Relative Index*, 11th ed. (Albany, N.Y., Forest Press, 1979).

[2]*Dewey Decimal Classification*, vol. 1, pp. xxi-lxxv.

[3]*Manual on the Use of the Dewey Decimal Classification*, prepared by John P. Comaromi, editor, et al. (Albany, N.Y., Forest Press, 1982).

[4]*Dewey Decimal Classification Additions, Notes and Decisions*, vol. 4, no. 1- (Albany, N.Y., Forest Press, 1980-).

[5]DC&, vol. 4, no. 4 (Winter 1983/84): 11-12.

[6]Malcolm Rigby, *Automation and the UDC, 1948-1980*, 2nd ed. (The Hague, FID, 1981). (FID 565)

[7]British Standards Institution, *UDC: International Medium Edition* (London, BSI, 1985). (BS 1000M:1985). Available in printed or machine-readable form.

[8]*Bibliographic Survey of UDC Editions* (The Hague, FID, 1982). (FID publication 573)

[9]*Extensions and Corrections to the UDC* (The Hague, FID, 1951-). Annual.

[10]*Meteorological and Geoastrophysical Abstracts* (Boston, American Meteorological Society, 1950-).

[11]W. Boyd Rayward, "The UDC and FID: A Historical Perspective." *Library Quarterly* 37 (July 1967): 259-278; A. C. Foskett, "The Universal Decimal Classification," in *The Subject Approach to Information*, 4th ed. (London, Bingley, 1982), pp. 349-371; *Principles of the UDC and Rules for Its Revision and Publication* (The Hague, FID, 1981). (FID 598); Geoffrey Robinson, *UDC: A Brief Introduction* (The Hague, FID, 1979). (FID 574)

SUGGESTED READING

Foskett, A. C. *The Subject Approach to Information.* 4th ed. London, Bingley, 1982. Chapters 17-18.

Manual on the Use of the Dewey Decimal Classification, prepared by John P. Comaromi, editor, et al. Albany, N.Y., Forest Press, 1982.

Osborn, Jeanne. *Dewey Decimal Classification, 19th Edition: A Study Manual.* Littleton, Colo., Libraries Unlimited, 1982.

Robinson, Geoffrey. *UDC: A Brief Introduction.* The Hague, FID, 1984. (FID 574). Also available in French (FID 612), Italian (FID 583), and Spanish (FID 608).

18
Library of Congress Classification

INTRODUCTION

The Library of Congress was founded in 1800. Its earliest classification system was by size (folios, quartos, octavos, etc.), subdivided by accession numbers. But by 1812 the collection had grown to about 3,000 volumes, and a better method of classification was needed. The solution was to arrange the works under eighteen broad subject categories similar to the Bacon-d'Alembert system used in the 1789 *Catalogue* of Benjamin Franklin's Library Company of Philadelphia. Soon after, in 1814, British soldiers burned the Capitol where the collection was housed. To re-establish it, Thomas Jefferson offered to sell Congress his library of around 7,000 volumes. Jefferson had cataloged and classified the works himself, using forty-four main classes and divisions based on a different interpretation of the Bacon-d'Alembert system. After some debate, Congress agreed to purchase the Jefferson books. Although many were destroyed in a later fire, the classification which came with them was used until the end of the nineteenth century. By that time it had undergone so much ad hoc modification, largely based on shelving and other physical limitations, that it was barely recognizable, and completely inadequate.

Many significant changes occurred at the Library of Congress near the turn of the century. In 1899 Dr. Herbert Putnam, the new Librarian, with many new staff appointments and a brand new building, decided to reorganize and reclassify his rapidly growing collection. Since it was to be moved into more adequate shelving areas, the time was right to develop a better, more detailed classification system. There were already in existence the first five editions of the *Dewey Decimal Classification* and the first six expansions of Cutter's *Expansive Classification*. LC classifiers studied both, as well as the German *Halle Schema* devised by Otto Hartwig. They did not adopt any in full, but the experience they gained was invaluable, and their debt, especially to Cutter, is implicit in the basic structure of their system. While the outline and notation of their main classes are very similar to those of the *Expansive*

Classification, there are no main classes I, O, W, X, or Y, as there are in the Cutter system.[1] All five letters do appear, however, as second or third symbols in the notation for various Library of Congress subclasses. The other major similarity to the *Expansive Classification* is in the structure of class "Z — Bibliography and Library Science," which was the first class devised, and was adopted from Cutter with only minor variations.

After Putnam and his Chief Cataloger, Charles Martel, determined the broad outlines of the new classification, different subject specialists were asked to develop each individual schedule, or portion of the system. Within a broad general framework set up to ensure coordination, each topic or form of presentation identified as a class or subclass was further organized to display the library's holdings and to serve anticipated research needs. Schedules comprising single classes or parts of classes were separately published as they were completed. Most of them first appeared between 1899 and 1940. Many have since gone through several editions. In one sense, the scheme represents a series of special classifications. Yet special libraries, with narrowly defined collecting and service goals, often find the LC Classification, which serves broader, more interdisciplinary uses, unsatisfactory for their purposes.

To keep the system functionally up-to-date, individual schedule volumes are frequently reviewed in committee. Revisions, reallocations, and additions keep it flexible and hospitable to new subjects or points of view. For example, recent interest in eastern religions and the increase in materials from Asia occasioned a reallocation in 1972 of the topic "Buddhism" from the span BL1400-1495 into a whole new subclass, BQ. Revisions were likewise made in subclass PL, particularly in the sections for Chinese, Japanese, and Korean literatures. Also recent are block revisions in the "D — General and Old World History" class. In subclass DZ, Hungary has been released at last from Austrian captivity. Number spans now reflect political changes in Albania, Bangladesh, Korea, Namibia, Somalia, and the like. A new triple-letter subclass "DJK — Eastern Europe" was developed in 1976. Further steps are underway to counter the old tendency to equate that region with the Soviet Union or the Balkan Peninsula. Intensified foreign acquisitions programs under PL480, the National Program for Acquisitions and Cataloging (NPAC) initiated by Title II of the Higher Education Act of 1965, the revised Copyright Law, and other developments, stimulate increased expansion and revision of the system.

Hundreds of different number-letter combinations compatible with the notation have not yet been employed, or have been retired in favor of new locations. The scheme will continue to accommodate for a long time the many new subjects and aspects of subjects not yet anticipated. It is particularly useful for large university and research collections because of its hospitality and inherent flexibility. It has been used effectively in smaller academic and public libraries, although its adaptability for broad classification is limited. Even special libraries frequently base their own more technical constructs on it, extending its schedules or parts of schedules to cover their unique materials. Some foreign libraries also use the system, although, in spite of LC's large foreign holdings, it is primarily designed from an American perspective.

In the MARC format call numbers based on LC classification that are assigned by LC are placed in field 050. Those assigned by other libraries are placed in field 090.

CLASSIFICATION TOOLS AND AIDS

The working schedules are contained in 37 separate volumes. Besides the basic schedules, there are a separately published partial index for P-PM sub-categories in the Language and Literature class, and a short general *Outline*, now in its fourth edition, which gives the secondary and tertiary subclass spans for most classes. Several volumes are devoted to subclass coverage of broad areas, such as related language and literature groups. They comprise:

A	General Works; Polygraphy (4th ed., 1973)
B-BJ	Philosophy; Psychology (3rd ed., 1979)
BL-BX	Religion (2nd ed., 1962)
BL-BQ	Religion: Religions, Hinduism, Judaism, Islam, Buddhism (3rd ed., 1984)[2]
C	Auxiliary Sciences of History (3rd ed., 1975)
D	General and Old World History (2nd ed., 1959; Reissue with supplementary pages, 1966)
E-F	American History (3rd ed., 1958; Reissue with supplementary pages, 1965)
G	Geography; Maps; Anthropology; Recreation (4th ed., 1976)
H-HJ	Social Sciences: Economics (4th ed., 1981)
HM-HX	Social Sciences: Sociology (4th ed., 1980)
J	Political Science (2nd ed., 1924; Reissue with supplementary pages, 1966)
K	Law (General) (1st ed., 1977)
KD	Law of the United Kingdom and Ireland (1st ed., 1973)
KDZ, KG-KH	Law of the Americas, Latin America, and the West Indies (1st ed., 1984)
KE	Law of Canada (1st ed., 1976)

KF	Law of the United States (Prelim. ed., 1969)
KK – KKC	Law of Germany (1st ed., 1982)
L	Education (4th ed., 1984)
M	Music; Books on Music (3rd ed., 1978)
N	Fine Arts (4th ed., 1970)
P-PZ	Language and Literature Tables (supersedes the tables in the P Schedules, 1982)
P-PA	General Philology and Linguistics; Classical Languages and Literatures (1st ed., 1928; Reissue with supplementary pages, 1968)
PA supplement	Byzantine and Modern Greek Literature; Medieval and Modern Latin Literature (1st ed., 1942; Reissue with supplementary pages, 1968)
PB-PH	Modern European Languages (1st ed., 1933; Reissue with supplementary pages, 1966)
PG	Russian Literature (in part) (1st ed., 1948; Reissue with supplementary pages, 1965)
PJ-PM	Languages and Literatures of Asia, Africa, Oceania; American Indian Languages; Artificial Languages (1st ed., 1935; Reissue with supplementary pages, 1965)
P-PM supplement	Index to Languages and Dialects (3rd ed., 1983)
PN, PR, PS, PZ	General Literature; English and American Literatures; Fiction in English; Juvenile Literature (2nd ed., 1978)
PQ, pt. 1	French Literature (1st ed., 1936; Reissue with supplementary pages, 1966)
PQ, pt. 2	Italian, Spanish, and Portuguese Literatures (1st ed., 1937; Reissue with supplementary pages, 1965)
PT, pt. 1	German Literature (1st ed., 1938; Reissue with supplementary pages, 1966)
PT, pt. 2	Dutch and Scandinavian Literatures (1st ed., 1942; Reissue with supplementary pages, 1965)
Q	Science (6th ed., 1973)

R   Medicine (4th ed., 1980)

S   Agriculture (4th ed., 1982)

T   Technology (5th ed., 1971)

U   Military Science (4th ed., 1974)

V   Naval Science (3rd ed., 1974)

Z   Bibliography; Library Science (5th ed., 1980)

A-Z   Outline (4th ed., 1978)

Updating is accomplished by a variety of publications, most of which are available directly from the Library of Congress.

1. **Revised editions of individual schedules.** As the above list shows, the various schedules differ widely in the number and kinds of revisions made. Pre-1970 volumes were letter-press printed on both sides of each leaf, and issued in beige paper covers. As changes came, some schedules were thoroughly revised and issued in new editions. In other cases, "reissues" showed the new material cumulated at the back in a separate sequence, with a separate index. Users had to remember to look in both sections each time they consulted one of these "reissues." Since 1970 all revisions show a new format. They are photo-offset from keyboarded copy, printed on only one side of each leaf, and bound in blue-and-white paper covers. Automated production techniques now make fully integrated revisions more feasible, so the confusing double-sequence reissues no longer appear. However, the new editions do not always render prior editions obsolete. A notable instance is the second edition of the PN, PR, PS, PZ schedule, which omits not only the first edition index entries for personal names, but also long-established, heavily-used author cutters from the *Additions and Changes* because they were never incorporated into the "official schedules."[3] Instructive prefaces are frequently dropped from new editions. When buying recent editions of the schedules, classifiers should check their older issues, to ensure that no valuable information would be inadvertently lost if they were discarded. All schedules and the *Outline* are sold individually by the Library's Cataloging Distribution Service at nominal prices.

2. **Library of Congress Additions and Changes.** This stapled paper publication reports quarterly on the latest adjustments in all schedules and schedule indexes of the LC Classification. Subscriptions may be placed with the Cataloging Distribution Service.

3. **Library of Congress Classification Schedules: A Cumulation of Additions and Changes.** These periodic cumulations of the quarterly *Additions and Changes* have been published since 1972 by Gale Research Company on contract with the Library of Congress.[4] The class and subclass coverage of each separate booklet corresponds to that of the basic schedule volumes. Each

new set updates previous cumulations from their final cutoff date to the close of a given year. Their chief value is to reduce and consolidate the number of places one must look to get full information about the system. Each new series or individual volume is available from the publisher.

4.   **Cataloging Service Bulletin.** This channel for recent decisions and experiments in technical processing at the Library of Congress has been offered since 1945.[5] It now has a regular quarterly publication schedule, carrying valuable data on LC classification and shelflisting practice, as well as other aspects of subject and descriptive cataloging.

5.   **Library of Congress Subject Headings.** There is no official comprehensive index to the LC classification scheme. Most of the schedules carry their own indexes, which are largely self-contained, although they occasionally refer to other schedules where related materials can be found on an indexed topic. For example, the index to class "T — Technology" provides the following sequence of entries under "Automobiles":

Automobiles: TL1-390
   Accidents: HE5614-5614.5
   Racing: GV 1029-1029.8

At best, this type of cross-schedule indexing is spotty. The class "H-HJ Social Sciences: Economics" index entries under "Automobiles" read:

Automobiles:
   Accounting: HF5686.A9
   and
      railways: HE1049
   Railway freight traffic: HE2321.A8
   Selling: HF5439.A8
   Shipping: HE595.A8
   Telegraph codes: HE7677.A8

The most obvious substitute for an official comprehensive index is *Library of Congress Subject Headings.*[6] While it was never designed to function as a true index, many entries and subdivisions refer in parentheses to one or more class numbers, often including terminology used in the schedules. In it, under the term "AUTOMOBILES" (including subdivisions and inverted modifications), there are about 60 specific LC class number associations. Two of these come from the "G — Geography, etc." schedule, one from the "U — Military Science" schedule, and the rest from "T — Technology." LC makes no effort to maintain class notations in *LCSH*, and it can be seen that in the heading "Automobiles" one would miss the entries from the H — HJ schedule. However, sometimes LC class notations relating to a given concept can be grouped more quickly through *LCSH* than through the many schedule indexes, as shown in the following example:

Schedule B-BJ— Philosophy; Psychology:

Hypnotism (Parapsychology): BF1111 +

Schedule BL-BX— Religion:

Hypnotism
 and religion: BL65.H9
 Moral theology
  Roman Catholic Church: BX1759.5.H8

Schedule H— Social Sciences:

Hypnotism and crime: HV6110

Schedule Q— Science:

Hypnotic conditions (Neurophysiology): QP425

Schedule R— Medicine:

Hypnotism and hypnosis
 Anesthesiology: RD85.A9
 Forensic medicine: RA1171
 Psychiatry: RC490

LCSH9 and supplements:

HYPNOTISM (BF1111-1156; Hypnotism and crime, HV6110;
 Psychiatry, RC490-499)
HYPNOTISM IN SURGERY (RD85.H9)

6. **LC Subject Catalog.** Subject access has been provided as part of the *National Union Catalog* since 1950. It was provided only for books from 1950 through 1974 in *Library of Congress Catalog, Books: Subjects.* From 1975 through 1982 the *Subject Catalog* contained entries for books, pamphlets, serials, maps, and atlases. Since January 1983, the subject catalog has been incorporated into *National Union Catalog. Books*, for which there is a subject index.

7. **Library of Congress Shelflist in Microform.** In 1978 the six and one-half million cards of the LC shelflist, arranged by call number, were offered for purchase in various microformats (35mm roll film, 16mm cartridge, and microfiche) as well as in Copyflo hard copy. The United States Historical Documents Institute, Inc. and University Microfilms International jointly sponsored the filming, and respectively sell different formats of the full shelflist, or selected portions of it. This tool can be used most effectively for fine-tuning class number and shelflist assignments through comparison of proposed numbers for new materials with those already grouped in a given area.

8. **Commercially prepared indexes.** Just as the Gale *Additions and Changes* cumulations and the LC shelflist reproductions are commercial aids based on official, publicly accessible LC data, so a number of new indexing ventures reflect similar trade manipulation of publications or automated processing available from the Library of Congress. They are designed to give broader scope and greater depth to the primary access materials on which they draw. Notable among these are:

Williams, James G., Martha L. Manheimer, and Jay E. Daily. *Classified Library of Congress Subject Headings.* 2nd ed. New York, Marcel Dekker, 1982. v. 1 — Classified List; v. 2 — Alphabetic List. Based on a computer tape of *LCSH8* (1975) with some changes based on comparing records against *LCSH9* upon its publication in 1980.

Elrod, J. McRee, Judy Inouye, and Ann Craig Turner. *An Index to the Library of Congress Classification. With Entries for Special Expansions in Medicine, Law, Canadiana, and Nonbook Materials.* Preliminary edition. Ottawa: Canadian Library Association, 1974. Based on schedule indexes, *Additions and Changes* through 1973, and some nonofficial Canadian, British, and American expansions of the LC Classification.

Olson, Nancy B. *Combined Indexes to the Library of Congress Classification Schedules.* Washington: United States Historical Documents Institute, 1974. These fifteen volumes comprise five major subsets based on schedule indexes to the close of 1973, proper names with associated LC class numbers from the *LC Catalog, Books: Subjects* for 1965-1969, and portions of the official LC shelflist as microfilmed on a variety of dates from early 1970 through mid-1974:
    Set I: Author/number index. Alphabetical by literary authors'
        names. 2v.
    Set II: Biographical subject index. Alphabetical by subjects'
        names. 3v.
    Set III: Classified index to persons. All entries from Set II
        arranged in LC class number order. 3v.
    Set IV: Geographical name index. Nouns only, in permuted
        alphabetical order. 1v.
    Set V: Subject keyword index. Includes all entries from Set IV as
        well as topical subjects. 6v.

9. **Texts and general discussions.** Through the years many perceptive discussions of the LC Classification System have appeared. The list of suggested readings at the end of this chapter gives those titles which are most likely to help introduce the scheme to the beginning student.

BASIC FEATURES

Since the LC Classification was developed as a utilitarian scheme for books at the Library of Congress, it is an enumerative, rather than a deductive, system. Among the basic features borrowed from C. A. Cutter are its order of main classes, its use of capital letters for main and subclass notation, its use of Arabic numerals for further subdivision, and its modification of the Cutter author-mark idea to achieve alphabetic subarrangements of various kinds. While most LC call numbers follow a simple, recurring letter-number-letter-number pattern, various other combinations sometimes reflect special situations, or more detailed subdivisions. Twenty large main classes represent the traditional disciplines, plus an additional class for general works.

All the LC schedules have similar, but not identical, sequencing arrangements and physical appearance. Within each sequence of class numbers the order proceeds as a rule from general aspects of the topic or discipline to its particular divisions and subtopics. Chronological sequences may trace historical events, publication dates, or other useful time frames. Geographical arrangements are frequently alphabetical, but just as frequently are given in a "preferred order," starting with the Western Hemisphere and the United States. Class "G—Geography, etc." is distinct from the history classes, although located next to them. This distribution is more effective than the DDC location of "910—Geography and Travel" within class "900—History." Neither scheme quite succeeds in solving the problem of ambiguous relationships between popular works of description and travel, and other, perhaps more scholarly, books on national or regional social life and customs. The user must search both the history and the geography shelves to find all available materials on these topics.

There are other significant differences from the Dewey Decimal theory of organizing some materials. In class "J—Political Science," which is largely devoted to constitutional history of various modern governments, the primary groupings are national or jurisdictional. Each topical aspect (e.g., political parties or electoral systems) is treated as a subdivision of the governmental unit under which it functions. In DDC materials are grouped first by topic (e.g., "324—The political process," *formerly* "329—Practical Politics") and then subdivided by geography or jurisdiction.

Similarly, the Library of Congress provides broad subclasses in class P for the various national literatures, subdividing next by chronology and then by individual author. Seldom, except for anthologies, does it group literary works by form. DDC also starts in its 800 class with a basic separation into national literatures, but it subdivides next by form, e.g., poetry, drama, fiction, etc. Only subordinately does it provide for time divisions or individual authors.

The LC preference for grouping national literatures by time period and author extends to class "B—Philosophy" but not to music or the graphic arts. In subclass "M—Music and Scores" works are classed first by form (e.g., opera, oratorio, symphony, chamber music), then by composer. There is no attempt to keep time periods, national schools, or genres of expression (e.g., classical, romantic, modern) distinct. Subclass "ML—Literature, History and Criticism of Music" does use national, chronological, and similar groupings. In class "N—Fine Arts" materials are grouped first by form (e.g., sculpture, drawing, painting), then by nationality or chronology, and finally by artist.

The major LC use of literary grouping by form formerly was its infamous subclass "PZ — Fiction in English; Juvenile Belles Lettres." Here a concession was made to a "reader interest" orientation which proved to be most controversial, and a stumbling block to the full use of LC Classification by other research libraries with large holdings in literature. Therefore, beginning July 1, 1980, LC discontinued use of PZ1, PZ3, and PZ4. American fiction is now classed in PS, English fiction in PR, and translations of fiction into English with the original national literature. Otherwise, LC's handling of literature has met with general approval. A recurring pattern of organization within each literature affords the shelf or shelflist browser a useful guide:

1. History and criticism, subdivided
    a. Chronologically
    b. Then by form
2. Collections or anthologies, subdivided by form
3. Individual authors, subdivided
    a. Chronologically
    b. Then alphabetically by author
        1) Collective works
        2) Individual works
        3) Biography and criticism

The LC Classification breaks the "Generalia" class familiar to DDC users into two classes at opposite ends of the alphabet. The "A — General Works" schedule employs for its subclasses rare instances of mnemonic notation. General encyclopedias are located in subclass AE, general indexes in AI, general museum publications in AM, and so forth. By contrast, the Z class, containing bibliographies and works on the book industries and on libraries, has no two-letter subclasses at all. While its subject bibliographies are arranged alphabetically by topic in the Z5001-Z8000 span, there is nothing mnemonic about their notation. The only other notable instances of mnemonic class letter associations are for class "G — Geography, etc.," class "M — Music," subclass "ML — Music Literature," and class "T — Technology."

SCHEDULE FORMAT

Most of the LC schedules exhibit certain common features of external and internal format. Many of these format features are missing from certain schedules, a reminder that the scheme was intentionally decentralized in its development. Subject specialists were encouraged to adopt standard modes of organization, but were never forced to maintain a rigid formal pattern.

EXTERNAL FORMAT

The gross physical format, or external appearance, of the schedules has already been described. Both old and new editions, regardless of typography or binding, tend to follow a familiar pattern of organization:

1. **A preface or prefatory note** nearly always follows the title page. As was said, these introductory remarks in recent editions have become briefer and less helpful for classification purposes than they formerly were.

2. **Brief synopses** next appear in over one-third of the schedules, to show the primary subdivisions contained in those volumes. In most cases these broad subclasses are readily identifiable by their brief double-letter notation, but the newly developed class "K — Law" is issued in double-letter subclass volumes with synopses that frequently show mnemonic triple-letter divisions. We can learn at a glance that the law of Ontario is found in subclass KEO, while that of Quebec is in KEQ. A similar mnemonic arrangement applies to the American states in subclass KF, but their notation is more complicated since several states share certain initial letters. Moreover the KF schedule is one of those which carries no synopsis. A typical synopsis is:

SYNOPSIS

H	SOCIAL SCIENCES (GENERAL)
HA	STATISTICS
HB	ECONOMIC THEORY
HC	ECONOMIC HISTORY AND CONDITIONS
HD	ECONOMIC HISTORY AND CONDITIONS
HE	TRANSPORTATION AND COMMUNICATIONS
HF	COMMERCE
HG	FINANCE
HJ	PUBLIC FINANCE

3. **An outline,** consisting not only of alphabetic subclasses, but of significant alphanumeric subspans, is present in nearly every schedule. In schedules without synopses the outlines tend to be briefer and to show broader subdivisions; in schedules with synopses, they are longer and more detailed. Occasionally, as in the schedule for class "J — Political Science," the "synopsis" is really an outline. These two kinds of preliminary overview lend a counterweight to the detail of the schedule indexes. They offer the user supplementary techniques for arriving quickly at any given portion of the schedules. The outline for the first two subclasses of class H appears in the schedule as follows:

OUTLINE

H		SOCIAL SCIENCES (GENERAL)
HA		STATISTICS
	29-31.9	Theory and method of social science statistics
	36-37	Organizations. Bureaus. Service
	38-39	Registration of vital events. Registration (General)
	154-4737	Statistical data
	154-155	Universal statistics
	175-4737	By region or country
HB		ECONOMIC THEORY
	71-74	Economics as a science. Relation to other subjects
	75-130	History of economics. History of economic theory
		Including special economic schools
	131-145	Methodology
	135-145	Mathematical economics. Quantitative methods
		Including econometrics, input-output analysis, game theory
	201-205	Value. Utility
	221-236	Price. Regulation of prices
	238-251	Competition. Production. Wealth
	501	Capital. Capitalism
	522-715	Income. Factor shares
	531-551	Interest. Usury
	601	Profit
	615-715	Entrepreneurship. Risk and uncertainty. Property
	801-843	Consumption. Demand
	846-846.8	Welfare theory
	848-3697	Demography. Vital events
	3711-3840	Business cycles. Economic fluctuations

One cannot assume that the numbers and spans given in a schedule outline will coincide precisely with those in the corresponding portion of the general *Outline* (4th edition). Decentralized classification and intermittent revisions of the different publications result in slightly varying "summaries" of schedule contents in print at the same time. The section of the H and HA subclasses in the fourth edition of the *Outline* reads like a synopsis:

SOCIAL SCIENCES

H	Social sciences (General)
HA	Statistics
	Including collections of general and census statistics of special countries. For mathematical statistics, *see* QA

4. **The schedule proper** enumerates specific class number assignments and sequences in their most explicit form. Page formatting devices, standard in most published schemes, demonstrate hierarchical subordinations and progressions. LC schedules show left-margin indentions, with nested running titles on nearly every page to demonstrate hierarchy. These devices are not so carefully worked out, nor so consistently displayed, as they are in the Dewey Decimal Classification. Size and quality of typeface also indicate levels of subordination in the pre-1970 letter-press LC schedules, as well as in DDC. But current production from typed copy permits the use of only two typographical devices (underlining and full capitals) to identify topics of greater generality or inclusiveness. Many broad headings not listed in the schedule outline, but which offer a useful survey of subtopics, are interpolated just ahead of the specific numbers which they embrace. They often carry no single class number of their own. For this and related reasons the LC scheme does not work well for classifying small general collections, or parts of collections. Nor are these spans very often accompanied by internal summary tables such as DDC uses.

Most schedules do carry internal tables at key junctures, to provide schematic patterns for further localized development of class numbers or sequences. While the LC system is basically enumerative (that is, its topical number assignments are usually not made until there is at least one book to go into the category), these generalized tables open up patterned arrangements which are usually not fully realized on the shelves.

A related space saver is the "Divide like" or "Subarranged like" note, which appears infrequently, but very specifically, in simple one-to-one equivalencies, without the complications encountered in the more abstractly contrived DDC notation. Scope notes and footnotes occasionally refer to auxiliary tables, etc., or they sometimes give useful instructions for number building. The following page from the "T — Technology" schedule shows most of these features:

TD   ENVIRONMENTAL TECHNOLOGY. SANITARY ENGINEERING

→   The promotion and conservation of the public health, comfort and convenience by the control of the environment
Cf. GF, Human ecology
    HC68, HC95-710, Environmental policy (General)
    HD3840-4730, Economic aspects (Government ownership, municipal industries, finance, etc.)
    QH75-77, Landscape protection
    RA565-604, Public health
    S622-627, Soil conservation
    S900-972, Conservation of natural resources
    TC801-978, Reclamation of land
    TH6014-7975, Building environmental engineering

(Schedule continues on page 416.)

	Periodicals and societies, by language of publication
1	English
2	French
3	German
4	Other languages (not A-Z)
5	Congresses
6	Exhibitions. Museums
——→	Subarranged like TA6
7	Collected works (nonserial)
9	Dictionaries and encyclopedias
12	Directories
	History
15	General works
16	Ancient
17	Medieval
18	Modern to 1800
19	Nineteenth century
20	Twentieth century
21-126	Country and city subdivisions. Table I[1]
——→	Including municipal reports of public sanitary works
	Under each country (except as otherwise specified):
	(1) .A1A-Z General works
	.A6-Z States, provinces, etc.
	(2) Local (Cities, etc.), A-Z
	Biography
139	Collective
140	Individual, A-Z
	General works
144	Early to 1850
145	1850-
146	Elementary textbooks
148	Popular works
151	Pocketbooks, tables, etc.
153	General special
155	Addresses, essays, lectures
156	Environmental and sanitary engineering as a profession
157	Study and teaching
.5	Research
158	Municipal engineering organization and management

——→ [1]For Table I, *see* pp. 263-265. Add country number in table to 0

    5. **Auxiliary tables** designed for use with more than one specific class notation or span are located externally to the schedules proper in many volumes. If, as in the "B — Philosophy" and "J — Political Science" schedules, they apply to only one subclass, they follow that subclass. Otherwise, they appear after the full schedule, immediately preceding the index. Sometimes a table number is given in parentheses beside an entry in the schedule, to warn the user that the entry should be further subdivided. More often a footnote cites the table with its page number, and occasionally indicates how the interpolation should be made. Such a footnote can be seen on the subclass TD page reproduced above. A part of the table to which it refers appears here:

T TABLES OF SUBDIVISIONS

TABLE I

HISTORY AND COUNTRY DIVISIONS

	History
15	General works
16	Ancient
17	Medieval
18	Modern
19	19th century
20	20th century

Special countries

Under each country with two numbers:

(1) General works

(2) Local or special, A-Z

The numbers for "Cities or other special," "Local or special," "Provinces or special" may be used in some cases for the local subdivision, in other cases for special canals, rivers, harbors, railroads, or bridges, as specified in the particular scheme to which this table is applied

Under both general and local subdivisions arrange as follows:

.A1-5 Official documents

.A6-Z Nonofficial. By author, A-Z

e.g. TD257.A5, 1966, Gt. Brit. Water Resources Board. Water supplies in South East England

TD264.T5P6, 1967, Port of London Authority. The cleaner Thames.

TD224.C3A53, 1963, California. Dept. of Water Resources. Alameda County investigation

21	America
22	North America
23	United States
.1	Eastern states. Atlantic coast
.15	New England
.2	Appalachian region
.3	Great Lakes region
.4	Midwest. Mississippi Valley
.5	South. Gulf states
.6	West
.7	Northwest
.8	Pacific coast
.9	Southwest
24	States, A-W ⟵
	e.g. .A4 Alaska
	.H3 Hawaii
25	Cities (or other special), A-Z
26	Canada
27	Provinces (or other special), A-Z
.5	Latin America
28-29	Mexico ⟵
30	Central America
31	Special countries, A-Z

This auxiliary Table I from the T schedule is "simple" because it carries only one sequence of numbers which can be interpolated directly into the corresponding number spans in the schedule. Other tables are "compound." That is, they supply more than one number sequence for the same list of subtopics. Number spans from the schedule and the table are matched according to the quantity of materials which the LC classifiers anticipate at any given location. The following excerpt from the "N—Fine Arts" external Tables I to III-A shows how spans of from one hundred to three hundred numbers can be distributed by reference to the same list of terms.

N   TABLES OF SUBDIVISIONS

                                  Tables I to III-A

I (100)		II (200)	III (300)	III-A (300)
01	America	01	01	01
	Latin America	02	02	02
02	North America	03	03	03
03	United States	05	05	05
.5	Colonial period; 18th (and early 19th) century	06	06	06
.7	19th century	07	07	07
04	20th century	08	08	08
05	New England	10	10	10
.5	Middle Atlantic States	.5	.5	.5
06	South	11	11	11
07	Central	14	18	18
08	West	17	23	23
09	Pacific States	19	25	25
10	States, A-W	25	35	35
11	Cities, A-Z	27	38	38
12	Special artists, A-Z	28	39	39
13	Canada	29	41	41
14	Mexico	31	44	44

For instance, the span "N5801-5896—Classical Art in Other [i.e. Non-Greek or Italian] Countries" is to be distributed according to Table I, starting from class number N5800. On the other hand, "NB1501-1684—Sculptured Monuments in Special Countries" uses Table II as a guide for adding country numbers to NB1500. Similarly, "ND2601-2876—Mural Painting in Special Countries" uses Table III to add country numbers to ND2600.

Geographical and chronological subdivisions are often relegated to auxiliary tables. Frequently the two concepts are combined, as in the above excerpt from the N schedule. But other principles of division may also be found in tabular form. A compound table external to subclass "JS—Local Government" contains such categories as "Periodicals," "Executive administration," "Legislative organization," and the like. The heavily-used PN, PR, PS, PZ schedule closes with an extensive set of simple and compound tables designed for use with literary author numbers, running the gamut from long spans for prolific, often translated and discussed authors to brief expansions of cutter designations for recent or little-published authors.

A few auxiliary tables, especially certain geographic lists from the H schedule, are said to "float." That is, they appear, usually in slightly variant forms, in other schedules. Thus the Table of Countries in One Alphabet from the H schedule shows up in mutation as an auxiliary table for schedules C, D, E-F, T, U, and V.

6. **A detailed index** accompanies each schedule except PA Supplement and Parts 1 and 2 each of the PQ and PT subclasses. These indexes vary in coverage and depth, but most of them list specific topics from their schedule. Cross references from synonyms or related terms, alphabetized and indented subordinate topical lists, and suggestions for placing related materials in other schedules are occasionally included. Excerpts from the class "T — Technology" and class "H — Social Sciences" indexes are given on page 408.

7. **Supplementary pages of additions and changes** appear at the back of many schedules published before 1970. These were discussed under "Revised editions of individual schedules" on page 407.

INTERNAL FORMAT

While Herbert Putnam and Charles Martel left the local arrangement of topical and form divisions very much to the discretion of their subject specialists, they nevertheless identified certain basic orientation features for use throughout the system. These organizational concepts were generally known as "Martel's Seven Points" of internal format. They could be incorporated into the schedules at any level of hierarchical subdivision appropriate within the given context. They encompassed:

1. **General form divisions.** The approach here was similar to Dewey's Form Division Table, which has evolved in recent DDC editions into the Table of Standard Subdivisions. It assumes that library materials can often be effectively grouped according to their mode of presentation. Examples are periodicals, society publications, collections, dictionaries or encyclopedias, conference, exhibition, or museum publications, annuals or yearbooks, directories, and documents. Because of their general application they belong near the beginning of any disciplinary or topical section, but the LC system imposes no rigid order upon their location. Their importance in subclass "L — Education (General)" is best observed in the following schedule outline:

L	EDUCATION (GENERAL)	
7-97	Periodicals.	Societies
101	Yearbooks	
106-107	Congresses	
111-791	Documents.	Reports
797-899	Exhibitions.	Museums
900-991	Directories	

By contrast, subclasses "LD-LG — Individual Educational Institutions" show no obvious use of the form division concept. Only in their auxiliary tables do a few of the forms emerge as useful ordering concepts.

2. **Theory. Philosophy.**

3. **History. Biography.**

4. **Treatises. General works.** Works falling under these three of Martel's Seven Points are often intermixed with those arranged according to physical form, and with other locally useful groupings, as the following excerpt shows:

QC	**PHYSICS**
1	Periodicals, societies, congresses, serial collections, yearbooks
3	Collected works (nonserial)
5	Dictionaries and encyclopedias
.3	Communication in physics
.45	Physics literature
.5	Abstracting and indexing
→ 6	Philosophy
	Unified field theories, *see* QC173.7-75
	Relativity physics, *see* QC173.5-65
.8	Nomenclature, terminology, notation, abbreviations
→	History
→ 7	General works
9	By region or country, A-Z
→	Biography
15	Collective
→16	Individual, A-Z
	e.g. Curie, Marie and Pierre, *see* QD22
	.E5 Einstein
	.N7 Newton
.2	Directories
	Early works
17	1501-1700
19	1701-1800

5. **Law. Regulation. State relations.** Until the publication in 1969 of the first "K — Law" subclass, this ordering principle was handy for grouping legal materials with their related topics, especially in the social sciences. The belated, still unfinished development of class K inverts the relationship. Whenever possible we now classify such works first as legal materials, and only subordinately as being discipline-oriented. For example, books dealing with government regulations for control of drugs as economic commodities were originally classed in HD9665.7-9. Those dealing with regulations for the manufacture, sale, and use of drugs were classed in RA402. Subclass "KF — Law of the United States" now places drug laws in KF3885-3894. In years to come, most works dealing with U.S. drug legislation and regulation will be placed there.

6. **Study and teaching. Research. Textbooks.** Unlike DDC, the LC scheme sometimes allows a unique place for textbooks, as well as for more theoretical works on how to study, teach, or research a topic. Thus under "QL — Zoology" there appears the following sequence:

QL   ZOOLOGY

          General works and treatises
41   Early through 1759
45   1760-1969
  .2   1970-
46   Pictorial works and atlases
  .5   Zoological illustrating
⟶   Textbooks
          Advanced
47   Through 1969
  .2   1970-
          Elementary
48   Through 1969
  .2   1970-
49   Juvenile works
          Cf. SF75.5, Domestic animals
50   Popular works
          For stories and anecdotes, *see* QL791-795
  .5   Zoology as a profession
⟶ 51   Study and teaching. Research
  .5   Problems, exercises, examinations
52   Outlines, syllabi
53   Laboratory manuals
          Cf. QL812, Anatomy
             QP44, Physiology
55   Laboratory animals
⟶   General works only. Prefer systematic divisions for particu-
          lar groups of animals.
          Cf. SF405.5-407, Breeding and care.
57   Audiovisual aids
58   Other special

In other disciplines LC Classification explicitly groups textbooks with general works and treatises. Under one subtopic we find:

QH   ECOLOGY

540   Periodicals, societies, congresses, serial collections, yearbooks
  .3   Collected works (nonserial)
  .4   Dictionaries and encyclopedias
⟶ 541   General works, treatises, and textbooks
  .13 Popular works
  .14 Juvenile works
  .145 Addresses, essays, lectures
⟶ .15 Special aspects of the subject as a whole, A-Z
      .M3 Mathematical models
      .R4 Remote sensing
⟶ .2   Study and teaching. Research
  .3   Biological productivity
  .5   By type of environment, A-Z

7. **Subjects and subdivisions of subjects.** Most modern classification systems are disciplinary rather than topical. That is, they normally proceed from broad general divisions of knowledge to narrower subdivisions, with more or less comprehensive coverage provided for each special topic in relation to the hierarchy. Any linear arrangement of books or other materials on shelves must resort to a series of cyclic progressions if it displays subject-related groupings based on logical considerations or practical associations. Just as Martel's fifth point reminds classifiers that "general works" should be shelved together, usually near the beginning of each new topical group, so this seventh point provides for further subject breakdown based on "literary warrant" or the amount of material requiring classification in such a group. One intermediate type which the LC system frequently places just after "general works" is a potpourri called "general special" or "special aspects." These works treat the topic from particular points of view. Sometimes, as in TD153 (*see* page 416) and QH541.15 (above), such books have a single class number. At other places they must be spread out over several pages of the schedules.

NOTATION

The typical LC class notation contains a mixed notation of one to three letters, followed by one to four integers, and possibly a short decimal. Decimal numbers were not used much until it became necessary to expand certain sections where no further integers were available. Decimals do not usually indicate subordination, but allow a new topic or aspect to be inserted into an established context. In the above excerpt from the "QH540-549 — Ecology" schedule the decimals belie the left-margin indentions of their associated topics. Clearly, "QH541.145 — Addresses, Essays, Lectures" is hierarchically equivalent to "QH541 — General Works, Treatises, and Textbooks."

Another method of expanding LC class notations is by means of mnemonic letter-number combinations, which look like Cutter's "Author numbers," but are derived from a different matrix (*see* chapter 19, "Creation of Complete Call Numbers"). These "cutter numbers" may represent geographic, personal, corporate, or topical names. They are subordinated to schedule notations where an instruction to subdivide "A-Z" appears. Since they are part of the class notation, most of the actual LC assignments, or at least a significant number of examples, are usually included within the schedule (*see* "QH541.15 — Special Aspects of Ecology as a Whole, A-Z" and "QC16 — Individual Biography of Physicists, A-Z" above). Geographic cutter numbers are generally omitted, however, unless they happen to be available in an auxiliary table to one or another of the schedules. In the excerpt from class T, Table I (page 417), the table number 24 is associated with American states "A-W," together with a rare inclusion of two examples. The class T user will find that auxiliary Table III is a complete list of state cutter numbers which corroborates the examples in Table I.

Alphabetic geographic sequences normally appear at subordinate places in the schedules, where they subdivide a single integer or decimal number. For broader disciplines or subjects, where the geographic arrangement covers an extensive number span, the organization follows a "preferred pattern" as was noted in the section on external format (page 418). The excerpt from class N,

Tables I to III-A, shows how such sequences begin with "home base" (i.e., the Western Hemisphere and the United States), following a pattern which covers the earth pretty much according to our American perceptions of the nearness and importance of our neighbors.

Library of Congress interpretation of "cutter numbers" is always decimal. In a typical letter(s)-number(s)/letter-number(s) combination, the primary letter(s)-number(s) group should be arranged first alphabetically, then by integer(s) until a fifth digit is introduced following a decimal point. All schedules make the basic ordering by integer quite evident, as when PR509 follows PR51, but precedes PR5018. The secondary letter-number(s) combination, by contrast, should be filed decimally. The Library of Congress carefully inserts a decimal point in front of it, even if, as at "QH541.15.M3 — Mathematical Models in Ecology," a decimal is already part of the primary notation. Some libraries using the LC system drop the cutter decimal from their notation, on the premise that users will remember to follow the convention. The practice may possibly cause confusion in long cutter number runs where it is not clearly understood that a class notation like PR4972.M33 should follow PR4972.M3 but precede PR4972.M5.

Occasionally a class notation, or series of notations, appears in the schedules in parentheses. These were formerly termed "shelflist numbers," but today more often are called "alternative class numbers." Some of them represent locations once actively used, but now retired by the Library of Congress. Class notation G1020, for instance, was assigned to school atlases in schedule G, third edition (1954). By 1966 the *Additions and Changes* showed it as G(1020) with an instruction to see G1019 for school atlases. In the 1976 fourth edition of class G, there is no G1020 at all.

Other class notations appear to have been reserved in parentheses for possible future use, and have since been activated. The span "PA2023 — 2027 — Congresses and Collections of Papers Dealing with Latin Philology and Language" was so reserved in the original 1928 edition of the P-PA schedule, but all parentheses were removed by 1962. Alternative class notations are nearly always accompanied by "prefer notes." Thus subclass SF (Animal culture) has an entry "SF(112) Weight tables, see HF5716.C2, etc." Libraries using the LC system are welcome to adopt these alternative class notations if their own classification needs are better realized by so doing.

Following are a few examples of number building using LC classification.

EXAMPLE 1

DC203.4	Ashton, John, b. 1834.
	English caricature and satire on Napoleon I . . . 1968.
	67-24349

D	History and Topography (except America)
DC	France
139-249	Revolutionary and Napoleonic period, 1789-1815
203-212	Biography of Napoleon
203	General works
.4	Caricature and satire

EXAMPLE 2

JX1977.8   Asamoah, Obed Y.
.G4   The legal significance of the declarations of the
                general assembly of the United Nations . . . 1966.
                                                                    67-81320

J   Political science
JX   International law
1901-1991   Procedure in international disputes. International
                    arbitration. Peace literature, etc.
1977   United Nations, 1946-
   .8   Special topics, A-Z
.G4   General Assembly

EXAMPLE 3

RA407.3   American Hospital Association
                    Comparative statistics on health facilities and popula-
                tion : metropolitan and nonmetropolitan areas. 1978 ed.
                . . . c1978.   78-7259

R   Medicine
RA   Public aspects of medicine
407-409   Medical statistics
407   General
.3-.5   By country
   .3   United States

CONCLUSION

Most libraries using the LC classification system will continue to appropriate officially assigned call numbers for any of their own materials which the
Library of Congress has already classified. However, it is a rare library which
holds only titles, editions, and issues available in the Library of Congress collection. Librarians and library users should be able to break down an LC call
number into its components. Classifiers should be able to create reasonably
consistent supplementary notations with which to fit their unique holdings into
the system. Users may stumble over special practices at local points, but the
general principles of arrangement are nearly always decipherable, especially if
a shelflist of LC call numbers is available to compare with the schedules.
Highly specific shelflisting (i.e., the rationale underlying many cutter
numbers, as explained in chapter 19) is, on the other hand, not always so easy
to explain. The perfectionist classifier, geared to the invariabilities of DDC,
must remember that the LC system is loosely coordinated and essentially
pragmatic. It aims first to class closely, then to identify uniquely, particular
works, or issues of works, using the most economical notation available within
its broad parameters of theory and practice.

NOTES

[1]A table comparing the main classes of the Cutter and the LC schemes is given on page 438.

[2]BL-BX, 2nd ed., is being superseded by three new schedules. BL-BQ, 3rd ed., was published in 1984. It will be followed by "BX" and "BR-BV."

[3]*Cataloging Service Bulletin*, no. 2 (Fall 1978): 45.

[4]*Library of Congress Classification Schedules: A Cumulation of Additions and Changes through* ... (Detroit, Gale Research Company). (These cumulations are completed periodically for each schedule. The exact dates of coverage vary, but they typically are published two years after the end of the cumulative time covered. For example, a cumulation of additions and changes for schedule "D" through 1983 was published in 1985.)

[5]Library of Congress, *Cataloging Service*, bulletin 1 (June 1945)-125 (Spring 1978); *Cataloging Service Bulletin*, no. 1 (Summer 1978)-date.

[6]Library of Congress, Subject Cataloging Division, *Library of Congress Subject Headings*, 9th ed. (Washington, D.C., The Library, 1980), 2 vol. and suppls. For a detailed discussion of this work, *see* chapter 22.

SUGGESTED READING

Chan, Lois M. *Immroth's Guide to the Library of Congress Classification*, 3rd ed. Littleton, Colo., Libraries Unlimited, 1980.

Foskett, A. C. *The Subject Approach to Information*. London, Bingley, 1982. Chapter 21.

Immroth, John Phillip. "Library of Congress Classification," in *Encyclopedia of Library and Information Science*, vol. 15, pp. 93-200. New York, Marcel Dekker, 1975.

Matthis, Raimund E., and Desmond Taylor. *Adopting the Library of Congress Classification System: A Manual of Methods and Techniques for Application or Conversion*. New York, R. R. Bowker, 1971.

Swanson, Gerald L. *Dewey to LC Conversion Tables*. New York, CCM Information Corporation, 1972.

19
Creation of
Complete Call Numbers

INTRODUCTION

Library call numbers serve a double function. The class notation portion groups related materials together. The second portion of the complete call number uniquely identifies different works in the same class. Traditionally, this second part of the call number is based on the main entry, which has been chosen for the work through descriptive cataloging. Various terms such as "author number," "book number," and "cutter number" have been applied, but "author number" does not allow for those works with title main entries, while "book number" implies that it cannot be applied to nonbook materials. "Cutter number" is also misleading because the LC method of deriving it differs from the original tables devised by C. A. Cutter. However, the name "cutter number" has come into general use in practice regardless of the classification scheme used. Its general usage is a tribute to C. A. Cutter who conceived the idea of using alphanumeric symbols to keep items in alphabetical order within a particular classification notation. In this text "cutter number" is used for any notation serving this function.

CUTTER NUMBERS DEVISED BY
C. A. CUTTER

Providing a classification notation with a supplementary cutter number enables the cataloger to design a fully unique call number for each title in a collection. The cutter numbers most often used with DDC class notations are taken from a set of tables devised by Charles Ammi Cutter. These tables equate surnames and other words with alphanumeric sequences. Cutter initially produced a table in a single alphabet of all consonants except "S," followed by an alphabet of vowels and the letter "S."[1] This "two-figure" table (most of its combinations consist of a capital letter plus two digits) was later expanded by Kate E. Sanborn to provide more differentiation among names for use with larger collections.[2] However, since she did not adhere to Cutter's schema, Cutter then developed his own expansion to permit growing libraries to assign more specific book numbers without disrupting the sequences they had already established from his two-figure table.[3] There are thus three different "cutter" tables. The Cutter-Sanborn version is perhaps the most widely used today, being preferred by many larger libraries because of its simpler design and notation.

While Cutter numbers are most commonly used to arrange material by main entries (usually authors' surnames, but occasionally forenames, corporate names, or titles), they are also used in some instances to alphabetize material by subject, as in the case of biography. To illustrate the use of each table, let us suppose that we wish to assign a book number for the English poet John Donne. The three tables carry the following sequences:

Cutter Two-figure Table

Doll	69	Foh
Dom	71	Folg
Doo	72	Foll

Cutter Three-figure Table

Donk	718	Folk
Donnet	719	Folke
Doo	72	Foll

Cutter-Sanborn Table

Donk	684	Fonti
Donn	685	Fontr
Donner	686	Foo

According to the Cutter two-figure table, the number for Donne is D71. By the Cutter three-figure table it is D718 (an expansion of the D71 assignment). But by the Cutter-Sanborn table it is D685. The above examples also demonstrate the typical three-column display used in the original form of the tables. In 1969 Paul K. Swanson of the Forbes Library, Northampton, Massachusetts, and Mrs. Esther M. Swift, editor of the H. R. Huntting Company, revised this arrangement into single continuous alphabets of two columns, with letters on the left corresponding to numbers on the right. The new arrangement appears to be easier to use.

The work letter (or workmark) is the first letter of the title of the work, exclusive of articles. It follows the cutter number on the second line of the call number. Thus, the complete Dewey Decimal call number of Henry James's novel *Wings of the Dove* is 813.4 J27w. Work letters do not inevitably ensure that a book will be placed in alphabetical sequence within the author grouping; this depends upon the sequence of acquisition of the books. One additional letter from the title may be added if necessary. Thus, a copy of James's *Washington Square* might be classified 813.4 J27wa. If the third acquisition is a volume entitled *The Works of Henry James*, it can be classified 813.4 J27wo.

With an author such as Erle Stanley Gardner, who began the title of all of his Perry Mason mysteries with *The Case of the* . . . , such a scheme is not feasible. Depending on the library's policy, the cataloger can choose one of several alternatives. For example, the cataloger can ignore completely the common phrase "the case of the" and proceed directly to the distinctive part of the title, or use two work letters: "c" for "case," plus an additional letter for the distinctive title (e.g., *The Case of the Mischievous Doll* might be assigned the work letters "cm").

Biographies and criticism of a specific author pose a particular problem of library policy. Two procedures are common. In the Dewey schedule, 928 is the biography number for literary figures (920 for Biography; 8 for Literature). Thus, biographies of authors might be classified in 928, with subdivision for nationality. Another way of classifying biography is to use the standard biography subdivision, 092. A third possibility is to classify biographies of authors with their work, in order to keep everything by and about a literary figure in one place. In such cases, a common method of distinguishing works "by" from works "about" an author is to insert an arbitrary letter – usually one toward the end of the alphabet – after the cutter number and to follow it with the initial of the author of the biography. This device puts all books about an author directly behind all books by that author. Thus, if the letter "z" is chosen as the biographical letter, a biography or criticism of Henry James by Leon Edel would be cuttered J27zE; and it would follow, in shelflist order, J27w. If James had written a novel beginning with the letter "z" only the work letter "z" would be used for the novel; thus, the novel would still come before all criticism and biography.

The problem of a variety of editions occurs most frequently in literature, but classic works in all other fields are also reprinted by the same or another publisher, especially now that paperbacks have revived many worthwhile books that have been long out of print.

One cataloging practice is to assign the date of publication as part of the call number to all editions of a single work issued by the same publisher, and to assign a number following the work letter to all editions of the same work published by different publishers. Thus, the first acquired copy of *Wings of the Dove* would be classified 813.4 J27w. If the library acquired a second copy of the novel, issued by a different publisher, the number would be 813.4 J27w2. Assume that the second publisher was Modern Library, and that the library received another edition of the novel, also published by Modern Library in 1955. The call number might then be 813.4 J27w2 1955. A completely different edition published by a third publisher would be classified 813.4 J27w3.

CUTTER NUMBERS DEVISED
BY LC

Library of Congress call numbers also consist, in general, of two principal elements: class notation and cutter number, to which are added, as required, symbols designating a particular work. While it is possible to use Cutter-Sanborn numbers with LC classification, most libraries prefer to use Library of Congress cutter numbers constructed from a table composed by LC for this purpose.

Library of Congress cutter numbers are composed of the initial letter of the main entry heading, followed by Arabic numerals representing the succeeding letters on the following basis:

```
1) After initial vowels
      for the second letter: b   d   l,m   n   p   r   s,t   u-y
                use number: 2   3    4    5   6   7    8     9

2) After the initial letter S
      for the second letter:  a   ch   e   h,i   m-p   t    u
                use number:   2    3   4    5     6    7-8   9

3) After the initial letters Qu
      for the third letter:   a   e   i   o   r   y
                use number:   3   4   5   6   7   9
      for names beginning Qa-Qt
                use: 2-29

4) After other initial consonants
      for the second letter:  a   e   i   o   r   u   y
                use number:   3   4   5   6   7   8   9

5) When an additional number is preferred
      for the third letter:  a-d   e-h   i-l   m   n-q   r-t   u-w   x-z
                use number:   2*    3     4    5    6     7     8     9
                (*optional for third letter a or b)
```

Letters not included in these tables are assigned the next higher or lower number as required by previous assignments in the particular class.

The arrangements in the following examples illustrate some possible applications of these tables:

```
1) Names beginning with vowels

     Abernathy  .A2      Ames       .A45     Astor     .A84
     Adams      .A3      Appleby    .A6      Atwater   .A87
     Aldrich    .A4      Archer     .A7      Austin    .A9

2) Names beginning with the letter S

     Saint      .S2      Simmons    .S5      Steel     .S7
     Schaefer   .S3      Smith      .S6      Storch    .S75
     Seaton     .S4      Southerland .S64    Sturges   .S8
     Shank      .S45     Springer   .S66     Sullivan  .S9
```

3) Names beginning with the letters Qu

Qadriri	.Q2	Quick	.Q5	Qureshi	.Q7
Quabbe	.Q3	Quoist	.Q6	Quynn	.Q9
Queener	.Q4				

4) Names beginning with other consonants

Carter	.C3(7)	Cinelli	.C5(6)	Cullen	.C8(4)
Cecil	.C4(2)	Corbett	.C6(7)	Cyprus	.C9(6)
Childs	.C45	Croft	.C7(6)		

( ) = if using two numbers

5) When there are no existing conflicting entries in the shelflist, the use of a third letter book number may be preferred:

Cabot	.C3	Callahan	.C34	Carter	.C37
Cadmus	.C32	Campbell	.C35	Cavelli	.C38
Caffrey	.C33	Cannon	.C36	Cazalas	.C39

The numbers are treated as decimals, thus allowing for infinite interpolation of the decimal principle.

Since the tables provide only a general framework for the assignment of numbers, the symbol for a particular name or work is constant only within a single class. Each entry must be added to the existing entries in the shelflist in such a way as to preserve alphabetic order in accordance with Library of Congress filing rules.[4]

Some points need further comment. Note first of all that the numeral "1" appears nowhere in the table. The Library of Congress avoids its use, and the use of zeros, as decimals to preserve alphabetic order. If, for instance, the name "Abbott" were given the cutter ".A1," a subsequent cutter at the same location for "Aamodt" would have to be, say, ".A09," while "Aagard" would go to ".A085" or something like it. While most type-fonts and computer print-chains distinguish between the digit zero and the capital letter "O," typewriters as a rule do not. In actual practice, LC shelflisters would more likely give "Abbott" a cutter such as ".A15" so later assignments for names such as "Aagard" and "Aamodt" could have ".A12" and ".A128," or similar decimals to insure space for unlimited further alphabetical expansion if needed.

All this brings out another trait of LC shelflisting. There is nothing sacrosanct about the above table. It has been officially changed as shelflisting problems were encountered and new needs were perceived. The present LC shelflist contains a jumble of old and new assignments. Recently devised numbers may reflect accommodation to outmoded practices, to avoid extensive re-shelflisting, rather than following current practice as outlined in the table. Cutter numbers assigned for the same person may also vary significantly from one class notation to another. The examples below illustrate such a variation:

TL561   Splaver, Sarah, 1921-
.S65   Some day I'll be an aerospace engineer . . . 1967.
                                                                 67-23997

. . . .

Z682   Splaver, Sarah, 1921-
.S735   Some day I'll be a librarian . . . 1967.
                                                                 67-23998

Since cutter numbers are used by the Library of Congress to extend some class notations, as well as for shelflisting alphabetically by main entry, many works have at least two cutter segments in their call numbers. One example is Niles M. Hansen's *French Regional Planning* (LC card number 68-14603) for which the LC call number HT395.F7H35 can be analyzed as follows:

H   Social sciences
HT   Communities. Classes. Races
395   Regional planning: countries or regions other than the
              United States, A-Z
.F7   France
H35   The cutter number for Hansen

While double cutters are commonplace, triple "cutters" are exceedingly rare. They have been used in class G for certain kinds of subject maps, but with a special disclaimer added. An example is the *Urban Atlas, Tract Data for Standard Metropolitan Statistical Areas: Hartford, Connecticut* from the U.S. Bureau of the Census (LC card number 75-603461). Its call number G1242.H3E25U5 1974 signifies:

G   Geography. Maps. Anthropology. Recreation
1242   Connecticut sub-area atlas
.H3   Hartford metropolitan area
E25   Statistical areas. Census tracts [see Table IV - Subject sub-
                divisions: "These numbers are not Cutter numbers and have
                no alphabetical significance."]
U5   Cutter number for United States. Bureau of the Census,
                the authority responsible for the atlas
1974   Date of atlas publication

In the few instances where double cutters are prescribed in the schedules to stand for two separate subdivisions of the subject, the second cutter is made to accommodate both the subject for which it stands and the alphabetical arrangement for which it stands. For example:

HD3561   Hydén, Göran, 1938-
.A6E227   Efficiency versus distribution in East African
                    cooperatives ... 1973.

                                                        73-980184

In the classification schedules under HD3441-3570.9, the notation run
assigned to industrial cooperation by country, the notation for the country is
first cuttered by ".A6" for general cooperative societies and then is subdivided
further "by state, province, etc." Thus, "E227" stands both for East Africa and
for the alphabetical arrangement of "Hydén" among other works on the
subject.

   Reserved cutter numbers. The LC schedules and tables frequently set
aside the first few ".A" or the last several ".Z" possibilities in a cutter sequence
for special purposes. Observe the example at "TD21-126 – Country and City
Subdivisions of Environmental Technology and Sanitary Engineering" on
page 416. Assume that class T, Table I and the internal table in the schedule
have been applied to derive the class number TD28.A1 for a general work on
sanitary engineering in Mexico. Let us suppose that the first book classified
here was written by a Ricardo Gomez. Using the LC cutter number table,
we would probably complete the full call number as TD28.A1G6, or
TD28.A1G65. A second work on the same topic by a Werner Goode might
then receive the call number TD28.A1G66, while still a third treatise by a
Ralph Goddard could be given something like TD28.A1G58.
   Assume now that we have a book on sanitary engineering in the Mexican
state of Aguascalientes. It cannot receive the usual cutter ".A3" or ".A33"
because the internal table at TD21-126 has "reserved" .A1 through .A5 for
general works and other possible future needs. Therefore we must accommodate the reservation by assigning the class number TD28.A68 or TD28.A7,
followed by an appropriate cutter number for main entry. Now suppose that
still another book covers sanitary engineering in the city of Aguascalientes.
Our class number will probably be TD29.A33, plus a second cutter for the
main entry.
   ".A" cutters are likely to be reserved for serials, society publications,
documents, etc., where these general forms of material have not been given
integer or decimal class numbers. Such special reservations are often called
"official" cutters. The following schedule excerpt, with two LC call number
assignments, illustrates this practice:

HA	STATISTICS
175-4010	By country
195-730	United States
730	Cities, A-Z

Under each:
.A1-5 Official
.A6-Z Nonofficial

. . . .

HA730	Houston, Tex. Division of Vital Statistics.
.H67A3	Facts about Houston : population, births, deaths, maternal and infant deaths . . . 1958. 77-350875

HA730	Houston, Tex. Chamber of Commerce. Census Tract
.H67H6	Division.
	1970 Census data for the Houston area . . . 1971
	78-31293

In both of the above call numbers ".H67," identifying the city of Houston, is a geographical extension of the class number. Publications of the city government's Division of Vital Statistics are considered to be "official publications." Therefore "A3" is added in accordance with schedule instructions and the LC shelflist entries, to serve as the cutter number for the main entry. Houston Chamber of Commerce publications, not being considered "official," have their cutters based on the traditional first word of the main entry.

".7" cutter reservations are most common in class P, where researchers like to have biography and criticism of an author shelved immediately following that author's works. In this class, separate integers frequently designate all authors of a given period whose surnames start with the same initial. The first cutter number is then based on the second letter of the surname (i.e., the letter beginning the cutter is the second letter of the author's name, followed by a number representing the third, or third and fourth, letter[s]). A second cutter, based usually on an auxiliary table of reserved numbers, identifies collected works, selections, titles of separate works, adaptations, translations, or biography and criticism. *The Selected Letters of Robinson Jeffers, 1897-1962* (LC card number 67-29318) carries the LC call number PS3519.E27Z53, exemplifying application of auxiliary Table IXa (or Table XL in the revised edition of Tables published in 1982).[5]

Workmarks, in the traditional sense of lowercase letters added to book numbers to alphabetize titles or writers of biographies, are not used by the Library of Congress. Lowercase letters do serve a few special purposes in LC call numbers. In subclass "PZ—Fiction in English. Juvenile Literature" a unique combination of upper- and lower-case letters (instead of second cutter numbers) alphabetizes the titles of a given author, while Arabic numerals (instead of dates) designate reissues or new editions. Thus Colin Spencer's *The Tyranny of Love* published in New York by Weybright and Talley (LC card number 68-28267) has the LC call number PZ4.S7446Ty3. Lowercase letters are also used following dates (see below).

Additions to LC call numbers. The adding of dates to LC call numbers has increased with multiple publication in more than one country, in different imprints, in paperback as well as hard cover, in later editions, and in reprints. The Library of Congress began in 1982 to add dates to all monographic call numbers.[6] One use of lowercase letters is to identify bibliographically distinct issues of the same title published in the same year. For example, when Brian Jackson's *Working Class Community: Some General Notions Raised by a Series of Studies in Northern England* was simultaneously published in London and New York by Routledge & Kegan Paul, and by Humanities Press (LC card number 68-101992) it was given the LC call number "HN398.Y6J3 — Social History and Conditions in Yorkshire" plus cutter number. Later that year (1968), a second New York issue by F. A. Praeger (LC card number 68-25543) received the same call number with an added element "1968b." [Note: LC card numbers do not necessarily show the precise order in which successive issues of the same title are to be shelflisted. Card numbers may be assigned in advance of publication, or other shelflisting conditions may dominate.] Another use of lowercase letters following dates is to distinguish among works on the same subject and published in the same year that have the same corporate body as main entry.[7]

A few other exceptional notations show up in some schedules. For example, dates are used not only as final elements, to distinguish issues of the same title. They occasionally become secondary elements of class numbers, taking precedence over cutter numbers. Class numbers "BX830-831 — Medieval and Modern Councils Within Roman Catholicism" use this device to arrange church councils by date of opening. An example is Xavier Rynne's *Vatican Council II* (LC card number 67-21527), which carries the LC call number BX830 1962 .R94. Also, in schedule "BL-BX — Religion" some Bible texts are so specifically classed that LC shelflisters add merely dates (no cutter numbers) to keep them in order. For example:

BS391.2   Bible. English. Revised Standard. Selections. 1975.
1975   Christianica : the basic teachings of the Christian faith ar-
           ranged for prayer and meditation . . . 1975.
                                    74-13005

BS	Bible
370-399	Selections. Quotations
390-391	English
391	General
.2	1951-
1975	The publication date of this anthology

CONCLUSION

Call numbers are of particular concern in libraries with open stacks where browsing allows patrons to find materials on similar subjects in proximity, to find works of one author on a subject together, and to find editions of a work together. Where there are closed stacks, an accession number can serve as well as a call number.

While use of cutter numbers is the most common method of creating complete call numbers, other means may sometimes be found more useful. In a science and technology collection, for example, where recency of material may be of utmost importance, subarrangement under each class notation may be by year of imprint. In very small general collections, on the other hand, one or more letters of the first word of the main entry may be added after the class notation, with no additional numbers given. This method, however, will usually not result in unique call numbers, which may be needed for circulation control.

NOTES

[1] Charles Ammi Cutter, *Two-Figure Author Table*, Swanson-Swift revision, 1969. Distributed by Libraries Unlimited, Inc., Littleton, Colo. (formerly distributed by H. R. Huntting Co.).

[2] *Cutter-Sanborn Three-Figure Author Table*, Swanson-Swift revision, 1969. Distributed by Libraries Unlimited, Inc., Littleton, Colo. (formerly distributed by H. R. Huntting Co.).

[3] Charles Ammi Cutter, *Three-Figure Author Table*, Swanson-Swift revision, 1969. Distributed by Libraries Unlimited, Inc., Littleton, Colo. (formerly distributed by H. R. Huntting Co.).

[4] *Cataloging Service Bulletin*, no. 3 (Winter 1979): 19-20.

[5] Library of Congress, *Classification — Class P-PZ: Language and Literature Tables* (Washington, D.C., The Library, 1982).

[6] *Cataloging Service Bulletin*, no. 19 (Winter 1982): 25-26.

[7] Library of Congress, *Cataloging Service*, bulletin 110 (Summer 1974): 6-8.

SUGGESTED READING

Comaromi, John P. *Book Numbers: A Historical Study and Practical Guide to Their Use.* Littleton, Colo., Libraries Unlimited, 1981.

Lehnus, Donald J. *Book Numbers: History, Principles, and Application.* Chicago, American Library Association, 1980.

20
Other
Classification Systems

INTRODUCTION

This chapter provides a brief overview of some of the more significant modern classifications besides DDC and LC. Those discussed are Cutter's Expansive Classification, Brown's Subject Classification, Bliss' Bibliographic Classification, and some special classifications. UDC was discussed at the end of the chapter on "Decimal Classification" (chapter 17), and Ranganathan's Colon Classification was used as an example in the discussion of faceted classification in chapter 16. While the classifications discussed here by no means exhaust modern classification research and practice, they do illustrate many of the problems and solutions, or failures, of both the seminal and the well-entrenched systems discussed in the contemporary literature.[1]

CUTTER'S EXPANSIVE CLASSIFICATION

The Expansive Classification, like the Dewey Decimal Classification, is the brainchild of an eminent library pioneer. Charles Ammi Cutter (1837-1903) was fifteen years older than Melvil Dewey (1851-1931) but took fifteen years longer to publish his scheme. Both men devised their systems as practical efforts to organize collections which they knew and served. Just as DDC came out of Dewey's student employment in the Amherst College Library, so Cutter's cataloging efforts in the Harvard College Library, and for much longer at the Boston Athenaeum, flowered into his Expansive Classification.

While the lives and achievements of the two men show many parallels, there are also significant differences. In classification, Dewey chose his pure decimal notation early on, making it such a key feature of his approach that it more or less governed all subsequent growth patterns. He saw that a simple basic design, easy-to-master mnemonic devices, and a certain sturdy inflexibility could provide a general system that would be applicable to the many libraries which were being established. With characteristic energy, he started a schedule of periodic revision to keep his system responsive to the rapidly changing cultural and publishing milieu. And he marketed his invention with zest and conviction. Cutter was of a more delicate physique and temperament, less exuberant, more institution-oriented. But he too, imbued with the gregarious optimism of his era, worked diligently to establish librarianship as a helping profession, with "scientific" organization as one of its basic assumptions.

Cutter's scheme stressed a sequence of "classifications," or expansions, from a very simple set of categories for a small library to an intricate network of interrelated, highly specific subdivisions for the library of over a million volumes.[2] He did not live to finish his ultimate seventh expansion, or to embark on a successive-edition program, but he did have the satisfaction of seeing the Library of Congress prefer many features of his scheme to that of his friendly rival. His willingness to take suggestions, and to compromise, worked to his credit and to the continuing influence of his system in spite of its limited adoption.

Cutter found the ten broad classes of DDC too narrow a base for large collections. He therefore turned to the alphabet, with its easily ordered sequence of up to twenty-six primary groupings. For collections which "could be put into a single room" his first "classification" used only seven letters, with an eighth double-letter subclass, as follows:

A Works of reference and general works which include several of the following sections, and so could not go to any one

B Philosophy and Religion

E Biography

F History and Geography and Travels

H Social sciences

L Natural sciences and Arts

Y Language and Literature

YF Fiction

If a small library should grow to require closer, more specific classes, Cutter's second classification, or expansion, introduced a mixed alphanumeric notation. It also subdivided the "F — History" and the new "G — Geography" classes by adding two Arabic numerals to the letter to signify identical geographic areas for each class. For example, F30 means History of Europe, while G30 means Geography of Europe. The second expansion holds fourteen main classes, some redefinition of the original seven, and further differentiation of two classes along geographic lines.

The third expansion completes all but "P — Vertebrates" of the base twenty-six divisions, and separates Religion from Philosophy, moving it to a second double-letter subclass. Part of the debt which LC Classification owes to Cutter can easily be traced through the following outline comparison:

Cutter's Expansive		Library of Congress	
A	General works	A	General works
B	Philosophy	B	Philosophy – Religion
BR	Non-Judaeo-Christian religions		
C	Judaism and Christianity	C	History – Auxiliary sciences
D	Ecclesiastical history	D	History (except America)
E	Biography	E-F	History of the Americas
F	History		
G	Geography	G	Geography – Anthropology
H	Social sciences	H	Social sciences
I	Sociology		
J	Political science	J	Political science
K	Law	K	Law
L	Natural sciences	L	Education
M	Natural history	M	Music
N	Botany	N	Fine arts
O	Zoology		
		P	Language and literature
Q	Medicine	Q	Science
R	Technology	R	Medicine
S	Engineering	S	Agriculture
T	Manufactures and Handicrafts	T	Technology
U	Defensive and preservative arts	U	Military science
V	Athletic and recreative arts	V	Naval science
W	Fine arts		
X	Languages		
Y	Literature		
YF	Fiction		
Z	Book arts	Z	Bibliography and Library science

The fourth expansion subdivides twelve main classes for the first time, increasing the double-letter subclasses to fifty. It also carries an extensive supplementary table expanding the double-digit geographic numbers from the F and G classes into a "place" or "local" list.

The fifth expansion introduces the twenty-sixth single-letter class "P – Vertebrates," and subdivides all remaining undivided classes, using many triple- and a few quadruple-letter sections.

The sixth "classification" introduces no new techniques – only new expansions of existing classes and subclasses.

The seventh classification was published in eighteen parts, edited and to some extent developed by William Parker Cutter after the originator's death.[3] All expansions were prepared on the theory that as a library outgrew its simpler modes of organization, partial dislocation and reclassification of the existing collection was preferable to complete reorganization. Although some books would have to be reclassed and relocated, not all would be, and certainly not all at once.

While it was never widely adopted, some sixty-seven American, Canadian, and British libraries have been identified as past or present Cutter System users.[4] Perhaps even more important is the influence it exerted on later, more popular classifications, such as that developed soon after at the Library of Congress.

BROWN'S SUBJECT CLASSIFICATION

Next in chronological development is a British scheme. James Duff Brown (1864-1914) was a Scottish counterpart of Dewey and Cutter, if somewhat younger. Coming to the profession from an early apprenticeship to publishers and booksellers, he became deeply involved in the public library movement in Great Britain. It is debatable whether his advocacy of open stacks was directly influenced by his travels in the United States, in 1893. Without benefit of a university education, his breadth of knowledge was legendary, and his interest in music resulted in several music reference tools which he either compiled or sponsored.

Brown recognized the lack of good organization of materials in most British libraries. To make open stack access feasible he and John Henry Quinn published in 1894 a "Classification of Books for Libraries in Which Readers Are Allowed Access to Shelves." Brown's own "Adjustable Classification" followed in 1898. As the name implies, it allowed for insertion of new divisions or topics as needed, but it was not worked out or indexed in much detail. Growing out of it, in 1906, was the first edition of the *Subject Classification*. In 1914, shortly after Brown's death, came a second edition, and in 1939 James Douglas Stewart issued a revised and enlarged third edition.[5]

The basic scaffold of Brown's *Subject Classification* consists of eleven main classes, expressing four broad divisional concepts in orderly sequence. Primary notation is alphabetical, with some classes assigned more than one capital letter, to cover all subtopics without making the notation unduly long:

A	Generalia	} Matter and Force
B C D	Physical Science	
E F	Biological Science	} Life
G H	Ethnological and Medical Science	
I	Economic Biology and Domestic Arts	
J K	Philosophy and Religion	} Mind
L	Social and Political Science	
M	Language and Literature	} Record
N	Literary forms	
O - W	History, Geography	
X	Biography	

Each initial letter is followed by three Arabic numerals. Sequence, rather than length of number reveals hierarchy, e.g.,

D600   METALLURGY
601   Smelting
602   Blast Furnaces
603   Open Hearth Furnaces
604   Ores

These schedule numbers may be expanded like decimals (without the decimal point) when new topics require insertion. The scheme allows several methods of building numbers: geographic numbers from the O-W classes may be attached to topical numbers when needed. There is a "Categorical Table" of "forms, etc. for the subdivision of subjects." Numbers from this table are attached after a period, which is not to be regarded as a decimal point. A plus sign is used to connect two facets from the same class. The underscore is used to "stack" parts of a number. Its purpose is to keep an extended notation compact.

While Brown's *Subject Classification*, like Cutter's *Expansive Classification*, never received the widespread adoption received by its American rivals, timing and the lack of a consistent, continuing update program may be the explanation, rather than the comparative merits of the four schemes. Brown's system stimulated research and development in British classification theory, much as Cutter's did in the United States. Both are now milestones of classification history, rather than popular modern schemes for arranging library materials.

BLISS' BIBLIOGRAPHIC CLASSIFICATION

Henry Evelyn Bliss (1870-1955) was Librarian of the College of the City of New York, where he spent some thirty years developing and testing his ideas on library classification. After several periodical articles and books, he finished publication of his magnum opus only two years before his death. [6]

A "bibliographic" classification is, in Bliss' terminology, one designed to organize documentary materials (i.e., library collections, chiefly in print format). The sequence of main classes nonetheless preserves the discipline (rather than topical) orientation which Bliss interpreted as the basic structure of knowledge. Paul Dunkin called it "a sort of reader interest classification for scholars." [7]

According to Bliss, it is important in classifying a book to decide in what main classes it falls. The literature on concrete topics like "bees" is not kept in one place (as Brown would try to do) but is distributed according to the "aspect" from which it is viewed. For example, a book on bees from a scientific aspect goes to class "G - Zoology," whereas a book on beekeeping is classed in "U - Useful Arts."

The Bliss system soon grew more popular in Great Britain than in the United States. [8] A British Committee for the Bliss Classification, which changed its name in 1967 to the Bliss Classification Association, draws its membership largely from libraries using the scheme. It publishes an annual

Bliss Classification Bulletin, formerly issued by H. W. Wilson, and has commissioned its chairman, Jack Mills, to edit a thoroughly revised and enlarged second edition in twenty separate parts. After various delays, the first volumes of this edition appeared in 1977.[9]

The second edition makes full use of principles which Bliss developed over the years but had little opportunity to apply consistently to his original edition. It also derives techniques of facet analysis, as well as of explicit citation and filing orders, from Ranganathan's monumental contributions to classification theory.

Second edition notation consists of capital letters and numerals, omitting zero because of its similarity to the letter O. Bliss wished to keep his numbers as brief as possible, consistent with full expression of the various aspects of a topic. He was not interested much in expressiveness, that is, showing position in the logical hierarchy of the system by the length or configuration of the individual class number. Rather, he tried to make his notation show flexibly, but specifically, all the auxiliary features (facets and arrays) which might be used to modify the basic subject of a work. He further strove to provide alternative locations and treatments so that the individual classifier could select the one most appropriate to the library's holdings.

The future of the *Bibliographic Classification* is dependent in large part on the timing and public acceptance of the new edition. That Bliss' theory and practice had many advantages is a fact recognized by anyone who knows it well enough to compare it with more widely accepted schemes. That it badly needed updating and further development is also clear. The gargantuan job of complete overhaul by a few aficionados on a shoestring budget, if finished, should permit future sequential revision of different class schedules as needed (somewhat resembling the present revision program at the Library of Congress). Meanwhile, some libraries using the original schedules are falling away.[10] Establishment of the Bliss scheme as a major contender for library adoption will require not only efficient, dedicated work, but a great deal of luck.

SPECIAL CLASSIFICATION SCHEMES

Classification schemes comprising the entire universe of knowledge must of necessity be general and cannot deal with specialties or fine detail. They are also largely inflexible, presenting the particular viewpoint of their designers (which in the case of DDC and LCC represents the late nineteenth century), and they often disperse subjects which, for the purposes of specialists, ought to be dealt with in close proximity (e.g., DDC has chemistry in 540 but chemical technology in 660, which is very unhelpful for a chemistry library). Even UDC, though providing for very fine detail, suffers from many of the faults inherited from DDC (e.g., the chemistry dispersal) and often has long notations.

Librarians of collections devoted mainly or exclusively to one specific field of knowledge, a discipline, or one of its subfields have therefore often found it necessary to design special classification schemes. The British Classification Research Group (CRG) was particularly active in designing special faceted classifications during the 1960s and 1970s, whereas in the

United States special classifications were more often the work of individuals and organizations.

Special classification schemes are mainly of two types: "general-special" schemes, which classify a special field or subject exhaustively while providing only very general class marks to peripheral or extraneous subjects, and "special" schemes, dealing only with a particular specialty in sometimes very fine detail, but leaving the classing of other subjects to one of the general schemes; hybrids of the two types are those schemes that expand an existing class of a general scheme or make use of an unused notation under which a special subject field is developed in detail.

Two examples of the latter type are widely used in U.S. libraries. *The National Library of Medicine Classification*[11] uses class W (which is vacant in LCC) and the medical parts of LCC's class Q for the entire biomedical field. Subdivision of W is by all letters of the alphabet, including even I and O (which are avoided by LCC because of possible confusion with the digits 1 and 0), followed by up to three digits used enumeratively and an occasional fourth digit used decimally, followed by more detailed subdivision using cuttering, e.g.,

WD 200   Metabolic diseases
WD 205.5.A5   Amino acid metabolism

Since NLM's W class notations now appear on MARC records for medical books, most medical libraries use the W special classification.

A Classification Scheme for Law Books[12] which expands class K of LCC has found wide acceptance in law libraries, due to the fact that LCC's own class K is still unfinished. Another expansion of LCC is for a highly specialized subject. *An Alternative Classification for Catholic Books*[13] takes a section of the LC classification that was not in use by LC when the schedule was developed in 1937 and develops it as Christian literature with three major subclasses: BQT, theology; BQV, canon law; and BQX, church history, all further subdivided by enumerative digits and cuttering. The introduction gives detailed instructions on how to integrate these schedules into either LCC or DDC when these are used to class other subjects in a library.

The following examples are representatives of the special type that combine a faceted structure and high flexibility with brief notations. The *London Education Classification*[14] fulfills a double role as a classification and thesaurus, and uses a letter notation, uppercase letters serving as facet indicators, e.g.,

Mab   Curriculum
Mabb   Curriculum development
Mabf   Curriculum classification

The *Physics and Astronomy Classification Scheme*[15] of the American Institute of Physics (AIP) uses a mixed notation of two decimal groups followed by a letter, e.g.,

84	Electromagnetic technology
84.30	Electronic circuits
84.30 L	Amplifiers

Except for two sections, the AIP scheme is identical with the *International Classification for Physics*,[16] and parts of it have been adopted by the Institution of Electrical Engineers in London for its *INSPEC Classification for Physics, Electrotechnology, Computers and Control.*[17] Thus, a physics library could choose among three major special schemes, all of which have the backing of professional societies.

The London Classification of Business Studies[18] has five major classes: management responsibility in the enterprise (A-G), environmental studies (J-R), analytical techniques (S-X), library and information science (Y), and auxiliary schedules (1-7). The notation consists of up to four uppercase letters, e.g.,

K	Industries
KCL	Alcoholic drinks industry
KCLB	Wine industry

and notations can be combined by an oblique stroke, e.g.,

EE/KCLB	Financial management in the wine industry

The scheme is used in about forty British libraries and more than twenty libraries elsewhere. The London Business School is responsible for updating and development of the scheme.

An example of a special scheme relying on another classification for extraneous subjects is the *Classification for Library and Information Science*,[19] designed by the CRG and used by *Library and Information Science Abstracts* (*LISA*) for the arrangement of entries. This scheme, too, makes use of a letter notation with capitals as facet indicators, resulting in notations such as TogsNjrFv, which expresses the topic "Online systems:centralized:Public libraries," or ZmRnM(57), "Databases:Information Services:By subject: Biology," with 57 taken from UDC for a subject not germane to the central topic of library and information science.

Special classifications are sometimes developed for extremely narrow subjects, such as the *Classification for London Literature*,[20] concerned with works only on that city, with decimal subdivisions for every place and event in its long history, e.g.,

10	Religion
12	St. Paul's Cathedral
12.4	Dome and roof

A bibliography of classification schemes and subject heading lists for hundreds of different subjects lists 2,250 items in several languages.[21]

A special classification scheme may initially have the advantage of being more detailed and more up to date than any of the general schemes, but it is unfortunately often the case that such schemes, once designed, are not further developed and therefore become obsolete and lacking in detail much quicker than general schemes. When adopting a special scheme, one must take care to choose a scheme that has a reasonably good chance of being further developed and updated — that is, one that is backed by an organization rather than being the one-time effort of a librarian in a special collection. Such homemade classification schemes are generally motivated by the fact that sooner or later almost any librarian will find that the scheme he or she uses, whether general or specific, is insufficiently detailed or does not contain a class notation for a new subject. It is then easy to succumb to the temptation to create a new subdivision or an entirely new scheme for the missing topics or for sections of a scheme that seem to be misplaced. The proper design of a special classification is, however, a task best left to someone thoroughly familiar with the theory and principles of classification design, and the novice should refrain from attempting this enterprise until some considerable experience has been gained. Many a hastily conceived and improperly designed special classification scheme has had to be abandoned sooner or later, to be replaced with an existing and proven scheme at great cost and inconvenience to the library and its users.

CONCLUSION

The classification systems briefly reviewed here differ from each other, and from the better known DDC and LC systems, in many ways. In basic theory of the organization of knowledge, some emphasize the specific subject approach, clustering these unitary topics in related sequences, whereas most start from a broad disciplinary orientation, subdividing hierarchically, so that the various aspects or unitary topics become scattered to different parts of the system. In providing a schedule framework to arrange books on shelves, some systems (the more traditional) are primarily enumerative, whereas most newer ones are synthetic or faceted. Some maintain a comparatively pure notation, whereas others use combinations of letters and Arabic numerals, while upper- and lower-case letters, roman numerals, Greek letters, and a variety of arbitrary relational signs and symbols appear in still others. Timeliness is a constant problem. Some systems maintain a serials program to announce additions and changes, or issue new editions at intervals of five to twenty-five years. Many have outlived their originators, but some suffer more than others from age and lack of funds or organized promotion. Each has unique attractive features; each has practical and theoretical problems. Some are more useful for shelf arrangement of books and related formats. Others are better suited to in-depth indexing of periodical articles, technical reports, books, and the like. Centripetal forces such as networking seem at the moment to favor general acceptance of one or two well-known, widely used schemes, overlooking functional disadvantages to achieve standardization and administrative coherence. Yet classification research, like that in all other areas of bibliographic organization, is very brisk and busy in the modern world of information science. Time may show that all the schemes we study and use today, regardless of their present achievements or popularity, are chiefly important for the historic part they play as heralds of still better solutions to the problems of subject access.

NOTES

[1]Four examples of specific applications using the systems discussed in this chapter, as well as DDC and LC, are given in Bohdan S. Wynar, *Introduction to Cataloging and Classification*, 5th ed., prepared with the assistance of John Phillip Immroth (Littleton, Colo., Libraries Unlimited, 1976), pp. 314-328.

[2]Charles Ammi Cutter, *Expansive Classification, Part I: The First Six Classifications* (Boston, Cutter, 1891-1893).

[3]Charles Ammi Cutter, *Expansive Classification, Part II: Seventh Classification*, largely edited by William Parker Cutter (Boston and Northampton, Mass., 1896-1911), 2v. with supplementary pages.

[4]Robert L. Mowery, "The Cutter Classification: Still at Work," *Library Resources & Technical Services* 20 (Spring 1976): 154.

[5]James Duff Brown, *Subject Classification: With Tables, Indexes, etc. for the Subdivision of Subjects*, 3rd ed., rev. and enl. by James Douglas Stewart (London, Grafton, 1939).

[6]Bliss' major works are the following: *The Organization of Knowledge and the System of the Sciences* (New York, Holt, 1929); *The Organization of Knowledge in Libraries*, 2nd ed. rev. and partly rewritten (New York, H. W. Wilson, 1939), *see* page 405 for further citations; *A Bibliographic Classification: Extended by Systematic Auxiliary Schedules for Composite Specification and Notation* (New York, H. W. Wilson, 1940-1953), 4v. in 3.

[7]Paul S. Dunkin, *Cataloging U.S.A.* (Chicago, American Library Association, 1969), p. 126.

[8]*See*, for instance: School Library Association (England), *The Abridged Bliss Classification: The Bibliographical Classification of Henry Evelyn Bliss Revised for School Libraries* (London, The Association, 1967).

[9]Bliss, H. E. *Bibliographic Classification*, 2nd ed., edited by Jack Mills and V. Broughton (London, Butterworths, 1977-).
   Class H: Anthropology, Human Biology, Health Sciences, 1981.
   Class I: Psychology, Psychiatry, 1978.
   Class J: Education, 1977.
   Class P: Religion, 1977.
   Class Q: Social Welfare, 1977.
   Introduction and Auxiliary Schedules, 1977.

[10]*See*, for instance: "Ibadan Abandons Bliss," *Library Association Record* 79 (May 1977): 241, which tells how the University of Ibadan (Nigeria), after using Bliss for twenty-five years, is converting to the LC scheme because of the inadequacy of outdated, unrevised Bliss schedules.

[11]*National Library of Medicine Classification: A Scheme for the Shelf Arrangement of Books in the Field of Medicine and Its Related Sciences* (Bethesda, Md., NLM, 1978).

[12]E. M. Moys, *A Classification Scheme for Law Books* (Hamden, Conn., Archon Books, 1968).

[13]Jeannette Murphy Lynn, *An Alternative Classification for Catholic Books*, 2nd ed. rev. by G. C. Peterson; supplement (1965) by Thomas G. Pater (Washington, D.C., Catholic University of America Press, 1965).

[14]D. J. Foskett and J. Foskett, *The London Education Classification: A Thesaurus/Classification of British Education Terms*, 2nd ed. (London, University of London Institute of Education Library, 1974).

[15]American Institute of Physics, *Physics and Astronomy Classification Schemes* (New York, AIP, 1977).

[16]International Council of Scientific Unions, Abstracting Board, *International Classification for Physics* (Paris, ICSU/AB, 1975).

[17]Institution of Electrical Engineers, *INSPEC Classification: A Classification Scheme for Physics, Electrotechnology, Computers and Control* (London, IEE, 1981).

[18]K. D. C. Vernon and V. Lang, *The London Classification of Business Studies*, 2nd ed. rev. by K. G. B. Bakewell and D. A. Cotton (London, Aslib, 1979).

[19]Classification Research Group, *A Classification of Library and Information Science* (London, CRG, 1965). (A second edition was published in 1975 but is not used by LISA.)

[20]Guildhall Library, *Classification for London Literature*, 3rd ed. (London, The Library, 1966).

[21]*Classification Systems and Thesauri, 1950-1982* (Frankfurt, West Germany, Indeks Verlag, 1982). (International Classification and Indexing Bibliography 1.)

SUGGESTED READING

Chan, Lois Mai. *Cataloging and Classification: An Introduction.* New York, McGraw-Hill, 1981. Chapter 14.

Foskett, A. C. *The Subject Approach to Information.* London, Bingley, 1982. Chapters 9, 13, 18-20.

21
Verbal Subject Analysis

INTRODUCTION

We have seen in the preceding chapters that classification provides a library with a systematic arrangement of materials according to their subject content, mode of treatment, or even their physical format. In addition to classification, there is another commonly used means of access to the intellectual contents of a library—namely indexing through the use of a subject heading list of controlled vocabulary terms and cross references. Whereas classification provides a logical, or at least a methodical, approach to the arrangement of documentary materials, subject headings give a more random alphabetic approach to the concepts inherent in those materials, thus adding another dimension to the linear arrangement characteristic of classification. The two techniques offer alternative, and to some extent complementary, modes of access to the collection, comprising that aspect of bibliographic control and access known as subject cataloging.

There are many theoretically sound objectives for subject cataloging. Shera and Egan summarized them as follows:

1. To provide access by subject to *all* relevant material.

2. To provide subject access to materials through all suitable *principles of subject organization*, e.g., matter, process, applications, etc.

3. To bring together references to materials which treat of substantially the *same subject* regardless of disparities in terminology, disparities which may have resulted from national differences, differences among groups of subject specialists, and/or from the changing nature of the concepts with the discipline itself.

4. To show *affiliations among subject fields*, affiliations which may depend upon similarities of matter studied, or method, or of point of view, or upon use or application of knowledge.

5. To provide entry to any subject field at any *level of analysis*, from the most general to the most specific.

6. To provide entry through any *vocabulary* common to any considerable group of users, specialized or lay.

7. To provide a *formal description of the subject content* of any bibliographic unit in the most precise, or specific, terms possible, whether the description be in the form of a word or brief phrase or in the form of a class number or symbol.

8. To provide means for the user to make *selection* from among all items in any particular category, according to any chosen set of criteria such as: most thorough, most recent, most elementary, etc.[1]

BASIC CONCEPTS AND STRUCTURE
OF SUBJECT HEADINGS

Subject heading has been defined as "an access point to a bibliographic record, consisting of a word or phrase which designates the subject of the work(s) contained in the bibliographic item."[2] Today, information analysts distinguish pre-coordinate indexing, by which appropriate terms are chosen and coordinated at the time of indexing, from post-coordinate indexing, with which coordination takes place after the encoded documents have been stored.[3] Libraries traditionally prefer the former method of compiling alphabetical subject catalogs. All standard published lists of "subject headings" were developed with pre-coordinate indexing techniques.

Obviously, subject headings have dual objectives: 1) to identify pertinent material on a given subject or topic, 2) to enable the inquirer to find material on related subjects. Both objectives pose problems of communication; both demand a set of terms that match, as far as possible, the terms likely to be in the minds of inquirers wishing to locate material on a given topic or in a given discipline. E. J. Coates warns:

> This would be fairly simple to achieve if there were an uncomplicated, one-to-one relationship between concepts and words: that is to say, if there were a single word corresponding to each separate concept and a single concept corresponding to each separate word. In fact, we have on the one hand concepts that can be rendered by any one of a number of words, and on the other hand, concepts for which no single word equivalent exists in the natural language.[4]

Modern subject heading practice has its roots in Charles A. Cutter's *Rules for a Dictionary Catalog.*[5] Immroth reminds us that Cutter's "rules for subject entries are the basis for two major American lists of subject headings—the *Library of Congress Subject Headings* and the *Sears List of Subject Headings.*"[6] Later theorists refined and expanded Cutter's work in various ways. David Judson Haykin, former Chief of the Library of Congress Subject

Cataloging Division, enumerates the principles on which the choice of terms for a subject list must rest.[7] They may be summarized as follows:

1. *The reader as focus.* The heading, in wording and structure, should be that which the reader will seek in the catalog, if we know or can presume what the reader will look under. In the face of a lack of sufficient objective, experimental data, we must rely for guidance in the choice of terms upon the experience of librarians and such objective findings as are available.

2. *Unity.* A subject catalog must bring together under one heading all the books which deal principally or exclusively with the subject, whatever the terms applied to it by the authors of the books, and whatever the varying terms applied to it at different times. [It] must [use] a term which is unambiguous and does not overlap in meaning other headings in the catalog, even where that involves defining the sense in which it is used.

3. *Usage.* The heading chosen must represent common usage or, at any rate, the usage of the class of reader for whom the material on the subject within which the heading falls is intended. Whether a popular term or a scientific one is to be chosen depends on several considerations. If the library serves a miscellaneous public, it must prefer the popular to the scientific term.

4. *Specificity.* The heading should be as specific as the topic it is intended to cover. As a corollary, the heading should not be broader than the topic; rather than use a broader heading, the cataloger should use two specific headings which will approximately cover it.

The following discussion touches on some of the most important problems encountered in construction and use of subject headings.

THE CHOICE OF SUBJECT HEADINGS

Linguistic usage determines correctness of form in natural language, as all grammarians and dictionary compilers well know. Language changes constantly, not only in response to new discoveries and formulations of knowledge, but also in response to dynamic forces of its own, some but not all of which have been codified by linguists. In choosing subject terms, librarians try to consider both the author's usage and the patron's needs and preferences. But authors and patrons are likely to use different terms for the same subject. Without a record of choices, the cataloger may enter the same subject under two or more different headings. Two types of decision are especially likely to miscarry: those for which more than one adequate term is available, and those for which no adequate term is available.

Selecting a term from among verbal equivalents. The cataloger or compiler of a subject heading list must sometimes choose one subject term from among several synonyms or very similar terms. Cutter suggests the following sequence of preferences when selecting from synonymous headings:[8]

1. *The term most familiar to the general public.* Cutter no doubt was thinking of the local library's public. We shall see that one of the major differences between *LCSH* and *Sears* is that *LCSH*, being designed for use in a comprehensive research library, favors scientific terminology (e.g., "ARACHNIDA *see also* SPIDERS"), whereas *Sears* tends to use more popular terms (e.g., "Arachnida *see* SPIDERS").

2. *The term most used in other catalogs.* Since patrons frequently change libraries, or consult more than one library catalog, it is comforting to find that terminology remains stable, even standardized, so long as it does not violate the usage of the local library's public. Broad automated networks, using consolidated machine-readable data bases, make reliably standardized terminology even more desirable. A different, but related, argument is that new concepts and terms are often introduced into the periodical literature before they form the topics of full-scale books. If a library's subject heading list does not yet include such a term, the cataloger might well consult the *New York Times Index,* or commonly-used periodical indexes and abstracting tools, to discover what usage, if any, has been established.

3. *The term that has fewest meanings.* The clear intent here is to avoid ambiguity wherever possible.

4. *The term that comes first in the alphabet.* This is the type of arbitrary, procedural decision which can and should be invoked when semantic considerations have been exhausted.

5. *The term that brings the subject into the neighborhood of other, related subjects.* It was previously noted that a serious drawback of alphabetic arrangement is its fragmentation of subject matter, and that most alphabetic subject lists indulge in some "classing." Here is Cutter's recognition that the technique is valid, but only after all other modes for choosing among synonymous terms have been exhausted.

Supplying a term which is not contained in a single word. Some concepts must be expressed by phrases (combinations of words). Phrase headings present certain disadvantages. As Coates indicates, most catalog users try to formulate search topics in single words, even when a phrase would be used in natural language.[9] Various uncertainties shadow the introduction of phrases into a controlled vocabulary. In determining the order of words, should a heading always retain the order of natural language, or should modifications and transpositions be allowed in the interests of brevity and clarity? Should a variety of syntactic forms be used, or should the syntax of phrase headings be confined to a few simple forms which occasionally make them seem awkward and artificial? Some theorists feel that, lacking cleanly enunciated rules, phrase-makers have produced a number of troublesome headings. Modern usage condones several varieties which different subject lists usually adapt to their own uses. The specific rules printed in *Sears List of Subject Headings* and in *Library of Congress Subject Headings* simplify but do not solve this problem, since they are purely arbitrary.[10] The problem of communication still exists. Many books are listed under subject headings that patrons would not immediately think of as the appropriate ones under which to search. For the most part they can be roughly categorized as follows. All examples are taken from either the *Sears* or the Library of Congress list:

1. *Modified nouns.* Modifiers can take different syntactic forms:
    a) Nouns preceded by adjectives or other modifiers, e.g., "Regional planning," "Furbearing animals," or "Country life"
    b) Nouns followed by adjectives or other modifiers, e.g., "Occupations, Dangerous," "Insurance, Malpractice," or "Molds (Botany)"

2. *Conjunctive phrases.* The conjunction is nearly always "and," e.g., "Mills and millwork," "Instrumentation and orchestration," or "Mind and body"

3. *Prepositional phrases.* "In" and "of" are most common, but other prepositions may be used to form phrases, e.g., "Segregation in education," or "Freedom of conscience"

4. *Serial phrases*, e.g., "Hotels, motels, etc.," "Rewards (Prizes, etc.)," or "Plots (Drama, fiction, etc.)"

5. *Complex phrase forms*, e.g., "Artificial satellites in telecommunication," "Glass painting and staining," "Libraries, College and university," "State aid to libraries," "Cities and towns, Ruined, extinct, etc.," "Justice, Administration of," "Music, Popular (Songs, etc.)," "Right and left (Political science)," or "Fortune-telling by tea leaves"

6. *Subdivided topical phrases*, e.g., "Book industries and trade— Exhibitions," "Mines and mineral resources—United States," or "Military service, Compulsory—Draft resistors"

THE NUMBER OF SUBJECT HEADINGS

The number of subject headings entered into a catalog for a single item depends on many factors. As long as most library catalogs are in card form, rapidly increasing bulk is both an economic and a use hazard. Maintenance costs (housing, filing, revising) are high, while users grow confused, or waste considerable time, moving from one point to another in a roomful of several thousand trays. The larger the number of subject entries provided, the greater is the cost of cataloging a title. On the other hand, the assignment of more headings per item makes the total resources of the library more available, and may bring out special aspects and bits of unusual or significant information.

The current trend toward storing catalogs in machine-readable data banks makes increasing the number of subject entries proportionately less expensive in time, effort, or cost of retrieval. Print-outs in either book form or microform occupy little space and can be consulted in one spot, as can a computer terminal giving online access. Moreover, the simultaneous display of either complete or truncated entries in an ordered column often makes filing practices self-evident. In the early 1980s the Library of Congress was adding about two subject entries per cataloged item. This was up from fewer than two entries per record prior to the implementation of *AACR 2*. The tendency over the decades prior to 1980 was to reduce the average number of subject entries. However, this trend has reversed, and more entries per record are being made.[11] Indexes and abstracting tools in science and technology, by contrast, tend to use specific subject entries to a point of minute analysis. Twenty to forty subject terms for one brief article are not rare. It is probable that subject analysis of library titles will expand with the increased use of automated bibliographic control. The computer is facilitating more, and better, studies of library use, to discern optimum types and quantities of subject headings for full subject retrieval. A Council on Library Resources (CLR) study of online catalog use of fifteen online catalogs showed that in catalogs with subject access, about 59 percent of all searches were for subject information rather than for "known items."[12] This is quite different from studies of card catalog use, which showed that over two-thirds of searches were known-item searches. The CLR study recommended that system designers implement keyword searching for subjects and browsing of the subject index or thesaurus. It also recognized that such systems can only find subject terms that exist in bibliographic records and recommended increased subject information in bibliographic records along with strict authority control to restrict the number of synonymous and related terms.[13]

LOCATION OF MATERIAL ON RELATED SUBJECTS

Consistency is one of the most important criteria for assigning subject headings. The cataloger should choose one subject term, and one alone, to index all materials on the same topic. References should then be made to the chosen heading from all other likely headings. They help the inquirer to locate available material on the topic, plus collateral topics, at the level of specificity and from the point of view most useful for the particular need. Cross references consist primarily of two types: *see* references refer from a name or term under which no items are entered to the relevant term under which items are listed, e.g., "Lunar expeditions *see* SPACE FLIGHT TO THE MOON"; *see also* references suggest that not only is the already located heading more or less relevant, but the user might wish to look under other, similar or closely related terms, e.g., "DEAFNESS *see also* HEARING AIDS." As with references for names, online catalogs have brought opportunities for more explanatory terminology than "see" and "see also." For example, an online display might say "Lunar expeditions. For material on this subject search under SPACE FLIGHT TO THE MOON" or "DEAFNESS. Related material on this topic may be found under HEARING AIDS." It is also possible for an online catalog to give no reference at all in a situation where a *see* reference would be given in a manual catalog. A user searching under "lunar expeditions" might be given automatically a list of the library's material that had been given the heading "space flight to the moon." This practice is called "invisible referencing." For terminology used in some thesauri, such as "broader term" and "related term," *see* chapter 24.

Hierarchical references move vertically, rather than horizontally, leading the user to topics at a different level of specificity. *See also* references of this type nearly always move "down" from a general term to one or more specific topics subsumed under it, e.g., "CRUELTY *see also* ATROCITIES." A few *see* references, however, move "up" from a specific term which is not used to the broader term which contains it, e.g., "Heirs *see* INHERITANCE AND SUCCESSION."

Coordinate references may be of either the *see* or the *see also* variety. The connections they make and the relationships they show are horizontal rather than vertical. They occasionally overlap in such ways that reciprocal or multilateral entries are deemed to be necessary. Some direct the user from a term not used (i.e., where no material is listed) to a synonymous or closely related term, where materials are listed, e.g.:

Synonymous terms:
   "Civic art   *see*   ART, MUNICIPAL"

Closely related terms:
   "REFORESTATION   *see also*   TREE PLANTING"
   "TREE PLANTING   *see also*   REFORESTATION"

Others suggest "associative" (not necessarily related) or "illustrative" (not, strictly speaking, synonymous) terms, e.g.:

Associative, unrelated terms:
   "CORRUPTION IN POLITICS   *see also*   LOBBYING"
   "LOBBYING   *see also*   CORRUPTION IN POLITICS"

Illustrative, non-synonymous terms:
   "Economic entomology   *see*   INSECTS, INJURIOUS
           AND BENEFICIAL"

Besides simple cross references, subject heading lists sometimes include scope notes to define and delimit a subject term. These may or may not suggest further terms for the user to consult. Some libraries copy these notes for guides to precede all subject entries under those given terms in their catalogs. Other libraries, wishing to avoid unnecessary catalog entries, keep one or more copies of the printed list near the catalog for public consultation. The following two examples come from *Sears*, but nearly verbatim scope notes for the same terms can be found in *LCSH*:

COMMUNITY AND SCHOOL
   Use for materials on ways in which the community at large, as distinct from government, may aid the school program.

MIGRANT LABOR
   Use for materials dealing with casual or seasonal workers who move from place to place in search of employment. Materials on the movement of population within a country for permanent settlements are entered under MIGRATION, INTERNAL.

Some lists include key headings or pattern headings, with instructions to the cataloger on how to construct other headings of similar form which have been omitted from the list for reasons of brevity. The following example is from *Sears*:

HIJACKING OF AIRPLANES
   Use same form for the hijacking of other modes of transportation.

To assure maximum consistency, a careful, up-to-date record of all subject term selections and cross references should be kept, either by checking the terms used and the additions made in a standard printed list, or by maintaining a separate subject authority file. Such a record can save the cataloger time in the long run, and provide the following summary information:

1.   Unused terms from which *see* references have been made.

2.   Scope notes describing a heading, or distinguishing its use in instances where one of its two or more meanings has been chosen.

3.   Less comprehensive, subordinate headings, to which *see also* references have been made from more comprehensive terms.

4.   More comprehensive, broad headings, from which *see also* references have been made to more specific headings.

5.   Coordinate headings from which and to which cross references have been made from related or associated headings.

THE CONCEPT OF SPECIFIC ENTRY

One of Haykin's principles on which the choice of terms for a subject list must rest was "specificity." The idea had been enunciated a half century earlier by Cutter:

> Enter a work under its subject heading, not under the heading of the class which includes that subject. . . . Put Lady Cust's book on "the cat" under "Cat," not under Zoology or Mammals, or Domestic animals. . . . Some subjects have no name. They are spoken of by a phrase or phrases not definite enough to be used as headings. It is not always easy to decide what is a *distinct* subject. . . . Possible matters of investigation . . . must attain a certain individuality as objects of inquiry and be given some sort of *name*, otherwise we must assign them class-entry.[14]

It should be noted that the concept of specific entry is not the same as the concept of coextensive entry. At least one recently developed system for subject analysis, PRECIS (discussed in greater detail in chapter 24), attempts to make subject headings coextensive with the concept/topics covered in the item analyzed. That is, the subject heading will cover all, but no more than, the concepts or topics covered in the item. A very simple example can be drawn by elaborating upon the idea from Cutter above. If one had a book about cats and dogs, the concept of *specific* entry would require two headings: CATS and DOGS. There is no one specific term to cover these two kinds of animal. In order to have a heading that is *coextensive* with the subject of the item the heading would have to be CATS AND DOGS.

A great weakness of the concept of specific entry is that subjects must be described in terms that are constantly changing. Material very often has to be cataloged before a suitable term has been added to any standard list. Many subjects now represent a cross-fertilization among once traditional disciplines. As Coates indicates,

> New subjects are being generated around us all the time, and while subjects may still be more or less distinct, there can be no hard and fast separation of the "distinct" subjects from the others.[15]

Not only do particular terms fluctuate in meaning, but a constant, obtrusive tendency of any alphabetic subject list based on the ideal of specific entry is to develop sequences of topical subdivisions or modifications which, as was previously noted, convert true random access into an inadvertent classing device. All such lists show marks of a split personality in this respect. The two most popular American lists, *LCSH* and *Sears*, are reviewed in the next two chapters; chapter 24 presents some indexing systems which have been proposed as supplements to, or replacements for, these two lists as a primary mode of subject access to organized library collections.

NOTES

[1]Jesse H. Shera and Margaret E. Egan, *The Classified Catalog* (Chicago, American Library Association, 1956), p. 10.

[2]*ALA Glossary of Library and Information Science* (Chicago, American Library Association, 1983), p. 220.

[3]A. C. Foskett, *The Subject Approach to Information*, 4th ed. (London, Clive Bingley; Hamden, Conn., Linnet Books, 1982), p. 86.

[4]E. J. Coates, *Subject Catalogues: Headings and Structure* (London, Library Association, 1960), p. 19.

[5]Charles Ammi Cutter, *Rules for a Dictionary Catalog*, 4th ed. (Washington, D.C., GPO, 1904).

[6]John Phillip Immroth, "Cutter, Charles Ammi," in *Encyclopedia of Library and Information Science*, vol. 6 (New York, Marcel Dekker, 1971), p. 382.

[7]David Judson Haykin, *Subject Headings: A Practical Guide* (Washington, D.C., GPO, 1951), pp. 7-9.

[8]Cutter, *Dictionary Catalog*, p. 19.

[9]Coates, *Subject Catalogues*, p. 19.

[10]For the development of phrase heading forms in *Sears List of Subject Headings* and in *Library of Congress Subject Headings see* chapters 22 and 23.

[11]Personal communication with Mary K. D. Pietris, Chief, Subject Cataloging Division, Library of Congress, June 1985.

[12]*Using Online Catalogs: A Nationwide Survey*, edited by Joseph R. Matthews, Gary S. Lawrence, and Douglas K. Ferguson (New York, Neal-Schuman Publishers, 1983), pp. 144-146.

[13]Ibid., pp. 177-179.

[14]Cutter, *Dictionary Catalog*, pp. 66-67.

[15]Coates, *Subject Catalogues*, p. 32.

SUGGESTED READING

Chan, Lois Mai, Phyllis A. Richmond, and Elaine Svenonius. *Theory of Subject Analysis: A Sourcebook*. Littleton, Colo., Libraries Unlimited, 1985.

Coates, E. J. *Subject Catalogues: Headings and Structure*. London, Library Association, 1960.

Foskett, A. C. *The Subject Approach to Information*. 4th ed. London, Bingley, 1982. Chapter 7.

Harris, Jessica Lee. *Subject Analysis: Computer Implications of Rigorous Definition*. Metuchen, N.J., Scarecrow Press, 1970.

Pettee, Julia. *Subject Headings: The History and Theory of the Alphabetical Approach to Books*. New York, H. W. Wilson, 1946.

22
Library of Congress
Subject Headings

INTRODUCTION

The official list of Library of Congress subject headings consists of terms, with cross references, which have been established over the years since 1897 for use in that library's subject catalogs. A basic two-volume ninth edition appeared in 1980.[1] Quarterly supplements announce changes, including cancelled terms, added new terms, and revisions. They are later cumulated into volumes spanning one or more years.[2] A fully updated list can be purchased each quarter on microfilm or microfiche.[3] It saves the bother of consulting several alphabets to find the most current status of any given term. Machine-readable tapes of the basic list and supplements were available for a while for headings established through 1979. However, the format proved to be unsuccessful, and further updates were not issued. The most recent edition of the MARC Authorities Format now allows for subjects to be formatted the way that names and series titles have been formatted. Authority records for names have been sent to subscribers since the late 1970s, and authority records for series titles have been available since the early 1980s. In the near future subject authority records also will be available from LC in the MARC Communications Format.

Though developed to give subject access to the vast collections of one particular library, this list can be, and has been, adopted by libraries of all sizes, including many with non-LC classification schemes. The National Library of Canada, for example, has for many years used it as basic, supplementing it with a special set of terms for Canadian material.[4] It is used by most large public libraries, college and university libraries, and special libraries that do not have more technical subject lists of their own. Since LC printed cards and MARC tapes usually carry Dewey Decimal classification numbers as well as LC call numbers, but have only LC subject headings, some smaller libraries also use the LC subject list. Others retain the shorter, less frequently revised *Sears* list as their primary source, but consult the LC list for suggestions when *Sears* cannot provide the specificity or the diversity they want.[5]

Supplementary grafting of portions of one list onto the other should be carefully monitored, to avoid inconsistencies or contradictions. For instance, LC uses the term "UNIVERSITIES AND COLLEGES—CHAPEL EXER-CISES," whereas *Sears* uses "COLLEGES AND UNIVERSITIES" but does not include the subdivision "Chapel Exercises." If a library using *Sears* headings wishes to use the subdivision, it should retain its *Sears* form of the primary segment, i.e., "COLLEGES AND UNIVERSITIES—CHAPEL EXERCISES," or else convert all its "COLLEGES AND UNIVERSITIES" headings to the LC form.

BACKGROUND

The current ninth edition of *LCSH* is heir to a long tradition of theory and practice which is generally held to begin with Charles Ammi Cutter's *Rules for a Dictionary Catalog*.[6] A brief review of Cutter's approach, and of the major developments stemming from his work can be found in chapter 21, "Verbal Subject Analysis." The purpose in the present chapter is to highlight trends leading directly to *LCSH* in its present form.[7]

On July 1, 1909, J. C. M. Hanson, Chief of the Catalog Division of the Library of Congress, addressed the Catalog Section of the American Library Association at its Bretton Woods Conference on "The Subject Catalogs of the Library of Congress."[8] He alluded to a two-volume subject catalog published by the Library in 1869, but called the subject heading developments of the intervening forty years too radical to permit a meaningful comparison. The many changes attendant upon the new classification scheme and the move into the new building required a new approach to subject indexing. LC catalogers agreed to start from the *ALA List of Subject Headings for Use in Dictionary Catalogs* (1895), which embodied much of Cutter's theory, and which originally formed an appendix to his *Rules*. It was designed for smaller libraries of "generally popular character," but with LC's printed card distribution plans, such an orientation was not altogether disadvantageous.

When the first cards carrying the new headings were published, subject terms were given only if an LC call number was available to print. Since many class schedules were still undeveloped, the list of subject headings grew slowly in the first decade. Proposed new headings were compared to those in the *ALA List* before final selection. Separate publication of the new list did not start until 1909, when the annotated and interleaved copies of the *ALA List* grew unwieldy. It was assumed from the first that cumulations of additions and changes would be issued periodically to supplement the main list, which itself appeared in parts until March 1914.

The practice of subordinating place to subject in scientific and technical headings, as well as under many economic and educational topics, was established at this time. But other subjects—historical, political, administrative, social, and descriptive—were to be subordinated to place, although Hanson admitted to "a number of subjects so nearly on the border line, that it has been difficult in all cases to preserve absolute consistency in decisions" (p. 387). Besides the place/subject versus subject/place precedents, other syntactic forms evolved:

> There is undeniably a strong tendency in the Library of Congress catalog to bring related subjects together by means of inversion of headings, by combinations of two or more subject-words, and even by subordination of one subject to another (p. 389).

Hanson recognized that subordination within the dictionary arrangement of his new subject list was a concession to the alphabetic-classed or systematic organization of the 1869 catalog. He argued:

> ... the student and the investigator ... are best served by having related topics brought together so far as that can be accomplished without a too serious violation of the dictionary principle (p. 390).

TYPES OF SUBJECT HEADINGS
(MARC field 650)

Library of Congress subject headings are constructed in a variety of ways, ranging from a single noun to complex descriptive phrases. As was discussed in chapter 21, Cutter enumerated six varieties according to their grammar or syntax.[9] They covered only primary headings, i.e., headings without further subdivision. The categories below are his, but the examples come from the current LC list:

1. A single word (e.g., "SKATING")
2. A noun preceded by an adjective (e.g., "ADMINISTRATIVE LAW")
3. A noun preceded by another noun used like an adjective (e.g., "ENERGY INDUSTRIES")
4. A noun connected with another by a preposition (e.g., "RADIOISOTOPES IN CARDIOLOGY")
5. A noun connected with another by "and" (e.g., "LIBRARIES AND SOCIETY")
6. A phrase or sentence (e.g., "SHOW DRIVING OF HORSE-DRAWN VEHICLES")

While Cutter did tolerate modifier inversions (e.g., "ETCHING, ANONYMOUS") "only when some other word is decidedly more significant or is often used alone with the same meaning as the whole name," he made no explicit provision for parenthetical qualifiers (e.g., "KAIROS (THE GREEK WORD)") or other such complicated forms as "INTERNAL COMBUSTION ENGINES, SPARK IGNITION," which, like subdivisions, are usually reminiscent of the alphabetico-classed approach. There are various alternative groupings. This discussion follows those used by Lois Mai Chan in her treatise on LC subject headings.[10]

SINGLE NOUN OR SUBSTANTIVE

Cutter's Rule No. 172 reads: "Enter books under the word which best expresses their subject, whether it occurs in the title or not." He worked primarily in terms of the simple concept-name relationship on which the noun forms of all languages are based. The Library of Congress over the years has experimented with slight variations of this single-word heading, for example, inclusion of an initial article (e.g., "THE WEST"), sometimes inverted (e.g., "STATE, THE") in the interests of clarity. Subject headings are no longer established with an English article in initial position. "THE WEST" has been changed to "WEST (U.S.)."[11]

Another variation was the distinction drawn, particularly in literature and art, between singular nouns (denoting the activity or the form, e.g., "ESSAY" and "PAINTING") and plural nouns (denoting the objects, e.g., "ESSAYS" and "PAINTINGS"). No new plural noun headings are being established, and some old plurals (e.g., "PAINTINGS") have been cancelled in favor of the singular form.

ADJECTIVAL HEADINGS

These headings start with a modifier followed by a noun or noun phrase (e.g., "MUNICIPAL OFFICIALS AND EMPLOYEES"). Chan lists nine types of modifiers, quoting Haykin to the effect that they require *see* references only when the modifier rather than the substantive carries the primary meaning.[12]

1. Common adjective (e.g., "DENTAL RECORDS")
2. Ethnic, national, or geographic adjective (e.g., "AFRO-AMERICAN LIBRARIANS")
3. Eponymic adjective (e.g., "BERNOULLIAN NUMBERS")
4. Participial modifiers (e.g., "APPLIED ANTHROPOLOGY" or "HEARING AIDS")
5. Common noun (e.g., "HOUSEHOLD PESTS")
6. Proper noun (e.g., "BERNSTEIN POLYNOMIALS" or "SHANGHAI GESTURE")
7. Common noun, possessive case (e.g., "SAILORS' SONGS")
8. Proper noun, possessive case (e.g., "BERGMANN'S RULE")
9. Combination (e.g., "WOMEN'S HEALTH SERVICES" or "ERHARD SEMINARS TRAINING")

CONJUNCTIVE PHRASE HEADINGS

Headings composed of two or more nouns, with or without modifiers, connected by "and" or ending with "etc." belong in this group. Those which are additive may comprise similar elements (e.g., "WIT AND HUMOR" or "HOTELS, TAVERNS, ETC."), or the elements may be contradictory (e.g., "RIGHT AND WRONG"). Headings of this type are now established only when a work being cataloged discusses a relationship between two topics from both perspectives and in such broad terms that the relationship could not be described by use of a main heading with a subdivision.[13] Some older additive headings, such as the former "BUDDHA AND BUDDHISM," have been separated, to the dismay of certain local catalogers with large files of material affected.[14]

PREPOSITIONAL PHRASE HEADINGS

Prepositions sometimes enable the subject cataloger to express single but complex ideas for which there is no one word. Some express reciprocal relationships for which an "and" phrase would be artificial (e.g., "PHOTOGRAPHY IN PSYCHIATRY" or "POLICE SERVICES FOR JUVENILES"). Some are inverted (e.g., "DRUG ABUSE, PREDICTION OF"). Prepositions so used include:

against (e.g., "OFFENSES AGAINST THE PERSON")
as (e.g., "ALFALFA AS FEED")
for (e.g., "CAMPS FOR THE HANDICAPPED")
from (e.g., "THEFT FROM MOTOR VEHICLES")
in (e.g., "HUMAN EXPERIMENTATION IN MEDICINE")
of (e.g., "FREE ELECTRON THEORY OF METALS")
on (e.g., "PLANTS, EFFECT OF HEAT ON")
to (e.g., "CERAMIC TO METAL BONDING")
with (e.g., "DOUBLE BASS WITH BAND")

Many of these circumlocutions are replaced when a simpler expression gains currency (e.g., "PSYCHOANALYSIS IN HISTORIOGRAPHY" was replaced by "PSYCHOHISTORY"). "As" headings for classes of persons have been restricted to persons not normally considered to have a profession (e.g., "CHILDREN AS COLLECTORS" or "ANIMALS AS ARTISTS"), or to situations involving two professions (e.g., "PHYSICIANS AS AUTHORS"). Old headings in which men or women are identified as professionals (e.g., "MEN AS NURSES" or "WOMEN AS TEACHERS") are being replaced by adjectival phrases (e.g., "MEN NURSES" and "WOMEN TEACHERS"). "In" headings are used broadly to designate persons from one particular discipline or activity treated *in* a different capacity (e.g., "MUSICIANS IN LITERATURE").[15]

PARENTHETICAL QUALIFIERS

Nouns or phrases in parentheses following primary terms have in the past occasioned a variety of linguistic ineptitudes. The Library of Congress no longer adds them to designate special applications of a general concept, although it has no plans to change established headings such as:

VIBRATION (MARINE ENGINEERING)

COOKERY (FROZEN FOODS)

EXCAVATIONS (ARCHAEOLOGY)

SYMMETRY (BIOLOGY)

ENVIRONMENTAL ENGINEERING (BUILDINGS)

For newly established situations, three different techniques are available:

1.   "In" and "of" headings:

INFORMATION THEORY IN BIOLOGY (*not* INFORMATION THEORY (BIOLOGY))

ANESTHESIA IN CARDIOLOGY (*not* ANESTHESIA (CARDIOLOGY))

ABANDONMENT OF AUTOMOBILES (*not* ABANDONMENT (AUTOMOBILES))

2.   Phrase headings:

COMBINATORIAL ENUMERATION PROBLEMS (*not* ENUMERATION PROBLEMS (COMBINATORIAL ANALYSIS))

INDUSTRIAL DESIGN COORDINATION (*not* DESIGNS (INDUSTRIAL PUBLICITY))

SERIALS CONTROL SYSTEMS (*not* CONTROL SYSTEMS (SERIALS))

3.   Subdivisions under a primary heading (preferred when practicable):

GEOGRAPHY – NETWORK ANALYSIS (*not* NETWORK ANALYSIS (GEOGRAPHY))

PUBLIC HEALTH – CITIZEN PARTICIPATION (*not* CITIZEN PARTICIPATION (PUBLIC HEALTH))

Where primary headings express concepts in more than one discipline, parenthetical qualifiers are used, although not always does more than one such qualifier appear with the potentially confusing word – e.g., "BANDS (MUSIC)."

Three situations are recognized in which it may be necessary to use parenthetical qualifiers:

1.   To specify a definition if several can be found in the dictionary (e.g., "ANALYSIS (PHILOSOPHY)")

2.   To remove ambiguity if other actual or possible terms or phrases exist (e.g., "CLUTTERING (SPEECH PATHOLOGY)")

3.   To make an obscure word or phrase more explicit (e.g., "PAPILLONS (DOGS)").[16]

INVERTED HEADINGS

We have already cited Haykin's emphasis on primary meaning in adjectival phrases. Inversions, while awkward syntactically (e.g., "AGED, WRITINGS OF THE, AMERICAN"), serve the alphabetico-classed function of subordinating specific descriptors under their broad generic categories (e.g., "EDUCATION, BILINGUAL" or "ASYLUM, RIGHT OF"). Here too, much inconsistency is apparent.

In the course of its efforts to modernize and systematize *LCSH*, the Library of Congress has made it a policy to create no more new inverted headings, with the following exceptions:

1.   Adjectives that represent:
    a) ethnic groups, e.g., MUSIC, KARNATIC
    b) nationalities, e.g., ART, FRENCH
    c) languages, e.g., PROSE POEMS, FRENCH
    d) time periods, e.g., LITERATURE, MODERN

2.   Situations where all the instances of the concept that already exist are in inverted form, e.g., INSURANCE, AERONAUTICAL

3.   A few other unique situations, e.g., PECCARIES, FOSSIL

LC occasionally changes an existing inverted heading, especially in cases where every instance of the concept but one is in direct order.[17]

SEMANTICS

Not only have syntactic forms of LC subject headings come under close scrutiny and revision in recent years, but *LCSH* terminology has been reconsidered. Word meanings, particularly their connotative aspects, mutate rapidly; social and political upheavals cause many changes, and scientific and technological developments account for many more. The problem of shifting terminology is particularly troublesome for a subject access list based on specific entry, avoidance of synonyms, and controlled cross references, designed for use with card or printed book catalogs.

A ringing complaint that *LCSH* terminology was obsolete and prejudicial came from Sanford Berman in 1971.[18] As Head of the Hennepin County, Minnesota, Library Catalog Department, Berman now edits the *HCL Cataloging Bulletin*, a bimonthly carrying lists of subject headings and cross references currently added to the HCL catalogs.[19] Most of these are more responsive to changes in usage than are the official additions and changes in *LCSH*.

Other writers have criticized the pedantic stance at the Library of Congress on conceptual and linguistic shifts. Doris Clack's 1975 analysis of black literature resources starts from a critique of LC subject analysis. She reminds us that:

> Inadequate subject analysis is not just a problem with black literature — though admittedly there the level of adequacy is critically low — nor has it only in recent years been brought to the attention of the library world.[20]

Clack devotes the bulk of her treatise to various lists of LC class numbers and subject terms from the black perspective. A classified "List of Relevant Subjects Included in the Library of Congress Classification Schedules and Appropriate Subject Headings" is followed by the list of "Relevant Library of Congress Subject Headings" (first in alphabetic, then in classified order) and then by lists of non-relevant LC class numbers and subject headings. Since her book was published the Library of Congress has made some changes. The one cited below involved changing approximately 12,000 cards:

> A basic function in the maintenance of a subject heading system is that of updating headings to conform to changing terminology or altered concepts. In general, the Library of Congress is and has been conservative in making changes since it involves altering reference structures surrounding a given heading as well as accommodating the change in both the card catalogs and the machine-readable data base. However, after a long period of great reluctance in effecting major changes, the Library has recently been involved in a number of changes represented in the following list . . .
>
> NEGROES. This heading discontinued February 1976.
> See AFRO-AMERICANS for later materials on the permanent residents of the United States. See BLACKS for later materials on persons outside the United States. . . .[21]

Reflecting a similar socio-linguistic revolution is Joan K. Marshall's 1977 critique of sex bias in *LCSH*.[22] She uses six principles developed by the American Library Association's Social Responsibilities Round Table Task Force Committee on Sexist Subject Headings to replace logically and consistently the guess-work which evolved over the years from Cutter's concern for the "convenience of the public." Basing her work on the six principles, she submits an alphabetical, annotated "Thesaurus for Nonsexist Indexing and Cataloging." As in the case of blacks, the Library of Congress has overhauled some of its more obsolete or offensive sexist headings. Annual *LCSH* supplements usually carry lists of the significant heading changes made during the year.

NEW HEADINGS

In addition to changing obsolete and outdated headings, the Library of Congress adds many new headings each year that reflect new topics appearing as the subjects of books cataloged at LC. *Cataloging Service Bulletin*, no. 19 (Winter 1982), began carrying a list of "new subject headings that represent popular trends or concepts."[23] The lists were not exhaustive and did not contain any scope notes or cross reference structure. For these it was necessary to wait until the new headings appeared in the quarterly supplement. This listing in *Cataloging Service Bulletin* was discontinued after no. 25 (Summer 1984) because of the beginning of a new publication: *Library of Congress Subject Headings Weekly Lists*.[24] This publication, available on subscription from the Cataloging Distribution Service, contains *all* new headings, changed headings, and cancelled headings approved by the LC Subject Cataloging Division, and includes reference structure and scope notes. These lists are issued long before the appearance of the headings in quarterly supplements or in the microform version of *LCSH*.

GENERAL PHYSICAL CHARACTERISTICS OF THE LIST

The present ninth edition carries a short introduction and a discussion of, and a list of, terms used by the Library of Congress in its Annotated Card Program for children's literature. The Annotated Card Program is discussed later in this chapter. The eighth edition had contained an extensive introduction that included lists of pattern headings and subdivisions with instructions for their use. Because the ninth edition was printed on short notice (funds became available if publication could proceed quickly) and much of the introductory matter was not in machine-readable form, most of it was omitted. However, in 1981, *Library of Congress Subject Headings: A Guide to Subdivision Practice* was published. It consisted of sections drawn from previous publications: introduction from the ninth edition, lists of subdivisions from the 1979 annual supplement, and scope notes for subdivisions from the eighth edition. The most recent aid to use of *LCSH* is the *Subject Cataloging Manual: Subject Headings*, published in 1984.[25] This looseleaf publication reproduces guidelines given to subject catalogers at LC and describes procedures those catalogers should use in various situations. The knowledge of LC subject heading practice that can be gleaned from this publication assists other catalogers to make their work mesh with that from LC, assists public service librarians to develop successful subject search strategies, and assists library school students in learning subject cataloging "rules."

FILING

The list proper is given in alphabetical order. Filing rules were revised for the eighth edition, to facilitate computer manipulation, and the revised rules continue to be used in the ninth edition and in the microfiche version. Basic arrangement is word by word. Numbers given in digits precede alphabetic characters in the order of increasing value. Initials separated by punctuation file as separate words. Abbreviations without interior punctuation file as single whole words:

> 4-H CLUBS
> A-36 (Fighter-bomber planes)
>   *See* MUSTANG (FIGHTER PLANES)
> A.D.C. *See* CHILD WELFARE
> A PRIORI
> A3D bomber *See* SKYWARRIOR BOMBER
> A4D bomber *See* SKYHAWK BOMBER
> Aage family *See* AGEE FAMILY
> ACI test *See* ADULT-CHILD INTERACTION TEST
> ACTH
> AK 8 MOVING-PICTURE CAMERA
> ALASKA
> ALGOL (COMPUTER PROGRAM LANGUAGE)

Punctuation of subject terms affects filing order more immediately than it does in lists such as *Sears*, which sacrifice categorical to straight alphabetical arrangement. LC subject headings which contain subordinate elements preceded by one or more dashes fall into three groups:

a) period subdivisions (MARC subfield $y), arranged chronologically according to explicit dates, regardless of whether a descriptive term is used,

b) form and topical subdivisions (MARC subfield $x), arranged alphabetically, and

c) geographical subdivisions (MARC subfield $z), arranged alphabetically.

The secondary subdivisions under "UNITED STATES—Foreign relations" faithfully illustrate all three groups in order:

a)   UNITED STATES—Foreign relations—Revolution, 1775-1783
      UNITED STATES—Foreign relations—1783-1865
      UNITED STATES—Foreign relations—Constitutional period, 1789-1809
      UNITED STATES—Foreign relations—War of 1898

b)   UNITED STATES — Foreign relations — Executive agreements
UNITED STATES — Foreign relations — Historiography
UNITED STATES — Foreign relations — Juvenile literature
UNITED STATES — Foreign relations — Law and legislation
UNITED STATES — Foreign relations — Speeches in Congress
UNITED STATES — Foreign relations — Treaties
c)   UNITED STATES — Foreign relations — Canada
UNITED STATES — Foreign relations — France
UNITED STATES — Foreign relations — Japan
UNITED STATES — Foreign relations — Russia

In actual practice these three groups generally collapse into two, for nearly all period subdivisions follow such topical subdivisions as "—Civilization," "—Economic conditions," "—Politics and government," or "—History." All period subdivisions have explicit dates to allow for computer filing:

UNITED STATES — History — 1849-1877
UNITED STATES — History — Civil War, 1861-1865
UNITED STATES — History — 1865-
UNITED STATES — History — 1865-1898
UNITED STATES — History — 1865-1921

Prior to 1974 period subdivisions were sometimes indicated only by descriptive terminology (e.g., UNITED STATES — History — Civil War), and one may still find these forms in old card catalogs.

All subject subdivisions (identified by dashes) file ahead of inverted modifiers, which are punctuated by commas. Inverted modifiers, in turn, file ahead of parenthetical qualifiers. Last of all come phrases which start with the primary term:

CHILDREN
CHILDREN — Attitudes
CHILDREN — Growth
CHILDREN — Quotations
CHILDREN, ADOPTED
CHILDREN, FIRST-BORN
CHILDREN, VAGRANT
CHILDREN (CHRISTIAN THEOLOGY)
CHILDREN (INTERNATIONAL LAW)
CHILDREN (ROMAN LAW)
CHILDREN AND ANIMALS
CHILDREN AND STRANGERS
CHILDREN AS WITNESSES
CHILDREN IN LITERATURE
CHILDREN OF WORKING MOTHERS

SYNDETIC (CROSS REFERENCE) FEATURES

All primary subject terms appear in boldface roman type. All subdivisions and cross reference tracings, as well as cross references interfiled with the main headings, are in lightface roman type. The directions "sa" (*see also*), "x" (refer from: *see* tracings), and "xx" (refer from: *see also* tracings) are given in lightface italics. The code "sa" means that the term on that line and all the terms that follow until the code changes are terms that are related in some way to the primary term (usually either more specific or on the same level of specificity), and that there should be an instruction in the catalog to "see also" the term(s). The code "x" is a tracing that identifies the term(s) under which one will find a reference to "see" this primary term. These terms are ones that will not be used as headings on bibliographic records. Only the term(s) to which they refer are so used. The code "xx" is a tracing that identifies the term(s) under which one will find a "see also" reference to this primary term. These terms are also related to the primary term in some way (usually they are either more general or on the same level of specificity). Note that the codes appear only once under a primary term and are implied for the headings that follow until the code changes. The following examples illustrate their usage:

EXAMPLE 1

ISOTOPE GEOLOGY
    sa   Radioisotopes in geology
    x   Nuclear geophysics
    xx   Radioactivity

The symbol "sa" is read just as it is written, i.e.,

ISOTOPE GEOLOGY
    sa   Radioisotopes in geology

is read as:

ISOTOPE GEOLOGY
  see also RADIOISOTOPES IN GEOLOGY

The "x" and "xx" symbols are read in inverted order, beginning with the element following the "x" or "xx." Thus,

ISOTOPE GEOLOGY
    x   Nuclear geophysics

is read as:

Nuclear geophysics
    see   ISOTOPE GEOLOGY

and

ISOTOPE GEOLOGY
    xx   Radioactivity

is read as:

RADIOACTIVITY
    see also ISOTOPE GEOLOGY

EXAMPLE 2

ART, MODERN (*Indirect*)
    sa   Gothic revival (Art)
             Neoclassicism (Art)
    x   Modern art
    xx   Arts, Modern

The "*sa* Gothic revival (Art)
    Neoclassicism (Art)"

means that if a local catalog has subject entries under the three headings "ART, MODERN," "GOTHIC REVIVAL (ART)," and "NEOCLASSICISM (ART)," then LC recommends a reference:

ART, MODERN
  see also
GOTHIC REVIVAL (ART)
NEOCLASSICISM (ART)

If the library lacks entries under "GOTHIC REVIVAL (ART)," then that heading would be omitted from the reference. The same would be true for "NEOCLASSICISM (ART)." If both headings were lacking, then the reference should not be made at all.

Suppose next that the local catalog has a different book under "ARTS, MODERN." The "*xx* Arts, Modern" reminds us that we should make a reference: "ARTS, MODERN *see also* ART, MODERN." If we check the subject list under "ARTS, MODERN" exactly such a reference can be found, among other *sa* listings, as follows:

ARTS, MODERN (*Indirect*)
   sa   Art, Modern
        Gothic revival (Art)
        Literature, Modern

On the other hand, assume that the local catalog has no materials under "ARTS, MODERN." Strictly speaking, it would be inaccurate to make a reference reading "ARTS, MODERN *see also* ART, MODERN." Some theorists argue that it is nonetheless "administratively justifiable" to make such *see also* references, on the assumption that the term referred from will eventually be activated.[26] Even if it is not, they say, the reference serves to move users from a term not included to one where there may be pertinent materials. Other libraries convert such ambiguous *see also* into *see* references, e.g., "ARTS, MODERN *see* ART, MODERN." If the term referred from is later activated, they then add the word "*also*" to the "*see*" on the card.

As for the *x* tracings, there is never any danger of ambiguity in converting them to the *see* references for which they stand. The "*x* Modern Art" means simply that the subject list includes, in proper alphabetic order, an entry which reads: "Modern Art *see* Art, Modern."

Authority records for subjects in MARC format contain only *x* and *xx* references (found in the 4xx and 5xx fields, respectively). In an automated system, if all appropriate *xx* references are made, the *sa* references are automatically taken care of.

One additional type of reference is found in *LCSH*: the general reference. A general *see also* reference was made in the past in order to suggest more specific headings that should also be sought. For example:

PLASTICS
   sa   *names of plastics*, e.g., Bakelite, Celluloid, Nylon,
          Plexiglas

These general references were given in the list in the past in order to save space. LC actually makes individual references in its catalogs, and it has abandoned the practice of making general references of this type for new headings, although existing general references of this type are being retained. General *see also* references continue to be made for references to subdivisions that are free-floating, references to categories of name headings, and references to groups of headings that all begin with the same word. Examples:

LAW
   sa   subdivision Law and legislation under topics

BASEBALL CLUBS
   sa   names of individual baseball teams

SCIENCE
   sa   headings beginning with the word Scientific[27]

A number of writers have criticized *LCSH*'s syndetic structure and its lack of ability to show hierarchical relationships. Coates wrote in 1960 that *LCSH* merely linked an "indeterminate selection" of related terms—that at times there was more than one level of hierarchy in a list under one primary term, while at other times intermediate hierarchical terms were omitted from the chain of references.[28] Sinkankis demonstrated in his 1972 study, in which he followed the "see alsos" under the heading "Hunting," that a user was quickly led away from the subject. By following the references he was led to "Migrant labor," "Pimps," "Liturgy and drama," and "Panic," among other terms.[29] Petersen wrote in 1983 that during a project to create the Art and Architecture Thesaurus, the designers chose to keep *LCSH* terms as a base and to modify and expand them. But the "see alsos" and "see also froms" in *LCSH* had to be ignored because they could not be converted to broader, narrower, and related terms. There were too many types of reference present.[30]

LC has recognized the problems but has generally not eliminated cross references created in the past; staff time has not been available for "clean-up" projects. However, beginning late in 1984, subject catalogers at LC put into effect a fairly strict policy for creating new cross references for all *new* headings created. The general rule is to make a *see also* reference from the class of which the heading is a class member (e.g., CINEMATOGRAPHY, *xx* PHOTOGRAPHY), to make a reference for a whole/part relationship (e.g., TOES, *xx* FOOT), and to make a reference for cases in which a specific heading is an instance or example of a broader category (e.g., ERIE, LAKE, *xx* LAKES—UNITED STATES). Broader term *xx*'s are made only from the next broader level in a hierarchy. Related terms (shown by a *sa* and *xx* involving the same heading) are used to link two headings not in the same hierarchy (e.g., a concept and an object). Related terms are required in the definition of each other, making the relationship obvious (for example, "BANKERS" and "BANKS AND BANKING").[31]

CLASSIFICATION AIDS

Many primary subject terms, and some subject subdivisions under those terms, are accompanied by LC classification notations. Sometimes more than one LC class notation is given, with a term from the schedule to show the various aspects of classification represented by the subject heading. Frequently a range of notations is supplied:

> CHESTNUT (*Indirect*) (*Botany, QK495.F14; Forestry, SD397.C5;*
> *Nut trees, SB401.C4*)
> *Example under* NUTS
> —Diseases and pests (*SB608.C45*)
> *sa names of pests, e.g.* CHESTNUT-BORER
>
> CHESTNUT-BLIGHT (*SB608.C45*)
> *Example under* PLANT DISEASES—EPIDEMICS
>
> HOBO SONGS (*M1977.H6; M1978.H6*)
>
> OPERA (*Indirect*) (*Aesthetics, ML3858; History and criticism,*
> *ML1700-2110*)

These notations are usually supplied when a term is first established. Occasionally they are added at a later time. But there is no systematic checking or revision of these notations once supplied. Thus, a classification notation could be changed or its meaning revised in the LC Classification Schedules, but it would not be changed in *LCSH*. Therefore, these notations are only a guide and should not be assigned without verification.

SCOPE NOTES

Scope notes are sometimes inserted into the full list between subject terms and their suggested cross references. Such notes specify the range of application for a term or draw distinctions between related terms. Some libraries copy these notes on cards and file them in the catalog just ahead of the subject entries under the same heading. Other libraries provide one or more copies of *LCSH* near the catalog for reference use by patrons doing subject searches. A typical example of an entry with a scope note is the following:

> SEXISM (*Indirect*)
>   Here are entered works on sexism as an attitude as well as works on attitude and overt discriminatory behavior. Works dealing solely with discriminatory behavior directed toward both of the sexes are entered under SEX DISCRIMINATION.
>   *sa*   Sex discrimination
>   Sex role
>   *x*   Sex bias
>   *xx*   Attitude (Psychology)
>   Prejudices
>   Sex (Psychology)
>   Sex role
>   Social perception
>   Note under SEX DISCRIMINATION

GEOGRAPHIC SUBJECT HEADINGS
(MARC field 651)

Geographic, jurisdictional, and physiographic names form a large part of any library's subject network. *LCSH*, like most general subject lists, did not until recently include more than a few key examples to illustrate modes of entry and types of subdivision. Starting in 1976, newly established geographical names were listed in *LCSH* supplements and then incorporated into *LCSH 9*. However, these names were not in *AACR 2* form; so no new ones were listed between 1979 and 1981. After establishing a policy for constructing geographic names in *AACR 2* form, the policy of printing the names was reinstated, and newly established names now appear in supplements and the microform cumulations. Many geographic names in *LCSH 9* are pre-*AACR 2* and should not be used. For example:

ARDINGLY, ENG.
BARAČKO LAKE, BOSNIA AND HERZEGOVINA
BYZANTINE EMPIRE
CAPE OF GOOD HOPE
CHICAGO
CLINTON, IOWA
CLOUD PEAK PRIMITIVE AREA, WYO.
FLINT RIVER WATERSHED, MICH.

Only those headings not requiring qualifiers can still be used in the form
shown above (e.g., BYZANTINE EMPIRE and CAPE OF GOOD HOPE).
The others shown above should now appear as:

ARDINGLY (WEST SUSSEX)
BARAČKO LAKE (BOSNIA AND HERZEGOVINA)
CHICAGO (ILL.)
CLINTON (IOWA)
CLOUD PEAK PRIMITIVE AREA (WYO.)
FLINT RIVER WATERSHED (MICH.)

Names of jurisdictions are established in the Descriptive Cataloging
Division and can be verified in Name Authorities. Therefore, they are printed
in *LCSH* only when needed in order to add a topical subdivision (e.g.,
CHICAGO (ILL.) — Haymarket Square Riot, 1886).

Since 1972 the Library of Congress has assigned to all material of local
historical or genealogical interest at least one subject heading in which a place
name is the first element. Place names reflecting political or jurisdictional
changes are incorporated as rapidly as the work-load permits. Such changes
usually have the greatest impact on descriptive cataloging, but many are also
important for establishing subject entries. Special attention has been given to
reconstructing headings for Taiwan, the People's Republic of China, Czecho-
slovakia, Poland, Germany, and Korea. Since 1975, LC accepts decisions of
the National Library of Canada on forms for Canadian corporate names,
including place names.

When the name of a country, state, city, etc., has been changed without
substantially affecting the jurisdictional area covered, LC's subject policy is to
make all subject entries under the new name regardless of the time period
covered. Subject entries under an old name are changed to the new name.
These changes are referred to as "linear name changes."[32] This policy is
followed regardless of whether the government changed the jurisdiction name
or the change was made to accommodate cataloging rules. Examples:

Old Form	Latest Name/form
Congo (Democratic Republic)	Zaire
British Honduras	Belize
Argentine Republic	Argentina
Germany, West (used only as a subject)	Germany (West)

With the implementation of *AACR 2*, the policy of using as a subject heading a term not used as an author entry was abandoned. For example, the subject heading "Germany, West" was used from 1975 through 1980 instead of "Germany (Federal Republic, 1949-)." With *AACR 2* the form is "Germany (West)" for both author and subject headings.[33]

GEOGRAPHIC SUBDIVISIONS
(MARC subfield $z)

The examples in the section on classification aids show how the LC subject list authorizes local catalogers to supply geographic subdivisions. The code word "Indirect" in parentheses after any entry tells us that place names may be added without having been spelled out in the list. Indirect subdivision means that the elements of the geographic name are to be arranged hierarchically, with a broader place name preceding the local name, e.g., "CHESTNUT—Oregon—Portland." Each sequential part of the subdivision is filed in its proper alphabetical order, regardless of its political, administrative, or regional scope.

Formerly, "direct" subdivision was allowed. This meant that the place name was written as it would be written to address a letter (e.g., OPERA—Santa Fe, N.M.). Late in 1976, "direct" subdivision was abandoned, although there are a few exceptions, which are well defined. The advantage of indirect subdivision is the collocation of material on one topic in one country or state, while direct subdivision separated such material by the first letters of the names of cities. On the other hand indirect subdivision can sometimes be difficult to apply (e.g., when a geographic entity falls within two countries), whereas direct subdivision allowed use of the established name without alteration.

The following are subdivided "direct" in exception to the "indirect" policy:

Names of countries
Names of geographical entities not wholly within one country
Names of first order subdivisions (e.g., states) of the United States, Soviet Union, Canada, and Great Britain. (While there are seven countries that are qualified by first-order subdivision rather than country under *AACR 2*, only four of these are subdivided indirectly this way.)
Inverted terms with name of the country, etc., first (e.g., —Italy, Northern)
Four cities: New York, Berlin, Washington, and Jerusalem. (Hong Kong and Vatican City are treated as countries.)
Islands "at a distance" from "owning" land masses.

The following list shows some results of the above policy:

CATHOLIC CHURCH—France—Paris
EXPEDITIONS—Pyrenees (France and Spain)
CHILDREN—Ontario—Toronto

CHILDREN—Australia—New South Wales [only two levels are allowed;
   so a city in New South Wales would follow "Australia—":
   CHILDREN—Australia—Newcastle (N.S.W.)]
EDUCATION—New York (N.Y.)
GEOLOGY—Islands of the Aegean
GEOLOGY—Indonesia—Ambon Island

For geographic subdivisions, as for geographic headings, local name
changes are observed. For instance, works which formerly would have
received the heading "BANKS AND BANKING—Leopoldville, Belgian
Congo" are now found under "BANKS AND BANKING—Zaire—Kinshasa."
The Library of Congress finds it less disruptive to keep subdivisions updated
en masse, although in practice all geographic subdivisions have not been
changed when a name is changed because of the difficulty of finding all
occurrences of, for example, "Belgian Congo" used as a subdivision. Its
dilemma is aggravated by critics on both sides of the issue. Some feel that all
headings should be changed immediately when a name change occurs. Others
object to the work involved in making such changes "regardless of the form of
the name used in the work cataloged."[34]
   If both local and topical, or form, subdivisions are established in the same
heading, the last provision for indirect subdivision prevails. For example, the
subject heading "Children" may be subdivided geographically. The subdivision
"costume" is not divided. Therefore, a correct heading would be:

CHILDREN—Illinois—Costume

The subdivision "Dental care" *is* divided. Therefore, a correct heading
would be:

CHILDREN—Dental care—Illinois

Other explanations and illustrations of geographic headings and
subdivision practice are issued from time to time. Their best sources are the
Cataloging Service Bulletin, the introductory pages of the *LCSH* paper supplements, and the *Subject Cataloging Manual: Subject Headings*.

HEADINGS OMITTED FROM *LCSH*

A troublesome corollary of the principle of specific entry is the inevitable,
and seemingly endless, proliferation of subject terms for individual members
of certain subject categories. Until recently the Library of Congress omitted
from its printed list a wide variety of such terms, which it nonetheless uses for
subject headings. The term "omitted" is not strictly correct: these terms were
included in the library's official records but were not spelled out in the printed
editions of *LCSH*. For a time they were referred to as "nonprint headings," but
this was a source of confusion because most catalogers associate "nonprint"
with audiovisual and other nonbook formats. In the *Subject Cataloging
Manual* they are referred to as "unprinted headings."[35] The only headings that
are now "unprinted" are:

"Most author headings, including anonymous works in general, motion
  pictures, radio and tv programs, etc. However, some personal and
  corporate headings are included in the list primarily for illustration.
Individually named art collections based on a personal name.
Regions of cities and metropolitan areas."[36]

There are also some music headings that are unprinted.[37] Even though
formerly unprinted headings are now being printed, one will not find all such
authorized headings in the lists. They are being added as used. Therefore,
many headings in such categories as family names, parks, buildings, and
mythological characters, that have been used by LC in the past, do not yet
appear in the printed *LCSH*.

FREE-FLOATING SUBDIVISIONS
(MARC subfield $x)

For many kinds of primary headings (both those dropped from *LCSH 8*
and those faithfully listed) there are a number of identical, or nearly identical,
subdivisions which can be applied as needed, whether or not they are all
written into the published *List*. These are collectively designated "free-
floating," but they may not be assigned indiscriminately, for they fall into different groups, each with its own rules and examples.

GENERAL FREE-FLOATING SUBDIVISIONS

General free-floating subdivisions are listed in *Library of Congress
Subject Headings: A Guide to Subdivision Practice*. This work also includes a
reprint of the scope notes for these subdivisions that appeared in the eighth
edition of *LCSH*. The subdivisions may be used as required within the limits
allowed by the scope notes. Because the scope notes date from 1974, some
have been superseded by more current policies.[38] The scope notes section
includes standard subdivision terms followed by scope notes and suggested
cross references, in similar format to the full subject list, except that scope
notes play a more prominent role than in the list proper. One example of a
commonly used division is:

STATISTICS, VITAL
   Use as a form subdivision under names of regions, countries,
cities, etc., as well as under names of ethnic groups, for
compilations of birth, marriage, and death statistics.
        sa   Mortality
               Population
               Statistics, Medical
        x   Vital statistics

A cumulative list of most commonly used subdivisions appeared in
Cataloging Service Bulletin.[39] This list updates the list in the *Guide* but does
not include scope notes and references.

PATTERN HEADINGS

Pattern headings are examples of a particular primary heading type which have been entered into the published *List* to show all the possible subdivisions which might be used with other specific headings of the same type. A very few may not even apply to the heading under which they are found. For instance, under "SHAKESPEARE, WILLIAM, 1564-1616" a scope note warns us:

> The subdivisions provided under this heading represent for the greater part standard subdivisions useable under all literary author headings and may not necessarily pertain to Shakespeare.

Besides personal names, several other categories of specific subjects have distinctive sets of subdivisions applicable to all examples of their genre. These include such categories as educational institutions, monastic and religious orders, languages, musical instruments, industries, military services, animals, diseases, philosophers, and sports. Most are represented by an example or two embedded in the published *List*, but for the uninitiated user they could be hard to find. The most current source for identifying pattern headings is the *Subject Cataloging Manual: Subject Headings*. The following table shows some of the pattern headings available:

SUBJECT FIELD	CATEGORY	PATTERN HEADING(S)
Philosophy and religion	Philosophers	Thomas, Aquinas, Saint
	Founders of religions	Jesus Christ
	Theological topics	Salvation
History and geography	Rulers, statesmen, etc.	Lincoln; Washington; Napoleon I
Recreation	Sports	Soccer
Social Sciences	Individual schools	Harvard University
The arts	Music compositions	Operas
Science and technology	Organs and regions of the body	Heart; Foot

Thus, if one were cataloging a work about "football" it would be appropriate to find "Soccer" in *LCSH* and choose appropriate subdivisions found there to be used with the heading "Football." General free-floating subdivisions are not usually printed under pattern headings, but they may also be used as appropriate.[40]

SUBDIVISIONS UNDER PLACE NAMES

To encourage correct expansion of geographic headings without identifying every unique possibility, LC developed three standard lists: one to use with specific names of regions, countries, states, etc.; one to use under names of cities; and a third to use under names of bodies of water. These lists are printed in *Library of Congress Subject Headings: A Guide to Subdivision Practice* and are supplemented in the *LCSH* 1982 supplement. They may also be found in *Subject Cataloging Manual: Subject Headings*. In the summer of 1985 the list for use under cities was cancelled, but card catalogs will continue to reflect the effects of its use for many years. The list for use under cities contained a number of terms that were (and still are) acceptable as subject headings alone and could be subdivided geographically "(*Indirect*)." When this situation occurred, the heading could not be divided down to the city level, but was used as a subdivision under the name of the city, e.g., CHICAGO (ILL.) – BUILDINGS (*not* BUILDINGS – ILLINOIS – CHICAGO, even though the heading "Buildings (*Indirect*)" was, and still is, in the list). This phenomenon was referred to as "the city flip."[41] Headings formerly treated under "the city flip" are now either given as subdivisions under the subdivision "History" for a city, or the city is given as an indirect subdivision under the term that was formerly a subdivision.[42]

PHRASE HEADINGS

In free-floating phrase headings it is the initial word which changes. This type is still limited to a very few pattern phrases. The following are listed in the *Subject Cataloging Manual*:

[personal name] in fiction, drama, poetry, etc.
    e.g., JESUS CHRIST IN FICTION, DRAMA, POETRY, ETC.

[topic or name heading (except personal names)] in literature
    e.g., HORSES IN LITERATURE

[topic or name heading (except personal names)] in art
    e.g., MANHATTAN (NEW YORK, N.Y.) IN ART

[name of city] Metropolitan Area ([geographical qualifier])
    e.g., CHICAGO METROPOLITAN AREA (ILL.)

[name of city] Region ([geographical qualifier])
    e.g., DALLAS REGION (TEX.)

[name of geographic feature] Region ([geographic qualifier, if part of the name as established])
    e.g., HIMALAYA MOUNTAINS REGION

[name of river] Estuary [Region, Watershed, or Valley] ([geographic qualifier, if part of name as established])
    e.g., KOBUK RIVER VALLEY (ALASKA)[43]

The local cataloger should not take any other "... IN ..." phrase found in *LCSH* as a pattern phrase. For example, the heading "COLOR IN CLOTH-ING" does not of itself give license to coin other phrases ending with "... IN CLOTHING." The Library of Congress formerly used pattern phrases of the form "... AS A PROFESSION" (e.g., "MEDICINE AS A PROFESSION"). It now uses the subdivision "— Vocational guidance" instead (e.g., "MEDICINE — Vocational guidance").

SUBJECT HEADINGS FOR
CHILDREN'S LITERATURE
(2nd MARC indicator 1 in 650 field)

Since 1965 the Library of Congress has issued a special service for children's catalogers. Known as the Annotated Card Program, it provides "more appropriate and in-depth subject treatment of juvenile titles."[44] A list of specially tailored subject headings is accompanied by a review of commonly used subdivisions, another of subdivisions and qualifiers not used, and general instructions for applying and modifying standard LC subject terms. The Library's printed cards carry the children's heading forms in brackets. In the MARC format they are tagged specifically as subject terms for children. Some comparative examples are:

LCSH 9	Annotated Card List
ACROBATS AND ACROBATISM	ACROBATS AND ACROBATICS
ALPINE FAUNA	ALPINE ANIMALS
FIRE-ENGINES	FIRE ENGINES
PHYTOGEOGRAPHY	PLANT DISTRIBUTION
PICTURE-BOOKS FOR CHILDREN	PICTURE BOOKS
ZOOGEOGRAPHY	ANIMAL DISTRIBUTION

CONCLUSION

In spite of perennial criticisms on grounds of its outdated terminology, illogical syntax, and general inefficiency for precise subject retrieval, *LCSH* is the most widely accepted controlled vocabulary list in use in English-language libraries today. The Library of Congress, with considerable prompting from interested bystanders, now and again assesses its virtues and disadvantages, in comparison with other, more scientifically constructed systems. PRECIS (Preserved Context Index System), inaugurated for the *British National Bibliography* in 1971, received perhaps the strongest consideration as an alternative to, if not a replacement for, *LCSH*. After cost studies, however, the decision went against any such replacement or supplement. Instead, more intensive efforts are under way to modernize and systematize the existing tool. Many of the features discussed in this chapter represent steps in that direction. For the foreseeable future, this venerable subject list gives every sign of retaining its vitality and preeminence for subject access to library collections.

NOTES

[1]Library of Congress, Subject Cataloging Division, *Library of Congress Subject Headings*, 9th ed. (Washington, D.C., The Library, 1980), 2v. and suppls.

[2]*Supplement to Library of Congress Subject Headings*, 1979-date.

[3]*Library of Congress Subject Headings in Microform* (current issue supersedes all previous issues).

[4]*Canadian Subject Headings* (Ottawa, National Library of Canada, 1978); *Canadian Subject Headings: Additions, Changes and Corrections to Canadian Subject Headings* (Ottawa, National Library of Canada, 1981).

[5]Minnie Earl Sears, *Sears List of Subject Headings*, 12th ed., edited by Barbara M. Westby (New York, H. W. Wilson, 1982).

[6]Charles A. Cutter, *Rules for a Dictionary Catalog*, 4th ed., rewritten (Washington, D.C., GPO, 1904; republished, London, The Library Association, 1953). The original version of this work was: Charles A. Cutter, "Rules for a Printed Dictionary Catalogue," in *Public Libraries in the United States of America: Their History, Condition, and Management*, United States Bureau of Education (Washington, D.C., GPO, 1876), Part II.

[7]For fuller information on the origin and development of the *LC Subject List*, see: Lois Mai Chan, *Library of Congress Subject Headings: Principles and Application*, 2nd ed. (Littleton, Colo., Libraries Unlimited, 1985); and Richard S. Angell, "Library of Congress Subject Headings — Review and Forecast," in *Subject Retrieval in the Seventies: New Directions*, edited by Hans (Hanan) Wellisch and Thomas D. Wilson (Westport, Conn., Greenwood Publishing Co., 1972), pp. 143-163.

[8]J. C. M. Hanson, "The Subject Catalogs of the Library of Congress," *Bulletin of the American Library Association* 3 (September 1909): 385-397. Further citations to this article will be documented only by page number, which will be included parenthetically in the text.

[9]Cutter, *Rules*, 4th ed., pp. 71-72.

[10]Chan, *Library of Congress*, pp. 48-59.

[11]*Subject Cataloging Manual: Subject Headings* (Washington, D.C., Library of Congress, 1984), H290, p. 1.

[12]David Judson Haykin, *Subject Headings: A Practical Guide* (Washington, D.C., GPO, 1951), pp. 21-22.

[13]*Subject Cataloging Manual*, H310, pp. 1-2.

[14]The two new headings replacing the older compound heading are BUDDHISM and GAUTAMA BUDDHA.

[15]*Subject Cataloging Manual*, H360, p. 1.

[16]*Subject Cataloging Manual*, H357, pp. 1-2.

[17]Personal communication with Mary K. D. Pietris, Chief, Subject Cataloging Division, Library of Congress, June 1985.

[18]Sanford Berman, *Prejudices and Antipathies: A Tract on the LC Subject Heads Concerning People* (Metuchen, N.J., Scarecrow, 1971).

[19]Hennepin County Library, Cataloging Section, *Cataloging Bulletin*, May 1973- .

[20]Doris H. Clack, *Black Literature Resources: Analysis and Organization* (New York, Marcel Dekker, 1975), p. 10.

[21]*Cataloging Service*, bulletin 119 (Fall 1976): 22, 24.

[22]Joan K. Marshall, comp., *On Equal Terms: A Thesaurus for Nonsexist Indexing and Cataloging* (Santa Barbara, Calif., American Bibliographical Center—Clio Press, 1977).

[23]*Cataloging Service Bulletin*, no. 19 (Winter 1982): 3.

[24]*Library of Congress Subject Headings Weekly Lists* (January 1984-).

[25]Library of Congress, Subject Cataloging Division, *Subject Cataloging Manual: Subject Headings*, Prelim. ed. (Washington, D.C., Library of Congress, 1984).

[26]See, for example, *Anglo-American Cataloging Rules: North American Text* (Chicago, American Library Association, 1967), p. 173, footnote 1.

[27]*Subject Cataloging Manual*, H373, pp. 1-3.

[28]E. J. Coates, *Subject Catalogues: Headings and Structure* (London, The Library Association, 1960).

[29]George M. Sinkankis, "A Study in the Syndetic Structure of the Library of Congress List of Subject Headings" (Pittsburgh, University of Pittsburgh, 1972).

[30]Toni Petersen, "The AAT: A Model for the Restructuring of LCSH," *Journal of Academic Librarianship* 9 (September 1983): 207-210.

[31]*Regional Institute on Library of Congress Subject Headings Handbook* (Chicago, American Library Association, 1984), p. 210.

[32]*Regional Institute ... Handbook*, p. 88.

[33]Ibid.

[34]*Cataloging Service*, bulletin 120 (Winter 1977): 10.

[35]*Subject Cataloging Manual*, H198, p. 1.

[36]*Regional Institute ... Handbook*, p. 113.

[37]*LCSH 9*, p. viii.

[38]*Regional Institute ... Handbook*, p. 24.

[39]*Cataloging Service Bulletin*, no. 26 (Fall 1984): 35-39.

[40]*Subject Cataloging Manual*, H1146, pp. 1-4.

[41]*Regional Institute ... Handbook*, p. 59.

[42]Personal communication with Mary K. D. Pietris, Chief, Subject Cataloging Division, Library of Congress, July 1985.

[43]*Subject Cataloging Manual*, H362, pp. 1-2.

[44]*LCSH 9*, p. xiii.

SUGGESTED READING

Chan, Lois Mai. *Library of Congress Subject Headings: Principles and Application*. 2nd ed. Littleton, Colo., Libraries Unlimited, 1985.

Foskett, A. C. *The Subject Approach to Information*. 4th ed. London, Bingley, 1982. Chapter 22.

23
Sears List of
Subject Headings

INTRODUCTION

The *Sears List of Subject Headings,* now in its twelfth edition, is widely used by small public libraries and by school libraries. It is very much smaller in scope and more general in treatment than *Library of Congress Subject Headings* (*LCSH*), which is commonly used in academic and research libraries. Its history of continuous publication is not so long-standing as that of the LC list, but its first edition is now over sixty years old:

> Minnie Earl Sears prepared the first edition of this work in response to demands for a list of subject headings that was more suitable to the needs of the small library than the A.L.A. and the Library of Congress lists. Published in 1923 the *List of Subject Headings for Small Libraries* was based on the headings used by nine small libraries that were known to be well cataloged. However, Minnie Sears early recognized the need for uniformity, and she followed the form of the Library of Congress subject headings with few exceptions. This decision was important and foresighted because it allowed a library to add Library of Congress headings as needed when not provided by the Sears List and to graduate to the full use of Library of Congress headings when collections grew too large for a limited subject heading list.[1]

The reliance of *Sears* editors and users on *LCSH* as a kind of sturdy big brother has never ceased. The following hypothetical situation should help make this clear. Suppose that a library using *Sears* acquires a book on the chemical effects of high energy radiation on matter. *Sears* offers the following headings:

RADIATION, which seems too broad
RADIATION — PHYSIOLOGICAL EFFECT, which seems too narrow
CHEMISTRY, PHYSICAL AND THEORETICAL, which seems much
  too broad
RADIOCHEMISTRY, which seems to fit the book's contents most
  closely.

However, the cataloger checks the library holdings for which the term
"RADIOCHEMISTRY" has been used, and finds that the new work has a
distinctly different focus. By consulting *LCSH* he or she learns that the difference is important enough to merit another heading "RADIATION CHEM-
ISTRY." A scope note carefully distinguishes it from "RADIOCHEMISTRY,"
making its application to the book at hand clear. The local library can
incorporate the borrowed term into its subject authority file, using the cross
references suggested by *LCSH* to relate it to existing *Sears* terminology.[2]

TERMINOLOGY

New headings for the twelfth edition of *Sears* were suggested by librarians
representing various sizes and types of libraries, and by H. W. Wilson
catalogers responsible for the Standard Catalog series and the *Book Review
Digest*. Wilson also publishes one special interest companion volume for
Canadian libraries.[3] *Sears* headings are based on *LCSH*, but modifications of
LC subject headings are made to meet the needs of smaller collections.
Included among these are many terms from LC's "Subject Headings for
Children's Literature." Terms considered by the editor to be sexist, racist, or
pejorative have been changed or eliminated. Aside from its comparative
brevity and simplicity, the following *Sears* differences from *LCSH* are worthy
of note:

    1. **More current terminology and spelling.** *Sears* uses
"CRISIS CENTERS" and "MOTION PICTURES"; *LCSH* uses
"CRISIS INTERVENTION (PSYCHIATRY)" and "MOVING-
PICTURES" as primary headings. Some more recently established
derivative headings, such as "SURREALISM IN MOTION
PICTURES," bear witness to its efforts to change.

    2. **Less emphasis on specificity.** *Sears* uses "SILK SCREEN
PRINTING"; *LCSH* uses only two narrower terms: "SCREEN
PROCESS PRINTING" and "SERIGRAPHY."

ELIMINATION OF RACIST, SEXIST, AND PEJORATIVE HEADINGS

The tenth edition of *Sears* was published in 1972, in the midst of considerable furor over the obsolescent, prejudicial terminology lingering in both
Sears and *LCSH*. A suggested list of terms relating to blacks was appended to
that edition. It reworded the older terms using "Negro" and related headings
which the editors presumably had not had time to expunge from the list

proper. The eleventh edition, published in 1977, eliminated the appendix and integrated the updated terms. For instance, "NEGRO POETRY" no longer appears anywhere in *Sears*, having fully given way to "BLACK POETRY."

Similar, though less sweeping, changes can be seen in older terminology which to modern ears would sound sexist. Thus, when the heading, "NEGRO ACTORS," was abandoned, it was replaced by "BLACK ACTORS AND ACTRESSES," while "AIR LINES—HOSTESSES" became "AIR LINES—FLIGHT ATTENDANTS."

Other headings with prejudicial connotations disappeared or underwent purification rites. The tenth edition's "JEWISH QUESTION" disappeared along with "WOMEN IN AERONAUTICS" and most other "WOMEN IN ..." and "WOMEN AS ..." headings. "UNDERDEVELOPED AREAS" was downgraded into a *see* reference to "DEVELOPING AREAS" in the eleventh edition and then changed to a *see* reference to "THIRD WORLD" in the twelfth edition. "INSANITY" was likewise converted into a *see* reference to "MENTAL ILLNESS—JURISPRUDENCE." "MAN, PRIMITIVE" became "MAN, NONLITERATE." (It is noted that "MAN" is to be used only in its anthropological and generic sense.)

PROBLEMS OF UPDATING TERMINOLOGY

Some linguistic change would have occurred, no doubt, regardless of the social climate. However, formal subject lists are notoriously conservative in their response to new terminology. In attempting to retain the goodwill of their constituents, they are understandably sensitive to the disruptions caused to a library's cataloging routines when an unduly large number of new subject forms are mandated at one time. Still, the argument that an obsolete form (e.g., "MOHAMMEDANISM" instead of the more acceptable "ISLAM") reflects usage in the bulk of the literature indexed is specious. Furthermore, it becomes misleading as new materials with new terminology are added. On the other hand, librarians fear not only the time and effort required to change large numbers of entries, but also the stresses placed on the filing apparatus when revised cards must be moved from one section of the catalog to another. As online catalogs become more numerous, this problem will be eased. However, the small libraries that use *Sears* are also the ones with the least amount of money to purchase online systems, and it will be a while longer before even a majority of them can boast online catalogs.

Various proposals have been advanced for coping with large-scale subject heading revision. Dowell (now Taylor) suggests three major options:[4]

1. For card catalogs, interfiling of "over-printed" cards (on which the subject term is printed above the main entry) or "highlighted" cards (on which one subject tracing is underlined for use as the filing element). Interfiling is seldom fully successful unless there is considerable erasing and retyping, although its purpose is to avoid just those problems. An analogous technique bypasses any marking of the subject entries themselves, preceding them instead with a "guide term" which, through typography or other marks of format and design, shows the full group of subject entries ranged behind or under it. The guide

term principle works better in book and microform catalogs, or machine-readable data bases, than for the more traditional card catalog.

2. Cross references connecting the old and revised heading forms. The *see also* references might well carry brief explanations, particularly showing the dates of publication, or of cataloging, covered by each form of the altered headings.

3. Changing old headings to the new forms. We have already suggested that the "interfiling" option for card catalogs usually requires some erasing and retyping of subject cards. The "full change" method extends such revisions to every entry affected by the new heading. Some libraries attempt to remove old markings and reword the entry. Others prepare complete new subject entries. Either mode involves labor that is both intensive and wasteful. As card catalogs gradually give way to online catalogs, the possibilities of quick, easy, and accurate subject heading change through computer programming looks more and more attractive.

SEARS' USE OF SUBJECT HEADING THEORY

The general philosophy of *Sears List of Subject Headings* is contained in two phrases, both of which the cataloger should remember as he or she makes specific application of the list to the individual materials in the library's collection.[5]

"The theory of specific entry" means that a specific heading is preferred to a general one. For a book about cats alone, "CATS" is preferred to "DOMESTIC ANIMALS." On the other hand, the headings "SIAMESE CATS" OR "SEAL-POINT SIAMESE CATS" would likely be too specific for most libraries, except possibly a veterinary library. The cataloger must know the collection, know its emphases, and know something of the way people use it, to be prepared to assign subject headings to it.

"The theory of unique heading" means that one subject heading, and one alone, is chosen for all items on that subject. The choice of subject headings must be logical and consistent. Cross references should be inserted in the catalog wherever it is anticipated that patrons are likely to approach the topic through different terminology. A few general principles or guidelines are useful for constructing subject headings:

1) Prefer the English word or phrase unless a foreign one best expresses the idea. *Sears*, for example, carries the reference "Laissez faire *see* INDUSTRY—GOVERNMENT POLICY."

2) Try to use terms that are used in other libraries as well, unless the library in question is highly specialized or otherwise unique.

3) Try to use terms that will cover the field, i.e., terms that will apply to more than one item.

4) Try to use no more than three subject headings per cataloged item. This rule is not tyrannical; some items may require more than three.

CROSS REFERENCES

Sears breaks down cross references into three main categories, and discusses each in some detail. Among them are seven varieties of *see* references, plus two broad classes of *see also* references.[6]

See references are considered essential to the success of the catalog. Yet the cataloger in a local library may not find necessary every *see* reference suggested in the list. For example, *Sears* proposes "Copybooks *see* HANDWRITING." But if the library's holdings on handwriting contain nothing about copybooks, then it is potentially misleading to put such a reference into the catalog. The most frequent and helpful varieties of *see* references direct the user from:

1)   Synonyms or terms so nearly synonymous that they would cover the same kind of material, e.g., "Chemical geology *see* GEOCHEMISTRY" and "Degrees of latitude and longitude *see* GEODESY."

2)   The second part of a compound heading, e.g., "Illusions *see* HALLUCINATIONS AND ILLUSIONS" and "Motels *see* HOTELS, MOTELS, ETC."

3)   The second part of an inverted heading, e.g., "Popular music *see* MUSIC, POPULAR (SONGS, ETC.)." *Sears* also suggests for this rather awkward subject heading, "Popular songs *see* MUSIC, POPULAR (SONGS, ETC.)" and "Songs, Popular *see* MUSIC, POPULAR (SONGS, ETC.)."

4)   Some inverted forms to the heading in normal order, e.g., "Libraries, Music *see* MUSIC LIBRARIES."

5)   Variant spellings (including initialisms) to the accepted spelling, e.g., "Gipsies *see* GYPSIES" and "K.K.K. *see* KU KLUX KLAN."

6)   Opposites when they are included without being specifically mentioned, e.g., "Disobedience *see* OBEDIENCE" and "Truth in advertising *see* ADVERTISING, FRAUDULENT."

7)   The singular to the plural when the two forms would not file together, e.g., "Goose *see* GEESE."

See also references pose theoretical and practical problems which jeopardize their efficacy. Yet both *Sears* and *LCSH* make heavy use of them. The above warning against making blind references simply because they are suggested in a standard list holds as true for *see also* references as it does for *see* references. There are two broad classes of *see also* references. We shall note that the second or "general" class proves especially resistant to adequate control:

1) Specific *see also* references. We found in chapter 21 that *see also* references normally move downward from a general term to a more specific term or terms, e.g., "CONSERVATION OF NATURAL RESOURCES *see also* ENERGY CONSERVATION; NATURE CONSERVATION." In this example the general term refers to two more specific terms. The user who pursues the reference by looking under "NATURE CONSERVATION" will find a still more specific downward reference to four more headings: "NATURE CONSERVATION *see also* LANDSCAPE PROTECTION; NATURAL MONUMENTS; RARE AND ENDANGERED SPECIES; WILDLIFE—CONSERVATION."

Sears also indulges in a high number of bilateral or duplicate references, where the movement is horizontal, between related subjects of more or less equal specificity. The following examples have been pruned of extraneous terms, to make their reciprocity more visible:

GODS *see also* MYTHOLOGY; RELIGIONS
MYTHOLOGY *see also* GODS
RELIGIONS *see also* GODS

MOLLUSKS *see also* SHELLS
SHELLS *see also* MOLLUSKS

2) General *see also* references. Here the more specific terms being referred to are so diverse or numerous that the standard list cites only one or two noteworthy illustrations, adding an "etc." to launch the cataloger on his or her own list of additional headings of similar format, as needed to describe the local library collection. The problem raised by these general or "blanket" references is one of control. When *Sears* uses "FORAGE PLANTS *see also* GRASSES . . . also names of specific forage plants, e.g. CORN; HAY; SOYBEAN; etc." but the only book in the library on a specific forage crop is on clover, it seems fairly obvious that the cataloger should change the illustration to read "FORAGE PLANTS *see also* GRASSES . . . also names of specific forage plants, e.g. CLOVER." Or perhaps the format could be simply "FORAGE PLANTS *see also* GRASSES; CLOVER."

If, on the other hand, there are books on several specific topics, not all of which serve as examples in the cross reference, should the cataloger add each new term at the time it first becomes a subject heading? That is, when the list gives "Illustrations *see* subjects with the subdivision *Pictorial Works*; e.g. ANIMALS—PICTORIAL WORKS; UNITED STATES—HISTORY—1861-1865, CIVIL WAR—PICTORIAL WORKS; etc." and the library which has subject entries for both referrals adds a book consisting largely of pictures of children, should the cataloger revise the reference entry by inserting "CHILDREN—PICTORIAL WORKS" as a third illustration?[7] Or can he or she depend on the "etc." to cover all subsequent examples? Most libraries follow the second option, thus throwing the burden of search on the user, who probably either will not understand the instructions or, after a bit of desultory searching, will give up. However well the user copes, valuable materials may be overlooked.[8]

Sears enumerates seven major types of general *see also* references:

1) Common names of different species of a class, e.g., "DOGS *see also* classes of dogs, e.g. GUIDE DOGS; HEARING EAR DOGS; etc.; also names of specific breeds, e.g. COLLIES; etc."

2) Names of individual persons, e.g., "PRESIDENTS – UNITED STATES *see also* names of presidents, e.g. LINCOLN, ABRAHAM; etc."

3) Names of particular institutions, buildings, societies, etc., e.g., "BRIDGES *see also* names of cities and rivers with the subdivision *Bridges* (e.g. CHICAGO (ILL.) – BRIDGES; HUDSON RIVER (N.Y.) – BRIDGES; etc.) also names of bridges, e.g. GOLDEN GATE BRIDGE (SAN FRANCISCO, CALIF.); etc."

4) Names of particular geographic features, e.g., "NATURAL MONU-MENTS *see also* WILDERNESS AREAS; also names of natural monuments, e.g. NATURAL BRIDGE (VA.); etc."

5) Geographic treatment of a general subject, e.g., "IMMIGRATION AND EMIGRATION *see also* ALIENS; ... also names of countries with the subdivision *Immigration and emigration* (e.g. UNITED STATES – IMMIGRATION AND EMIGRATION; etc.); names of countries, cities, etc. with the subdivision *Foreign population* (e.g. UNITED STATES – FOREIGN POPULATION; etc.); and names of nationality groups, e.g. MEXICAN AMERICANS; MEXI-CANS – UNITED STATES; etc."

6) Form divisions, e.g., "INDEXES *see also* SUBJECT HEADINGS; also subjects with the subdivision *Indexes*, e.g. NEWSPAPERS – INDEXES; PERIODICALS – INDEXES; SHORT STORIES – INDEXES; etc."

7) National literatures, e.g., "ESSAYS *see also* AMERICAN ESSAYS; ENGLISH ESSAYS; etc.; also general subjects with the subdivision *Addresses and essays*, e.g. AGRICULTURE – ADDRESSES AND ESSAYS; UNITED STATES – HISTORY – ADDRESSES AND ESSAYS; etc."

STRUCTURE OF SUBJECT HEADINGS

Like LC subject headings, *Sears* terms consist of a variety of forms, ranging from a single noun to different kinds of complex descriptive phrases:[9]

1) The single noun is the most desirable form of subject heading if it is specific enough to fit the item at hand and the needs of the library. This point was discussed earlier under "Theory of Specific Entry." In general, if there is a significant difference between the singular and plural forms, the plural is preferred (e.g., "MOUSE *see* MICE"). However, there are situations where the singular form is used to cover abstract ideas or general usage (e.g., "SONATA" as a musical form), while the plural designates individual examples of the form, frequently collected into anthologies or the like.

2)   The modified noun takes at least three forms: a) normal word order (e.g., "HEALTH MAINTENANCE ORGANIZATIONS"), b) inverted word order (e.g., "ARTIFICIAL SATELLITES, RUSSIAN"), and c) explanatory modifier added in parentheses (e.g., "HOTLINES (TELEPHONE COUN-SELING)"). There is usually no reliable way of predicting which form of modification will be used. Some topics, such as "EDUCATION," exhibit a luxuriant variety of forms (e.g., "ADULT EDUCATION," "EDUCATION, SECONDARY," and "PRISONERS—EDUCATION"). Some theorists try to justify these "inconsistencies," but for the most part they seem to be the result of habit and a reluctance to make extensive unnecessary changes.

3)   The compound heading is usually two nouns joined by "and," but the nouns are sometimes also modified (e.g., "COAL MINES AND MINING"). The terms are conjoined for various reasons:

a)   To link related topics. Usually both ideas are covered in a single treatise, e.g., "ANARCHISM AND ANARCHISTS," "BICYCLES AND BICYCLING," "CLOCKS AND WATCHES," and "PUPPETS AND PUPPET PLAYS."

b)   To link opposites. Again, the pairs are often discussed together, e.g., "CORROSION AND ANTICORROSIVES," "GOOD AND EVIL," and "JOY AND SORROW."

c)   To dispel ambiguity when the primary term is susceptible to more than one interpretation, e.g., "FILES AND FILING." The second term is added to distinguish storage files from the tools used by carpenters and mechanics. *LCSH*, as might be expected, is even more precise with these homonyms. It uses two subject headings: "FILES AND FILING (DOCUMENTS)" and "FILES AND RASPS."

In most cases, usage dictates the order of terms, but when that fails, alphabetical order is preferred. If a library should acquire enough materials under one of two such terms (e.g., "FRATERNITIES AND SORORITIES") to make searching difficult or tiresome, the cataloger might consider splitting the subject heading into its two components, with linking cross references. For example, *LCSH* has broken its former heading "ANTIGENS AND ANTIBODIES" into "ANTIGENS" and "IMMUNOGLOBULINS."

4) The phrase heading may be prepositional (e.g., "COST OF LIVING"), serial (e.g., "PLOTS (DRAMA, FICTION, ETC.)"), or an intriguing combination of forms (e.g., "INSECTS AS CARRIERS OF DIS-EASE" or "LIFE SUPPORT SYSTEMS (MEDICAL ENVIRONMENT)").

TYPES OF SUBDIVISIONS

Subject subdivisions indicate a specialized aspect of a broad subject or point of view, e.g., "RADIO—REPAIRING." They are set off from the primary heading by a dash, and are presumably distinguishable from inverted modifiers, which restrict or narrow the topic, e.g., "RADIO, SHORT WAVE." Yet *Sears* no longer separates the two categories, but interfiles them in straight alphabetical order, letter by letter to the end of each word, disregarding punctuation.[10] The only concession it makes to categorical filing is in alphabetizing all punctuated headings together under the primary entry word, following them with all phrase headings in a second alphabet, e.g.:

COOKERY
COOKERY, FRENCH
COOKERY — MAINE
COOKERY, MICROWAVE
COOKERY, OUTDOOR
COOKERY, QUANTITY
COOKERY — SOUTHERN STATES
COOKERY — VEGETABLES
Cookery for institutions, etc. *see* COOKERY, QUANTITY
COOKERY FOR THE SICK

The primary purpose of the subject subdivision is to group related materials in the catalog under one topic if it is quite broad, or if there is much written about it, e.g., "EDUCATION." That is, linguistic random access is partially replaced by a modified classing device. A patron seeking all available materials on "PHOTOGRAPHY" in a card catalog, for instance, would have to examine several different trays of cards from one end of the catalog to the other if subdivisions, inverted modifiers, and phrase headings were not clustered under that word in the standard lists.

Subdivisions may be compounded under a given topic. As many as three are used for such a subtopic as "UNITED STATES — HISTORY — 1861-1865, CIVIL WAR — MEDICAL AND SANITARY AFFAIRS." In it are displayed several of the different types of subdivisions:

1) Form divisions are used, like the Dewey Decimal Classification form divisions, to indicate the physical (e.g., "... — BIBLIOGRAPHY") or philosophical (e.g., "... — RESEARCH") form of the work. The twelfth edition of *Sears* gives a table of general form subdivisions which may be used by the cataloger to divide practically any subject heading in the list.[11] It may also be useful in some libraries to add form subdivisions that describe the physical format of nonbook materials. When this is desirable, *Sears* calls for using the general material designations given in *AACR 2*, e.g., "CATHEDRALS — SLIDE." The twelfth edition of *Sears* was the first to give suggestions for the handling of nonbook materials.[12]

2) Special topic divisions cannot so readily be transferred from one subject to another. *Sears* lists a basic group which, although not quite universal, may be applied by the cataloger to appropriate subject entries.[13] Still other subdivisions are specially tailored to bring out important aspects of individual topics, e.g., "CHILDREN — CARE AND HYGIENE" or "AIRPLANES — PILOTING." One could not reasonably use "CHILDREN — PILOTING" or "AIRPLANES — CARE AND HYGIENE." Such divisions are listed in full in the body of the list, being for the most part non-transferrable.

3) Time divisions, which apply most frequently to history, define a specific chronology for the primary topic. Some consist merely of dates (e.g., "EUROPE — HISTORY — 1789-1900"). Often the date or dates are followed by a descriptive phrase (e.g., "CHURCH HISTORY — ca. 30-600, EARLY CHURCH"). Prior to the twelfth edition the descriptive phrase preceded the dates in such headings. The change in position was made to facilitate filing in chronological order both manually and by machine. Occasionally the chronological designation is an inverted qualifier rather than a subdivision. It may be used without dates (e.g., "CIVILIZATION, ANCIENT"), but more often dates are added (e.g., "GETTYSBURG (PA.), BATTLE OF, 1863" and "WORLD WAR, 1939-1945").

4) Geographic divisions are of two forms: a) area — subject, e.g., "CHICAGO (ILL.) — FOREIGN POPULATION," and b) subject — area, e.g., "GEOLOGY — BOLIVIA." *Sears* adds parenthetical instructions to those headings in its list which may be divided by place, e.g., "GEOLOGY (May subdiv. geog.)." It should be noted that the form of such geographic subdivisions should be according to *AACR 2*: "CHICAGO (ILL.)," not just "CHICAGO" as appeared in editions preceding the twelfth. Under some headings the instructions are more detailed, e.g., "PARKS (May subdiv. geog. country or state) *see also* AMUSEMENT PARKS; ... also names of cities with the subdivision *Parks*, e.g. CHICAGO (ILL.) — PARKS; etc." Or the place term might be an inverted modifier, e.g., "ETHICS (May subdiv. geog. adjective form, e.g. ETHICS, JAPANESE; ETHICS, JEWISH; etc.)."

Area — subject situations are less conspicuous in the list, but play an important role in most library catalogs. Instructions may take the form: "ITALY ... May be subdivided like U.S. except for *History*." A similar example is: "NEUTRALITY *see also* names of countries with the subdivision *Neutrality*, e.g. UNITED STATES — NEUTRALITY; etc."

Subject headings in the fields of science, technology, economics, education, and the arts usually are subdivided by place. Those in history, geography, politics, and the social sciences usually are made subdivisions under place.[14] It is assumed that the real subject of a book about Colorado history, and the one the patron will most likely consult, is "COLORADO," not "HISTORY." In *Sears*, the subject entry, "HISTORY," is used only for general works on history as an intellectual discipline. If the subject is an institution such as a library the real subject might be either the institution or the area, depending on the type of area. *Sears* will specify, e.g., "LIBRARIES (May subdiv. geog. country or state)." Subdivision by city is thus precluded, and the *see also* note includes the phrase " . . . names of cities with the subdivision *Libraries* (e.g. CHICAGO (ILL.) — LIBRARIES)." This means that a discussion of the libraries of a state or country will fall under the topical heading, e.g., "LIBRARIES — CANADA" and "LIBRARIES — QUÉBEC (PROVINCE)." By contrast, a discussion of the libraries of a local jurisdiction will fall under the place heading, e.g., "QUÉBEC (QUÉBEC) — LIBRARIES."

Individual works of belles-lettres (e.g., novels, plays, and poetry) are not usually assigned subject headings. It is assumed that patrons are more likely to seek access to these materials through author or title. Reference librarians also find certain published indexes, such as H. W. Wilson's *Fiction Catalog* and F. W. Faxon's series of indexes to full-length plays, sufficient. If not, they make, or request the catalogers to make, special demand files. In the list of form subdivisions supplied by *Sears* " . . . —FICTION" appears as a suggested option for libraries that prefer to make subject headings for fictionalized history or biography. Thus, a novel about the Six Day War in the Middle East might be given the subject heading, "ISRAEL-ARAB WAR, 1967—FICTION."

Literary anthologies are far more likely to receive subject headings. As discussed above, plural nouns (e.g., "SONATAS") are used to differentiate collections of actual works from discussions of the form, for which the singular noun would be used. In situations where plural and singular words are not normally distinguished, the subdivision "...— COLLECTED WORKS" is available for the cataloger to add as needed (e.g., "POETRY—COLLECTED WORKS").[15]

PHYSICAL CHARACTERISTICS AND FORMAT OF *SEARS*

The twelfth edition of *Sears* opens with a preface which gives its historical setting and identifies the authoritative sources and the new features incorporated in it. It is followed by an explanatory essay which has become a *Sears* tradition, undergoing considerable expansion in scope and detail over the years. This essay is called "Principles of the Sears List of Subject Headings."[16] It treats both the theoretical and practical aspects of subject heading work. It merits the careful reading, not only of those planning to use the *Sears* list, but of anyone wishing to gain knowledge of traditional subject list usage.

In the list proper, the right half of each page is blank. All entries, references, and instructions are confined to the left columns, to leave space for the local cataloger to add any new headings, references, or comments needed to convert the volume into an authority file. Subject entries are printed in boldface type. *See* references appear in lightface type in the same alphabet. Filing in *Sears* has already been discussed under "Types of Subdivisions." The following excerpt shows the various elements which may be included under a subject entry, although not every entry requires all of these elements:

Children's poetry 808.81; 811; 811.08; etc.
    Use for collections of poetry for children by one or more
    authors. Materials on poetry written by children are
    entered under **Child authors**
    See also **Children's songs; Lullabies; Nursery rhymes**
    x Poetry for children
    xx **Children's literature; Poetry — Collected works**

Dewey Decimal numbers, which had long accompanied subject headings in the list, were dropped from the ninth and tenth editions. Since DDC schedules are edited and printed by an entirely different publisher, various objections had been raised to the gratuitous, unofficial association of certain DDC numbers with the subject entries. It was feared that *Sears* might be used as a substitute index to the DDC schedules, or worse yet, as a substitute for the schedules themselves. However, upon catalogers' insistence, the eleventh edition once again carried them, with admonitions about the differences between classification and subject heading work, as well as strong recommendations that both the DDC index and the schedules be consulted before any classification is done. They continue to appear in the twelfth edition. The above example shows the associated DDC numbers in their customary place, on the same line with the subject entry. Note that three numbers are specifically included, together with an "etc." to remind the user that he or she might profitably seek further in the Dewey Decimal Classification to find the best number for the particular need.

Scope notes are an exception, rather than the rule, but the one in the example above is typical. The reader receives first a positive instruction on appropriate use of the entry. Then comes a negative instruction (albeit stated positively) on the kinds of material which should be placed under a different entry.

The words "See also" in italics normally follow the scope note, or, if there is no scope note, the entry proper. They precede a list in boldface of closely related headings which the user might like to explore. Each boldface entry in this list is a legitimate subject heading. Reference to these *see also* headings might very well lead to further *see also* headings which could help expand or modify the search to reveal the full range of materials available in the particular collection. But a *see also* reference should never be made unless the catalog actually has material under the heading referred to.

The letter *x* before one or more terms means that a *see* reference is recommended from each such term to the heading under which the *x* appears. Terms preceded by an *x* are never used as subject headings. The letters *xx* before one or more terms mean that a *see also* reference should be made from each such term used in the catalog to the heading under which the *xx* appears. Thus, *Sears* suggests the following cross references for the subject entry, "CHILDREN'S POETRY," but the local cataloger is expected to consider each on its merits, in view of the terminology used by the library's clientele and the presence of other subject entries in the catalog:

CHILDREN'S POETRY *see also* CHILDREN'S SONGS
                              LULLABIES
                              NURSERY RHYMES

Poetry for children *see* CHILDREN'S POETRY

CHILDREN'S LITERATURE *see also* CHILDREN'S POETRY

POETRY — COLLECTED WORKS *see also* CHILDREN'S POETRY

The *x* and *xx* are tracings of a sort, to help the cataloger fit the most appropriate specific subject entries to each individual item in the collection and keep track of their interrelationships. The "*x* Poetry for children" under "CHILDREN'S POETRY" is there as a reminder that a user might very well go first to the P's, looking under "Poetry for children." If so, a simple reference could save both time and frustration. "POETRY – COLLECTED WORKS" is in boldface under the "*xx* CHILDREN'S LITERATURE; POETRY – COLLECTED WORKS." It might be a subject entry in the catalog, but according to the theory of specific entry it is too broad for a work confined to children's poetry. However, the "*xx* POETRY – COLLECTED WORKS" serves the dual purpose 1) of reminding the cataloger to make a "POETRY – COLLECTED WORKS *see also* CHILDREN'S POETRY" reference, and 2) of helping anyone who has access to the printed list to work back to the broader heading, where some entries may lead to poetry anthologies which actually contain some poetry for children. In most libraries the *see also* reference will be filed after all the subject entries bearing the heading "POETRY – COLLECTED WORKS."

Sears supplies two pages of minute instructions for Checking and Adding Headings.[17] Here the technique of checking all terms in the list which have been transferred to the local catalog, and the uses of the blank right-hand columns to record the headings and cross references added by the local cataloger, are fully explained. Many smaller libraries find this type of subject authority file the simplest and quickest to prepare. There is one serious drawback, however. When a new edition of *Sears* appears, all checks and entries must be laboriously recopied, or the library's subject control will suffer. If the older edition is retained for its authority records, all new headings and changes must be entered, making it increasingly messy and difficult to read. If the new edition is adopted without reviewing and checking former practices, inconsistencies will soon weaken the power of the subject access structure.

Sears includes a list of "Headings to Be Added by the Cataloger."[18] Eight varieties of proper names, and five each of corporate names and common names, are identified, for which there is no attempt to include all possibilities in the printed list. One or two obvious names of each variety can be found in the list proper, to serve as examples, or because important or typical subdivisions have been given. The cataloger is also reminded that general *see also* references imply other specific names which the cataloger is to add as needed, using available reference sources to establish correct entry forms.

Closely related are the "Key Headings" or prominent specific names where full displays of possible subdivisions are listed, not just for those names, but for most or all names of the same type.[19] Eight key entries are given, exemplifying four major categories of headings and subdivisions to be added by the cataloger:

Persons

PRESIDENTS – UNITED STATES   (to illustrate subdivisions which
                                      may be used under presidents,
                                      prime ministers, and other
                                      rulers)

SHAKESPEARE, WILLIAM   (to illustrate subdivisions which
                                      may be used under any volum-
                                      inous author)

Places

UNITED STATES   (to illustrate subdivisions under
OHIO   geographic names, except for
CHICAGO (ILL.)   historical periods)

Languages and Literatures

ENGLISH LANGUAGE   (to illustrate subdivisions which
ENGLISH LITERATURE   may be used with any language
                                      or literature)

Wars

WORLD WAR, 1939-1945   (to illustrate subdivisions which
                                      may be used under any war or
                                      battle)

There are two additional sections in *Sears*. The "List of Subdivisions"
really includes three lists of differing generality.[20] Reference was made to these
in the discussion of "Types of Subdivision." They are followed by the full
printed list, which occupies the bulk of the volume.

Instead of issuing quarterly supplements, as does *LCSH, Sears* updates its
usage by successive editions at intervals of five to seven years. The relatively
limited scope of *Sears*, for use in small- and medium-sized libraries, makes
comprehensive revision more manageable for both editors and users. The
results are possibly more coherently integrated. However, nine, seven, or even
five years is a long time to wait for the updated version of a subject access tool
in today's rapidly developing bibliographic environment. The Library of
Congress's quarterly supplements to its subject heading list and its publication
of the "Weekly Lists" permit (if they do not always ensure) early professional response on the part of one enormous library to inevitable, but generally
unpredictable, shifts in publishing interests and emphases. While they may
absorb and distribute better the shocks of linguistic and epistemological
change, they quickly clutter one's work space with their numerous partial
revisions, at least in their paper formats. Actually neither approach
monopolizes all the advantages. What matters is that every viable subject access mode remain under constant surveillance and revision, offering a dynamic
compromise between rigid custom and assimilative change.

CONCLUSION

The assigning of subject headings is a discipline that inevitably seems complicated and bewildering to the neophyte cataloger. Unlike other cataloging disciplines, it has no logical progression other than the linguistic development of knowledge itself. Even the assigning of a classification number to a book is less forbidding, for the novice usually has some sort of previous orientation to the Dewey system, and can see, if dimly, the divisions of knowledge and why they should exist. Subject headings are, however, not difficult once the cataloger learns to handle them. Both *Sears* and *LCSH* are quite explicit in their directions; both contain lists of general subdivisions with specific instructions for their use. If followed consistently, they will provide useful reference guides for the user, including the reference librarian.

A beginning cataloger should study the subject list used in the local library. It would be helpful to choose a subject in which he or she is personally interested, tracing it throughout the list, and observing the interrelation of *see also*, *x*, and *xx* references. There are other aids, such as the reference tools in the library. They amplify subjects and clarify aspects not immediately understood, especially in an age when no one can expect to know everything. The library's shelflist and public catalog are also helpful. The former can suggest subject headings if the cataloger has a classification number in mind, since most shelflists nowadays consist of full unit records, with tracings for the subject entries of each cataloged item. The public catalog can suggest classification numbers if the would-be cataloger has a subject heading in mind. Neither is a completely reliable crutch. Books are very often written about new subjects and about more than one subject. The vagaries of past and present individual catalogers, however experienced, may mislead. Yet both resources are generally helpful; both serve to characterize the practices of the local library. To become a successful cataloger, one must know what is current local practice, and work within that frame of reference. Major changes should not be put into effect until the reasons for what is done are fully understood, and the reactions of other users and fellow librarians can be anticipated.

NOTES

[1]Minnie Earl Sears, *Sears List of Subject Headings*, 12th ed., edited by Barbara M. Westby (New York, H. W. Wilson, 1982), p. 7.

[2]For further discussion of the hazards and techniques of integrating *LCSH* headings into a *Sears* authority file, *see* the introduction to chapter 22, "Library of Congress Subject Headings," especially p. 460.

[3]Ken Haycock and Lynne Isberg Lighthall, comps., *Sears List of Subject Headings: Canadian Companion*, 2nd ed. (New York, H. W. Wilson, 1983).

[4]Arlene Taylor Dowell, *Cataloging with Copy: A Decision-Maker's Handbook* (Littleton, Colo., Libraries Unlimited, 1976), pp. 118-124, 128-129.

[5]For more detailed discussion of the theory of subject headings, refer to chapter 21, "Verbal Subject Analysis." *See also Sears*, pp. 12-14.

[6]The list of reference types is copied from *Sears*, pp. 25-27, but the examples are changed, to give alternative insights.

[7]Note that the example given is a *see*, rather than a *see also*, reference. The principle involved is the same.

[8]*Sears*, pp. 26-27, offers some advice on this problem.

[9]For a review of the structure of LC headings, and further comment on some of the points mentioned here, *see* "Types of Subject Headings" in chapter 22, and "The Choice of Subject Headings" in chapter 21.

[10]*See* pp. 468-469 to compare the filing used by *LCSH* with that found in *Sears*. Chapter 26 presents still other filing options.

[11]*Sears*, p. 38.

[12]*Sears*, pp. 24, 40.

[13]*Sears*, pp. 38-39.

[14]*Sears*, p. 20.

[15]*Sears*, p. 23.

[16]Much of the foregoing discussion is based on this essay.

[17]*Sears*, pp. 34-35.

[18]*Sears*, p. 36.

[19]*Sears*, p. 37.

[20]*Sears*, pp. 38-40.

SUGGESTED READING

Foskett, A. C. *The Subject Approach to Information*. 4th ed. London, Bingley, 1982. Chapter 23.

"Principles of the Sears List of Subject Headings," in *Sears List of Subject Headings*. 12th ed. Edited by Barbara M. Westby. New York, H. W. Wilson, 1982. pp. 11-32.

24
Other Types of
Verbal Analysis

INTRODUCTION

For well over a century libraries have provided subject retrieval from their holdings through the use of pre-coordinate lists of integrated and cross-referenced topical headings. The preceding chapters have discussed *Sears* and *LCSH*, which remain the most universally recognized linguistic tools for analyzing library collections. But recent developments in information science, with its many similarities to, and differences from, library science, offer new modes of indexing which throw both practical and theoretical light on traditional subject lists. Some of the rival techniques are offered as supplements, or even substitutes, for traditional subject catalogs. This chapter reviews those enterprises most pertinent to library subject retrieval and explains briefly the applications of the more successful ones.

RECENT DEVELOPMENTS IN
DOCUMENT INDEXING

The word "index" still connotes book and periodical indexes more often than it does subject catalogs for library collections. However, library indexes and catalogs are nearly as old as alphabets, being present in some form with almost every organized collection of written records as far back as the early Mesopotamian and Egyptian archives. In the final years of the nineteenth and the early years of the twentieth centuries, catalogers frequently made numerous "analytics" to significant informational works in their libraries. Books were expensive. The high cost of acquisitions and the relative scarcity of printed materials were countered with efforts to exploit collections intensively. Librarians were a captive labor force, often with "disposable time" on the job. And what more profitable "pick-up work" could there be than making analytic indexes to anthologies and treatises? If the cards followed standard cataloging practices they were filed into the official catalog. If they were less carefully constructed, they might be kept in a desk drawer or a shoe box in the reference department. John Rothman points to a continuing reciprocity between library classification and indexing:

> Although indexing is often clearly differentiated from catalog-ing and classification, there is considerable overlapping in practice, and the development of new cataloging techniques or new classification systems is bound to affect indexing practices. Thus the development of the Dewey and other decimal classification systems for library catalogs was paralleled by the development of decimal, coded, and faceted topical indexing systems.[1]

COORDINATE INDEXING

The post-World War II information explosion dramatized the values of good indexing. Older methods which had gone into eclipse were revived and improved. New theories sprang up to support other techniques. A major departure from the relatively simple hierarchical use of subordinate divisions and inverted modifiers in traditional subject heading lists was the idea of post-coordinate searching, in which the searcher could play a more active role. A coordinate index consists of a list of subject terms in a standard format. Each term is independent of all others, except for cross references, and is designed to retrieve all documents for which it is specifically relevant. A user can stop at the single-term level of search if he or she is satisfied with the results. However, true coordinate searching moves on to a second level. Taking two or more terms which together delimit a still more specific search topic, and com-paring the records indexed under each, the searcher retrieves only those items which have been indexed under all the chosen terms.

Suppose the searcher is looking for material on the use of solar energy for drying grain. The index might offer the terms "Solar energy," "Heat engines," and "Grain." Perhaps five document citations emerge because they are all entered under all three terms. The searcher makes the matches and consults those documents. In a traditional subject catalog this type of post-coordinate searching is awkward and difficult. The underlying assumption is that the list itself is pre-coordinate. That is, the assimilation and matching of concepts has already been done by the cataloger, and is implicit in the terminology of the list. Thus, *LCSH* offers the subject heading, "SOLAR ENERGY IN AGRICULTURE," with a *see also* reference from "AGRICULTURE," as the one correct subject identifier for the above items. If *Sears* were used, the sub-ject entry or entries would be broader. Probably both "SOLAR ENERGY" and "GRAIN" would be assigned, but there would be no way of matching the two concepts to specify the available items except by comparing subject entries under each term, or examining full unit entries to find those on which both terms were traced.

In post-coordinate indexing, the coordination of terms is the responsi-bility of the searcher, rather than of the subject cataloger. The terms are usually single nouns, and the specific document citations frequently take the form of accession numbers (rarely hierarchical class or call numbers). In 1953

Mortimer Taube introduced what he called the Uniterm index, to emphasize its post-coordinate use of single terms as opposed to composite headings.[2] It was primarily a manual system, using cards with headings displayed at the top, and ten columns in which document accession numbers could be entered according to the number's final digit. For example, documents 56A, 306, 96, 1176, and 1006 might all be listed in column 6 of each of the three cards bearing the Uniterms "Solar energy," "Heat engines," and "Grain." The technique, known as terminal digit posting, has been most successful in its computerized applications, where some of the tediousness and error-proneness of manual listing is forestalled. The CROSS (Computer Rearrangement of Subject Specialties) Index of Biosciences Information Service (BIOSIS) is one example. The searcher must still make the visual comparisons and match the reference numbers under the chosen headings. Precision of search and in-depth subject retrieval are the obvious rewards, but any extensive search involves eyestrain, mental fatigue, and an inordinate amount of time.

To overcome the disadvantages of a visual search, other modes of post-coordinate indexing soon developed. Mechanical scanning devices are based on the fact that cards may be precisely gridded for punched holes to replace the columns of written or printed numbers. Two or more of these punched cards (e.g., the three carrying the headings "Solar energy," "Heat engines," and "Grain") may be laid together and held up to the light, or otherwise probed, to extract the reference numbers which they index in common. Various brands of these cards have been marketed. Foskett prefers to call them all optical coincidence cards, but he recognizes other popular names such as "peek-a-boo," "peephole," and "feature" cards.[3]

HIERARCHIC OR SUBORDINATION INDEXING

The subsuming of narrower terms or subdivisions under broader terms is familiar to librarians in many contexts. We spoke in previous chapters of its use for library subject catalogs. Book indexes frequently indent secondary words under primary ones, and make use of see and see also references. The New York Times Index, and most of the H. W. Wilson indexes, such as Readers' Guide to Periodical Literature, do the same. The rapid growth of machine-readable data bases which analyze periodical articles, books, report literature, patents, and the like for rapid retrieval in nearly all disciplines has led to the publication of search-oriented thesauri to aid users with their search strategies. The term, thesaurus, is endemic to discussions of subject retrieval. Its general meaning is little different from "subject heading list," although it is likely to cover a limited discipline or cross-disciplinary area, whereas Sears and the LC list are designed for unrestricted application. These thesauri also tend to hybridize or blend hierarchical classification with syndetic (cross referencing) structures even more than Sears and LCSH do. In place of see, see also, x, and xx, they usually tag entries and references with names or mnemonic initials.

One very simple example of such a search strategy manual is the Thesaurus of Psychological Index Terms.[4] Its users' guide explains:

Each *Thesaurus* term is listed alphabetically, cross-referenced, and displaced with its broader, narrower and related terms. An array term, representing an extremely broad conceptual area, is denoted by a slash (/). . . .

The *Use* reference directs the user from a term that cannot be used in indexing or searching to a preferred term. . . .

> Scholastic Aptitude
> *Use* Academic Aptitude

The *Used for* reference is the reciprocal reference for the *Use* reference, as seen with:

> AVOIDANCE CONDITIONING
> *Used for* Conditioning (Avoidance)

The *Broader-Narrower* term designators are reciprocals and are used to indicate the genus-species hierarchical relationships, as in these examples:

> PSYCHOMOTOR DEVELOPMENT
> *Broader* Motor Development
>   Physical Development
>   Psychogenesis

> INTERPERSONAL INTERACTION
> *Narrower* Bargaining
>   Conflict
>   Conversation
>   Cooperation

A *Related* term designator is used to show relationships that are semantic or conceptual but not hierarchical. Related term references serve to broaden the perspective of searchers or indexers by directing them to terms they have not considered but which may have a bearing on their subject matter interest as in this example:

> STRESS
> *Related* Anxiety
>   Disasters
>   Endurance

In the *Thesaurus of ERIC Descriptors* each descriptor (main term) is accompanied by one or more notations: UF—*Used for*; NT—*Narrower term*; BT—*Broader term*; RT—*Related term*.[5] "Use" is the mandatory reciprocal of UF, putting the non-postable terms (*see* references) into place. SN precedes a scope note. Under postable terms two more kinds of information are given.

The date is the "add" (first entry) date. Search strategies for materials entered into the data base prior to that time should in most instances use different terminology. Posting counts (the number of citations available when the *Thesaurus* was published) are given for both the *Current Index to Journals in Education* and *Resources in Education*. Examples of *Thesaurus* entries are given below:

```
Dressmakers
    Use Seamstresses

Drill Presses
    Use Machine tools

DRINKING              May 1974
        CIJE: 45      RIE: 42
    SN   Consumption of alcoholic
            or other beverages
    UF   Social Drinking
    BT   Activities
    RT   Alcohol Education
         Alcoholic Beverages
         Alcoholism
         Health
         Health Education
         Recreational Activities
```

A final, more complex example comes from the *INSPEC Thesaurus* of the Institution of Electrical Engineers.[6] It uses the following abbreviations:

UF: *Used for*	indicates the 'lead-in' term from which reference is made
NT: *Narrower Term*	indicates a more specific term, one level lower in the hierarchy
BT: *Broader Term*	indicates a more general term, one level higher in the hierarchy
TT: *Top Term*	indicates the most general term in the hierarchy
RT: *Related Term*	indicates conceptual relationships between terms, not related hierarchically
CC: *Classification Code*	version of the INSPEC classification code as used in INSPEC Magnetic Tape Services. This indicates the subject area in which the particular term is commonly used.
FC: *Full Classification Code*	full version of the INSPEC classification code as input to the data base. This indicates the subject area in which the particular term is commonly used.

Two examples of *INSPEC Thesaurus* listings follow:

DIELECTRIC THIN FILMS
see also ferroelectric thin films; insulating thin films;
optical films; piezoelectric thin films
NT ferroelectric thin films
    piezoelectric thin films
BT thin films
TT films
RT dielectric materials
    insulating thin films
    optical films
    polymer films
CC A7755 B2830
FC a7755 + rb2830-x

dielectric triodes
USE space-charged limited devices

The programs written to retrieve information from computer-stored data bases nearly all make use of the Boolean logic operators "and," "or," and "not." With these machine-manipulated instructions, search commands which are highly sophisticated and very powerful examples of post-coordinate searching can be executed. For example, someone using the ERIC data base might want to examine material on the consumption of alcohol in clubs, at social gatherings, and the like, but not have to wade through all those discussing related problems of health. Using the *ERIC Thesaurus*, he or she could construct the search command "(Drinking *or* Alcoholic Beverages) *and* ((Activities *or* Recreational Activities) *not* (Health *or* Health Education))." Since the commands within parentheses are executed first, all documents indexed under the following rubrics would be retrieved:

Drinking *and* Activities *but not* Health
Drinking *and* Activities *but not* Health Education
Drinking *and* Recreational Activities *but not* Health
Drinking *and* Recreational Activities *but not* Health Education
Alcoholic Beverages *and* Activities *but not* Health
Alcoholic Beverages *and* Activities *but not* Health Education
Alcoholic Beverages *and* Recreational Activities *but not* Health
Alcoholic Beverages *and* Recreational Activities *but not* Health
    Education

As library catalogs go online, the allowable number of subject entries may increase, since the old storage and filing difficulties in large card files will likely prove less expensive and troublesome. Search programs built upon Boolean operators could then enhance subject retrieval, giving it a precision, breadth, and depth not possible in manual searching.

THE PRESERVED CONTEXT INDEXING SYSTEM (PRECIS)

In chapter 15 chain indexing was discussed in connection with classified catalog access. Chain indexes, while bearing a format resemblance to keyword indexes, usually are built upon a more selective, indexer-controlled vocabulary. They delete unnecessary context, and all subheadings are super-ordinate terms. Key entries are as specific as possible. Where they are hierarchically subordinate to broader terms in the search vocabulary, the next broader term is added for context. This type of alphabetical chain index was used for subject access to *The British National Bibliography* (*BNB*) from 1950 to 1970. Since then, a different system, based on a set of working procedures, rather than an established list of terms, has been used. It is called PRECIS, an acronym for Preserved Context Indexing System. Derek Austin states:

> The system is firmly based upon the concept of an open-ended vocabulary, which means that terms can be admitted into the index at any time, as soon as they have been encountered in literature. Once a term has been admitted, its relationships with other terms are handled in two different ways, distinguished as the syntactical and the semantic sides of the system.[7]

The Library of Congress developed its Machine Readable Cataloging (MARC) tapes in the mid-1960s. *BNB*, which is now part of the Bibliographic Services Division of the British Library, launched its cooperative UK/MARC Project in 1968. But *BNB* was not satisfied with the subject access provided by existing MARC fields, such as the title, DDC, and LC classification and subject heading fields. Drawing on its twenty-year chain indexing experience, it constructed a new system which, since the revisions adopted in 1974, has become a serious rival to traditional subject lists and catalogs.[8] Phyllis Richmond ran a two-year comparison of PRECIS with *Library of Congress Subject Headings* (*LCSH*) and with KWIC index retrieval from the sample titles. (*See* pp. 516-518 for a discussion of KWIC indexing.) She concluded that PRECIS can make subject material more accessible, both quantitatively and qualitatively, than either of the other two techniques:

> The indexing produced in these operations cannot be duplicated in either LCSH or . . . Keyword-in-Context methodology or even with both used together. . . . Aside from differences in the terminology used to convey concepts, which may be as much a matter of taste as of customary usage, the two greatest problems in all indexing are ambiguity and semantic confusion occasioned by inadequate context accompanying terms of dubious ancestry. These terms include homonyms, homographs, metaphor, allusion, neologisms and, of course, public words with private meanings. Lack of context in subject headings and the general unwillingness to add clarifying terms to titles in the various processes of indexing by title ensure the continuation of both problems. PRECIS stops them dead in their tracks.[9]

Austin often starts his descriptions of PRECIS with a series of negative points, to dispel misconceptions. It is not a fully computer-generated program, but requires human processing for preparation of input. It is not a subject heading list, but is characterized by a set of established procedures rather than a set of accepted terms. Also, it is not a library classification, although its computerized thesaurus, like those of the hierarchical indexing systems examined above, embodies certain principles of classification. PRECIS operates with an open-ended vocabulary, so that terms can be adopted as soon as they appear in the literature. Entries are pre-coordinated, context-dependent strings of terms in which each term is semantically defined and syntactically related by *see* and *see also* references to synonyms and other associated words of different specificity. A Reference Indicator Number (RIN) is the computer address where the particular term, plus all references to it, may be accessed.

From established index strings, with their separate terms and RINs, all of the verbal parts of a PRECIS index can be generated. For reasons of bulk and cost, actual bibliographic citations are not included in such indexes. Instead, citations are usually sequenced and systematically grouped elsewhere by serial number according to a classification scheme. For bibliographic records in the MARC Project, *BNB* provides each index string with a packet of subject data consisting of the string itself, a DDC number, an LC class number, LC subject headings as required, and the pertinent RINs to ensure appropriate cross references. A Subject Indicator Number (SIN) is then assigned as a computer address for each packet. The indexer does not write the chosen subject terms or strings on the worksheet of the item being cataloged. Rather, he or she tags the worksheet with the appropriate SINs and the document retrieval number. If a new topic, with new references, is needed in the thesaurus, the indexer makes the various necessary subject decisions, assigning corresponding RINs and SINs. The computer can perform all subsequent manipulation, such as alphabetizing, responding to subject requests, and generating output, at high speed.

Suppose, for instance, that an item to be cataloged is about the training of personnel in the cotton industries in India. The indexer would start by establishing a context-dependent, hierarchical concept string such as: "India – Cotton industries – Personnel – Training." The terms form a sequence in which, much as in a traditional subject heading, each is directly related to the next one in the string. Standard permutation (e.g., a KWIC index) would generate entries under each term as follows:

INDIA. Cotton industries. Personnel. Training
COTTON INDUSTRIES. Personnel. Training. India
PERSONNEL. Training. India. Cotton industries
TRAINING. India. Cotton industries. Personnel

Simple permutation indexes are most successful in retrieving natural language forms, such as book and article titles, or loosely controlled terminology such as that used in the indexes to the Library of Congress Classification schedules. For indexing subject materials with a controlled vocabulary and a high degree of entry concentration at given levels of specificity, something more sophisticated is needed. Indeed, simple transposition of each term to the entry position could raise serious ambiguities, as in the entry below under "Personnel," where directly dependent terms in the original string are no longer adjacent, which raises the question of whether the personnel are doing, or receiving, the training.

> INDIA. Cotton industries. Personnel. Training
> COTTON INDUSTRIES. India. Personnel. Training
> PERSONNEL. India. Cotton industries. Training
> TRAINING. India. Cotton industries. Personnel

To meet this inherent danger as economically and elegantly as possible, PRECIS uses a two-line print-out which can be diagramed:

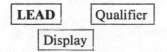

The Lead, as the filing element, is printed in boldface. The Qualifier position carries any broader term which gives the Lead context. Each successive Qualifier term broadens that context. The Display represents hierarchic movement in the opposite direction. Each successive Display term narrows the context. Not all entries must have Qualifier or Display terms attached. If the topic has no broader, or narrower, context, those positions are blank. Setting our example into the print-out matrix gives entries as shown below.

When organizing terms into entries, indexers strive for consistency of lead concepts, and of the input order of qualifiers and displays. They can use either conventional visual code markings (e.g., a check-mark or "tick" marks the lead in such a compound term as "cotton industries"), or they can assign machine-readable manipulation codes for computer handling in automated systems.

> INDIA
>   Cotton industries. Personnel. Training
>
> COTTON INDUSTRIES. India
>   Personnel. Training
>
> PERSONNEL. Cotton industries. India
>   Training
>
> TRAINING. Personnel. Cotton industries. India

The dollar sign ($) is a standard UK/MARC convention to distinguish certain instructions from the succeeding concept terms to which they apply. With it, two connective codes ("v" and "w") provide a defense against ambiguity in permuted entries. Thus, for such a topic as "the erosive effects of wind on rock" the indexer would code the lead terms in the string as follows:

rocks

erosion $v by $w of

winds

The three resulting index entries would be:

ROCKS
    Erosion by winds

EROSION. Rocks
    By winds

WINDS
    Erosion of rocks

Three other codes, called theme interlinks, identify the thematic role of each term in a given string. An "x" identifies the first element of any separate theme, while "y" identifies each component of any theme coded by a previous "x," and "z" identifies concepts common to all those themes which occur at the beginning or the end of a given string. Suppose the indexer is coding a document on two themes which share a common component, e.g., "Water as a contaminant of lubricating oils" and "Measuring the viscosity of lubricating oils." The terms would be coded:

(z) lubricating oils	(common term)
(x) contaminants $w of	(theme 1 term)
(y) water	(context dependent term in theme 1)
(x) viscosity	(theme 2 term)
(y) measurement	(context dependent term in theme 2)

The indexer has decided against using the term "measurement" in the lead, and accordingly has not ticked it. Index entries developed from this coding would include:

LUBRICATING OILS
    Contaminants. Water

CONTAMINANTS. Lubricating oils
    Water

WATER. Contaminants of lubricating oils

LUBRICATING OILS
Viscosity. Measurement

VISCOSITY. Lubricating oils
Measurement

The table of codes and role operators, reproduced in Fig. 24.1 on page 512,[10] gives the codes used to organize index strings. All operators except connectives and theme interlinks have syntactic or semantic roles in a string. Syntactic relationships give the overall meaning of the string by determining the order in which its component terms are set down. Semantic relationships exist between a specific concept and the group of interconnected ideas to which it belongs. *See* and *see also* references evolve from these connections. Syntactic and semantic operators provide the precision and consistency which allow permutation without loss or distortion of meaning.

In indexing for computer manipulation, primary operators identify the basic components of a compound subject and regulate the order in which they are written down. Secondary operators can appear between primary operators to increase specificity, but they cannot start a string. Secondary codes for "differences," being semantic rather than syntactic, identify the adjectives that fix a given term's connotation. A primary nine-character code precedes each subject element in the string. The function of each of the nine characters may be summarized as shown below.

1st — The primary code tag ($)

2nd — Theme interlink (no syntactical function)

x — The first concept in a subtheme

y — An element of a subtheme

z — An element of the common theme

3rd — The primary or secondary operator. Determines not only format but typography and punctuation. Terms introduced by numerical operators appear in the string in numerical order. Alphabetic operators follow other rules which determine their order in the string.

4th — Focus in lead

0 — Not a lead term

1 — A lead term

(Character summarization continues on page 513.)

Fig. 24.1. PRECIS operators and codes.

SCHEMA OF OPERATORS

Primary operators

Environment of core concepts	0	Location
Core concepts	1	Key system. *Thing when action not present. Thing towards which an action is directed, e.g. object of transitive action, performer of intransitive action.*
	2	Action; Effect of action
	3	Performer of transitive action *(agent, instrument)*; Intake; Factor
Extra-core concepts	4	Viewpoint-as-form; Aspect
	5	Selected instance, *e.g. study region, sample population*
	6	Form of document; Target user

Secondary operators

Coordinate concepts	f	'Bound' coordinate concept
	g	Standard coordinate concept
Dependent elements	p	Part; Property
	q	Member of quasi-generic group
	r	Assembly
Special classes of action	s	Role definer; Directional property
	t	Author-attributed association
	u	Two-way interaction

Note on prefixes to Codes. The codes in the left-hand panel are marked as instructions, as opposed to data, by their preceding symbols. These are shown as dollar signs ($) to reflect current practice in many PRECIS files, but any non-alpha-numeric character will serve the same purpose. The draft version of the *UNIMARC Manual* (referring to PRECIS data in Field 670) states that "signs used as subfield codes (in UNIMARC, the $) *should be avoided*".

CODES IN PRECIS STRINGS

Primary codes

Theme interlinks	$x	1st concept in coordinate theme
	$y	2nd/subsequent concept in theme
	$z	Common concept
Term codes †	$a	Common noun
	$c	Proper name (class-of-one)
	$d	Place name

Secondary codes

Differences

Preceding differences *(3 characters)*   *1st and 2nd characters :*

	$0	Non-lead, space generating
	$1	Non-lead, close-up
	$2	Lead, space generating
	$3	Lead, close-up

3rd character = number in the range 1 to 9 indicating level of difference

Date as a difference	$d	
Parenthetical differences	$n	Non-lead parenthetical difference
	$o	Lead parenthetical difference
Connectives	$v	Downward-reading connective
	$w	Upward-reading connective

Typographic codes †

$e	Non-filing part in italic preceded by comma
$f	Filing part in italic preceded by comma
$g	Filing part in roman, no preceding punctuation
$h	Filing part in italic preceded by full point
$i	Filing part in italic, no preceding punctuation

† These codes are also used in the thesaurus

5th—Substitute phrase (when permutation requires a change of grammar)

0—Not a substitute

1-9—A substitute, suppressing the designated number of earlier terms when a later term appears as lead

6th—Appearance or nonappearance of a term

0—Do not print under preceding or following concept

1—Print under preceding, but not under following concept

2—Do not print under preceding concept; print under following concept

3—Print under both preceding and following concept (represents "standard" case)

7th—Not yet used (0)

8th—The term code tag ($)

9th—The term code. Identifies type of term:

a—Common noun

c—Proper name: person or institution

d—Place name[11]

The codes and subject terms used for the topic "training of personnel in the cotton industries in India" would be:

```
$z 0 103 0$d   India
$z 1 103 0$a   cotton industries
$z p 103 0$a   personnel
$z 2 103 0$a   training
```

As entered into the computer, the full string would be:

$z01030$dIndia$z11030$acotton industries$zp1030$apersonnel
$z21030$atraining

The computer can be programmed to read such a string far easier and quicker than can the human eye. However, the coded strings can be visually analyzed as well. For the initial subject term of the above string, the first and second manipulation characters ($z) identify "India" as an element of the common theme. The third character (0) sets the environment or location as the broadest term in the string. Character 4 (1) ensures its use as a lead term. Character 5 (0) shows that there is no need to suppress earlier terms when they appear as a lead. Character 6 (3) represents a "normal" case in which the subject term is tagged to print under both the preceding and the following concept. The following concept in this string is "cotton industries," but there is no preceding concept. Character 7 (0) is presently meaningless. The eighth and ninth characters ($d) form a "term" code identifying the term as a place name.

PRECIS strings sometimes include secondary codes consisting of only two characters, the $ tag and a differencing code or connective. Such a code applies only to the string element immediately following it. One of its functions is to ensure context dependency where one or more permutations requires reformatting in a non-standard way. The example "erosive effects of wind on rock" requires a type of reformatting called "predicate transformation." The fully coded string, using the secondary connective codes "$v" and "$w" to tag the reciprocal prepositions "by" and "of," would appear as follows:

$z11030$arocks$z21030$aerosionvbywof$z31030$awinds

PRECIS indexing has been applied successfully to all sorts of subject disciplines and formats: films, instructional aids, books, periodical articles, abstracts, technical reports, etc. In this brief review, many of its technical requirements and possibilities have been omitted. For instance, little or nothing has been said about the generation of cross-references. While it is a complex tool, developed to perform a complex job, its designers claim that beginners can learn to construct simple strings in a matter of hours. They freely admit that, like any human-based indexing system, it can never ensure that different indexers will arrive systematically at the same entries for the same document. However, it provides a climate of semantic control which fosters adaptability and creativity without degenerating into anarchy. At the same time, its syndetic structure, as represented in its three-part entry print-out, allows full statement of a compound subject under any of its significant terms without loss of either meaning or concepts. More than in any other known system of subject indexing, terminological access is both controlled and presented in a logical context.

There has been strong pressure in both Canada and the United States for libraries to adopt PRECIS as either a replacement for or a supplement to traditional subject headings. Valentina de Bruin reported in 1976, as one reason for the University of Toronto's decision to abandon *LCSH* in favor of PRECIS:

> growing dissatisfaction among the staff with LC subject access, especially since it is realized that in a machine-readable environment we are tied to subject headings that resist change simply because they were not designed in the first place to be machine-readable and machine-manipulable. (Here I would like to acknowledge our great debt to *LCSH*, which, manifestly, has done a great job through the years. Gratitude, not denigration, is the keyword.)[12]

G. Donald Cook, addressing "The Practical Possibilities of PRECIS in North America," found that PRECIS assigned an average of 5.52, as compared to *LCSH*'s 4.09, distinctive words per bibliographic record. The average PRECIS string, without its manipulation codes, is some 25 percent longer than the average *LCSH* entry for the same record. He warned that in neither system would all such words serve as useful access points, but he affirmed that, with permutation, access through PRECIS is triple that through *LCSH*.[13]

In response to this type of comment, the Library of Congress conducted a feasibility study on the addition of PRECIS to its existing subject heading system. While the study admittedly could not show the future level of public demand for PRECIS, it indicated that a suitably designed retrieval system using Boolean logic with existing MARC fields (title, subject, fixed fields, and the geographic area code) would usually give access to the same words provided in analogous PRECIS strings. Moreover, it was believed that the number of subject headings per record would likely increase, once the 3x5-inch card ceased to dominate record formats. For those libraries wishing to continue their card catalogs, PRECIS entries, with their two-line formats, would waste space and PRECIS strings would be hard to read and interpret. But the major drawback was the anticipated cost. Forty-five additional catalogers and editors would be needed. Work space, salaries, and related costs would amount to approximately $1,000,000 per year. In view of the lack of user demand, the Library did not feel justified in asking Congress for the money to support two subject heading/indexing systems.[14] Not everyone is content with the decision,[15] but there is no evidence that it will be reconsidered.

An indexing technique similar to PRECIS is POPSI (Postulate-based Permuted Subject Indexing). This approach was developed at the Documentation Research and Training Centre in Bangalore, India, where Ranganathan was the director until his death. It is often thought to be a particular string index language associated with the Colon Classification. However, it can be applied to different languages, according to the postulates recognized. The postulates comprise the definitions and the rules of grammar or syntax, which control associative as well as hierarchical relationships. Both POPSI and PRECIS are rotated pre-coordinate indexing systems, but whereas PRECIS developed out of a set of linguistic terms and a thesaurus, POPSI indexing developed directly from classification schedules and chain indexing.[16]

THE NEPHIS INDEXING SYSTEM

NEPHIS (NEsted PHrase Indexing System) is another string indexing system, designed by Timothy C. Craven. As with PRECIS, the indexer constructs an input string of indexing terms that are coextensive with the subject treated and the parts of which are permuted by a computer to produce multiple access points for the various parts of the string. A normal NEPHIS input string takes the basic form of a noun phrase into which other phrases are "nested" or imbedded. The indexer needs to know only four special characters, $<$, $>$, ?, and @; these characters, when inserted into the input string, signal to the computer what parts of the string are to be displayed as access points and how to display the other parts of the string. The symbols $<$ and $>$ are used to set off a nested phrase; the symbol ? is used to indicate connectives, both forward- and backward-reading, depending on whether the string ends in a $<$ or a $>$; and the symbol @ is used to suppress unwanted permutations.

A typical input string, taken from the title of a document (or formulated in a title-like form after analysis of the subject), would be, in NEPHIS-coded form:

@Case studies? of <Psychosocial aspects? of <Adaptability? of
<Adults? in <United States >> ? to <Transitions>>>.

This instructs the NEPHIS program to generate the following permutations:

Psychosocial aspects of Adaptability of Adults in United
States to Transitions. Case studies.

Adaptability of Adults in United States to Transitions.
Psychosocial aspects. Case studies.

Adults in United States. Adaptability to Transitions.
Psychosocial aspects. Case studies.

United States. Adults. Adaptability to Transitions.
Psychosocial aspects. Case studies.

Transitions. Adaptability of Adults in United States.
Psychosocial aspects. Case studies.

The NEPHIS system is simpler to learn and use than PRECIS but is not
quite as versatile, and it is primarily intended for smaller collections. NEPHIS
programs have been written for microcomputers and are thus applicable to
materials ranging from private files to those of multimedia libraries. More
information on NEPHIS can be found in many articles by its inventor.[17]

AUTOMATIC INDEXING METHODS

Indexers, like other human beings, are fallible, often are inconsistent, are
subject to extraneous influences on their work, operate at a slow pace, and are
therefore the most expensive component of an indexing operation. The idea of
replacing human indexers by feeding part or all of a text into a machine that
would assign index terms automatically, impartially, and with unfailing
consistency and accuracy arose, therefore, quite early in the computer age.
Success has, however, largely eluded the best efforts of many investigators and
inventors.

KWIC AND KWOC INDEXING

The earliest automatic indexing method relying on the power of
computers to perform repetitive tasks at high speed was invented by Hans
Peter Luhn, an IBM engineer, who in 1958 produced what became known as
KWIC (Key Word In Context) indexing. Luhn reported his system in 1960.[18]
On the assumption that titles of scientific and technical articles generally
include words indicating the most significant concepts dealt with, he wrote a
program that printed strings of title words, each word appearing once in
alphabetical order in the center of a page, with all other words to the left or
right of the center word printed in the order in which they appeared in the title;
when the right-hand margin was reached, the rest of the title (if any) was

"wrapped around" to the left-hand margin and continued inward. A user had only to scan the left-justified middle column for a desired keyword and could, when the word was found, read the rest of the title "in context." The method worked indeed fully automatically (i.e., without any human intervention other than the keyboarding) and resulted in a quickly and inexpensively produced display of potentially sought terms. Most KWIC programs also employ so-called stop lists to eliminate common words such as articles, prepositions, and conjunctions from the middle column where they presumably would not be sought. A specimen of a typical KWIC index is shown in Fig. 24.2. This earliest and rather crude form of automatic indexing has, ironically, remained the only one that has proven itself to be practical and is still being used.

Fig. 24.2. Sample from a KWIC index.

.CHEMICAL	ABSTRACTS.	CRANEJ-55-CA
NT STATUS OF BIOLOGICAL	ABSTRACTS.	[illegible]
TITLES OF PAPERS AND	ABSTRACTS.	EASTJC-55-TPA
CHEMICAL	ABSTRACTS. YESTERDAY, TODAY AND TOMO	CRANEJ-57-CAY
ERENCE SERVICES THROUGH	ACADEMIC PUBLIC LIBRARY PRACTICE AND	BOTHS -55-DRS
ICAL INFORMATION OF THE	ACADEMY OF SCIENCES OF THE USSR.	MIKHAI-58-FAI
INFORMATION OF THE USSR	ACADEMY OF SCIENCES.	CHERVP-55-EIM
IFIC INFORMATION OF THE	ACADEMY OF THE USSR.	PANOD -55-ISI
A MACHINE SYSTEM FOR	ACCEPTING, STORING, AND SEARCHING EN	CORRR -54-MSA
RANDOM	ACCESS ADDRESSING SCHEMES.	LUHNHP-56-RAA
NG A LARGE SCALE RANDOM	ACCESS MEMORY.	MOLAJJ-58-PIS
DRESS SYSTEM FOR RANDOM	ACCESS STORAGE.	LUHNHP-53-ASR
AL SYSTEM PROVIDES FAST	ACCESS TO PUNCHED CARD DATA FILE.	DRILJH-52-MES
THE	ACCESSIBILITY OF KNOWLEDGE. II	ENDEAV-52-AKI
ODING CAUSES OF ILLNESS	ACCORDING TO A DIAGNOSIS FOR TABULAT	PUBLHS-44-MCC
IN CONTENT OF ABSTRACTS	ACCORDING TO USE.	FLEIM -56-VCA
IBM PUNCHED CARD	ACCOUNTING IS ADAPTED TO MAKE SCHOLA	PUBLWE-56-IPA
RGINAL-PUNCHED CARDS ON	ACCOUNTING MACHINES.	OHLHH -57-LPM
EMICAL PROPERTIES USING	ACCOUNTING MACHINES.	VALEVH- -IPC
INTERRELATED LOGIC	ACCUMULATING SCANNER.	ANDRDD- -ILA
THE	ACQUISITION OF GOVERNMENT PUBLICATIO	WILCJW-55-AGP
	ACQUISITIONS.* SOURCES AND TECHNIQUE	JACKEB-52-AST
THE	ACS PUNCHED-CARD COMMITTEE. AN INTER	PERRJW-49-APC
DOCUMENTATION IN	ACTION.	KENTA -56-DA
	ADAMO II.	MAREE -56-AI
	ADDRESS SYSTEM FOR RANDOM ACCESS STO	LUHNHP-53-ASR
RANDOM ACCESS	ADDRESSING SCHEMES.	LUHNHP-56-RAA
CUMENTATION IN RESEARCH	ADMINISTRATION.	SCOTEW-51-RDR
	ADMINISTRATION OF TECHNICAL INFORMAT	INDUEC-59-ATI
INSTITUTE ON THE	ADMINSTRATION AND USE OF TECHNICAL R	SPECLA-52-IAU
CATALOGER-S VIEW OF THE	AEC LIBRARY PROGRAM.	CHESCF-49-CVA
INS AS APPLIED TO U. S.	AEC REPORTS.	MARHI -[illegible]-SCI
	AEC TECHNICAL INFORMATION PROGRAM.	THOMAF-50-ATI
ECHNICAL INFORMATION BY	AEC.	GRAYDE-51-DTI
L. L. CARD CATALOGUE OF	AERODYNAMIC MEASUREMENTS.	VESSHF- -TML
L. L. CARD CATALOGUE OF	AERODYNAMIC MEASUREMENTS.	STAPLE-54-MLL
PORT LITERATURE USED BY	AERODYNAMICISTS.	WILSCW- -RLU
R INDEXING DOCUMENTS ON	AERODYNAMICS.* AN EXPERIMENT IN RETR	WRIGRC- -CPI
TION IN THE ENGINEERING	AERONAUTIC AND METAL FIELDS.	MACRLF- -CMD
MCES OF TRANSLATIONS OF	AERONAUTICAL INTEREST IN NATO COUNTR	[illegible]-56-STA
	AERONAUTICAL DOCUMENTATION IN FRANCE	FRENGM-56-ADF
	AERONAUTICAL DOCUMENTATION IN THE U.	LOWRWK-56-ADU
R APPLICATIONS TO SOUTH	AFRICAN CONDITIONS.	SPOHOH-53-SRD
BAILEY-S	AFRICIAN-ORIENTAL CATALOGUE OF DICTI	BAILBS-55-BAC
	AGRICULTURAL RESEARCH SERVICE.	USDEAG-57-ARS
E PRESENT CONDITIONS OF	AIR FORCE INFORMATION SERVICES IN IT	GARITB-56-PCA
CT READING LIST FOR THE	AIR UNIVERSITY PERIODICAL INDEX- AN	JOHNRK-56-[illegible]
ABSTRACT ARCHIVE OF	ALCOHOL LITERATURE.	JELLEM-48-AAA
	ALGEBRAIC REPRESENTATION OF STORAGE	FAIRRA- -ARS
AN	ALGEBRAIC THESAURUS.	PARKRA-56-AT
THE FUNCTIONING OF THE	ALL-UNION INSTITUTE OF SCIENTIFIC TE	MIKHAI-58-FAI
FIELD OF PETROLEUM AND	ALLIED SUBJECTS.	BAILMF- -PCD
S ON CLASSIFICATION AND	ALLIED SUBJECTS.	JOURDO-56-BPC
	ALPHA-NUMERIC CHARACTER READER.	STONW -56-ACR
	ALPHABETIC SUBJECT INDEXES AND COORD	GULLCD-53-ASI

An adaptation of the KWIC method, known as KWOC (Key Word Out Of Context), simply prints the sought words in the left-hand margin instead of in the middle of the page, the rest of the title (or the entire title, including the keyword itself) being printed to the right or beneath the keyword (*see* Fig. 24.3).

KWIC and KWOC indexing have, however, some severe limitations: only words that appear in titles can be sought, while the article itself may deal with many other concepts not mentioned in the title; since there is absolutely no vocabulary control (other than the elimination of stop-list words), synonymous terms are not available to users as potential access points for

Fig. 24.3. Sample from a KWOC index.

```
THEORY          VARIETY GENERATION REINTERPRETATION SHANNONS MATHEMATICAL THEORY OF COMMUNICATION.   28-1-19
THESAURUS       PROBLEMS OF THESAURUS CONSTRUCTION.                                                   28-4-211
TOPOLOGY        APPLICATION FUNCTION DESCRIPTORS DEVELOPMENT INFORMATION SYSTEM TOPOLOGY.             28-5-259
TOWARD          TOWARD NATIONAL INFORMATION SYSTEM SOCIAL SCIENCE DATA FILES.                         28-6-313
TRANSFER        EARLY WARNING SYSTEM FOR RAPID IDENTIFICATION AND TRANSFER OF NEW TECHNOLOGY.         28-3-170
TRANSFER        RULES OF REVIEWS IN INFORMATION TRANSFER.                                             28-3-175
TRANSFORMATION  TWO-WAY IRREVERSIBLE PRIVACY TRANSFORMATION.                                          28-5-301
TRANSLATION     COMPUTERIZED RUSSIAN TRANSLATION AT ORNL.                                             28-1-26
TRENDS          DATA BASES HISTORY DEVELOPMENTS AND TRENDS 1966 THROUGH 1975.                         28-2-71
TRUNCATE        RELATIONSHIP AUTHOR NAMES ENTRIES ONLINE UNION CATALOG TRUNCATE.                      28-2-115
TWO-WAY         TWO-WAY IRREVERSIBLE PRIVACY TRANSFORMATION.                                          28-5-301
UNCONVENTIONAL  UNCONVENTIONAL USES ONLINE INFORMATION RETRIEVAL SYSTEMS.                             28-1-13
UNION           RELATIONSHIP AUTHOR NAMES ENTRIES ONLINE UNION CATALOG TRUNCATE.                      28-2-115
UNITED          SERIALS AUTOMATION UNITED STATES BIBLIOGRAPHIC HISTORY *R PITKIN.                     28-4-233
UNIVERSE        INDUSTRIAL SPECIAL LIBRARY UNIVERSE BASE LINE STUDY.                                  28-3-135
UNIVERSITY      IDENTIFIER METHOD MEASURING USE MODELING CIRCULATION USE BOOKS UNIVERSITY LIBRARY.    28-2-96
USE             IDENTIFIER METHOD MEASURING USE MODELING CIRCULATION USE BOOKS UNIVERSITY LIBRARY.    28-2-96
USE             IDENTIFIER METHOD MEASURING USE MODELING CIRCULATION USE BOOKS UNIVERSITY LIBRARY.    28-2-96
USERS           SEMANTIC DIFFERENTIAL ACCESS USERS ATTITUDES BATCH IR SYSTEM ERIC.                    28-5-268
USES            UNCONVENTIONAL USES ONLINE INFORMATION RETRIEVAL SYSTEMS.                             28-1-13
USING           CLUSTERING LARGE FILES OF DOCUMENTS USING THE SINGLE LINK METHOD.                     28-6-341
USING           COMPARING ALGORITHMS DOCUMENT RETRIEVAL USING CITATION LINKS.                         28-4-192
VARIATIONS      SOCIODEMOGRAPHIC CORRELATES INTERCOUNTY VARIATIONS PUBLIC LIBRARY OUTPUT.             28-6-360
VARIETY         VARIETY GENERATION REINTERPRETATION SHANNONS MATHEMATICAL THEORY OF COMMUNICATION.    28-1-19
VEIT            COMMUNITY COLLEGE LIBRARY *R VEIT.                                                    28-2-123
VOIGHT          ADVANCES IN LIBRARIANSHIP 6 *R VOIGHT HARRIS.                                         28-2-127
VOIGHT          ADVANCES IN LIBRARIANSHIP 7 *R VOIGHT HARRIS.                                         28-5-304
VOSPER          NATIONAL INTERNATIONAL LIBRARY PLANNING *R IFLA VOSPER NEWKIRK.                       28-2-125
WARNING         EARLY WARNING SYSTEM FOR RAPID IDENTIFICATION AND TRANSFER OF NEW TECHNOLOGY.         28-3-170
WESTERN         HISTORY OF LIBRARIES IN WESTERN WORLD *R JOHNSON HARRIS.                              28-2-124
WORLD           HISTORY OF LIBRARIES IN WESTERN WORLD *R JOHNSON HARRIS.                              28-2-124
WORLD           WORLD DIRECTORY OF MAP COLLECTIONS *R RISTOW.                                         28-4-232
WRIGHT          ORAL ANTECEDENTS OF GREEK LIBRARIANSHIP *R WRIGHT.                                    28-6-371
YEAR            LOTKAS LAW YEAR BY YEAR *L.                                                           28-1-65
YEAR            LOTKAS LAW YEAR BY YEAR *L.                                                           28-1-65
```

searching (i.e., there are no *see* references, say, from AGRICULTURE to FARMING or from SODIUM CHLORIDE to SALT); and many titles are not representative of the subject dealt with or are on purpose written to catch the attention of prospective readers without indicating the subject at all, e.g., "On the care and construction of white elephants" (on cataloging) or "The money-eating machines" (on computer management). In addition, lengthy KWIC indexes are tiresome to scan, especially when they are printed in small type and in all capitals, as is often the case. Thus, contrary to the pun intended by the acronym KWIC, such indexes are neither quick for the user nor really indexes to concepts dealt with in texts but rather are listings of words that authors happened to put into titles. On the other hand, since the introduction of KWIC indexes, titles of scientific and technical articles have become more indicative of their contents because authors and editors became aware of the fact that inexpressive titles would be overlooked in KWIC and similar indexing techniques.[19] In the social sciences and humanities, however, the custom of authors to give catchy and uninformative titles to their papers is continuing unabatedly.

EXTRACTION OF WORDS

KWIC indexing was only the first of the so-called derivative indexing methods, all of which are based on the principle of extracting words from machine-readable text—a title, an abstract, or even the full text of a document. Automatic extraction of words is generally coupled with *truncation* in searching, that is, the possibility of searching for a word stem without regard to its prefixes or suffixes, in order to retrieve a maximum of potentially useful occurrences of that word. Thus, a physicist looking for the presence of the concept "pressure" may search for *PRESS* (the asterisks indicating that prefixes and suffixes are also to be searched), which may give:

COMPRESS
COMPRESSION
IMPRESSION
SUPPRESSION
PRESS
PRESSER
PRESSES
PRESSURE
PRESSURIZE
PRESSURIZATION
PRESSWORK

While truncation (or "stemming") does increase recall, it lowers precision because it may result in unwanted and irrelevant items being retrieved (the latter known as "false drops"). This may occur because of at least two phenomena: a) homonyms cannot be detected by mere extraction methods — that is, in the example just cited, IMPRESSION, SUPPRESSION, and PRESSWORK do not pertain to "pressure" in the physical sense, while PRESS may pertain both to mechanical equipment and to newspapers, the latter being of no interest to a physicist; b) the elimination of "common" words by a stop list may also result in false drops whenever relationships are of importance, e.g., a Boolean search for TEACHERS *and* STUDENTS *and* EVALUATION will retrieve both teachers' evaluation of students and students' evaluation of teachers, because the elimination of the crucial words "of" and "by" makes it impossible to know who does what to whom.

For a time it was tried to correct the lack of indicators of relationships in derivative indexing by so-called *links* and *roles*, the former making explicit which words were linked to each other in a relationship, while the latter indicated functions (e.g., acting "as" or "for" something). These devices led indeed to higher precision, but they had to be assigned at the input stage by human beings. As that greatly diminished any gains made by automatic extraction of terms, the method was soon abandoned.

TERM FREQUENCY METHODS

On the assumption that terms (other than common words) to be indexed are those occurring either very frequently in a text (and therefore indicating concepts dealt with) or very seldom (indicating a topic mentioned expressly only once or twice in the title or first paragraph but then being referred to by "it" or "this" and the like), methods were designed to perform automatic indexing on the basis of frequency of occurrence and co-occurrence of terms, using probabilistic models. Some investigators tried to couple such methods of determining how often a term is used (term frequency methods) with term weighting, i.e., assigning different degrees of importance to terms on the basis of what terms are used in a search request or on the basis of where and how terms appear (e.g., in the title, in an abstract, or in the first or last paragraph of a text, and whether they are italicized or capitalized), all of which can to some extent be determined automatically. While these methods are of interest to statisticians and mathematicians, and some have produced acceptable results under tightly controlled laboratory conditions when applied to very limited subject fields, they have as yet not found any practical large-scale application.

LINGUISTIC METHODS

A quite different approach to automatic indexing is by syntactic and semantic analysis. The former is concerned with the automatic recognition of significant word order in a phrase or sentence and with inflections, prefixes, and suffixes that indicate grammatical relationships, while the latter approach seeks to analyze noun phrases automatically with the aid of stored dictionaries and other linguistic aids (thus having affinities to automatic translation). The two methods are also often used in conjunction. Most research in this direction has been performed in the Soviet Union, Germany, France, and Japan, while relatively little interest in purely linguistic methods has been shown by English-speaking researchers.[20]

COMPUTER-AIDED INDEXING

As indicated above, except for KWIC and KWOC indexing, none of the other automatic indexing methods has been applied on a large scale. For the time being, the large access services and data bases still use human indexers and abstractors, even though their work is far from perfect or consistent, because none of the methods of automatic indexing invented so far has shown itself to be able to compete in terms of indexing quality or economic viability. According to Lancaster,[21] automatic indexing methods are now no longer the focus of interest of researchers, but computers will increasingly aid information retrieval in various other ways. Microcomputers are now widely used by indexers in *computer-aided* indexing, relying on stored dictionaries of synonyms and homonyms, lists of authors' names for automatic verification, lists of trade names and names of chemical compounds, plants and animals, etc. They are also used to take the drudgery out of indexing by automatically arranging entries in alphabetical order or subordinating subheadings and cross references in exact sequence under a heading, and by performing many other functions that previously had to be done manually and therefore were quite expensive and often subject to errors.

SWITCHING LANGUAGES

We have made a cursory examination of a number of subject access systems available for use in modern library cataloging. Most are self-contained, providing their own categories and terminology, with syntactical rules designed to express complex or multi-faceted concepts. Each exhibits both strengths and weaknesses. Not one has yet proved sufficient to meet all needs, nor demonstrably better than all others in every situation. In consequence, a movement toward "switching languages" has emerged. Eric Coates tells us:

The problem is thus to devise a mechanism for making index information, originally input in a particular indexing language, immediately usable by another institution employing a different indexing
language. A possible answer to this problem has for some time been
exercising French documentalists of the Groupe d'Etude sur l'Information Scientifique of the CNRS at Marseilles. The Groupe proposes what is variously called a mediating indexing language, an
intermediate indexing language, or, by appropriating a term from
another discipline (a procedure which in the long run indexers and
vocabulary controllers may come to rue) a switching language.[22]

The information explosion, together with rapid developments in automation, made intercommunication among subject disciplines, libraries, and
nations both a possibility and a growing necessity. With a multilateral translation program, materials already indexed would be more readily available,
while libraries and information centers could avoid future duplication by join-
ing systems of shared cataloging without discarding or revamping their own
catalogs and indexes.

Many enthusiasts favored an umbrella classification, a coarse approach
recognizing only two to four hierarchical levels, for use by several agencies to
construct a cumulative thesaurus or to share indexing on a general level. One
example is the Committee on Scientific and Technical Information's *COSATI
Subject Category List*, a scheme of 22 broad research-oriented topical areas,
each with one or two levels of subdivision. It is used by a number of government agencies and research organizations to order their abstracting and indexing tools, and for similar purposes. But the problems of depending on such an
ad hoc system are obvious. Lacking breadth as well as specificity, it does not
provide a satisfactory universal switching language.

Another effort, backed by the Fédération Internationale de Documentation (FID) and Unesco, has produced a subject code schedule called the Broad
System of Ordering (BSO).[23] It is basically a classification system designed to
serve as a switching mechanism between various indexing languages. Its
proponents claim:

A classification, more than any other form of indexing language, is
amenable to easy, predictable, yet at the same time fully controlled
updating. This is the essential ground upon which it is the preferred
form of indexing language for the universal switching application.
That existing universal classifications have failed, or are visibly
failing, precisely in this respect does not vitiate the argument.[24]

Criteria established for BSO include flexibility, structural simplicity, and
easy manipulation in either manual or automated information systems. In its
present form it is an umbrella mechanism for shallow indexing and collocation
of large blocks of related information, rather than for retrieving specific
documents from different in-depth indexing systems.

Several other illuminating experiments have taken place. The interested
student will have no trouble finding descriptions of most of them in the

literature.[25] Whether a single switching language can perform equally well at all levels of specificity remains to be seen. Meanwhile there are other, less ambitious attacks on the problem. Linda C. Smith reports an effort to "map" a portion of the *Medical Subject Headings* (MeSH), which the National Library of Medicine uses in its preparation of *Index Medicus*, to three other controlled vocabularies, namely, *Subject Headings for Engineering* (SHE), used in *Engineering Index*; the *NASA Thesaurus*, used for *Scientific and Technical Aerospace Reports* (STAR); and *Subject Headings Used by the USAEC*. She explains:

> The alternative to a master switching language is to work with the individual vocabularies themselves, identifying terms from the two vocabularies used to index identical concepts and establishing such terms as equivalent for searching. While this device has been variously labelled in the literature as a table of equivalents or concordance, the mechanism to be used in converting from terms in one vocabulary to those in another is more rigorously defined by the mathematical concept of mapping. Since it is possible to mechanize only that which can be explicitly defined, it is useful to view the mapping as an algorithm for translating the terms of one vocabulary into equivalent terms used by another.[26]

This particular effort was only partially successful. Test searches showed that *Index Medicus* alone could retrieve 81 percent of the materials retrieved through mapping all four sources. Where the mapping increased the number of documents retrieved, some loss of precision occurred. The experiment did suggest possible alternative approaches to the clerical conversion of terms from one index language to another. This and other programs for machine translation and automated index transformations are still in the developmental stage.

NOTES

[1]John Rothman, "Index, Indexer, Indexing," in *Encyclopedia of Library and Information Science*, Vol. 11 (New York, Marcel Dekker, 1974), p. 289.

[2]Mortimer Taube and Associates, *Studies in Coordinate Indexing* (Washington, D.C., Documentation, Incorporated, 1953).

[3]A. C. Foskett, *The Subject Approach to Information*, 4th ed. (London, Clive Bingley; Hamden, Conn., Linnet Books, 1982), p. 436.

[4]*Thesaurus of Psychological Index Terms*, 4th ed. (Washington, D.C., American Psychological Association, 1985).

[5]*Thesaurus of ERIC Descriptors*, 8th ed. (New York, Macmillan Information; London, Collier Macmillan, 1980).

[6]*INSPEC Thesaurus,* 1985 [ed.] (London, Institution of Electrical Engineers, 1985).

[7]Derek Austin, "Progress in Documentation: The Development of PRECIS; A Theoretical and Technical History," *Journal of Documentation* 30 (March 1974): 47. In addition to this excellent article, the serious student is referred to: Derek Austin, *PRECIS: A Manual of Concept Analysis and Subject Indexing,* 2nd ed. (London, British Library, 1984); *The PRECIS Index System: Principles, Applications, and Prospects,* Proceedings of the International PRECIS Workshop, ed. by Hans H. Wellisch (New York, H. W. Wilson, 1977); and M. Mahapatra and S. C. Biswas, "PRECIS: Its Theory and Application—an Extended State-of-the-Art Review from the Beginning up to 1982," *Libri* 33 (December 1983): 316-330.

[8]Derek Austin and Jeremy A. Digger, "PRECIS: The Preserved Context Index System," *Library Resources & Technical Services* 21 (Winter 1977): 13-30; Derek Austin, "PRECIS: Theory and Practice," *International Cataloguing* 13 (January/March 1984): 9-12.

[9]Phyllis A. Richmond, "PRECIS Compared with Other Indexing Systems," in *The PRECIS Index System,* p. 113.

[10]Austin, *PRECIS Manual,* p. 307.

[11]Austin, *PRECIS Manual,* pp. 184-195.

[12]Valentine De Bruin, "PRECIS in a University Library," in *The PRECIS Index System,* p. 143.

[13]C. Donald Cook, "The Practical Possibilities of PRECIS in North America," in *The PRECIS Index System,* p. 189.

[14]*Library of Congress Information Bulletin* 37 (March 3, 1978): 154.

[15]*See,* for instance: Mary Dykstra, "The Lion That Squeaked: A Plea to the Library of Congress to Adopt the British PRECIS System, and to Reconsider the Decision to Overhaul the LC Subject Headings," *Library Journal* 103 (September 1, 1978): 1570-1572.

[16]G. Bhattacharyya and A. Neelameghan, "Postulate-Based Subject Heading for Dictionary Catalogue System," in Documentation Research and Training Centre, *Annual Seminar* 7 (1969): 221-254; and G. Bhattacharyya, "Chain Procedure and Structuring of a Subject," *Library Science with a Slant to Documentation* 9 (1972): 585-635.

[17]Some of the articles on NEPHIS, all by Timothy C. Craven, are "NEPHIS: A Nested-Phrase Indexing System," *Journal of the American Society for*

Information Science 28 (1977): 107-114; "Need a Subject Index? Use NEPHIS," *Creative Computing* 4, no. 6 (1978): 94-95; "A Government Publication Index Using Direct NEPHIS Coding of Titles," *Journal of Information Science* 2 (1980): 13-21.

[18]Hans Peter Luhn, "Keyword in Context Index for Technical Literature (KWIC Index)," *American Documentation* 11 (1960): 288-295.

[19]J. J. Tocatlian, "Are Titles of Chemical Papers Becoming More Informative?" *Journal of the American Society for Information Science* 21 (1970): 345-350.

[20]Hans H. Wellisch, "Vital Statistics on Abstracting and Indexing Revisited," *International Classification* 12 (1985): 11-16.

[21]F. W. Lancaster, "Trends in Subject Indexing from 1957 to 2000," in *New Trends in Documentation and Information: Proceedings of the 39th FID Congress, 1978* (London, Aslib, 1980), pp. 223-233.

[22]Eric J. Coates, "Switching Languages for Indexing," *Journal of Documentation* 26 (June 1970): 103.

[23]Eric J. Coates, et al., *BSO, Broad System of Ordering: Schedule and Index* (The Hague, IFLA; Paris, Unesco, 1978).

[24]Eric J. Coates, et al., *The BSO Manual: The Development, Rationale and Use of the Broad System of Ordering* (The Hague, FID, 1979), p. 35.

[25]For example: Karen Sparck Jones, "CLUMPS, Theory of," in *Encyclopedia of Library and Information Science*, Vol. 5 (New York, Marcel Dekker, 1971), pp. 208-224.

[26]Linda C. Smith, "Systematic Searching of Abstracts and Indexes in Interdisciplinary Areas," *Journal of the American Society for Information Science* 25 (November-December 1974): 344.

SUGGESTED READING

Austin, Derek. "PRECIS: Theory and Practice." *International Cataloguing* 13 (January/March 1984): 9-12.

Foskett, A. C. *The Subject Approach to Information*. 4th ed. London, Bingley, 1982. Chapters 14-15, 24-27.

Part IV
ORGANIZATION

25
Centralized Processing, Networking, and Online Systems

INTRODUCTION

Because of such problems as the growth in volume of published materials, the emphasis on rapid transfer of documents and bibliographic records from producer to consumer, and the resultant need for more and better library service, traditional patterns of cataloging and processing are changing significantly. Most libraries and library systems of any size have either centralized their technical services or entered into cooperative arrangements with other libraries. Smaller institutions usually purchase most of their processing from commercial vendors or non-commercial suppliers such as the Library of Congress. In fact, for nearly all American libraries, LC has long been the primary source of bibliographical data, since most other vendors, as well as cooperative and locally centralized processors, merely repackage or reformat LC products. Generally, original cataloging is undertaken only if the Library of Congress has for some reason not cataloged the work at hand. Major processing offices usually have two production lines operating side-by-side. The bigger one, staffed by well-trained technicians called "copy catalogers," works from LC records in machine-readable form, reproduced on printed cards or proofslips, in the *National Union Catalog*, or elsewhere. Only a handful of professionally trained "original catalogers" prepare the non-LC records.

TYPES OF PROCESSING CENTERS

Historically, each library service unit was responsible for its own ordering, cataloging, and the physical preparation of materials. Administrative efforts to increase efficiency and economy gradually substituted larger, or more coordinated, programs which took various experimental forms. The introduction and rapid growth of automation, while essentially unrelated, soon exercised a powerful influence over the development and success of those programs.

CENTRALIZED PROCESSING

In integrated library systems serving an entire region, county, municipality, university, public school district, commercial enterprise, or government agency, a central processing office normally handles the acquisition and preparation of materials for all public service branches. Subunits may do a final checking of records and file those records in their branch catalogs, but if any significant revision of the work is needed, it usually goes back to the central office. Although this type of organization is by no means new, it received strong emphasis with the rapid growth of library systems after World War II.

The term "centralized processing" may be broadly defined as any consolidated effort to bring under one control the technical operations necessary to prepare library materials for access and use at different service points. In the ensuing discussion several comments will be made which apply equally well—perhaps with some slight modification—to cooperative efforts and even to commercial sources of cataloging. The reader can carry over such observations into those discussions where they have a bearing.

Processing centers take a variety of forms, but can generally be grouped into broad categories according to one or more notable characteristics. Grouping by type of services rendered gives: 1) centers responsible for acquisition and complete technical processing, down to the physical marking and/or jacketing, 2) centers that order, catalog, and classify, and 3) centers that only catalog and classify.

There are, of course, advantages to setting up a processing center for a group of libraries or branches. They include:

1. Increased efficiency in handling more material at less cost

2. Higher quality cataloging

3. Centralization and simplification of business routines

4. Better deployment of staff through specialization

5. Use of more sophisticated equipment

6. Opportunities to create union catalogs

But there are problems as well. Local variations in practice have to be identified and coordinated, or, if necessary, eliminated. Economic justification must be carefully determined, both before and after decision-making, to ensure that it is real, not imaginary. Many descriptive reports of individual centers lack critical self-appraisal and follow-up studies, especially in their cost analyses. Efficiency of operation is often the function of size. The "optimum" volume of processing in a given center should be determined. Combining several different types of libraries (e.g., school and public) within one system may lead to problems which even a highly structured organization cannot solve. We often learn as much from our failures as from our more successful attempts at consolidation.

COOPERATIVE SYSTEMS

The chief trait differentiating cooperative from centralized processing is that the cooperative approach involves several independent libraries or systems. Each member usually continues to perform some of its own technical service work, depending on exchange of data to achieve broader coverage, or leaving a sizeable portion of its processing to be performed as a group project. Again, better use of resources, personnel, and equipment, as well as higher discounts on bulk purchases, are anticipated. The need for more standardization in ordering, cataloging, and processing may become either an advantage or a disruptive factor.

There are a number of cooperative arrangements in which several libraries share a single terminal connected to a bibliographic utility. Several libraries with small budgets and small staffs can pool resources to share one membership in a utility. Some such libraries may use the terminal only a few hours a month; others may use it one day a week. The librarians must commute to the location of the terminal and must schedule terminal time carefully.[1]

COMMERCIAL PROCESSING

Over a century ago, Charles C. Jewett, librarian of the Smithsonian Institution, proposed "A Plan for Stereotyping Catalogues by Separate Titles. . . ." The Smithsonian was at that time a copyright depository. As it produced bibliographic records, they could, he suggested, be preserved on stereotype plates for a variety of applications, including the printing of cards for sale to other libraries on demand. While Jewett's proposal did not itself endure, it presaged the marketing of printed cards undertaken by the Library of Congress in 1901. Neither venture was "commercial" in the strict sense. However, they were later imitated by a host of business concerns. Barbara Westby defines "commercial cataloging" as "centralized cataloging performed and sold by a non-library agency operating for profit."[2] In most cases it is a by-product of other commercial interests, e.g., the Standard Catalog compilations of H. W. Wilson, the vending emphasis of a book jobber such as Baker & Taylor, or the promotional activities of a corporation like the Society for Visual Education.

The Wilson Printed Catalog Card Service supplied many school and public libraries with simple but adequate card copy at nominal cost for widely-read books from 1938 to 1975. During that period over one hundred other distributors and publishers followed the Wilson example of supplying a packet of cards with each book sold. In 1976 Dowell listed in *Cataloging with Copy* fifteen commercial processing services and five additional commercial sources of card sets.[3] Technological advances have caused considerable changes in the scene since then. Some of the services are no longer in business. Most of the others have radically changed their character. They have supplemented their print services with microform and/or online data retrieval systems. Changes are occurring so rapidly that no reliable recommendations of particular systems or services can be made, but the Commercial Processing Services Committee of the Resources and Technical Services Division (RTSD) does offer a set of guidelines that any cataloger interested in making an intelligent choice should apply.[4]

UNION CATALOGS

Union catalog projects are not, strictly speaking, a type of processing arrangement, but they are essential to a successful processing center, and can be the *sine qua non* of a bibliographic research center. For example, the Bibliographical Center for Research (BCR) in Denver started in 1936 with a WPA grant to develop a union catalog based on a depository set of Library of Congress cards marked to show the holdings of member libraries in the Rocky Mountain area. The catalog was designed chiefly to serve BCR as a clearinghouse for regional interlibrary loans. In 1975, after a period of waning membership and reduced revenues, new objectives were announced, including the brokerage of OCLC services, with aid to members in other, related fields of communication, systems study, and network stimulation. The union catalog and interlibrary loan (ILL) services continued, but were de-emphasized in favor of newer forms of cooperation. As at BCR, most union catalog projects in printed card form are now valued primarily for having fostered early efforts at library cooperation which are presently coming to fruition in many kinds of consortia and networks.

BIBLIOGRAPHIC SERVICES OF THE
LIBRARY OF CONGRESS

In 1975 the Card Division of the Library of Congress changed its name to the Cataloging Distribution Service.[5] The change reflected a trend from print to machine-readable format (i.e., MARC tapes) in its distribution of bibliographic records. The print formats are still widely used. This distribution of print formats includes the sale of Alert Service cards as well as printed cards, the Cataloging-in-Publication (CIP) program, the publication of book catalogs and cataloging tools, including the *National Union Catalog* (*NUC*), various bibliographies, the *Library of Congress Classification* schedules, *Library of Congress Subject Headings, New Serial Titles*, etc.

LIBRARY OF CONGRESS CARDS

LC printed cards offer complete coverage for materials, both foreign and domestic, cataloged by the Library. LC is of course the copyright depository for domestic works. Two federal legislative acts significantly increased LC's coverage of foreign materials starting in the early 1960s. One authorized certain foreign countries to pay some of their debts to the United States by sending printed materials. The other authorized LC to acquire, catalog, and distribute bibliographic records for all materials of research value published in foreign countries. The thrust of the legislation benefited not only the Library of Congress, but all American research libraries.

Most of today's card output is produced on demand from MARC tapes, and packaged by machine through use of automated optical scanning equipment, although orders for non-MARC cards must still be filled manually from inventory stocks. The pamphlet, *Catalog Cards*, available on request, gives information on how to open an account and interpret the various order codes and pricing structures. Standard order slips of the kind reproduced below are furnished free to subscribers; multiple order forms compatible with LC optical character recognition devices are available from all major library supply houses.

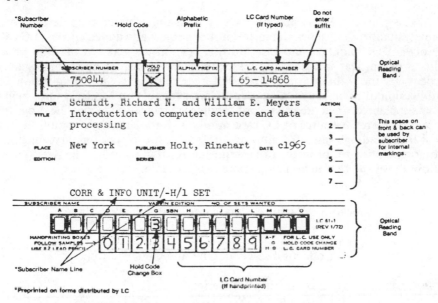

Ordering by LC card number rather than by author or title is more economical, and usually more satisfactory. This number can be found in standard bibliographies and book selection tools, such as the *Cumulative Book Index (CBI)*, the *Weekly Record (WR)*, the *American Book Publishing Record (BPR)*, *Library Journal (LJ)*, etc. It is also included, along with CIP data, on the title-page verso of most current books.

CDS ALERT SERVICE

The CDS Alert Service is a notification service that issues subject selections of bibliographic records produced at LC. The notices are printed on 3x5-inch white lightweight card stock. They are sent weekly to subscribers, and the content depends upon a subscriber's profile. The subscriber chooses from any of over 1,800 subject categories identified in the *CDS Alert Directory* and/or any of 22 broad subject categories (which are basically the class letters of the LC classification). With this service the subscriber receives full LC cataloging for the subject areas of interest. Subscribers may choose to receive English-language records only, non-English records only, or both, and may also choose to receive only MARC records, only non-MARC records (i.e., records in the nonroman alphabets that are not yet being input to MARC), or both. CIP records are included, thus providing three to six months' advance notice of a book's publication. The pamphlet *CDS Alert Service*, describing the procedures for ordering, is available on request.

Depository card sets were formerly maintained by many research libraries, but the *NUC* now serves the same purpose at very real economy of both filing time and storage space.

CATALOGING-IN-PUBLICATION

Most current American books carry a partial bibliographic description, namely author, title, series statement, notes, subject and added entries, LC call number, DDC number, and LC card number, on the verso of the title page. This program was initiated in 1971. Publishers cooperate by sending galley proofs to the Library of Congress for preliminary cataloging prior to publication of their books. CIP records are available on MARC tapes, being later supplanted when the full record becomes machine-readable. The program is useful as a ready source of LC card numbers, for assistance in establishment of name headings, and for libraries doing "fast-cat" preliminary, or full, cataloging prior to, or instead of, acquiring full LC records. The illustration below shows the format and appearance of CIP data.

Library of Congress Cataloging-in-Publication Data

Wynar, Bohdan S.
    Introduction to cataloging and classification.

    (Library science text series)
    Bibliography: p. 597
    Includes index.
    1. Cataloging. 2. Anglo-American cataloguing rules.
3. Classification--Books. I. Taylor, Arlene G.,
1941-   . II. Title.
Z693.W94 1985   025.3   85-23147
ISBN 0-87287-512-1
ISBN 0-87287-485-0 (pbk.)

LC PUBLICATIONS DISPLAYING CATALOGING

A wealth of bibliographic information can be obtained from the printed catalogs of the Library of Congress. The *Catalog of Books Represented by Library of Congress Printed Cards Issued to July 31, 1942* has been continued by cumulative serial publication of the *NUC*. A separate retrospective set is entitled *National Union Catalog, pre-1956 Imprints*. Library of Congress book catalogs include *Audiovisual Materials; Music, Books on Music, and Sound Recordings; Monographic Series;* and the *Subject Catalog*. Since January 1983 *Monographic Series* and *Subject Catalog* are no longer published separately but are incorporated into the *National Union Catalog. Books,* which is published in microfiche, is issued monthly and features a register of full records and four separate cumulative indexes for name, title, subject, and series. Likewise, *Audiovisual Materials* is no longer published in book form but is published quarterly in microform as *National Union Catalog. Audiovisual Materials* in the same format as *National Union Catalog. Books*. Also published in microfiche format are *National Union Catalog. Cartographic Materials; National Union Catalog. Register of Additional Locations;* and *National Union Catalog. U.S. Books*.

MACHINE-READABLE CATALOGING (MARC)

The importance of the Library of Congress for setting catalog practice became even more evident with the introduction of the MARC Distribution Service. The initial study began in 1964; since that time, extensive experimentation has proceeded in the MARC I and MARC II, the Retrospective Conversion (RECON), the Cooperative Machine-readable Cataloging (COMARC), and the British UK/MARC pilot projects.[6]

At first, records were available only for English-language monographs, but now there are formats available for archival materials, audiovisual materials, films, machine-readable data files, manuscripts, maps, music, and serials as well as for books. In addition, over 130 roman-alphabet languages and several nonroman-alphabet languages are now being input. The MARC data base now includes well over 2 million records.

The Conversion of Serials (CONSER) automated data base was sponsored by the Council on Library Resources, using the online facilities of OCLC, and distributed through the MARC Distribution Service—Serials. Starting in mid-1976 with nearly 30,000 LC/MARC serial records, and accepting input from 14 North American libraries, it amassed over 200,000 records in its initial two years. Only one-third of them were authenticated by the Library of Congress and the National Library of Canada (the Designated Centers of Responsibility), but the number of verifications increased each year. Original plans were for LC to take over full support at the close of the two-year pilot program, but when it ran into difficulties in expanding its automation capacity, OCLC agreed to retain the data base, assuming managerial responsibility as well.

More recent projects include REMARC, a retrospective conversion project, and two cooperative cataloging projects with Harvard University and the University of Chicago. The REMARC data base has been in creation by Carrollton Press since 1980. The goal is to convert to MARC format over 5 million titles cataloged by LC between 1897 and 1968 (the year that most English-language LC cataloging of monographs became available in MARC format). Carrollton is also converting some items cataloged by LC since 1968 that were not input into the MARC data base by LC (e.g., foreign-language items that were phased into the MARC program throughout the 1970s). The projects with Harvard University and the University of Chicago involve direct input of bibliographic records into the LC data base by staff at the two universities. These records become part of the MARC data base and are distributed along with LC records to MARC subscribers.

The growth and nearly universal acceptance of the MARC formats, and even more, the publication of *AACR 2*, have highlighted the need for machine-readable authority records. A MARC format for name authority records was developed in the late 1970s, and LC began inputting name authority records in 1978. (The MARC authorities format is discussed and illustrated in chapter 27.) All new names and series titles are currently entered into the LC data base in the MARC authorities format, and many records have been retrospectively converted.

It is possible to obtain a subscription to one or more of the MARC tape services. One can receive only books, films, maps, or serials, or any combination of these. Also available are CONSER records and Name Authorities. *Machine Readable Cataloging*, available on request, describes this service.

ONLINE BIBLIOGRAPHIC NETWORKING

Various definitions of networking spell out theoretical criteria or conditions. In practice, however, the term covers any systematic interchange of materials, bibliographic data, services, information, or occasionally, the transfer of such resources from a central office to a number of libraries. "Network" has been used to describe multi-library organizations designed to facilitate inter-library loan, reference, duplicate exchange, processing, and the like. Our concern in this section is with the last named activity.

There are at present three major online bibliographic networks in the United States: OCLC Online Computer Library Center, the Research Libraries Information Network (RLIN), and the Western Library Network (WLN). The Network Development Office of the Library of Congress uses the term "bibliographic utility" for these and other online processing systems of individual libraries such as that of the University of Chicago, and Northwestern University's NOTIS (Northwestern On-line Totally Integrated System).[7] This term distinguishes originators of computerized cataloging from bibliographic service centers, e.g., the Southeastern Library Network (SOLINET) and the New England Library Information Network (NELINET), which serve as regional brokers, providing intermediate communication, training, and service for participating libraries. The possibility of such a service center's becoming a utility is not precluded if it later assumes the responsibility of maintaining some component of a national library network data store.[8]

Bibliographic utilities seek to make catalog data widely and conveniently available, to foster processing speed and efficiency, to reduce the staff and cost of technical operations, and to facilitate resource sharing. Emphasis varies with the types of library a utility is designed to serve. RLIN, for example, caters to the needs of major research libraries, while OCLC appeals to a wider spectrum. As most bibliographic utilities evolved, their goals broadened to include support for different library functions.

Although the objectives of the three major bibliographic utilities are similar, their services, costs, and operating procedures differ considerably. Each offers unique features that involve advantages and disadvantages for different members. The library that has potential access to more than one network must consider carefully such factors as cost, size of data base, adaptation to its needs, types of service contracts, training and support arrangements, and the membership among neighboring libraries. If and when a national library network data store is completed, it will provide an interface to the data bases of all utilities regardless of an individual library's primary affiliation.

OCLC ONLINE COMPUTER LIBRARY CENTER

This oldest and largest of the bibliographic networks was incorporated in 1967 as the Ohio College Library Center, establishing an online, shared cataloging system with an online union catalog to the academic libraries of Ohio. Online operations began in 1971 and expanded rapidly. By the mid-1980s there were over 5,000 member libraries throughout the country, cataloging 94 percent of their incoming materials through use of the existing online records, and inputting their original catalog records for cooperative use by other members. In 1978 it changed its name to the acronym OCLC, Inc., downplaying the former regional connotation. At the same time, the governing structure was altered to allow libraries outside Ohio equal participation in its governance. In 1981 it changed the official name to "OCLC Online Computer Library Center" in response to the fact that many people thought "OCLC" should stand for something. A Users' Council, elected from participants grouped in the regional service networks, chooses from among its members six of the fifteen who serve on the Board of Trustees. The Users' Council also advises the Board, which is the corporation's governing body.

OCLC serves individual libraries for the most part through broker networks such as AMIGOS, NELINET, SOLINET, SUNY, and BCR. Although there are scattered independent members, the western states and Europe each have a regional service center maintained by OCLC itself. The original Ohio libraries have now formed OHIONET. The brokers negotiate group contracts on behalf of their affiliates, perform profiling and staff training according to each one's specific needs, handle billing and other business procedures, and offer general assistance in effective utilization of OCLC services. Most regional networks are financed through membership fees plus surcharges on OCLC's first-time use charges.

The primary OCLC service has always been the Online Cataloging Subsystem. Because of its widespread use, it is described briefly here, but this overview is not intended to be a full introduction to its operation.[9] A library using the subsystem has access to a data base that numbers over 12 million bibliographic records, for which there are over 150 million locations listed. LC MARC tapes and additional cataloging by affiliates are constantly expanding the data base at the rate of about 8,000 records per week. An authorized library staff member at any one of the terminals connected to the system via dedicated line or dial access may access any record, then edit the data to agree with the book being processed, and add holdings statements, locations, or other in-house data, requesting catalog cards as specified in the library's pre-determined profile. Cards are produced offline at OCLC headquarters in Dublin, Ohio, and shipped daily to members. They come arranged in packs according to member specifications, ready for immediate filing in local catalogs. Other products available from the system include magnetic tapes carrying records in the MARC format.

The data base may be searched by personal or corporate author (including added as well as main entries), author/title, title, series title, LC card number, OCLC control number, ISBN, ISSN, or CODEN. These searches may be modified in several ways, e.g., by type of material or by date of publication. As yet there is no subject access to the file, chiefly because of the enormous computing power needed to provide it on so large a data base for so many simultaneous users. OCLC continues to study subject access and intends to make it available as soon as it becomes economically feasible.

All records appear in MARC formats. There are, of course, standard protocols for cataloging at the OCLC terminals. For one, member libraries are obliged to follow the *Anglo-American Cataloguing Rules* (*AACR 2*). They are also requested, when inputting original cataloging, to check all name and series headings in the LC MARC authority file, which is available online through OCLC. Headings found in the authority file that are coded as being *AACR 2* are to be input in that form into original cataloging. However, the system is highly flexible, allowing members to adapt local records to meet local practices and conventions.

Quality control exists in published standards to which participating libraries are expected to adhere. Participants are encouraged to report any errors they find in the data base. OCLC staff members check and correct the master records from these reports. Certain authorized libraries have been able to correct errors directly since 1984. Unnecessary duplication of records has been a problem. James Schoenung reported in 1981 that 17 percent of the records in his study could be eliminated without the loss of a unique title.[10] LC records, when received replace some duplicates, and OCLC staff eliminate others when they are reported.

Consultation of training manuals and, above all, hands-on use are needed to gain skill in tagging worksheets and operating the terminals. Most people who have been properly trained find the techniques simple to master. Suggested sources for further information include OCLC's *Online Systems. Cataloging: User Manual* and other texts produced by participating networks. It must be remembered, however, that the Online Catalog Subsystem is constantly developing and changing. Only recent tools should be used. In fact, it is often necessary to supplement published manuals with the serial, *OCLC*

Technical Bulletins, and their accompanying documentation to learn the latest instructions for using the system.

Although the subsystem was originally designed specifically for cataloging support, online access to a bibliographic data base of over 12 million records is in fact a general service resource. Other subsystems have been introduced which interface with it or use it as a point of reference. Other subsystems offered are serials control, acquisitions, and interlibrary loan. Experience with these subsystems has led to the conclusion that some operations (e.g., serial check-in) are best handled at the local level. The rapid development of microcomputers has made such designs quite feasible, and OCLC has created a number of software packages that allow certain tasks to be completed at the local level with an interface to OCLC's Online Union Catalog (OLUC) where needed. OCLC's adoption of the IBM PC as an official terminal (adapted especially for use with OCLC and called the M300 Workstation) has made development and use of local software packages easier.

RESEARCH LIBRARIES INFORMATION NETWORK (RLIN)

RLIN resulted from adoption of Stanford University's Bibliographic Automation of Large Library Operations (BALLOTS) by the Research Libraries Group (RLG). RLG, Inc., was originally formed in 1974 by Columbia, Harvard, and Yale universities and the New York Public Library. Harvard withdrew at the time RLIN was formed, to be replaced by Stanford University. Membership neared 70 in 1985. Several hundred other institutions purchase RLG's services (e.g., "search only" access to RLIN).

The corporate objective is to foster interinstitutional support of scholarly communication and instruction in a rapidly changing climate of increasing costs and shrinking resources. Voting officers are elected annually by the member institutions to a Board of Directors. Together with the President — RLG's executive officer whom the Board elects and who then serves on the Board ex officio — they establish policies, programs, budgets, and fee structures, and appoint committees. Over them is a Board of Governors, to which each member library sends a representative. At its quarterly meetings it reviews the actions of the Board of Directors, as well as those of other officers and committees.

The primary programs of RLG are shared access to materials, collection management and cooperative development, preservation of research materials, and provision of sophisticated bibliographic tools. The bibliographic component, originally known as BALLOTS but now called RLIN, consists of a computerized set of data files and data manipulation programs. Like OCLC, the RLIN system can transmit data in either a "full-face" (covering an entire screen) or a "line-by-line" mode, depending on the user's hardware. It provides catalog worksheets, printed cards, and magnetic tapes in the U.S. MARC communications format; a variety of other acquisitions and in-process forms; and interlibrary loan capabilities.

Unlike OCLC, RLIN preserves a separate bibliographic record for every title cataloged by each library. Thus each library has online access to its own records showing whatever local changes may have been made. Local holdings, etc., are available to each local library, and selected data are available from records of other institutions.

All entries are in one of the MARC formats, including added copy cataloging and record maintenance. One of RLIN's strengths is its powerful query potential. Search terms can be used singly or in any sequence. They comprise LC card numbers, all or part of call numbers, and LC subject headings. Truncation searching on main and added entry words includes personal surnames and names of corporate bodies and geographic entities. The Boolean logic operators "and," "or," and "not" help tailor search strategies. All searches are interactive and can be negotiated or changed as searching progresses. Searching is also available on authority records. If a library has reason to believe an item will be cataloged by a national agency, brief bibliographic information can be keyed in once. It then is automatically searched against all new records entering the system.

The RLIN data base is considerably smaller than that of OCLC. The cost for first-time use of records for cataloging is comparable to that of OCLC, but fixed costs for telecommunications are substantially higher to some areas of the country. In spite of these drawbacks, RLIN is now a serious competitor in the field of networking. Its programs have a strong appeal to research libraries.

WESTERN LIBRARY NETWORK (WLN)

WLN was initiated by the State Library of Washington to give public and private libraries of the state a comprehensive bibliographic control system. While online operations began only in 1977 with ten pilot libraries, it has developed rapidly to become the most complete, though still the smallest, of the three major U.S. bibliographic utilities. Using equipment at both the Washington State Data Processing Service in Olympia and the Washington State University Computing Center in Pullman, it can be accessed online either by leased telephone lines or by dial-up. Its first out-of-state clients, the Alaska State Library at Juneau and the University of Alaska Library at Fairbanks, joined in the spring of 1978. By mid-1979 WLN extended its coverage to much of the Pacific Northwest, with state, public, academic, community college, and special libraries participating. While WLN gives first priority to libraries in its region, it agreed in early 1979 to sell its software to the National Library of Australia (NLA) in Canberra. Since then it has sold its software to others, including the University of Illinois at Urbana-Champaign and the Southeastern Library Network (SOLINET). But WLN has determined to restrict membership to the Pacific Northwest. In 1985 it changed its name from Washington Library Network to Western Library Network to reflect its regional character.

Like its two counterparts, WLN reached a point where its growing constituency called for representation in its administrative decisions. There is no talk of its breaking away from the State Library of Washington as NELINET and SOLINET did from their parent institutional structures; however, it expanded the governance of one of its major components, the Washington Library Network Computer Service, to include representatives from other states.

Like RLIN, WLN is well on its way to becoming a "full service" network. Its Bibliographic Subsystem provides catalog support services notable for their quality control. All LC MARC formats are used. WLN, like the other networks, conforms to Library of Congress policy in adopting *AACR 2* headings. Headings are linked to a network-wide authority data base that is more sophisticated than those of either OCLC or RLIN. When a cataloger is ready to enter original cataloging into the data base, a check command is given, whereupon each heading is checked automatically against the authority file. A code is returned to tell the cataloger whether each heading is identical to a heading already in the authority file, is identical to a *see* reference in the file, or does not match any term in the authority file. If a heading matches a *see* reference, the form referred to is given on the screen so that the cataloger can determine which form to delete or alter.[11]

Local catalog records can be accessed and edited online as in RLIN. Passwords, which may be changed as a precaution against unauthorized use, give access to specific files. Authorized participants are intensively trained in MARC tagging and input/edit techniques. Modifications in either bibliographic or authority data are automatically reviewed by the central Bibliographic Maintenance staff, who alone carry the right to replace existing records with modified records.

The Inquiry Module uses algorithms that are both powerful and flexible enough to support reference services as well as the Bibliographic Subsystem. They include subject and keyword, as well as author (personal and corporate names), title (including keyword and uniform titles), series, LC card number, ISBN, and ISSN search keys. Boolean operators expand the search capabilities.

Book catalogs, COM catalogs, printed cards, and processing kits are producible offline, to fit the individual client's profile. A COM union catalog in quarterly issues is supplemented with biweekly local library accessions lists. Holdings information facilitates interlibrary loan and other searches. In addition to the Bibliographic Subsystem, WLN supports acquisitions and interlibrary loan subsystems.

Part of the success of the WLN system can be attributed to its adoption of the system design with a quadraplanar data structure developed at the University of Chicago, although never fully utilized there.[12] At a demonstration to the Library of Congress, WLN representatives showed:

> The redundant storage of data is minimized in the system by interrelating the principal files: holdings, authorities, bibliographic, and local data. Thus, an individual institution may hold data unique to it, while more general data will be stored in the central system to be implemented at the level most appropriate for its operation.[13]

CANADIAN NETWORK CATALOGING

Canadian efforts toward computer-based network cataloging were sparked largely by the University of Toronto Library Automation Systems (UTLAS). In 1963 the Ontario New Universities Library Project started work on computer-produced book catalogs representing the initial library collections for five new campuses in the province.[14] The project was to facilitate selection, acquisition, and cataloging, while remaining flexible in its record format, access, and products. Implementation in 1965 led to the University's participation in the Library of Congress MARC project. By 1970 it was producing cards from MARC tapes for sale to clients, including in 1971 the College Bibliocentre, a processing center for nineteen colleges of applied technology. It started supplying computer-based systems and services to libraries in 1973.

Membership in UTLAS has been primarily among Canadian libraries, although UTLAS signed an agreement in 1981 with a Japanese firm to broker its services in Japan, and an UTLAS branch office was opened in New York in 1984.[15]

The UTLAS Catalogue Support System (CATSS) provides original, derived, and shared cataloging of monographs, serials, AV materials, government documents, and other formats. Like the other utilities, CATSS provides online interactive editing with generation of various offline products: cards, book and COM catalogs, lists, and forms. Like RLIN, UTLAS maintains online separate copies of every record produced by every user. However, these are kept in separate files, which can be searched, but not altered, by other users. Like WLN, UTLAS offers online verification of headings for authority control.

Searching of CATSS includes keyword capabilities along with the ability to "browse" personal and corporate names, titles, series, and subjects. One can also search LCCNs, ISBNs, and other control numbers. Boolean capabilities assist in narrowing keyword searches.

The University of Toronto closed its public card catalogs as of June 30, 1976. Its retrospective holdings records are now available on COM fiche, supplemented periodically by cumulations of new cataloging.[16]

COOPERATION

The obvious duplication of resources and effort among the utilities has been of concern for some time. It has been felt that there should be some means for exchanging data across utilities. However, there are political, technical, and economic factors that must be taken into account. In 1980 a study of this subject was completed by Battelle Institute under a grant from the Council on Library Resources. It recommended either batch processing of search requests to be exchanged among the utilities, or allowing a user of one utility direct online access to the others. The recommendations were not implemented, but the report drew attention to the need for cooperation. As a result there have been policy changes, and cooperative projects have been initiated.[17] In 1982, for example, OCLC began allowing partial membership and tapeload membership status. At reduced cost over full membership, this allows members of other networks (particularly RLIN) to have access to the OCLC data base. Partial members may use noncataloging subsystems or search the data base without entering their cataloging. For tapeload members, the location identifier is added to the OCLC master record for records on the library's archive tapes which are run against the OCLC data base. Most of RLG's full members have become tapeload members of OCLC. Similarly,

RLIN has loaded some OCLC tapes. A number of RLG members that were formerly OCLC members desired access to the records they had created on OCLC. By loading their archive tapes into RLIN, they were allowed that access. WLN has a somewhat different approach. Any library or system that purchases the WLN software agrees to allow its archive tapes to be run against the WLN data base for the purpose of adding to WLN any records not already in the file.[18]

Another cooperative venture that has implications for improved cataloging is the Linked Systems Project (LSP). RLIN, WLN, and LC have been working on this since 1980. The goal is to be able to exchange data in an online mode through a standard network interconnection (SNI). OCLC has been contributing expertise to the project but is not committed to actually linking. Several library system vendors, however, have made known their intention to use SNI when it is operational.[19]

GENERAL CONSIDERATIONS

In most libraries, the professional cataloger's role with respect to online cataloging procedures is supervisory and managerial, although it is not uncommon for professionals to edit machine records, to revise nonprofessionals' input, and to use the data base in problem solving routines. Even direct supervision of terminal operators is considered paraprofessional in many libraries. The essential professional contribution is to organize policies and procedures to make the most efficient use of the system.

Research shows that use of an online cataloging system does not always result in major organizational or procedural change.[20] However, the introduction of such a tool into a traditional catalog department is potentially a powerful change agent. It should at least stimulate revaluation of long-standing policies and procedures. The measures taken by librarians to adapt their operations to the new environment affect their success in reducing per-unit cataloging costs, speeding the flow of materials through the processing department, and achieving related objectives. Some of the factors to be considered when utilizing network services and designing efficient interface procedures are described below.

Cataloging Networks as a General Bibliographic Resource

Library managers should encourage use of the data base for pre-order verification, for location spotting in ILL work, for public service uses such as citation verification, and for bibliographic problem solving. It is unfortunate that many libraries overlook these potential uses of the system, since cataloging networks usually do not charge extra for them.[21] Charges generally occur only when the system is used for cataloging, except for terminals reserved exclusively for public service use. Not only can full use of the system improve such tasks as pre-order searching, but it can foster goodwill and acceptance by introducing more staff to use of the terminals. Staff resistance to online cataloging comes most often from those who do not use the terminals in their jobs. It is generally good policy to introduce the full staff to the fundamentals of terminal operation, encouraging them to use the system as part of their daily routines if possible.

It is true, however, that administrative emphasis on full utilization of the system complicates matters such as terminal placement, scheduling, and decisions to purchase additional ones. These problems are cited most often where use has been restricted to the catalog department. On the other hand, noncataloging uses seldom require large amounts of terminal time, in comparison to cataloging use. It is usually possible to schedule these functions, either with an "interrupt priority" or with one or more terminals completely unscheduled for catalog production.

Unfortunately, sometimes a perceived encroachment on cataloging time is actually the result of inefficient, wasteful cataloging procedures. Time must be treated as a valuable resource if the system is to provide optimum support to all appropriate technical and public service functions. Cataloging routines should proceed in a manner that conserves terminal time. This point will be further discussed in the section on procedural design.

Also related to maximizing use of some online cataloging systems is the decision to acquire a library's archive tapes, the machine-readable records of all transactions the library makes on the system. While cards are the principal system product for the great majority of libraries, the possibility of owning, very inexpensively, a machine-readable record of a library's holdings is an important byproduct. Even though there may be no immediate need for the archive tapes, it is a good idea to place a subscription when a library joins such an online system. In many libraries machine-readable bibliographic products such as COM and online catalogs are making use of these tapes.

Cataloging Policy

It is more convenient to edit copy to local standards with online cataloging than when using printed cards from LC or other sources. Still, a high degree of local variation from standard LC practice tends to slow work-flow, due largely to the need to consult local authority files and shelflist records.

To profit most from online cataloging, it is a good idea to review all local variations from standard practice at the time a library enters the system. This is not to suggest that all variations are misguided. Many local prerogatives are necessary because of inconsistent precedents over the years on the part of LC itself. Others may be justified by special local conditions. However, librarians should review all such variations in the light of their costs and their effects on processing efficiency. Any decision will affect online cataloging in areas such as terminal staffing, policies on the use of other libraries' records, and the organization of authority (integration) procedures.

The majority of titles added to a member library's collections will be cataloged in accordance with records existing in the data base. Policies related to accepting and modifying records created by another institution are now among the most critical ones a library makes — even more important than those related to original cataloging. Arlene Taylor Dowell's *Cataloging with Copy* is a detailed examination of copy-cataloging which is still timely, although based on the use of non-machine-readable techniques.[22]

Procedural Design

Local cataloging procedures related to online networking fall into five general groups:

1) The pre-cataloging search for copy, either as an acquisitions or as a cataloging responsibility
2) Cataloging with exact-match LC copy from the data base
3) Cataloging with LC copy which requires editing and/or with non-LC copy from the data base
4) Inputting original cataloging
5) Dealing with the offline products from the central office.

For best results, these functions must be well coordinated to avoid duplicate effort. They must be assigned to appropriate staff, with proper supervision and revision. They must also be integrated into an organizational structure designed to fit the new conditions resulting from network membership. Many issues arise when catalogers set up interface procedures with an online system. Among them are the following:

1) To what extent should clerical operators be restricted to using exact copy, or be allowed to edit "near copy" at the terminal?
2) To what extent should they be allowed to accept non-LC records?
3) What information should the pre-order search, or a special pre-catalog search, provide them?
4) How should the Acquisitions Department sort and route incoming items in accordance with the availability and type of data base copy?
5) Where should authority work take place for name, series, and subject entries?
6) To what extent must the shelflist be consulted in the course of cataloging?
7) What amount of revision is needed for each type of terminal operation?
8) Who should perform the revision?

Obviously, the above questions are interrelated. For example, appropriate revision of clerical operators' work will depend on the amount of editing and authority determination they may perform, and on the type of copy they are permitted to use. Collectively, the answers to such questions will decide a library's program for interfacing with the network. The system's efficiency helps determine whether the library meets its goals for network participation. To reduce turn-around time, cut the cost spiral, and improve cataloging quality, the interface must be as efficient as possible.

No single combination of procedures and policies would fit the majority of situations, since each interface emerges from the meshing of network capabilities with unique library conditions. A few simple guidelines may be useful, however, when setting up or evaluating such procedures:

1) **Conserve terminal time.** The point has been made that cataloging should be designed to avoid needless waste of time. Techniques can be used such as batching offline activities (particularly authority processing), avoiding unnecessary transcription (such as nonproductive printing of information from the terminals), and avoiding unnecessary call-ups of records (e.g., using a second or third call-up to produce cards if all the processing information is available the first time).

2) **Coordinate authority procedures.** One task that an online cataloging system does not do for a library is to ensure that the cataloging it initiates is compatible with that already existing at the library. Authority control is still largely manual and, if poorly executed, can nullify the advantages of online operation. Establishing authority records for names, for series, and for subjects should be handled as separate processes. A decision on whether to do any one of them before, during, or after cataloging at the terminal should be carefully weighed.

3) **Take advantage of the special capabilities of the system.** Major differences between online cataloging and the manual techniques it replaces are the speed of copy work and that of card production. It is no longer necessary to backlog bibliographic records while waiting for cards to arrive or for typists to produce them. With appropriate priorities, a library can expedite books for which exact LC copy is available, thus considerably reducing the familiar cataloging gap. Some of these capabilities are:

1) Priority staffing such that the copy-cataloging work remains fully staffed regardless of attrition in the department as a whole.

2) Special staff assignments on a temporary basis to meet peak load conditions in copy-cataloging work.

3) Expeditious sorting of recently acquired books according to the types of catalog copy available. Some libraries follow a "first in, first out" rule, which mixes all categories of materials regardless of their difficulty, or the availability of catalog copy.

4) Frequent recycling of arrearages for which catalog copy is likely to become available.

As has been previously said, it is a good idea to revaluate continuously a library's procedures in the light of systems capability within the network. Such changes inevitably include the constant growth of the data base and the evolution of operating procedures and subsystems. In the volatile network environment no cataloging interface can become so immutable as the techniques it replaces long appeared to be.

ONLINE PUBLIC ACCESS CATALOGS

Although experimentation with online public-access catalogs (OPACs) began in the 1960s, they did not become really functional until the 1980s. OPACs are now at the stage of development at which card catalogs were at the beginning of the twentieth century, when there was little agreement on size of cards, amount and order of data to be included, etc. OPACs have been developed locally in libraries and commercially. Some have expanded out of circulation systems that became fully functional in the 1970s. Others have been designed solely to serve as OPACs. Still others have grown up as one component of multipurpose systems that incorporate acquisitions and serials control functions as well as circulation and catalog functions. OPACs all differ in the way in which data are displayed, the amount of data displayed, and the manner in which a user must interact with them. There are varying amounts of authority control from none at all to a complete authority record for every heading fully linked to the bibliographic records. OPACs also provide for very different kinds of access ranging from those that essentially duplicate the access points available in a card catalog to those that offer sophisticated levels of searching using keywords, Boolean operators, truncation, and qualifiers.

OPACs differ further in the way in which bibliographic records are entered. Some allow direct downloading of records from the bibliographic utility to which the library belongs. Most allow loading of records from archive tapes, but the tapes usually must first be processed to eliminate superseded records, consolidate duplicates, etc. Some OPACs require direct input of records in a mode that has come to be known as "conversational cataloging," where the inputter is prompted for each line of the record.

Although there has been some research on existing OPACs,[23] more is needed along with more experimentation before standards can be set for future design.

FUTURE PROSPECTS

Trends in computer technology and progress in developing bibliographic standards are encouraging. Recent advances in computer technology indicate that minicomputers have the capacity to operate local online catalogs and other processing functions, such as acquisitions and serials control, at reasonable cost. Advances in telecommunication make possible distributed networks, consisting of a series of separate individual library catalogs interconnected by telecommunications links. Such a configuration is especially attractive in areas where many libraries engage in extensive resource sharing and coordinated collection development.

Even with local online catalogs, libraries still find the large network data bases valuable as sources for extended record searching. It appears that cataloging will continue in much the same way as today, except for the transfer of the edited machine-readable record into the local online data base rather than to card stock. Closing of card catalogs, at least in the larger libraries, will be the next major step in the evolution of materials processing toward quality improvement and control in standardized entry, descriptive detail, filing, physical preparation, and economical production of records.

The professional cataloger's contribution to an exclusively online situation is sometimes questioned. It is possible that many libraries that acquire only standard trade books and accept existing cataloging without modification will no longer need professional processing staff. On the other hand, there will likely be greater coordination of the national cataloging effort. The Library of Congress cannot maintain timely coverage of the world's entire publication output. Other libraries at home and abroad will no doubt take responsibility for cataloging in specific languages or subject categories. Consistently high standards will be kept in relatively few cataloging centers throughout the world. The number of professional catalogers may well be reduced, but the highly skilled bibliographer with special language or subject competency will be in greater demand than ever. Moreover, public service librarians are finding that in-depth knowledge of catalog codes and conventions, machine search strategies, and MARC or other machine-readable formats immeasurably increases their effectiveness in reference work, information exchange, bibliographic problem solving, and implementation of online public-access catalogs.

NOTES

[1]OCLC, *Annual Report 1983/84* (Dublin, Ohio, OCLC, 1984), pp. 15-16.

[2]Barbara M. Westby, "Commercial Services," *Library Trends* 16 (July 1967): 46.

[3]Arlene Taylor Dowell, *Cataloging with Copy: A Decision-Maker's Handbook* (Littleton, Colo., Libraries Unlimited, 1976), pp. 248-257.

[4]American Library Association, Resources and Technical Services Division, Commercial Processing Services Committee, "Guidelines for Selecting a Commercial Processing Service," *Library Resources & Technical Services* 21 (Spring 1977): 170-173.

[5]*Cataloging Service*, bulletin 113 (Spring 1975): 7-8.

[6]Henriette D. Avram, *MARC: Its History and Implications* (Washington, D.C., Library of Congress, 1975).

[7]Library of Congress, Network Development Office, "A Glossary for Library Networking," *Network Planning Paper*, no. 2 (Washington, D.C., The Library, 1978): 7.

[8]Ibid., p. 22.

[9]For a general description and comparison of the three major utilities *see* Dennis Reynolds, *Library Automation: Issues and Application* (New York, R. R. Bowker, 1985), pp. 55-63, 327-360.

[10]James Gerald Schoenung, "The Quality of the Member-Input Monographic Records in the OCLC On-Line Union Catalog," (Ph.D. Thesis, Drexel University, 1981), p. 129.

[11]Arlene G. Taylor, Margaret F. Maxwell, and Carolyn O. Frost, "Network and Vendor Authority Systems," *Library Resources & Technical Services* 29 (April/June 1985): 199.

[12]Maurice J. Freedman, "Some Thoughts on Public Libraries and the National Bibliographic Network," *Journal of Library Automation* 10 (June 1977): 128.

[13]*Library of Congress Information Bulletin* 36 (December 30, 1977): 845.

[14]Gordon H. Wright, "The Canadian Mosaic—Planning for Shared Partnership in a National Network," *ASLIB Proceedings* 30 (February 1978): 96-102; and Harriet Velazquez, "University of Toronto Library Automation System," *Online Review* 3 (September 1979): 254.

[15]Reynolds, *Library Automation*, p. 63.

[16]Valentine DeBruin, "Sometimes Dirty Things Are Seen on the Screen: A Mini-Evaluation of the COM Microcatalogue at the University of Toronto Library," *Journal of Academic Librarianship* 3 (November 1977): 256-266.

[17]Reynolds, *Library Automation*, pp. 349-350.

[18]Ibid., pp. 350-352.

[19]Ibid., pp. 353-354.

[20]Joe A. Hewitt, *OCLC, Impact and Use* (Columbus, Ohio State University Libraries, Office of Educational Services, 1977), pp. 122-124.

[21]Ibid., pp. 60-61.

[22]Dowell, *Cataloging with Copy*.

[23]*See*, for example: Jean Dickson, "An Analysis of User Errors in Searching an Online Catalog," *Cataloging & Classification Quarterly* 4 (Spring 1984): 19-38; Karen Markey, "Subject-Searching Experiences and Needs of Online Catalog Users: Implications for Library Classification," *Library Resources &*

Technical Services 29 (January/March 1985): 34-51; Joseph R. Matthews and Gary S. Lawrence, "Further Analysis of the CLR Online Catalog Project," *Information Technology and Libraries* 3 (December 1984): 354-376; Arlene G. Taylor, "Authority Files in Online Catalogs: An Investigation of Their Value," *Cataloging & Classification Quarterly* 4 (Spring 1984): 1-17.

SUGGESTED READING

Dickson, Jean. "An Analysis of User Errors in Searching an Online Catalog." *Cataloging & Classification Quarterly* 4 (Spring 1984): 19-38.

Dowell, Arlene Taylor. *Cataloging with Copy: A Decision-Maker's Handbook.* Littleton, Colo., Libraries Unlimited, 1976.

Matthews, Joseph R., and Gary S. Lawrence. "Further Analysis of the CLR Online Catalog Project." *Information Technology and Libraries* 3 (December 1984): 354-376.

Reynolds, Dennis. *Library Automation: Issues and Applications.* New York, R. R. Bowker, 1985. Chapters 2-4, 10-14.

Taylor, Arlene G., Margaret F. Maxwell, and Carolyn O. Frost. "Network and Vendor Authority Systems." *Library Resources & Technical Services* 29 (April/June 1985): 195-205.

26
Filing

INTRODUCTION

Neophyte catalogers are surprised to discover many alternative filing codes. They learn not only that choice of catalog arrangement (dictionary or divided) affects filing decisions, but that choice of entry is to some extent interactive with filing questions. Arbitrary groupings, exceptions from strict alphabetical order, and other complexities are directly related to the forms of subject headings and other catalog entries. Filing problems resulting from entry conflicts between the old *ALA Cataloging Rules* and *AACR* are a major impetus to the closing of such large catalogs as those of The New York Public Library and the Library of Congress. Some libraries attempt to interfile old and new forms of the same entry, while others file all forms exactly as they appear. In either case, ample use of references is necessary.

Before the advent of online catalogs, some people thought that filing would become a nonissue in online catalogs. However, we are now learning that when more than ten or so entries are retrieved in response to a search, they need to appear on the screen in some logical order. Catalog users are not happy with responses in which the entries appear in the order in which the items happened to be acquired by the library. Filing order is somewhat less of a problem, however, in online, book, and microform catalogs than it is in card catalogs. It is easier to scan one or more columns of entries and to discern their order than it is to determine the order of cards.

Research libraries have long adhered to one or another of various kinds of "categorical filing," particularly in those parts of their catalogs where relatively large numbers of highly formalized entries are concentrated. Categorical filing is based on the assumption that the user knows enough about a subject to prefer a partially classified arrangement over straight adherence to the alphabet. Less scholarly libraries generally prefer a simpler and therefore more readily grasped alpha-arrangement. Even the big academic and research collections are gradually succumbing to popular demand, and to the requirements of computer filing. For instance, the Library of Congress used to arrange its entries for individual books and groups of books of the Bible in

549

canonical order, as part of an intricate categorical arrangement.[1] Today, those entries are filed alphabetically:

Former Arrangement	Present Arrangement
Bible. O.T. Pentateuch	Bible. N.T. Acts ....
" " Genesis	" " Colossians ....
" " Exodus	" " 1 Corinthians ....
" " Leviticus	" " 2 Corinthians ....
" " Numbers	" " Ephesians ....
" " Deuteronomy	" " Epistles ....
[etc.]	[etc.]
Bible. N.T. Gospels	Bible. O.T. Amos ....
" " Matthew	" " Apochryphal books ....
" " Mark	" " 1 Chronicles ....
" " Luke	" " 2 Chronicles ....
[etc.]	[etc.]

Some libraries adopt published filing codes, e.g., the *ALA Filing Rules*.[2] Others develop sets of rules tailored to their own preferences. In almost every case questions arise which cannot be answered by a simple appeal to the alphabet.

FAMILIAR FILING DILEMMAS

In the first place, there is a significant difference between alphabetizing straight through to the end of a phrase entry, and observing the breaks in the string which occur at the end of each word. Most filers know the admonition "nothing before something," or "blank to Z." It means that library catalogs are generally arranged letter-by-letter to the end of each word. However, not all files in libraries are based on this premise. Reference librarians have to remember that the *American Peoples Encyclopedia*, the *Americana*, and the *World Book* are arranged word-by-word, while *Britannica*, *Collier's*, and *Compton's* prefer uninterrupted letter-by-letter filing to the close of the entry phrase. The differences are in some areas important, e.g.:

Word-by-word	Letter-by-letter
New Hampshire	Newark (N.J.)
New Haven (Conn.)	Newcastle (N.S.W.)
New York (N.Y.)	Newfoundland
New York (State)	New Hampshire
New Zealand	New Haven (Conn.)
Newark (N.J.)	Newman, Arthur
Newcastle (N.S.W.)	Newport (Isle of Wight)
Newfoundland	NEWSPAPERS
Newman, Arthur	New York (N.Y.)
Newport (Isle of Wight)	New York (State)
NEWSPAPERS	New Zealand

In entries containing dates, early historical periods usually precede later ones. However, codes differ on whether longer periods should precede or follow shorter ones starting with the same year. The *ALA Filing Rules* and the *Library of Congress Filing Rules*[3] both say to arrange periods of time beginning with the same year in chronological order. They give examples from which the following selection was made:

UNITED STATES – HISTORY – CONFEDERATION, 1783-1789
UNITED STATES – HISTORY – 1783-1865
UNITED STATES – HISTORY – CONSTITUTIONAL PERIOD,
    1789-1809
UNITED STATES – HISTORY – 1865-
UNITED STATES – HISTORY – 1865-1898
UNITED STATES – HISTORY – WAR OF 1898
UNITED STATES – HISTORY – 1898-
UNITED STATES – HISTORY – 20TH CENTURY

The *ALA Rules for Filing Catalog Cards*, second edition,[4] called for arranging periods of time beginning with the same year so that the longest period would file first, e.g.,

UNITED STATES – HISTORY – 1783-1865
UNITED STATES – HISTORY – CONFEDERATION, 1783-1789
UNITED STATES – HISTORY – 1898-
UNITED STATES – HISTORY – WAR OF 1898

If there are two or more editions or impressions of a work, edition dates or numbers may be added to the entry line, solely as filing elements. Again, codes differ on whether the earliest or latest should file first. The *ALA Filing Rules* say to arrange editions in straight chronological order, with earliest date first, e.g.,

Briscoe, Herman Thompson
    General chemistry for colleges. [c1935]
    General chemistry for colleges. [c1938]
    General chemistry for colleges. 3d ed. [1943]
    General chemistry for colleges. 4th ed. [1949]

In the list below, the latest ones come first, on the assumption that they are the ones the user is most likely to want.

Imagism and the imagists. 3rd ed.
Imagism and the imagists. [1st ed.]

Principles of cardiac surgery. 1979 ed.
Principles of cardiac surgery. [1967 ed.]

Numbers or digits in catalog entries give further challenges. Under current sets of rules, character strings beginning with numerals (whether arabic or nonarabic) are arranged before character strings beginning with letters, e.g.,

The 24th Congress of the CPSU and its contribution to
   Marxism-Leninism.
XXIVth International Congress of Pure and Applied Chemistry,
   main section lectures presented at ....
Twenty-four dramatic cases of the International Academy of Trial
   Lawyers.
The twenty-fourth session of the International Labour Conference ....

According to the *ALA Filing Rules*, numerals precede character strings, and all such character string/numeral combinations are interfiled regardless of the type of entry, e.g.,

HENRY I, KING OF ENGLAND, 1068-1135
HENRY V, KING OF ENGLAND, 1367-1413
Henry VIII and his wives.
HENRY VIII, KING OF ENGLAND, 1491-1547
Henry VIII's fifth wife.
Henry the Eighth and his court.
Henry the Fifth of England.

However, under *LC Filing Rules* fields with identical leading elements are subgrouped in the order of person, place, thing, title. Thus, while numerals precede character strings, the person entries are all grouped before the title entries, e.g.,

HENRY I, KING OF ENGLAND, 1068-1135
HENRY V, KING OF ENGLAND, 1367-1413
HENRY VIII, KING OF ENGLAND, 1491-1547
Henry VIII and his wives.
Henry VIII's fifth wife.
Henry the Eighth and his court.
Henry the Fifth of England.

In prior rules, however, numerals were most often filed as spelled, and spelled "as spoken," in whatever language the entry appeared. Many catalogs and other sources still file numerals in this way. Interpretation becomes most critical when the primary filing element of a title is expressed on the chief source of information in numerals. For instance, it is conceivable, though not very likely, that the two delightful books (one by Walter Sellar, the other by Reginald Arkell) entitled *1066 and All That* are lost forever to the patron who cannot transcribe "1066" appropriately. More hazardous is the alphabetizing of titles which start with a number in the 100s. They are collocated together, usually with interspersed entries and a guide card starting with the words "one hundred." Nevertheless, as the file grows, interpretations become increasingly difficult. The following selections were gleaned, in the order shown here, from a research library catalog. To indicate the inconsistencies in this list, the words in brackets indicate how the numbers should be "spoken" according to the 1968 ALA rules for filing.

An Equivocal File of Entries under Various Forms of "100"

100 American drawings. [one hundred]
One hundred and eleven poems.
One hundred and fifty years of collecting ....
One hundred and forty years of the Tennant companies ....
119 years of the Atlantic. [one hundred and nineteen]
One hundred & one ballades.
101 nudes. [one hundred and one]
One hundred and sixty cat proverbs & proverbial similes.
One hundred and two H-bombs.
100 classical studies for flute. [one hundred]
150th commemorative recital. [one hundred and fiftieth]
One hundred fifty years; a history of publishing ....
150 years of British steam locomotives. [one hundred and fifty]
The 158-pound marriage. [one hundred and fifty-eight]
140 Jewish marshals, generals and admirals. [one hundred and forty]
101 American vacations from $25 to $250. [one hundred and one]
One hundred one-act plays.
101 best nature games and projects. [one hundred and one]

As displayed here the problems are fairly obvious; in a large file of several hundred entries they become more elusive. However, filing numerals first can also cause problems for users. How would a user who has heard a title spoken (e.g., 100 classical studies for flute) know whether to look in the numerical section or the alphabetical section? References and/or added entries are required, regardless of the method of filing.

Extensive use of acronyms and initialisms has in recent years aggravated the familiar problem of how to file abbreviations. Computerized filing throws new light on the difficulties encountered in traditional approaches. In the past, initials were most often treated as one-letter words, regardless of whether spaces or punctuation intervened. For machine-readable data bases it is easier to file strings of letters, or letters-and-numbers, lacking spacing or punctuation as multicharacter words. It is immaterial whether they consist entirely of capitals (e.g., FORTRAN) or of a combination of upper and lower case (e.g., MeSH or Unesco). Nor does pronounceability affect the filing, as it did under previous sets of filing rules that required that one determine whether or not an acronym or initialism was pronounced as a word in order to decide where to file it.

Abbreviated titles of respect or position (e.g., Mr., Dr., St.) formerly were filed as if spelled out in full. But social pressures, as well as the computer, have effected changes. For example, *Webster's New International Dictionary* (second edition) defined "Mrs." as "the form of Mistress when used as a title."[5] The problems ensuing from that edict were impressive. Fortunately, *Webster's* third edition substitutes a more contemporary (and considerably more round-about) explanation which in effect recognizes the abbreviation at its face value. Meanwhile, many libraries had already decided to file "Mrs." and "Ms." as written. Under both of the 1980 sets of filing rules (ALA and LC) abbreviations are arranged exactly as they are written.

Initial articles are usually suppressed as filing words, especially in titles. The practice extends to all languages using articles, since even in inflected languages the number of articles is relatively limited. They can be tabulated for manual filing, or programmed out of machine filing. But homonyms (e.g., the French article "la," as in "la belle epoque," and the British interjection, as in "La! she was a lady") must be differentiated. Also, articles which initiate proper names (e.g., "La Crosse, Herman Thomas" and "Los Angeles (Calif.)") are always filed for American or English names, and for other languages as well where usage so dictates.

In dictionary catalogs the order of entries with identical wording, which nonetheless are punctuated differently, must be decided. The conventional arrangement is: author, subject, title. In practice, it is highly unusual to find an author entry, a subject entry, and a title entry, all with exactly the same wording; the question bears more often on different kinds of entries which start with the same word. Application of the "authors first" guideline leaves unanswered the ordering of surnames and given name entries which start alike (e.g., "Thomas ..."). The *LC Filing Rules* file given name entries (e.g., "Francis, of Assisi, Saint" and "Francis Xavier, Saint") ahead of the same word used as a surname (e.g., "Francis, Connie"). The *ALA Filing Rules* reverse that preference, interfiling all entries, regardless of type, character by character to the end of the character string. However, many card catalogs are still filed according to the 1968 *ALA Rules*, according to which all surname entries come first, followed by all other entries that begin with the same word.

Many libraries, particularly large ones with comprehensive collections by and about certain versatile writers, have separated out main and added entries for those persons into at least two categories. However, the original edition of the *ALA Rules* discouraged the practice:

> Arrange in one file all the entries, both main and secondary, for a person as author, joint author, compiler, editor, illustrator, translator and general added entry. Subarrange alphabetically by the title of the book. *Note:* An earlier practice, still followed in some libraries, is to arrange the secondary author entries in a separate alphabet after the main author entries. This practice is not recommended because users of the catalog overlook entries so filed.[6]

It was observed in chapter 1 that divided catalogs permit a simpler filing scheme than do dictionary catalogs. The simplifications obviously depend on the way in which the division is made. Most commonly, subject entries are alphabetized separately from author and title entries. Persons (e.g., "Shakespeare, William") who are both authors and subjects of books have entries in each catalog, rather than having all the entries about them collocated immediately behind all the entries by them. Titles that happen to be identical with a subject heading (e.g., *Freedom of the Press*) are similarly located in a separate file. There is perhaps less danger of the title entries' being misfiled or overlooked, but closely related titles and subjects are divorced from each other.

Cross-references are likewise automatically multiplied in a divided catalog. In either type of catalog there is seldom any doubt about where to file a *see* reference, but there are definitely two schools of thought on the location of *see also* references. Most catalogers place them immediately after those entries from which they lead, on the theory that the user will have exhausted a search at that point, and be most ready for new suggestions. However, both sets of 1980 filing rules (ALA and LC) say categorically to file *see also* references before the first entry under the same word or words.

THE 1980 FILING RULES

The first edition of the *A.L.A. Rules for Filing Catalog Cards* was published in 1942. A Subcommittee of the American Library Association's Editorial Committee was established exactly twenty years later to prepare a revision which would correlate with the 1967 publication of the *Anglo American Cataloging Rules*. The second edition of filing rules, like the first, was primarily designed for a dictionary catalog.[7] Except for the surname-first groupings in cases of identical entry words, single-alphabet arrangements were preferred over categorical considerations in nearly all cases. Machine filing experiments undoubtedly influenced the trend toward straight alphabetization. Yet the *ALA Rules* were designed for the manually filed catalogs which would continue to predominate for at least another two decades.

The Filing Committee of the Resources and Technical Services Division was appointed in the early 1970s to look into rules for computer filing. However, contact was maintained with the committee that was developing *AACR 2* so that the new rules would be applicable for *AACR 2* entries. The new *ALA Filing Rules* were thought to be so different from the earlier two sets of ALA rules that they were considered to be a new work, not another edition.[8] The introduction states that they are applicable to any bibliographic displays, not just card formats, and that they can be used to arrange records formulated according to any cataloging rules.[9]

The brief summary of the *ALA Filing Rules* that follows is designed to show the rules that a filer in a modest collection would be most likely to use. In cases where the *LC Filing Rules* vary significantly, this is brought to the reader's attention.

GENERAL RULES

As already mentioned, filing is character by character to the end of each word and word by word to the end of the filing element. This is a result of applying the "nothing files before something" principle, with spaces, dashes, hyphens, diagonal slashes, and periods all considered to be "nothing." Also, as already mentioned, numerals precede letters. In addition, letters of the English alphabet precede letters of nonroman alphabets.

Modified letters (e.g., *Ł*) are filed as if they were the plain English equivalent, and diacritical marks are ignored. Punctuation and nonalphabetic signs and symbols (except those noted above as equivalent to "nothing," ampersands, and certain such marks in numeric character strings) are also ignored.

Examples of the Basic ALA Rules

10 ans de politique social en Pologne
$20 a week
112 Elm Street
150 science experiments step-by-step
1918, the last act
130,000 kilowatt power station
A.
A.A.
A.B.C. programs
Aabel, Marie
AAUN news
$$$ and sense
Camp-fire and cotton-field
Camp Fire Girls
Campbell, Thomas J.
Campfire adventure stories
LIFE
Life — a bowl of rice
"Life after death"
LIFE (BIOLOGY)
Life, its true genesis
LIFE — ORIGIN
Life! physical and spiritual
Life, Spiritual. *See* SPIRITUAL LIFE
LIFE STYLES
Muellen, Abraham
Muellenbach, Ernst
Mullen, Allen
Müllen, Gustav
Mullen, Pat
New York
Newark
% of gain
One hundred best books
Parenting guidebook
Rolston, Brown
Rolvaag, Ole Edvart
Rølyat, Jane
Zookeeper's handbook
π Σ A: A history

The *LC Filing Rules* differ on the treatment of nonroman alphabet letters: these are to be romanized for filing.

Note that under previous rules, hyphenated prefixes and compound words written both as separate words (or hyphenated) and as single words (e.g., campfire, camp-fire) were interfiled as the single word. Under the new rules a hyphen is regarded as a space.

Ampersands

Ampersands may be ignored or, optionally, may be spelled out in their language equivalents, e.g.,

Without option	With option
Art and beauty	Art and beauty
ART AND INDUSTRY	Art & commonsense
Art & commonsense	ART AND INDUSTRY
L'art et la beauté	L'art et la beauté
L'art et les artistes	L'art & la guerre
L'art & la guerre	L'art et les artistes

Under *LC Filing Rules* the ampersand has the lowest filing value in alphanumeric order, e.g.,

Art & commonsense
L'art & la guerre
Art and beauty
ART AND INDUSTRY
L'art et la beauté
L'art et les artistes

TREATMENT OF ACCESS POINTS

If access points are not identical they are filed character by character and word by word according to the general rules. The major exceptions are for initial articles, certain kinds of numerals, and certain additions to names (e.g., relators and terms of honor and address). For explanation of these exceptions, see below.

When access points consist of a name and a title, they are filed as two separate elements. The title portion files with all other titles under the same name heading.

Identical Access Points

When arranging identical access points, first consider the function of the access point. As mentioned earlier, *see* and *see also* references precede the entries of their type. In addition, main and added entries are interfiled but precede subject references and subject entries, e.g.,

Philadelphia. Free Library.   [corporate name entry]
Annual report ...

Philadelphia Free Library   [title added entry]
Wagner, Robert L.
The Philadelphia Free Library ...

PHILADELPHIA. FREE LIBRARY [subject entry]
Bruns, Suzanne.
A history of the Philadelphia Free
Public Library ...

As mentioned earlier, *LC Filing Rules* call for arranging entries with identical leading elements in the order: person, place, thing, title. "Thing" includes corporate body entries. Thus in the example above the title added entry would follow the subject entry.

Subarrangement of identical access points *with equivalent functions* in the *ALA Filing Rules* is determined by consideration of secondary data elements. For records with author or uniform title main entry, the next element considered is the title, followed by the date of publication, distribution, etc. For records with title main entry (not uniform title) the next element considered is the date. If the access point is a personal or corporate name added entry, the next element considered is the title, followed by the date. If the access point is a title added entry, the next element considered is the author or uniform title main entry, if there is one, followed by the date. If the access point is a series or subject added entry, the next element considered is the author or uniform title main entry, if there is one, followed by the title, followed by the date.

Examples Arranged by ALA Filing Rules

(examples are invented)

Love.
James, Samuel.
Love ...

Love and beauty.
Adams, Harriet.
Love and beauty ...

Love and beauty.
Hansen, Sigurd.
Love and beauty ...

LØVE (DENMARK)
Friis Møller, Jens.
Life in a Danish town ...

Love, Harold G., 1878-1926.
    The chemical industry ...

Love, Harold G., 1911-
Symposium on the Social Organization of Anthropoid
        Apes (1st : 1954 : Berkeley, Calif.)
    Anthropoid apes and their society ...

Love, Harold G., 1911-
    Behavior of nocturnal primates ...

Love, Harold G., 1911-
    The primates of Africa ...

    Love, Harold G., 1911-
Atkins, Francis Harrison.
    Psychological studies of the great apes ...

    LOVE, HAROLD G., 1911-
Coffin, Lyle Warner.
    Harold Love ...

    LOVE, HAROLD G., 1911-
Driscoll, Maynard.
    Cousins, once removed ...

    LOVE, HAROLD G., 1911-   —BIBLIOGRAPHY
Hennesey, Judy.
    Books by and about Harold Love ...

    LOVE (THEOLOGY)
Adam, Karl.
    Love and belief ...

The above entries would have a somewhat different order under the *LC
Filing Rules* because of the arrangement of fields with identical leading
elements in the order of person (forename, then surname), place, thing
(corporate body, then topical subject heading), title.

Examples Arranged by LC Filing Rules

(examples are invented)

Love, Harold G., 1878-1926.
    The chemical industry ...

Love, Harold G., 1911-
Symposium on the Social Organization of Anthropoid
        Apes (1st : 1954 : Berkeley, Calif.)
    Anthropoid apes and their society ...

Love, Harold G., 1911-
    Behavior of nocturnal primates ...

Love, Harold G., 1911-
    The primates of Africa ...

    Love, Harold G., 1911-
Atkins, Francis Harrison.
    Psychological studies of the great apes ...

    LOVE, HAROLD G., 1911-
Coffin, Lyle Warner.
    Harold Love ...

    LOVE, HAROLD G., 1911-
Driscoll, Maynard.
    Cousins, once removed ...

    LOVE, HAROLD G., 1911-   — BIBLIOGRAPHY
Hennesey, Judy.
    Books by and about Harold Love ...

    LØVE (DENMARK)
Friis Møller, Jens.
    Life in a Danish town ...

    LOVE (THEOLOGY)
Adam, Karl.
    Love and belief ...

    Love.
James, Samuel.
    Love ...

    Love and beauty.
Adams, Harriet.
    Love and beauty ...

    Love and beauty.
Hansen, Sigurd.
    Love and beauty ...

SPECIAL RULES

Abbreviations

As mentioned earlier, abbreviations are arranged as written.

Examples

Concord (Mass.)
The Concord saunterer
Concord (Va.)
CONCORD (VT.)

Doctor come quickly
Doktor Brents Wandlung
Dr. Christian's office
Dr. Mabuse der Spieler [in German]

Initial Articles

Initial articles that form integral parts of place names and personal names are filed as written. Initial articles at the beginning of corporate names, title, and subject headings are ignored unless they begin with a personal name or place name.

Examples

Las cartas largas.
El chico.
The Club.
Der Club.
Club 21 (New York)
Club accounts
The Club (London)
El-Abiad, Ahmed H., 1926-
El Campo (Tex.)
The El Dorado Trail.
The John Crerar Library today.
La Fontaine, Jean de, 1621-1695.
Las Hurdes (Spain)
Laš, Michal.
Lasa, Jose Maria de.

Initials, Initialisms, and Acronyms

The filing of initials, initialisms, and acronyms depends upon the spacing and punctuation between the characters. If they are separated by spaces, dashes, hyphens, diagonal slashes, or periods, they are filed as if each character were a separate word. If they are separated by other marks or symbols or are not separated, the group of characters is filed as a single word.

Examples

A.
A.A.
A., A.J.G.
A apple pie
A.B.
A.B.C. programs
Aabel, Marie
AAUN news
The ABC about collecting
ABM. See ANTIMISSILE MISSILES
U.N.E.S.C.O. See UNESCO and Unesco.
Unesco
UNESCO bibliographical handbooks
Unesco fellowship handbook

Names and Prefixes

A prefix that forms part of the name of a person or place is filed as a separate word unless it is joined to the rest of the name without a space or is separated from it only by an apostrophe.

Examples

De Alberti, Amelia
De la Roche, Mazo
De Marco, Clara
De senectute
Defoe, Daniel
Del Mar, Eugene

EL ALAMEIN, BATTLE OF, 1942 [place name]
El Dorado (Ark.) [place name]
El-Wakil, Mohamed Mohamed [personal name]
Elagin, Ivan
Elam, Elizabeth
Eldorado (Neb.)
Elwell, Floyd

MacAlister, James
Mach, Ernst
MACHINERY
MacHugh, Angus
Maclaren, Ian
MacLaren, J

Maclaren, James
M'Bengue, Mamadou Seyni
McHenry, Lawson
McLaren, Jack
Mead, Edwin Doak
M'Laren, J. Wilson

Under previous ALA filing rules names beginning with the prefixes M' and Mc were filed as if written Mac, and many card catalogs are still filed that way.

Numerals

Numerals are arranged according to their value from lowest to highest, but there are some difficulties in reading numbers with punctuation, decimals, fractions, and nonarabic notation, and superscript/subscript numerals. If punctuation is for readability, it is treated as if it did not exist. Other punctuation is treated as a space. Decimals are arranged digit by digit, and if they are not combined with a whole integer, they precede the numeral 1. Fractions are arranged as if they are characters in the order numerator, line (treated as space), denominator (e.g., 2½ is filed: 2 space 1 space 2). Nonarabic numerals are interfiled with their arabic equivalents. Superscript/subscript numerals are filed as if on the line and as if preceded by a space.

Examples

.300 Vickers machine gun mechanism
1:0 für Dich
1¼ yards of silk
1.3 acres
1³ is one
⅓ of an inch
2 x 2 = 5
3.2 beer for all
3:10 to Yuma
3 point 2 and what goes with it
$20 a week
XX Century cyclopaedia and atlas
20 humorous stories
XXth century citizen's atlas of the world
200 years of architectural drawing
2000 A.D., a documentary

Dates

Dates in titles are filed as numerals. Dates in a chronological file, such as subdivisions of subjects or personal names with dates, are arranged chronologically, with B.C. dates preceding A.D. dates. Historic time periods that are generalized or expressed only in words are filed with the full range of dates for the period (e.g., "18th century" is equivalent to 1800-1899). Subject period subdivisions are filed chronologically even when words (e.g., the name of a war) precede the dates. Geologic time periods are arranged alphabetically.

Examples

    UNITED STATES—HISTORY
    UNITED STATES—HISTORY—COLONIAL PERIOD,
        CA.1600-1775
    UNITED STATES—HISTORY—FRENCH AND INDIAN
        WAR, 1755-1763
    UNITED STATES—HISTORY—REVOLUTION, 1775-1783
    UNITED STATES—HISTORY—REVOLUTION, 1775-1783—
        CAMPAIGNS AND BATTLES
    UNITED STATES—HISTORY—CONFEDERATION,
        1783-1789
    UNITED STATES—HISTORY—1783-1865
    UNITED STATES—HISTORY—1865-
    UNITED STATES—HISTORY—1865-1898
    UNITED STATES—HISTORY—WAR OF 1898
    UNITED STATES—HISTORY—1898-
    UNITED STATES—HISTORY—20TH CENTURY
    UNITED STATES—HISTORY—1933-1945
    UNITED STATES—HISTORY—BIO-BIBLIOGRAPHY
        [alphabetical]
    UNITED STATES—HISTORY—DICTIONARIES
    UNITED STATES—HISTORY—PHILOSOPHY
    UNITED STATES—HISTORY—STUDY AND TEACHING

Under the *ALA Filing Rules*, subjects with subdivisions and those with qualifiers are interfiled ignoring punctuation. The *LC Filing Rules*, however, are more inclined to categorize entries. Topical subject headings are grouped so that the leading element alone is first, followed by entries in the form leading element—subject subdivision. These are followed by entries in the form leading element, additional word(s). The last group is entries in which the leading element is followed by a parenthetical qualifier.

Examples

    COOKERY
    COOKERY—DICTIONARIES
    COOKERY—YEARBOOKS
    COOKERY, AMERICAN
    COOKERY, AMERICAN—BIBLIOGRAPHY
    COOKERY, CHINESE
    COOKERY, INTERNATIONAL
    COOKERY (APPLES)
    COOKERY FOR DIABETICS

Subordinate elements that follow a dash are also grouped according to the *LC Filing Rules*. The order is period subdivision, form and topical subdivisions, and geographical subdivisions. This is the order in which *LCSH 9* is arranged, and it is further discussed with examples in chapter 22 of this text.

ALTERNATE FILING RULES

The *ALA Filing Rules* summarized above were a response to a feeling that traditional practices were too complex, too awkward, and too concerned with fine theoretical distinctions. Not everyone agrees, as is evidenced by the fact that many libraries have not fully implemented the changes. There are two major considerations: 1) it would be prohibitively expensive to re-file a card catalog for a collection of, say, a million volumes or more; and 2) there is a direct relationship between the size of the collection and the need for a fine-tuned filing system. John Rather argues the case for meaningful complexity:

> Filing arrangement is the capstone of the system of bibliographic control that begins with descriptive cataloging and includes subject analysis and classification. The entire effort to achieve bibliographic control necessarily reaches its fulfillment in the means of displaying catalog information to users. If the arrangement of the file violates the form or meaning of the headings, users will be hampered in their efforts to use the catalog successfully.[10]

The primary issue is categorical versus alphabetical filing. Research libraries hold that the *ALA Filing Rules* to some extent "violate the form or meaning of the headings." The 1968 *ALA Rules* were also criticized for this even though that set of rules maintained more categorization than do the current *ALA Filing Rules*. The 1968 *ALA Rules* Subcommittee claimed:

> An attempt was made to develop an alternative code of rules based on a consistent regard for punctuation, but that method also proved to be not entirely satisfactory, because of lack of consistency in punctuation.[11]

The Subcommittee's reference was a major 1942 rule requiring that subject entries beginning with the same initial element be arranged by type as signified by differing marks of punctuation in the manner still called for by the *LC Filing Rules* and described above.

The Subcommittee held that many of the disadvantages of alpha arrangements could be overcome by adding state or country designations after all city names, and using parenthetical explanatory terms after all homonyms or homonymous phrases. Movement has been made in this direction with LC's implementation of *AACR 2*, which calls for making additions to nearly all local place and jurisdictional names. The following examples compare the arrangements achieved by applying first one, then the other, of the 1942, 1968, and 1980 versions of the ALA rules to the same group of entries:

1942 ALA Rules

Love, David T.
LOVE, DAVID T.
Love, Zachary
The Love Corp.
Love County (Okla.)
LOVE   [subject]
LOVE—LETTERS
LOVE—QUOTATIONS
LOVE, MATERIAL
LOVE (THEOLOGY)
Love   [title]
Love and beauty
LOVE POETRY
Love songs, old and new
Love your neighbor

1968 ALA Rules

Love, David T.
LOVE, DAVID T.
Love, Zachary
LOVE   [subject]
Love   [title]
Love and beauty
The Love Corp.
Love County (Okla.)
LOVE—LETTERS
LOVE, MATERIAL
LOVE POETRY
LOVE—QUOTATIONS
Love songs, old and new
LOVE (THEOLOGY)
Love your neighbor

1980 ALA Filing Rules

Love   [title]
LOVE   [subject]
Love and beauty
The Love Corp.
Love County (Okla.)
Love, David T.
LOVE, DAVID T.
LOVE—LETTERS
LOVE, MATERIAL
LOVE POETRY
LOVE—QUOTATIONS
Love songs, old and new
LOVE (THEOLOGY)
Love your neighbor

The 1942 *ALA Rules* responded to the wide diversity of filing practices by including alternatives or variants for 60 percent of the rules. The 1968 Subcommittee opted for simplicity in this respect as well, developing a consistent code derived from one basic principle, with as few exceptions as possible. The 1980 Committee made the rules simpler still by eliminating the exceptions. However, those who want more categorization have a choice. The *LC Filing Rules* provide for this option, even with computerization in mind. The field tags, indicators, and subfield codes of the MARC format allow adequate identification of elements in headings so that a computer program has been written and is in use at LC that sorts using the *LC Filing Rules*.[12]

SHELFLIST FILING

The notation of most modern classifications, whether pure or mixed, includes arabic numerals (both integers and decimals) which are filed in normal mathematical sequence. A typical series of class numbers from the DDC schedules, which use a pure decimal notation, could appear as follows:

DDC Class Number Order

001	- Knowledge
010	- Bibliography
016	- Subject bibliographies
070.01	- Theory of journalism
070.1	- News media
070.17	- Printed media
070.172	- Newspapers
070.19	- Radio and television
070.4	- Journalistic activities
070.41	- Editing
070.509	- History of publishing
070.59	- Kinds of publishers
078	- Journalism in Scandinavia
100	- Philosophy
101	- Theory of philosophy
110	- Metaphysics
	[etc.]

Class number notation for the Library of Congress system is mixed. In its simplest form it consists of one to three roman alphabet letters followed by one to four integers. However, decimals both in pure numeric form and in alphanumeric form may be introduced at various points. A typical sequence might be:

LC Class Number Order

DJ288	- Netherlands history under Queen Juliana, 1948-
DJ401	- Local history in the Netherlands
DJ401.G35	- Goeree-en-Overflakke
DJ401.G4	- Groningen
DJK1	- Serials on Eastern European history
DJK24	- Social life and customs in Eastern Europe
DJK46	- Eastern European history by period
DJK46.4	- The Bulgars

T20	- History of technology in the 20th century
T26.G3	- History of technology in Germany
T26.G5B5	- History of technology in Berlin
TP572	- Directories of brewing and malting
TP573.A1	- General histories of brewing and malting
TP573.5	- Biography of brewers and malters
TP573.5A1	- Collective biography of brewers and malters
TP574	- Schools of brewing and malting
TP1107	- Exhibitions of plastics and plastics manufacture
TP1130	- Handbooks, manuals, tables, etc. of plastics
TP1135	- Plastics plants and equipment
	[etc.]

Cutter number notation also varies with the system. Libraries which use DDC may use cutter numbers assigned through use of the Cutter two- or three-figure alphanumeric tables or the Cutter-Sanborn tables. Two-figure Cutter and Cutter-Sanborn numbers can be filed in straight integer sequence, but those from the three-figure Cutter table must be arranged decimally, as shown:

DDC call numbers with three-figure Cutter book numbers

333 D189	- A work on land economics by an author surnamed Falkinson
333 D19	- A similar work by an author surnamed Fallaby
333 D191	- A similar work by an author surnamed Fallentz
333 D21	- A similar work by an author surnamed Famareus
333 D218	- A similar work by an author surnamed Fantine

Workmarks consisting of lowercase letters, and most often corresponding to the first significant word of the item's title, may be added to the cutter number as follows:

DDC call numbers with workmarks

515.33 R41i - Introduction to Differential Calculus, by an author
                surnamed Richmond
515.33 R41m-Mean Value Theorems, by the same author
515.33 R41t - Total and Directional Derivatives, by the same author

Many smaller libraries using DDC bypass the Cutter tables in favor of adding one to three or more capital letters from the main entry word of the item to the DDC class number. These book symbols are of course arranged alphabetically as follows. In such libraries congested files are rare, so that lowercase workmarks are not often needed:

DDC call numbers with alphabetic book numbers

799.1 ROB - A book on fishing by an author surnamed Robb
799.1 ROBE - A similar book by an author surnamed Robertson
799.1 ROBI - A similar book by an author surnamed Robinson

The Library of Congress assigns its own unique cutter numbers to materials, as discussed in chapter 24—Library of Congress Classification. Many LC call numbers include two cutter numbers, of which only the final one is, or incorporates, the number for the particular item. The official shelflist at the Library of Congress will show, with or without intervening entries, the following arrangement:

Library of Congress Shelflist Arrangement

HC59.7.B7	- Broekmeijer, M. W. J. M. *Fiction and truth about the decade of development.* (66-25082)
HC59.7.C28	- Caiden, Naomi. *Planning and budgeting in poor countries.* (73-12312)
HC59.7.C6	- Committee for Economic Development. *How low income countries can advance their growth.* (66-29453)
HN438.C5G2	- Galpern, A. N. *The religions of the people in sixteenth-century Champagne.* (75-35993)
HN438.P3R8	- Rudé, George F. E. *Paris and London in the eighteenth century.* (73-148267)
HN438.P6H52	- Higonnet, Patrice L. R. *Pont-de-Montvert; social structure and politics in a French village, 1700-1914.* (70-133209)

What needs to be remembered when filing LC call numbers is that the classification part of the notation up to the period files as integers, but any cutter numbers after the period file as decimals.

HN4
HN5
HN15
HN23
HN43
HN59

but   HN438.C15
HN438.C23
HN438.C4
HN438.C43
HN438.C5
HN438.C59

Dates or edition numbers may be added as a third element to either DDC or LC call numbers to distinguish among different issues of the same title. These might be filed in either chronological or retrospective order, just as in catalog filing, but the majority of libraries prefer chronological shelflist filing. Location symbols of various kinds may also accompany call numbers of some materials. The shelflist filing of such additions is purely a matter of local preference.

CONCLUSION

The final results of the filing debates are by no means settled. Still, progress has been made. Perhaps universal standardization should not be our goal, given the diverse objectives of different libraries and types of libraries.

NOTES

[1]*A Catalog of Books Represented by Library of Congress Printed Cards Issued to July 31, 1942* (Ann Arbor, Mich., Edwards Brothers, 1943); vol. 14, pp. 3-13 gives full explanation of the arrangement.

[2]*ALA Filing Rules* (Chicago, American Library Association, 1980).

[3]*Library of Congress Filing Rules* (Washington, D.C., Library of Congress, 1980).

[4]*ALA Rules for Filing Catalog Cards*, 2nd ed. (Chicago, American Library Association, 1968).

[5]*Webster's New International Dictionary of the English Language*, 2nd ed., unabr. (Springfield, Mass., G. & C. Merriam, 1959), p. 1605.

[6]*A.L.A. Rules for Filing Catalog Cards* (Chicago, American Library Association, 1942), p. 25.

[7]*See* Pauline Seely, "ALA Filing Rules—New Edition," *Library Resources & Technical Services* 11 (Summer 1967): 377-379; and Pauline Seely, "ALA Rules for Filing Catalog Cards: Differences between 2d and 1st Editions (Arranged by 2d Rule Numbers)," *Library Resources & Technical Services* 13 (Spring 1969): 291-294.

[8]For a critique of the *ALA Filing Rules* see Hans H. Wellisch, "The *ALA Filing Rules*: Flowcharts Illustrating Their Application, with a Critique and Suggestions for Improvement," *Journal of the American Society for Information Science* 34 (September 1983): 313-330.

[9]*ALA Filing Rules*, pp. 1-2.

[10]John C. Rather, "Filing Arrangement in the Library of Congress Catalogs," *Library Resources & Technical Services* 16 (Spring 1972): 240-261.

[11]*ALA Rules*, 2nd ed., p. vi.

[12]*LC Filing Rules*, pp. 6-7.

SUGGESTED READING

Carothers, Diane Foxhill. *Self-Instruction Manual for Filing Catalog Cards.* Chicago, American Library Association, 1981.

Gorman, Michael. "Fear of Filing: Daunted Librarians Have Ally in New Rules." *American Libraries* 12 (February 1981): 71-72.

Wellisch, Hans H. "The *ALA Filing Rules*: Flowcharts Illustrating Their Application, with a Critique and Suggestions for Improvement." *Journal of the American Society for Information Science* 34 (September 1983): 313-330.

27
Catalog Management

INTRODUCTION

Efficiency of bibliographic retrieval, and the quality of bibliographic description, are affected not only by the care and standards used to catalog each item, but by several other important factors. One is the recording of local decisions and practices and keeping the department files and records current; another is the organization and routines facilitating each phase of the process; a third is the continuing maintenance and editing of the catalog. Each of these factors should be carefully evaluated and efficiently administered. Here we will consider briefly the major responsibilities, summarizing those features for which patterns of implementation may vary from library to library. Organizational structure, including the specification of staff duties, is not within the scope of this text.[1]

Cataloging, as we know, is usually divided into two kinds of activity: description and subject analysis. These activities are in turn subdivided. Descriptive cataloging records the essential identifying bibliographic and physical details of an item. It also establishes non-topical access points through selection of entries and forms of heading. In the course of selecting access terms, it is necessary to do authority work, which requires identifying a name or title to such an extent that it can be distinguished from any other person or entity or work that may have a similar name or title, while at the same time drawing together all manifestations of the same name or title. It is also necessary to make provision for references from forms of name or title not selected as the heading form.

Subject access is generally provided in two complementary modes: by shelf arrangement and by descriptive terms. Both of these modes exhibit categories indicative of topical content, as well as other categories showing literary or publication form. The first mode consists of assigning unique call numbers to each item, using the notation of a systematic classification scheme, plus other identifiers for the specific piece. The other aspect of subject cataloging is choosing linguistic terms to characterize the item's content. These terms are in most libraries selected from a pre-coordinated "subject heading list."

Since these, like non-topical access points, use a controlled vocabulary, references again provide bridges from terms not chosen to those chosen.

CATALOGING RECORDS AND FILES

A catalog department maintains files essential for accuracy, efficiency, standardization, and record keeping. Until recently, such files were nearly always formatted on cards or slips. Technology now offers new formats, which have been successfully introduced into many libraries. From the cataloger's, as well as the user's, viewpoint each embodies certain advantages, as well as some less attractive features.

ALTERNATIVE CATALOG FORMATS

The historical development and present uses of various catalog formats were briefly reviewed in chapter 1, "Principles of Cataloging." Although the dictionary catalog on 3x5-inch cards still predominates in most libraries, active vendor merchandizing of proprietary machine-readable data bases now brings alternative catalogs within the reach of smaller public and school libraries or systems. In many cases the existing card catalog remains in use, while another format is adopted to supplement and continue it.

Book catalogs may be produced in two ways, as was noted in chapter 1. In photoreproduction the book pages carry images of catalog cards, filed in order and reduced in size, but still in most cases quite legible. Varied type faces, type sizes, and local characteristics are all preserved. The original card catalog should, of course, be carefully groomed before it is photographed. Many manual operations, such as correcting errors, retyping poor quality cards, and checking the filing, are unavoidable prerequisites. Computer-based book catalogs have also been produced with varying degrees of success. Entries in such works are less likely to reflect a card-type appearance, being amenable to a denser column-and-line presentation.

Book catalogs are frequently limited to author (or main entry) lists, or to subject lists. They are far more compact and easy to scan than are card files, but they cannot be continuously cumulated, as can card lists. Periodically cumulated reprints are possible, but expensive. Most libraries prefer to supplement the latest book edition with a card file, an acquisitions list, or some other means of showing recent additions to the collection. The human tendency to overlook, or neglect to search, more than one file makes multiple access lists an ever-present hazard.

Computer output microform (COM) catalogs, like the other alternatives, are primarily a technological innovation. Still, their impact on cataloging procedures is significant.[2] While initially expensive, COM per-unit cost is significantly reduced by mass production. Particularly in large libraries, where many service points need ready and full information about the entire collection, extra issues of the catalog at minimum cost are a real benefit. To be sure, other expenses, such as the purchase or lease of reading machines, and the keyboarding of all bibliographic records for the computer's data base, must be met. COM catalogs, like book catalogs, cannot be continuously expanded and updated. New cumulations must be reissued from time to time. Or supplements must provide the records for incoming materials in a separate alphabetical file, and possibly in a different format. Moreover, since microforms cannot be read with the naked eye, some simple form of indexing must accompany them. Microfiche indexing is more precise and easier to use than film indexing, which depends on sequential searching, but both are somewhat awkward. Another drawback is the reluctance of many people to work with microforms, which require different reading skills and attitudes than do print materials. Yet COM catalogs have increased in number. Many large public systems, such as those in Hennepin County (Minnesota), St. Louis County (Missouri), Chicago, and Los Angeles County (California), now use them.

At the initial conversion stage, the machine-readable records may be stored in a large network data base, in commercial automated service facilities, on archival tapes, or in the in-house computers of individual libraries. Whatever the storage arrangements, COM catalogs, in either fiche or film, at various reduction ratios, can be issued in batch mode—that is, at times when online demands for computer power are minimal. Record and format quality depends on the needs and budget of the library. There are grades of difference, at varying prices. For example, the use of lower as well as upper case type faces, or the inclusion of special characters, will raise the cost of production, but will also result in a more pleasing, and usually a more readable, appearance.

The number of online machine-readable catalogs in libraries is growing rapidly. Some administrators now feel that it will be ultimately more satisfactory to wait until they can put their bibliographic records directly online, rather than adopting interim solutions in the forms of book or COM catalogs.

In some institutions computers were installed before their proponents knew precisely what would be their most effective applications. Librarians were thus encouraged to experiment with online catalogs to help absorb the computer potential and the fixed costs. More recently, various commercial services contract their hardware and software to libraries for the development of such products as online circulation systems, acquisitions systems, shelflists, and catalogs. A third source has come in the form of spin-offs from the large multi-institutional data bases that some cataloging networks, such as RLIN, supply. The future may provide further approaches, as well as new production technologies. The online catalog retains the continuous expansion features of the card catalog, along with the compactness, speed, and ease of access characteristic of book and COM catalogs. Cost is still prohibitive for many libraries but will probably go down, rather than up, as computer services are expanded and refined.

All of the files discussed in the remainder of this section can and do exist in card, COM, or online formats. (The only one likely to appear in book format is the catalog department manual, which is beginning to be found also online.)

THE SHELFLIST

The shelflist is a complete record of all titles in a collection, arranged by call number as the library materials are found on the shelves. Its primary purpose is to provide an official inventory record of the collection. Its classified arrangement shows what titles have been placed in a specific class notation. It serves, then, as an important classification aid, for catalogers consult it to verify their library's past use of each notation. The shelflist also displays, within certain limitations, related materials more general and more specific on either side of the notation referred to. In addition, it furnishes the matrix on which unique cutter numbers and workmarks are assigned, to differentiate titles collocated in the same class.

If the shelflist is in card format, the cataloger inserts a temporary hold slip, or other place marker, for each new item entered, to avoid duplication of call numbers, and to provide some information (not necessarily full cataloging) until the permanent record is made. That permanent record very likely will be a unit card, showing the entire bibliographic description plus tracings. Multiple volumes and copies, including location symbols for duplicates in reference, in children's rooms, branches, and the like, are noted. This information makes it not only easier, but more accurate, to browse the shelflist than to go directly to the shelves, where a number of items may be out in circulation, or otherwise displaced. The shelflist is thus useful not only to catalogers, but to reference staff and knowledgeable patrons. For these reasons many libraries make their shelflists available to the public. Others keep the official shelflist in the catalog office, perhaps placing a less detailed one near the card catalog.

Some libraries keep on their shelflist cards brief records of costs, accession numbers, acquisition dates, sources, missing and withdrawn copies, or anything else considered pertinent to the current status of each title. A typical "full information" shelflist card is shown in Fig. 27.1. It indicates that two copies of volume 1 have been purchased, but one is missing. In addition, the purchase source, date, and price of each volume and copy are shown. On an official card, of which this card is a copy, the cataloger has checked the tracings which were actually used. In this particular library, no series card was made.[3]

If the library has an online system searchable by call number, this can serve as the shelflist. This is more likely to occur in situations where there is an integrated system that is used for acquisition functions as well as for cataloging. In such a system a record is initiated with the order of an item. Dates, costs, etc., are part of the record and can be maintained for as long as the item is part of the system or even after the item is withdrawn or reported missing. Some libraries, however, maintain a card form shelflist as a backup to the online system.

Fig. 27.1. Sample shelflist card.

```
QA          Bellman, Richard Ernest, 1920–
427              Methods of nonlinear analysis [by] Richard Bellman.
.B4         New York, Academic Press, 1970–73.

                 2 v.  illus.  24 cm.   (Mathematics in science and engineering, v.
              61, 1–2)   $18.00 (v. 1)

                 Includes bibliographical references.
v.1, c.1    Baker & Taylor    11–5–74    $18.00    msg 9–30–75
v.2, c.1       "      "      "        "         $30.00
              1. Nonlinear theories.  2. Differential equations, Nonlinear.
            3. Numerical analysis.   1. Title.  II. Series.

            QA427.B4                      515'.35                  78–91424
            ISBN 0–12–084902–X (v. 2)                               MARC

v.1, c.2    Academic Press    12–9–79    $36.00

                                          ◯        rev
            Library of Congress                     70 [r73e3]
```

OFFICIAL CATALOGS

Some libraries maintain an official card catalog, kept in the technical services area. Essentially, it is a tool of convenience, duplicating to some extent the information found in the public catalog or in the shelflist. Frequently, it is limited to one main entry per cataloged title. It often serves as the authority file, including information on the choice of all non-subject and subject added entries, explanatory cards, and cross references. Usually, it identifies materials held in departmental libraries or special collections. Since it is not open to the public, it may show additional non-bibliographic details for the guidance of the staff, such as administrative decisions on the use of analytics, and other notes which might be missed in the department manual.

The shelflist approach is classificatory, showing the location of materials as they stand on the shelves. The official catalog, with its alphabetic approach, is complementary, but the high cost of keeping one prevents many libraries from indulging in a dispensable file. Such factors as library size, building layout, a decision to separate technical processes from public service areas, or responsibility for servicing more than one library unit are most likely to precipitate a separate official catalog. In any case, an online system usually obviates the need for an official catalog since terminals can be located in the technical services area regardless of its distance from the public services area.

AUTHORITY FILES

The purpose of an authority file, or files, is to standardize and control a library's use of non-subject entries, subject headings, and their respective cross references. In many smaller libraries its upkeep has often been more honored in the breach than in the observance. Such libraries obviously depend on their prime cataloging sources (e.g., the Library of Congress) to suggest cross references and to keep the use of heading forms in standard order. The inconsistencies that inadvertently creep in, through rule changes, error, and the like, are remedied if and when found. In a limited operation there may be some economic justification for this ad hoc approach. However, in larger libraries, where inconsistent and erroneous entries cause mis-filing, result in loss of entries in online catalogs, and otherwise obscure valuable entries in extensive files, the interest in authority files has escalated in the last decade.[4] As discussed in chapter 25, there is work toward exchanging data online in the Linked Systems Project. The first kind of data to be exchanged is authority data.

Many libraries use the public catalog, or the official catalog, as their authority list, but some information that should be available to the acquisitions or catalog librarian does not lend itself to inclusion in a public file. Moreover, the introduction of *AACR 1* in 1967, and even more of *AACR 2* in 1978, stimulated soul searching about authority records among libraries great and small.

It is important to note the difference between the existence of an authority file and the processes of creating and using an authority file. *Authority work* is "the process of determining the form of a name, title, or subject concept that will be used as a heading on a bibliographic record; determining cross references needed to that form; and determining relationships of this heading to other authoritative headings."[5] The record of that work is given in a printed or machine-readable unit that is entered into the authority file. The file is then used for the process of *authority control*, i.e., for maintaining the consistency of headings in a bibliographic file. In increasing numbers of online systems, the process of *authority control* is becoming at least partially automated; but the process of *authority work* remains highly tied to human endeavor.

Western Library Network (WLN), University of Toronto Library Automation Systems (UTLAS), a number of commercial suppliers of online systems, and some locally developed in-house systems have well-developed authority control programs. Some commercial suppliers of bibliographic services, such as Blackwell North America, provide magnetic tape processing in which a library's archive tapes from a bibliographic network may be edited to change older forms of heading to new forms. Online Computer Library Center (OCLC) and Research Libraries Information Network (RLIN) provide their members with LC's authority file online but give no control over headings in their data bases. In the systems that provide automated authority control, incoming headings on bibliographic records are automatically checked against the machine-readable authority file. When a heading matches one in the authority file, the bibliographic record is linked to the authority record. When a heading does not match, it is either referred to the cataloger for checking, or the system creates a mini-authority record for it.[6]

Most libraries that maintain authority files still do so in card form. Name authority files bring together in an alphabetic list all name headings, personal, corporate, or geographic, which are used in a given catalog as main, added, analytic, or subject entries. Authority records for series, uniform titles, and topical subjects may be added, turning the list into a general authority file. Or they may be handled in other, separate files.

The steps suggested below demonstrate the essential features of localized authority work.[7] The process followed for names, uniform titles, and series is different from that used for subjects. We will begin by discussing the process used for names, uniform titles, and series. First, it is important to understand the process of verification, which here means determining the existence of an author or other entity, and the accepted form of heading to use. Verification often involves consulting a number of bibliographic sources or reference tools. The name or title is first recorded as it appears in the work being cataloged. The item's title, date, and the location of the name, if it is not on the chief source of information, are noted. The next step usually is to check the LC authority file (LCAF) either online through the utility in which the library holds membership or in the microfiche version. If the name or title is in the LCAF and is coded as being in *AACR 2* form, the record is copied for the local file. If the name or title is not in the LCAF or is not coded as being in *AACR 2* form, *AACR 2* is consulted for the appropriate rules for form. If verification problems emerge, such as the existence of different names or different forms of the same name, further sources of information must be consulted. These might be other works by the same author, *National Union Catalog, Cumulative Book Index, Book Publishers' Record, New Serial Titles*, reliable directories or biographical dictionaries, or other reference sources. The one or more sources used as authoritative should be cited on the authority record, together with any pertinent cross references. References should then be made as well as a revised authority record for any conflicting heading that had to be changed in the process of creating the authority heading for the name or title in hand. Fig. 27.2 shows one format that an authority card might take. Fig. 27.3 shows this name authority record in MARC format. In the MARC authorities format the authorized heading is given in the 1xx field. "See from" references (those preceded by an "x" in a manual file) are given in 4xx fields. If there are "see also from" references, they are given in 5xx fields. Notes are given in 6xx fields.

Subject authority work usually represents the adaptation of one or more generalized subject heading lists to the needs of a particular library. LC and *Sears* lists are sometimes marked and annotated to show local practice and are thus used directly as the authority file. *Sears* has consistently, throughout its many editions, supplied a blank one-half page alongside each column of subject terms and references, for the local library to record new decisions on subject usage as they are made. The hindrance to this method is the work entailed in transferring hand-written emendations into the new edition when it is published. Yet the need to transfer is possibly a spur to thorough revision from time to time of the library's subject practice.

Fig. 27.2. Sample name authority card.

```
Van Buren, Ariane.

LCAF: n 79022593

Work cat.:  Nuclear or not? 1978 (a.e.): t.p. (Ariane
van Buren), jkt. (E. Ariane van Buren, research assoc.,
International Inst. of Environment & Development)


x Buren, Ariane van
x Van Buren, E. Ariane
```

Fig. 27.3. MARC authority record.

ARN: 256371	Rec stat: n	Entrd: 840818	Used: 840818
Type: z	Geo subd: n	Govt agn: _ Lang:	Source:
Roman: _	Subj: a	Series: n Ser num: n	Head: aab
Ref status: a	Upd status: a	Auth status: a	Name: a
Enc lvl: n	Auth/Ref: a	Mod rec:	Rules: c

```
1 010      n  79022593
2 040      DLC $c DLC
3 100 10   Van Buren, Ariane.
4 400 10   Buren, Ariane van
5 400 10   Van Buren, E. Ariane
6 670      Nuclear or not? 1978 (a.e.) $b t.p. (Ariane van Buren) jkt.
(E. Ariane van Buren, research assoc., International Inst. of
Environment & Development)
```

If the subject authority file is maintained on cards, the process involves verifying a heading as being the latest terminology through checking the list and any supplements to the list. In the case of *LCSH*, the latest microfiche version may be checked. It is then necessary to determine which of the headings following the *sa* and *xx* codes are already represented in the catalog. The cataloger must also choose from the recommended terms following the *x* code those that will be used locally. Fig. 27.4 is an example of a subject authority card, indicating its source.

Fig. 27.4. Sample subject authority card.

```
LITERATURE AND SCIENCE   (PN55; English literature,
   PR149.S4)

   sa   LITERATURE AND TECHNOLOGY
        SCIENCE FICTION

   x    Poetry and science
        Science and literature
        Science and poetry

   xx   SCIENCE AND THE HUMANITIES


                         ◯               LC 9th ed.
```

IN-PROCESS FILES

Certain areas of acquisitions and cataloging overlap. Each library's requirements must be studied to avoid duplication of record keeping, verification, etc. This is a continuous administrative responsibility. Some file, whether maintained by the cataloger or by the order librarian, must show "books in process." Its records continuously trace the status of each item from the time it is received in the library until it goes to the shelf, with its permanent catalog cards filed. Libraries that use multiple order forms can reserve one section for the in-process record. Others use the original requisition slip, once the book has been invoiced. Since the correct main entry may not be established until the book is cataloged, most libraries arrange their in-process files by title rather than by author. If printed cards are ordered separately from the works they describe (e.g., card orders from the Library of Congress), a separate file may be necessary for those card sets that arrive ahead of the books. In online systems a record can be created at the time an item is ordered, and this record can then have various kinds of information added to it as it goes through processing. The end result is a complete bibliographic record that can be part of an online catalog or can be used to produce catalog cards for other printed products.

CATALOG DEPARTMENT MANUALS

The purpose of a department manual is to codify all pertinent decisions and procedures. A copy should be readily available to every member of the library staff, and it should contribute to the in-service training of every new cataloging employee. Even public service staff should be able and willing to consult it on problems of local catalog interpretation and use. It is most effective in looseleaf format, so the various tagged and indexed sections can be withdrawn and replaced by updated material as needed. Foster recommends that it give complete coverage of responsibilities and practices, and that it be easy to use, to read, and to revise. He gives the following points to remember during its preparation:

1. Arrange material in logical order so that related information is found together.

2. Use precise and concrete words, not abstract words. And illustrate whenever possible.

3. Be alert to details. Write the manual so that there is no question about procedures and so that the newcomer can easily understand and follow each routine.

4. But do not over-detail. Too much detail provides no room for individual variation and will not allow for minor changes without complete rewriting.

5. Anticipate future revisions and additions.

6. Before adding a new procedure into the manual, test it out to discover and correct unforeseen problems.

7. Take advantage of auxiliary sources, particularly publications from the Library of Congress and, if the library is part of a network, publications distributed by network headquarters.[8]

CATALOGING ROUTINES

We know that most cataloging performed in the United States today derives from LC copy in either print or machine-readable form.[9] Since the Library of Congress uses ISBD and *AACR 2*, most present-day descriptive cataloging embodies the precepts of these two compatible and internationally recognized paradigms. Local catalogers may use the description as it stands or may alter it to reflect differences in a copy of an item received locally, to correct occasional errors made on LC copy, to adjust headings to fit the local authority file, or to add name or title added entries.

As for subject analysis, the Library of Congress provides with most of its records a suggested DDC class number, as well as its own full call number, with possible alternative LC and DDC class numbers for such materials as bibliographies, biographies, and the separate parts of a monographic series. It also shows the subject headings it has chosen for the work. Local catalogers may use LC decisions as they stand, or modify them to reflect variations in edition, impression, or format, to complete the DDC class numbers, to adjust official LC call numbers to their local shelflists, to substitute *Sears* or other subject list terms for the LC subject headings, and to omit, add, or change other tracings. Original cataloging is usually necessary for a work without an available record from the Library of Congress or some other reliable bibliographic agency.

USE OF WORK FORMS

Whether the task is copy cataloging or original cataloging, work forms are useful to routinize procedures and ensure full coverage of essential points. In print format they are sheets, cards, or slips pre-printed to exhibit the standard categories of information that catalogers must consider. Many catalogers use typewriters. For them, some form of the 3x5-inch card (actually 7.5x12.5 cm.) or a larger work slip may be sufficient. Some libraries use one part of the multiple copy order forms available from library supply houses, but these leave little room for corrections and additions. If printed cards are purchased, especially from the Library of Congress or a commercial vendor, necessary changes to fit the local item may be made directly on the card set, or perhaps on one unit card, which can then be reproduced to give added copies for secondary entries, departmental or branch libraries, and shelflists.

Other catalogers prefer to use longhand on work sheets which are forwarded to typists for card production or inputting into machine-readable files. If the cataloging is based primarily on a large union file of machine-readable records, and done at a terminal, the operator usually can call up prepared work forms. These are filled in in substantive detail directly at the keyboard. Where the MARC format is used, pre-selected fields and tags are changed or expanded as needed. On the other hand, the cataloger may prefer to start in longhand on a printed form (*see* Fig. 27.5), handing the completed sheet to a terminal operator for inputting. Fig. 27.6 shows the MARC record for the item in Fig. 27.5.

Fig. 27.5. An OCLC participant's work form.

Type: *a* Bib lvl: *m* Govt pub: *i* Lang: *eng* Source: *d* Illus: *ab*
Repr: Enc lvl: *I* Conf pub: *∅* Ctry: *fr* Dat tp: *s* M/F/B: *1∅*
Inax: *∅* Mod rec: Festschr: *∅* Cont: *b*
Desc: *a* Int lvl: Dates: *1984,*

---

010 LCCN   043 Geog. area code *a-io---*

---

040 Cat. Source *IVE $c IVE*   050 _ LC call no.

---

020 ISBN   082 _ Dewey Class

---

041 _ Lang.   ⟨090⟩/ 092 Local call no.
                                           TK5101 $b .B37 1984

1*00* *1∅* Main entry *Battu, Daniel Pierre,*

24_ _ _ Uniform title

---

245 *1∅* Title *Telecommunication services for the transfer of*
information and data : $b a case study in Indonesia / $c
prepared by Daniel Pierre Battu and John B. Rose.

250   Edition

---

260 *∅* Imprint *Paris : $b General Information Programme*
and UNISIST, United Nations Educational, Scientific and
Cultural Organization, $c 1984.

300   Collation *vii, 83 p. : $b ill., maps ; $c 30 cm.*

4*90* *1* _ Series *PGI ; $v 84/WS/10*

5*04*   Note *Bibliography: p. 67-68.*

5___   Note

5___   Note

6*50* *∅* Subject *Telecommunication systems.*

6*50* *∅* Subject *Telecommunication policy $z Indonesia.*

6___ _ Subject

7*00* *1∅* Added entry *Rose, John B.*

7___ _ _ Added entry

8*30* _ *∅* Series traced *PGI (Series) ; $v 84/WS/10.*
           differently

---

910 _ _ User option

Fig. 27.6. OCLC record produced from preceding work form.

```
OCLC: 11851699        Rec stat: c Entrd: 850326          Used: 850408
Type: a Bib lvl: m Govt pub: i Lang:  eng Source: d Illus: ab
Repr:     Enc lvl: I Conf pub: 0 Ctry:  fr  Dat tp: s M/F/B: 10
Indx: 0 Mod rec:    Festschr: 0 Cont: b
Desc: a Int lvl:    Dates: 1984,
   1 010
   2 040      IVE $c IVE
   3 043      a-io---
   4 090      TK5101 $b .B37 1984
   5 049      IVEA
   6 100 10  Battu, Daniel Pierre.
   7 245 10  Telecommunication services for the transfer of information
and data : $b a case study in Indonesia / $c prepared by Daniel Pierre
Battu and John B. Rose.
   8 260 0   Paris : $b General Information Programme and UNISIST,
United Nations Educational, Scientific and Cultural Organization, $c
1984.
   9 300      vii, 83 p. : $b ill., maps ; $c 30 cm.
  10 490 1   PGI ; $v 84/WS/10
  11 504     Bibliography: p. 67-68.
  12 650  0  Telecommunication systems.
  13 650  0  Telecommunication policy $z Indonesia.
  14 700 10  Rose, John B.
  15 830  0  PGI (Series) ; $v 84/WS/10.
```

DESCRIPTIVE CATALOGING

Most libraries follow the Library of Congress in conforming to ISBD and *AACR* requirements, or some modification thereof. *AACR 2* outlines three levels of description, with increasing detail included at each of the two higher levels. It also offers options throughout, which frequently have to do with adding further details to the record. Main and added (non-subject) entries are determined in accordance with *AACR 2*, or perhaps with some adjustments for established practice. Any changes from LC practice, or *AACR 2* options exercised, should be described in the catalog department manual. All new headings should be recorded in the local authority list, along with cross references as indicated. Authority control was discussed earlier.

ASSIGNING CALL NUMBERS

After examining the item to be cataloged in the light of the classification schedules used by the library, a cataloger usually consults the shelflist to see if the class number chosen, or its possible alternative, has been previously used for similar or different materials. When the appropriate class number is selected, the distinguishing book number, with any necessary additions, such as workmark, edition date, or location symbol, is added. The full call number is recorded in the shelflist, on the item proper (with volume and copy number if needed), and on the work form. If catalog and shelflist are in card form, a temporary slip should be inserted in the shelflist, with possibly another in the catalog main entry position, pending arrival of permanent cards. Libraries using non-card catalogs frequently maintain card shelflists for recent additions, until a new cumulated non-card issue is available. In machine-readable files new entries are likely to be held or "saved" online until an authorized reviser has approved them, but this routine does not take so long that a temporary substitute is considered necessary.

ASSIGNING SUBJECT HEADINGS

The subject heading list and subject authority file used by the library must be consulted for consistent selection and recording of accepted headings and references. Obsolete terminology may be caught and changed at once, although it is usually better to postpone major overhauls to a designated time, in order to expedite new cataloging in progress. The work form for the particular item can carry instructions for the typist or keyboard operator to use when preparing added entries, tracings, new references, subject analytics, and the like. At this point the item, with its work form, is generally ready for final preparation. In most libraries the work form must be manually translated by a typist into cards (or a machine-readable record), pockets, and labels before the work travels to the preparations department for final processing. Other libraries have this step performed by commercial suppliers, by a network central office, or by in-house automated printers.

CARD CATALOG MAINTENANCE

Like any ongoing function, a catalog is subject to wear and tear, obsolescence, inadvertent clerical and professional errors, inconsistency, and a variety of related ills. It therefore requires continual editing and maintaining, although libraries, being traditionally shorthanded, often neglect or postpone the responsibility, to the detriment of effective service. As collections grow, the efforts needed to keep a card catalog in satisfactory condition tend to increase exponentially. Outdated and disreputable cards, filing backlogs, and blind cross references (from headings once used but incompletely or inaccurately withdrawn) are among the major maintenance problems encountered. Attention to physical elements such as repair of damaged drawers or replacement of worn and soiled cards is important. Tray labels, guide cards, and instructions for use inside and outside the file should be altered whenever improvements are possible. Expansion inevitably requires occasional shifting of cards.

Catalog editing is needed to eliminate unnecessary entries, to suggest improvements, and to plan for future growth and development. Old entries may not have been pulled during cancellation of a title. Inconsistent headings, misleading or blind references, filing errors, missing cards, wrong call numbers, etc. all cause perplexity and ill will. The normal, rapid obsolescence of terminology mandates constant surveillance to modify or expand existing terms and references. The intricacies of connecting references between old and new headings, as established according to changes in rules of entry, must be adjudicated. Changes in filing rules also present problems. Some entries may need to be refiled, to keep pace with shifting needs of the library and its users. Foster describes a number of grooming functions that should be assigned as full- or part-time responsibilities, depending on the size and age of the catalog.[10]

MAINTENANCE OF OTHER TYPES OF CATALOGS

Maintenance of book, COM, and online catalogs involves editing, as discussed above, to guard against obsolescence of terminology. References must be maintained, and old name and title entries must sometimes be changed when there are conflicts with new entries to the catalog. In addition, for COM and online catalogs there must be concern for maintenance of the equipment necessary for their use.

REPRODUCING CATALOG CARDS

Catalog cards can be produced by typing each one individually. More often, however, they are purchased in sets from LC or from a number of other suppliers. One of the most common sources of such sets is the utility of which the library may be a member. But card sets may also be produced from MARC records by the library's own computer. It is also possible to photocopy a set from one master unit card by either using copy received through LC's CDS Alert Service, adapting information from CIP or NUC, or typing one copy of one's original cataloging.[11]

RECLASSIFICATION AND RECATALOGING

There is inevitably a certain amount of recataloging to be performed in any library. Recataloging may be either a mass production affair or an individualized, single item performance. During the 1960s and early 1970s many medium-sized and larger libraries, especially academic ones, mounted full conversion projects from DDC to LC classification. Large-scale conversion was sometimes undertaken on special collections or a selected part of a collection. In the course of most such efforts, brief, inaccurate, or obsolete cataloging could be caught and redone. Many collections were at the same time weeded and surveyed for needed new materials.

More commonly, however, recataloging is performed on individual items for which the former records prove unsatisfactory. Class numbers within a given classification scheme (e.g., DDC or LC) may need changing because the schedules have been revised or because of new interpretations and needs within the collection. Recataloging on a greater or lesser scale is also the consequence of adopting a new or revised descriptive cataloging code. For instance, *AACR 2* calls for many more corporate names to be entered directly under the body's own name rather than subordinately under a higher body than was done under earlier rules (e.g., "Library of Congress" *not* "United States. Library of Congress"). Catalogers whose libraries are not yet ready to close their card files and start new ones based strictly on the changed rules must decide what to do about superseded usages, particularly changed headings for already used entries that are likely to be used again. Not all practices have been officially standardized to meet this dilemma. Some attempt to solve it with full sets of *see also* references linking old and new forms of headings in unified or split files without actually recataloging the older works. Others refile old headings under guide-cards carrying the new heading forms, leaving *see* references at the old positions to assist users who still search under those outdated forms. Still other libraries recatalog under the new forms, particularly if there are only a limited number of entries under the obsolete forms.

CLOSING CARD CATALOGS

In 1965 studies were made at the New York Public Library which confirmed that a staggering number of the cards (actually 29 percent) in the public catalog of the Research Libraries Division were illegible, damaged, dirty, badly worn, or otherwise unfit to remain. The problem was aggravated by the fact that some entries had been there for over one hundred years. It was a dramatic instance of a malaise that was reaching epidemic proportions in many long-established research libraries. Besides the deterioration problem, upkeep and maintenance were expensive and unsatisfactory. Space, lighting, and furniture pose real logistics problems in files of over ten million cards. Labor costs for filing and revising have increased considerably since the 1960s.

The NYPL studies led to a decision to photograph the existing catalog prior to discarding it in favor of conversion to book format.[12] All new cataloging would be made available in a combination of card and book formats from a store of machine-readable records.[13]

The NYPL venture, along with other, similar experiments, encouraged the Library of Congress to announce in late 1977 that it would soon implement a similar solution to its card catalog proliferation.[14] LC's original plans were to "freeze" its existing files on January 1, 1980. The particular point in time was intentionally orchestrated to the appearance of *AACR 2*, but other research libraries, fearful of the consequences of so "precipitous" an action, persuaded the Library of Congress to postpone the change until January 1, 1981.

The Library proposed to abandon at the same time its practice of "superimposition," by which it retained most of its established headings regardless of rule changes, following *AACR* dictates only for those headings being established for the first time. Superimposition had been an attempt to avoid the Herculean task of updating all forms rendered obsolete by the new rules. But even with liberal use of cross references, it confounded catalogers and catalog users alike, with its legacy of inconsistent access forms in a single file. Starting in 1981, with all obsolete headings officially frozen in a searchable, but defunct, catalog, headings for new materials were established according to *AACR 2* regardless of whether a given entry was identified differently in the old catalog. In situations where libraries have closed old catalogs, complete bibliographic access to all the records in *both* catalogs under many personal, corporate, and geographic headings requires that the search be conducted under heading forms that differ from one catalog to the other. The kind and number of cross references to be used in one or both catalogs have occasioned much discussion.

Not all librarians in 1981 were convinced that a step as radical as closing one catalog and starting afresh on another was the best solution to problems of catalog lag. For the most part, only large research collections tried it. Most libraries maintained one catalog, using combinations of interfiling, split files, cross references, and revising old headings.

The advent of online catalogs is precipitating more catalog closings than did *AACR 2*. Once an online system can provide as many access points as does the card or other printed catalog, the old catalog can be closed. Most online catalogs do not have a distinct "opening" date. Several years' worth of entries appear in both the closed catalog and the online catalog. However, all new entries after a certain date appear only in the online catalog. In order to circumvent the necessity of keeping the old catalog for access to older materials, many libraries have embarked on retrospective conversion projects in which they convert every record in their shelflists to machine-readable form. This is often done through a utility by searching for the records in the data base and, when a match is found, adding that record to the library's archive tape. Retrospective conversion can also be done by a commercial service on contract.[15]

NOTES

[1]Other reliable texts are available for this purpose. *See*, for example, Marty Bloomberg and G. Edward Evans, *Introduction to Technical Services for Library Technicians*, 5th ed. (Littleton, Colo., Libraries Unlimited, 1985); and Donald L. Foster, *Managing the Catalog Department*, 2nd ed. (Metuchen, N.J., Scarecrow, 1982).

[2]Ellen Altman, "Reactions to a COM Catalog," *Journal of Academic Librarianship* 3 (November 1977): 267-268; Richard W. Meyer and Bonnie Juergens, "Computer Output Microfiche Catalogs: Some Practical Considerations," *Journal of Micrographics* 11 (November 1977): 91-96; and William Saffady, *Computer-Output Microfilm: Its Library Applications* (Chicago, American Library Association, 1978).

[3]For additional examples of shelflist cards and explanations, *see* Bloomberg and Evans, *Technical Services*.

[4]*See*, for instance, S. Michael Malinconico, "Bibliographic Data Base Organization and Authority File Control," *Wilson Library Bulletin* 54 (September 1979): 36-45.

[5]Arlene G. Taylor, "Authority Files in Online Catalogs: An Investigation of Their Value," *Cataloging & Classification Quarterly* 4 (Spring 1984): 1.

[6]For more detailed information on automated authority control *see* Arlene G. Taylor, Margaret F. Maxwell, and Carolyn O. Frost, "Network and Vendor Authority Systems," *Library Resources & Technical Services* 29 (April/June 1985): 195-205.

[7]For procedures used to establish a name authority card file at the Simmons College Library, *see* Edith K. Baecker and Dorothy C. Senghas, *A Little Brief Authority: A Manual for Establishing and Maintaining a Name Authority File* (Boston, Dedoss Associates, 1978).

[8]Foster, *Managing the Catalog Department*, pp. 211-212.

[9]For discussion of adapting copy in the cataloging process, *see* Arlene Taylor Dowell, *Cataloging with Copy: A Decision-Maker's Handbook* (Littleton, Colo., Libraries Unlimited, 1976).

[10]Foster, *Managing the Catalog Department*, pp. 15-21.

[11]Surveys of card reproduction can be found in Dowell, *Cataloging with Copy*, pp. 17-19; and Bloomberg and Evans, *Technical Services*.

[12]S. Michael Malinconico and James A. Rizzolo, "New York Public Library Automated Book Catalog Subsystem," *Journal of Library Automation* 6 (March 1973): 3-36.

[13]James W. Henderson and Joseph A. Rosenthal, *Library Catalogs: Their Preservation and Maintenance by Photographic and Automated Techniques* (Cambridge, Mass., The M.I.T. Press, 1968), p. ix.

[14]"LC to Freeze Card Catalog," *Library of Congress Information Bulletin* 36 (November 4, 1977): 743-744; "Freezing the Library of Congress Catalog," *Library of Congress Information Bulletin* 37 (March 3, 1978): 152-156; and "Information on Freezing the Catalog Updated," *Library of Congress Information Bulletin* 37 (July 21, 1978): 415-419.

[15]For in-depth discussions of retrospective conversion, *see* Ruth C. Carter and Scott Bruntjen, *Data Conversion* (White Plains, N.Y., Knowledge Industry Publications, 1983); and Dennis Reynolds, *Library Automation: Issues and Applications* (New York, R. R. Bowker, 1985), pp. 280-324.

SUGGESTED READING

Bloomberg, Marty, and G. Edward Evans. *Introduction to Technical Services for Library Technicians.* 5th ed. Littleton, Colo., Libraries Unlimited, 1985. Chapters 24-25.

Burger, Robert H. *Authority Work: The Creation, Use, Maintenance, and Evaluation of Authority Records and Files.* Littleton, Colo., Libraries Unlimited, 1985.

Dowell, Arlene Taylor. *Cataloging with Copy: A Decision-Maker's Handbook.* Littleton, Colo., Libraries Unlimited, 1976. Chapters 1, 8.

Foster, Donald L. *Managing the Catalog Department.* 2nd ed. Metuchen, N.J., Scarecrow, 1982.

Intner, Sheila S. *Access to Media: A Guide to Integrating & Computerizing Catalogs.* New York, Neal-Schuman, 1984.

Reynolds, Dennis. *Library Automation: Issues and Applications.* New York, R. R. Bowker, 1985. Chapter 10.

Taylor, Arlene G., Margaret F. Maxwell, and Carolyn O. Frost. "Network and Vendor Authority Systems." *Library Resources & Technical Services* 29 (April/June 1985): 195-205.

Cataloging and Classification Aids

Fortunately, many aids are available today to help the cataloger with the various difficult aspects of his or her work. Library interest in bibliography and biography provides important reference tools that help the cataloger verify personal names and corporate bodies. More specific tools are designed for classification and choice of subject headings. Still different tools furnish complete cataloging records, as prepared by the Library of Congress, or perhaps another cataloging source, for individual works.

The beginning cataloger must know the principles and rules underlying the techniques of cataloging and classification before he or she can make intelligent use of these aids. For this reason, introductory cataloging courses emphasize original cataloging, in which the student does both the descriptive and subject cataloging from scratch, even though a shelflist and pre-processed bibliographic records (when available) are generally used in an on-the-job situation. The cataloging aids listed below are by no means the only ones available. They suggest only some of the landmark titles available for consultation, indicating the range of information and specialization within the field.

CODES, SCHEDULES, AND MANUALS

CLASSIFICATION AND SHELFLISTING

Cutter, C. A. *Two-Figure Author Table* (Swanson-Swift Revision), 1969; *Three-Figure Author Table* (Swanson-Swift Revision), 1969; and *Cutter-Sanborn Three-Figure Author Table* (Swanson-Swift Revision), 1969. Distributed by Libraries Unlimited, Littleton, Colo.

Dewey, Melvil. *Dewey Decimal Classification and Relative Index.* 19th ed. Albany, N.Y., Forest Press, 1979. 3 v.

Library of Congress. Decimal Classification Division. *Dewey Decimal Classification: Additions, Notes and Decisions.* Albany, N.Y., Forest Press, 1959- . (Irregular).

Library of Congress. Subject Cataloging Division. *L.C. Classification—Additions and Changes.* Washington, D.C., The Library, 1928- . (Quarterly).

Library of Congress. Subject Cataloging Division. *Library of Congress Classification: Classes A-Z.* var. eds. Washington, D.C., The Library, 1917- . 37v.

Library of Congress Classification Schedules: A Cumulation of Additions and Changes through.... Detroit, Gale, 1974- .

Manual on the Use of the Dewey Decimal Classification. Prepared by John P. Comaromi, editor, et al. Albany, N.Y., Forest Press, 1982.

Olson, Nancy B. *Combined Indexes to the Library of Congress Classification Schedules.* Washington, D.C., United States Historical Documents Institute, 1974. 15v.

Swanson, Gerald L. *Dewey to LC Conversion Tables.* New York, CCM Information Corp., 1972.

DESCRIPTION, ENTRY, AND HEADING

American Library Association. Committee on Cataloging: Description and Access. *Guidelines for Using AACR 2 Chapter 9 for Cataloging Microcomputer Software.* Chicago, The Association, 1984.

Anglo-American Cataloguing Rules. 2nd ed. Chicago, American Library Association, 1978.

Cartographic Materials: A Manual of Interpretation for AACR 2. Chicago, American Library Association, 1982.

Library of Congress. *Bibliographic Description of Rare Books.* Washington, D.C., The Library, 1981.

Maxwell, Margaret F. *Handbook for AACR 2.* Chicago, American Library Association, 1980.

FILING

ALA Filing Rules. Chicago, American Library Association, 1980.

Carothers, Diane Foxhill. *Self-Instruction Manual for Filing Catalog Cards.* Chicago, American Library Association, 1981.

Library of Congress Filing Rules. Washington, D.C., Library of Congress, 1980.

SUBJECT HEADINGS

Haycock, Ken, and Lynne Isberg Lighthall, comps. *Sears List of Subject Headings: Canadian Companion.* 2nd ed. New York, H. W. Wilson, 1983.

Library of Congress. Subject Cataloging Division. *Library of Congress Subject Headings.* 9th ed. Washington, D.C., The Library, 1980.

Library of Congress. Subject Cataloging Division. *Library of Congress Subject Headings Supplement.* Washington, D.C., The Library, 1908- . (Quarterly, plus microform quarterly cumulations).

Library of Congress. Subject Cataloging Division. *Library of Congress Subject Head-ings Weekly Lists*. Washington, D.C., The Library, 1984- .

Library of Congress. Subject Cataloging Division. *Subject Cataloging Manual: Sub-ject Headings*. Washington, D.C., The Library, 1984.

National Library of Canada. *Canadian Subject Headings*. Ottawa, The Library, 1978.

National Library of Canada. *Canadian Subject Headings: Additions, Changes and Corrections to Canadian Subject Headings*. Ottawa, The Library, 1981.

Scars, Minnie Earl. *Sears List of Subject Headings*. 12th ed. Edited by Barbara M. Westby. New York, H. W. Wilson, 1982.

TERMINOLOGY

ALA Glossary of Library and Information Science. Chicago, American Library Association, 1983.

Harrod, Leonard Montague. *The Librarians' Glossary*. 4th ed. Boulder, Colo., West-view Press, 1977.

CURRENT INFORMATION AND UPDATING

Cataloging & Classification Quarterly. Binghamton, N.Y., Haworth Press, 1979- . (Quarterly).

Cataloging Service Bulletin, no. 1- . Washington, D.C., The Library of Congress, 1978 . (Quarterly). Supersedes *Cataloging Service*, bulletins 1-125 (1945-1978).

Library of Congress Information Bulletin. Washington, D.C., The Library, 1942- . (Weekly).

Library Resources & Technical Services. Chicago, American Library Association, 1957- . (Quarterly).

GENERAL TEXTBOOKS

Bloomberg, Marty, and G. Edward Evans. *Introduction to Technical Services for Library Technicians*. 5th ed. Littleton, Colo., Libraries Unlimited, 1985.

Chan, Lois Mai. *Cataloging and Classification: An Introduction*. New York, McGraw-Hill, 1981.

Chan, Lois Mai. *Immroth's Guide to the Library of Congress Classification*. 3rd ed. Littleton, Colo., Libraries Unlimited, 1980.

Chan, Lois Mai. *Library of Congress Subject Headings: Principles and Applications*. 2nd ed. Littleton, Colo., Libraries Unlimited, 1985.

Dowell, Arlene Taylor. *Cataloging with Copy: A Decision-Maker's Handbook.* Littleton, Colo., Libraries Unlimited, 1976.

Dunkin, Paul S. *Cataloging U.S.A.* Chicago, American Library Association, 1969.

Foskett, A. C. *The Subject Approach to Information.* 4th ed. London, Bingley, 1982.

Foster, Donald L. *Managing the Catalog Department.* 2nd ed. Metuchen, N.J., Scarecrow Press, 1982.

Hagler, Ronald, and Peter Simmons. *The Bibliographic Record and Information Technology.* Chicago, American Library Association, 1982.

Haykin, David J. *Subject Headings: A Practical Guide.* Washington, D.C., GPO, 1951.

Intner, Sheila S. *Access to Media: A Guide to Integrating & Computerizing Catalogs.* New York, Neal-Schuman, 1984.

Osborn, Jeanne. *Dewey Decimal Classification, 19th Edition: A Study Manual.* Littleton, Colo., Libraries Unlimited, 1982.

Reynolds, Dennis. *Library Automation: Issues and Applications.* New York, Bowker, 1985.

SPECIALIZED TEXTBOOKS

Comaromi, John P. *Book Numbers: A Historical Study and Practical Guide to Their Use.* Littleton, Colo., Libraries Unlimited, 1981.

Dodd, Sue A. *Cataloging Machine-readable Data Files.* Chicago, American Library Association, 1982.

Frost, Carolyn O. *Cataloging Nonbook Materials: Problems in Theory and Practice.* Littleton, Colo., Libraries Unlimited, 1983.

Lehnus, Donald J. *Book Numbers: History, Principles, and Application.* Chicago, American Library Association, 1980.

Olson, Nancy B. *Cataloging of Audiovisual Materials: A Manual Based on AACR 2.* 2nd ed. Mankato, Minn., Minnesota Scholarly Press, 1985.

Rogers, JoAnn V. *Nonprint for Media Collections: A Guide Based on AACR 2.* Littleton, Colo., Libraries Unlimited, 1982.

Smiraglia, Richard P. *Cataloging Music: A Manual for Use with AACR 2.* Lake Crystal, Minn., Soldier Creek Press, 1983.

Weihs, Jean, with Shirley Lewis and Janet Macdonald. *Nonbook Materials: The Organization of Integrated Collections.* 2nd ed. Ottawa, Canadian Library Association, 1979.

NATIONAL BIBLIOGRAPHIES AND CATALOGS

Books in Series. 3rd ed.-   . New York, Bowker, 1980- .

Books in Series in the United States. 1st-2nd eds. New York, Bowker, 1977-1979.

Library of Congress. *Catalog of Books Represented by Library of Congress Printed Cards.* Ann Arbor, Mich., Edwards Brothers, 1942-1955. 191 v. (Title varies).

Library of Congress. *Library of Congress Catalog, Books: Subjects.* 1950-1982. (Various publishers).

Library of Congress. *Library of Congress Catalogs: Monographic Series.* Washington, D.C., The Library, 1974-1982.

Music, Books on Music and Sound Recordings. Washington, D.C., Library of Congress, 1973- .

Name Authorities Cumulative Microform Edition. Washington, D.C., Library of Congress, (current year).

National Union Catalog: A Cumulative Author List Representing Library of Congress Printed Cards and Titles Reported by Other American Libraries. Washington, D.C., Library of Congress, 1956-1982.

National Union Catalog: Audiovisual Materials. Washington, D.C., Library of Congress, 1983- . (Available only on microfiche; includes indexes for names, titles, subjects, and series).

National Union Catalog: Books. Washington, D.C., Library of Congress, 1983- . (Available only on microfiche; includes indexes for names, titles, subjects, and series).

National Union Catalog: Cartographic Materials. Washington, D.C., Library of Congress, 1983- . (Available only on microfiche; includes indexes for names, titles, subjects, and series).

National Union Catalog: Pre-1956 Imprints. London, Mansell, 1968-1984.

New Serial Titles: A Union List of Serials Commencing Publication after December 31, 1949. Washington, D.C., Library of Congress, 1953- .

Union List of Serials in Libraries of the United States and Canada. 3rd ed. New York, H. W. Wilson, 1965. 5 v.

These tools are undoubtedly among the most important of all cataloging aids, useful particularly for verifying entries and providing authoritative descriptive cataloging and classification. While they represent a considerable financial investment, even a medium-sized library would find these basic sets, supplements, and current volumes invaluable as both cataloging and reference tools. Several foreign national bibliographies and catalogs published by the British Library, the Bibliothèque Nationale, etc. might also be useful.

Bibliography

Consult "Cataloging and Classification Aids," pages 591-595, for a listing of general and specialized textbooks and of bibliographic tools.

Austin, Derek. *PRECIS: A Manual of Concept Analysis and Subject Indexing.* 2nd ed. London, British Library, 1984.

Avram, Henriette D. *MARC: Its History and Implications.* Washington, D.C., Library of Congress, 1975.

Batty, C. D. *Introduction to Colon Classification.* Hamden, Conn., Archon Books, 1966.

Berman, Sanford. *Prejudices and Antipathies: A Tract on the LC Subject Heads Concerning People.* Metuchen, N.J., Scarecrow, 1971.

Bliss Bibliographic Classification. 2nd ed. Edited by Jack Mills and Vanda Broughton with the assistance of Valerie Lang. Boston, Butterworths, 1977- .

Brown, James Duff. *Subject Classification: With Tables, Indexes, etc., for the Subdivision of Subjects.* 3rd ed., rev. and enl. by James Douglas Stewart. London, Grafton, 1939.

Buchanan, B. *Theory of Library Classification.* London, Bingley, 1979.

Burger, Robert H. *Authority Work: The Creation, Use, Maintenance, and Evaluation of Authority Records and Files.* Littleton, Colo., Libraries Unlimited, 1985.

Cannan, Judith Proctor. *Special Problems in Serials Cataloging.* Washington, D.C., Library of Congress, 1979.

Clack, Doris H. *Black Literature Resources: Analysis and Organization.* New York, Marcel Dekker, 1975.

Coates, E. J. *Subject Catalogues: Headings and Structure.* London, Library Association, 1960.

Cutter, Charles Ammi. *Expansive Classification, Part I: The First Six Classifications.* Boston, C. A. Cutter, 1891-1893.

Cutter, Charles Ammi. *Expansive Classification, Part II: Seventh Classification.* Edited by William Parker Cutter. Boston, 1904.

Cutter, Charles Ammi. *Rules for a Dictionary Catalog.* 4th ed., rewritten. Washington, D.C., GPO, 1904.

Dowell, Arlene Taylor. *AACR 2 Headings: A Five-Year Projection of Their Impact on Catalogs.* Littleton, Colo., Libraries Unlimited, 1982.

Encyclopedia of Library and Information Science. Edited by Allen Kent and Harold Lancour. New York, Marcel Dekker, 1968-1985.

Fédération Internationale de Documentation. *Universal Decimal Classification.* Abridged English Edition. 3rd rev., 1961. London, British Standards Institution, 1963.

Fédération Internationale de Documentation. *Universal Decimal Classification. Complete English Edition.* 4th international ed. London, British Standards Institution, 1943-   . (In progress).

Hagler, Ronald. *Where's That Rule? A Cross-Index of the Two Editions of the Anglo-American Cataloguing Rules.* Ottawa, Canadian Library Association, 1979.

Harris, Jessica Lee. *Subject Analysis: Computer Implications of Rigorous Definition.* Metuchen, N.J., Scarecrow Press, 1970.

Herdman, M. M. *Classification: An Introductory Manual.* 3rd ed., rev. by Jeanne Osborn. Chicago, American Library Association, 1978.

Hunter, Eric J. *AACR 2: An Introduction to the Second Edition of Anglo-American Cataloguing Rules.* Rev. ed. London, C. Bingley; Hamden, Conn., Linnet Books, 1979.

International Conference on AACR 2, Florida State University, 1979. *The Making of a Code: The Issues Underlying AACR 2.* Chicago, American Library Association, 1980.

International Conference on Cataloguing Principles, Paris, 9th-18th October 1961. *Report.* London, International Federation of Library Associations, 1963.

International Federation of Library Associations. International Office for UBC. *Examples of ISBD(M) Usage in European Languages.* London, IFLA Committee on Cataloguing, 1976.

International Federation of Library Associations and Institutions.
The following ISBDs have been published by the IFLA International Office for UBC in London:

ISBD(A): International Standard Bibliographic Description for Older Monographic Publications (Antiquarian). 1980.

ISBD(CM): International Standard Bibliographic Description for Cartographic Materials. 1977.

ISBD(G): General International Standard Bibliographic Description: Annotated Text. 1977.

ISBD(M): International Standard Bibliographic Description for Monographic Publications. Rev. ed. 1978.

ISBD(NBM): International Standard Bibliographic Description for Non-Book Materials. 1977.

ISBD(PM): International Standard Bibliographic Description for Printed Music. 1980.

ISBD(S): International Standard Bibliographic Description for Serials. 1977.

International Federation of Library Associations and Institutions. *Names of Persons. National Usages for Entry in Catalogues.* 3rd ed. London, IFLA International Office for UBC, 1977.

Library of Congress. Automated Systems Office. *MARC Formats for Bibliographic Data.* Washington, D.C., The Library, 1980- .

Library of Congress. Network Development and MARC Standards Office. *LSP/SNI Protocol Specification.* Washington, D.C., The Library, 1985.

Library of Congress. Network Development and MARC Standards Office. *USMARC Format for Holdings and Locations.* Washington, D.C., The Library, 1984.

Lubetzky, Seymour. *Cataloging Rules and Principles: A Critique of the ALA Rules for Entry and a Proposed Design for Their Revision.* Washington, D.C., Processing Department, Library of Congress, 1953.

Lubetzky, Seymour. *Code of Cataloging Rules, Author, and Title; an Unfinished Draft ... with an Explanatory Commentary by Paul Dunkin.* Washington, D.C., American Library Association, 1960.

Malinconico, S. Michael, and Paul J. Fasana. *The Future of the Catalog: The Library's Choices.* White Plains, N.Y., Knowledge Industry Publications, 1979.

Marshall, Joan K., comp. *On Equal Terms: A Thesaurus for Nonsexist Indexing and Cataloging.* Santa Barbara, Calif., American Bibliographical Center — Clio Press, 1977.

Osborn, Andrew. *Serial Publications: Their Place and Treatment in Libraries.* 3rd ed. Chicago, American Library Association, 1980.

Painter, Ann F., comp. *Reader in Classification and Descriptive Cataloging.* Washington, D.C., NCR Microcard Editions, 1972.

Pettee, Julia. *Subject Headings: The History and Theory of the Alphabetical Approach to Books.* New York, H. W. Wilson, 1946.

The PRECIS Index System: Principles, Applications, and Prospects. Proceedings of the International PRECIS Workshop. Edited by Hans H. Wellisch. New York, H. W. Wilson, 1977.

Ranganathan, Shiyali Ramamrita. *Colon Classification.* 6th rev. ed. London, Asia Publishing House, 1963.

Robinson, Geoffrey. *UDC: A Brief Introduction.* The Hague, FID, 1979. (FID 574).

Shera, Jesse H., and Margaret E. Egan. *The Classified Catalog: Basic Principles and Practices.* Chicago, American Library Association, 1956.

Subject Retrieval in the Seventies: New Directions: Proceedings of an International Symposium. Edited by Hans Wellisch and Thomas D. Wildon. Westport, Conn., Greenwood, 1972.

Using Online Catalogs: A Nationwide Survey. Edited by Joseph R. Matthews, Gary S. Lawrence, and Douglas K. Ferguson. New York, Neal-Schuman Publishers, 1983.

Vickery, B. C. *Faceted Classification: A Guide to the Construction and Use of Special Schemes.* London, Aslib, 1960.

Glossary of Selected Terms
and Abbreviations

Defined in this glossary are selected basic terms for students of cataloging, including a number of terms and identifiers used in descriptive cataloging, classification, subject heading work, filing, document indexing, networking, and other topics treated in this text. Consult the *AACR 2* Glossary (Appendix D) and Abbreviations (Appendix B) for additional terms used in the rules. Fuller discussion of a few of the terms included here may be found in Phyllis A. Richmond's "AACR 2—A Review Article," in *Journal of Academic Librarianship*, vol. 6, no. 1 (March 1980), pp. 30-37.

Access point. *See* **Choice of access points.**

Accession number. A number assigned to each item as it is received in the library. Accession numbers may be assigned through continuous numbering (e.g., 30291, 30292) or a coded system (67-201, 67-202, etc.).

Accompanying materials. Dependent materials, such as answer books, teacher's manuals, atlases, portfolios of plates, slides, and phonodiscs.

Add instructions. Notes in classification schedules that specify what digits to add to what base number; they replace divide-like notes in DDC.

Added entry. A secondary access point; i.e., any other than the main entry. An added entry record often duplicates the main entry record except that it has an additional heading to represent in the catalog a subject, joint author, illustrator, editor, compiler, translator, collaborator, series, etc. (Subject entry is excluded from this definition in LC usage.)

Analytical entry. An entry for a part of a work or for a whole work contained in a series or a collection for which a comprehensive entry is made. Name-title analytics may be made in the form of added entries.

Anonymous work. One in which the author's name does not appear anywhere in the book; a work of unknown authorship.

Area. A major section of a catalog entry; e.g., edition area or physical description area.

601

Artifact. *See* **Realia.**

Author. The person chiefly responsible for the intellectual or artistic content of a work; e.g., writer of a book, compiler of a bibliography, composer of a musical work, artist, photographer, etc.

Author number. *See* **Cutter number.**

Authority control. The process of maintaining consistency in form of headings in a bibliographic file or catalog through reference to an authority file.

Authority file. A record of the correct forms of names, series, subjects, or uniform titles used in the catalog.

Authority record. A printed or machine-readable unit that registers the decisions made during the course of authority work.

Authority work. The process of determining the form of a name, title, or subject concept that will be used as a heading on a bibliographic record; of determining references needed to that form; and of determining relationships of the heading to other headings.

Auxiliary table. A generalized subdivision table appended to a classification schedule for use in building specific class numbers where indicated in the schedule proper.

BALLOTS. Bibliographic Automation of Large Library Operations using a Time-sharing System, at Stanford University, now reorganized into RLIN.

Bibliographic control. The process of maintaining bibliographic records each of which contains enough information to identify an item; of arranging and providing access to those records; and of providing access to the items represented by the records.

Bibliographic record. A catalog entry in card, microtext, machine-readable, or other form carrying full cataloging information for a given item in a library.

Bibliographic service center. A regional broker, providing intermediate communication, training, and service for libraries participating in an online bibliographic network.

Bibliographic utility. An online processing center based on a machine-readable data base of catalog records.

Bibliography. A list of writings on a given subject or by a given author.

Book number. *See* **Cutter number.**

Books in sets. *See* **Monographs in collected sets.**

Boolean operators. The terms "and," "or," and "not" as used to construct search topics through post-coordinate indexing.

Broad classification. A scheme that omits detailed subdivision of its main classes, or that facilitates the use in smaller libraries of only its main classes and subdivisions.

BSO. Broad System of Ordering, a classification developed for a proposed worldwide information network covering the whole field of knowledge.

Call number. The notation used to identify and locate a particular item on the shelves; it consists of the classification notation and cutter number, and it may also include a workmark and/or a date.

CAN/MARC. A machine-readable bibliographic record format for monographs and serials compatible with LC-MARC, developed by the National Library of Canada.

Catalog. A list of books, maps, recordings, coins, or any other medium that composes a collection. It may be arranged by alphabet, by number, or by subject. It may be in the form of cards, book, computer output microform (COM), or computer online.

Cataloging. The process of describing an item in the collection, conducting subject analysis, and assigning a classification number. *See also* **Descriptive cataloging** and **Subject cataloging**.

Catchword indexing. *See* **Keyword indexing**.

Categorical filing. The preference in some areas of a filing system for partially classified arrangements over a straight alphabetical sequence.

Centralized processing. Any cooperative effort that results in the centralization of one or more of the technical processes involved in getting material ready for use in a library.

Chain index. A direct and specific index based on the extracted vocabulary of a classification system. It retains all necessary context but deletes unnecessary context; all subheadings are superordinate terms.

Chief source of information. The source in an item that is prescribed by the rules as the major source of data for use in preparing a bibliographic description.

Choice of access points. The process of selecting the main entry or heading and any added entries under which an item is to be listed in the catalog.

CIP. Cataloging in Publication, a program sponsored by the Library of Congress and cooperating publishers; a partial bibliographic description is provided on the verso of the title page of a book.

Classification notation. The notation assigned to an item of a collection to show the subject area and to indicate its location in the collection.

Classification schedule. The printed scheme of a particular classification system.

Classified catalog. A catalog arranged in the order of symbols, numbers, or other notations that represent the various subjects or aspects of subjects covered by the items owned by the library.

Close classification. The use of minute subdivisions for arranging materials by highly specific topics.

Closed stacks. Library collections not open to public access or limited to a small group of users.

CODEN. A system of unique letters assigned for ready identification of periodicals and serials, now administered by Chemical Abstracts Service (CAS).

Coextensive subject entry. A principle of subject entry, by which a term, phrase, or set of terms defines precisely the complete contents, but no more than the contents, of an item.

Collation. *See* **Physical description area.**

Collection. Three or more works or parts of works by one author published together, or two or more works or parts of works by more than one author published together. Each work in a collection was originally written independently or as part of an independent publication.

Collocation. The process of bringing together in a catalog records for names, titles, or subjects that are bibliographically related to one another.

COM. Computer Output Microform.

COMARC. Cooperative MARC, an experimental program in which LC worked to develop modes of cooperation with outside libraries and network utilities in building high-quality bibliographic data bases and authority records.

Compiler. One who brings together written or printed matter from the works of various authors or the works of a single author.

Computer-produced catalog. *See* **COM; Online catalog.**

CONSER. Conversion of Serials project, a shared national data base of serial records from selected libraries, now maintained by OCLC.

Continuation. 1) A work issued as a supplement to an earlier one. 2) A part issued in continuance of a book, a serial, or a series.

Coordinate indexing. Information retrieval through the use of related terms in a catalog or data base to identify concepts.

Corporate body. An organization or group of persons who are identified by a name and who act as an entity.

Cross reference. A reference made from one entry in a catalog to another; e.g., *see* reference and *see also* reference.

Cutter number. The symbols, usually a combination of letters and numbers, used to distinguish items with the same classification number in order to maintain the alphabetical order (by author, title, or other entry) of items on the shelves; sometimes called author number or book number. The word "cutter" is derived from the widespread use of the *Tables* first devised by C. A. Cutter for use in such alphabetical arrangement.

Dash. A symbol of punctuation and separation which in printing consists of a single line and in typing is made by striking the hyphen key twice in succession. In descriptive cataloging the dash usually appears with one space on either side; for subject subdivisions no spaces are used.

DDC. Dewey Decimal Classification.

Descriptive cataloging. The phase of the cataloging process concerned with the identification and description of library material, the recording of this information in the form of a catalog entry, and the choice of name and title access points for the resultant bibliographic record.

Dictionary catalog. A catalog arranged in alphabetical order with entries for names, titles, and subjects all interfiled.

Divide-like note. A place in a classification schedule referring the user to another location where analogous sequencing and notation set a pattern.

Divided catalog. A catalog in which different types of entries are separated into different sections. Usually the subjects are separated from other entries. Order is usually alphabetical in each section, but the subject section may be in classified order.

Edition. In the case of books, all the impressions of a work printed at any time or times from one setting of type; also, one of the successive forms in which a literary text is issued either by the author or by a subsequent editor. In the case of nonbook materials, all the copies of an item made from one master copy.

Edition area. Includes the following elements: named and/or numbered edition statement, and statement of responsibility relating to a particular edition, if any.

Editor. One who prepares for publication or supervises the publication of a work or collection of works or articles that are not his own. Responsibility may extend to revising, providing commentaries and introductory matter, etc.

Element. A sub-section of an area in the catalog entry; for example, the alternative title is an element of the title and statement of authorship area.

Entry. A representation of a bibliographic record at a particular point in a catalog. There can be one or more entries for any one heading. *See also* **Heading.**

Entry word. The word by which the entry is arranged in the catalog, usually the first word (other than an article) of the heading. Also called "filing word."

Enumerative classification. A classification that attempts to assign a designation for every subject concept required in the system.

Expansive classification. A scheme in which a set of coordinated schedules gives successive development possibilities from very simple (broad) to very detailed (close) subdivision.

Explanatory reference. A reference that gives the detailed guidance necessary for effective use of the headings involved.

Faceted classification. A classification constructed from the combination, in prescribed sequence, of clearly defined, mutually exclusive, and collectively exhaustive aspects, properties, or characteristics of a class or specific subject.

FID. Fédération Internationale de Documentation (International Federation for Documentation).

Filing word. *See* **Entry word.**

Fixed location. The assignment of each item in a collection to a definite position on a certain shelf.

Form division. *See* **Standard subdivision.**

Form heading. A subject list term that refers to the literary or artistic form, or the publication format of a work rather than to its topical content.

Form of entry. The specific spelling and wording used to record an access point on a catalog record.

Free-floating subdivision. A sub-heading that can be added to headings in a published list, as needed, whether or not it is written in the published list following those headings.

Generalia class. That part of a classification system designed to hold materials of a general nature, usually covering many diverse topics.

Geographic name. The place name usually used in reference to a geographic area. It is not necessarily the political name. *See also* **Political name.**

GMD. General Material Designation, a term that is given in the catalog record to indicate the class of material to which an item belongs (e.g., motion picture).

Guide card. A labeled card with a noticeable projection that distinguishes it from other catalog cards. It is inserted in a card catalog to help the user find a desired place or heading in the catalog.

Hanging indention. This form of indention is used in traditional bibliographic record format when the main entry is under title; the title begins at first indention and all succeeding lines of the body of the record begin at second indention.

Heading. The "official" uniform mode of representing the name of a person, corporate body, geographic area, title of a work, or subject. Usually provided at the top of each catalog record or at the top of a column, page, or screen on which several entries for the heading may appear.

Hierarchical classification. A classification that attempts to arrange subjects according to a "natural" order—proceeding from classes to divisions to subdivisions.

Hierarchical notation. In classification, the use of symbol groups of varying combinations and lengths to reflect a hierarchy of topics and subdivisions.

Holdings note. One note in the bibliographic record for a serial that tells which parts of the serial are held by the library. *See also* **Numeric and/or alphabetic, chronological, or other designation area.**

IFLA. International Federation of Library Associations.

IFLAI. International Federation of Library Associations and Institutions. Formerly IFLA.

ILL. Interlibrary Loan.

Imprint. *See* **Publication, distribution, etc., area.**

Indentions. Designated spaces or margins at which parts of a catalog record begin; used especially in typing cards.

Index. A tool that exhibits the analyzed contents of a bibliographic entity or a group of such entities, as contrasted with a library catalog, which lists and describes the holdings of a particular collection.

INTERMARC. A French-language format for bibliographic exchange for monographs; similar to LC-MARC formats. *See also* **UNIMARC.**

ISBD. International Standard Bibliographic Description, an internationally accepted format for the representation of descriptive information in bibliographic records. ISBDs developed so far include: **ISBD(A)**, ISBD for Older Monographic Publications (Antiquarian); **ISBD(CM)**, ISBD for Cartographic Materials; **ISBD(G)**, General; **ISBD(M)**, ISBD for Monographic Materials; **ISBD(NBM)**, ISBD for Nonbook Materials; **ISBD(PM)**, ISBD for Printed Music; **ISBD(S)**, ISBD for Serials.

ISBN. International Standard Book Number, a distinctive and unique number assigned to a book. ISBNs are used internationally; the U.S. agency for ISBNs is R. R. Bowker Company.

ISDS. International Serials Data System, a network of national and international centers sponsored by UNESCO. The centers develop and maintain registers of serial publications; this includes the assignment of ISSNs and key title.

ISSN. International Standard Serial Number, a distinctive number assigned by ISDS.

Joint author. A person who collaborates with one or more associates to produce a work in which the individual contributions of the authors cannot be distinguished. *See also* **Shared authorship.**

Key heading. *See* **Pattern heading.**

Keyword indexing. Use of significant words from a title or a text as index entries.

KWIC indexing. Key Word In Context, a format for showing index entries within the context in which they occur.

KWOC indexing. Key Word Out of Context, the use of significant words from titles for subject index entries, each followed by the whole title from which the word was taken.

LC. Library of Congress or Library of Congress Classification.

LC-MARC. *See* **MARC.**

LCSH. Library of Congress Subject Headings.

Leaf. A single thickness of paper; i.e., two pages.

Literary warrant. The development of certain parts of a classification scheme in response to the volume of materials available for classification.

LSP. Linked Systems Project, a joint project of LC, RLIN, and WLN; the goal is to be able to exchange data among systems in an online mode through a standard network interconnection (SNI).

Machine-readable data base. A collection of discrete records or files on punched tape or cards, magnetic tape or disk, or in another form, which can be identified, deciphered and displayed by machine.

Machine-readable data file. A body of coded information that can be read only by a machine (usually a computer).

Main class. A principal division of a classification scheme.

Main entry. 1) The major access point chosen; the other access points are added entries. 2) A full catalog entry headed by the access point chosen as main entry, which gives all the information necessary for the complete identification of a work. This entry also bears the tracing of all the other headings under which the work is entered.

Manufacturer. The agency that has made the item being cataloged (e.g., printer of a book).

Map series. A group of map sheets having the same scale and cartographic specifications, identified collectively by the producing agency, that, when the series is completed, will cover a given geographic area.

MARC. Machine-readable Cataloging, a program of the Library of Congress, which distributes machine-readable cataloging in LC format.

Material specific details area. Includes elements needed in the bibliographic description of certain special materials. *See* **Mathematical data area, Musical presentation statement,** and **Numeric and/or alphabetic, chronological, or other designation area.**

Mathematical data area. Includes the following elements in description of cartographic material: scale, projection, and optionally, coordinates and equinox.

Microfiche. A flat sheet of photographic film designed for storage of complete texts in multiple micro-images, and having an index entry visible to the naked eye displayed at the top.

Microfilm. A length of photographic film containing sequences of micro-images of of texts, title pages, bibliographic records, etc.

Microform. Usually a reproduction photographically reduced to a size difficult or impossible to read with the naked eye; some microforms are not reproductions but original editions. Microforms include microfilm, microfiche, microopaques, and aperture cards.

Mixed notation. A notation that combines two or more kinds of symbols, such as a combination of letters and numbers.

Mnemonic devices. Devices intended to aid or assist the memory.

Monograph. A complete bibliographic unit; it may be issued in successive parts at regular or irregular intervals, but it is *not* intended to continue indefinitely. It may be a single work or a collection that is not a serial.

Monographic series. A series of monographs with a collective title.

Monographs in collected sets. Collections or compilations by one or more authors issued in two or more volumes.

MRDF. *See* **Machine-readable data file.**

Musical presentation statement. A statement in a chief source of information for music that indicates its physical form.

NAL. National Agricultural Library, Washington, D.C.

Name authority file. A file of the name (author) headings used in a given catalog, and the references made to them from other forms.

Name-title added entry. An added entry that includes the name of a person or corporate body and the title of a work. It serves to identify a work that is included in the larger work that is being cataloged, to identify a work that is the subject of the work being cataloged, to identify a larger work of which the work being cataloged is part, or to identify another work to which the work being cataloged is closely related (e.g., an index).

NLA. The National Library of Australia, Canberra.

NLM. The National Library of Medicine, Washington, D.C.

Nonbook materials. Term used to designate collectively maps, globes, motion pictures, filmstrips, videorecordings, sound recordings, etc.

Notation. A system of numbers and/or letters used to represent a classification scheme.

Note area. Reserved for recording catalog data that cannot be incorporated in the preceding parts of the record. Each note is usually recorded in a separate paragraph.

NUC. The *National Union Catalog*, a publication in the Library of Congress Catalogs series.

Numeric and/or alphabetic, chronological, or other designation area. The publication record of a serial. It does not necessarily indicate the volumes or parts of a serial held by a library. *See also* **Holdings note.**

OCLC. Online Computer Library Center, a library network. Among other services, it provides a machine-readable data base for cataloging.

Online catalog. A catalog based on and giving direct access to machine-readable cataloging records.

Online retrieval. Direct use of a computer to access stored data.

Open entry. A part of the descriptive cataloging not completed at the time of cataloging. Used for uncompleted works such as serials, series, etc.

Open stacks. A library collection where all users are admitted directly to the shelves.

Other title. A title other than the title proper (and parallel title); e.g., a subtitle.

Parallel title. The title proper written in another language or in another script.

Pattern heading. A representative heading from a category of terms that would normally be excluded from a subject heading list (e.g., names of individuals), included as an example of normal subdivision practice within that category.

Periodical. A publication with a distinctive title, which appears in successive numbers or parts at stated or regular intervals and which is intended to continue indefinitely. Usually each issue contains articles by several contributors. Newspapers and memoirs, proceedings, journals, etc., of corporate bodies primarily related to their internal affairs are not included in this definition. *See also* **Serial** and **Monograph.**

Phonograph records. *See* **Sound recordings.**

Physical description area. The section of a catalog entry that includes extent of an item, dimensions, and other physical details.

Place name. *See* **Geographic name.**

Plate. An illustrative leaf that is not included in the pagination of the text; it is not an integral part of a text gathering; it is often printed on paper different from that used for the text.

Political name. The proper name of a geographical area according to the law. This name often changes with a change in government.

Post-coordinate indexing. The grouping of a large number of entries under simple concepts in such a way that the user can combine them to locate material on the compound subjects in which he or she is interested.

PRECIS. Preserved Context Indexing System, a British technique for subject retrieval in which an open-ended vocabulary can be organized according to a scheme of role-indicating operators for either manual or computer manipulation.

Pre-coordinate indexing. The combination of subject terms at the time of indexing for use in the retrieval of materials on complex concepts.

Preliminaries. The title page or title pages, the verso of each title page, the cover, and any pages preceding the title page.

Processing center. A central office where the materials of more than one library are processed and distributed. Such a center may also handle the purchasing of materials for its constituents.

Producer. Person or agency responsible for financial and administrative production of a motion picture or machine-readable data file, and for its commercial success.

Pseudonym. A false name assumed by an author to conceal identity.

Pseudo-serial. A frequently reissued and revised publication which at first publication is usually treated as a monographic work.

Publication, distribution, etc., area. Includes the following elements: place of publication, distribution, etc.; name of publisher, distributor, etc.; date of publication, distribution, etc.; and sometimes place of manufacture, name of manufacturer, and date of manufacture.

Publisher. The person, corporate body, or firm responsible for issuing printed matter.

Pure notation. A notation that consistently uses only one kind of symbol (e.g., either letters *or* numbers, but not both).

Realia. Actual objects (artifacts, specimens, etc.) rather than replicas.

RECON. Retrospective Conversion of Library of Congress records to MARC format, an experimental project on the results of which LC determined that it was not economically feasible to make a complete conversion of its existing card catalogs.

Record. *See* **Bibliographic record.**

Relative index. An index to a classification scheme that not only provides alphabetical references to the subjects and terms in the classification but also shows some of the relations between subjects and aspects of subjects.

Relative location. A classificatory arrangement of library materials, allowing the insertion of new material in its proper relation to that already on the shelves.

Reprint. A new printing of an item either by photographic methods or by resetting the type for substantially unchanged text.

Retrospective conversion. The process of changing information in eye-readable bibliographic records into machine-readable form.

RLG. Research Libraries Group, a consortium formed originally by Columbia, Harvard, and Yale universities, and the New York Public Library, now consisting of over sixty large research libraries, but minus Harvard.

RLIN. Research Libraries Information Network, a regional bibliographic network based at Stanford University, resulting from the reorganization of its BALLOTS system under the aegis of RLG.

Romanization. The representation of the characters of a nonroman alphabet by roman characters. *See also* **Transliteration.**

Scope note. A statement delimiting the meaning and associative relations of a subject heading or a classification notation.

Score. An arrangement of all of the parts of a piece of music one under another on different staves. A series of staves on which is written music composed originally for one instrument is not considered a score. Thus, "piano score" is used to designate, not music written originally for the piano, but music written originally for instrumental or vocal parts that has been arranged for the piano.

SCORPIO. Subject-Context Oriented Retriever for Processing Information Online, a text retrieval facility in operation at the Library of Congress.

Secondary entry. *See* **Added entry.**

See also **reference.** A reference indicating related entries or headings.

See **reference.** A direction from a heading not used to a heading that is used.

Serial. A publication issued in successive parts at regular or irregular intervals and intended to continue indefinitely. Included are periodicals, newspapers, proceedings, reports, memoirs, annuals, and numbered monographic series. *See also* **Periodical** and **Monograph.**

Series. A number of separate works, usually related in subject or form, that are issued successively. They are usually issued by the same publisher, distributor, etc., and in uniform style, with a collective title.

Series area. The area of a catalog record that gives series information.

Series authority file. A file of series entries used in a catalog with the record of references made to them from other forms.

Series title. The collective title given to volumes or parts issued in a series.

Shared authorship. More than one author is responsible for the work.

Shelflist. A record of the items in a library; entries are arranged in the order of the items on the shelves.

s.l. Place of publication, distribution, etc., unknown (*sine loco*).

s.n. Name of publisher, distributor, etc., unknown (*sine nomine*).

SNI. Standard Network Interconnection. *See also* **LSP.**

Sound recordings. Aural recordings, including discs (i.e., phonograph records), cartridges, cassettes, cylinders, etc.

Specific entry. A principle observed in most library subject lists, by which material is listed under the most specific term available, rather than under some broader heading.

Standard number and terms of availability area. Includes ISBN or ISSN and, optionally, price or other terms on which the item is available.

Standard subdivisions. Divisions used in DDC that apply to the form a work takes. Form may be physical (as in a periodical or a dictionary) or it may be philosophical (such as a philosophy or history of a subject). Formerly called form divisions.

Statement of responsibility. A statement in the item being described that gives persons responsible for intellectual or artistic content, corporate bodies from which the content emanates, or persons or bodies responsible for performance.

Subject authority file. A file of the subject headings used in a given catalog, with the record of the references made to them.

Subject cataloging. The assignment of classification numbers and subject headings to the items of a library collection.

Subject entry. The catalog entry for a work under the subject heading.

Subject heading. A word or group of words indicating a subject.

Subject subdivision. A restrictive word or group of words added to a subject heading to limit it to a more specific meaning.

Subtitle. A secondary title, often used to expand or limit the title proper.

Superimposition. A Library of Congress policy decision that only entries being established for the first time would follow *AACR 1* rules for form of entry, and that only works new to LC would follow *AACR 1* rules for choice of entry. When LC adopted *AACR 2*, the policy of superimposition was dropped.

Switching language. A mediating or communication indexing language used to establish subject indication equivalencies among various local indexing languages.

Syndetic structure. An organizational framework in which related names, topics, etc., are linked to each other via connective terms such as *see* and *see also*.

Synthetic classification. A classification that assigns designations to single, unsubdivided concepts and gives the classifier generalized rules for combining these designations for composite subjects.

Thesaurus. A specialized authority list of terms used with automated information retrieval systems; very similar to a list of subject headings.

Title and statement of responsibility area. The section of a catalog entry that gives the title of a work and information on its authorship.

Title page. A page that occurs very near the beginning of a book and that contains the most complete bibliographic information about the book, such as the author's name, the fullest form of the book's title, the name and/or number of the book's edition, the name of the publisher, and the place and date of publication.

Title proper. The title that is the chief name of an item; excludes any parallel title or other title information.

Tracing. The record on the main entry record of all the additional entries under which the work is listed in the catalog.

Transliteration. A representation of the characters of one alphabet by those of another. *See also* **Romanization.**

UDC. Universal Decimal Classification.

UK/MARC. A machine-readable bibliographic record format compatible with LC-MARC, developed by British National Bibliography for use in the United Kingdom.

Uniform title. The title chosen for cataloging purposes when a work has appeared under varying titles.

UNIMARC. Universal MARC format, first developed in 1977 by the Library of Congress to be an international communications format for the exchange of machine-readable cataloging records between national bibliographic agencies; the second edition, published in 1980, is being used for international exchange of bibliographic data.

Union catalog. A catalog that lists, completely or in part, the holdings of more than one library or collection.

Unit record. The basic catalog record, in the form of a main entry, which when duplicated may be used as a unit for all other entries for that work in the catalog by the addition of appropriate headings.

UTLAS. University of Toronto Library Automated Systems, a computer-based bibliographic network offering its data base and services to a variety of Canadian libraries.

Verification. Determining the existence of an author and the form of name as well as the correct title of a particular work; in short, using bibliographic sources to verify (i.e., prove) the existence of an author and/or work.

Vernacular name. A person's name in the form used in reference sources in his own country.

Verso of the title page. The page immediately following the title page; i.e., the page on the back side of the title page.

Videorecording. A recording originally generated in the form of electronic impulses and designed primarily for television playback. The term includes videocassettes, videodiscs, and videotapes.

Volume. In the bibliographical sense, a major division of a work distinguished from the other major divisions of that work by having its own chief source of information.

WLN. Western Library Network, a regional bibliographic network based at the State Library of Washington, now servicing libraries in Alaska, Idaho, Oregon, and Washington.

Work form. A card or other form that often accompanies a book throughout the cataloging and preparation processes. The cataloger notes on the work form any directions and information needed to prepare catalog entries, cross references, etc.

Workmark. A letter (or letters) placed after the cutter number. A workmark may consist of one or two letters, the first of which is the first letter of the title of a work (exclusive of articles). Also called work number.

Worksheet. *See* **Work form.**

Author/Title/Subject Index